VIDEO
CAPSULE REVIEWS

Desmond Ryan

A FIRESIDE BOOK
Published by Simon & Schuster, Inc.
NEW YORK

A Fireside Book
Published by Simon & Schuster, Inc.
Simon & Schuster Building
Rockefeller Center
1230 Avenue of the Americas
New York, New York 10020

Some of the reviews in this book have been published in different form in *The Philadelphia Inquirer*

FIRESIDE and colophon are registered trademarks of Simon & Schuster, Inc.
Designed by Farrand Booth Associates
Manufactured in the United States of America

10 9 8 7 6 5 4 3 2

Library of Congress Cataloging in Publication Data

ISBN: 0-671-49182-2

Preface

This guide was prompted by interruptions. Movie critics grow accustomed to telephone calls from readers who want to settle a bet made at the office water cooler over some contested point of film trivia. But in recent years—as video cassette recorders have become a prime and often preferred way of seeing a movie—the questions have changed along with viewing habits. Today, the callers want information and opinion on the bewildering array of movies available for home consumption.

Video Capsule Reviews is an attempt to respond to that need. I would be the first to admit that squeezing a movie into a critical nutshell is a rash and, in some ways, impertinent undertaking. The intent is simply to advise and inform as concisely as possible.

The videotape sales and rental market is in a constant state of flux and expansion. The movies I have chosen for the guide represent the history of the industry from the silent era to the present. In doing the choosing, I have tried to tailor the capsules to the way people use their recorders. Most surveys show that they prefer to rent films or tape them off the air from cable and network television—a practice that has been ruled legal by the Supreme Court if the film is for purely private consumption.

The heavy emphasis in this guide is on movies released in the seventies and eighties. These films make up the dominant portion of the videotape market. And, because they reflect changes in attitudes to the depiction of sex and violence, there is a greater need to discuss their content. This is especially the case if children are going to watch.

I have also included films—such as *The Empire Strikes Back* and *Indiana Jones and the Temple of Doom*—that can reasonably be expected to come onto the videotape rental market in the presumed lifespan of this guide.

Where a film is exceptional in terms of sex and violence, it is noted in the capsule as a supplement to the Motion Picture Association of America (MPAA) rating.

The arrangement of each capsule is:
(1) The title of the film.
(2) The year of its release.
(3) A combined description of the content and an opinion of the film's merit.
(4) The MPAA rating, where applicable, that it was given when first issued.
(5) A critic's rating of one to five stars.
(6) The director **(D)**.
(7) The writer **(W)**.
(8) The cinematographer **(Ph)**.
(9) The composer of the musical score **(M)**.
(10) The four leading performers **(Cast)**.

The star ratings are:
One Star——Poor.
Two Stars——Fair.
Three Stars——Good.
Four Stars——Very Good.
Five Stars——Excellent.

The MPAA categories, as employed at movie theaters, are:

G—Suitable for all ages.

PG—Parental Guidance Suggested.

PG-13—Not suitable for children under 13.

R—Restricted to those over seventeen or accompanied by an adult.

X—No one under 17 admitted.

The MPAA ratings system was amended in the summer of 1984 after an avalanche of criticism of the PG rating given *Indiana Jones and the Temple of Doom* and *Gremlins*. Many parents and critics felt these Steven Spielberg productions were too violent for children. Hence the new PG-13 rating.

Hollywood's rating system is, I suppose, better than nothing. The trouble is that a G or an X is the kiss of death at the box office. Therefore almost all movies now released are given an R, PG, or the new PG-13. These designations do not tell you the reason.

Another point to bear in mind is that movies reflect changing times. What was deemed pornographic and controversial a decade ago now rates an R. If, for example, *Last Tango in Paris*, which caused uproar in 1973, were released today it would probably be as an R.

The MPAA has been justly criticized for its *laissez-faire* attitude toward violence. It takes only one common four-letter word to receive an R. What it takes in terms of mayhem is never quite clear. In general, you're likely to find far more violence than sex in the PG category. The way things are was graphically illustrated by the first film given the new PG-13 rating—John Milius' violent fantasy *Red Dawn*.

Desmond Ryan
Philadelphia, 1984

VIDEO
CAPSULE REVIEWS

A

THE ABOMINABLE DOCTOR PHIBES. (1971) Vincent Price gives out bad phibes indeed in a horror film that's a must for anyone who's just gotten a doctor's bill. Enraged at the physicians who treated his late wife, Phibes dreams up bizarre ways of killing them. His method is based on resurrecting Egyptian plagues whose treatment is not covered by Medicare. Price enjoyed himself hugely.

★★★

D: Robert Fuest; W: William Goldstein and James Whiton; Ph: Norman Warwick; M: Basil Kirchen.
Cast: Vincent Price, Joseph Cotten, Hugh Griffith, Terry-Thomas.

ABSENCE OF MALICE. (1981) Sally Field's reporter commits enough ethical violations to get her kicked out of a dozen city rooms in the course of an entertaining but dishonest newspaper drama. It bulges with issues that cannot be adequately addressed and it rebuts the heroic reporter image that goes back to the thirties deadline pictures. An innocent businessman is the victim of a sensational story and it is the reporter who is left with ink on her face.
PG. ★★★
D: Sidney Pollack; W: Kurt Luedtke; Ph: Owen Roizman; M: Dave Grusin.
Cast: Paul Newman, Sally Field, Bob Balaban, Josef Summer.

ACCIDENT. (1967) Dirk Bogarde, Harold Pinter and Joseph Losey, the three imposing talents who collaborated on *The Servant*, reteamed with results that are almost as good. An Oxford student is killed in a car crash. His girlfriend becomes the object of a double mid-life crisis afflicting two teachers, Bogarde and Stanley Baker. Pinter's uncanny ear for speech and Losey's sensitive direction make the most of what would be a mundane situation in lesser hands.

★★★★

D: Joseph Losey; W: Harold Pinter; Ph: Gerry Fisher; M: John Dankworth.
Cast: Dirk Bogarde, Stanley Baker, Jacqueline Sassard, Michael York.

ACE IN THE HOLE. (1951) Billy Wilder's withering look at the media and the way stories are manipulated sometimes makes *Absence of Malice* seem like a defense of journalism. It's set at a biting, satirical extremity with Kirk Douglas bribing a sheriff to slow down a rescue operation so that he can milk the story and return to the journalistic big time.

★★★

D: Billy Wilder; W: Wilder, Walter Newman and Lesser Samuels; Ph: Charles Lang, Jr.; M: Hugo Friedhofer.
Cast: Kirk Douglas, Jan Sterling, Bob Arthur, Porter Hall.

ADAM'S RIB. (1949) The barbed affection that the imperturbable Tracy and the brittle Hepburn brought to their partnership is deployed in a juicy court-room comedy in which they play married lawyers on opposite sides of a case. An ingenious, if formula vehicle, but the chemistry between the two stars makes it work flawlessly and this is one of the best their partnership produced. Judy Holliday is the wronged wife who shoots her husband, an act Hepburn turns into a feminist vindication.

★★★★

D: George Cukor; W: Ruth Gordon, Garson Kanin; Ph: George J. Folsey; M: Miklos Rosza.
Cast: Spencer Tracy, Katharine Hepburn, Tom Ewell, Judy Holliday.

THE ADVENTURES OF DON JUAN. (1948) Despite the title and the star, this is no more than a routine Errol Flynn swashbuckler enlivened by his refusal to take any of it too seriously. Don Juan has to save the Queen of Spain.

★★★

D: Vincent Sherman; W: George Oppenheimer; Ph: Elwood Bredell; M: max Steiner.
Cast: Errol Flynn, Viveca Lindfors, Romney Brent, Ann Rutherford.

THE ADVENTURES OF ROBINSON CRUSOE. (1953) You could hardly name an odder couple than Luis Bunuel and Daniel Defoe. Nonetheless, the master surrealist's version of the classic is surprisngly literal and his view of Crusoe rather spiritual. The script is occcasionally unfortunate —(Crusoe to Friday: "Someday, if you're good, I'll teach you to smoke"). Trademark Bunuel appears in Crusoe's fever-ridden dream.

★★★

D: Luis Bunuel; W: Bunuel and Phillip Roll; Ph: Alex Phillips; M: Anthony Collins.
Cast: Dan O'Herlihy, James Fernandez.

1

THE ADVENTURES OF SHERLOCK HOLMES' SMARTER BROTHER. (1975) Reunion of some of the *Young Frankenstein* team —minus Mel Brooks— and that means the humor is very elementary. Gene Wilder is one of those comic actors who needs someone else to direct him. There is no restraint here and even the good gags are flogged to death. The celebrity of Sherlock hangs over his jealous brother like a London fog and he tries to prove himself by recovering some documents lost by the Foreign Secretary. For those who find the ida of Queen Victoria cursing funny. We were not amused.
PG.   ★★
D and W: Gene Wilder; Ph: Gerry Fisher; M: John Morris.
Cast: Gene Wilder, Madeline Kahn, Marty Feldman, Dom DeLuise.

ADVISE AND CONSENT. (1962) Alan Drury's sprawling novel dealt with the repercussions that follow the nomination of a Secretary of State and its expose style was something of a revelation to Americans who then had a purer notion of their elected leaders. Otto Preminger imposed some order and the actors had a field day.
                                                 ★★★
D: Otto Preminger; W: Wendell Mayes; Ph: Sam Leavitt; M: Jerry Fielding.
Cast: Henry Fonda, Don Murray, Charles Laughton, Walter Pidgeon.

THE AFRICAN QUEEN. (1951) Rose Sayer and Charlie Alnutt are two of the most likeable and unlikely lovers in movies. She is a spinster missionary and he a booze-sodden captain of a ramshackle riverboat, *The African Queen*. The chemistry between Hepburn and Bogart, the humor they brought out in their characters and the delicacy with which they convey the transition from friction to fondness and then love made this a wonderful movie instead of a well-done adventure. They are cast together by the outbreak of war in 1914 and make a perilous journey that culminates in an attack on a German gunboat.
                                               ★★★★★
D: John Huston; W: Huston and James Agee; Ph: Jack Cardiff; M: Allan Gray.
Cast: Katharine Hepburn, Humphrey Bogart, Robert Morely, Peter Bull.

AGAINST ALL FLAGS. (1952) Piracy on the Spanish Main and Errol Flynn's farewell to the swashbuckler. He looks like he's had enough in a very standard outing that pits him against pirate leader Anthony Quinn.
                                                 ★★

D: George Sherman; W: Aeneas Mackenzie and Joseph Hoffman; Ph: Russell Metty; M: Hans Salter.
Cast: Errol Flynn, Anthony Quinn, Maureen O'Hara, Mildred Natwick.

AGATHA. (1978) Agatha Christie never revealed the answer to one of her biggest mysteries. What did she do and where did she go for 11 days in 1926, a disappearance that attracted frenzied press converage. *Agatha* is a haunting speculation involving love and revenge that is weakened by the fact that Vanessa Redgrave is given so little time to establish the character before the disappearing act. Many arguments over the final print and creative control—including lawsuits—may explain this.
PG.   ★★★
D: Michael Apted; W: Kathleen Tynan and Arthur Hopcraft; Ph: Vittorio Storaro; M: Johnny Mandel.
Cast: Dustin Hoffman, Vanessa Redgrave, Timothy Dalton, Helen Morse.

THE AGONY AND THE ECSTASY. (1965) The camera cannot reveal the creative processes of the painter; only its results. The vast labor and genius invested in the ceiling of the Sistine chapel makes a work that is better to look at than listen to. The film opens with a collage of the Renaissance master's great achievements and then recounts his bickering with Pope Julius II. Heston is a stalwart, manly Michelangelo, whose homosexuality is never mentioned, and Rex Harrison has more to work with as the cantankerous pontiff.
                                                 ★★★
D: Carol Reed; W: Philip Dunne; Ph: Leon Shamroy; M: Alex North.
Cast: Charlton Heston, Rex Harrison, Diane Cilento, Harry Andrews.

AIR FORCE. (1942) Wartime propaganda produced more than its share of jingoistic bombs, but Howard Hawks contribution to the cause is right on target. He loved the air and the biography of a B-17 nicknamed Mary Ann gave him every opportunity. The film tells the story of the plane and the crew. The combat, some borrowed from newsreel footage, has impact. William Faulkner wrote some of the dialogue as his contribution.
                                                 ★★★
D: Howard Hawks; W: Dudley Nichols and William Faulkner; Ph: James Wong Howe; M: Franz Waxman.
Cast: John Garfield, John Ridgely, George Tobias, Harry Carey.

AIRPLANE II. (1982) A severe case of joke-lag awaits the viewer of this feeble sequel. The best gags—the pederast pilot and the sub-titled jive talk—are repetitions of jests in the original, a fact which puts the film's humor in a holding pattern. The supporting parody framework is missing in Ken Finkelman's idea of a commercial shuttle lost in space. The movie is trapped in a similar vacuum of ideas.

PG. ★★
D and W: Ken Finkelman; Ph: Joe Biroc; M: Richard Hazard.
Cast: Robert Hayes, Julie Hagerty, William Shatner, Peter Graves, Lloyd Bridges.

AIRPORT. (1970) There's a mad bomber to cope with, but no amount of critical bombardment could do in the series that took off with a diverting piece of schlock. There are enough problems to confound a traffic controller, let alone a director. The first of the series is the best, which, of course, isn't saying a great deal. Helen Hayes played a stowaway and won an Oscar.

★★
D and W: George Seaton; Ph: Ernest Laszlo; M: Alfred Newman.
Cast: Burt Lancaster, Dean Martin, Jean Seberg, Helen Hayes.

AIRPORT 1975. (1974) The sequel propels a Boeing 747 down a runway of cliches and toward a midair collision over Utah, a calamity that allows everyone except the Mormon Tabernacle Choir to get into the act. Dismal even by the low aspirations of the disaster genre, this one has stewardess Karen Black trying to land the crippled plane under the remote guidance of her pilot-lover. Complete with sick child and singing nun.

PG. ★★
D: Jack Smight; W: Don Ingalls; Ph: Philip Lathrop; M: John Cacavas.
Cast: Charlton Heston, Karen Black, George Kennedy, Helen Reddy.

AL CAPONE. (1959) Playing Capone can scar an actor's reputation because the part is an open invitation to overdo it and because it's difficult to add anything new to our perception of the gangster. Rod Steiger surmounted the challenge with perhaps the most provocative of the competing portrayals of Capone. Otherwise, the movie is a competent and straightforward rehashing of Capone's career in the Prohibition era and his eventual imprisonment.

★★★

D: Richard Wilson; W: Marvin Wald and Henry Greenberg; Ph: Lucien Ballard; M: David Raksin.
Cast: Rod Steiger, Fay Spain, Murvyn Vye, Nehemiah Persoff.

ALEXANDER NEVSKY. (1938) Sergei Eisenstein's epic can claim primacy on two fronts. It is perhaps the finest propaganda film ever made and it boasts, for my money at least, the best film score ever written. With Hitler threatening in the West, Eisenstein told the story of Alexander Nevsky, a 13th century prince who united Russia against the invading Teutonic knights. By today's standards the film is slowly paced and under-characterized, but Prokofiev's music is stunning and apposite and the battle on the ice is one of the most spectacular scenes in movies.

★★★★★
D: Sergei Eisenstein; W: Eisenstein and Pyotr Pavlenko; Ph: Eduard Tisse; M: Sergei Prokofiev.
Cast: Nikolai Cherkasov, Nikolai Okhlopkov, Alexandr Abrikosov, Dmitri Orlov.

ALEXANDER THE GREAT. (1956) A military career of uninterrupted victory that was unique in its scope becomes a rather solemn history lesson. Richard Burton does his best to make it an interesting one in the title role and the screenplay is quite serviceable. By the time he died at the tender age of 33, Alexander's empire extended to India.

★★★
D and W: Robert Rossen; Ph: Robert Krasker; M: Mario Nascimbene.
Cast: Richard Burton, Frederic March, Danielle Darrieux, Claire Bloom.

ALFIE. (1966) Michael Caine was an obscure English actor doing lower class roles. He became a star by doing a lower class role as a cockney skirt-chaser seasoned in the fine art of chatting up the "dollies" and "the birds". He narrates his experiences as a sort of Casanovan manifesto and the enormously popular film still boasts one of Caine's most memorable creations.

★★★
D: Lewis Gilbert; W: Bill Naughton; Ph: Otto Heller; M: Sonny Rollins.
Cast: Michael Caine, Vivien Merchant, Shirley Anne Field, Millicent Martin.

ALI BABA AND THE FORTY THIEVES. (1944) Benighted Arabiana that shows how dumb things can get when done seriously. A much-wronged prince becomes a leader of the thieves and faces a dilemma presented by their code and his love on the way to regaining his throne.

★★

D: Arthur Lubin; W: Edmund Hartmann; Ph: George Robinson; M: Edward Ward.
Cast: Jon Hall, Maria Montez, Scotty Beckett, Turhan Bey.

ALICE DOESN'T LIVE HERE ANYMORE. (1975) Ellen Burstyn, a woman liberated from a rotten marriage, uses her new freedom of choice to try to resume a career as a singer. Martin Scorsese, in one of his more benign moods, makes her journey across America as raunchy and funny as possible. Credibility goes out the window when Kris Kristofferson enters as a rancher who's prepared to give up everything for her.

R. ★★★

D: Martin Scorsese; W: Robert Getchell; Ph: Kent Wakeford.
Cast: Ellen Burstyn, Kris Kristofferson, Alfred Lutter, Diane Ladd.

ALICE'S RESTAURANT. (1969) One of the better youth-movement movies from that down period in Hollywood when it seemed that anyone with long hair and blue jeans was allowed to direct a film. It was inspired by Arlo Guthrie's record which sang of the alternative life-style that was such an issue of the times. As such, it now has documentary value.

★★★

D: Arthur Penn; W: Penn and Venable Herndon; Ph: Michael Nebbia; M: Arlo Guthrie.
Cast: Arlo Guthrie, Pat Quinn, James Broderick, Geoff Outlaw.

ALIEN. (1979) The old fifties sci-fi formula—the monster aboard the spaceship returning to earth—given the virtuoso, high-tech treatment by Ridley Scott. After the benevolence of the Spielberg/Lucas school, Scott gave us a monster of unredeemed savagery and a neat role reversal that puts Sigourney Weaver in the heroic role instead of a square-jawed cipher. The crew's response to the alien presence is sometimes incredible but Scott moves things at a pace that sweeps objections aside. Terrific special effects by Brian Johnson and Nick Allder and a deliciously creepy score from Jerry Goldsmith

R. ★★★★

D: Ridley Scott; W: Dan O'Bannon; Ph: Derek Vanlint and Denys Ayling; M: Jerry Goldsmith.

Cast: Sigourney Weaver, Tom Skerritt, John Hurt, Veronica Cartwright.

ALL ABOUT EVE. (1950) "You're far too short for that gesture," sneers critic George Sanders at scheming actress Anne Baxter. But not too short to try to use Bette Davis as a stairway to stardom. Davis is terrific as the aging actress who will not be stepped upon in this vastly entertaining and supremely catty film. It is a film that takes neither the "Theater" nor theater people with absolute seriousness and it's worth it just for Davis' use of a celery stalk to make a widely understood gesture in Sanders' direction. Four major Oscars, all deserved.

★★★★★

D and W: Joseph L. Mankiewicz; Ph: Milton Krasner; M: Alfred Newman.
Cast: Bette Davis, George Sanders, Anne Baxter, Celeste Holm, Gary Merrill, Hugh Marlowe.

ALLEGRO NON TROPPO. (1979) Some warhorses of the classical repertoire are liberally and ingeniously animated. Not *Fantasia*, but then what is? There are some rather tedious comedic cadenzas between the purely musical episodes.
PG. ★★★
D: Bruno Bozzetto.

ALLIGATOR. (1980) A crock. John Sayles's tongue-in-cheek script attacks corporate greed. But it's corporate greed that's behind this shabby piece of exploitation. A baby alligator turns into a huge one in sewers polluted by business. It shows a rare discernment in finding the guilty among its victims. Quite slick until the alligator leaves the sewers and then much gory silliness.
R. ★★
D: Lewis Teague; W: John Sayles; Ph: Joseph Mangine; M: Craig Hundley.
Cast: Robert Forster, Michael Gazzo, Dean Jagger, Robin Riker.

ALL MY SONS. (1948) A war profiteer suffers domestic losses. An adaptation of Arthur Miller's play in which a returning veteran discovers that his father was responsible for peddling defective airplanes to the military.

★★★

D: Irving Reis; W: Chester Erskine; Ph: Russell Metty; M: Leith Stevens.
Cast: Edward G. Robinson, Burt Lancaster, Mady Christians, Howard Duff.

ALL QUIET ON THE WESTERN FRONT. (1930) The Nazis were loud critics of Lewis

Milestone's pacifist tale of young German recruits encountering the brutal realities of the war in 1916. In truth, the sincerity and the emotional power inherent in the material have given Milestone's work its place among the great anti-war movies. The acting is not especially striking but that does not detract from the film's impact.

★★★★

D: Lewis Milestone; W: Del Andrews and Maxwell Anderson; Ph: Arthur Edeson; M: David Broekman.
Cast: Lew Ayres, Louis Wolheim, John Wray, Raymond Griffith.

ALL SCREWED UP. (1976) Sex, money, machismo and the oppression of the workers served up with customary flair by Lina Wertmuller. The Italian title literally translates as "Everything in its Place and Nothing in Order". Everything really is neatly in place in this a series of effective and mostly comic vignettes about two farm boys living in a Milan workers commune and toiling in a slaughterhouse. Among Wertmuller's best.

PG. ★★★★

D and W: Lina Wertmuller; Ph: Giuseppe Rotunno; M: Piero Piccioni.
Cast: Luigi Diberti, Lina Polito, Nino Bignamini, Giulana Calandra.

ALL THAT HEAVEN ALLOWS. (1955) Second time around for the stars of *Magnificent Obsession*. Tears are manipulatively jerked from the affair of an older woman and her gardener that violates local notions of propriety.

★★★

D: Douglas Sirk; W: Peg Fenwick; Ph: Russell Metty; M: Frank Skinner.
Cast: Rock Hudson, Jane Wyman, Agnes Moorehead, Conrad Nagel.

ALL THE KING'S MEN. (1949) Broderick Crawford bulled his way through the movie to an Oscar in a thinly disguised look at Huey Long, who ruled Louisiana like a feudal lord in the thirties. At the heart of this knowledgeable reading of the way power corrupts and absolute power corrupts absolutely is a keen understanding of how a sytem changes a man's values. In the transition from populist to power-broker, Crawford's Willie Stark changes his ends as much as the means.

★★★★

D and W: Robert Rossen; Ph: Burnett Guffey; M: Louis Gruenberg.
Cast: Broderick Crawford, John Ireland, Joanne Dru, Mercedes McCambridge.

ALL THE PRESIDENT'S MEN. (1976) Alan Pakula made no effort to glamorize the numbing tedium that is the reality of successful investigative reporting, and the journalistic coup of the century — the uncovering of Watergate — is made engrossing by the enormity of the subject. A riveting detective story and a judicious pairing of Hoffman's neurotic intensity and Redford's cool in the parts of the two reporters whose discoveries brought down a President.

PG. ★★★★★

D: Alan Pakula; W: William Goldman; Ph: Gordon Willis; M: David Shire.
Cast: Robert Redford, Dustin Hoffman, Jason Robards, Martin Balsam.

ALL THIS AND WORLD WAR II. (1977) A juxtaposition of Beatles tunes with the most traumatic historical development of this century. It's rather like playing Beethoven on a kazoo. The Lennon-McCartney songs are sung by the likes of the Bee Gees and Frankie Valli, which is an insult in itself. Newsreel footage of World War II leaves one wondering what the London Blitz has to do with "Once There Was a Way" or "Help" to do with the Afrika Corps. A gratuitous affront to people who lived through the war and a demeaning use of some great music.

PG. ★

D: Susan Winslow; M: John Lennon, Paul McCartney.

ALOHA, BOBBY AND ROSE. (1975) Lower class young lovers on the lam. Floyd Mutrux aimed for a note of high tragedy, but wound up with little more than pathos. A mechanic pulls a fake hold-up that ends in a real killing and flees to Mexico with a young divorcee. The characters are not arresting and the movie is vacuuous.

PG. ★★

D and W: Floyd Mutrux; Ph: William A. Fraker; M: Various artists.
Cast: Paul Le Mat, Dianne Hull, Tim McIntire, Leigh French.

THE AMAZING COLOSSAL MAN. (1957) The special effects and other necessary tricks are more appalling than amazing, which is a distinct drawback in a sci-fi fantasy about an army officer radiated during an atomic explosion. Instead of getting sick he gets big at the rate of 10 ft a day. He earns our undying esteem by tearing up Las Vegas before the army takes care of him.

★★

D: Bert Gordon; W: Gordon and Mark Han-

na; Ph: Joe Biroc; M: Albert Glasser.
Cast: Glenn Langan, William Hudson, Cathy Downs, James Seay.

AMERICAN HOT WAX. (1978) Supposedly an account of the career of Alan Freed, the disc jockey who claimed to have coined the term "rock and roll" and rode its popularity in a highly successful career. The film ignores both his rise and fall—in a payola scandal—and concentrates on his heyday. That allows a "let's put on a show" musical. There are more deserving candidates for martyrdom.
PG.   ★★
D: Floyd Mutrux; W: John Kaye; Ph: William A. Fraker; M: Kenny Vance.
Cast: Tim McIntire, Fran Drescher, Jay Leno, Laraine Newman.

AN AMERICAN IN PARIS. (1951) George Gershwin's jauntily romantic songs and rich scoring wear down any resistance one might have to the more fanciful aspects of the musical. Gene Kelly is a Paris-based painter caught between a millionairess and Leslie Caron. Happily he finds time to do a lot of dancing and the choreography is often stunning in its creativity and execution.
                                                ★★★★
D: Vincente Minnelli; W: Alan Jay Lerner and Alan Lin; Ph: Alfred Gilks; M: George Gershwin.
Cast: Gene Kelly, Leslie Caron, Oscar Levant, Georges Guetary.

AMERICATHON. (1979) In the 1990s America needs $400 billion to stave off an attempt to buy the country by the United Arab-Jewish Republic and a telethon is staged. Telethons are marked by unconscionable length and performers desperately trying to fill the time. So is *Americathon* and it is a shambles that doesn't have the redeeming excuse of a worthy cause.
PG.   ★
D: Neil Israel; W: Israel, Michael Mislove and Monica Johnson; Ph: Gerald Hirschfeld; .
Cast: Harvey Korman, Fred Willard, John Ritter, Peter Riegert.

AMIN—THE RISE AND FALL. (1982) Not so much a film as a passage through an abbatoir. It is dedicated to the half million souls said to have died under the Ugandan dictator's regime and its idea of homage is to reenact their deaths as gruesomely as possible. Amin's coup and his reign of terror are chronicled without any real effort at as-

sessment. Extremely violent.
R.   ★
D and W: Sharad Patel; Ph: Harvey Harrison.
Cast: Joseph Olita, Geoffrey Keen, Dennis Hills, Leonard Trolley.

THE AMITYVILLE HORROR. (1979) Strictly for the terminally credulous. The book about the terrifying things that began to happen when a family moved into a Long Island house where a murder had been committed was repudiated fact-by-alleged-fact in *Newsday.* The film presents the repossessed house as if it were all true and a lot of people believed it.
R.   ★
D: Stuart Rosenberg; W: Sandor Stern; Ph: Fred J. Koenekamp; M: Lalo Schifrin.
Cast: James Brolin, Margot Kidder, Rod Steiger, Don Stroud.

AMONG THE LIVING. (1941) A taut and thoughtful suspense film that surmounted its B movie origins. Albert Dekker plays twin brothers, one of whom emerges from an insane asylum to commit murder. A finely turned Cain and Abel variation.
                                                ★★★
D: Stuart Heisler; W: Garrett Fort and Lester Cole; Ph: Theodor Sparkuhl
Cast: Albert Dekker, Susan Hayward, Frances Farmer, Harry Carey.

THE AMSTERDAM KILL. (1978) Robert Mitchum sleepwalking through an international tale of corruption in the U.S. Drug Enforcement Agency in what amounts to a filmed narcotic. He is an agent who was once an addict and who is hired to bust up an Amsterdam-based heroin ring. No Dutch treat.
R.   ★★
D: Robert Clouse; W: Clouse and Gregory Teifer; Ph: Alan Hume; M: Hal Schaffer.
Cast: Robert Mitchum, Bradford Dillman, Richard Egan, Keye Luke.

ANATOMY OF A MURDER. (1959) Considered rather risque in its dialogue and in the evidence introduced in court, Otto Preminger's dissection of a murder case wears its years well. The most notable reason is James Stewart's sincere but down-on-his luck lawyer Paul Biegler. He undertakes the defense of a man accused of murder. The victim may or may not have raped the murderer's wife.
                                                ★★★
D: Otto Preminger; W: Wendell Mayes; Ph:

Sam Leavitt; M: Duke Ellington.
Cast: James Stewart, Lee Remick, Ben Gazzara, Arthur O'Connell.

AND JUSTICE FOR ALL. (1979) Norman Jewison's attack on our cumbersome legal system is scathing but there are too many counts in the indictment for one movie. He also offers a wild stylistic mix of everything from black comedy to straightforward liberal sincerity. Al Pacino is a lawyer defending a kennel full of underdogs and the film lurches through a series of vignettes. In effect, it is revolving door justice seen through a revolving door.
R. ★★
D: Norman Jewison; W: Valerie Curtin and Barry Levinson; Ph: Frank Holgate; M: Dave Grusin.
Cast: Al Pacino, Jack Warden, John Forsythe, Lee Strasberg.

AND NOW FOR SOMETHING COMPLETELY DIFFERENT. (1971) The first Monty Python movie is an anthology of skits from their long-running television show. If you're a fan, you've probably seen such classics as "The Upper Class Twit of the Year" and equally devastating pieces. That's no reason to avoid a second helping of the group in their prime.
PG. ★★★★
D: Ian MacNaughton; Ph: David Muir .
Cast: (Also writers) John Cleese, Graham Chapman, Eric Idle, Micahel Palin, Terry Gilliam, Terry Jones.

THE ANDROMEDA STRAIN. (1971) Michael Crichton went on to a successful directing career of his own, but this version of his best-seller was entrusted to Robert Wise. Wise does well by the story which takes the old plot idea of deadly organisms from outer space causing a plague and dresses it up with contemporary technology. The suspense is well managed as scientists struggle against stiff odds and an approaching deadline.
★★★
D: Robert Wise; W: Nelson Gidding; Ph: Richard Kline; M: Gil Melle.
Cast: Arthur Hill, David Wayne, James Olson, Kate Reid.

ANDY WARHOL'S FRANKENSTEIN. (1974) The idea is a tongue-in-cheek version of the horror classic, but other parts of the body are flung all over the screen in one of the most revolting and specifically bloody films ever made. The baron wants to create a master race by cobbling together bodies and mating them. In seeking to be outrageous Warhol winds up being merely nauseating. Originally shot in 3-D.
X.
D and W: Paul Morrissey; Ph: Luigi Kueveillier; M: Claudio Gizzi.
Cast: Joe Dallesandro, Monique Van Vooren, Udo Kier, Arno Juerging.

ANGEL. (1984) The ads proclaimed that she was a high school student by day and a hooker by night. By any measure, this is unrelieved sleaze that makes precious little attempt to establish this bizarre proposition before straying into a silly murder plot and a milieu of Sunset boulevardiers.
R. ★
D: Robert Vincent O'Neill; W: O'Neill and Joseph Cala; Ph: Andy Davis; M: Craig Saffin.
Cast: Donna Wilkes, Cliff Gorman, Dick Shawn, Rory Calhoun.

ANIMAL CRACKERS. (1930) A much loved, riotous comedy from the Marx Brothers that shows its stage origins—it was a Broadway hit before it became their second movie. But who cares when Groucho, as Captain Spaulding, and his cohorts offer a guide on how to ruin the life of a socialite? Don't miss "Hooray for Captain Spaulding", a number whose sentiments you will share.
★★★★
D: Victor Heerman; W: Morris Ryskind; Ph: George Folsey; M: Bert Kalmar and Harry Ruby.
Cast: Groucho, Chico, Harpo and Zeppo Marx, Margaret Dumont.

ANIMAL FARM. (1952) A painstaking and literal-minded animated version of George Orwell's trenchant political allegory. Farm animals rise in revolution but socialism is betrayed by despotic pigs. Much is lost in this translation and Orwell's ending is changed.
★★
D: John Halas; W: Lothar Wolff and John Halas; M: Matyas Seiber.
Cast: (Voices)Maurice Denham.

ANNIE. (1982) That you do not need an insulin shot to negotiate the 128 minutes of the musical about an orphan and a surly millionaire is a credit to John Huston's arms-length direction. Made at a cost that would have fed the hungry for the entire Depression, the film finds Huston approaching the

material like a grandfather telling a children's story in some embarrassment. Decent work from Finney and Burnett in overblown and contrived circumstances.
PG. ★★
D: John Huston; W: Carol Sobleski; Ph: Richard More; M: Charles Strouse.
Cast: Albert Finney, Carol Burnett, Aileen Quinn, Bernadette Peters.

THE ANNIVERSARY. (1968) Bette Davis camping up a storm in an eye-patch. A macabre and occasionally funny exercise in black humor with Davis reduced to one good eye and lavishing a corrupt form of mother love on three sons. Her cruel wiles overwhelm their attempts to escape the fold. Davis is the only reason to catch it.
★★
D: Roy Ward Baker; W: Jimmy Sangster; Ph: Harry Waxman; M: Philip Martell.
Cast: Bette Davis, Jack Hedley, Sheila Hancock, James Cossins.

ANOTHER COUNTRY. (1984) A splendidly executed drama that takes place in another world—the exclusive private school where the English upper classes are trained for a life of future privilege. It opens in yet another world —Moscow in 1984— where a man who was educated in that system looks back on a life of espionage and high treason. The conception is that such an inexplicable betrayal of class and country can actually be explained through the school-days of two traitors. It is highly convincing and memorably acted.
PG. ★★★★
D: Marek Kanievska; W: Julian Mitchell; Ph: Peter Biziou.
Cast: Rupert Everett, Colin Firth, Michael Jenn, Robert Addie.

ANOTHER MAN, ANOTHER CHANCE. (1977) But not another movie of the calibre of Lelouch's *A Man and a Woman*, made a decade earlier. A sepia-drenched, nostalgic view of the west with puns on the genre that only a French movie buff would love. Caan is a widower with a son and Bujold a new widow making her way in an alien environment. The film's few good moments belong to her and the loneliness she conveys as a stranded woman. Caan has little to do and the arthritic screenplay does not help matters.
PG. ★★
D and W: Claude Lelouch; Ph: Jacque Lefrancois; M: Francis Lai.

Cast: James Caan, Genevieve Bujold, Francis Huster, Jennifer Warren.

THE APE. (1940) Boris Karloff comes up with a cure for polio that would amaze Jonas Salk. The serum needs spinal fluid drained from human beings and for reasons too batty to enlarge upon the scientist goes after it while dressed as an ape.
★
D: William Nigh; W: Curt Siodmak and Richard Carroll; Ph: Harry Neumann.
Cast: Boris Karloff, Maris Wrixon, Gertrude Hoffman, Henry Hall.

APOCALYPSE NOW. (1979) Francis Ford Coppola's Vietnam epic is a reworking of Conrad's *Heart of Darkness* with a burned-out killer dispatched to terminate a renegade American colonel who has set himself up as a warlord in Cambodia. The savagery and futility of war and what it does to man's nobler instincts is presented in often stunning images, but it remains only a depiction. There is no underlying point of view from Coppola and that makes *Apocalypse Now* a fitfully brilliant film instead of the work of art it could have been. Everyone is a barbarian at the beginning of the movie; the dramatic process of degeneration is missing.
R. ★★★
D: Francis Ford Coppola; W: Coppola and John Milius; Ph: Vittorio Storaro; M: Carmine Coppola.
Cast: Marlon Brando, Martin Sheen, Robert Duvall, Frederic Forrest.

THE APPLE DUMPLING GANG. (1975) Agreeable Disney Western. Three orphans discover a gold-mine and Bill Bixby and Susan Clark enter a platonic marriage to give them a home and protect them from predators. The marriage ceremony ends in a handshake, setting a new record for Disney reticence on sex. The mood is spoofing, but Don Knotts and Tim Conway are wearing as the incompetent outlaws.
G. ★★
D: Norman Tokar; W: Don Tait; Ph: Frank Phillips; M: Buddy Baker.
Cast: Bill Bixby, Susan Clark, Don Knotts, Tim Conway.

AROUND THE WORLD IN EIGHTY DAYS. (1956) The passage of time has drained some of the vitality from Mike Todd's mammoth, all-star production and it now plays more like a stately progress. Inspired by Jules Verne and blessed with David Niven's light urbanity as Phineas Fogg, it is still a pleasant enough trip that needs a scorecard to note all the familiar faces crammed into its 3 hours, 18 minutes. Fogg bets his London cronies that he can make the trip in the given time.

★★★

D: Michael Anderson; W: S. J. Perelman, James Poe and John Farrow; Ph: Lionel Lindon; M: Victor Young.
Cast: David Niven, Shirley MacLaine, Robert Newton, Charles Boyer.

ARROWSMITH. (1932) Ronald Colman's Dr. Martin Arrowsmith is a country physician who encounters romantic and professional conflicts when he comes to an institute to do research on tropical diseases. John Ford's version of the Sinclair Lewis novel is incisive and compassionate.

★★★

D: John Ford; W: Sidney Howard; Ph: Ray June; M: Alfred Newman.
Cast: Ronald Colman, Helen Hayes, A.E. Anson, Richard Bennett.

THE ASPHALT JUNGLE. (1950) As so often happens in John Huston's films, greed disrupts and ruins the best-laid plans of criminals. In his well-observed and influential caper film, Huston makes his point lightly. A master criminal rounds up a crooked attorney and a disparate as well as desperate gang for a jewel robbery. The gangsters are drawn and acted with depth and, in some cases, sympathy.

★★★★

D: John Huston; W: Huston and Ben Maddow; Ph: Harold Rosson; M: Miklos Rozsa.
Cast: Sterling Hayden, Louis Calhern, Sam Jaffe, James Whitmore.

THE ATOMIC CAFE. (1982) An hilarious and slightly terrifying documentary about nuclear madness that collects military films and government pronouncements from the period between Hiroshima and the end of the fifties. The deft editing and shrewd choices offer a panorama of military and bureaucratic stupidity and remind us that lying was in fashion long before Watergate.

★★★★

D: Kevin Rafferty, Pierce Rafferty and Jayne Loader; M: Rick Eaker.

AT THE EARTH'S CORE. (1976) A feeble version of the Edgar Rice Burroughs science fantasy about a geological expedition that winds up at the center of the earth and amid much silliness involving sub-strata denizens. The film's chief tension lies in guessing which monster will burst through the wall hiding the studio commissary. Doug McClure shows all the animation of a pet rock and Peter Cushing, who usually brings a touch of class to films like this, makes a fool of himself. The special effects are creaky and the monsters seem to be made out of vinyl and Michelin tires.

PG. ★★

D: Kevin Connor; W: Milton Subotsky; Ph: Alan Hume; M: Mike Vickers.
Cast: Doug McClure, Peter Cushing, Cy Grant, Keith Barron, Caroline Munro.

AUTHOR! AUTHOR! (1982) At the time, Neil Simon was writing second-rate Neil Simon so this woeful and anti-woman comedy seemed redundant. Al Pacino deserved some applause for trying something light but the part of a Broadway playwright saddled with the offspring of several marriages doesn't suit his brooding screen presence. The film would have you believe that women can't stand children.

PG. ★★

D: Arthur Hiller; W: Israel Horovitz; Ph: Victor J. Kemper; M: Dave Grusin.
Cast: Al Pacino, Tuesday Weld, Dyan Cannon, Alan King.

AUTUMN SONATA. (1978) Ingmar Bergman emerged from the emotional nadir of *The Serpent's Egg* to invest this extraodinary study of a mother/daughter relationship with universal scope. The essence of the film contrasts the disparity between what parent and child are supposed or obliged to feel and the addled mixture of love and hate that can exist in reality. The daughter invites the mother, who has just lost her lover to a lingering disease, to visit the parsonage she shares with her husband.

R. ★★★★

D and W: Ingmar Bergman; Ph: Sven Nykvist.
Cast: Liv Ullmann, Ingrid Bergman, Halvar Bjork.

AVALANCHE. (1978) Tycoon Rock Hudson builds a ski resort in the wrong place and it disappears under tons of snow. Unfortunately, there is a long stretch of film about as interesting as a ski slope in August before this happens. Saint Bernards may enjoy it, but a stiff belt of brandy is advisable for two-legged viewers.

PG. ★

D: Corey Allen; W: Allen and Claude Pola; Ph: Pierre-William Glenn; M: William Kraft.
Cast: Rock Hudson, Mia Farrow, Robert Forster, Jeannette Nolan.

AVALANCHE EXPRESS. (1979) In order to escape the Soviets, a Russian mole working for the CIA has to burrow his way out of avalanches and various other attempts at assassination aboard a Milan-to-Rotterdam express. The plot makes intelligence agent a contradiction in terms and Mark Robson's last outing as a director deserves a place under its own pile of rocks.
PG. ★
D: Mark Robson; W: Abraham Polonsky; Ph: Jack Cardiff; M: Allyn Ferguson.
Cast: Robert Shaw, Lee Marvin, Linda Evans, Maximilian Schell.

THE AVIATOR'S WIFE. (1980) A teen-aged girl says that she would prefer her life to be like a novel and it's clear that the characters are an open book to Eric Rohmer. Another in his series called "Comedies and Proverbs", it is an essay on the distance between what people say and what they actually do. A neurotic young secretary detests the idea of marriage but wants the commitment it represents.
★★★★
D and W: Eric Rohmer; Ph: Bernard Lutic.
Cast: Philippe Marlaud, Marie Riviere, Anne-Laure Meury, Mathieu Carriere.

THE AWAKENING. (1980) A mummy movie in which the curse falls on a mummy-to-be. Charlton Heston, a manly Egyptologist bashes in the door of an ancient tomb and his pregnant wife begins to feel spasms. The rest is a variation on the possessed child motif that ignores the camp associations of mummies and treats words as if they should be embalmed instead of spoken.
R. ★★
D: Mike Newell; W: Allan Scott, Chris Bryant and Clive Exton; Ph: Jack Cardiff; M: Claude Bolling.
Cast: Charlton Heston, Susannah York, Jill Townsend, Stephanie Zimbalist.

B

THE BABE RUTH STORY. (1948) A foul tip rather than a home run that the greatest of all baseball legends deserved. The Babe's career is traced with William Bendix lumbering through the part and adding nothing to our perception of the athlete. Not that it's his fault.
★★
D: Roy del Ruth; W: Bob Considine and George Callahan; Ph: Philip Tunnura; M: Edward Ward.
Cast: William Bendix, Claire Trevor, Charles Bickford, William Frawley.

BABES IN ARMS. (1939) The first of the Mickey Rooney-Judy Garland partnerships in the "Hey, kids, let's put on a show!" vein. A hyper-kinetic Rooney, unrestrained by Busby Berkely, leads a gang of children, all the progeny of ex-vaudevillians, in a revue that will raise money to stave off parental bankruptcy. Believe it or not, it's a hit. Rooney even throws in a Clark Gable imitation.
★★★
D: Busby Berkeley; W: Jack McGowan and Kay Van Riper; Ph: Ray June; M: Rodgers and Hart.
Cast: Mickey Rooney, Judy Garland, Charles Winninger, Douglas MacPhail.

BABES IN TOYLAND. (1961) The efforts of the villainous Barnaby to spread misery in Toyland, cut Tom Thumb down a size or two and marry Mary Contrary himself. The Disney version of the Victor Herbert tale is flamboyant and rather lifeless despite the elaborate production numbers.
★★
D: Jack Donohue; W: Joe Rinaldi, Ward Kimball and Lowell S. Harley; Ph: Edward Colman; M: Victor Herbert.
Cast: Ray Bolger, Tommy Sands, Ed Wynn, Annette Funicello.

BABY BLUE MARINE. (1976) "It was another time. There was innocence," intones the narrator. Jan-Michael Vincent, by an unlikely means, goes home as a war hero even though he has been thrown out of boot camp. Small-town America in World War II is lovingly recreated, but the film views its characters with an ironic sophistication that is misplaced in the context.
PG.
★★
D: John Hancock; W: Stanford Whitmore; Ph: Laszlo Kovacs; M: Fred Karlin.

Cast: Jan-Michael Vincent, Glynnis O'Connor, Katherine Helmond, Bert Remsen.

BABY DOLL. (1956) The steam still rises from this earthy collaboration of Tennessee Williams and Elia Kazan. Time Magazine called it filthy and religious groups and right-wingers were up in arms. Today, with controversy long gone, we can view it as a cutting and accurate study of lust and corruption and one that Williams wrote beautifully. Carroll Baker, the girl-bride in her crib, is married to a cotton worker and the object of lustful advances from one of his enemies.
★★★★
D: Elia Kazan; W: Tennessee Williams; Ph: Boris Kaufman; M: Kenyon Hopkins.
Cast: Carroll Baker, Karl Malden, Eli Wallach, Mildred Dunnock.

BABY FACE NELSON. (1957) Mickey Rooney certainly has the right features even if he has too many years on him for the part. They didn't give Don Siegel much of a budget but he gave fans of the traditional rise-and-fall-and-go-down-shooting gangster movie their money's worth.
★★
D: Don Siegel; W: Irving Shulman and Daniel Mainwaring; Ph: Hal Mohr; M: Van Alexander.
Cast: Mickey Rooney, Cedric Hardwicke, Carolyn Jones, Chris Dark.

BABY IT'S YOU. (1983) John Sayles' strong suit is talk, but here he frames his dialogue in a logically developed narrative. Trenton, N.J., in the sixties is the scene of a high school romance where the boy and girl come from different classes. She is a Jewish princess and he a greaser with ambitions as a lounge singer. Familiar terrain, but Sayles' writing and directing elevate the material and he makes the wise decision to discuss what happened to them after graduation.
PG.
★★★★
D and W: John Sayles; Ph: Michael Balhaus;
Cast: Rosanna Arquette, Vincent Spano, Liane Curtis, Claudia Sherman.

THE BACHELOR PARTY. (1957) An evening intended for traditional stag carousing turns into depressing introspection for the participants. Each man confronts domestic and sexual problems and the essential drabness of his existence. Paddy Chayefsky wrote it as a television play and the acting and observation lift the film above the aridity of the idea.

★★★

D: Delbert Mann; W: Paddy Chayefsky; Ph: Joseph La Shelle; M: Paul Madeira.
Cast: Don Murray, E.G. Marshall, Jack Warden, Philip Abbott.

BACHELOR PARTY. (1984) Burn your invitation. Tom Hanks made a grotesquely bad boys-night-out picture before his big *Splash* with Daryl Hannah. Distasteful and always dumb jokes on everything from suicide to the single life.
R.   ★

D: Neal Israel; W: Israel and Pat Proft; Ph: Hal Trussell; M: Robert Folk.
Cast: Tom Hanks, Adrian Zmed, Tawny Kitaen, George Grizzard.

BACK ROADS. (1981) A road movie as leisurely and pleasant as the title suggests. Martin Ritt, who directed Sally Field in *Norma Rae*, guides her again in the story of an Alabama hooker and a ham-and-eggs fighter. It's typical of the film's humor when she notes that he spends more time on his back than she does. Beneath the earthy repartee, *Back Roads* explores the consequences of going through life without goals.
R.   ★★★

D: Martiin Ritt; W: Gary Devore; Ph: John A. Alonzo; M: Henry Mancini.
Cast: Sally Field, Tommy Lee Jones, David Keith, Miriam Colon.

BACK TO BATAAN. (1945) John Wayne is a marine officer who rallies freedom fighters in the Phillipines after Bataan is cut off. One of his more plodding propaganda films.

★★

D: Edward Dmytryk; W: Ben Barzman and Richard Landau; Ph: Nicholas Musuraca; M: Roy Webb.
Cast: John Wayne, Anthony Quinn, Beulah Bondi, Leonard Strong.

THE BAD AND THE BEAUTIFUL. (1952) Hollywood tried to bare its soul and discovered that it didn't have one. But Vincente Minnelli's look at the dream factory rebuts the contention that Hollywood people who make movies should not make movies about people who make movies. The story is told in flashbacks with Kirk Douglas as a director and the reminiscences of those who feel wronged by him.

★★★

D: Vincente Minnelli; W: Charles Schnee; Ph:

Robert Surtees; M: David Raksin.
Cast: Kirk Douglas, Walter Pidgeon, Lana Turner, Dick Powell.

BAD DAY AT BLACK ROCK. (1954) A film of excruciating and escalating suspense with Spencer Tracy leading a fine cast and setting a low-key tone that only adds to the tension. He is a one-armed veteran who disembarks from a train and finds himself in a quagmire of ill-feeling and guilt among the people of the small town. John Sturges is particularly adroit at suggesting the pettiness of such a community and how it can be corrupted into something much worse.

★★★★

D: John Sturges; W: Millard Kaufman and Don McGuire; Ph: William Mellor; M: Andre Previn.
Cast: Spencer Tracy, Robert Ryan, Ernest Borgnine, Lee Marvin.

BADLANDS. (1974) Terrence Malick's reticent, detached style, which later made *Days of Heaven* so extraordinary was here deployed in far more chilling fashion. Mallick wrote a fictional account of Charles Starkweather, a young psychotic who went on a killing spree in the midwest in 1959 and died in the electric chair. His companion is a 15-year-old girl and one of the victims is her father. Sissy Spacek and Martin Sheen are coldly effective as the fugitives.
R.   ★★★

D and W: Terrence Malick; Ph: Brian Probyn; M: George Tipton.
Cast: Martin Sheen, Sissy Spacek, Warren Oates, Ramon Bieri.

THE BAD NEWS BEARS. (1976) When it comes to discussing the American passion for winning, no one beats Michael Ritchie. And no one does a grudging curmudgeon as well as Walter Matthau. Add a bunch of foul-mouthed little leaguers and you have a baseball comedy that's a diamond in the rough. The best pitcher on the team is a girl, played with nonchalant aplomb by Tatum O'Neal.
PG.   ★★★

D: Michael Ritchie; W: Bill Lancaster; Ph: John A. Alonzo; M: Jerry Fielding.
Cast: Walter Matthau, Tatum O'Neal, Vic Morrow, Joyce Van Patten.

THE BAD NEWS BEARS IN BREAKING TRAINING. (1977) The boisterous Little League team, still given to foul tips and fouler language, return without their star pitcher

(Tatum O'Neal) or coach (Walter Matthau). This is a Triple-A franchise following a World Series champion to the plate. Michael Ritchie's keen eye for parent-child relationships is also missing from the line-up in a weak sequel that finds the team visiting the Astrodome for an exibition game.
PG. ★★
D: Michael Pressman; W: Paul Brickman; Ph: Fred J. Koenekamp; M: Craig Safan.
Cast: William Devane, Jack Haley, Clifton James.

THE BAD SEED. (1956) Patty McCormack repeated her stage role from a play by Maxwell Anderson. She is a child of outward innocence and boundless evil and the film is a stylish entry into what was to later become the province of hacks. It is still eerie and disquieting to watch the child casually plotting murder. Not surprisingly, the ending appended to the film had more to do with censorship pressure than what had gone before.
★★★
D: Mervyn LeRoy; W: John Lee Mahin; Ph: Harold Rosson; M: Alex North.
Cast: Patty McCormack, Nancy Kelly, Henry Jones, Eileen Heckart.

BAD TIMING. (1980) Nicholas Roeg's enigmatic and disjointed perusal of the love-and-death relationship of a stuffy psychiatrist and a free-loving woman who makes him obsessively jealous. It's like a maze with many dead-ends and little satisfaction when you finally emerge. Roeg's sleight of hand does not atone for the pompous, windy screenplay and a sadistically miscast Art Garfunkel.
★★
D: Nicholas Roeg; W: Yale Udoff; Ph: Anthony Richmond; M: Richard Hartley(dir.).
Cast: Art Garfunkel, Theresa Russell, Harvey Keitel, Denholm Elliott.

BALL OF FIRE. (1942) An arch variation of the Snow White story concocted by Billy Wilder and Charles Brackett. Barbara Stanwyck, a moll on the run, finds refuge with seven professors who have closeted themselves in an ivory tower in order to prepare a dictionary. Gary Cooper finds her more interesting than words.
★★★
D: Howard Hawks; W: Billy Wilder and Charles Brackett; Ph: Gregg Toland; M: Alfred Newman.

Cast: Gary Cooper, Barbara Stanwyck, Oscar Homolka, Henry Travers.

BAMBI. (1942) For a dismaying number of people who saw Walt Disney's animation classic in their childhood, the death of Bambi's mother is a still an alarming and wrenching memory. And it still upsets small children. Apart from that, *Bambi* represents Disney at his most techniquely imaginative and overbearingly cute. Bambi grows up with various gleefully realized forest friends and gets married.
★★★★
D: Walt Disney; W: Larry Morey; M: Frank Churchill.

BANANAS. (1971) Only Woody Allen would conceive of Howard Cosell doing a South American political assassination as a Wide World of Sports event. Only Howard Cosell would agree to do it. Woody escapes life as a Chaplinesque product tester to become the top revolutionary banana in a South American republic. The pace of the jokes is hectic and there are many more hits than misses.
★★★★
D: Woody Allen; W: Allen and Mickey Rose; Ph: Andrew Kostikyan; M: Marvin Hamlisch.
Cast: Woody Allen, Louise Lasser, Carlos Montalban, Jacobo Morales.

BANDOLERO. (1968) James Stewart poses as an executioner to free his brother from the noose and the sheriff pursues them to Mexico. Pretty much a waste of Stewart and an exemplar of the violent strain that was beginning to make itself felt in westerns.
★★
D: Andrew McLaglen; W: James Lee Barrett; Ph: William Clothier; M: Jerry Goldsmith.
Cast: James Stewart, Dean Martin, George Kennedy, Raquel Welch.

THE BAND WAGON. (1953) One of the numbers is "That's Entertainment" and the high spirited musical certainly lives up to it. The thin but serviceable plot casts Fred Astaire as a Hollywood has-been, a role he soon belies with his brilliant dancing. He goes to Broadway to attempt a comeback and to romance Cyd Charisse. There is room on this accomodating bandwagon for spoofs of both Mickey Spillane and Orson Welles
★★★★
D: Vincente Minnelli; W: Adolph Green and Betty Comden; Ph: Harry Jackson; M: Adolph Deutsch.

Cast: Fred Astaire, Cyd Charisse, Jack Buchanan, Oscar Levant.

BANG THE DRUM SLOWLY. (1973) John Hancock took the title literally; the pulse is slow and the tears are jerked unabashedly. Athletes have to undergo a form of death when their skills erode and they retire. Robert De Niro faces the real thing prematurely as a catcher with a New York team who has a terminal disease. The overwrought but still affecting drama concentrates on his relationship with the team's best pitcher as he faces the inevitable.

★★★

D: John Hancock; W: Mark Harris; Ph: Richard Shore; M: Stephen Lawrence.
Cast: Robert De Niro, Michael Moriarty, Vincent Gardenia, Phil Foster.

THE BANK DICK. (1940) W.C. Fields begins by breaking into a kid's piggy bank — and leaving an IOU —and then breaking up a bank robbery by mistake. The misadventures of Egbert Souse, town drunk and layabout, are not connected, but this contains some of the funniest work in indivudual scenes Fields ever put on film. It is W.C. ranged against those who are supposed to love him and against the whimsical blows of fate. And who could dislike a man who proudly declares, "I never smoked a cigarette until I was nine."

★★★★★

D: Eddie Cline ; W: Mahatma Kane Jeeves (Fields); Ph: Milton Krasner; M: Charles Previn.
Cast: W.C. Fields, Franklin Pangborn, Shemp Howard.

BANK HOLIDAY. (1938) Carol Reed's skilled handling of humor and far-fetched melodrama holds together a string of vignettes of the English of various classes enjoying a national holiday. A young nurse has the difficult task of telling a husband of his wife's death and then has a premonition about him while she is on an outing.

★★★

D: Carol Reed; W: Rodney Ackland and Roger Burford; Ph: Arthur Crabtree.
Cast: Margaret Lockwood, John Lodge, Hugh Williams, Rene Ray.

BARBARELLA. (1968) Derived from the French comic strip and something that Jane Fonda probably doesn't find very funny these days. It's a tacky piece of science fiction with Fonda as a 40th century astronaut embroiled with various odd types. The movie's continued camp following owes more to the dubious pleasure of comparing the worked-out, super-political feminist of today with Barbarella.

★★

D: Roger Vadim; W: Terry Southern; Ph: Claude Renoir; M: Bob Crewe and Charles Fox.
Cast: Jane Fonda, John Phillip Law, Anita Pallenberg, Milo O'Shea.

THE BARBARIAN AND THE GEISHA. (1958) The experiences of Townsend Harris, the first American consul to Japan in the mid-nineteenth century, told at the pace of a geisha tea ceremony. John Huston evinced no sign of what to do with the story and his old friend John Wayne is excruciatingly out of place—in both senses.

★★

D: John Huston; W: Charles Grayson; Ph: Charles Clarke; M: Hugo Friedhofer.
Cast: John Wayne, Eiko Ando, Sam Jaffe, Norman Thomson.

THE BARBARY COAST. (1935) On the the waterfront in San Francisco with Edward G. Robinson, who always did excellently by gangsters with charm. In this handsome recreation of life in the notorious district in the last century, Robinson is a local king-pin who discovers that it is one thing to make a star and another to make her love you.

★★★

D: Howard Hawks; W: Ben Hecht and Charles MacArthur; Ph: Ray June; M: Alfred Newman.
Cast: Edward G. Robinson, Miriam Hopkins, Joel McCrea, Walter Brennan.

THE BAREFOOT CONTESSA. (1954) Hollywood considered it a barefaced lie, but for Joseph L. Mankiewicz it's the unalloyed truth. Ava Gardner is discovered as an unshod flamenco dancer and finds stardom and misery in Hollywood, courtesy of the sleazes she encounters.

★★

D and W: Joseph L. Mankiewicz; Ph: Jack Cardiff; M: Mario Nascimbene.
Cast: Ava Gardner, Humphrey Bogart, Edmond O'Brien, Marius Goring.

BAREFOOT IN THE PARK. (1967) Robert Redford and Jane Fonda in a fifth floor walk-up in Greenwich Village. They are newly-weds and there is no elevator and there are points in Neil Simon's play when the dialogue represents a step-down from his best.

It's still breezy fun with Redford reprising the role that was a smash hit for him on Broadway.

★★★

D: Gene Saks; W: Neil Simon; Ph: Joseph La Shelle; M: Neal Hefti.
Cast: Robert Redford, Jane Fonda, Charles Boyer, Mildred Natwick.

BARRY LYNDON. (1976) In purely visual terms, Stanley Kubrick's version of Thackeray's picaresque novel is one of the most beautiful movies ever made. It goes beyond the re-creation of the rhythms of life in the eighteenth century to the evocation of the way the intellectuals of the Age of Reason viewed the world. These aspects tend to overwhelm Thackeray's hack work about an Irishman propelled from the sod into the maelstrom of the Seven Years War. The stately pace of the film is reinforced by baroque music and John Alcott's voluptuous photography which makes great use of natural light.

PG. ★★★★★

D and W: Stanley Kubrick; Ph: John Alcott; M: Leonard Rosenman (musical director).
Cast: Ryan O'Neal, Marisa Berenson, Patrick Magee, Hardy Kruger.

BATMAN. (1966) The Joker's on you in an attempt to capitalize on the then popular television series. The only real difference between large and small screen is in the production values and the wry balance of humor and camp that distinguishes the *Superman* films is nowhere in sight. The fearless duo challenges four of the favorite villains who plot to take over the world.

★★

D: Leslie Martinson; W: Lorenzo Semple, Jr.; Ph: Howard Schwartz; M: Nelson Riddle.
Cast: Adam West, Burt Ward, Cesar Romero, Lee Meriwether.

BATTLE BENEATH THE EARTH. (1968) Tunnelvision is yours in an offering that posits a Chinese plot to invade California by burrowing all the way with a laser beam and thus jeopardizing the hot tub industry. Fear not, our guys are waiting to slug it out.

★

D: Montgomery Tully; W: L. Z. Hargreaves; Ph: Kenneth Talbot; M: Ken Jones.
Cast: Kerwin Matthews, Vivienne Ventura, Robert Ayres, Peter Arne.

BATTLE BEYOND THE STARS. (1980) Cheerful hokum and not a bad chip off the *Star Wars* meteor. John Sayles' often arch script puts *The Seven Samurai* in outer space with mercenaries of various species gathering to defend a planet from heavily armed invaders. Richard Thomas is far too sober for Sayles' writing, which includes an amusing interplanetary discussion on the contents of a hot dog. Robert Vaughn repeats his burned-out gunslinger from *The Magnificent Seven*, from which Sayles also borrows.

PG. ★★

D: James T. Murakami; W: John Sayles; Ph: Daniel Lacambre; M: James Horner.
Cast: Richard Thomas, Robert Vaughn, George Peppard, John Saxon.

BATTLE CRY. (1954) The Marine Corps may have inspired a few good films, but this flag-waver is not among them. A group of recruits go off to boot camp and clamber over every cliche—including "turning boys into men"—on their way to combat. An intrusive narration by James Whitmore, more sex than most soldiers ever saw and Leon Uris' turgid script (adapted from his novel) makes the movie seem longer than World War II.

★★

D: Raoul Walsh; W: Leon Uris; Ph: Sid Hickox; M: Max Steiner.
Cast: Van Heflin, James Whitmore, Tab Hunter, Dorothy Malone.

BATTLE FOR THE PLANET OF THE APES. (1973) The fifth and, mercifully the last in the series really scraped the bottom of the cage. Various factions among the dominant apes squabble amongst themselves and humans live as mutants in ruined cities. But who cared by this time?

★★

D: J. Lee Thompson; W: John William Corrington and Joyce Corrington; Ph: Richard H. Kline; M: Leonard Rosenman.
Cast: Roddy McDowall, Claude Akins, Natalie Trundy, Severn Darden.

THE BATTLE OF CHILE. (1977) An impassioned left-wing polemic that is as subtle as a Peking wall-poster, the documentary chronicles the rise and fall of Salvatore Allende. Despite its inordinate length and Marxist stance, it is an absorbing piece beneath all the windy rhetoric. The Chilean director released a third installment in 1980 dealing with the capitalist conspiracy against Allende.

★★★

D and W: Patricio Guzman.

THE BATTLE OF THE BULGE. (1965) An intransigent division of Panzers disrupts the American advance in the Ardennes in 1944. The original running time ran to 167 minutes and the film itself bulges like a beer-drinker's stomach. Henry Fonda and Robert Shaw lend some class to the long, noisy proceedings.

★★

D: Ken Annakin; W: Philip Yordan, Milton Sperling and John Melson; Ph: Jack Hildyard; M: Benjamin Frankel.
Cast: Henry Fonda, Robert Shaw, Robert Ryan, Dana Andrews.

BATTLE TAXI. (1955) Never within hailing distance of an exciting war film. During the Korean conflict, when helicopters had not soared to their fashionable Vietnam heights, a pilot thinks it's demeaning to have to fly them. An assortment of episodes in the craft changes his mind.

★★

D: Herbert L. Strock; W: Malvin Ward.
Cast: Sterling Hayden, Arthur Franz, Marshall Thompson.

THE BEAST FROM 20,000 FATHOMS. (1953) A much-imitated monster movie in the *Oh, Godzilla* school where the awakened monster is released from an Arctic deep freeze. It decides to take Manhattan and Coney Island, too. The resurrected dinosaur takes an awfully long time to start chomping on the Big Apple and Ray Harryhausen's effects aren't worth the wait.

★★

D: Eugene Lourie; W: Lou Morheim and Fred Freiburger; Ph: Jack Russell; M: David Buttolph.
Cast: Paul Christian, Paula Raymond, Cecil Kellaway, Kenneth Tobey.

THE BEAST MUST DIE. (1974) But first you must decide which one is the werewolf and the movie pauses while you digest the evidence. A rich hunter wires his retreat for snooping and then invites his guests, one of whom has been known to bay at the moon.

★★

D: Paul Annett; W: Michael Winder; Ph: Jack Hildyard; M: Douglas Gamley.
Cast: Peter Cushing, Calvin Lockhart, Anton Diffring, Charles Gray.

THE BEAST WITH FIVE FINGERS. (1946) The work of diverse hands, including, of all people, Luis Bunuel. The great Spanish filmmaker reportedly contributed his talents to the filming of the hand whose fingers are

pointed at Peter Lorre. In an otherwise mundane five finger exercise, Lorre is in his element coping with the unwelcome attentions of a disembodied hand that belongs to a dead concert pianist. Still plays pretty well too.

★★★

D: Robert Florey; W: Curt Siodmak; Ph: Wesley Anderson; M: Max Steiner.
Cast: Peter Lorre, Andrea King, Robert Alda, J. Carroll Naish.

BEATLEMANIA, THE MOVIE. (1981) Sergeant Pepper should take those responsible, line them up against the wall and shoot them. An execrable collage of sixties newsreel footage with four young men clumsily imitating the Fab Four. It's an unconvincing illusion that makes one yearn for the reality.
PG.

★

D: Joseph Manduke; Ph: King Baggot; M: Paul McCartney and John Lennon.
Cast: Mitch Weissman, Tom Teeley, David Leon, Ralph Castelli.

BEAT STREET. (1984) A breakdancing movie that breaks down into four rather offensive plots that argue in favor of covering subways with graffiti as an artistic statement. The dumb goings-on are sprayed between the crevices left by the production numbers which are loud and energetic and not much else.
PG.

★

D: Stan Lathan; W: Andy Davis, Paul Golding and David Gilbert; Ph: Tom Priestly, Jr.; M: Harry Belafonte and Arthur Baker.
Cast: Rae Dawn Chong, Guy Davis, Jon Chardiet, Leon W. Grant.

BEAU GESTE. (1939) Percy Wren's story of brothers in the French Foreign Legion fighting Arabs and an in-house sadist—done with a vengeance by Brian Donlevy—was a popular silent film starring Ronald Colman. It was also filmed in 1966 with Telly Savalas and Guy Stockwell. The Gary Cooper version has by far the most style and spirit.

★★★

D: William Wellman; W: Robert Carson; Ph: Theodore Sparkuhl; M: Alfred Newman.
Cast: Gary Cooper, Ray Milland, Robert Preston, Brian Donlevy.

BEAU—PERE. (1981) Bertrand Blier, the director of *Get Out Your Handkerchiefs*, takes material that should be approached with a caution usually found only in bomb squads. A 14-year-old girl takes the place of her dead mother in the affections of her step-father. In Blier's adaptation of his novel, the father thinks he's in control of the situation even as he is flagrantly manipulated.

★★★

D and W: Bertrand Blier; Ph: Sacha Vierny; M: Philippe Sarde.
Cast: Patrick Dewaere, Ariel Besse, Maurice Ronet, Nathalie Baye.

BECKET. (1964) The division between church and state was never more dramatic and ultimately tragic than in the feud between Henry II and Thomas à Becket. What begins as friendship sours when Becket is made an archbishop and issues of principle arise. The acting transcends the inevitable glibness the film brings to vastly complicated history.

★★★

D: Peter Glenville; W: Edward Anhalt; Ph: Geoffrey Unsworth; M: Laurence Rosenthal.
Cast: Richard Burton, Peter O'Toole, Donald Wolfit, John Gielgud.

BEDAZZLED. (1967) Dudley Moore is the right height for a short-order cook in an uneven but often devilishly funny spoof on the Faust legend. His revue partner, Peter Cook, is the Devil, offering to make seven wishes come true in exchange for you know what. Non-stop gags of the sort that proved forerunners to the Monty Python films.

★★

D: Stanley Donen; W: Dudley Moore and Peter Cook; Ph: Austin Dempster; M: Peter Cook.
Cast: Peter Cook, Dudley Moore, Eleanor Bron, Raquel Welch.

THE BEDFORD INCIDENT. (1965) The strength of a sobering look at the possible beginning of World War III lies in its location—on the front line. There the strains of command are compounded by the awful consequences of making the wrong decision. Instead of Presidents and Presidiums, the scenario traces the pressures on a dictatorial destroyer captain playing an incredibly dangerous game with a Russian submarine. Richard Widmark is outstanding and *The Bedford Incident* is far more realistic and plausible than some of the more touted nuclear war films.

★★★★

D: James Harris; W: James Poe; Ph: Gilbert Taylor; M: Gerald Schurrmann.
Cast: Richard Widmark, Sidney Poitier, James MacArthur, Eric Portman.

THE BED SITTING ROOM. (1969) It is not difficult to see why Richard Lester's holocaust comedy bombed in atomic proportions at the box office. Its humor springs from *The Goon Show* and posits a post-nuclear Britain in which people turn into objects and the jokes only occasionally work. Unless you enter into the spirit of goonery tinged with a blacker wit, this is best left in the closet. It dealt a severe blow to Lester's career, from which he has happily now recovered.

★★

D: Richard Lester; W: John Antrobus; Ph: David Watkin; M: Ken Thorne.
Cast: Ralph Richardson, Rita Tushingham, Michael Hordern, Dudley Moore.

BEDTIME FOR BONZO. (1951) Political historians may find some explanation for the presence of James Watt in President Reagan's cabinet in this comedy about a scientist (Reagan) who brings up a chimp as a child. Given the chumpish chimp shows on network television—who can forget the immortal *Mr. Smith*?—Reagan has probably taken more than his fair share of abuse for Bonzo's antics. His first smart political decision was to disarm his future enemies by refusing to do the sequel.

★★

D: Frederick de Cordova; W: Lou Breslow and Val Burton; Ph: Carl Gurthrie; M: Frank Skinner.
Cast: Ronald Reagan, Diana Lynn, Walter Slezak, Lucille Berkely.

THE BEING. (1983) A throwback to the fifties with an environmental twist. Radioactive waste is the pollutant that sends a killer loose in an Idaho town. He's not a very prepossessing monster and the film's attempts at humor are labored.
R.

★★

D and W: Jackie Kong; Ph: Robert Ebinger; M: Don Preston.
Cast: Martin Landau, Jose Ferrer, Dorothy Malone, Ruth Buzzi.

BELL, BOOK AND CANDLE. (1955) The occult, in a refreshing change from the post-*Exorcist* fashion, is played for fun in this version of the Broadway comedy about a witch (Novak) who finds where her heart really lies. A good cast tries alchemy without ever turning the dross of the script into gold and this is pleasant rather than bewitching entertainment. The supporting work from Ernie Kovacs and Hermione Gingold spices the brew.

★★★

D: Richard Quine; W: Daniel Taradash; Ph: James Wong Howe; M: George Duning.
Cast: James Stewart, Kim Novak, Ernie Kovacs, Jack Lemmon, Hermione Gingold.

THE BELLES OF ST. TRINIANS. (1954) Ronald Searle's popular cartoon about mischievous school-girls made a very successful transition to the screen and was a box office hit. The girls are funny enough as they run wild through the bankrupt school but the real lesson in the art of screen comedy is delivered by Alistair Sim, who appears in drag as the beleaguered headmistress.
★★★
D: Frank Launder; W: Launder, Sidney Gilliat and Val Valentine; Ph: Stan Pavey; M: Malcolm Arnold.
Cast: Alistair Sim, Joyce Grenfell, Hermione Baddely, Irene Handl.

BELLE STARR. (1940) One of the greatest snow-jobs ever mounted by Hollywood and a misty-eyed look at the most notorious woman outlaw in the history of the West. Gene Tierney is no dumbell but she hardly seems persuasive as the woman who takes up a life of crime in vengeance against the damn Yankees. She marries Randolph Scott and they engage in a righteous war against carpetbaggers and other Northern miscreants.
★★
D: Irving Cummings; W: Lamar Trotti; Ph: Ernest Palmer; M: Alfred Newman.
Cast: Randolph Scott, Gene Tierney, Dana Andrews, John Shepperd.

A BELL FOR ADANO. (1945) Henry King's acute and touching version of John Hersey's celebrated novel. John Hodiak is especially effective as the American major charged with the administration of a small Italian town and coping with his love for a local girl. A generally thoughtful look at the problem of picking up the pieces and the pain of reconciliation after the war.
★★★
D: Henry King; W: Lamar Trotti and Norman Reilly; Ph: Joseph La Shelle; M: Alfred Newman.
Cast: John Hodiak, Gene Tierney, William Bendix, Richard Conte.

THE BELL JAR. (1979) A textbook example of why some novels —in this case poet Sylvia Plath's autobiographical account of a young woman's nervous breakdown—do not work on the screen. The depiction of mental disturbance visually is always tricky and Larry Peerce's direction excludes the necessary first person narrative and the wry wit in Plath's book. Esther is a college student who is torn between the desire to be a poet and the enticement of marriage and children. An honest, but doomed endeavor for both the character and the film-makers.
R.
★★
D: Larry Peerce; W: Marjorie Kellogg; Ph: Gerald Hirschfeld; M: Gerald Fried.
Cast: Marilyn Hassett, Anne Jackson, Julie Harris, Barbara Barrie.

THE BELLS OF SAINT MARY'S. (1945) The bells on the box office cash registers were ringing merrily for *Going My Way* and, as sequels go, Bing Crosby's return as Father O'Malley has its charm. He and Ingrid Bergman, the Mother Superior, have to raise funds in a poor parish.
★★★
D: Leo McCarey; W: Dudley Nichols; Ph: George Barnes; M: Robert Emmett Dolan.
Cast: Bing Crosby, Ingrid Bergman, Henry Travers, William Gargan.

BELOVED INFIDEL. (1959) Scott Fitzgerald, in his final drink-sodden years in Hollywood. He would have been amused at the idea of having Gregory Peck play him. It's a game effort but a basically calamitous piece of miscasting. Deborah Kerr is a little more comfortable—but not much—as Sheila Graham, the gossip columnist who has an affair with the writer.
★★
D: Henry King; W: Sy Bartlett; Ph: Leon Shamroy; M: Franz Waxman.
Cast: Gregory Peck, Deborah Kerr, Eddie Albert, Philip Ober.

BEND OF THE RIVER. (1952) The turns of the plot in the western are derivative, but James Stewart is as reliably professional as ever. In the Oregon of the 1840s he escorts a wagon train and leaves behind a past he would rather forget. The new country is less than welcoming with both whites and Indians registering their hostility to the new arrivals.
★★★
D: Anthony Mann; W: Borden Chase; Ph: Irving Glassberg; M: Hans Salter.
Cast: James Stewart, Arthur Kennedy, Rock Hudson, Julia Adams.

BENEATH THE PLANET OF THE APES. (1970) With the second Apes film the series degenerated into monkey business. The point and social commentary—not to mention the freshness and originality of *Planet of the Apes*—disappeared. James Franciscus lands in an attempt to find out what happened to the first expedition and is caught up in a conflict between the apes and a mutant race.

★★

D: Ted Post; W: Paul Dehn; Ph: Milton Krasner; M: Leonard Rosenman.
Cast: James Franciscus, Kim Hunter, Maurice Evans, Linda Harrison.

BENEATH THE TWELVE MILE REEF. (1953) A Florida family is wary of Greek divers bearing sponges. A standard effort involving two lovers whose families hate each other that is quite diverting when the characters are immersed in pursuit of sponges. Robert Wagner takes on an octopus in the main special effects sequence.

★★

D: Robert D. Webb; W: A.J. Bezzerides; Ph: Edward Cronjager; M: Bernard Herrmann.
Cast: Robert Wagner, Terry Moore, Gilbert Roland, J. Carrol Naish.

BEN-HUR. (1925) The story behind this $4 million extravaganza—an immense budget for the time—is an epic all to itself. Production began with the literal rather than promised cast of thousands in Rome in 1923 and then resumed in Hollywood the following year with a new creative team. What resulted was an immense and wooden retelling of Lew Wallace's tale of a life-long feud between a Jewish nobleman and his Roman nemesis. Its best scenes, not surprisingly, are the chariot race and the sea battle.

★★★

D: Fred Niblo; W: Bess Meredyth and Carey Wilson; Ph: Karl Struss.
Cast: Ramon Novarro, Francis X. Bushman, Carmel Myers, May McAvoy.

BEN-HUR. (1959) Even in 1959, the remake of the epic cost $15 million and economics and perhaps changing taste would make the mounting of such a spectacle out of the question today. As with the silent version, it is the set pieces—the sea battle and a chariot race that is one of the most exciting contests in all movies—that stay with the viewer. In an orgy of self-congratulation, Hollywood heaped Oscars on it and Charlton Heston certainly deserved his for his work in the lead. Ben Hur loses home and family, is enslaved and eventually triumphs. The full version of the film runs 217 minutes and that accounts for a pace that suggests a gallery powered by exhausted rowers.

★★★★

D: William Wyler; W: Karl Tunberg; Ph: Robert Surtees; M: Miklos Rozsa.
Cast: Charlton Heston, Jack Hawkins, Stephen Boyd, Hugh Griffith.

BENJI. (1974) Having scaled the heights of muttdom, showbiz division, as Higgins, the dog on television's long-running *Petticoat Junction*, Benji took to the big screen. The director, Joe Camp, said he wanted a dog who could say more with his face than humans could with their mouths. His dialogue gives Benji a big assist. Benji foils a kidnap scheme in a film that makes Disney seem hard-nosed.

G. ★★

D and W: Joe Camp; Ph: Don Reddy; M: Euel Box.
Cast: Peter Breck, Christopher Connelly, Patsy Garrett, Tom Lester.

BERSERK. (1968) The producers somehow conned Joan Crawford to take part in a horror film and perhaps the fact that the script was written with a coat-hanger attracted her. It is about the only implement not used in killing off various members of a traveling circus.

★★

D: Jim O'Conolly; W: Herman Cohen and Aben Kandel; Ph: Desmond Dickinson; M: Patrick John Scott.
Cast: Joan Crawford, Diana Dors, Ty Hardin, Judy Geeson.

BEST DEFENSE. (1984) Eddie Murphy had what was billed as a strategic guest appearance in another one of Dudley Moore's dreadful choices of material. For the viewer, a strategic withdrawal is strongly advised. Moore is an engineer who designs a tank that Murphy, an army lieutenant, has to test. The jokes here should try out for an army training film.

R. ★

D: Willard Huyck; W: Huyck and Gloria Katz; M: Patrick Williams.
Cast: Dudley Moore, Eddie Murphy, Kate Capshaw, Helen Shaver.

BEST FRIENDS. (1982) The movie's writers are married to each other. So they wrote a film about two screenwriters who live together and agonize over whether to make the final commitment. It's obviously intended as a wry look at the place of marriage in

contemporary relationships. But the couple agonizes over it as if only death could break up the union and divorce was impossible. In California?
PG.   ★★
D: Norman Jewison; W: Barry Levinson and Valerie Curtin; Ph: Jordan Croneweth; M: Michel Legrand.
Cast: Burt Reynolds, Goldie Hawn, Jessica Tandy, Barnard Hughes.

THE BEST LITTLE WHOREHOUSE IN TEXAS. (1982) You know a musical is in trouble when the best number is done by Charles Durning, the pudgy character actor. He steals the movie, but it's not worth taking. Colin Higgins, in telling the story of golden-hearted whores at the local cathouse, finds himself selling the idea that it's fun to be a prostitute. Burt Reynolds is the good ole boy sheriff and Dolly Parton, the saintly madame fending off reformers. It's an inert romance.
R.   ★
D: Colin Higgins; W: Higgins, Larry L. King and Peter Masterson; Ph: William A. Fraker; M: Carol Hall.
Cast: Burt Reynolds, Dolly Parton, Dom DeLuise, Charles Durning .

THE BEST MAN. (1964) One of the best films about the American political process. Gore Vidal, a witty and trenchant observer of human ambition and weakness, adapted his own stage melodrama and Franklin Schaffner made it work very well on the screen. It examines the fight for the party's presidential nomination between a liberal (Henry Fonda) and an anti-communist (Cliff Robertson).
                                               ★★★★
D: Franklin Schaffner; W: Gore Vidal; Ph: Haskell Wexler; M: Mort Lindsey.
Cast: Henry Fonda, Cliff Robertson, Lee Tracy, Margaret Leighton.

THE BEST OF ENEMIES. (1961) David Niven and Alberto Sordi are opposing officers in North Africa in 1941 who come to like each other in spite of everything. The target is the futility of war and the point is that it would not happen so often if we knew and understood one another a little better. It has been said many times before and with more finesse, but Niven and Sordi give it the correct light flavor.
                                               ★★★
D: Guy Hamilton; W: Jack Pulman; Ph: Giuseppe Rotunno; M: Nino Rota.

Cast: David Niven, Alberto Sordi, Michael Wilding, Amedeo Nazzari.

THE BEST OF WALT DISNEY'S TRUE-LIFE ADVENTURES. (1975) Disney's ventures into the animal kingdom began with *Seal Island* in 1949 and ended 11 years later with *Jungle Cat*. Some of the cuteness of the studio's animated animals spilled over into the filming of the real thing. Music and editing were used to make their behavior seem human. There are, for all that, many good moments in this well-chosen anthology.
G.   ★★★
D: James Algar; W: Algar, Winston Hibler and Ted Sears; Ph: Alfred G. Milotte and others; M: Paul Smith, Buddy Baker and Oliver Wallace.
Cast: Winston Hibler(narrator).

THE BEST THINGS IN LIFE ARE FREE. (1956) Predictably, the best things in the musical are the songs that made the team of DeSylva, Brown and Henderson a hit in the twenties. The good-humored and rather stilted reprise of their career is mercifully interrupted by such winners as "Birth of the Blues" and "Button up Your Overcoat".
                                               ★★
D: Michael Curtiz; W: William Bowers and Phoebe Ephron; Ph: Leon Shamroy; M: Lionel Newman.
Cast: Gordon MacRae, Ernest Borgnine, Dan Dailey, Sheree North.

THE BEST YEARS OF OUR LIVES. (1945) The irony suggested in the title is that, for many men, the war offered escape and excitement as well as danger. At the same time, peace was supposed to hold great promise. William Wyler follows three veterans back to the often wrenching adjustments of civilian life with a candor that was much praised in its day.
                                               ★★★
D: William Wyler; W: Robert Sherwood; Ph: Gregg Toland; M: Hugo Friedhofer.
Cast: Myrna Loy, Frederic March, Dana Andrews, Teresa Wright.

BETRAYAL. (1983) Harold Pinter's silences are worth the ten-minute speeches of other playwrights. In the expanded version of his play, he demonstrates the power of what is left unsaid. He is a pioneer explorer in the terrain between what is said and what is meant and this brilliant dissection of a broken marriage and adultery is one of his most accessible scripts. Ben Kingsley is the cuck-

olded husband and Pinter shows what can be done with basically soap opera ingredients.
R. ★★★★★
D: David Jones; W: Harold Pinter; Ph: Mike Fash; M: Dominic Muldowney.
Cast: Ben Kingsley, Jeremy Irons, Patricia Hodge.

THE BETSY. (1978) An alternately preposterous and incestuous saga of a Detroit auto-making dynasty that makes only gross points. It covers the industry from its early days to the present through the life of Loren Hardeman (Laurence Olivier in one of his most demeaning roles). Multi-million dollar decisions seem to be based solely on oedipal hatreds and if Detroit really worked like this, we'd all be cycling to work.
R. ★
D: Daniel Petrie; W: William Bast and Walter Bernstein; Ph: Mario Tosi; M: John Barry.
Cast: Laurence Olivier, Robert Duvall, Tommy Lee Jones, Katharine Ross.

BETWEEN THE LINES. (1977) Silver's second film is a warm and funny celebration of sixties counter-culture. It's not a sentimental dirge to lost innocence, even though the time is the mid-seventies and much has changed for the staff of the Back Bay Mainline, an alternative newspaper in Boston. The loose plot allows members of the ensemble their full measure and the film has a touching sense of people who have seen a special time in their lives pass and found nothing to replace it.
R. ★★★★
D: Joan Micklin Silver; W: Fred Barron; Ph: Kenneth Van Sickel.
Cast: John Heard, Lindsay Crouse, Jeff Goldblum, Jill Eikenberry.

BEYOND A REASONABLE DOUBT. (1956) Fritz Lang's farewell to American filmmaking is a despairing view of humanity encompassed in a thriller whose initial cleverness eventually becomes contrivance. A novelist, at the suggestion of his newspaper editor father-in-law, has himself framed for a murder. The idea is to expose the methods of an ambitious prosecutor. But did the novelist actually do it?
★★★
D: Fritz Lang; W: Douglas Morrow; Ph: William Snyder; M: Herschel Burke Gilbert.
Cast: Dana Andrews, Joan Fontaine, Sidney Blackmer, Philip Bourneuf.

BEYOND THE FOREST. (1949) Some-times a single line will make a movie live forever. Here it is Bette Davis, declaring with Olympian contempt, "What a dump!" And what a film! The melodrama surrounding the line is best described as distraught and no collector of great camp should miss Davis's stormy passage. She's a bitch who wrongs her husband and has an affair with a rich businessman from Chicago.
★★
D: King Vidor; W: Lenore Coffee; Ph: Robert Burks; M: Max Steiner.
Cast: Bette Davis, Joseph Cotten, David Brian, Ruth Roman.

BEYOND THE LIMIT. (1983) In a provincial Argentinian town, a boozy British consul marries a prostitute. He is cuckolded by a young doctor who is suspected of leftist connections by the local police chief. John Mackenzie gave Graham Greene's novel the look of *Missing*, but the emotional core is absent. There are so many moral dilemmas in the film that Mackenzie loses his way in trying to follow them all.
R. ★★★
D: John Mackenzie; W: Christopher Hampton; Ph: Phil Meheux; M: Paul McCartney.
Cast: Michael Caine, Richard Gere, Bob Hoskins, Elpidia Carrillo.

BEYOND THE POSEIDON ADVENTURE. (1979) And beneath contempt. Most of the action, appropriately, takes place in the bilges of the capsized vessel and the sequel proves that rats have much to teach us about the correct attitude toward sinking ships. Michael Caine leads the salvage effort, searching for money and finding caricatures, and Telly Savalas is an international crook trying to thwart him. Karl Malden says it all inside the ship: "It's a floating time bomb."
PG. ★
D: Irwin Allen; W: Nelson Gidding; Ph: Joseph Biroc; M: Jerry Fielding.
Cast: Michael Caine, Telly Savalas, Karl Malden, Sally Field.

THE BIBLE. (1966) Actually the first part of Genesis. We should all get down on our knees and thank God that it didn't go any further. John Huston played Noah and directed with the care of a man who is late for the ark and feels the first drops of rain. He's still the best part of the film, which he also narrates. It is not a movie to send you dashing to read the book.
★★
D: John Huston; W: Christopher Fry; Ph:

Giuseppe Rotunno; M: Toshiro Mayuzumi.
Cast: John Huston, Richard Harris, Stephen Boyd, George C. Scott.

THE BIG BRAWL. (1980) Chop-sockey, Chicago style, starring Jackie Chan, one of Bruce Lee's heirs unapparent. 1938 mobsters prey upon Chinese immigrants and try to take over Chan's father's restaurant. Mostly martial arts fights interrupted by silly plot.
R. ★
D and W: Robert Clouse; Ph: Robert Jessup; M: Lalo Schifrin.
Cast: Jackie Chan, Jose Ferrer, Kristine De Bell, Ron Max.

THE BIG BUS. (1976) Disaster movies and their ludicrous excesses are spoofed, but how do you top the singing nuns and ailing kids in the real thing? *Airplane* managed with non-stop zaniness, but *The Big Bus* never gets out of the depot. A nuclear powered bus on its way from New York to Denver goes off course in more than one sense. Good cast, weak script and permanently pre-empted by *Airplane*.
PG. ★★
D: James Frawley; W: Fred Freeman, Lawrence J. Cohen; Ph: Harry Stradling, Jr.; M: David Shire.
Cast: Joseph Bologna, Stockard Channing, John Beck, Ned Beatty.

THE BIG CHILL. (1983) In only his second effort as a director, Lawrence Kasdan placed himself in some very select company with a compassionate and sardonic discussion of refugees from the sixties. These men and women have to live with a double dose of disillusion because they left college with such unusually high ideals. They are reunited at the funeral of one of the old gang and the weekend is time of communal shock, recrimination and release. Kasdan balances the anger and the laughter effortlessly and catharsis has never been so wryly humorous.
R. ★★★★★
D: Lawrence Kasdan; W: Kasdan and Barbara Benedek Ph: John Bailey; M: Various artists.
Cast: Tom Berenger, Glenn Close, Jeff Goldblum, William Hurt.

THE BIG COUNTRY. (1958) A western that in visual scale and scoring lives up to its billing. Its strong suit is the sense of the grandeur and vastness of the landscape and the greed of the men who wish to own it.

Jerome Moross' vibrant music is as much a star as any on the big names. Gregory Peck is a sailor who doesn't feel at home on the range and who finds himself in the midst of a range war between two families dominated by belligerent patriarchs. The plot and the acting never quite measure up to the ambitious conception.
★★★
D: William Wyler; W: Sy Bartlett, James Webb, Jessamyn West and Robert Wilder; Ph: Franz Planer; M: Jerome Moross.
Cast: Gregory Peck, Charlton Heston, Jean Simmons, Burl Ives.

THE BIG FIX. (1978) An off-beat private eye story where the characters are far more arresting than the developments. Richard Dreyfuss' Moses Wine is a refugee from sixties counter culture forced to relive the old days when a former girl-friend asks him to investigate some dirty tricks in a Congressional election. Some neat twists on the genre's conventions but too much heavy-handed nostalgia for the sixties.
PG. ★★★
D: Jeremy Paul Kagan; W: Roger L. Simon; Ph: Frank Stanley; M: Bill Conti.
Cast: Richard Dreyfuss, Susan Anspach, Bonnie Bedelia, John Lithgow.

THE BIG HEAT. (1953) Glenn Ford's quest for revenge when the mob kills his wife with a bomb intended for him could have been strictly police routine. Fritz Lang turned it into a prized *film noir* in its bleak, cynical view of life and the dazzling technique with which it is staged. Ford's Detective Dave Bannion is thrown off the force, but he never gives up in his efforts to nail the head of the local mob.
★★★★
D: Fritz Lang; W: Sydney Boehm; Ph: Charles Lang; M: Daniele Amfitheatrof.
Cast: Glenn Ford, Gloria Grahame, Alexander Scourby, Lee Marvin.

BIG JIM McLAIN. (1952) Made at the height of the Cold War and a grim domestic atmosphere, it again shows that John Wayne's weaker efforts often involve political pointscoring. He's a government agent in Hawaii busting up a communist spy ring.
★★
D: Edward Ludwig; W: James Edward Grant; Ph: Archie Stout; M: Emil Newman.
Cast: John Wayne, Nancy Olson, James Arness, Alan Napier.

THE BIG LIFT. (1950) Mostly a let-down with American pilots braving the commnunist blockade of Berlin. Montgomery Clift is lost in the ponderous debate over the issues and a lackluster plot involving his romance with a German girl.

★★

D and W: George Seaton; Ph: Charles Clarke; M: Alfred Newman.
Cast: Montgomery Clift, Paul Douglas, Cornell Borchers, O.E. Hasse.

BIG RED. (1961) Norman Tokar's first film for Disney (he was to become an in-house stalwart for the studio) is a modest and unassuming exercise in the boy meets dog, boy loses dog genre. Walter Pidgeon, as the initially sour kennel owner, gives the film an anchor and the Canadian scenery is imposing.

★★

D: Norman Tokar; W: Louis Pelletier; Ph: Edward Colman; M: Oliver Wallace.
Cast: Walter Pidgeon, Gilles Payant, Emile Genest, Janette Bertrand.

THE BIG SCORE. (1983) Crude and ineffective try at a black Dirty Harry picture. Fred Williamson is no Clint Eastwood when it comes to playing a rogue cop who doesn't like the liberal court system. Frank Hooks is a cop who goes after a drug dealer and then finds himself out on the street looking for revenge.

R. ★

D: Fred Williamson; W: Gail Morgan Hickman; Ph: Joao Fernandes; M: Jay Chat Taway.
Cast: Fred Williamson, John Saxon, Nancy Wilson, Richard Roundtree.

THE BIG SKY. (1952) Kirk Douglas goes up the Missouri River as a fur trapper in the early nineteenth century and Howard Hawks allows him to take his time. Douglas is engaging enough to disarm objections to the leisurely flow of the story and the scenery is captivating.

★★★

D: Howard Hawks; W: Dudley Nichols; Ph: Russell Harlan; M: Dmitri Tiomkin.
Cast: Kirk Douglas, Arthur Hunnicutt, Elizabeth Threatt, Dewey Martin.

THE BIG SLEEP. (1946) There are people around who saw Howard Hawks' film in 1946 and are still trying to figure out the plot. Hawks, the writers and even Raymond Chandler admitted to being equally puzzled. And so, The

Big Sleep is a movie that howdunit can be more important than whodunit. Humphrey Bogart left a lasting imprint on Phillip Marlowe and the private eye movie. Nothing that is said is what it seems as Marlowe investigates a case of blackmail and trips over an assortment of bodies.

★★★★

D: Howard Hawks; W: Leigh Brackett, William Faulkner and Jules Furthman; Ph: Sid Hickox; M: Max Steiner.
Cast: Humphrey Bogart, Lauren Bacall, Martha Vickers, John Ridgely.

THE BIG SLEEP. (1977) Michael Winner extradited Philip Marlowe from L.A. to London, a transition that makes Robert Mitchum look slightly ridiculous in the title role. Mitchum does a very fine Marlowe but the California seediness is painfully absent. The plot, this time around, is clearer. Try Mitchum in *Farewell My Lovely*.

R. ★★

D and W: Michael Winner; Ph: Robert Paynter; M: Jerry Fielding.
Cast: Robert Mitchum, Sarah Miles, Richard Boone, Candy Clark.

THE BIG STORE. (1941) The Marx Brothers have the run of a department store when private detective Groucho comes to investigate skulduggery. Generally regarded as one of the weakest pieces of movie Marxism, it was the last the brothers made at MGM. There are a few funny scenes and, of course, Margaret Dumont.

★★★

D: Charles Reisner; W: Sid Kuller, Hal Fimberg and Ray Golden; Ph: Charles Lawton; M: George Stoll.
Cast: Groucho, Chico and Harpo Marx, Margaret Dumont.

BIG WEDNESDAY. (1978) John Milius dropped his macho guard long enough to wave goodbye to the heyday of surfing. It is well above the run-of-the-dune beach movie and probably takes surfing too seriously. Three young surfers come of age in the sixties and seventies and face assorted crises like the draft. Surfing should never be taken this mystically, but Milius made an often touching movie.

PG. ★★★

D: John Milius; W: Milius and Dennis Aaberg; Ph: Bruce Surtees; M: Basil Poledouris.
Cast: Jan-Michael Vincent, Gary Busey, William Katt, Patti D'Arbanville.

BILL COSBY—HIMSELF. (1983) Live performance by the versatile comedian that was filmed in Toronto in 1981. He mugs his way through familiar terrain—the disasters that beset us in ordinary life. A good reflection of his talent and one that does not wear out its welcome in the brisk 105 minute running time.
PG.   ★★★
D and W: Bill Cosby; Ph: Joseph Wilcox.

BILLION DOLLAR BRAIN. (1967) Michael Caine's third outing as the eccentric British agent Harry Palmer. Harry is more than a match for espionage opposition, but a poor loser to Ken Russell's hostile and often incomprehensible direction. Of interest only to that dwindling band of diehards who wonder what Russell would do in such a genre. Palmer is confronted with a nutty American tycoon who wants to subvert communism. Filmed in Finland.
                                        ★★
D: Ken Russell; W: John McGrath; Ph: Billy Williams; M: Richard Rodney Bennett.
Cast: Michael Caine, Oscar Homolka, Francoise Dorleac, Karl Malden.

BILLY JACK. (1971) Tom Laughlin's crude but timeless appeal to unarticulated teenage resentment of The System. It is not hard to see why such simplistic nonsense found a huge audience, but it surely is depressing. He is the Vietnam vet helping the kids take on bigots who don't like a "Freedom School".
                                        ★★
D: Tom Laughlin ; W: Laughlin and Delores Taylor; Ph: Fred Koenekamp; M: Mundell Lowe.
Cast: Tom Laughlin, Delores Taylor, Bert Freed, Clark Howat.

BILLY LIAR. (1963) One of the mysteries of movies is why Tom Courtenay didn't go on to a brilliant international career after his hilarious work in *Billy Liar*. He is a British Walter Mitty, a lowly and very bored clerk who avenges himself against life's many trials and indignities by drifting off into fantasy. It is one of the landmark British comedies of the sixties and its sustaining idea hasn't dated at all.
                                        ★★★★
D: John Schlesinger; W: Keith Waterhouse and Willis Hall; Ph: Denys Coop; M: Richard Rodney Bennett.
Cast: Tom Courtenay, Julie Christie, Wilfred Pickles, Mona Washbourne.

BILLY TWO HATS. (1974) An odd-ball western featuring Gregory Peck, as a Bible-thumping Scottish outlaw, and the Sinai desert masquerading as Mexico. The producers even built a western town from scratch on the outskirts of Tel Aviv. The movie is on the fringe of interest. Jack Warden is a vengeful lawman chasing Peck and a young half-breed after a bank robbery.
PG.   ★★
D: Ted Kotcheff; W: Alan Sharp; Ph: Brian West; M: John Scott.
Cast: Gregory Peck, Desi Arnaz, Jr., Jack Warden, Sian Barbara Allen.

THE BINGO LONG TRAVELING ALL-STAR AND MOTOR KINGS. (1976) An illuminating and exuberant glimpse at one of the darker chapters in American sports—the exclusion of blacks from major league baseball. The film stays on the pitcher's mound and shuns the soap box and the outrage of hindsight. It is easy-going and funny and catches the feel of what life on the road must have been like for great black ball players like Satchell Paige and Josh Gibson.
PG.   ★★★★
D: John Badham; W: Hal Barwood, Matthew Robbins; Ph: Bill Butler; M: William Goldstein.
Cast: Billy Dee Williams, Richard Pryor, James Earl Jones, Rico Dawson.

BIRDMAN OF ALCATRAZ. (1962) John Frankenheimer and Burt Lancaster labor mightily and quite successfully against the inherent problem of making a prison sentence interesting without resorting to riots and escapes. It's the true story of Robert Stroud, who spent forty years turning himself into an authority on birds. His collisions with authority and his passion for his calling keep things going.
                                        ★★★
D: John Frankenheimer; W: Guy Trosper; Ph: Burnett Guffey; M: Elmer Bernstein.
Cast: Burt Lancaster, Karl Malden, Thelma Ritter, Edmond O'Brien.

THE BIRDS. (1963) Like most Alfred Hitchcock films, *The Birds* can be taken on several levels. It is superficially a splendidly filmed, if ineptly written suspense story in which—for no accountable reason—the bird population of Bodega Bay in California sets upon the human inhabitants. The tension as they gather at a playground climber is excruciating. Hitchcock placed some very abrupt changes of mood in *The Birds* and beneath the surface is his bleak view of life and the fragility of our most entrenched assumptions about it.

★★★★

D: Alfred Hitchcock; W: Evan Hunter; Ph: Robert Burks; M: Bernard Herrmann.
Cast: Tippi Hedren, Rod Taylor, Jessica Tandy, Suzanne Pleshette.

BITE THE BULLET. (1975) An action western with an incisive view of some American values. An endurance horse race is the arena for discussing an attitude voiced by one of the characters: "If you're not the first and the best, if you don't win, then you're not American." Crisply written and directed and Gene Hackman is the anchor of the film as a cowboy indifferent to victory.
PG.   ★★★
D and W: Richard Brooks; Ph: Harry Stradling; M: Alex North.
Cast: Gene Hackman, Ian Bannen, Candice Bergen, Jan-Michael Vincent.

BITTERSWEET LOVE. (1976) The cruel realities of the problem of incest are evaded in a soppy treatment of a thoroughly implausible idea. Husband and pregant wife discover they are half-brother and half-sister. The consistently half-witted script plays as if it were rejected for *Days of Our Lives* and the score sounds as if it were written for Mantovani's funeral.
PG.   ★★
D: David Miller; W: Adrian Morrall and D.A. Kellogg; Ph: Stephen Katz; M: Ken Wannberg.
Cast: Lana Turner, Robert Lansing, Scott Hylands, Meredith Baxter Birney.

BLACK AND WHITE IN COLOR. (1977) Jean-Jacques Annaud's wryly observed anti-war film stunned everyone by winning the best foreign film Oscar over heavy competition (notably *Cousin, Cousine* and *Seven Beauties*). Set in colonial Africa in 1914, it finds French and Germans living amiably together and in mutual contempt for the natives. The arrival of news of the outbreak of war changes everything. The dying, of course, is done by the natives and the mood of the film grows increasingly somber. If its points are obvious, they remain inarguable and well-presented.
★★★★
D: Jean-Jacques Annaud; W: Annaud and Georges Conchon; Ph: Claude Agostini; M: Pierre Bachelet.
Cast: Jean Carmet, Catherine Rouvel, Jacques Dufilho, Jacques Spiesser.

BLACK BEAUTY. (1946) An also-ran. Anna Sewell's 1879 tale of the girl who loves and loses her horse and who is finally saved from a fire by the animal is given a half-hearted run-through.
★★
D: Max Nosseck; W: Lillie Hayward and Agnes Christine Johnston; Ph: Roy Hunt ; M: Dmitri Tiomkin.
Cast: Mona Freeman, Richard Denning, Evelyn Ankers, Charles Evans.

THE BLACK BIRD. (1976) An ill-fated attempt to pluck the memory of *The Maltese Falcon*. George Segal has to carry the load as Sam Spade's son, but the pathetic satire keeps getting caught between sly references to the great original and sustaining itself as a full-length comedy, Elisha Cook, Jr., the cheap gunsel in the 1941 film, and Lee Patrick, Spade's secretary, return to what is essentially a humorous vacuum. A game, klutz performance from George Segal is also wasted.
PG.   ★★
D and W: David Giler; Ph: Philip Lathrop; M: Jerry Fielding.
Cast: George Segal, Stephane Audran, Elisha Cook, Jr., Lee Patrick.

BLACKBOARD JUNGLE. (1955) Now chiefly celebrated for its theme song—Bill Haley's "Rock Around the Clock"—Richard Brooks' charged drama of juvenile delinquency retains something more than historic interest. Turn back the clock to a time when the idea of youthful disgruntlement and rebellion against one's parents and teachers was an alarming new development. Even if the novelty has worn off, Brooks' direction makes an arresting look at the way we were. Vic Morrow is the leading thug in a school where Glenn Ford is trying to teach.
★★★
D and W: Richard Brooks; Ph: Russell Harlan; M: Bill Haley and the Comets.
Cast: Glenn Ford, Anne Francis, Louis Calhern, Vic Morrow.

BLACK CHRISTMAS. (1975) No, this is not a soul version of the Bing Crosby film. Originally released as *Silent Night, Evil Night* and atrocious by any name. A sorority house is terrorized by an inventive murderer on Christmas Eve. Margot Kidder drinks a lot as one of the sisters. You can't blame her and at least she went on to better things than this Canadian schlock.
R.   ★

D: Bob Clark; W: Roy Moore; Ph: Reg Morris; M: Carl Zittrer.
Cast: Olivia Hussey, Keir Dullea, Margot Kidder, Marian Waldman.

THE BLACK HOLE. (1980) The spaceship Cygnus is stationed on the edge of a black hole and there is a large gap in the middle of the Disney space epic where the plot should be. The humans act like androids and much of the action is given over to robots. Maximilian Schell is the Captain Nemo-style mad scientist who does not welcome visitors. The special effects are quite impressive but the final plunge into the black hole is a bad trip burdened with bogus mysticism.
PG.   ★★
D: Gary Nelson; W: Jeb Rosebrook and Gerry Day; Ph: Frank Phillips; M: John Barry.
Cast: Maximilian Schell, Anthony Perkins, Ernest Borgnine, Yvette Mimieux.

THE BLACK LEGION. (1937) A sincere indictment of the Ku Klux Klan with a factory worker—and the audience—having their eyes opened to the true nature and purpose of the society. The worker joins after a setback at the factory.
                                          ★★★
D: Archie Mayo; W: Abem Finkel, Robert Lord and William Wister Haines; Ph: George Barnes.
Cast: Humphrey Bogart, Erin O'Brien Moore, Dick Foran, Ann Sheridan.

THE BLACK ROSE. (1950) Thomas Costain's sprawling novel of a Saxon soldier of fortune who ventures to the Far East because of his disgust with the Normans became a sprawling film. It turns into a rather slow road to China and gets downright silly once the adventurer(Tyrone Power) and his trusty companion arrive. He returns with the secret of gunpowder, but *The Black Rose* lacks the spark of great adventure.
                                          ★★
D: Henry Hathaway; W: Talbot Jennings; Ph: Jack Cardiff; M: Richard Addinsell.
Cast: Tyrone Power, Orson Welles, Jack Hawkins, Cecile Aubry.

THE BLACK SHIELD OF FALWORTH. (1954) Tony Curtis, Hollywood's knight, loose in medieval England and armed with a Brooklyn accent. He's miscast but game as a wronged young man seeking vengeance and justice in a quite enjoyable version of Howard Pyle's rousing *Men of Iron*.
                                          ★★★
D: Rudolph Mate; W: Oscar Brodney; Ph:

Irving Glassberg; M: Joseph Gershenson.
Cast: Tony Curtis, Janet Leigh, David Farrar, Barbara Rush.

THE BLACK STALLION. (1978) Carroll Ballard invested Walter Farley's popular children's story with an almost mystical quality that guarantees its appeal to all ages. A spellbinding film whose magic springs from an understanding of how childhood fantasies conflict with the demands of reality and induce a sense of loss in later life. A boy loses his father in a shipwreck and is saved by the stallion he befriended on the voyage. They are marooned on an idyllic island and then rescued. Superlative photography.
G.   ★★★★★
D: Carroll Ballard; W: Melissa Mathison and Jeanne Rosenberg; Ph: Caleb Deschanel; M: Carmine Coppola.
Cast: Kelly Reno, Mickey Rooney, Teri Garr, Clarence Muse.

THE BLACK STALLION RETURNS. (1983) In this sequel to the sumptuously beautiful Carroll Ballard film, Arabs make off with the beloved black, thus fueling our anti-OPEC sentiments. The film is a stolid, predictable adventure with Kelly Reno crossing the Altantic in search of the lost steed. The Arabs want the stallion to enter it in a vital horse race, but the sequel barely places.
PG.   ★★★
D: Robert Dalva; W: Richard Kletter and Jerome Kass; Ph: Carlo Di Palma; M: George Delerue.
Cast: Teri Garry, Kelly Reno, Vincent Spano, Allen Goorwitz.

BLACK SUNDAY. (1977) One of the first post-Vietnam films to focus on a veteran unhinged by the war. John Frankenheimer's polished thriller is a taut and skilled piece of popular film-making that builds inexorably to an Arab terrorist attack on the Super Bowl. The movie succeeds in plunging the viewer into its outlandish premise and Bruce Dern's trademark psychotic propels the film toward an exciting climax on the big day.
R.   ★★★★
D: John Frankenheimer; W: Kenneth Ross, Ernest Lehman, Ivan Moffat; Ph: John Alonzo; M: John Williams.
Cast: Bruce Dern, Robert Shaw, Marthe Keller.

THE BLACK SWAN. (1942) Swordplay and swashbuckling to the hilt and some arch lines and situations dreamed up by the worldly and cynical Ben Hecht set the tone for a classic pirate movie. Henry Morgan takes over as governor of Jamaica and finds his authority disputed by Tyrone Power. George Sanders as Redbeard and Maureen O'Hara's flaming red hair add to the color.

★★★★

D: Henry King; W: Ben Hecht and Seton J. Miller; Ph: Leon Shamroy; M: Alfred Newman.
Cast: Tyrone Power, Maureen O'Hara, Laird Cregar, George Sanders.

THE BLACK WINDMILL. (1974) A secret agent exercise that is not sufficiently secretive in its plotting to reach a sustained level of tension. Michael Caine is a hardened professional whose son is kidnapped by a couple running guns to IRA terrorists. Don Siegel loves these one-man-against-the-world scenarios and he manages the complex elements well enough, even if the end is exceedingly anticlimactic.

PG. ★★★
D: Don Siegel; W: Leigh Vance; Ph: Outsama Rawi; M: Roy Budd.
Cast: Michael Caine, Donald Pleasence, Delphine Seyrig, Clive Revill.

BLAZING SADDLES. (1974) Not all the cylinders in the Colt .45 were loaded when Mel Brooks fired this barrage at the western. It is not the best of his parodies—the honor belongs to *Young Frankenstein.* Cleavon Little is the sheriff, but the town doesn't want to be saved by a black. Every conceivable western cliche is inverted. Sometimes the results are merely vulgar —cowboys eating beans around a campfire and breaking wind. Sometimes they are hilarious, such as the pastor's sermon, Frankie Laine's opening song and Madeline Kahn's fine spoof of Marlene Dietrich.

R. ★★★
D: Mel Brooks; W: Brooks, Norman Steinberg, Richard Pryor, Andrew Bergman and Alan Uger; Ph: Joseph Biroc; M: John Morris.
Cast: Mel Brooks, Harvey Korman, Cleavon Little, Gene Wilder.

BLITHE SPIRIT. (1945) One of the more successful of the ghost stories so popular in this era, largely because Noel Coward is the ghost-writer. David Lean's translation of the play is diligent rather than inspired. A novelist who makes the mistake of dealing with a medium (blithely batty Margaret Rutherford) finds himself sharing a house with his second wife and the ghost of his first.

★★★

D: David Lean; W: Noel Coward; Ph: Ronald Neame; M: Muir Mathieson.
Cast: Rex Harrison, Constance Cummings, Kay Hammond, Margaret Rutherford.

THE BLOB. (1958) A giant and growing mass of what looks like strawberry Jello rolls into town, but nobody believes Steve McQueen when he sounds the alarm. A brain of gelatinous consistency helps in making it all the way through. Sci-fi mediocrity now remembered as McQueen's first leading role.

★★

D: Irving Yeaworthy; W: Kate Phillips and Theodore Simonson; Ph: Thomas Spalding; M: Ralph Carmichael.
Cast: Steve McQueen, Aneta Corseaut, Olin Howlin, Earl Rowe.

BLOOD ALLEY. (1955) The mention of communism in the presence of John Wayne was like waving a red flag at a bull. And this rather hysterical tirade against the commies responds like a provoked bull. It's a crude makeshift adventure with Wayne leading his charges to freedom in Hong Kong and its minimal suspense is undermined by its virulent political stance.

★★

D: William Wellman; W: A.S. Fleischmann; Ph: William Clothier; M: Roy Webb.
Cast: John Wayne, Lauren Bacall, Paul Fix, Joy Kim.

BLOOD AND SAND. (1941) Rita Hayworth makes a pass at a bullfighter(Tyrone Power) who is not a very convincing matador in the remake of Rudolph Valentino's huge hit of the twenties. This clumsiness at least makes the scene in which he is gored credible. Otherwise Power is on the horns of a dilemma, caught between Hayworth and ever-faithful Linda Darnell. The movie is saved from being a gore-bore by Mamoulian's spirited direction and the colorful and atmospheric photography.

★★★

D: Rouben Mamoulian; W: Jo Swerling; Ph: Ernest Palmer; M: Alfred Newman.
Cast: Tyrone Power, Rita Hayworth, Linda Darnell, Anthony Quinn.

SIDNEY SHELDON'S BLOODLINE. (1979) A two-hour fashion show that makes *Sidney Sheldon's Clothesline* a better title. The heiress to a large pharmaceutical fortune and an even larger wardrobe struggles for control of the company over a board and family who have odd vices to go along with unbridled greed. There is a nasty misogynist subplot involving pornography and "snuff" films and it leaves you with the feeling imparted by an anesthetic that won't wear off.

R.   ★

D: Terence Young; W: Laird Koenig; Ph: Freddie Young; M: Ennio Morricone.

Cast: Audrey Hepburn, Ben Gazzara, James Mason, Irene Papas.

BLOOD WEDDING. (1981) Quite simply, one of the best dance films ever made. Carlos Saura, the director of *Cria*, and Antonio Gades, the renowned dancer, combine for an incandescent flamenco version of Lorca's suitably passionate play. The flamenco here is light years removed from tourist-trap stomping. Saura also solves the usual problem of how much of the audience and its response to include. He shoots a dress rehearsal with only a remarkably fluent camera as the viewer. The charged tension of the dancing is dazzling.

★★★★★

D: Carlos Saura; W: Federico Garcia Lorca; Ph: Teo Escamilla.

Cast: Antonio Gades, Cristina Hoyos, Juan Antonio Jimenez, Pilar Cardenas.

BLOW OUT. (1981) Although encumbered by Brian De Palma's fascination with killing women, *Blow Out* is a pointed, relevant and technically sophisticated thriller. A sound technician accidentally records evidence which proves that a Presidential candidate's accident was in fact a murder. The treatment of politics is peremptory, but the dark paranoia of the technician's efforts to make himself and his recordings heard are very well done. John Travolta dispensed with the sexual trappings and gave his strongest performance in films here.

R.   ★★★

D and W: Brian De Palma; Ph: Vilmos Zsigmond; M: Pino Donaggio.

Cast: John Travolta, Nancy Allen, John Lithgow, Dennis Franz.

THE BLUE ANGEL. (1930) When Josef von Sternberg went to Berlin to create the creepily atmospheric tale of the downfall of a stuffy professor he was supposed to make it a vehicle for Emil Jannnings. But he chose a then unknown Marlene Dietrich to play the nightclub singer whose charms seduce the professor and a new sensuality was born on the screen. When she sings "Falling in Love Again," it is easy to understand the teacher's doomed passion. The camera work and production design contribute to a feeling of uniquely Teutonic decay. Edward Dmytryk remade it in 1959 with catastrophic results.

★★★★★

D: Josef von Sternberg; W: Robert Liebmann, Karl Zuckmayer and Karl Vollmoeller; Ph: Gunther Rittau; M: Frederick Hollander.

Cast: Emil Jannings, Marlene Dietrich, Kurt Gerron, Hans Albers.

THE BLUE BIRD. (1940) The first version of a children's story that proved fraught with peril for grown film-makers. Shirley Temple's fans stayed away in droves from the good-looking but clumsily Teutonic and inert allegory of a little girl's search for the bird of happiness.

★★

D: Walter Lang; W: Ernest Pascal; Ph: Arthur Miller; M: Alfred Newman.

Cast: Shirley Temple, Spring Byington, Nigel Bruce, Eddie Collins.

THE BLUE BIRD. (1976) Maurice Maeterlinck's supposedly ageless fairy tale seems positively senile in this clumsy third version from George Cukor. A joint American-Soviet venture about children seeking the bird of happiness emerges as a star-crossed combination of Slavic solemnity and Hollywood tackiness. Harry Andrews would like to forget he played an oak tree in this one. Funereal and no fun for kids

G.   ★★

D: George Cukor; W: Hugh Whitemore, Alfred Hayes and Alexei Kapler; Ph: Freddie Young; M: Irwin Kostel, Lionel Newman.

Cast: Elizabeth Taylor, Jane Fonda, Harry Andrews.

BLUE COLLAR. (1978) Paul Schrader's directing debut is a sometimes powerful film about the powerless —assembly line workers in Detroit. The frustrations of a numbing existence governed by the companies and unions are well caught in the lives of three men. They become involved in the robbery of their own union and the discovery of corruption and Schrader veers between wild comedy and violent gloom.

R.   ★★★

D: Paul Schrader; W: Schrader and Leonard Schrader; Ph: Bobby Byrne; M: Jack Nitzsche.

Cast: Richard Pryor, Harvey Keitel, Yaphet Kotto, Ed Begley, Jr.

THE BLUE LAGOON. (1949) The ineffably named Victorian novelist Henry Devere Stacpoole produced a book that was for many years considered racy. In the first version of the story of two children growing up on a desert island, adventure took precedence over sexual curiosity with the shipwrecked youngsters taking on smugglers.

★★★

D and W: Frank Launder; Ph: Geoffrey Unsworth; M: Clifton Parker.
Cast: Donald Houston, Jean Simmons, Noel Purcell, Cyril Cusack.

THE BLUE LAGOON. (1980) Still waters run shallow in the remake. Brooke Shields, despite a knowing face, wonders about the emergence of her "boobies". The story of the two castaways discovering each other depends for its interest on a Victorian attitude to sex that is no longer relevant. A sexual awakening that strikes the modern eye as perfectly natural is supposed to be the point of tension. Not surprisingly, its solemn treatment of puberty was a big hit with those going through it.

R. ★★
D: Randal Kleiser; W: Douglas Day Stewart; Ph: Nestor Almendros; M: Basil Poledouris.
Cast: Brooke Shields, Christopher Atkins, Leo McKern, William Daniels.

THE BLUE MAX. (1966) The Blue Max is Germany's ultimate medal, but much of the writing deserves a Purple Heart. Despite the muddy plot, the photography of combat in the air is briliantly executed and its spirit amply captured by Jerry Goldsmith's score. Heavy slogging on the ground with James Mason doing yet another "good" German and poor-boy George Segal making it out of the infantry trenches to become an heroic fighter pilot.

★★

D: John Guillermin; W: Gerald Hanley, David Pursall and Jack Seddon; Ph: Douglas Slocombe; M: Jerry Goldsmith.
Cast. James Mason, George Segal, Ursula Andress, Jeremy Kemp.

THE BLUES BROTHERS. (1980) John Belushi and Dan Aykroyd brought their popular *Saturday Night Live* creations to the screen for a multi-million dollar extravaganza of car chases and crashes. They are trying to reunite their band and save an orphanage. The characters are too limited for a feature-length film, but there are a few amusing moments, including the brothers' act in a country and western bar.

PG. ★★

D: John Landis; W: Landis and Dan Aykroyd; Ph: Stephen Katz; M: Ira Newborn.
Cast: John Belushi, Dan Aykroyd, James Brown, Kathleen Freeman.

BLUE THUNDER. (1983) John Badham's helicopter epic is so deafening that you can't hear yourself think—and that's precisely the idea. A wild fusion of hair-raising high-tech stunts and brain-numbing plot, it deals with technology allowing government to encroach on personal privacy. But *Blue Thunder* is a thunderous celebration of that technology. Roy Scheider, who has few rivals in this kind of film, is a Vietnam veteran piloting an advanced police helicopter and discovering a conspiracy in high places. Good fun if you don't think about it.

R. ★★★
D: John Badham; W: Don Jakoby and Dan O'Bannion; Ph: John Alonzo; M: Arthur B. Rubinstein.
Cast: Roy Scheider, Warren Oates, Daniel Stern, Candy Clark.

BOB AND CAROL AND TED AND ALICE. (1969) Paul Mazursky's bow as a director is very much of its time and, in its better scenes, catches the climate of sexual uncertainty of the late sixties. With high good humor—and with inspired work from Dyan Cannon and Elliott Gould—he dissects two marriages. Both are under pressure from changes in the air and the sense that marriage means missing out on something. Mazursky unfolds it in vignettes and the note of coyness that creeps in occasionally is the only irritant besides a miscast Natalie Wood.

★★★

D: Paul Mazursky; W: Mazursky and Larry Tucker; Ph: Charles Lang; M: Quincy Jones.
Cast: Elliott Gould, Dyan Cannon, Robert Culp, Natalie Wood.

BOBBY DEERFIELD. (1977) A racing driver lives with the terrible risks he takes on the track by reducing his responses to the outside world and denying his emotions. He meets his antithesis in a dying woman. She is played by Marthe Keller in a performance so bad that it becomes the film's nemesis. Instead of seeking every medical recourse available, the driver holds her hand and the film as a whole is neutral rather than moving. It is redeemed to some degree by its all too brief racing sequences and a beautifully done balloon race.

PG. ★★

D: Sydney Pollack; W: Alvin Sargent; Ph: Henri Decae; M: Dave Grusin.
Cast: Marthe Keller, Al Pacino, Annie Duperey, Walter McGinn.

BODY AND SOUL. (1981) The boxing movie suffers a black eye in a remake that should have been stopped in the first round. Leon Isaac Kennedy stars as a black Rocky, who abandons a medical career to punch his way to the top of the welterweight division. The awful screenplay isn't even bantamweight and Kennedy goes beyond stupidity to create something that is at once prurient and sentimental.
R.   ★
D: George Bowers; W: Leon Isaac Kennedy; M: Webster Lewis.
Cast: Leon Isaac Kennedy, Jayne Kennedy, Perry Lang, Peter Lawford.

BODY HEAT. (1981) The steam generated by the erotic scenes should not obscure a work of bleak vision and considerable skill from Lawrence Kasdan. His accomplished debut is a very contemporary version of a forties *film noir* with only a few moments where he gets lost in the murky terrain. William Hurt's Ned Racine is a cool but not too bright lawyer who happens into a consuming passion for Kathleen Turner during a stupefying heat wave. "You're not too smart. I like that in a man," she tells him and she's not kidding. What happens is not original, but the treatment is.
R.   ★★★
D and W: Lawrence Kasdan; Ph: Richard Kline; M: John Barry.
Cast: William Hurt, Kathleen Turner, Richard Crenna, Ted Danson.

THE BODY SNATCHER. (1945) A potent and well-made horror piece about a doctor whose curiosity gets the better of his ethics in nineteenth century Edinburgh. He makes a covenant with a coachman (Boris Karloff) to rob graves for specimens and it comes back to haunt him in a much admired climax. The film wears its years gracefully. It is based on the short story by Robert Louis Stevenson.
★★★★
D: Robert Wise; W: Philip MacDonald and Carlos Keith; Ph: Robert de Grasse; M: Roy Webb.
Cast: Boris Karloff, Henry Daniel, Bela Lugosi. Edith Atwater.

THE BOLD AND THE BRAVE. (1956) A rather timid war effort with a trio of American soldiers fighting their way through Italy in 1944 and stopping for a little romance. Much is a made of the fact that one of them is a religious fanatic. There is a diverting crap game scene with Mickey Rooney.
★★
D: Lewis Foster; W: Robert Lewis; Ph: Sam Leavitt; M: Herschel Burke Gilbert.
Cast: Wendell Corey, Mickey Rooney, Don Taylor, Nicole Maurey.

BONNIE AND CLYDE. (1967) The sixties went back to the thirties and consummated Hollywood's long romance with the gangster. Freed from the Depression-era constrictions which dictated that crime must not be seen to pay, Arthur Penn was free to take any tack he chose. He opted for a startlingly original approach filled with jittery contrasts—the central one being the just plain folks who happen to rob banks and kill people. The period is richly evoked to frame the dark humor and ironic view of what is and is not perceived to be moral. Warren Beatty and Faye Dunaway bring off their parts flawlessly and the support is brilliant. It was the attitudes to justice housed in *Bonnie and Clyde* rather than its considerable violence that established it as towering achievement in its own right and a film whose influence is still felt today.
★★★★★
D: Arthur Penn; W: Robert Benton and David Newman; Ph: Burnett Guffey; M: Charles Strouse.
Cast: Warren Beatty, Faye Dunaway, Gene Hackman, Estelle Parsons.

LES BONS DEBARRAS. (1980) From an unusual French quarter—the Laurentian mountains of Quebec. A girl on the brink of adolescence becomes expert at manipulating the love and guilt of parents for her own ends. Her tragedy is that she understands this technique more than herself. Poorly organized and full of digressions into vignettes of the hard life of a poverty-stricken region.
★★
D: Frank Mankiewicz; W: Rejean Ducharme; Ph: Michel Brault.
Cast: Charlotte Laurier, Marie Tifo, Germain Houd, Louise Marleau.

BOOM! (1968) The loud thud you hear is that of several reputations hitting the ground. It is found on a Mediterranean island where a millionairess spends her last summer dying of tuberculosis and using up more handkerchiefs than Camille. Tennessee Williams' dialogue creaks with overweight as a poet who is supposed to represent the angel of death shows up as the woman's final lover. One of the sorriest of the Taylor-Burton collaborations.

★★

D: Joseph Losey; W: Tennessee Williams; Ph: Douglas Slocombe; M: John Barry.
Cast: Richard Burton, Elizabeth Taylor, Noel Coward, Michael Dunn.

BOOMERANG. (1947) Elia Kazan adopted a documentary style that was certainly appropriate because the film is based on a real case. A minister is found dead and a man is accused. However, the public prosecutor comes to believe in his innocence and has to face pressure from the leading citizens. Kazan makes it a vocal plea for idealism and sticking to one's principles.

★★★

D: Elia Kazan; W: Richard Murphy; Ph: Norbert Brodine; M: David Buttolph.
Cast: Dana Andrews, Jane Wyatt, Lee J. Cobb, Cara Williams.

THE BORDER. (1982) Tony Richardson managed to capture the futility, corruption and hypocrisy that surrounds attempts to control immigration from Mexico, but he has no real viewpoint. What could have been an indictment of a system that supports agribusiness becomes a lurid melodrama involving a guard (Jack Nicholson) who is both appalled and compromised by what he sees. Nicholson admirers and lovers of first-rate screen acting should not miss a performance that transcends the mediocrity of the movie.

R. ★★

D: Tony Richardson; W: Deric Washburn, Walon Green and David Freeman; Ph: Ric Waite; M: Ry Cooder.
Cast: Jack Nicholson, Valerie Perrine, Harvey Keitel, Warren Oates.

BORDERLINE. (1980) The complexities of the immigration issue give way to Charles Bronson's limited repertoire of expressions and conventional manhunt tension. He is a border guard seeking the murderer of one of his deputies.

R. ★★

D: Jerrold Freedman; W: Freedman and Steve Kline; Ph: Tak Fujimoto ; M: Gil Melle.
Cast: Charles Bronson, Bruno Kirby, Karmin Murcelo, Ed Harris.

BORN FREE. (1965) The true story of a Kenya game warden and his wife who raised a lion cub named Elsa and then had to retrain it so that—as an adult—she could survive in the wilds. The lion's share of the praise, quite predictably, goes to the animals who are caught in handsome photography.

★★★

D: James Hill; W: Gerald L.C. Copley; Ph: Kenneth Talbot; M: John Barry.
Cast: Virginia McKenna, Bill Travers, Geoffrey Keen.

BORN YESTERDAY. (1950) A twist on Pygmalion with Judy Holliday's Billie establishing the dumb blonde as a screen archetype. Broderick Crawford decides that his image and his dame need upgrading, so he hires William Holden to confer some class on Billie. Inevitably, instruction leads to something else. Suavely directed by George Cukor and Holliday won a deserved Oscar for her performance.

★★★

D: George Cukor; W: Albert Mannheimer; Ph: Joseph Walker; M: Frederick Hollander.
Cast: Judy Holliday, Broderick Crawford, William Holden, Howard St John.

THE BOSTON STRANGLER. (1968) Tony Curtis, so justly maligned on so many occasions, does have some credits to be proud of and this is one of them. His Albert De Salvo, a schizophrenic responsible for a sensational series of murders of young women, is wholly convincing. De Salvo lived the normal humdrum life of a plumber and another existence as a murderer. He could not remember the latter. The attempt to dramatize his state of mind is not wholly successful, but what a refreshing change from all the mad killer movies of the seventies. Henry Fonda is the dogged detective pursuing the perplexing crimes.

★★★★

D: Richard Fleischer; W: Edward Anhalt; Ph: Richard Kline; M: Lionel Newman.
Cast: Tony Curtis, Henry Fonda, George Kennedy, Mike Kellin.

BOTANY BAY. (1952) Hugh Tallant is an American medical student framed for highway robbery and dispatched to Australia on a convict ship in the 1790s. His nemesis is a brutal ship captain, done with more class than the film deserves by James Mason. An unusual setting—the Australian penal colony—but the plot is rather weary.

★★

D: John Farrow; W: Jonathan Latimer; Ph: John Seitz; M: Franz Waxman.
Cast: Alan Ladd, James Mason, Patricia Medina, Cedric Hardwicke.

BOULEVARD NIGHTS. (1979) A journeyman gang melodrama that crawls along at the speed of one of the "low riders" popular in the L.A. barrio. Michael Pressman's effort is more honorable than the customary exploitation but the characters are superficial. A man tries to save his younger brother from gang life.
R. ★★
D: Michael Pressman; W: Desmond Nakano; Ph: John Bailey; M: Lalo Schifrin.
Cast: Richard Yniguez, Danny De La Paz, Marta Du Bois, James Victor.

BOUND FOR GLORY. (1976) Hal Ashby's beautiful and evocative re-creation of the Depression and the Dust Bowl captures the life and spirit of Woody Guthrie, the peerless voice of the downtrodden. Arranged like a leisurely and discursive folk song, the movie concentrates on the events that formed Guthrie's politics. Carrradine is excellent and his voice has the same scrawny eloquence as Guthrie's. Wexler's sumptuous photography won a deserved Oscar.
PG. ★★★★★
D: Hal Ashby; W: Robert Getchell; Ph: Haskell Wexler; M: Leonard Rosenman.
Cast: David Carradine, Melinda Dillon, Ronnie Cox.

THE BOUNTY. (1984) David Lean wanted to make the third film of this rich story into two three-hour movies. The task of making one fell to New Zealand's Roger Donaldson and the view of the mutiny is rather revolutionary. In this account, Captain Bligh is as courageous as he is unmoving and Fletcher Christian is headstrong and occasionally foolish. This allows screenwriter Robert Bolt a great deal more leeway in pushing the mutiny and its origins into a realistic grey area. A brave voyage that consistently prefers thought and discussion to action.
PG. ★★★
D: Roger Donaldson; W: Robert Bolt; Ph: Arthur Ibbetson; M: Vangelis.
Cast: Anthony Hopkins, Mel Gibson, Laurence Olivier, Edward Fox.

BOXCAR BERTHA. (1972) Martin Scorsese's second effort doesn't bear the personal imprint of *Mean Streets*, which he made in 1973 and which marked him as a major talent. His direction of the Depression era drama is able and judicious. Barbara Hershey takes up with gangsters and the film makes the usual points about the responsibility of economic conditions for her behavior.
★★★
D: Martin Scorsese; W: Joyce and John Corrington; Ph: John Stephens; M: Gilb Guilbeau.
Cast: Barbara Hershey, Barry Primus, David Carradine, Bernie Casey.

THE BOY FRIEND. (1971) The anorectic Twiggy gave it the old college try, but the demands of the lead in the Sandy Wilson musical about a stage company in Portsmouth in the twenties are really beyond her. Ken Russell's overblown direction and inflation of the numbers doesn't help.
★★
D and W: Ken Russell; Ph: David Watkin; M: Ian Whittaker.
Cast: Twiggy, Christopher Gable, Max Adrian, Tommy Tune.

THE BOYS FROM BRAZIL. (1978) Gregory Peck abandoned his good-guy image to give a snorting, manic account of Joseph Mengele, the doctor who killed Jews by the thousand at Auschwitz. Peck and an equally absorbing Laurence Olivier are wasted in an inane and incredible plot about breeding a new Fuhrer. The premise is interesting, but the assertion that a new Hitler could find the same amenable climate as pre-war Germany is ludicrous. The movie is limply paced and draws attention to its deficiencies.
R. ★★
D: Franklin Schaffner; W: Heywood Gould; Ph: Henri Decae; M: Jerry Goldsmith.
Cast: Gregory Peck, Laurence Olivier, James Mason, Lili Palmer.

THE BOYS IN COMPANY C. (1978) Like the American involvement in Southeast Asia, Sidney Furie's movie gets in deeper trouble the longer it spends in Vietnam. Five young marines go through boot camp in an excellent opening, but when they get to the war, the film is carried away by its own anger. One of the few traditional war movies about Vietnam.
R. ★★★
D: Sidney J. Furie; W: Furie and Richard Natkin; Ph: Godfrey Godar; M: Jaime Mendoza-Nava.
Cast: Stan Shaw, Andrew Stevens, James Canning, Michael Lembeck.

BRAINSTORM. (1983) A terrific idea that suffers from arrested development, Douglas Trumbull's speculation on the invention of a device that allows the wearer to experience the thoughts and emotions of others is long on high tech flair and short on character. If such a Thoughtman were marketed by a corporation like Sony the collision between ethics and technology would be shattering. Trumbull makes some well-taken points about the domination of machines, but his works suffers from the same thing. Natalie Wood died during the filming, but Trumbull managed to finish it without visible damage.
PG. ★★★
D: Douglas Trumbull; W: Phillip Frank Messina and Robert Stitzel; Ph: Richard Yuricich; M: James Horner.
Cast: Natalie Wood, Christopher Walken, Louise Fletcher, Cliff Robertson.

BRANNIGAN. (1975) One of the sorriest efforts of Wayne's final years casts him as a Chicago detective showing British bobbies how real justice is dispensed. The punch-ups take place in scenic spots around London and Wayne never looks anything but old and out-of-place. He is sent there to demean Scotland yard and extradite a mobster.
PG ★★
D: Douglas Hickox; W: Christopher Trumbo and Michael Wayne; Ph: Freddie Cooper; M: Dominic Frontiere.
Cast: John Wayne, Richard Attenborough, John Vernon, Mel Ferrer.

BRASS TARGETS. (1978) War "faction" built around gold and speculation. The bullion is aboard a train and the conjecture is that the death of General George Patton was not an accident but linked to a robbery organized by renegade American officers. They are willing to kill their own men, but the film takes little interest in revealing them. George Kennedy's Patton is cartoon apoplexy that has the misfortune to go up against George C. Scott's classic portrait. Five star foolishness.
PG. ★★
D: John Hough; W: Alvin Boretz; Ph: Tony Imi; M: Laurence Rosenthal.
Cast: George Kennedy, Robert Vaughn, Sophia Loren, John Cassavetes.

THE BRAVADOS. (1958) Henry King, who directed Gregory Peck in the superb *The Gunfighter*, guides him in another grimly moralistic western that's almost as good. Peck relentlessly pursues and kills the men he believes murdered his wife. When he catches the last of them, he learns the terrible truth of their innocence. A powerful and sobering rebuttal to the usual frontier vengeance posture.
★★★★
D: Henry King; W: Philip Yordan; Ph: Leon Shamroy; M: Lionel Newman.
Cast: Gregory Peck, Joan Collins, Stephen Boyd, Albert Salmi.

BREAD AND CHOCOLATE. (1978) Franco Brusati's much praised scrutiny of migrant workers in a society that considers them an inferior necessity —in this case an Italian waiter in Switzerland. He moves from broad and pointed humor as the waiter tries to land a permanent job to a scathing denunciation of the plight of uprooted Italians. Things end on a note of maudlin anger. He should have trusted his rapier wit to make his case.
★★★
D: Franco Brusati; W: Brusati, Nino Manfredi and Iaia Fiastri; Ph: Luciano Tovoli; M: Daniel Patrucci.
Cast: Nino Manfredi, Anna Karina, Johnny Dorelli, Paolo Turco.

BREAKER MORANT. (1980) A superbly acted story of enduring relevance that ponders the issue of the application of peacetime moral and legal standards to wartime conduct. Three Australian officers are accused of committing atrocities during the Boer War. Unlike the traditional court martial picture, *Breaker Morant* says that the issue is not guilt or innocence but how blame is to be apportioned. Morant, an Aussie folk hero, changed his attitude to the enemy when his best friend was tortured and Bruce Beresford pleads his case without sermonizing.
PG. ★★★★★
D: Bruce Beresford; W: Beresford, Jonathan Hardy and David Stevens; Ph: Don McAlpine; M: Phil Cuneen.
Cast: Jack Thompson, Edward Woodward, John Waters, Charles Tingwell.

BREAKHEART PASS. (1976) A western whodunit that is itself done in by Charles Bronson's impersonation of a wooden Indian. A troop train on its way to a fort beset by a diptheria epidemic has a murderer on board. Bronson is a Federal undercover agent trying to put an end to the strangeness on the train, but his inert acting is merely a strain.
PG. ★★

33

D: Tom Gries; W: Alistair MacLean; Ph: Lucien Ballard; M: Jerry Goldsmith.
Cast: Charles Bronson, Richard Crenna, Jill Ireland, Ben Johnson.

BREAKING AWAY. (1979) A brilliant and refreshing response to the thrice-familiar question: "Is there life after high school?" Four blue collar Indiana 19-year-olds grapple with the answer in a college town that heightens their resentment of opportunities denied them. The screenplay is a font of invention and as funny as it is accurate. Peter Yates showed an unerring eye for both the truth and youthful capacity for fantasy and self deception. One of the best American films about growing up.
PG. ★★★★★
D: Peter Yates; W: Steve Tesich; Ph: Matthew F. Leonetti; M: Patrick Williams(adaptor).
Cast: Dennis Christopher, Dennis Quaid, Jackie Earle Haley, Danile Stern.

BREAKING POINT. (1976) The proprietor of a judo parlor witnesses a Mafia killing and is forced to assume a new identity after testifying. An interesting premise done in by vigilantism, comic book thugs and dialogue like: Hero: "I have to stand up for what I believe in." Wife: "You have to do what you have to do."
R. ★
D: Bob Clark; W: Robert Swaybill and Stanley Mann; Ph: Marc Champion; M: David McLey.
Cast: Bo Svenson, Robert Culp, John Colicos, Belinda Montgomery.

BREAKOUT. (1975) Based on, but not noticeably inspired by a real-life escape from a Mexican prison. Robert Duvall is wrongly incarcerated and Charles Bronson, showing surprising signs of life and even movement in his face, masterminds his escape by helicopter. Several gratuitously violent scenes and a truly offensive view of rape.
PG. ★★
D: Tom Gries ; W: Howard B. Keitsek; Ph: Lucien Ballard; M: Jerry Goldsmith.
Cast: Charles Bronson, Robert Duvall, Jill Ireland, Randy Quaid.

BREATHLESS (A BOUT DE SOUFFLE). (1959) Jean-Luc Godard was 29 when he made his debut in a film whose importance in the history of the cinema is equalled by the enormous influence it had on other directors—both in and out of France. Its style, attitude and technique were a revelation even though it was filmed on a shoestring budget and at a breathless pace. Jean-Paul Belmondo, also in his debut, is Michel, an idler who steals a car and kills a cop. In Paris, he finds Jean Seberg and more than he bargained for. Godard redefined the way movies treated characters and their impulses.

★★★★★
D and W: Jean-Luc Godard; Ph: Raoul Coutard; M: Martial Solal.
Cast: Jean-Paul Belmondo, Jean Seberg, Henri-Jacques Huet, Van Doude.

BREATHLESS. (1983) Underground filmmaker Jim McBride dived into the commercial mainstream and promptly drowned with a lifeless remake of the New Wave classic by Jean-Luc Godard. He goes to great lengths to keep Jesse, the hustler, and his girl, at a distance from the audience. Jesse shoots a highway patrolman and takes up with a foreign student. Gere does the sullen aspect of the anti-hero well enough, but he should have attended Belmondo's charm school. Without that appeal, the movie is as doomed as he is.
R. ★★
D: Jim McBride; W: McBride and L.M. Kit Carson; Ph: Richard Kline; M: Jack Nitzsche.
Cast: Richard Gere, Valerie Kaprisky, Art Metrano, John P. Ryan.

THE BRIDE OF FRANKENSTEIN. (1935) Perhaps a hellish subject but the talent on both sides of the camera proved a marriage made in heaven and produced a classic of the genre. Besides the virtuosity of technique, James Whale and his writers invested the tale with just the right amount of leavening humor. It is a level of judgement that has eluded the scores of imitations the film has inspired down through the years. The performances are in perfect harmony with the balance Whale strikes. Dr. Pretorius forces the baron to bring the monster back to life and a mate is created with dire repercussions.

★★★★★
D: James Whale; W: William Hurlbut and John Balderston; Ph: John Mescall; M: Franz Waxman.
Cast: Boris Karloff, Colin Clive, Ernest Thesiger, Valerie Hobson.

THE BRIDES OF FU MANCHU. (1966) Fu is no stranger to excess and there are a dozen of the ladies. Christopher Lee sneers a lot and and the girls, all daughters of international leaders, find him less than an ideal husband. A camp trifle.

★★

D: Don Sharp; W: Sharp and Harry Alan Towers; .
Cast: Christopher Lee, Douglas Wilmer, Howard Marion-Crawford, Tsai Chin.

THE BRIDGE. (1959) A masterly indictment of the futility of war that dispassionately reviews the fate of a group of teenagers recruited during the collapse of the Third Reich. The corruption of the goals the German youths believe in only adds to the power of the film. The boys are assigned to the defense of a bridge threatened by advancing Americans.

★★★★★

D: Bernhard Wicki; W: Michael Mansfield and Karl-Wilhelm Vivier; Ph: Gerd Von Bonin; M: Hans-Martin Majewski.
Cast: Fritz Wepper, Michael Hinz, Frank Glaubrecht, Volker Lechtenbrink.

THE BRIDGE ON THE RIVER KWAI. (1957) David Lean's epic of moral ambiguities. In Siam in 1943 British prisoners of war are driven to forced labor by their Japanese captors. A war of wills develops between the colonels on both sides. Alec Guinness' Colonel Nicholson first suffers mightily in pleading the Geneva convention and then succumbs to an obsession with building the bridge as a method of maintaining the morale of his abused men. The drama measures the realities and some of the absurdities that men face in war against "the rules."

★★★★

D: David Lean; W: Pierre Boulle, Carl Foreman and Michael Wilson; Ph: Jack Hildyard ; M: Malcolm Arnold.
Cast: Alec Guinness, William Holden, Jack Hawkins, Sessue Hayakawa.

THE BRIDGES AT TOKO-RI. (1954) The on-ground and airborne conflicts of two jet pilots during the Korean war. Grace Kelly is insufferably sacrificial, but the rest is decently done and the flight sequences are exciting. Based on the popular James Michener novel.

★★

D: Mark Robson; W: Valentine Davies; Ph: Loyal Griggs; M: Lyn Murray.
Cast: William Holden, Grace Kelly, Mickey Rooney, Fredric March.

A BRIDGE TOO FAR. (1977) The massive salaries paid to some of the stars in the cast got all the attention and obscured the fact that Richard Attenborough made a superb anti-war war film about the debacle at Arnhem. Goldman's script is a model of spare lucidity in recounting the fate of 35,000 paratroopers stranded behind German lines in an ill-fated attempt to take some key bridges. The movie has a keen sense of military foolishness and never loses its compassion and precise observation despite the huge canvass.
PG. ★★★★★
D: Richard Attenborough; W: William Goldman; Ph: Geoffrey Unsworth; M: John Addison.
Cast: Michael Caine, Sean Connery, Laurence Olivier, Robert Redford.

BRIEF ENCOUNTER. (1945) Noel Coward's perceptive study of two people torn between passion and obligations to others profits from David Lean's sensitive direction and the memorable acting of Celia Johnson and Trevor Howard. Perhaps more importantly, the oppressiveness of English middle class life and its sedate rhythms—all of which are calculated to mask emotion—provides a backdrop that explains the two lovers and what they finally decide to do.

★★★

D: David Lean; W: Noel Coward, Lean and Anthony Havelock-Allan; Ph: Robert Krasker; M: Music of Rachmaninoff.
Cast: Trevor Howard, Celia Johnson, Cyril Raymond, Everley Gregg.

A BRIEF VACATION. (1975) Vittorio de Sica's last work as a director is a fitting testament to his artistry and compassion. A woman whose life is one of unrelieved drudgery is given a brief vacation in a sanitarium. The lover she meets there is no more than a catalyst that precipitates a basic change in her perception of herself and her life. Florinda Bolkan is deeply moving and this remains one of de Sica's most eloquent pleas against poverty.
PG. ★★★★
D: Vittorio de Sica; W: Cesare Zavatinni; Ph: Ennio Guarnieri; M: Manuel de Sica.
Cast: Florinda Bolkan, Renato Salvatori, Daniel Quenaud, Jose Maria Prada.

BRIGADOON. (1954) Two Americans— Gene Kelly and Van Johnson—discover a magical village in the Scottish highlands that wakes up once a century. The endearing score is in place, but the musical is more stodgy than magical and Vincente Minnelli didn't find the right tone.

★★★

D: Vincente Minnelli; W: Alan Jay Lerner; Ph: Joseph Ruttenberg; M: Alan Jay Lerner and Frederick Loewe.
Cast: Gene Kelly, Van Johnson, Cyd Charisse, Jimmy Thompson.

BRIGHAM YOUNG. (1940) A mounted sermon as the Mormons make their way to the promised land of Utah. The subject promises little and delivers less and Henry Hathaway brings a respectful dullness to the proceedings. The travails of the Mormons, led by Brigham Young in their flight from persecution, are interrupted with a romance that is suposed to liven things up.

★★

D: Henry Hathaway; W: Lamar Trotti; Ph: Arthur Miller; M: Alfred Newman.
Cast: Tyrone Power, Dean Jagger, Linda Darnell, Brian Donlevy.

BRIMSTONE AND TREACLE. (1982) Sting, the lead singer of the Police, is a London layabout who cajoles his way into a miserable household consisting of husband, wife and spastic daughter. He disrupts the marriage and rapes the helpless cripple. Even nastier than it sounds.

R.   ★

D: Richard Loncraine; W: Dennis Potter; Ph: Peter Hannan; M: The Police.
Cast: Sting, Denholm Elliott, Joan Plowright, Suzanna Hamilton.

BRING ME THE HEAD OF ALFREDO GARCIA. (1974) Warren Oates motors around Mexico with a man's head in a burlap sack. Their only company is a swarm of flies and the dialogue tends to be one-sided. Garcia proves not to have a good head on his shoulders when he seduces a millionaire's daughter. The father's response is to literally put a price on his head. Thoroughly nauseating and possibly Peckinpah's worst.

R.   ★

D: Sam Peckinpah; W: Peckinpah and Gordon Dawson; Ph: Alex Phillips, Jr.; M: Jerry Fielding.
Cast: Warren Oates, Gig Young, Isela Vega, Robert Webber.

BRITANNIA HOSPITAL. (1982) The hospital and its striking workers become a microcosm of everything that ails British society.

Lindsay Anderson decides it's a terminal illness and it would not do justice to the level of ferocity to call it satire. No one is spared, from the upper classes to the black radicals, in a bleak vision of a collapsing society. There are some operating room scenes that are not for the squeamish.

R.   ★★★★

D: Lindsay Anderson; W: David Sherwin; Ph: Mike Fash; M: Alan Price.
Cast: Leonard Rossiter, Graham Crowden, Malcolm McDowell, Joan Plowright.

BROADWAY DANNY ROSE. (1984) Woody Allen's bittersweet homage to the marginal players on the fringes of show business. Veteran comedians from the borscht belt sit around the Carnegie Deli in New York and try to outdo one another in telling stories about Broadway Danny, agent to the downtrodden in a a tough business. Who else will take on the one-armed juggler and the dreadful Italian lounge singer Lou Canova? Allen creates a Danny who is several steps away from his usual screen personality and the wit is gentle.

PG.   ★★★★★

D and W: Woody Allen; Ph: Gordon Willis.
Cast: Woody Allen, Mia Farrow, Nick Apollo Forte, Sandy Baron.

BROKEN ARROW. (1950) A western of incalculable influence and one that is more admirable for what it did than what is actually in it. Here, Indians are people with rights and feelings instead of bloodthirsty savages slaughtering decent white folks. James Stewart is an Indian scout who takes a conciliatory approach to Cochise and eventually marries an Indian girl. The need to make a case that is now inarguable slows things down measurably, but *Broken Arrow* occupies an honored place in the history of the genre.

★★★

D: Delmer Daves; W: Michael Blankfort; Ph: Ernest Palmer; M: Alfred Newman.
Cast: James Stewart, Jeff Chandler, Debra Paget, Will Geer.

BROKEN LANCE. (1954) The Brothers Karamazov go west. Actually, this is a western version of *House of Strangers* and its main claim to attention is Spencer Tracy's star turn as the bitter and curmudgeonly patriarch who presides over a cattle barony in Arizona. He has to cope with the enmity of his contentious sons.

★★★

D: Edward Dmytryk; W: Richard Murphy; Ph: Joe MacDonald; M: Leigh Harline.
Cast: Spencer Tracy, Robert Wagner, Jean Peters, Richard Widmark.

BRONCO BILLY. (1980) Clint Eastwood had considerable fun at his own expense, even to the point of bombing at the box office. Suavely directed and consistently appealing, *Bronco Billy* cherishes the fantasy of a New Jersey shoe salesman who goes west to become a cowboy and adhere to a B-movie white hat code of honor. Eastwood, playing off the macho image of his other movies, does Billy with poker straightness. He runs a Wild West show and tries to help out an heiress.
PG. ★★★★
D: Clint Eastwood; W: Dennis Hackin; Ph: David Worth; M: Snuff Garrett.
Cast: Clint Eastwood, Sondra Locke, Geoffrey Lewis, Scatman Crothers.

THE BROWNING VERSION. (1951) Terence Rattigan's dissection of a life that has failed in almost everything that counts is vividly and compassionately acted by Michael Redgrave. He is a schoolmaster on the verge of retirement whose wife is cheating and who is treated with more unkindness than is his due by his colleagues.
★★★
D: Anthony Asquith; W: Terence Rattigan; Ph: Desmond Dickinson.
Cast: Michael Redgrave, Jean Kent, Nigel Patrick, Brian Smith.

BRUBAKER. (1980) A reformist Arkansas prison warden unearths the bodies of murdered convicts at the Cummins Prison Farm in 1968. This powerful rendering of a true story pits the warden against a system of entrenched corruption and brutality where the convicts are used for slave labor. Resistance to the point of murder dogs Brubaker's efforts to establish the truth. An extraordinary prison film that is marred only by its occasional refusal to let the action speak for itself.
R. ★★★★
D: Stuart Rosenberg; W: W.D. Richter; Ph: Bruno Nuytten; M: Lalo Schifrin.
Cast: Robert Redford, Yaphet Kotto, Jane Alexander, Murray Hamilton.

BRUTE FORCE. (1947) A tough, violent prison movie with an undercurrent of symbolism. The prison, terrorized by the sadistic Captain Munsey, is a microcosm of the world at large and the doctor is given to saying that there is no escape. He means that in the most general sense. Burt Lancaster, as the convict leader, solidified his reputation in ignoring the doctor's warning and leading a doomed escape.
★★★
D: Jules Dassin; W: Richard Brooks; Ph: William Daniels; M: Miklos Rozsa.
Cast: Hume Cronyn, Burt Lancaster, Charles Bickford, Ella Raines.

BUCK ROGERS IN THE 25TH CENTURY. (1979) An odd merging of comic strip heroics and sexual double-entendres that —one hopes— will be over the heads of the kids. Gil Gerard is an inflexible Buck, frozen cryogenically and defrosted in time to save the earth five centuries hence. He can't save the film from its split personality and special effects, which are a rip-off of *Battlestar Galactica*, itself a theft from *Star Wars*.
PG. ★★
D: Daniel Haller; W: Glen A. Larson and Leslie Stevens; Ph: Frank Beascoehea; M: Stu Phillip.
Cast: Gil Gerard, Pamela Hensley, Erin Gray, Henry Silva.

BUDDY, BUDDY. (1981) The surefire combination of Lemmon and Matthau—in their first film together since *The Front Page* —fizzled. Lemmon does his neurotic and Matthau his sour misanthrope as, respectively, a man bent on suicide and a Mafia hit man whose plans he disrupts. The script does not extend them beyond trademark characterizations or develop the comic possibilities.
PG. ★★
D: Billy Wilder; W: Wilder and I.A.L. Diamond; Ph: Harry Stradling, Jr.; M: Lalo Schifrin.
Cast: Jack Lemmon, Walter Matthau, Paula Prentiss, Klaus Kinski.

THE BUDDY HOLLY STORY. (1978) Gary Busey captured Holly's obsessive perfectionism and gawky vulnerability in an excellent biography of the influential rocker who was killed in a plane crash. The approach to the creator of such standards as "That'll Be the Day" is itself standard and the better for it. A fine sense of what the late fifties were really like and a refusal to indulge in cheap melodrama. Busey sings Holly's songs without aping him.
PG. ★★★★
D: Steve Rash; W: Robert Gittler; Ph: Steven Larner; M: Joe Renzetti(director).

Cast: Gary Busey, Don Stroud, Charles Martin Smith, Bill Jordan.

BUFFALO BILL AND THE INDIANS, OR SITTING BULL'S HISTORY LESSON. (1976) Unbalanced by Robert Altman's pressing desire to do the teaching. Paul Newman is wonderful as the shambles behind the legend. Bill Cody is seen as the nation's first superstar, a fabrication of the hopes and greed of those around him and a man driven to believe in an unattainable image of himself. All this is heavily italicized in Burt Lancaster's narration as Ned Buntline.
PG.   ★★★
D: Robert Altman; W: Altman and Alan Rudolph; Ph: Paul Lohmann; M: Richard Baskin.
Cast: Paul Newman, Burt Lancaster, Joel Grey, Kevin McCarthy.

BUG. (1975) No one who relishes the idea of a swarm of overgrown cockroaches setting fire to Bradford Dillman's chest should pass up this one. Mutated bugs with the ability to start fires emerge after an earthquake and kill Dillman's wife. Watch now and spray later if you like truly ludicrous horror films.
PG.   ★
D: Jeannot Szwarc; W: William Castle and Thomas Page; Ph: Michael Hugo; M: Charles Fox.
Cast: Bradford Dillman, Joanna Miles, Richard Gilliand, Janie Smith.

THE BUGS BUNNY/ROAD RUNNER MOVIE. (1979) What's up here, doc, is a Grade A compilation of the best of Bugs chosen—on the occasion of the immortal rabbit's 40th anniversary—by his creator, Chuck Jones. It was originally called *The Great American Chase* and much of it is devoted to the pursuit of Bugs. As usual, the Bugs footage is more entertaining than the repetitious Road Runner material. Prime fare for Bugsians.
G.   ★★★
D: Chuck Jones; W: Jones and Michael Maltese; M: Carl Stalling and Milt Franklyn.

BUGS BUNNY, SUPERSTAR. (1976) A superior anthology of some of the best of Bugs and also a documentary about the animators who created the world's favorite rabbit and his gallery of staple companions. They tell rabbit tails out of school at Termite Terrace on the Warner Brothers lot. Here you can learn that the carrot-eating trademark was suggested by a Clark Gable gesture in *It Happened One Night*.
G.   ★★★

BUGSY MALONE. (1977) If there is one thing worse than adults behaving like children, it is kids pretending to be adults. Alan Parker's pastiche of the gangster movie begins by being appallingly cute and becomes throroughly grotesque. Set in New York in 1929 with child hoodlums singing and dancing. "If it rained the day they gave out brains, Roxie Robinson wouldn't even have gotten wet," opines the narrator. Neither would the creators of this Lilliputian fantasy.
G.   ★
D and W: Alan Parker; Ph: Michael Seresin, Peter Biziou; M: Paul Williams.
Cast: Jodie Foster, Scott Baio, Florrie Digger.

BULLITT. (1968) Steve McQueen is in top form as a San Francisco detective and it helps a rather muddled plot. He conceals the death of a witness and investigates collusion between politicians and hoods. All of this takes a back seat to the car chase at the climax, directed with great flair by Peter Yates.
                    ★★★
D: Peter Yates; W: Harry Kleiner and Alan Trustman; Ph: William Fraker; M: Lalo Schifrin.
Cast: Steve McQueen, Robert Vaughn, Jacqueline Bisset, Don Gordon.

BUNNY LAKE IS MISSING. (1965) So is the point of Otto Preminger's ponderous thriller. Carol Lynley goes to pick up her child at school one day and there is no trace of the little girl. To the usual kidnap ingredients, the film adds the notion that the kid never existed in the first place. Far beneath the skills of the cast.
                    ★★
D: Otto Preminger; W: John and Penelope Mortimer; Ph: Denys Coop; M: Paul Glass.
Cast: Laurence Olivier, Carol Lynley, Keir Dullea, Noel Coward.

THE BURNING. (1981) A cast of unknowns makes a permanent bid for anonymity in a rip-off of *Friday the 13th* that spares expense but not a revolting level of gore. The

same plot and, if you can credit it, even less taste with a literally burned-out handyman seeking vengeance. He is initially frightened by some kids who brandish a worm-infested skull that presumably belongs to the screenwriter.
R.
D: Tony Maylam; W: Peter Lawrence and Bob Weinstein; Ph: Harvey Harrison; M: Rick Wakeman.
Cast: Brian Matthews, Leah Ayres, Brian Backer, Larry Joshua.

BURNT OFFERINGS. (1976) A bad best-seller reduced to a charred remnant. A house is possessed—not by a mortgage banker, but an evil spirit. Oliver Reed and Karen Black take the house for the summer for a ridiculously low rent and an agreement to feed the strange old lady in the attic. Strictly bargain basement horror with Bette Davis doing a high camp turn and Reed rearranging his eyebrows into boring configurations.
PG. ★★
D: Dan Curtis; W: William F. Nolan and Curtis; Ph: Jacques Marquette; M: Robert Colbert.
Cast: Oliver Reed, Karen Black, Bette Davis, Lee Montgomery.

BUS STOP. (1956) It's fashionable to say that people stopped saying Marilyn Monroe was just a sex symbol when she revealed allegedly hidden gifts as Cherie, who will not rest until she makes it to Hollywood. In fact, the attentive eye could see the talent in some of her earlier outings. Here she had more room and used it. She takes up with a loud rodeo cowboy and tries to escape the life of a cafe singer.
★★★
D: Joshua Logan; W: George Axelrod; Ph: Milton Krasner; M: Alfred Newman.
Cast: Marilyn Monroe, Don Murray, Arthur O'Connell, Betty Field.

BUSTER AND BILLIE. (1974) The nostalgia for a Southern childhood—Georgia in1948—is as thick as grits in the romance of a high school hero and the girl who "puts out." The tenderness is contrived and the attraction of opposites not especially plausible, but Jan-Michael Vincent and Joan Goodfellow make more of their roles than one might expect. The movie comes apart in reaching for a nobly tragic conclusion.
R. ★★

D: Daniel Petrie; W: Ron Turbeville; Ph: Mario Tosi; M: Al DeLory.
Cast: Jan-Michael Vincent, Joan Goodfellow, Pamela Sue Martin, Clifton James.

THE BUSTER KEATON STORY. (1957) A bust and a misnomer since very little of the purported biography of a wonderful comedian defers to the facts of his fascinating and sad life. Donald O'Connor is pathetic in the lead in a view of Keaton that emphasizes the consequences of his alcoholism.
★
D: Sidney Sheldon; W: Sheldon and Robert Smith; Ph: Loyal Griggs; M: Victor Young.
Cast: Donald O'Connor, Rhonda Fleming, Ann Blyth, Peter Lorre.

BUSTIN' LOOSE. (1981) An old school bus proves a rather ramshackle vehicle for Richard Pryor's humor. He is a Philadelphia parolee who leaves the usual blizzard of blue lines at home when he agrees to take a bunch of emotionally disturbed kids aross the country. Pleasant enough, but not his style. The R rating is for some language.
R. ★★
D: Oz Scott; W: Roger L. Simon; Ph: Dennis Dalzell; M: Mark Davis.
Cast: Richard Pryor, Cicely Tyson, Robert Christian, Alphonso Alexander.

BUTCH AND SUNDANCE: THE EARLY DAYS. (1979) Prequel is a Hollywood coinage that sounds like a shampoo. Here it is a device for making another film about the famous outlaws even though they were last seen in Bolivia. They left large boots to fill and this slight story of their youth is slighted further by Richard Lester's casual direction. It traces their entry into crime and belabors conflicts between outlawry and family life.
PG. ★★
D: Richard Lester; W: Allan Burns; Ph: Laszlo Kovacs; M: Patrick Williams.
Cast: Tom Berenger, William Katt, Jeff Corey, John Schuck.

BUTCH CASSIDY AND THE SUNDANCE KID. (1969) More than just a western with wit, George Roy Hill's movie is an expansion of the form to accomodate ironic humor. It has a gaiety that never wears off and that has much to do with the chemistry—an abused term in Hollywood—between Paul Newman and Robert Redford. Outlawry was never presented with such sophisticated high spirits and the trail that takes the pair from a bank hold-up to South America holds many surprises and richly original characters.

★★★★★

D: George Roy Hill; W: William Goldman; Ph: Conrad Hall; M: Burt Bachrach.
Cast: Paul Newman, Robert Redford, Katharine Ross, Strother Martin.

BUTLEY. (1974) A virtuoso piece from Alan Bates, who brought his hit performance as the cruel and witty college English teacher from stage to screen with no loss of power. In the American Film Theater production, Ben Butley cuts himself shaving in the morning and the rest of the day is spent pondering the wounds he has inflicted on himself and others. This was Harold Pinter's debut as a film director and it's a fine one.

R. ★★★

D: Harold Pinter; W: Simon Gray; Ph: Gerry Fisher.
Cast: Alan Bates, Jessica Tandy, Richard Callaghan, Susan Engel.

C

CABARET. (1972) Bob Fosse was born to choreograph and direct a musical that packs a visceral punch and has some serious things to say about decadence and the price of some ambitions. It remains one of the finest post-war musicals and is further distinguished by its intelligence. Drawn from the Christopher Isherwood stories of life in Berlin before the war, *Cabaret* offers Liza Minnelli's galvanic Sally Bowles, the singer in the Kit Kat Klub and and an equally memorable Joel Grey as the master of ceremonies.
R. ★★★★★
D: Bob Fosse; W: Jay Presson Allen; Ph: Geoffrey Unsworth; M: John Kander.
Cast: Liza Minnelli, Joel Grey, Michael York, Helmut Griem.

THE CABINET OF CALIGARI. (1919) A landmark that exerted a very considerable influence because of its expressionist technique and its striking and quite successful attempt to place the viewer in the perception of a madman. What seems to be a form of reality is actually a dream. A doctor controls a somnambulist and makes him commit murder.
★★★★
D: Robert Wiene; W: Carl Mayer and Hans Janowitz; Ph: Willy Hameister.
Cast: Werner Krauss, Conrad Veidt, Lil Dagover, Friedrich Feher.

THE CABINET OF CALIGARI. (1962) The same title but in plot, not to mention imagination and power, there isn't any viable connection between this and the silent classic. Glynis Johns comes under the menacing influence of Caligari in his mansion and it's all revealed to be a nightmare in the end. There are better ways to pass a night.
★★
D: Roger Kay; W: Robert Bloch; Ph: John Russell; M: Gerald Fried.
Cast: Glynis Johns, Dan O'Herlihy, Dick Davalos, Lawrence Dobkin.

CADDIE. (1976) A self-consciously noble treatment of a woman who flees a domestic situation worthy of a Victorian melodrama to make a life on her own as a barmaid in Australia in the twenties. The pigginess of Australian manhood at the time makes things even more extreme but Helen Morse, in the title role, manages to downplay the feminist symbolism.
★★★

D: Donald Crombie; W: Joan Long; Ph: Peter James; M: Patrick Flynn.
Cast: Helen Morse, Jack Thompson, Takis Emmanuel, Melissa Jaffer.

CADDYSHACK. (1980) A subpar attempt to find humor among a group of caddies working at a snooty country club. Jokes include excrement in the swimming pool, which is hastily evacuated to the music from *Jaws*. It proves to be the kind of movie that has a sewage bill instead of a budget. Rodney Dangerfield, as a boorish contractor, is the only reason to sit through it.
R. ★
D: Harol Ramis; W: Ramis and Bryan Doyle-Murray.
Cast: Chevy Chase, Rodney Dangerfield, Ted Knight, Michael O'Keefe.

THE CAINE MUTINY. (1954) Naval law and tradition give the captain absolute command of his ship, but what happens if his control over his mind begins to erode? Herman Wouk's novel encountered some heavy weather on its way to the screen and the direction is occasionally ponderous. However, Bogart's Captain Queeg whose paranoia causes a mutiny and whose executive officer is then court-martialed, anchors the film magnificently.
★★★
D: Edward Dmytryk; W: Stanley Roberts; Ph: Franz Planer; M: Max Steiner.
Cast: Humphrey Bogart, Fred MacMurray, Jose Ferrer, Van Johnson.

CALAMITY JANE. (1953) Doris Day out west in a light-hearted and likeable musical that finds Calamity having to ditch some of her masculine ways to tame Wild Bill Hickock. Feminists might object, but there is a quaint charm and the songs include that ubiquitous fifties perennial "Secret Love."
★★★
D: David Butler; W: James O'Hanlon; Ph: Wilfrid Cline; M: (Songs) Sammy Fain and Paul Webster.
Cast: Doris Day, Howard Keel, Allyn McLerie, Phil Carey.

CALIFORNIA SPLIT. (1974) A chronicle of two gamblers that explores the comic possibilities rather than their compulsions or the emptiness of their lives. Robert Altman's rambling, almost plotless film is often very funny with Elliott Gould and George Segal hustling their way through various dives and scrapes on the way to a big score in Reno. Altman had more and better things to say about greed and the American dream in *Nashville*.

R. ★★★
D: Robert Altman; W: Joseph Walsh; Ph: Paul Lohmann; .
Cast: Elliott Gould, George Segal, Gwen Welles, Ann Prentiss.

CALIFORNIA SUITE. (1978) Neil Simon is more at home in the comedy of the drawing room than in bedroom farce. Four playlets set in a luxury Los Angeles hotel and the final score is two out of four. By far the best of the quartet finds Maggie Smith as an Oscar nominee and Michael Caine as her gay husband engaging in a catty fight. Farces involving and wasting Bill Cosby, Richard Pryor and Walter Matthau are mere embarrassments.

PG. ★★★
D: Herbert Ross; W: Neil Simon; Ph: David M. Walsh; M: Claude Bolling.
Cast: Alan Alda, Jane Fonda, Maggie Smith, Michael Caine.

CALIGULA. (1980) With its hardcore sex and nauseating violence, the dress uniform for watching this revolting epic is a raincoat and a brown paper bag. There are 2-½ hours of incest, perversion, beheadings, rape and torture courtesy of *Penthouse* publisher Bob Guccione. On top of that, it's wildly inaccurate as history.

★
D: Tinto Brass; W: Bob Guccione; Ph: Silvano Ippoliti; M: Paul Clemente.
Cast: Malcolm McDowell, John Gielgud, Peter O'Toole, Helen Mirren.

CALL ME MADAM. (1953) Ethel Merman in full voice, which you can take as a promise or a threat. She is a Washington hostess who is made ambassador to Lichtenburg and who establishes more than diplomatic relations with the foreign minister. An inventive Irving Berlin score.

★★
D: Walter Lang; W: Arthur Sheekman; Ph: Leon Shamroy; M: Irving Berlin.
Cast: Ethel Merman, George Sanders, Donald O'Connor, Vera-Ellen.

CALL NORTHSIDE 477. (1948) The natural drama of a reporter's dogged determination to prove the innocence of a washerwoman's son is sapped to some degree by the documentary approach adopted by Henry Hathaway. The story is true and James Stewart is particularly persuasive as the hard-nosed legman who won't give up.

★★★
D: Henry Hathaway; W: Jerome Cady and Jay Dratler; Ph: Joe MacDonald; M: Alfred Newman.
Cast: James Stewart, Richard Conte, Lee J. Cobb, Helen Walker.

CAMELOT. (1967) How not to handle a musical. Joshua Logan directed the film of the popular Lerner and Loewe musical like a man trying to yank Excalibur out of the stone. The musical rambles hither and yon for well over three hours and it doesn't help to have standards like "How to Handle a Woman" and "If Ever I would Leave You" when there's nobody around who can sing. Richard Harris, as King Arthur, does his weary and tremulous croaking. The story traces the tragic triangle of Arthur, Queen Guinevere and Lancelot. The acting is accomplished, but in this context it doesn't matter.

★★
D: Joshua Logan; W: Alan J. Lerner; Ph: Richard Kline; M: Frederick Loewe.
Cast: Richard Harris, Vanessa Redgrave, Franco Nero, David Hemmings.

CAN–CAN. (1960) Can't muster much of an impact. Frank Sinatra, who knows a thing or two about litigation, constantly defends nightclub owner Shirley MacLaine from charges of indecency stemming from the risque dance. One of the Cole Porter songs is "C'est Magnifique." It isn't.

★★
D: Walter Lang; W: Dorothy Kingsley and Charles Lederer; William Daniels; M: Cole Porter.
Cast: Frank Sinatra, Shirley MacLaine, Louis Jourdan, Maurice Chevalier.

THE CANDIDATE. (1972) Michael Ritchie's best films share an interest in the American obsession with winning and its personal price—whether it's a beauty contest (*Smile*) or Little League (*The Bad News Bears*). A senatorial election in California and a committed performance from Robert Redford allowed Ritchie to scrutinize the inner workings of big-time politics. *The Candidate* is an honest and insightful look at a superficial man pushed into office by the faddishness of the contemporary political process. It is not a film of blinding revelation, but much of what it says is still on the money.

★★★★

D: Michael Ritchie; W: Jeremy Larner; Ph: Victor Kemper; M: John Rubinstein.
Cast: Robert Redford, Peter Boyle, Don Porter, Allen Garfield.

CANDLESHOE . (1977) A comedy/drama from Disney and one of the few intelligent family films the studio made in the seventies. Jodie Foster is an American kid trying to pass as heiress in England so that she can find a treasure stashed in a sprawling mansion. Enough suspense to entertain children and it won't stupefy parents. The cast is excellent and doesn't condescend to its young audience. The sentimentality and cuteness common to Disney in this period is restrained.

G. **★★★**

D: Norman Tokar; W: David Swift, Rosemary Anne Sisson; Ph: Paul Beeson; M: Ron Goodwin.
Cast: David Niven, Helen Hayes, Jodie Foster, Leo McKern.

CANNERY ROW. (1982) Common sense would argue that John Steinbeck is the most important presence along Cannery Row, the stretch of Monterey waterfront whose hard times he chronicled. David Ward evicts the author and replaces compassion with sentimentality. Nick Nolte, a former major leaguer, and Debra Winger, a waitress and part-time hooker, are supposed to hold the movie together. But when you make a film about lives of quiet desperation in this manner, you end up with a quietly desperate movie.

PG. **★★**

D and W: David Ward; Ph: Sven Nykvist; M: Jack Nitzsche.
Cast: Nick Nolte, Debra Winger, Audra Lindley, Frank McRae.

THE CANNONBALL RUN. (1981) Asinine comedy is given a new definition when car chases are interrupted by proctology jokes. The screenplay is by a former editor of *Car and Driver* magazine and it has all the wit of a classified ad for an Edsel. Burt Reynolds leads various contestants in a cross country race that requires avoiding speeding tickets and risking injury to innocent people. Intelligent viewers are in similar peril.

PG. **★**

D: Hal Needham; W: Brock Yates; Ph: Michael Butler.
Cast: Burt Reynolds, Farrah Fawcett, Dom DeLuise, Roger Moore.

CANNONBALL RUN II. (1984) If you find it hard to imagine a film worse than *The Cannonball Run*, your search is over. Not so much a pit stop as a stop in the absolute pits, it features marquee names from the past and present who jeopardize their futures by appearing with Burt Reynolds here. The cross-country road race idea is aborted in favor of a dead-end involving an Arab sheik.

PG. **★**

D: Hal Needham; W: Needham, Albert Ruddy and Harvey Miller; Ph: Nick McLean; M: Snuff Garrett.
Cast: Burt Reynolds, Dom DeLuise, Dean Martin, Shirley MacLaine.

THE CANTERBURY TALES. (1971) One of the towering achievements of medieval literature is reduced to a dirty joke by Pier Paolo Pasolini. He chooses the bawdiest tales—the Miller's, the Steward's and the Wife of Bath's—and omits everything that makes Chaucer's work a masterpiece. The dubbing into English is very poor.

★

D and W: Pier Paolo Pasolini; Ph: Tonino Delli Colli.
Cast: Hugh Griffith, Laura Betti, Tom Baker, Ninetto Davoli.

CAPONE. (1975) if you got Sam Peckinpah drunk and asked him to make a commercial for the National Rifle Association, it would probably look like this. Ben Gazzara growls his way through the standard and familiar events in Al Capone's rise and fall in Chicago in the twenties and thirties. When somebody doctors his soup, Capone shouts, "Poison! What kinda way is that to kill a person?" The rest of the script is equally inspired and the film is exceptionally bloody.

R. **★**

D: Steve Carver; W: Howard Browne; Ph: Vilis Lapenieks; M: David Grisman.
Cast: Ben Gazzara, Susan Blakely, Harry Guardino, John Cassavetes.

CAPRICE. (1967) A spoof of the cosmetics industry that strikes with the impact of a powder puff. Doris Day, playing Doris Day with her usual effusiveness and conviction, gets involved in industrial espionage and narcotics. Feeble-minded plotting and Richard Harris, playing an agent, obviously knows it.

★★

D: Frank Tashlin; W: Tashlin and Jay Jayson; Leon Shamroy; M: Frank de Vol.

Cast: Doris Day, Richard Harris, Edward Mulhare, Ray Walston.

CAPRICORN ONE. (1978) Peter Hyams came up with a clever premise —the faking of a landing on Mars—but his script is flabbily written and increasingly outlandish. Elliott Gould's investigative reporter finds out what's going on with NASA, but believing how he did it is harder than crediting the bizarre inspiration of *Capricorn One.* Hyams' trademark attention to production design and sound and a startling climax do much to compensate.
PG. ★★★
D and W: Peter Hyams; Ph: Bill Butler; M: Jerry Goldsmith.
Cast: Elliott Gould, Hal Holbrook, James Brolin, Sam Waterston.

CAPTAIN BLOOD. (1935) Not recognizable as history, but richly satisfying as swashbuckling at its best. After small roles, Errol Flynn established himself as a star by showing his affinity for this kind of role. He is Peter Blood, a young doctor who is forced into a life of piracy. Michael Curtiz' direction equalled Flynn's flair and it's all topped off with a bracing score by Erich Korngold.
★★★★
D: Michael Curtiz; W: Casey Robinson; Ph: Hal Mohr; M: Erich Wolfgang Korngold.
Cast: Errol Flynn, Olivia De Havilland, Basil Rathbone, Lionel Atwill.

THE CAPTAIN FROM CASTILE. (1947) Score one for Alfred Newman's brilliant music, which is far more rousing than anything else in a prolix, Tyrone Power potboiler. He is a disenfranchised nobleman whose nemesis follows him to the New World. If the writing and narrative had been anywhere near the fine production values, it might have made for a more memorable adventure.
★★
D: Henry King; W: Lamar Trotti; Ph: Charles Clarke; M: Alfred Newman.
Cast: Tyrone Power, Jean Peters, Cesar Romero, Lee J. Cobb.

CAPTAIN HORATIO HORNBLOWER, R.N. (1951) Gregory Peck, fearless on the quarterdeck and flustered in the presence of women, is a convincing Hornblower, the fictional hero of C.S. Forester's popular series of novels about a naval officer during the Napoleonic wars. The writers took plot ideas from several of the books and spliced them into one film and it looks peremptory. Hornblower falls in love with his admiral's widow,

is captured and escapes from France. The film's tone is afflicted with post-war British patriotism.
★★★
D: Raoul Walsh; W: Ivan Goff, Aeneas Mackenzie and Ben Roberts; Ph: Guy Green; M: Robert Farnon.
Cast: Gregory Peck, Virginia Mayo, Robert Beatty, James Robertson Justice.

CAPTAIN JANUARY. (1936) Captain Marvel couldn't help this Shirley Temple outing. A literal orphan of the storm, she lights up the life of Guy Kibbee, a lighthouse keeper. The burning question here is whether a beacon or a boarding school is the fit place for a child. A dim viewing even for devout Templetonians.
★★
D: David Butler; W: Sam Hellman, Gladys Lehman and Harry Tugend; Ph: John Seitz; M: Louis Silvers.
Cast: Shirley Temple, Guy Kibbee, Slim Summerville, Buddy Ebsen.

THE CAPTAIN'S TABLE. (1958) An effective and unpretentious little English comedy tailored to John Gregson. A shipping line ups him from tramp steamers to the captaincy of its flagship liner and he has to cope with social problems undreamed of in his old life.
★★★
D: Jack Lee; W: John Whiting and Bryan Forbes; Ph: Christopher Challis; M: Frank Cordell.
Cast: John Gregson, Peggy Cummins, Donald Sinden, Reginald Beckwith.

THE CAR. (1977) Most of us are killed by car payments rather than cars in real life, but this is what you might call a repossession movie. The car in question has it in for people with a malevolence not generally found outside truckers on the New Jersey turnpike. James Brolin is a lawman, a legal Mr. Goodwrench tracking down the beserk automobile. The car won't go near a cemetery, presumably because it's a tow-away zone after midnight. More a lube job than a movie.
PG. ★
D: Elliot Silverstein; W: Dennis Shryack, Michael Butler and Lane Slate; Ph: Gerald Hirschfeld; M: Leonard Rosenman.
Cast: James Brolin, Kathleen Lloyd, John Marley, Ronny Cox.

CARBON COPY. (1981) It says here that a wealthy WASP executive would give up his life-style to go to Watts, take a menial job and live with a black kid who claims to be his

son. *Carbon Copy* is a blueprint for a bad movie because it goes beyond absurdity to hypocrisy. It pretends to skewer bigotry while indulging in racial stereotypes and jokes. The fact that the compromise at the conclusion would have logically been offered at the beginning is a final idiocy.
PG. ★
D: Michael Schultz; W: Stanley Shapiro; Ph: Fred Koenekamp; M: Bill Conti.
Cast: George Segal, Denzel Washington, Jack Warden, Susan Saint James.

CARLTON BROWNE OF THE FO. (1958) The FO is the British foreign office and the film is also known under the title *Man in a Cocked Hat.* Wearing it is Terry-Thomas, who turns in one of his patented upper class twit numbers as an incompetent diplomat sent to patch things up in a British colony. Peter Sellers is on hand and he should have been given more to do.
★★
D and W: Roy Boulting; Ph: Max Greene; M: John Addison.
Cast: Terry-Thomas, Peter Sellers, Ian Bannen, Thorley Walters.

CARMEN JONES. (1954) The straightforward transfer of opera to the screen has enjoyed a checkered history. Otto Preminger and Oscar Hammerstein tried something different—a wholesale update and transfer of Bizet's beloved work. Now it's in the South and bullfighters give way to boxers. Harry Belafonte and Dorothy Dandridge are dubbed (by Marilyn Horne and Vern Hutcherson). The treatment gives new life to the story.
★★
D: Otto Preminger; W: Oscar Hammerstein; Ph: Sam Leavitt ; M: Georges Bizet.
Cast: Harry Belafonte, Dorothy Dandridge, Olga James, Pearl Bailey.

CARNY. (1980) A cheerless journey on the road with a carnival, whose show people are perceived as somehow outside the corruption of mainstream American life. Everyone preys on the carnival—cops, politicians and criminals. But since the carnival itself is a lot of pandering and confidence tricks, it's hard to share this film's assertion of moral superiority. A small town girl drives a wedge between a clown and his partner.
R. ★★★
D: Robert Kaylor; W: Thomas Baum; Ph: Harry Stradling, Jr.; M: Alex North.
Cast: Gary Busey, Jodie Foster, Robbie Robertson, Kenneth McMillan.

CAROUSEL. (1956) The life and times of Billy Bigelow, a carnival worker who goes wrong for all the right reasons, became a musical that is more to be treasured for the wonderful songs—including standards like "If I Loved You"—than its ideas. It is expensively produced and, given the story, rather over-produced.
★★★
D: Henry King; W: Phoebe and Henry Ephron; Ph: Charles G. Clarke; M: Richard Rodgers.
Cast: Gordon MacRae, Shirley Jones, Cameron Mitchell, Barbara Ruick.

CARRIE. (1976) Brian De Palma's stylish but fatuous horror film features a tainted child who is armed with the power of telekinesis—the ability to move inanimate objects. De Palma sorely needs the gift here. Adapted from Stephen King's novel, the film is a vengeance fantasy for wronged teenagers, but De Palma is either resigned to or defeated by the material. The ending has a certain gory panache and Sissy Spacek and John Travolta, happily, went on to better things.
R. ★★
D: Brian De Palma; W: Laurence D. Cohen; Ph: Mario Tose; M: Pino Donaggio.
Cast: Sissy Spacek, John Travolta, Piper Laurie, Amy Irving.

CAR WASH. (1977) A deluge that consists largely of vulgar drivel and a cast of mostly unknown actors making a successful effort to hold on to their anonymity. The characters serve as pegs for predictable jokes, which, like the cars, never get clean. Richard Pryor's appearance as an evangelist is the high point of a low movie.
PG. ★
D: Michael Schultz; W: Joel Schumacher; Ph: Frank Stanley; M: Norman Whitfield.
Cast: Richard Pryor, Franklyn Ajaye, Richard Brestoff.

CASABLANCA. (1943) To a generation faced with the sundering of relationships in wartime the appeal of *Casablanca* was irresistible. As time has gone by, its magnetism has grown even more powerful. There may be greater American films, but surely none is more beloved than this timeless pairing of Humphrey Bogart and Ingrid Bergman. Rick came to Casablanca for "the waters" and to nurse his cynicism and selfishness. Ilsa comes there to rekindle the passion of their pre-war affair and to reawaken Rick's innate decency. From these modest ingredients, the stars fashioned one of the most poignant relationships in screen history because they invested the characters with such enduring truth. They will always have Paris. We're better off. We'll always have *Casablanca*.

★★★★★

D: Michael Curtiz; W: Julius Epstein, Philip Epstein and Howard Koch; Ph: Arthur Edeson; M: Max Steiner.
Cast: Humphrey Bogart, Ingrid Bergman, Claude Rains, Paul Henried.

CASANOVA. (1976) A disappointment, especially after Fellini showed he had regained his master's touch in *Amarcord*. His account of the 18th century libertine celebrates the stoop-and-conquer sexual meandering for which Casanova's name is a synonym. This overlong (163 minutes) work leaves the suspicion that the guilt-ridden, woman-hating vision of sex has more to do with Fellini than Casanova. The director's artistic license reduces Casanova to a merely licentious figure.

R. ★★

D: Federico Fellini; W: Fellini and Barnadino Zapponi; Ph: Giuseppe Rotunno; M: Nino Rota.
Cast: Donald Sutherland, Cicely Browne, Tina Aumont.

CASEY'S SHADOW. (1978) A dark horse and a very good one. Martin Ritt's directness and honesty on a track noted for ungoverned sentimentality does wonders for a children's story about a Cajun boy's love for a thoroughbred horse. Walter Matthau, who is wonderful on the screen with kids, anchors the movie as a horse trainer. All the ingredients are here—including the triumphant race—but they were rarely better served.

PG. ★★★★

D: Martin Ritt; W: Carol Sobieski; Ph: John A. Alonzo; M: Patrick Williams.
Cast: Walter Matthau, Alexis Smith, Robert Webber, Murray Hamilton.

CASINO ROYALE. (1967) We now have Sean Connery as James Bond in his middle years in *Never Say Never Again* and "Never again" is a more fitting response to a star-encrusted and tepid send-up of Bond. David Niven is an old Bond brought out of retirement and Woody Allen is his nephew and not nearly as funny as the situation suggests. There were—count 'em—five directors to toss in their ideas on male-Bonding.

★★

D: John Huston, Ken Hughes, Val Guest,

Robert Parrish, Joseph McGrath; W: Wolf Mankowitz, John Law and Michael Sayers; Ph: Jack Hildyard; M: Burt Bachrach.
Cast: Deborah Kerr, David Niven, Orson Welles, Peter Sellers.

THE CASSANDRA CROSSING. (1976) The express train carrying a virulent plague approaches a bridge that is about to collapse, a fate that befalls the film's plot before it leaves the station. The acting is on a level that makes you resent the fact that anyone on board was spared. The movie sacrifices its potential suspense by concentrating on the consequences of the disease instead of the search for a cure.

R. ★★

D: George Cosmatos; W: Tom Mankiewicz, Robert Katz, George Cosmatos; Ph: Ennio Guarnieri; M: Jerry Goldsmith.
Cast: Richard Harris, Sophia Loren, Ava Gardner, Burt Lancaster.

CAT BALLOU. (1965) A satirical western that skewers the genre and its conventions without losing its underlying affection for a screen tradition. A double helping of Lee Marvin is of enormous comic assistance. Marvin, playing off his countless frontier villainies, plays a gunslinger who drinks ten times faster than he draws. He also plays the noseless nemesis. The plot is a slight matter of his being called to defend Jane Fonda from predators and it's one that provides a great deal of room for Marvin. He quite deservedly won the Oscar. The title song becomes annoying after a while.

★★★★

D: Eliot Silverstein; W: Walter Newman and Frank Pierson; Ph: Jack Marta; M: Frank de Vol.
Cast: Jane Fonda, Lee Marvin, Michael Callan, Dwayne Hickman.

CATCH–22. (1970) Joseph Heller's superb satire of war and the military machine is arguably impossible to capture on film. It is a vision of utter lunacy with an officer trying to get out of more missions by proving himself to be insane to people who are certifiably crazy. Alan Arkin is a believable Yossarian but Mike Nichols adopts an episodic style and surreal overtones that makes things extremely uneven.

★★★

D: Mike Nichols; W: Buck Henry; Ph: David Watkin.
Cast: Alan Arkin, Martin Balsam, Richard Benjamin, Art Garfunkel.

THE CAT FROM OUTER SPACE. (1978) Pre-*E.T.* Disney fare with an extraterrestrial feline who lands his flying saucer and needs gold to make repairs. Norman Tokar, in his fourteenth movie for Disney, didn't come up with another *Candleshoe*, but he had some fun with the cat's powers to influence sporting events to make bets pay off.
G. ★★★
D: Norman Tokar; W: Ted Key; Ph: Charles F. Wheeler; M: Lalo Schifrin.
Cast: Ken Berry, Sandy Duncan, McLean Stevenson, Harry Morgan.

CAT ON A HOT TIN ROOF. (1958) Big Daddy is dying of a cancer that is an emblem of the corrosion in his family. Richard Brooks did very well by Tennessee Williams' melodrama and encouraged his actors to go for broke. Paul Newman is exceptional as Big Daddy's son, drinking to escape domination and unable to make love to his gorgeous wife (Elizabeth Taylor). Burl Ives is equally memorable as the patriarch.
★★★
D and Adapted: Richard Brooks; Ph: William Daniels.
Cast: Paul Newman, Burl Ives, Elizabeth Taylor, Jack Carson.

CAT PEOPLE. (1942) The two versions of this story demonstrate the superiority of the power of suggestion over the modern insistence on explicitness in sex and violence. In Jacques Tourneur's film everything depends on discretion and the way imagination and inference can be used to create fear and tension in an audience. The young woman is a Serbian who thinks she is under an ancient compulsion to become more than a little catty.
★★★
D: Jacques Tourneur; W: De Witt Bodeen; Ph: Nicholas Musuraca; M: Roy Webb.
Cast: Simone Simon, Kent Smith, Tom Conway, Jane Randolph.

CAT PEOPLE. (1982) Another sermon from Paul Schrader on all the bad things that can happen to people who indulge in sex. Especially those who enjoy it. His bloody remake of the Tourneur film often catnaps and the sluggish pace opens up all sorts of questions. Schrader is caught somwhwre between a routine horror film and metaphoric statement and he keeps showing what the audience should be allowed to infer.
R. ★★
D: Paul Schrader; W: Alan Ormsby; Ph: John Bailey; M: Giorgio Moroder.

Cast: Nastassja Kinski, Malcolm McDowell, John Heard, Annette O'Toole.

CATTLE ANNIE AND LITTLE BRITCHES. (1981) A light-hearted western comedy that finds two teenaged girls believing everything they read in Ned Buntline's dime novels. Their reading inspires them to go West and take up with the Dalton-Doolin gang. Most of the amiable humor comes from the contrast between myth and reality and Burt Lancaster makes it work. It is the kind of western where no one really dislikes his enemies and it's likeable on its own terms.
PG. ★★★
D: Lamont Johnson; W: David Eyre and Robert Ward; Ph: Larry Pizer; M: Tom Slocum and Richard Greene.
Cast: Burt Lancaster, Rod Steiger, Amanda Plummer, Diane Lane.

CAVEMAN. (1981). An idea that should have stayed under a rock. Carl Gottlieb lifted the stone and offered Ringo Starr and John Matuszak grunting and panting after Barbara Bach. There is no dialogue, which suits a film that is unspeakable.
PG. ★
D: Carl Gottlieb; W: Gottlieb and Rudy De Luca; Ph: Alan Hume; M: Lalo Schifrin.
Cast: Ringo Starr, Barbara Bach, John Matuszak, Dennis Quaid.

CELESTE. (1982) The last days of Marcel Proust as he desperately tries to find the strength to finish *Remembrance of Things Past* are the basis for a profound look at the craft of writing. Percy Adlon gets around the usual problem—the fact that writing is non-cinematic—by showing us a symbiotic relationship between Proust and his young housekeeper. He pillages her memories and transforms them for his masterpiece. These insights are offered in a very moving depiction of the courage of a dying artist.
★★★★
D and W: Percy Adlon; Ph: Jurgen Martin; M: Music of Cesar Franck.
Cast: Jurgen Arndt, Eva Mattes, Norbert Wartha.

CHAINED HEAT. (1983) From the producers of *The Concrete Jungle* and proof that there ought to be capital punishment for certain movies. John Vernon, the dean in *Animal House*, finds himself in a real one as a corrupt warden of a women's prison. He takes his pick of the inmates and films his sessions with them on videotape. Elsewhere

a great deal of gratuitous and specific violence and acting best done in solitary confinement.
R.
D: Paul Nicholas; W: Vincent Mongol and Nicholas; Ph: Mac Ahlberg; M: Joseph Conlon.
Cast: Linda Blair, John Vernon, Tamara Dobson, Stella Stevens.

THE CHAIRMAN. (1969) The Chinese have developed a method of dramatically increasing crop yields and Gregory Peck is an agent dispatched to find out about it. A transmitter in his head can be detonated, but there is nothing explosive about this off-beat thriller. There is a lot of talk of little significance.
★★
D: J. Lee Thompson; W: Ben Maddow; Ph: John Wilcox; M: Jerry Goldsmith.
Cast: Gregory Peck, Anne Heywood, Arthur Hill, Alan Dobie.

THE CHALLENGE. (1982) The challenge is to make an up-scale, intelligent martial arts film and it is one gauntlet director John Frankenheimer should have declined to pick up. The characters are all obsessed with some ancient swords and it is hard to get as exercised as they are over who owns them. The issue divides two brothers and one of them hires Scott Glenn, an American drifter, to help him. Frankenheimer's flair for action is the film's strong point.
R. ★★
D: John Frankenheimer; W: Richard Maxwell and John Sayles; Ph: Kozo Okazaki; M: Jerry Goldsmith.
Cast: Toshiro Mifune, Scott Glenn, Donna Kei Benz, Atsuo Nakmura.

THE CHAMP. (1979) Franco Zeffirelli directed this mawkish remake as if nothing had changed since 1931 —in boxing or the world at large. If the tale had been reset to take account of the corruption and venality of the current boxing scene, there might have been some point to the exercise. Instead, Jon Voight embarrasses himself and dies long before the bell for the last round sounds. Stylishly made but unforgivably soppy.
PG. ★
D: Franco Zeffirelli; W: Walter Newman; Ph: Fred J. Koenekamp; M: Dave Grusin.
Cast: Jon Voight, Faye Dunaway, Ricky Schroeder, Jack Warden.

CHAMPION. (1949) One of the true heavyweights among boxing movies, largely because of Kirk Douglas' forceful presence. His champion, in a motif resumed in *Raging Bull,* is ruined by the very qualities and drives that make him such a fearsome commodity in the ring. It is drawn from a Ring Lardner story and Douglas' memorable work is grittily framed by Mark Robson
★★★★
D: Mark Robson; W: Carl Foreman; Ph: Franz Planer; M: Dmitri Tiomkin.
Cast: Kirk Douglas, Marilyn Maxwell, Arthur Kennedy, Paul Stewart.

THE CHANGELING. (1980) Peter Medak, the director of *The Ruling Class,* goes for similar flamboyance in an above average ghost story. George C. Scott, a composer who has lost his wife and child in an auto accident, leases a Victorian mansion to write music. Instead he finds himself righting some wrongs done seventy years before. Medak has a lot of fun with the tricks of the horror trade.
R. ★★★
D: Peter Medak; W: William Gray and Diana Maddox; Ph: John Coquillon; M: Rick Wilkins.
Cast: George C. Scott, Trish Van Devere, Jean Marsh, Melvyn Douglas.

A CHANGE OF SEASONS. (1980) Anthony Hopkins takes his mid-life crisis into a hot tub with Bo Derek and also drowns in the sea of inanity that is Erich Segal's screenplay. He is a college professor re-asserting his virility with a younger woman, prompting his wife to have her own vengeful fling. Painfully unfunny repartee mixed with Segalian homilies about sexuality.
R. ★★
D: Richard Lang; W: Erich Segal, Fred Segal and Ronni Kern; Ph: Philip Lathrop; M: Henry Mancini.
Cast: Anthony Hopkins, Bo Derek, Shirley MacLaine, Michael Brandon.

CHAN IS MISSING. (1982) An off-beat delight filmed on a shoestring by Hong Kong's Wayne Wang. He took his cameras into San Francisco's teeming Chinatown neighborhood and the plot—a taxi-driver's search for an immigrant who owes him money—takes a back seat to the gallery of characters Wang presents. The director puts an easy spontaneity on the screen that is very diverting.
★★★
D and W: Wayne Wang; Ph: Michael Chin; M: Robert Kikuchi.

Cast: Wood Moy, Marc Hayashi, Laureen Chew, Judy Nihei.

CHAPTER TWO. (1980) Neil Simon's autobiographical study of a writer trying to adjust to life after losing his wife is a case of private grief elevated to public lamentation. James Caan is the wrong choice because his often effective laconic style becomes mere woodeness. He whines and dines Marsha Mason and is suspicious of happiness. The first marriage is an undocumented idyll that should have been explored to give the film some balance.
PG. ★★
D: Robert Moore; W: Neil Simon; Ph: David M. Walsh; M: Marvin Hamlisch.
Cast: James Caan, Marsha Mason, Joseph Bologna, Valerie Harper.

CHARADE. (1964) Glossy, well-mounted international suspense where the settings are as important as the rather silly plot. Audrey Hepburn is the widow of man who has left her with a problem. Four of his colleagues think she knows something important, but Cary Grant is there to step in.
★★★
D: Stanley Donen; W: Peter Stone; Ph: Charles Lang, Jr.; M: Henry Mancini.
Cast: Audrey Hepburn, Cary Grant, Walter Matthau, James Coburn.

THE CHARGE OF THE LIGHT BRIGADE. (1936) With Hollywood's customary regard for historic detail, the futile cavalry charge against the guns takes place in India instead of the Crimea. But who cares about details when Errol Flynn is leading the way? The climax is a tremendous piece of action filmmaking.
★★★
D: Michael Curtiz; W: Michael Jacoby and Rowland Leigh; Ph: Sol Polito; M: Max Steiner.
Cast: Errol Flynn, Olivia De Havilland, Patric Knowles, Donald Crisp.

CHARIOTS OF FIRE. (1981) A magnificent achievement that celebrates the striving of the human spirit and combines a fluent lyricism with worldly observation. Hugh Hudson goes far beyond the use of sports as a metaphor of life to make the story of two British athletes and their preparations for the 1924 Olympics a mirror of a society that still cherished the values of honor and patriotism. Essentially, he discusses how the perception of those values can be altered by personal prejudices and goals. One runner is a Jew with much to prove and the other a devout missionary who runs for God. The England of the twenties is meticulously re-created and the cast is splendid. *Chariots of Fire* won a deserved Oscar for Best Picture.
PG. ★★★★★
D: Hugh Hudson; W: Colin Welland; Ph: David Watkin; M: Vangelis.
Cast: Ian Charleson, Ben Cross, Ian Holm, Lindsay Anderson.

CHARIOTS OF THE GODS. (1974) A ride for the credulous in the film version of Erich Von Daeniken's book which argues that most of the wonders and remaining mysteries of the ancient world can be attributed to legions of extra-terrestials who dropped in to help out. The scientific level is set early when the narrator wonders if there is any life existing on "stars," where life in any form is demonstrably impossible. Even more daft is the insistence that these "Gods" who dropped in would all look exactly like us.
G. ★
D: Harold Reigl; Ph: Ernst Wild; M: Peter Thomas.

CHARLEY'S AUNT. (1941) A happy, if not especially imaginative filming of the popular stage farce that is worth a look for Jack Benny's inspired work. He is an Oxford undergraduate who has to pretend to be an old lady to help some friends out.
★★★
D: Archie Mayo; W: George Seaton; Ph: Peverell Marley; M: Alfred Newman.
Cast: Jack Benny, Kay Francis, James Ellison, Anne Baxter.

CHARRO. (1969) Elvis Presley couldn't act, which didn't matter to his fans and which the rest of us tolerated for his singing. Somebody had the bright idea of putting the Pelvis in a straight western as a man wrongly accused of taking a cannon. Predictably, the movie fires a blank and it's just about the worst in the undistinguished Presley canon.
★
D and W: Charles Marquis Warren; Ph: Ellsworth Fredericks; M: Hugo Montenegro .
Cast: Elvis Presley, Ina Balin, Barbara Werle, Lynn Kellogg.

CHE! (1969) A simple-minded biography that begins with the counter-culture saint of the sixties lying dead on a slab. Omar Sharif never injects any life into him, but the fault lies more with the script's insistence on reducing complicated political issues to a clod's level. In a sadistic piece of casting, Jack Palance does Fidel Castro with cheekbones.

★

D: Richard Fleischer; W: Michael Wilson and Sy Bartlett; Ph: Charles Wheeler; M: Lalo Schifrin.
Cast: Omar Sharif, Jack Palance, Cesare Danova, Robert Loggia.

THE CHEAP DETECTIVE. (1978) Neil Simon learned little about how to do it from his first whodunit parody, *Murder By Death*. Peter Falk, trapped somewhere between Colombo and an outright Bogart imitation, in a gentle send-up of favored moments from films like *The Maltese Falcon* and *Casablanca*. He is on the trail of the murderer of his partner. More of a cheap gunsel than anything else.
PG. ★★
D: Robert Moore; W: Neil Simon; Ph: John A. Alonzo; M: Patrick Williams.
Cast: Peter Falk, John Houseman, Nicol Williamson, Louise Fletcher.

CHEECH AND CHONG'S NICE DREAMS. (1981) More drug humor turns out to be junk in the third effort from the stoned team. They make a fortune selling drugs and then lose it and their ragged idea of wit is best witnessed after the ingestion of a suitable number of sleeping pills.
R. ★
D: Thomas Chong; W: Chong and Richard Marin; Ph: Charles Correll; M: Harry Betts.
Cast: Richard Marin, Thomas Chong, Stacy Keach, Evelyn Guerrero.

CHEECH AND CHONG'S THE CORSICAN BROTHERS. (1984) Cheech and Chong abandoned the dope humor, but still came up with junk. They are twin brothers who feel each other's pain when one of them is struck. One scene is enough to put the viewer in the same boat. The comedy is set in the eighteenth century and it's a costume piece that deserves a shroud.
PG. ★
D: Thomas Chong; W: Chong and Richard Marin; Ph: Harvey Harrison; M: Geo.
Cast: Thomas Chong, Richard Marin, Roy Dotrice, Shelby Fiddis.

CHEYENNE AUTUMN. (1964) It would be gratifying to declare John Ford's final western a fitting valedictory for a man who left such an enduring stamp on the genre. It would also not be the truth. Perhaps it is the nobility of purpose that infuses the film which vitiates his story-teller's gift . He takes a true and lamentable episode and chronicles the exodus of the Cheyenne from their reservation. Compassion sustains it in this central event, but there are too many digressions that subtract rather than add to the emotional impact of the piece. It has the Ford look, which, of course, makes it worth lookiing at.

★★★

D: John Ford; W: James R. Webb; Ph: William Clothier; M: Alex North.
Cast: Richard Widmark, Carroll Baker, Dolores del Rio, James Stewart.

CHILDREN OF THE DAMNED. (1964) The sequel to the harrowing *Village of the Damned* is forced to harp on the origninal idea of aliens taking up residence in the minds of children and using their innocence to their own advantage. This amounts to no more than repetition that quickly palls. Six of the kids are in grave danger from the curious authorities.

★★

D: Anton Leader; W: John Briley; Ph: David Boulton; M: Ron Goodwin.
Cast: Ian Hendry, Alan Badel, Barbara Ferris, Alfred Burke.

THE CHINA SYNDROME. (1979) Like the reactor at the core of the movie, *The China Syndrome* is in constant danger of overloading. But it manages, with surprising success, to cram a thriller format with the technology of nuclear power, the controversy it provokes, the uses of the media and the compromises of principle involved. Jane Fonda, a reporter, witnesses a near disaster at a nuclear plant and becomes a catalyst to the action when she persuades an engineer (Jack Lemmon) to go public with his doubts about the plant's safety. Lemmon's particular flair for bringing distraught people to sympathetic life is especially useful in a riveting and provocative drama.
PG. ★★★★
D: James Bridges; W: Bridges, Michael Gray and T.S. Cook; Ph: James Crabe; M: Stephen Bishop.
Cast: Jane Fonda, Jack Lemmon, Michael Douglas, Scott Brady.

CHINATOWN. (1974) "Nothing is what it really seems in Chinatown," says private eye J.J. Gittes. Nor is it in this ingeniously wrought thriller set in Los Angeles in the thirties. Robert Towne's screenplay begins with a simple case of marital infidelity and plunges Gittes into a dense thicket that touches on everything from incest to municipal corruption. Towne deserved his Oscar for keeping everything clearly in focus and Roman Polanksi delights in setting up the private eye cliches and then turning them into something different. Full of bizarre and arresting surprises and eloquently acted.

R. ★★★★
D: Roman Polanksi; W: Robert Towne; Ph: John A. Alonzo; M: Jerry Goldsmith.
Cast: Jack Nicholson, Faye Dunaway, John Huston, John Hillerman.

CHISUM. (1970) Late and not great John Wayne that looks back to his heroic roles rather than toward the kind of curmudgeonly western he was later to favor. The emphasis is very much on action instead of acting with Wayne as John Chisum, a Texas cattleman beset by rivals and more than holding his own.

★★
D: Andrew V. McLaglen; W: Andrew Fenady; Ph: William Clothier; M: Dominic Frontiere.
Cast: John Wayne, Forrest Tucker, Ben Johnson, Patrick Knowles.

THE CHOIRBOYS. (1978) The adaptation of Joseph Wambaugh's hard-edged novel has all the organization of a police blotter after a busy Saturday night at the station house. A veritable convention of cops, all suffering private hurts behind their public uniforms, demands to be heard. There is neither time nor room for anyone to establish anything more than the unhappiness of a policeman's lot. Unhappiest of all was Wambaugh, who had his name removed from the credits.

R. ★
D: Robert Aldrich; W: Christopher Knopf; Ph: Joseph Biroc; M: Frank de Vol.
Cast: Charles Durning, Lou Gossett, Jr., Perry King, Randy Quaid.

C.H.O.M.P.S. (1980) Needlessly childish kids' fare about a robot dog designed to protect property, hence the acronym title —Canine Home Protection System. The usual bad guys pursue the device. Blander than Disney, the film originally got a PG for having the dog utter a word kids hear in the playground every day. It was excised.

G. ★★
D: Don Chaffey; W: Dick Robbins and Duane Poole; Ph: Charles F. Wheeler.
Cast: Valerie Bertinelli, Wesley Eure, Conrad Bain, Larry Bishop.

THE CHOSEN. (1982) A young man is forced to choose betwen succeeding his father as the leader of a strict Hasidic community and the wider experience of life he craves. Jeremy Paul Kagan had a tougher choice in deciding how hard to be on the sect and its ways and how to make it accessible. He takes things at face value and explores rather than questions. Set in New York in the forties, the film's central conflicts seem remote. Rod Steiger is exceptional as the boy's father.

PG. ★★★
D: Jeremy Paul Kagan; W: Edward Gordon; Ph: Arthur Ornitz; M: Elmer Bernstein.
Cast: Rod Steiger, Robby Benson, Maximillian Schell, Barry Miller.

A CHRISTMAS STORY. (1983) An exercise in nostalgia that found a ready audience and it's not without a certain corny charm. Or surprises. This was actually directed by the man responsible for *Porky's*. His atonement uses the narration of humorist Jean Shepherd, who reminisces about a Christmas in the forties. A little boy dreams of getting a Red Ryder air rifle as a present.

PG. ★★
D: Bob Clark ; W: Clark, Jean Shepherd and Leigh Brown; Ph: Reginald Morris; M: Carl Zittrer and Paul Zaza.
Cast: Melinda Dillon, Darren McGavin, Peter Billingsley, Ian Petrella.

CHRISTINE. (1983) A Plymouth Fury takes its name seriously and is repossessed by an evil spirit. It comes into the loving hands of a high school loser who restores the car to its pristine 1957 state. John Carpenter does well by Stephen King's creation and has some sly observations about our love for wheels, but this is still basically the same nonsense as *The Car*. Worth a look if you enjoy Carpenter's undeniable style in horror.

R. ★★★
D: John Carpenter; W: Bill Phillips; Ph: Donald Morgan; M: John Carpenter.
Cast: Keith Gordon, John Stockwell, Alexandra Paul, Robert Prosky.

CHU CHU AND THE PHILLY FLASH. (1981) The Alan Arkin family, which appears in unseemly numbers in a calamitous piece of whimsy about San Francisco street peo-

ple, may want to watch this film. Why anyone else, including Carol Burnett, would wish to suffer through it is anyone's guess. The film-makers think that being a bum in urban America is fun and that street people just need a little luck to get back on their feet.
PG ★
D: David Lowell Rich; W: Barbara Dana; Ph: Victor J. Kemper; M: Peter Rugolo.
Cast: Alan Arkin, Carol Burnett, Jack Warden, Danny Aiello.

CINDERELLA LIBERTY. (1973) Before the clock chimes midnight, a simple and good-hearted sailor has fallen for a prostitute and feels paternal instincts for her fatherless son. A downbeat love story that pits James Caan and Marsha Mason against a schizophrenic posture in the movie. Conscious sleaziness and maudlin sentimentality are not good bedmates.
★★
D: Mark Rydell; W: Darryl Ponicsan; Ph: Vilmos Zsigmond; M: John Williams.
Cast: James Caan, Marsha Mason, Kirk Calloway, Eli Wallach.

CIRCLE OF DECEIT. (1982) Ranks with *The Year of Living Dangerously* as a searing indictment of war and the way its events are reported in the media. Volker Schlondorff gives an unsparing view of the mindless savagery in Lebanon as a backdrop to the way one man perceives the carnage and how he is changed by it. A German magazine reporter goes to the Middle East to lose his own troubles in larger calamities. He finds a private hell instead of escape.
★★★★
D: Volker Schlondorff; W: Schlondorff and Jean-Claude Carriere; Ph: Igor Luther; M: Maurice Jarre.
Cast: Bruno Ganz, Hanna Schygulla, Jean Carmet, Jerzy Skolimowski.

CIRCLE OF IRON. (1978) Upscale chopsocky with some imposing names on both sides of the camera and a story penned by the late Bruce Lee. The usual nonsense about a warrior enduring several tests in a quest is dressed up with claptrap reductions of Eastern philosophies.
R. ★★
D: Richard Moore; W: Stirling Silliphant and Stanley Mann; Ph: Ronnie Taylor.
Cast: David Carradine, Jeff Cooper, Roddy McDowell, Eli Wallach.

CIRCLE OF TWO. (1981) Richard Burton, a sixty-year-old painter, falls for a teenager.

Admirers of *Lolita* will be forgiven for shouting "Bah, Humbert!" at what Jules Dassin makes of it. The May-December romance ends up in a cinematic fall. Tatum O'Neal finds the artist asleep at a dirty movie and it's a shame she woke him up.
★★
D: Jules Dassin; W: Thomas Hedley; Ph: Laszlo George.
Cast: Richard Burton, Tatum O'Neal, Michael Wilcott, Robin Gammell.

THE CITADEL. (1938) King Vidor's remorselessly uplifting but nobly acted version of A.J. Cronin's novel about a young doctor who learns the difference between hypocrisy and the real meaning of his hippocratic oath. He begins by treating Welsh miners and then moves to lucrative practice in London's Harley Street and caters to rich patients. A good sermon.
★★★
D: King Vidor; W: Ian Dalrymple, Frank Ward and Elizabeth Hill; Ph: Harry Stradling; M: Louis Levy.
Cast: Robert Donat, Rosalind Russell, Ralph Richardson, Rex Harrison.

CITIZEN KANE. (1941) Orson Welles' first film has retained first place on almost any thinking man's list of the great achievements of American cinema. The language of movies was never the same after *Citizen Kane* and it remains technically dazzling today. Charles Foster Kane dies uttering the most famous last word in all of film—"Rosebud." Welles bends time and perception as a reporter tries to piece together a portrait of Kane that is culled from those who knew him and thus colored by individual prejudice. Kane is a thinly veiled version of Wiliam Randolph Hearst. The film touches brilliantly on a panorama of themes from the corrupting power of wealth to the vanity of human wishes. Welles aged into the part, beginning as the vital Kane and ending in his death in Xanadu. His only problem was that after such a debut, nothing he could subsequently do could possibly top *Citizen Kane*. But it is a problem shared by other directors who learned so much from one film.
★★★★★
D: Orson Welles; W: Herman J. Mankiewicz; Ph: Gregg Toland; M: Bernard Herrmann.
Cast: Orson Welles, Dorothy Comingore, Joseph Cotten, Everett Sloane.

CITIZEN'S BAND. (1977) Jonathan Demme's erratic effort is also known under

the title *Handle With Care*. Whatever you call it, the film is an uncomfortable mixture of low comedy built around the CB radio craze and a study of some off-beat characters in a small western town. A bigamous trucker copes with a conspiracy by his wives and two combative brothers vie for time amid vignettes of what Demme and Brickman think is funny. This includes cow droppings, prostitutes who use CB radios to drum up business, and masturbation.
PG. ★★
D: Jonathan Demme; W: Paul Brickman; Ph: Jordan Croneworth; M: Bill Conti.
Cast: Paul Le Mat, Candy Clark, Bruce McGill, Robert S. Blossom.

CITY BENEATH THE SEA. (1953) Anthony Quinn and Robert Ryan are deep sea divers looking for treasure, but there is little of value beyond the macho vitality they bring to routine roles.
★★
D: Bud Boetticher; W: Ramon Romero and Jack Harvey; Ph: Charles Boyle.
Cast: Anthony Quinn, Robert Ryan, Mala Powers, Suzan Ball.

CITY LIGHTS. (1931) A further testament to Charlie Chaplin's ability to fuse arrantly mawkish sentimentality with inspired comedy. There are some wonderful set pieces— the unveiling of the Statue of Prosperity and Charlie swallowing a whistle with riotous results. He gets involved with a blind flower girl and a millionaire and is sent to prison for stealing money to pay for an operation that will restore the former's sight. No dialogue even though sound had been around for two years.
★★★★
D and W: Charlie Chaplin; Ph: Robert Totheroh.
Cast: Charles Chaplin, Virginia Cherrill, Harry Myers.

CITY OF THE WALKING DEAD. (1983) Terrible Italian rip-off of George Romero. Monsters, created by nuclear fall-out, invade a city and attack the inhabitants and only a bullet in the head will kill them. Although this got away with an R, its gore is gruesome. So is the dialogue.
R. ★
D: Umberto Lenzi; W: Pierre Regnoli and Tony Corti; Ph: Hans Burnam; M: Stelvio Cipriani.
Cast: Hugo Stiglitz, Laura Trotter, Mel Ferrer, Rosaria Omaggio.

CITY ON FIRE. (1979) Charred lives. A refinery fire that spreads to threaten a city of one million people provides an excuse for endless shots of burning human flesh. The fire is started by a disgruntled maintenance man and the results belong in a crematorium.
R. ★
D: Alvin Rakoff; W: Jack Hill, David Lewis and Celine La Freniere; Ph: Rene Verzier and Frank Lenk; M: William McCauley.
Cast: Barry Newman, Henry Fonda, Ava Gardner, Shelley Winters.

CLAIR DE FEMME. (1980) The answer to a question that would not occur to many people: What kind of love story would Costa-Gavras, the master of the political movie, make? It's macabre, surreal and strangely moving. Romy Scheider has just lost her small daughter in an accident and Yves Montand's wife is dying of cancer. The dialogue occasionally sounds like philosophical assertion more than real speech, but the two leads lend humanity to Costa-Gavras' mournful vision of love.
★★★
D and W: Costa-Gavras; Ph: Ricardo Aranovich; M: Jean Musy.
Cast: Yves Montand, Romy Schneider, Romolo Valli, Lila Kedrova.

CLASH OF THE TITANS. (1981) Whom the Gods would destroy they first make sit through this relentlessly pompous exploration of the legend of Perseus. Familiar and embarrassed-looking stars play the Olympian deities looking down on human doings. The strong suit was supposed to be Ray Harryhausen's monsters, but the work is dated and clumsy. Harry Hamlin is prematurely petrified in the role of Perseus and flying horses couldn't drag one back for a second viewing.
PG. ★
D: Desmond Davis; W: Beverly Cross; Ph: Ted Moore; M: Laurence Rosenthal.
Cast: Harry Hamlin, Judi Bowker, Burgess Meredith, Maggie Smith.

CLASS. (1983) What happens when a classy director turns his hand to themes usually found in teen sex-ploitation pictures? Very little of note. Lewis John Carlino offers the usual juvenile jokes and grafts on an unbelievable tale of a boy having an affair with his room-mate's mother. And she's no middle aged frump looking for renewal, but the smashing Jackie Bisset. Teenagers worried about acne may believe this fantasy, but nobody else will. In fairness to the participants, it should be added that the studio cut the film.

R. ★

D: Lewis John Carlino; W: Jim Kouf and David Greenwalt; Ph: Ric Waite; M: Elmer Bernstein.
Cast: Jacqueline Bisset, Rob Lowe, Andrew McCarthy, Cliff Robertson.

THE CLASS OF MISS McMICHAEL. (1978) A teacher of troubled kids in London is a beatific figment of the screenwriter's imagination, despite Glenda Jackson's brave effort to put some grittiness in the character. Oliver Reed is the heavy, a principal who believes in the old ways. Miss McMichael counters with saintly liberalism.

PG. ★★

D: Silvio Narizzano; W: Judd Bernard; Ph: Alex Thomson; M: Stanley Myers.
Cast: Oliver Reed, Glenda Jackson, Michael Murphy, John Standing.

CLEOPATRA. 1963) Joseph Mankiewicz took over the direction of the incredibly expensive, Taylor-made epic from Rouben Mamoulian. His version actually ran far longer than the 254-minute edition. The love affair of the two stars tended to overshadow the one in the movie and it shows in their acting. As history, it provides a romanticized account of Cleopatra's ill-starred relationships with Caesar and Mark Antony. Ill-starred in its making, it does offer commanding spectacle like the Battle of Actium and Cleopatra's entry into Rome. The dramatic pulse is lost in the pomp and only Rex Harrison's Caesar lingers in the memory.

★★★

D: Joseph L. Mankiewicz W: Mankiewicz, Ranald MacDougall and Sidney Buchman: Ph: Leon Shamroy; M: Alex North.
Cast: Richard Burton, Elizabeth Taylor, Rex Harrison, Pamela Brown.

CLEOPATRA JONES. (1973) The people behind the picture said they wanted to give black women a new role model. It deserved total recall. Tamara Dobson, wearing earrings the size of steering wheels, in a misguided comic-strip about a narcotics agent with super-woman skills. Acting was not among them, as she reaffirmed in the sequel. Shelley Winters is especially pathetic as Dobson's adversary.

★

D: Jack Starrett; W: Max Julien and Sheldon Keller.

Cast: Tamara Dobson, Shelley Winters, Bernie Casey, Brenda Sykes.

CLEOPATRA JONES AND THE CASINO OF GOLD. (1975) Stella Stevens is a lesbian drug dealer in Hong Kong and uses a sword to decapitate those who displease her. Unfortunately, she missed the director and the writer of a sequel to *Cleopatra Jones*. Tamara Dobson is the Amazon American agent whose acting is less than amazing. Too dumb for adults and certainly too violent for children.

R. ★

D: Chuck Bail; W: William Tennant; Ph: Alan Hume; M: Dominic Frontierre.
Cast: Tamara Dobson, Stella Stevens, Norman Fell, Albert Popwell.

CLOAK & DAGGER. (1984) Henry Thomas, the boy who cried for *E.T.*, is mired in a boy-who-cried wolf variation. A good idea about the duality of the way sons see fathers gets lost on the streets of San Antonio. Thomas, living a desperate fantasy life after his mother's death, has imaginary adventures. Then he comes upon real-life espionage.

PG. ★★

D: Richard Franklin; W: Tom Holland; Ph: Victor J. Kemper; M: Brian May.
Cast: Henry Thomas, Dabney Coleman, Michael Murphy, Christina Nigra.

THE CLOCK. (1945) An unabashed wartime romance that reached a lot of hearts, chiefly because of Judy Garland's touching performance. Her husband, Vincente Minnelli, set the right mood, even if his affection for the material gets the better of him on occasion. Garland meets and marries a soldier on leave in New York for two days.

★★★

D: Vincente Minnelli; W: Robert Nathan and Joseph Schrank; Ph: George Folsey; M: George Bassman.
Cast: Judy Garland, Robert Walker, James Gleason, Keenan Wynn.

THE CLOCKMAKER. (1973) A middle-aged clockmaker is thrown out of the comfortable rut of his existence when his son is accused of murder. An accomplished adaptation of the Georges Simenon novel, the film perceives the crime and its consequences through a peripheral figure. It also explores the spiritual reassessment that events force on the clockmaker, who is brilliantly rendered by Philippe Noiret.

★★★★

D: Bernard Tavernier; W: Jean Aurenche and Pierre Bost; Ph: Pierre William Glenn.
Cast: Philippe Noiret, Jean Rochefort, Jacues Denis, Jacques Hiling.

A CLOCKWORK ORANGE. (1971) Stanley Kubrick's vision of the near-future shocked many people where his far future (*2001*) perplexed them. Its impact has increased rather than diminished because events and social trends have tended to support Kubrick's view of amoral alienation in youth. Malcolm McDowell is Alex, a young man who revels in violence in a society that allows him to run amok. Finally, he is arrested and brainwashed in scenes that are intentionally repulsive.

★★★★
D and W: Stanley Kubrick; Ph: John Alcott; M: Walter Carlos.
Cast: Malcolm McDowell, Michael Bates, Adrienne Corri, Patrick Magee.

CLOSE ENCOUNTERS OF THE THIRD KIND. (1977) Pre-*E.T.* or Steven Spielberg's first, sumptuously mounted argument on behalf of benevolent extra-terrestial life. Always a superb orchestrator of tension, Spielberg uses it here to generate enormous anticipation and he delivers in the film's spectacular climax. As a humble utility worker who becomes obsessed with making contact with the aliens, Dreyfuss has an earthy intensity that suits the film. In many ways, Spielberg made a homage to the fifties science fiction while positing a kindly disposed alien culture instead of the usual hostilities. There are some weaknesses of plot and evasions of matters that should be explained, but this is a movie whose celebrated end justifies the means used to get there.
PG. ★★★★★
D and W. Steven Spielberg; Ph: Vilmos Zsigmond; M: John Williams.
Cast: Richard Dreyfuss, Teri Garr, Francois Truffaut, Melinda Dillon.

CLUNY BROWN. (1946) Not the best of Lubitsch, largely because the English upper classes are a sitting duck for the satirist. Even so, he had some good fun at their expense in a suave comedy about a Czech refugee in pre-war Britain who causes havoc at a country house when he takes up with the maid.
★★★
D: Ernst Lubitsch; W: Samuel Hoffenstein and Elizabeth Reinhardt; Ph: Joseph La Shelle; M: Cyril Mockridge.

Cast: Charles Boyer, Jennifer Jones, Peter Lawford, Helen Walker.

COAL MINER'S DAUGHTER. (1980) Before succumbing to the *A Star is Born* syndrome and turning into a grand old soap opera, Michael Apted's spirited account of the life and trials of Loretta Lynn is excellent. So is Sissy Spacek throughout. Lynn's dirt poor Kentucky childhood is movingly reconstructed. Then the film trots out the marital woes, pills and breakdowns. It relies on shorthand references to the penalties on stardom rather than examining what led to Lynn's travails.
PG. ★★★
D: Michael Apted; W: Tom Rickman; Ph: Ralph D. Bode; M: Owen Bradley(md).
Cast: Sissy Spacek, Tommy Lee Jones, Levon Helm, Jennifer Beasley.

COAST TO COAST. (1980) Not quite the retread road movie the title suggests, although it does have the requisite amount of mobile mayhem. The old device of throwing two incompatible people together on the road is brightened by Dyan Cannon's winning account of Madie Levrington. Her husband puts her in a mental institution to avoid divorce costs and she escapes with the help of a trucker who has more than his share of problems.
PG. ★★★
D: Joseph Sargent; W: Stanley Weiser; Ph: Mario Tosi; M: Charles Bernstein.
Cast: Dyan Cannon, Robert Blake, Quinn Redeker, Michael Lerner.

THE COCKLESHELL HEROES. (1955) Inspired by an almost suicidal wartime operation that saw a handful of commandos sneak into Bordeaux harbor in canoes and blow up German shipping with limpet mines. They paid the price when they were captured. The cast is well chosen even if the script leans heavily on formulaic characters.
★★★
D: Jose Ferrer; W: Bryan Forbes and Richard Maibaum; Ph: John Wilcox; M: John Addison.
Cast: Trevor Howard, Jose Ferrer, Anthony Newley, Dora Bryan.

THE COCOANUTS. (1929) For their first movie the Marx Brothers stuck with material they had proven on the stage.They were to become infinitely more inventive in front of a camera, but this lively send-up of real estate wheeling and dealing in Florida still has an antique charm.
★★★

D: Robert Florey; W: George S. Kaufman and Morris Ryskind; Ph: George Folsey; M: Irving Berlin.
Cast: The Marx Brothers, Margaret Dumont, Oscar Shaw, Mary Eaton.

COMA. (1978) A polished thriller from Michael Crichton that touches a primal fear. In a Boston hospital, healthy young patients keep lapsing into comas and a woman physician enlists another doctor in her search for the cause. The explanation is as malevolent as you can imagine. Crichton, an ex-doctor, is a born story-teller and he has captured the mechanical anonymity of high-tech medicine.
PG. ★★★
D and W: Michael Crichton; Ph: Victor J. Kemper; M: Jerry Goldsmith.
Cast: Genevieve Bujold, Michael Douglas, Richard Widmark, Elizabeth Ashley.

THE COMANCHEROS. (1961) Michael Curtiz's final film is a western of large scale that proves how at home he was on the range. John Wayne hunting down a band of renegade whites who will stoop to anything to turn a dollar and Stuart Whitman as his gambling ally. Slam-bang climax, but not one of Wayne's most memorable westerns.
★★★
D: Michael Curtiz; W: James Edward Grant and Clair Huffaker; Ph: William H. Clothier; M: Elmer Bernstein.
Cast: John Wayne, Stuart Whitman, Ina Balin, Nehemiah Persoff.

COME BACK CHARLESTON BLUE. (1972) The second film inspired by the Harlem police novels of Chester Himes and not up to *Cotton Comes to Harlem*. Godfrey Cambridge and Raymond St. Jacques return as Coffin Ed and Gravedigger to combat heroin traffic on their turf. This may be the movie that inspired the subtitled black dialogue joke in *Airplane!*. Some of it is hard to follow, as is the fragmented plot. There's lots of action and shooting from the lip and hip, but little sense.
★★
D: Mark Warren; W: Peggy Elliott and Bontche Schweig (Ernest Kinoy); Ph: Dick Kratina; M: Donny Hathaway.
Cast: Godfrey Cambridge, Raymond St. Jacques, Peter de Anda, Jonelle Allen.

COME FILL THE CUP. (1951) Playing a drunk is one of the challenges that separates actors of high calibre from the common run.

There are many pitfalls and temptations to rank overplaying. James Cagney's alcoholic journalist is even better than Ray Milland's work in *The Lost Weekend*, but the film surrounding his moving performance is not its equal. He loses his job and his hold on life and an ex-alcoholic tries to help him through the many nights of desperate craving.
★★★
D: Gordon Douglas; W: Ivan Goff and Ben Roberts; Ph: Robert Burks; M: Ray Heindorf.
Cast: James Cagney, Gig Young, James Gleason, Raymond Massey.

COMES A HORSEMAN. (1978) Alan Pakula uses western archetypes for a fascinating discussion of what happened to the west. In Montana, after World War II, a cattle baron seeks to extend his empire and meets the resistance of a woman rancher. This standard situation is used to examine the pillaging of the land and the passing of a way of life. Gorgeously photographed and infused with a love of the West.
PG. ★★★★
D: Alan Pakula; W: Dennis Lynton Clark; Ph: Gordon Willis; M: Michael Small.
Cast: Jane Fonda, Jason Robards, James Caan, George Grizzard.

THE COMIC. (1969) An early and commendable directing effort from Carl Reiner in a subject he knows intimately —comedy. The tragedy behind the clown's mask in a great silent film comedian also gave Dick Van Dyke an opportunity to show his range and versatility and Mickey Rooney is wonderful as his companion. Buster Keaton is said to be the figure who provided the inspiration.
★★★
D: Carl Reiner; W: Reiner and Aaron Rubin; Ph: W. Wallace Kelley; M: Jack Elliott.
Cast: Dick Van Dyke, Mickey Rooney, Cornel Wilde, Michele Lee.

COMIN' AT YA. (1981) A sleeper that revived interest in the 3-D process despite the fact that its screenplay is a sleeping pill. A man pursues white slavers in Texas and the viewer is supposed to dodge the swords, arrows, snakes and so on that come through the screen.
R. ★
D: Ferdinando Baldi; W: Gene Quintano, Lloyd Battista and Wolf Lowenthal; Ph: Fernando Arribas; M: Carlo Savina.
Cast: Gene Quintano, Tony Anthony, Victoria Abril, Richard Palacios.

COMING HOME. (1978) Hal Ashby's elegiac appraisal of the way the Vietnam war changed two soldiers and one woman: a loyal military wife, a gung-ho officer and a crippled veteran. The central transition—Jane Fonda's graduation from docility to independence and an affair with the veteran—amplifies our perception of the other changes. There are some redundant scenes, but the tone of quiet understatement gives *Coming Home* an often overpowering presence.
R.   ★★★★
D: Hal Ashby; W: Waldo Salt and Robert C. Jones; Ph: Haskell Wexler.
Cast: Jane Fonda, Jon Voight, Bruce Dern, Robert Carradine.

THE COMPETITION. (1980) The contest in question is between young piano virtuosos. Their hopes of a solo career depend on winning competitions and when the film adheres to its avowed subject, it is fascinating and revelatory. But Hollywood will not allow music without romance and it saps the tension and vitality. Richard Dreyfuss gives a driven account of a man who, at thirty, is getting over the hill by competition standards.
PG.   ★★★
D and W: Joel Oliansky; Ph: Richard H. Kline; M: Lalo Schifrin(md).
Cast: Richard Dreyfuss, Lee Remick, Amy Irving, Sam Wanamaker.

THE COMPLEAT BEATLES. (1983) One of the problems with trying to assemble a complete documentary about the Beatles is the bewildering legal issue of who owns the rights to what piece of film. The makers, using everything legally at hand, have put together a pleasing collage of news footage and concert material chronicling the rise of the Fab Four. More than 50 Beatles songs in good sound.
                                                   ★★★
D: Patrick Montgomery; W: David Silver; M: The Beatles.
Cast: Malcolm McDowell (narrator).

COMPULSION. (1959) The great lawyer Clarence Darrow was doubly blessed by the fact that actors of commensurate talent played him in movies. Spencer Tracy did the honors in court in *Inherit the Wind*. Orson Welles did equally well in a fictional version of the notorious Leopold and Loeb case in the twenties. Two rich young men killed for the intellectual temptation of the perfect crime. Welles' court scenes are wonderful and E.G. Marshall is a pleasing foil as the dogged prosecutor. A generally fascinating study of the criminal impulse.
                                                   ★★★★
D: Richard Fleischer; W: Richard Murphy; Ph: William C. Mellor; M: Lionel Newman.
Cast: Orson Welles, E.G. Marshall, Dean Stockwell, Bradford Dillman.

CONAN THE BARBARIAN. (1982) The centerpiece is a giant, hydraulically operated snake. No one could figure out how to put a similar mechanism inside Arnold Schwarzenegger and his demeanor remains unchanged throughout. More a barbarian version of *Death Wish* than a sword and sorcery fantasy and very violent. Conan goes after someone called Thulsa Doom and says he lives only to kill his enemies and listen to the lamentations of their women. A loud groan is in order from the viewer.
R.   ★
D: John Milius; W: Oliver Stone; Ph: Duke Callaghan; M: Basil Poledouris.
Cast: Arnold Schwarzenegger, James Earl Jones, Max Von Sydow, Sandahl Bergman.

CONAN THE DESTROYER. (1984) This time Arnold Schwarzenegger punches out a horse and a camel, presumably for showing him up as an actor. There is an attempt at some humor, but Conan the Comedian is just as silly and only slightly less violent than *Conan the Barbarian*. Disco queen Grace Jones and Wilt Chamberlain join him in search of knick-knacks that control the universe. Wilt wears one expression—we used to see it when Bill Russell dunked on him—but at least that's one more than Schwarzenegger can muster.
PG.   ★
D: Richard Fleischer; W: Stanley Mann; Ph: Jack Cardiff; M: Basil Poledouris.
Cast: Arnold Schwarzenegger, Grace Jones, Wilt Chamberlain, Mako.

THE CONCERT FOR BANGLADESH. (1972) A no-frills and quite effective concert film commemorating a gathering of talent at Madison Square Garden the previous year to raise money for refugees. The artists include Ravi Shankar, Bob Dylan and George Harrison. A must for nostalgic music buffs.
                                                   ★★★
D: Saul Swimmer; Ph: Saul Negrin.
Cast: Eric Clapton, George Harrison, Bob Dylan, Ravi Shankar.

THE CONCRETE JUNGLE. (1983) Women in prison with all the usual cliches safely behind bars with them. An ingenue is set up by her boyfriend-drug dealer and sent off to a violent penitentiary.
R. ★
D: Tom De Simone; W: Alan Adler; Ph: Andrew Friend; M: Joe Conlan.
Cast: Jill St. John, Tracy Bregman, Barbara Luna, June Barrett.

THE CONDEMNED OF ALTONA. (1963) A German ship-builder is dying of cancer after the war, a metaphor that the film bludgeons home as emblematic of a national condition. He attempts to settle up with his two sons, one an insane Nazi who roams the estate. Based on a Sartre play.
★★
D: Vittorio de Sica; W: Abby Mann and Cesare Zavatinni; Ph: Robert Girardi; M: Music of Shostakovich.
Cast: Sophia Loren, Frederic March, Maximilian Schell, Robert Wagner.

CONDORMAN. (1981) A prime example of the Disney struggle for identity, this is a spy comedy that is roughly two decades behind the times. It uses the hoary plot idea of a comic-book artist forced to emulate his hero's stunts in real life. Both he and the film hit the ground harder than Icarus.
PG ★★
D: Charles Jarrott; W: Marc Stirdivant; Ph: Charles Wheeler; M: Henry Mancini.
Cast: Michael Crawford, Oliver Reed, Barbara Carrera, James Hampton.

CONDUCT UNBECOMING. (1975) Lust versus the honor of the regiment in British India in 1878. The film of the play retains a stagey quality which heightens the intensity of the court martial scenes. A newly arrived officer is accused of assaulting a widow and is tried by a kangaroo court of his peers. The exposure of this sort of hypocrisy has been done with more substance elsewhere.
PG. ★★★
D: Michael Anderson; W: Robert Enders; Ph: Bob Huke; M: Stanley Myers.
Cast: Michael York, Stacey Keach, Trevor Howard, Susannah York.

CONFESSIONS OF A NAZI SPY. (1939) What we may find obvious in a fictional account of an international Nazi spy ring was not so clear to the world when Anatole Litvak made a movie that amounts to a warning. The Nazis themselves were extremely upset at the exposure and made all kinds of threats. Apart from that, it's still an exciting suspense tale.
★★★★
D: Anatole Litvak; W: Milton Krims and John Wexley; Ph: Sol Polito.
Cast: Edward G.Robinson, Francis Lederer, George Sanders, Paul Lukas.

CONFESSIONS OF A WINDOW CLEANER. (1974) Weak-minded British sex comedy that depends entirely on the single entendre and stops just this side of soft-core porn. A young man finds every open window a symbolic invitation from the lady inside. The *Carry On* films did this kind of thing with a lot more zest.
R. ★
D: Val Guest; W: Guest and Christopher Wood; Ph: Norman Warwick; M: Sam Sklair.
Cast: Robin Askwith, Anthony Booth, Sheila White, Dandy Nichols.

A CONNECTICUT YANKEE IN KING ARTHUR'S COURT. (1949) He's from Hartford and—courtesy of a bump on the head—he wakes up in Camelot. Bing Crosby sings amiably and proves who he is by dazzling King Arthur and his court with modern technology. A good one for children.
★★★
D: Tay Garnett; W: Edmund Beloin; Ph: Ray Rennahan; M: Victor Young.
Cast: Bing Crosby, Rhonda Fleming, William Bendix, Cedric Hardwicke.

THE CONQUEROR. (1956) On paper the idea of casting John Wayne in an eastern about Genghis Khan is absurd. On celluloid, it's hilarious and blessed with a script that makes it a prime contender as the silliest epic ever made. With lines like "I shall keep you, Bortai, in response to my passion," *The Conqueror* subjugates the cast under an avalanche of immortally bad dialogue. Wayne romances a tigress in between the battles, which are quite well staged. An irresistibly bad movie.
★
D: Dick Powell; W: Oscar Millard; Ph: Joseph La Shelle; M: Victor Young.
Cast: John Wayne, Susan Hayward, Pedro Armendariz, Agnes Moorehead.

CONQUEST. (1937) A lavish production for Garbo that imprisons her in a stately costume drama. It deals with Napoleon's relationship with his Polish mistress, Countess Marie Walewska. Its strong suit is

Charles Boyer's Napoleon because he was able to do more than Garbo in the confining circumstances.

★★★

D: Clarence Brown; W: Samuel Hoffenstein, Salka Viertel and S.N. Behrman; Ph: Karl Freund.
Cast: Greta Garbo, Charles Boyer, Reginald Owen, Alan Marshal.

THE CONQUEST OF SPACE. (1955) We have the reality of what really happened with the Apollo missions to measure against fifties speculation. George Pal's special effects are passable, but the plot about an attack of conscience during an expedition to Mars is as dopey as the conclusion.

★★

D: Byron Haskin; W: James O'Hanlon; Ph: Lionel Lindon; M: Van Cleeve.
Cast: Eric Fleming, Walter Brooke, William Hopper, Ross Martin.

CONQUEST OF THE PLANET OF THE APES. (1972) Going ape for the fourth time and running out of things to do with the initial idea. Smart simian Roddy McDowall rallies his kind in 1990 when American is going fascist and apes are monkeys non grata.

★★

D: J. Lee Thompson; W: Paul Dehn; Ph: Bruce Surtees.
Cast: Roddy McDowall, Ricardo Montalban, Don Murray, Natalie Trundy.

CONRACK. (1974) A white school teacher undertakes the education of a group of backward black kids in a backwater Southern island community. Jon Voight's work has immense charm and presence, enough to ease the slight condescension in the fact that the white teacher is the source of all knowledge and wisdom. The teacher supposedly learns from his pupils and has to cope with the entrenched attitudes of his superiors who don't like his freewheeling methods. The kids, recruited in Georgia on location, are wonderful.
PG. ★★★
D: Martin Ritt; W: Irving Ravetch and Harriet Frank; Ph: John Alonzo; M: John Williams.
Cast: Jon Voight, Paul Winfield, Hume Cronyn, Madge Sinclair.

CONTINENTAL DIVIDE. (1981) The divisions owe more to the convenience of the script than real life in Lawrence Kasdan's homage to screwball comedy. John Belushi made a manful effort to escape his clown image as a newsman with the hardest nose in Chicago. He falls for an environmentalist in the Rockies, allowing room for some mildly amusing city vs. country jokes. Kasdan didn't know what to do with the situation he concocted and the ending is silly.
PG. ★★★
D: Michael Apted; W: Lawrence Kasdan; Ph: John Bailey; M: Michael Small.
Cast: John Belushi, Blair Brown, Allen Goorwitz, Carlin Glynn.

CONTRACT. (1981) Even when the marriage is made in heaven the wedding can be hell. A Polish response to *A Wedding* with booze loosening the tongues and dismantling defenses of various family members. Their bickering is set against the realities of life in Poland with venal ordinary folk colliding with the communist system. The sardonic humor makes up for the rambling style.

★★★

D and W:: Krzystof Zanussi; Slawomir Idziak; Ph: Wojclech Kilar.
Cast: Maja Komorowska, Tadeusz Lomnicki, Leslie Caron, Magda Jaroszowna.

THE CONVERSATION. (1974) A harrowing character study of a surveillance expert (Gene Hackman) who assumes he can be a professional and take no responsibility for the information he surreptitiously steals. Francis Ford Coppola's absorbing film owes something to Antonioni's *Blow-Up* and Kafka and a lot to the Watergate revelations. And yet it's a truly original work that tightens the screws inexorably as Hackman discovers his conscience and a murder. His wires become a web that entangles him.
PG. ★★★★
D and W: Francis Ford Coppola; Ph: Bill Butler; M: David Shire.
Cast: Gene Hackman, John Cazale, Allen Garfield, Frederic Forrest.

CONVOY. (1978) Nothing to convey. Kris Kristofferson, the star, admitted it was "mindless," but he was biased in its favor. *Convoy* celebrates a truckers demonstration of the sort popular during the energy crisis. As the truckers discovered, once the protest was staged there was nowhere to go. *Convoy* finds the same situation and opts for dumb cops, mayhem and chases. Negatory.
PG. ★
D: Sam Peckinpah; W: B.W.L. Norton; Ph: Harry Stradling, Jr.; M: Chip Davis.
Cast: Kris Kristofferson, Ali MacGraw, Ernest Borgnine, Burt Young.

COOGAN'S BLUFF. (1968) A slight variation on the stranger-in-town with Eastwood cast as an Arizona deputy sheriff hounding his quarry in Manhattan. "We don't treat people like that in New York," says a miffed probation officer after the deputy slaps a prisoner around. The movie makes much of how people get treated in the Big Apple with Eastwood finding it rotten to the core. Much sneering at the counter-culture in a film that formed the basis for the *McCloud* TV series.

★★★

D: Don Siegel; W: Howard Rodman, Dean Riesner, Herman Miller; Ph: Bud Thackery; M: Lalo Schifrin.
Cast: Clint Eastwood, Lee J. Cobb, Susan Clark, Tisha Sterling.

COOLEY HIGH. (1975) Nostalgia for black Edwin Cooley High School in Chicago, circa 1964. The movie begins as a low comedy, which ignores the fact that slum schools aren't funny, and abruptly changes to maudlin sentimentality. It focuses on a kid who wants to be a Hollywood screenwriter and his friend, the inevitably doomed basketball hot-shot. Nice acting in a losing cause.
PG. ★★
D: Michael Schultz; W: Eric Monte; Ph: Paul Von Brack; M: Freddie Perren.
Cast: Glynn Turman, Lawrence Hilton-Jacobs, Garrett Morris, Cynthia Davis.

COOL HAND LUKE. (1967) Even the eggs, which Paul Newman devours in a contest, are hard-boiled in a first-rate prison drama. Newman is wonderful as the truculent hero whose "crime" is vandalizing parking meters and who becomes a figure of redeeming pride in a brutal Southern prison. The sixties vision of the nobility of personal independence infuses the drama but the point is not belabored. The usually appalling George Kennedy did nobly as the prison guard and won an Academy Award.

★★★★

D: Stuart Rosenberg; W: Donn Pearce and Frank Pierson; Ph: Conrad Hall; M: Lalo Schifrin.
Cast: Paul Newman, George Kennedy, Jo Van Fleet, J.D. Cannon.

COONSKIN. (1975) Civil rights activists denounced Ralph Bakshi's third feature — a sophisticated piece of animation about life in Harlem—but it is really an indictment of entrenched racism. The animation is interspersed with live footage and the portrait of three rural blacks visiting the ghetto is unsparing. Lots of four-letter words.
R. ★★★★
D and W: Ralph Bakshi; Ph: William A. Fraker; M: Chico Hamilton.
Cast: Barry White, Charles Gordone, Philip Thomas, Scat Man Crothers.

CORVETTE SUMMER. (1978) Boy loses car. Boy meets girl. Boy loses virginity. Boy gets car. Not a smash-'em-up car movie, but an innocuous and fragmented tale of a California misfit (Mark Hamill) who hooks up with an aspiring call-girl on the way to Las Vegas to retrieve his stolen Corvette.
PG. ★★
D: Matthew Robbins; W: Robbins and Hal Barwood; Ph: Frank Stanley; M: Craig Safan.
Cast: Mark Hamill, Annie Potts, Eugene Roche, Kim Milford.

COTTON COMES TO HARLEM. (1970) There's actually a bale of it and something everyone wants hidden inside. Taken from Chester Himes' tough tales of two Harlem detectives, Gravedigger Jones and his partner Coffin Ed, this is spirited and hard-nosed police work and one of the better black oriented films of the early seventies.

★★★

D: Ossie Davis; W: Davis and Arnold Perl.
Cast: Godfrey Cambridge, Raymond St. Jacques, Calvin Lockhart, Judy Pace.

COUNTDOWN AT KUSINI. (1976) An African political thriller in which, for once, the whites are the stereotypes. Ossie Davis is no Costa-Gavras and the film lacks both coherence and judgment and is of poor technical quality. Corporate exploiters who are gouging huge profits hire a mercenary to kidnap a guerrilla leader. An inept romance and a liberal journalist tossed in for bad measure.
PG. ★★
D: Ossie Davis; W: Davis, Al Freeman, Jr., and Ladi Ladebo; Ph: Andrew Laszlo; M: Manu Dibango.
Cast: Ossie Davis, Ruby Dee, Greg Morris, Tom Aldredge.

THE COUNTERFEIT TRAITOR. (1962) If there is one thing harder than treason, it is surely the notion of being wrongly assumed to be a traitor. In one of his more unsung outings, William Holden gives genuine depth and poignance to the plight of a Swedish businessman who is strong-armed into becoming a double agent. Excellent and off-beat wartime suspense.

★★★

D and W: George Seaton; Ph: Jean Bourgoin; M: Alfred Newman.
Cast: William Holden, Lilli Palmer, Hugh Griffith, Werner Peters.

COUNTESS DRACULA. (1972) The secret of long life is not diet and exercise. It's baths filled with the blood of virgins. Try it and you can pass yourself off as your own daughter. Lurid and silly, even by blood-sucking standards.

★★

D: Peter Sasdy; W: Jeremy Paul; Ph: Ken Talbot.
Cast: Ingrid Pitt, Nigel Green, Sandor Eles, Patience Collier.

THE COUNTRY DOCTOR. (1936) The travails of practicing medicine in rural Canada disappear when a rural physician finds himself busy delivering the Dionne quintuplets. A hit in its time and Henry King's direction managed to be warm without being unctuous.

★★★

D: Henry King; W: Sonya Levien; Ph: John Seitz; M: Louis Silvers.
Cast: Jean Hersholt, June Lang, Slim Summerville, Michael Whalen.

THE COUNTRY GIRL. (1954) Although Bing Crosby's drunken performer marinating in booze and self-pity is surely the finest of his career, the Oscar went to Grace Kelly as his long-suffering wife. After becoming a Hollywood queen, she went off to be a real-life princess. The film itself is a mawkish melodrama with William Holden getting involved in the booze-wrecked marriage.

★★★

D and W: George Seaton; Ph: John Warren; M: Victor Young.
Cast: Grace Kelly, Bing Crosby, William Holden, Anthony Ross.

COUP DE TETE. (1980) A sardonic comedy from the maker of *Black and White in Color*. The obsession with winning is dissected through the efforts of small French town to win a soccer championship at any cost. The late Patrick Dewaere is the town layabout they need to play right-wing and he alternates between being a bum and a hero.

★★★

D: Jean-Jacques Annaud; W: Annaud and Francis Veber; Ph: Claude Agostini; M: Pierre Bachelet.
Cast: Patrick Dewaere, France Dougnac, Jean Bouise, Michel Aumont.

COUP DE TORCHON. (1982) Bertrand Tavernier makes a colonial town in French West Africa on the eve of World War II a microcosm of the social and political conditions that contribute to the growth of fascism. It is also a shrewd study of evil that never takes to the pulpit. The incomparable Philippe Noiret is a slovenly police chief who decides to retaliate against his tormentors and doesn't know when to stop.

★★★★

D: Bertrand Tavernier; W: Tavernier and Jean Aurenche; Ph: Pierre William Glenn; M: Philippe Sarde.
Cast: Philippe Noiret, Isabelle Huppert, Stephane Audran, Guy Marchand.

COUSIN, COUSINE. (1975) Opening with a marriage feast full of relatives and devoid of kinship, Jean-Charles Tacchella's witty satire of middle class values never loses its bite and elan. Two cousins are driven to adultery by the expectations of those around them in a film that is an unabashed celebration of romantic love and a wryly affectionate view of family life.

★★★★★

D and W: Jean-Charles Tacchella; Ph: Georges Lendi; M: Gerard Anfosso.
Cast: Marie-France Pisier, Victor Lanoux, Marie-Christine Barrault.

THE COWBOYS. (1972) Some of John Wayne's finest war films—such as *The Sands of Iwo Jima*—cast him as a mature man charged with turning boys into men so that they would have a chance in combat. *The Cowboys* takes up the same motif on the frontier when a cattleman loses his regular crew and takes on some callow boys. Along the way, they become men in the school of hard knocks. Wayne did this kind of role with an infallible instinct and this is one of his better late westerns. John Williams' score is as exuberant as it is derivative.

★★★

D: Mark Rydell; W: Irving Ravetch and Harriet Frank, Jr.; Ph: Robert Surtees; M: John Williams.
Cast: John Wayne, Roscoe Lee Brown, Bruce Dern, Colleen Dewhurst.

CRASH DIVE. (1943) Before he went off to join the armed services amid much publicity, Tyrone Power went underwater to fight the Germans and squabble over the love of Anne Baxter with his new captain. Uninspiring, which is fatal to propaganda.

★★

D: Archie Mayo; W: Jo Swerling; Ph: Leon Shamroy; M: Emil Newman.
Cast: Tyrone Power, Dana Andrews, Anne Baxter, James Gleason.

THE CREATURE FROM THE BLACK LAGOON. (1954) An amphibious twist on the beauty-and-the-beast theme and a quite effective monster liven up an early 3-D production. A scientific expedition discovers more than it wants when it finds an ancient merman. Noteworthy for the photography and the care taken to make the gilled creature convincing. There were two sequels.

★★

D: Jack Arnold; W: Harry Essex and Arthur Ross; Ph: William Snyder.
Cast: Julie Adams, Richard Carlson, Richard Denning, Antonio Moreno.

CREEPSHOW. (1982) With movies increasingly turning to comic strips for inspiration, it was inevitable that someone should try a film that *is* a comic. The line between laughter and fear in horror is very difficult to draw, especially when you are using a child's crayon. Stephen King and George Romero collaborated on four non-descript and occasionally infantile episodes.

R. ★

D: George Romero; W: Stephen King; Ph: Michael Gornick; M: John Harrison.
Cast: Hal Holbrook, Adrienne Barbeau, Fritz Weaver, Carrie Nye.

CRIME SCHOOL. (1938) The lesson is heavy-handed when Humphrey Bogart meets the Dead End Kids and the film strays into a *cul-de-sac*. Bogie runs a reform school and the message is that bad kids are made worse by harsh treatment.So is this subject.

★★

D: Lewis Seiler; W: Crane Wilbur and Vincent Sherman; Ph: Arthur Todd.
Cast: Humphrey Bogart, Gale Page, Billy Halop, Huntz Hall.

THE CRIMSON PIRATE. (1952) Burt Lancaster has a dumb companion but this is one of the smartest and most amusing pirate spoofs ever done. Lancaster and Nick Cravat show off their acrobatic skills in some breath-taking stunts and lead a rebellion against a tyrant. They are helped by ingenious inventions and the high spirits are infectious.

★★★★

D: Robert Siodmak; W: Roland Kibbee; Ph: Otto Heller; M: William Alwyn.
Cast: Burt Lancaster, Nick Cravat, Eva Bartok, Torin Thatcher.

CRITIC'S CHOICE. (1963) Not mine. Bob Hope is supposed to be a Broadway critic who makes John Simon seem like an industry flack. His wife, Lucille Ball, writes a play, presenting him with a dilemma that is a lot more boring than it should have been.

★★

D: Don Weis; W: Jack Shers; Ph: Charles Lang; M: George Duning.
Cast: Bob Hope, Lucille Ball, Marilyn Maxwell, Rip Torn.

CROSS CREEK. (1983) A genteel, gorgeously photographed account of Marjorie Kinnan Rawlings, who found herself as a writer by giving up the city for the hard life in the Florida swamps. Films about writers often tend to be self-defeating and an honorable attempt succumbs here. It can be enjoyed for the vitality of the people she meets in a strange new world and her relationships and learning experience. It does not genuinely enlarge our understanding of Rawlings.

PG. ★★★

D: Martin Ritt; W: Dalene Young; Ph: John Alonzo; M: Leonard Rosenman.
Cast: Mary Steenburgen, Rip Torn, Peter Coyote, Dana Hill.

CROSSED SWORDS. (1978) A prissy, straightforward retelling of Mark Twain's *The Prince and the Pauper* that finds Ernest Borgnine being tossed into a pigsty. He is outhammed by Oliver Reed, who plods around Tudor England in a blue funk as Miles Hendon. George C. Scott has a wonderful vignette in his brief appearance as the vagabond king and hints at what might have been. The familiar ingredients of the story—Prince Edward's ill-fated switch of identity with a pauper who is his double—are intact.

PG. ★★

D: Richard Fleischer; W: George MacDonald Fraser; Ph: Jack Cardiff; M: Maurice Jarre.
Cast: Oliver Reed, Mark Lester, Ernest Borgnine, George C. Scott.

CROSSFIRE. (1947) Richard Brooks' novel *The Brick Foxhole* posited a murder of a homosexual. The screen version, presumably reasoning that anti-semitism was an easier target than homophobia, changed the victim to a Jew. It allowed for a sermon that intrudes upon a well-made thriller and Robert Ryan stands out.

★★★

D: Edward Dmytryk; W: John Paxton; Ph: J. Roy Hunt; M: Roy Webb.
Cast: Robert Mitchum, Robert Ryan, Robert Young, Gloria Grahame.

CROSS OF IRON. (1977) The irony here is that the hellishness of war should be argued by a director who has always chosen to inhabit the theater of blood. James Coburn leads a German unit in retreat from the Russian front and Peckinpah handles the killing with his customary sensual obsession. The trouble is his trademark technique has been done to death by imitators and the blood obscures the rather mundane moral. Routine performances and some strange accents from James Mason and David Warner.

R. ★★

D: Sam Peckinpah; W: Julius J. Epstein; Ph: John Coquillon; M: Ernest Gold.
Cast: James Coburn, James Mason, David Warner, Maximilian Schell.

THE CROWD ROARS. (1932) And so do the engines in Howard Hawks' well-staged auto-racing film. Off the track, it's a run-of-the mill story of a big brother trying to keep kid brother away from the dangerous sport.

★★★

D: Howard Hawks; W: Kubec Glasmon, John Bright and Niven Busch; Ph: Sid Hickox; M: Leo Forbstein.
Cast: James Cagney, Joan Blondell, Ann Dvorak, Eric Linden.

THE CRUEL SEA. (1952) Life aboard the tiny escort vessel *Compass Rose* as it fights the Battle of the Atlantic. Adapted from Nicholas Monsarrat's best-selling novel, which was in turn based on his wartime experiences, Charles Frend's stirring film was made without the need for propaganda. Jack Hawkins, at his understated best, is the captain and the film is superb in both its seagoing sequences and its depiction of the enormous strain such service imposed.

★★★★

D: Charles Frend; W: Eric Ambler; Ph: Gordon Dines; M: Alan Rawsthorne.
Cast: Jack Hawkins, Donald Sinden, John Stratton, Denholm Elliott.

CRUISING. (1980) A policeman poses as a homosexual to hunt a psychotic killer preying on New York gays. The sex, which plays like a training film for proctologists, will turn the stomachs of heterosexuals. The violence will outrage homosexuals. Graphic murders and even autopsies make the film both offensive and pointless and it aroused a great deal of controversy when it was released. The film's central fault is that it is about killing rather than the killer.

R ★

D and W: William Friedkin; ; Ph: James Contner; M: Jack Nitzsche.
Cast: Al Pacino, Paul Sorvino, Karen Allen, Richard Cox.

CUBA. (1979) A boring romance between counter-intelligence expert Sean Connery and an old flame is set against the backdrop of Cuba on the brink of the Castro revolution. What went on during the downfall of Batista would surely furnish an absorbing movie, but Richard Lester chose not to make it.

PG. ★★

D: Richard Lester; W: Charles Wood; Ph: David Watkin; M: Patrick Williams.
Cast: Sean Connery, Brooke Adams, Jack Weston, Hector Elizondo.

CUJO. (1983) Saint Bernards, rushing brandy to climbers stranded in the Alps, enjoy one of the most benign images in dogdom. That's one reason why the version of Stephen King's horror novel doesn't work when bat bites dog and turns the proceedings into the story of a rabid monster . Apart from the dog, there are several red herrings that disappear from the film which is slow arriving at the scenes where a mother and her young son are trapped in their car while the mad dog slobbers all over the fender. The mother, Dee Wallace, is more famous for her maternal role in *E.T.*

R. ★

D: Lewis Teague; W: Don Carlos Dunaway and Lauren Currier; Ph: Jan DeBont; M: Charles Bernstein.
Cast: Dee Wallace, Danny Pintauro, Daniel Hugh-Kelly, Ed Lauter.

THE CULPEPPER CATTLE CO. (1972) A self-conscious western that worried a great deal about looks and authenticity and did not give much thought to plot and character. A humdrum tale of a youth who becomes a man by enduring the privations and dangers of a cattle drive.

★★

D: Dick Richards; W: Eric Bercovici and Greg Prentiss; Ph: Lawrence Edward Williams and Ralph Woolsey; M: Tom Scott and Jerry Goldsmith.
Cast: Gary Grimes, Billy "Green" Bush, Luke Askew, Bo Hopkins.

THE CURSE OF THE WEREWOLF. (1961) A quite presentable addition to the werewolf collection, which has had more than its share of howlers down through the years. Oliver Reed goes for sheer menace as a beggar lad in 18th century Spain who grows up to discover he has more than a five o'clock shadow and some unusual appetites. From the Hammer films factory.

★★

D: Terence Fisher; W: John Elder; Ph: Arthur Grant; M: Benjamin Frankel.
Cast: Oliver Reed, Clifford Evans, Catherine Feller, Yvonne Romain.

CURTAINS. (1963) Yet another threat to mental health with a young actress committed to an insane asylum—a fate which should justly befall the director and writer of this prurient little horror flick. All the usual blood and voyeurism as the actress seeks vengeance against the movie producer who had her confined. She should do it in real life. Her weapon of choice is a sickle; the film is a sickie.

R.

D: Jonathan Stryker; W: Robert Guiza, Jr.; Ph: Robert Paynter; M: Paul Zaza.
Cast: Samantha Eggar, John Vernon, Linda Thorson.

CUTTER AND BONE. (1981) A violent, off-beat work from the talented Czech director Ivan Passer, who does some unconventional things with predictable ingredients. John Heard makes a bitter and crippled Vietnam veteran more than the cliche it had become by this time. Although he drinks so much that finding his walking stick is an adventure, he witnesses a murder in Santa Barbara, Calif. Passer has the foreigner's fine eye for the telling detail in the American scene.

R. ★★★

D: Ivan Passer; W: Jeffrey Alan Fiskin; Ph: Jordan Cronenweth; M: Jack Nitzsche.
Cast: Jeff Bridges, John Heard, Lisa Eichhorn, Ann Dusenberry.

D

DADDY LONG LEGS. (1955) The director took the title literally and allowed the length of the film (125 minutes) to exceed the life of the story. The flimsy variation on the Cinderella theme has Leslie Caron as an orphan and Fred Astaire as her anonymous benefactor. She made an accomplished dancing partner for Astaire and the film is at its modest best when they take the floor.

★★

D: Jean Negulesco; W: Phoebe and Henry Ephron; Ph: Leon Shamroy; M: Alex North.
Cast: Fred Astaire, Leslie Caron, Thelma Ritter, Terry Moore.

DAFFY DUCK'S MOVIE: FANTASY ISLAND. (1983) When it comes to acting, Daffy has it all over Ricardo Montalban. And Speedy Gonzalez makes a much better Tattoo. The take-off on the television show is an excuse to trot out the familiar gallery of Looney Tunes characters for eighty minutes of fun.

G. ★★★

D: Fritz Freleng; W: Freleng, John Dunn and David Detiege; M: Rob Walsh et al.

DAISY KENYON. (1947) The eternal triangle turns out to be a tiresome piece of geometry that wastes the talents of the cast. Joan Crawford diehards may relish her turn as a woman torn between a married lover and her new husband, but others will be deterred by the cumbersome direction.

★★

D: Otto Preminger; W: David Hertz; Ph: Leon Shamroy; M: David Raksin.
Cast: Joan Crawford, Henry Fonda, Dana Andrews, Ruth Warrick.

DAISY MILLER. (1974) James Ivory has shown that Henry James' delicate ironies can be translated to the screen. Peter Bogdanovich merely shows what can go wrong in this version of James' novella about an American girl who scandalizes turn-of-the-century Rome with her unconventional behavior. A beautiful production comes unglued as soon as Cybil Shepherd opens her mouth and the role is cruel exposure of her many limitations as an actress.

G. ★★

D: Peter Bogdanovich; W: Frederic Raphael; Ph: Alberto Spagnoli; M: Various composers.
Cast: Cybil Shepherd, Barry Brown, Cloris Leachman, Mildred Natwick.

THE DAM BUSTERS. (1955) A British war movie that breaks through many of the stereotypes. It gives a fascinating account of the preparations for a hazardous bombing mission against a system of dams in the Ruhr that are vital to the German industrial output. Richard Todd leads the mission and Michael Redgrave designs the special bombs that are its only hope of success. The story is based on a raid that took place in 1943.

★★★★

D: Michael Anderson; W: R.C. Sheriff; Ph: Erwin Hiller; M: Leighton Lucas.
Cast: Richard Todd, Michael Redgrave, Basil Sydney, Derek Farr.

DAMIEN—OMEN II. (1978) Another empty puff of smoke from Hollywood's dark satanic mills and painfully lacking in the flair of Richard Donner's original. Once again the idea hinges on Damien, the Devil's minion, having foolish guardians who cannot believe evidence of his evil. The plot has something to do with the Third World and remains badly underdeveloped. Unique only in listing a raven trainer in the credits.

R. ★

D: Don Taylor; W: Stanley Mann and Michael Hodges; Ph: Bill Butler; M: Jerry Goldsmith.
Cast: William Holden, Lee Grant, Jonathan Scott-Taylor, Robert Foxworth .

DAMNATION ALLEY. (1976) Armageddon for airheads. The survivors of a nuclear attack try to reach Albany, N.Y., across a desolate wasteland. They make the trip in what appear to be armed Winnebagos. The highlight is a duel with armor-plated cockroaches. A noisy, non-contribution to the holocaust film.

PG. ★★

D: Jack Smight; W: Lukas Heller and Alan Sharp; Ph: Harry Stradling, Jr.; M: Jerry Goldsmith.
Cast: George Peppard, Jan-Michael Vincent, Dominique Sanda, Paul Winfield.

THE DAMNED. (1969) When family relationships have to carry the additional burden of metaphor—in this case the cancer of Nazism—the results are often worthy of condemnation. Visconti didn't improve matters by taking a lurid approach to an already extreme situation. Dirk Bogarde, who excels in evoking decadence, is a corrupt munitions tycoon in pre-war Germany.

★★

D: Luchino Visconti; W: Visconti, Nicola Badalucco and Enrico Medioli; Ph: Armando Nannuzzi; M: Maurice Jarre.
Cast: Dirk Bogarde, Ingrid Thulin, Helmut Berger, Renaud Verley.

DAMN YANKEES. (1958) The Washington Senators are long gone but they live on in the Broadway musical. Tab Hunter, a casting way out of left field, is the fan who contracts with the Devil to realize his fantasy of playing in the big leagues and making an impact. Bob Fosse's choreography, Gwen Verdon's debut and Ray Walston's engaging Lucifer are the hits, but parts of it call for a seventh inning stretch.

★★★

D: Stanley Donen and George Abbott; W: George Abbott; Ph: Harold Lipstein; M: Jerry Ross and Richard Adler.
Cast: Tab Hunter, Gwen Verdon, Ray Walston, Russ Brown.

DANGEROUS. (1935) Bette Davis took her first Oscar for an overwrought performance as a booze-sodden actress. As often happens with the Academy Awards, it was really an afterthought honoring another film—her work in *Of Human Bondage*. She is not a memorable drinker and there is nothing else to recommend a tacky movie .

★★

D: Alfred Green; W: Laird Doyle; Ph: Ernest Haller.
Cast: Bette Davis, Franchot Tone, Margaret Lindsay, Allison Skipworth.

DARBY O'GILL AND THE LITTLE PEOPLE. (1959) Blarney-encrusted Disney fantasy full of storybook Irishisms but not without charm. A storyteller who is about to lose his job, falls down a well into the kingdom of the little people and eventually wins the right to have three wishes granted. Handsomely done with first-rate special effects.

★★★

D: Robert Stevenson; W: Lawrence E. Watkin; Ph: Winton C. Hoch; M: Oliver Wallace.
Cast: Albert Sharpe, Janet Murno, Sean Connery, Jimmy O'Dea.

DARBY'S RANGERS. (1958) The formation, training and active service of the commando unit headed by William Darby (James Garner). It stands slightly apart from the common run of war movies in favoring the relations of the Americans and their sometimes reluctant British hosts over the beachstorming heroics.

★★★

D: William Wellman; W: Guy Trosper; Ph: William Clothier; M: Max Steiner.
Cast: James Garner, Jack Warden, Edward Byrnes, Venetia Stevenson.

THE DARK CRYSTAL. (1982) Muppetmaster Jim Henson created a brave new world and had the courage to ignore the commercial exigencies of this one. He fashioned a richly imagined allegory and his brave new world has no people in it. Working in the area between animation and live action, he conjured various species in a quest story that returned the children's film to calmer days. A surviving member of an elfin race called Gelflings must return a fragment of crystal to an ominous castle guarded by the nasty Skeksis.
PG. ★★★★
D: Jim Henson and Frank Oz; W: David Odell; Ph: Oswald Morris; M: Trevor Jones.
Cast: (Voices) Stephen Garrick, Lisa Maxwell, Billie Whitelaw, Percy Edwards.

DARK PASSAGE. (1947) The theme song is "Too Marvelous For Words", but the film falls far short of that description. Humphrey Bogart and Lauren Bacall were stuck with a fairly absurd story of a fugitive who undegoes plastic surgery, hides out in a woman's apartment and manages to find the real killer of his wife. Darkly and sometimes impenetrably directed by Delmer Daves.

★★

D and W: Delmer Daves; Ph: Sid Hickox; M: Franz Waxman.
Cast: Humphrey Bogart, Lauren Bacall, Agnes Moorehead, Bruce Bennett.

DARK STAR. (1975) John Carpenter went on to make a string of horror hits like *Halloween* after this low-budget and low-minded satire of *2001*. Surfers and drug-users become astronauts and roam the heavens looking for planets to bomb. Off-beat and off-target.
G. ★★
D: John Carpenter; W: Dan O'Bannon and Carpenter; Ph: Douglas Knapp.
Cast: Brian Narelle, Dre Pahich, Cal Kuniholm, Dan O'Bannon.

DARK VICTORY. (1939) A triumph for Bette Davis and one of the all-time, three hankie tear-jerkers. Davis' Judith Traherne is one of the roles that define her craftsmanship on the screen. Certainly, one aspect of her art was her ability to elevate material that threatened to drag her down. She is an heiress who discovers that she is dying of a brain tumor.

★★★

D: Edmund Goulding; W: Casey Robinson; Ph: Ernest Haller; M: Max Steiner.
Cast: Bette Davis, George Brent, Humphrey Bogart, Ronald Reagan.

DARLING. (1965) John Schlesinger's look behind the scenes at what was then deemed the swinging London lifestyle. What he finds is vanity and vacuity which is embodied in the drifting but upward career of a model who sleeps around judiciously. Julie Christie at the height of her beauty managed to make the emptiness fascinating and the slick style Schlesinger adopted was much imitated in the sixties.

★★★

D: John Schlesinger; W: Frederick Raphael; Ph: Ken Higgins; M: John Dankworth.
Cast: Julie Christie, Laurence Harvey, Dirk Bogarde, Roland Curram.

THE DARWIN ADVENTURE. (1972) Of necessity, Charles Darwin and his earth-shaking discoveries is a journey of the mind. Here it's the voyage of the *Beagle* to South America and the biography makes a stab at incorporating Darwin's entire life. It is predictably superficial and innocuous and you are better off taping a re-run of the fine PBS series on Darwin.

★★

D: Jack Couffer; W: William Fairchild; Ph: Denys Coop and others; M: Marc Wilkinson.
Cast: Nicholas Clay, Susan Macready, Ian Richardson, Robert Flemyng.

DAS BOOT. (1982) The U-Boat is suspended beneath the surface with its lethal load of torpedoes and what follows requires a suspension of moral revulsion rather than disbelief. Life and death aboard a submarine has never been portrayed in such harrowing detail and this is not a film for claustrophobics. The story is told entirely from the German side and the weary captain and his crew are seen as victims of a crazed war machine. Very few movies make you live and smell war with the impact of *Das Boot*.

★★★★

D and W: Wolfgang Petersen; Ph: Jost Vacano; M: Klaus Doldinger.

Cast: Jurgen Prochnow, Herbert Gronemeyer, Klaus Wennemann, Hubertus Bengsch.

DAVEY CROCKETT AND THE RIVER PIRATES. (1956) More splicing of episodes from the television series and the two stories don't hang together in a way that makes sense. The first is broadly comic with Davey racing the self-styled king of the river to New Orleans and being self-consciously righteous about fair play. The second is dull stuff about white men pretending to be Indians.

★★

D: Francis D. Lyon; W: Lawrence E. Watkin; Ph: Charles Boyle; M: Paul J. Smith.
Cast: Fess Parker, Buddy Ebsen, Jeff York, Kenneth Tobey.

DAVEY CROCKETT, KING OF THE WILD FRONTIER. (1955) The coonskin hero's popularity was such in the mid-fifties that Walt Disney dispatched him to a new marketing frontier. The studio spliced together three episodes from the television series, covering Crockett from his scouting days to the Alamo. The section dealing with Andrew Jackson's duplicity is surprising in this context and could have used more development.

★★

D: Norman Foster; W: Foster and Tom Blackburn; Ph: Charles P. Boyle; M: George Bruns.
Cast: Fess Parker, Buddy Ebsen, Basil Ruysdael, Hans Conreid.

DAVID AND BATHSHEBA. (1951) A bible film that lands with a thump despite the lavish scenery. David's lust for Bathsheba leads him to arrange the death of her husband and bring down the punishment of God on his people. God should have saved some wrath for the film.

★★

D: Henry King; W: Philip Dunne; Ph: Leon Shamroy; M: Alfred Newman.
Cast: Gregory Peck, Susan Hayward, Raymond Massey, Kieron Moore.

DAWN OF THE DEAD. (1979) A gruesome sequel to the cult horror film *Night of the Living Dead*. The zombies, or flesh-eating undead, are on the march again. They trap four people in a shopping mall and some critics actually discern a satiric intention on George Romero's part. All I see is a slick horror merchant who knows what the zombies in the theater want. There's plenty of it, including a beheading and some inventive cannibalism.

★

D and W: George Romero; Ph: Michael Gornick; M: The Goblins.
Cast: David Emge, Ken Foree, Scott Reinger, Gaylen Ross.

THE DAWN PATROL. (1938) In many ways the remake is superior to the 1930 Howard Hawks film. Both catch the futility of war and the genuine agony of sending men into the air against terrible odds. Errol Flynn's bravado and David Niven's boozy pilot capture the mad bravery and there is an especially touching scene when they get drunk and wistful. Some of the air footage from the Hawks film was used again.

★★★★

D: Edmund Goulding; W: Dan Tothero and Seton Miller; Ph: Tony Gaudio.
Cast: Errol Flynn, Basil Rathbone, David Niven, Melville Cooper.

A DAY AT THE RACES. (1937) Thoroughbred lunacy from the Marx Brothers, if not up to the standard of their very best work. Groucho is a vet practising on expensive patients and the high points include a seduction interrupted by paperhangers and a tip-peddling scene at the track.

★★★★

D: Sam Wood ; W: Robert Pirosh, George Seaton and George Oppenheimer; Ph: Joseph Ruttenberg; M: Franz Waxman.
Cast: Groucho, Chico and Harpo Marx, Margaret Dumont.

DAY FOR NIGHT. (1973) Francois Truffaut's exuberant Valentine to the arduous art of making movies is perhaps the finest of the many homages the theme has prompted. The director made the film with the ingenious stroke of appearing as a director making a film. It's called *Meet Pamela* and the tribulations of getting it made make a film-within-a-film of boundless charm and considerable understanding of the many pitfalls involved in a necessarily collaborative art form.

★★★★★

D: Francois Truffaut; W: Truffaut, Jean-Louis Richard and Suzanne Schiffman; Ph: Pierre William Glenn; M: Georges Delerue.
Cast: Jacqueline Bisset, Valentina Cortese, Jean-Pierre Aumont, Jean-Pierre Leaud.

DAY OF THE ANIMALS. (1977) Tail-end of the *Jaws* imitations. Girdler directed one

of the worst of them in *Grizzly* and, after exhausting all the other possibilities, decided to try a movie in which the entire animal kingdom goes beserk. The animals, their instincts and appetites, twisted by environmental damage, take on a party of hikers. The possible ironies here on the theme of what man has done to nature are lost in setpiece carnage.

PG.

★

D: William Girdler; W: William and Eleanor Norton; Ph: Tom McHugh; M: Lalo Schifrin.
Cast: Christopher George, Lynda Day George, Leslie Nielsen, Richard Jaeckel.

THE DAY OF THE DOLPHIN. (1973) Mike Nichols actually persuaded the crusty George C. Scott to converse with dolphins in baby talk like "Pa loves Pha." This may be terrific if you're a dolphin, but the conversation is wearing on the land-bound. Scott is a dolphin trainer who discovers that his charges are to be corruptly used in a plot against the President. The movie is by turns righteous about the glum political atmosphere of the time and meanly whimsical. Dolphins may be smarter than men; they don't, after all, make movies like this.

★★

D: Mike Nichols; W: Buck Henry; Ph: William A. Fraker; M: Georges Delerue.
Cast: George C. Scott, Fritz Weaver, Paul Sorvino, Trish Van Devere.

THE DAY OF THE JACKAL. (1973) A compelling, if coldly impersonal movie that bases its tension on an event that we know did not happen—the assassination of Charles de Gaulle. In adapting the Frederick Forsythe novel, Zinnemann opted for the juxtaposition of the killer's meticulous preparations and the equally thorough international police hunt for him. The film is at pains to keep the audience's sympathies at a distance and it is one of the better exercises in the "what if?" genre.

★★★★

D: Fred Zinnemann; W: Kenneth Ross; Ph: Jean Tournier; M: Georges Delerue.
Cast: Edward Fox, Michel Lonsdale, Alan Badel, Eric Porter.

THE DAY OF THE LOCUST. (1975) Hollywood is a common metaphor for the American dream and it's brilliantly used in an adaptation of the Nathanael West novel. In the late thirties, failures, freaks and whores gather on the fringes of the film industry. A studio head describes his life as "Grown men mak-

ing mudpies to sell to the great unwashed." Against this none too grand illusion are measured the paltry hopes of a studio artist and an extra who wants to be a star.
R. ★★★★
D: John Schlesinger; W: Waldo Salt; Ph: Conrad Hall; M: John Barry.
Cast: William Atherton, Karen Black, Donald Sutherland, Burgess Meredith.

DAY OF THE TRIFFIDS. (1963) Richly imagined science fiction novels, particularly ones as successful as John Wyndham's, create expectations that movies don't often fulfill. The adaptation is a good one that does not, as you might surmise, become ridiculous when plants start attacking people. The ingenious Wyndham idea is that the population of the earth is blinded by a meteor shower. The few people not affected have to take on the no-longer placid plants.
★★★
D: Steve Sekely; W: Philip Yordan; Ph: Ted Moore; M: Ron Goodwin.
Cast: Howard Keel, Nicole Maurey, Kieron Moore, Janette Scott.

DAYS OF HEAVEN. (1978) Terrence Malick, the creator of *Badlands*, infused a humble tragedy with a sense of the country's harsh grandeur and a vision of exquisite lyricism. Three urban migrants find work with a rich Texas farmer, whom they believe to be dying. He falls for the migrant girl, but the triangle that springs up is kept at arm's length by Malick, who is far more concerned with the look of the film. On that level, it is nothing short of ravishing.
PG. ★★★★
D and W: Terrence Malick; Ph: Nestor Almendros; M: Ennio Morricone.
Cast: Richard Gere, Brooke Adams, Sam Shepard, Linda Manz.

DAYS OF WINE AND ROSES. (1963) The irony of the title becomes even crueller in a powerful study of alcoholism that takes the trouble to calibrate the steps by which drinking becomes first a problem and then a calamity. Jack Lemmon, a San Francisco public relations man, recruits his wife into his drinking bouts with terrible consequences. Great comic actors are usually very good in serious roles, a proposition that Lemmon demonstrated here and reiterated on many subsequent occasions.
★★★★
D: Blake Edwards; W: J.P. Miller; Ph: Philip Lathrop; M: Henry Mancini.

Cast: Jack Lemmon, Lee Remick, Charles Bickford, Jack Klugman.

THE DAY THE EARTH CAUGHT FIRE. (1961) Sweat it out in London as the temperature goes up and up and up. Fleet Street newshounds make the discovery that nuclear testing by both superpowers has moved the earth closer to the sun. In the big heat, the world prepares for the worst. Well-done and quite frightening, the film avoids many of the disaster cliches with an intelligent screenplay.
★★★
D: Val Guest; W: Guest and Wolf Mankowitz; Ph: Harry Waxman; M: Monty Norman.
Cast: Edward Judd, Janet Munro, Leo McKern, Arthur Christiansen.

THE DAY THE EARTH STOOD STILL. (1951) One of the landmark science fiction pictures of the fifties even though it has to overcome the fact that it is a parable about the Cold War. Michael Rennie is perfect as a visiting alien who sets up his flying saucer in Washington and stations a massive robot to guard it. His quest is for world peace, but Robert Wise keeps things fluent and does not succumb to pomposity.
★★★★
D: Robert Wise; W: Edmund H. North; Ph: Leo Tover; M: Bernard Herrmann.
Cast: Michael Rennie, Patricia Neal, Sam Jaffe, Billy Gray.

THE DAY THEY ROBBED THE BANK OF ENGLAND. (1960) And who would have more cause to do it than the Irish? The attempt on the impregnable bastion of British money is made in 1901 and it's an extremely well-executed caper movie.
★★★
D: John Guillermin; W: Howard Clewes and Richard Maibaum; Ph: Georges Perinal; M: Edwin Astley.
Cast: Peter O'Toole, Aldo Ray, Elizabeth Sellars, Kieron Moore.

D.C. CAB. (1983) Capital punishment whose makers redefine the meaning of hack. A Washington cab company is the setting for a string of unrelated jokes that are as dirty and ramshackle as the taxis in the fleet. The humor has a mean streak as wide as the Capitol Beltway and Joel Schumacher resolutely avoids the abrupt racial contrasts in Washington that might have given *D.C. Cab* a worthwhile destination.
R. ★

D and W: Joel Schumacher; Ph: Dean Cundey; M: Giorgio Moroder.
Cast: Mr. T, Max Gail, Charlie Barnett, Irene Cara.

D-DAY, THE SIXTH OF JUNE. (1956) Taking the opposite tack to *The Longest Day*, Henry Koster tries the personal approach in which the epic events affect a triangle of lovers. Dana Wynter is torn between a British officer and an American captain and what happens on the beaches of Normandy takes the decision out of her hands.

★★★

D: Henry Koster; W: Ivan Moffat and Harry Brown; Ph: Lee Garmes; M: Lyn Murray.
Cast: Robert Taylor, Richard Todd, Dana Wynter, Edmond O'Brien.

DEAD AND BURIED. (1981) A tacky and third rate resurrection that rips off George Romero's Living Dead series. Murder stalks the streets of a small town called Potters Bluff, but the dead don't rest in peace. Nothing new and poorly executed.

R. ★

D: Gary Sherman; W: Dan O'Bannon and Ronald Shusett; Ph: Steve Poster; M: Joe Renzetti.
Cast: James Farentino, Jack Albertson, Melody Anderson, Dennis Redfield.

DEAD END. (1937) The Dead End Kids, before they were turned into comedians, played a pivotal role in William Wyler's serious and influential look at the roots of crime. Although you can find fragments of the same argument in *The Public Enemy*, Wyler and Humphrey Bogart made a forceful case for the way surroundings—a New York slum —shape criminal behavior. They emphasized it by juxtaposing the slum with a rich neighborhood. The sets are very striking and Bogart's Baby Face Martin confirmed his command of the sort of role he was to make his own.

★★★★

D: William Wyler; W: Lillian Hellman; Ph: Gregg Toland; M: Alfred Newman.
Cast: Humphrey Bogart, Sylvia Sidney, Joel McCrea, Wendy Barrie.

DEADLINE—U.S.A. (1952) A newspaper editor's crusade against crime is threatened by both external pressures—the murder of a witness—and internal troubles. Humphrey Bogart is the crusty newsman and Richard

Brooks, in one of the pictures that made his name, scorns the usual hard-nosed nonsense. The final edition of the paper has the last word and *Deadline—U.S.A.* belongs among the more thoughtful journalistic melodramas.

★★★

D and W: Richard Brooks; Ph: Milton Krasner; M: Cyril J. Mockridge.
Cast: Humphrey Bogart, Ethel Barrymore, Kim Hunter, Ed Begley.

THE DEADLY AFFAIR. (1968) One of the most effective of the films made from John le Carré's morally complex novels. (This one is *Call for the Dead*). James Mason, in one of his finest later roles, is Charles Dobbs, a British security agent. After a suicide in the Foreign Office, he encounters obstacles in his investigation and resigns to pursue it on his own. Mason is consummately good in the ethical dilemmas posed by le Carré and Sidney Lumet fashioned a provocative thriller.

★★★★

D: Sidney Lumet; W: Paul Dehn; Ph: Frederick Young; M: Quincy Jones.
Cast: James Mason, Simone Signoret, Harry Andrews, Maximilian Schell.

DEADLY BLESSING. (1981) There is something irresistible in Ernest Borgnine, a religious fanatic to the far right of Jerry Falwell, bellowing, "You are a stench in the nostrils of God." Humans will find the smell pretty bad too. Wes Craven, the sicko director of *The Hills Have Eyes*, throws a snake in a woman's bubble bath to spice up the silly incantations.

R. ★

D: Wes Craven; W: Glen Besest; Ph: Robert Jessup; M: James Horner.
Cast: Ernest Borgnine, Lois Nettleton, Maren Jensen, Sharon Stone.

DEADLY EYES. (1983) Rats eat grain impregnated with chemicals and get big enough to eat people. Far more revolting than you can imagine.

R. ★

D: Robert Clouse; W: Lonon Smith; M: Anthony Green.
Cast: Scatman Crothers, Sam Groom, Sara Botsford, Lisa Langlois.

DEADLY FORCE. (1983) The people who made *Vice Squad* should have been back walking the streets. Instead they got to make another sleazy venture with the ineffably named Wings Hauser. Hauser is the hero instead of the perverse pimp in this dimwitted stroll, but the plot is signalled by semaphore and involves a tedious trek around Los Angeles in search of a mass killer. The most laughable aspect of the movie is the fact that his estranged wife is covering the murders as a TV newswoman.

R. ★

D: Paul Aaron; W: Barry Schneider, Robert Vincent O'Neil and Ken Barnett; Ph: Norman Leigh and David Myers; M: Gary Scott.
Cast: Wings Hauser, Joyce Ingalls, Paul Shenar, Al Ruscio.

DEAD MEN DON'T WEAR PLAID. (1982) A clever splice of life and one of Steve Martin's better screen efforts. Through ingenious editing, he is a private eye who gets to converse with stars of the forties in some of their most famous moments. Did you know that when Burt Lancaster lay on his bed in *The Killers*, Martin was making him a cup of coffee? Sometimes it works and at others it falls flat.

PG. ★★★

D: Carl Reiner; W: Reiner, George Gipe and Steve Martin; Ph: Michael Chapman; M: Miklos Rosza.
Cast: Steve Martin, Rachel Ward, Carl Reiner, Reni Santori.

THE DEAD ZONE. (1983) Second sight and clairvoyance are treated without much insight in David Cronenberg's adaptation of Stephen King's novel. It is faint praise to say that this is one of the better horror films inspired by King's conglomerate. A fine and eerily accurate performance from Christopher Walken is wasted in a diffuse script. He acquires the unwelcome gift, but Cronenberg goes off in several directions in speculating on the possible consequences.

PG. ★★

D: David Cronenberg; W: Jeffrey Boam; Ph: Mark Irwin; M: Machael Karmen.
Cast: Christopher Walken, Brooke Adams, Tom Skerritt, Herbert Lom.

DEAL OF THE CENTURY. (1983) The unscrupulous international arms industry is such an inviting target that it is hard to imagine a film-maker coming up with a total bomb on the subject. William Friedkin did the unthinkable in a pretty unspeakable picture where ideas fly around like shrapnel. Chevy Chase gets involved in Latin American politics as an arms dealer and the running gag is that

he keeps shooting himself in the foot. So does the movie.

PG. ★

D: William Friedkin; W: Paul Brickman; Ph: Richard Kline; M: Arthur B. Rubinstein.
Cast: Chevy Chase, Sigourney Weaver, Gregory Hines, Vince Edwards.

DEAR DETECTIVE. (1978) An easy-going blend of mystery and wit. Annie Girardot is a detective stuck with investigating minor crimes until she gets her big break with a major murder. She also has an affair with a professor who despises the police. Philippe De Broca manages the ensuing complications adroitly. Hollywood remade the story in 1979 with Brenda Vaccaro in the lead. The French version is vastly preferable.

★★★

D: Philippe De Broca; W: De Broca and Michel Audiard; Ph: Jean-Paul Schwartz; M: Georges Delerue.
Cast: Annie Girardot, Philippe Noiret, Catherine Alric, Hubert Deschamps.

DEATH HUNT. (1981) Based on the true story of the biggest manhunt in Canadian history. A rugged trapper (Charles Bronson) leads his pursuers on an unmerry chase across the Yukon in 1931. Bronson doesn't have to say much, which is always a plus, and Lee Marvin drinks a lot as the sergeant of the mounties leading the chase.

R. ★★

D: Peter Hunt; W: Michael Grals and Mark Victor; Ph: James Devis; M: Jerrold Immel.
Cast: Charles Bronson, Lee Marvin, Ed Lauter, Angie Dickinson.

DEATH OF A SALESMAN. (1951) Laslo Benedek did more than point the camera at the stage in bringing Arthur Miller's American tragedy to the screen. Willie Loman, bitter and 60, looks back in anger and Benedek uses judicious and well-chosen flashbacks to illustrate Loman's misery. Frederic March's Loman is profoundly moving.

★★★★

D: Laslo Benedek; W: Stanley Roberts (adaptor); Ph: Franz Planer; M: Arthur Miller.
Cast: Frederic March, Mildred Dunnock, Kevin McCarthy, Cameron Mitchell.

DEATH ON THE NILE. (1978) An Agatha Christie mystery that finds the actors taking things with varying degrees of seriousness. They range from the cool professionalism of David Niven to Angela Lansbury's swooning

campiness. Everyone, of course, has a motive for murder, some of them exceedingly far-fetched. An heiress on a cruise up the Nile is dispatched with a derringer. Peter Ustinov's first Poirot film.
PG. ★★
D: John Guillermin; W: Anthony Shaffer; Ph: Jack Cardiff; M: Nino Rota.
Cast: Peter Ustinov, David Niven, Bette Davis, Mia Farrow.

DEATH RACE 2000. (1975) A transcontinental road race in which competitors score points by the number of pedestrians they run over. Perhaps a viable fantasy for Manhattan drivers, but a gory, stupid movie. Listen closely and you will hear a pre-Rocky Sylvester Stallone declare, "I want to win this race in the name of hate." That catches the tone of the movie, which is a black comedy that gets lost in the dark.
R. ★
D: Paul Bartel; W: Robert Thom; Ph: Tak Fujimoto ; M: Paul Chihara.
Cast: David Carradine, Sylvester Stallone, Simone Griffeth, Mary Woronov.

DEATH SHIP. (1980) The captain of a luxury liner is being forced to retire from the job. He is played by George Kennedy, who, unfortunately, is still working in movies. On any thinking man's list of the all-time dumb movies, *Death Ship* turns out to be a vessel possessed by departed Nazis which rams the liner. Surviving passengers climb on board the ship with ludicrous consequences.
R. ★
D: Alvin Rakoff; W: John Robins; Ph: Rene Verzier.
Cast: George Kennedy, Sally Ann Howes, Richard Crenna, Nick Mancuso.

DEATHSTALKER. (1984) Third-rate, low budget sword and sorcery that is distinctly lacking in magic. Richard Hill sleepwalking through the hero's role doesn't help the routine rehash of warrior against wizard. A fair amount of sex and violence.
R. ★
D: John Watson; W: Howard Cohen; Ph: Leonardo Rodriguez Solis; M: Oscar Cardozo Campo.
Cast: Richard Hill, Barbi Benton, Richard Brooker, Bernard Ehard.

DEATHTRAP. (1982) Sidney Lumet's able adaptation of the Broadway hit cannot dispense with its staginess. Michael Caine, a playwright confronting failure for the first time, and Christopher Reeve, a student who has written an obvious potential hit, are both better than the script deserves. Caine decides to murder Reeve and steal the play, plunging the film into an often irritating labyrinth of twists and turns.
PG. ★★★
D: Sidney Lumet; W: Jay Presson Allen; Ph: Andrzej Bartkowiak.
Cast: Michael Caine, Christopher Reeve, Dyan Cannon, Irene Worth.

DEATH WATCH. (1979) Bertrand Tavernier's first English language film is a riveting rebuttal to the rosy look of the future to be found in some concurrent American science-fiction. Premature death has been eliminated so that when a young novelist learns she is dying she becomes the center of a media event. A reporter, who is both ambitious and duplicitous, deceives her at great cost to both of them.
★★★★
D: Bertrand Tavernier; W: Tavernier and David Rayfield; Ph: Pierre William Glenn.
Cast: Harvey Keitel, Romy Schneider, Harry Dean Stanton, Max Von Sydow.

DEATH WISH. (1974) An influential and repulsive vigilante movie that amounts to white exploitation. The film's contention is that a liberal is a conservative who hasn't been mugged yet. We are invited to believe that, in the beginning, Charles Bronson is a pillar of the ACLU. He starts exacting vengeance for the murder of his wife and the sexual abuse of his daughter by slaughtering muggers and becoming a media hero. A fantasy for the harried city dweller, but its underlying arguments are frightening.
R. ★
D: Michael Winner; W: Wendell Mayes; Ph: Arthur J. Ornitz; M: Herbie Hancock.
Cast: Charles Bronson, Vincent Gardenia, Hope Lange, Stuart Margolin.

DEATH WISH II. (1982) By an absurd coincidence, an architect who lost his wife now loses his daughter and housekeeper. This allows Charles Bronson to stalk the killers in Los Angeles in a crude piece of exploitation that reduces the vast complexities of the justice system to the caveman level. In an otherwise comatose script, a character wonders if this attitude—taken to its logical extreme—would allow one citizen to gun down another because he has long hair. Very violent.
R. ★

D: Michael Winner; W: David Engelbach; Ph: Richard Kline and Tom Del Ruth; M: Jimmy Page.
Cast: Charles Bronson, Jill Ireland, Robin Sherwood, Silvana Gillardo.

THE DEEP. (1977) Rescued from the shallows of B-moviedom by the extraordinary craftsmanship and technique of the underwater sequences by photographers Al Giddings and Stan Waterman. Submerged for about one third of the running time, the movie gets into trouble when it comes up for air. Nolte and Bisset are a young couple whose innocent skin-diving involves them in huge cache of morphine lying in a wreck. Shaw's Romer Treece is a fine variation on his shark-obsessed hunter in *Jaws*.
PG. ★★★
D: Peter Yates; W: Peter Benchley, Tracy Keenan Wynn; Ph: Christopher Challis, Al Giddings, Stan Waterman; M: John Barry.
Cast: Robert Shaw, Nick Nolte, Jacqueline Bisset, Lou Gossett.

THE DEEP SIX. (1958) The Quaker man of conscience confronted with the dilemma of a just war or act of violence is a Hollywood staple. What gets deep-sixed here is Alan Ladd's predicament when he enters the submarine service armed with a conscience and a reluctance to fight. Scruples don't last very long, but the film does.
★★
D: Rudolph Mate; W: John Twist, Martin Rackin and Harry Brown; Ph: John Seitz; M: David Buttolph.
Cast: Alan Ladd, William Bendix, Efrem Zimbalist, Jr., Dianne Foster.

THE DEER HUNTER. (1979) The definitive distillation of the Vietnam experience begins with the searing image of men standing before the inferno of a blast furnace before their departure for the hell of war. The fate of three working class men from a Pennsylvania mill town is a microcosm of the American tragedy broadened by the vivid imagery of Michael Cimino's landmark film. The narrative divides into three segments: the peaceful pleasures of the men, the horror and insanity of the war and the homecoming. Robert De Niro is the redemptive force who tries to save his friend from madness in Saigon and the rest of the cast approaches the exalted level of acting he sets.
R. ★★★★★
D: Michael Cimino; W: Deric Washburn; Ph: Vilmos Zsigmond; M: Stanley Myers.

Cast: Robert De Niro, John Savage, John Cazale, Christopher Walken.

DEFIANCE. (1980) A western on New York's Lower East Side and quite a good one. Jan-Michael Vincent is a merchant seaman who moves into a run-down neighborhood and stands up to the local gang. Ultimately, the community follows suit. John Flynn knows his plot is standard vigilante exploitation, but he is understated in his direction and the actors follow his sense of restraint.
PG ★★★
D: John Flynn; W: Thomas Michael Donnelly; Ph: Ric Waite; M: Basil Poledouris.
Cast: Jan-Michael Vincent, Theresa Saldana, Art Carney, Rudy Ramos.

THE DEFIANT ONES. (1958) Stanley Kramer's condemnation of racism is labored when set against the likes of *Brubaker*. Even so, it's a forthright piece and one of the few pictures Tony Curtis can be genuinely proud of. A black convict and a white prisoner escape in the South and, because they are literally and figuratively chained together, must learn to live with prejudice and work as a team.
★★★
D: Stanley Kramer; W: Nedrick Young and Harold Jacob Smith; Ph: Sam Leavitt; M: Ernest Gold.
Cast: Sidney Poitier, Tony Curtis, Theodore Bikel, Charles McGraw.

DELIVERANCE. (1972) John Boorman delivered James Dickey's novel with primal force. Four men from Atlanta embark on a canoe trip in rough country in the macho friendship of a beer commercial. Locals take after them and the trip literally becomes a survival course. *Deliverance* is best taken for its comments on instincts and masculinity and the environmental arguments can be ignored. The characters are well defined and the tension at the end is nerve-wracking.
R. ★★★★
D: John Boorman; W: James Dickey; Ph: Vilmos Zsigmond; M: Eric Weissberg.
Cast: Burt Reynolds, Jon Voight, Ned Beatty, Ronny Cox.

DEMETRIUS AND THE GLADIATORS. (1954) What lion can survive the blinding dazzle of Victor Mature's teeth? Man and beast go down before Demetrius, a Greek slave forced to fight and temporarily seduced away from Christianity by Susan Hayward. Tacky sequel to *The Robe* that is pretty silly outside the arena. Jay Robinson throws in a high camp Caligula.

★★

D: Delmer Daves; W: Philip Dunne; Ph: Milton Krasner; M: Franz Waxman.
Cast: Victor Mature, Susan Hayward, Michael Rennie, Debra Paget.

DEMON SEED. (1977) Julie Christie lent new meaning to the idea of a personal computer in this glib tale of a machine that wishes to reproduce itself. The computer is called Proteus IV and its efforts to procreate Proteus V are consummated in the basement by means of a brass valve. For those into screws and bolts erotica. Anyone looking for a probing essay on rampant technology should try elsewhere.

R.   ★★

D: Donald Cammell; W: Robert Jaffe, Roger O. Hirson; Ph: Bill Butler; M: Jerry Fielding.
Cast: Julie Christie, Fritz Weaver, Gerrit Graham.

DERSU UZALA. (1975) Visually stunning Oscar winner from Akira Kurosawa that celebrates the friendship of a hunter who lives at one with nature and a Russian surveyor. Set in Siberia at the turn of the century, the film chronicles the life of the hunter as a symbol of natural man, who has lost his wife and children to smallpox.

G.   ★★★★

D: Akira Kurosawa; W: Kurosawa and Yuri Nagibin; Ph: Asakardu Nakai; M: Isaak Shvarts.
Cast: Maxim Munzuk, Yuri Solomin.

THE DESERT FOX. (1951) An already sympathetic account of General Rommel in World War II is made the more so by James Mason's excellence in the lead. Rommel's tactical brilliance is documented and he emerges as a "good" German—thereby justifying the stance of the picture. His resistance to Hitler and participation in the plot against the Fuhrer culminate in his forced suicide.

★★★

D: Henry Hathaway; W: Nunnally Johnson; Ph: Norbert Brodine.
Cast: James Mason, Jessica Tandy, Cedric Hardwicke, Luther Adler.

THE DESERT RATS. (1953) James Mason scored such a success as Rommel in *The Desert Fox* that he inspired and appeared in this account of a band of Australian soldiers at the siege of Tobruk. He makes only a brief contribution at an interrogation. Despite its artificial origins, *The Desert Rats* is a first-rate war film with Richard Burton and Robert Newton in particuarly good form.

★★★

D: Robert Wise; W: Richard Murphy; Ph: Lucien Ballard; M: Leigh Harline.
Cast: Richard Burton, James Mason, Robert Newton, Robert Douglas.

DESIRE. (1936) A delightful contrast between Gary Cooper's open and slightly naive Americanism and Marlene Dietrich's European sensuality. In one of her sexier light outings, she is a thief who co-opts Cooper into her plans by the most reliable method at her disposal.

★★★

D: Frank Borzage; W: Edwin Justus Mayer, Waldemar Young and Samuel Hoffenstein; Ph: Charles Lang; M: Frederick Hollander.
Cast: Gary Cooper, Marlene Dietrich, John Halliday, William Frawley.

DESIREE. (1954) On the battlefront with Marlon Brando as Napoleon. Once again, he proves that even in trash he is an actor of rare and hypnotic fascination. *Desiree* purports to be an account of Napoleon's passion for a girl he met in Marseilles in 1794. Diverting claptrap.

★★

D: Henry Koster; W: Daniel Taradash; Ph: Milton Krasner; M: Alex North.
Cast: Marlon Brando, Jean Simmons, Merle Oberon, Michael Rennie.

DESK SET. (1957) An efficiency expert, armed with all manner of new technology, invades the bailiwick of a super-efficient researcher. The most efficient aspect of the comedy is its maximum use of the electrifying partnership of Spencer Tracy and Katharine Hepburn. No screen pairing was better at managing the transition from hostility to love. *Desk Set* is not their best, but it remains amusingly pertinent and rather far-sighted for all of us trapped in the computer age.

★★★★

D: Walter Lang; W: Phoebe and Henry Ephron; Ph: Leon Shamroy; M: Cyril Mockridge.
Cast: Spencer Tracy, Katharine Hepburn, Gig Young, Joan Blondell.

DESPERATE JOURNEY. (1942) Well done wartime propaganda with the point bludgeoned home by Errol Flynn, who was, of course, the nemesis of the Axis powers all by himself. The Germans don't stand a chance when Flynn, a prisoner, bids for freedom.

★★

D: Raoul Walsh; W: Arthur Horman; Ph: Bert Glennon.
Cast: Errol Flynn, Ronald Reagan, Alan Hale, Nancy Coleman.

DESTINATION GOBI. (1953) The Pentagon, which is used to throwing around billions, has to come up with sixty saddles. They are payment to a Mongol chief who comes to the aid of a group of stranded American sailors in their fight with the Japanese. He even finds them a Chinese junk and the film is far from garbage. Its humor and locale are off the beaten track.

★★★

D: Robert Wise; W: Everett Freeman; Ph: Charles Clarke; M: Sol Kaplan.
Cast: Richard Widmark, Don Taylor, Casey Adams, Murvyn Vye.

DESTINATION MOON. (1950) In its day, George Pal's speculative voyage to the moon caught the imagination of moviegoers and it is an important landmark in the development of science ficiton. Its chief contribution lay in advancing—however modestly—the notion of simulating reality in outer space. The voyage itself is conceived of as a capitalist gesture and turns into a rather dull trip. *Destination Moon* is a document of the way we thought it would be.

★★★

D: Irving Pichel; W: Rip van Ronkel, Robert Heinlein and James O'Hanlon; Ph: Lionel Lindon; M: Leith Stevens.
Cast: Warner Anderson, John Archer, Tom Powers, Dick Wesson.

DESTINATION TOKYO. (1944) Underwater with Cary Grant as the suave commander coping with John Garfield and the dangers of life aboard a submarine. The film builds, with more deliberation than necessary, to a climactic raid on Tokyo harbor.

★★★

D: Delmer Daves; W: Daves and Albert Maltz; Ph: Bert Glennon; M: Franz Waxman.
Cast: Cary Grant, John Garfield, Alan Hale, Dane Clark.

DESTRY RIDES AGAIN. (1939) "See What the Boys in the Backroom Will Have" is huskily belted out by Marlene Dietrich in a number that shows up frequently in affectionate anthologies. This western deserves to be remembered for more than the famous offer. It is a spry, light-hearted and action-packed exercise that plays as much on Jimmy Stewart's droll side as Dietrich's sensuality. He has to tame a tough town and guess who?

★★★★

D: George Marshall; W: Gertrude Purcell, Felix Jackson and Henry Myers; Ph: Hal Mohr; M: Frank Skinner.
Cast: Marlene Dietrich, James Stewart, Brian Donlevy, Charles Winninger.

THE DETECTIVE. (1968) A hard-bitten *policier* enriched by the gritty New York locations. Frank Sinatra is married and none too happily to a nymphomaniac and assigned to a homosexual murder case. The film makes its points about a policeman's lot without shouting from the rooftops and Sinatra conveys a man doing his job and making a terrible mistake in the midst of private misery.

★★★

D: Gordon Douglas; W: Abby Mann; Ph: Joseph Biroc; M: Jerry Goldsmith.
Cast: Frank Sinatra, Lee Remick, Ralph Meeker, Jack Klugman.

DETECTIVE STORY. (1951) It's actually several stories brought together during a night at a tough New York precinct, focussing on a tougher cop. Kirk Douglas' Jim McLeod hates criminals with a passion —and occasionally a punch— in a way that Dirty Harry would approve. The detective's attitude is rather glibly explained but Douglas gives him a powerhouse presence.

★★★

D: William Wyler; W: Wyler and Philip Yordan; Ph: Lee Garmes.
Cast: Kirk Douglas, William Bendix, Eleanor Parker, Cathy O'Donnell.

THE DEVILS. (1971) Perhaps the Devil made him do it, but Ken Russell's version of the stage play is infernally bad. John Whiting based his study of witchcraft on Aldous Huxley's *The Devils of Loudon* and both are honorable and fascinating treatments of the supposed mass posssession that overwhelms a 17th century convent. Russell's additions to a compelling drama are both superflous and revolting.

★

D and W: Ken Russell; Ph: David Watkin; M: Peter Maxwell Davies.
Cast: Oliver Reed, Vanessa Redgrave, Dudley Sutton, Max Adrian.

THE DEVIL'S BRIGADE. (1968) A *Dirty Dozen* imitation that gives very short measure. Canadian commandos and the sweepings of U.S. Army jails are brought together under the reluctant gaze of William Holden to train for a dangerous World War II mission. They dislike each other, a point reiterated with great tedium. A French Canadian soldier calls Claude Akins a "merde" and a companion tells him it's a compliment. The appraisal suits a pedestrian undertaking.

★

D: Andrew McLaglen; W: William Roberts; Ph: William Thier; M: Alex North.
Cast: William Holden, Claude Akins, Cliff Robertson, Vince Edwards .

THE DEVIL'S DISCIPLE. (1959) If General Burgoyne had been as smart as he is in Laurence Olivier's reading we would still be hearing Cockney accents on the streets of Manhattan. In a so-so version of George Bernard Shaw's light piece on the American revolution, a rogue (Kirk Douglas) is assumed to be a rebel by the British. The memorable moments belong to Olivier. He makes off with the trial scene while seated and saying nothing.

★★★

D: Guy Hamilton; W: John Dighton and Roland Kibbee; Ph: Jack Hildyard; M: Richard Rodney Bennett.
Cast: Kirk Douglas, Burt Lancaster, Laurence Olivier, Eva Le Gallienne.

DEVIL'S ISLAND. (1940) A conscientious and rather strident expose of conditions at the infamous French penal colony that followed the fashion for airing the brutality of prison life. Boris Karloff is a physician who is exiled to the island for treating a fugitive and confronts a sadistic warden.

★★★

D: William Clemens; W: Don Ryan and Kenneth Gamet.
Cast: Boris Karloff, James Stephenson, Ned Harrigan, Robert Warwick.

THE DEVIL'S PLAYGROUND. (1978) The first work of the talented Australian director

Fred Schepisi is a semi-autobiographical study of life in a seminary. The tone is one of rueful compassion for both the boys and the priests who teach them instead of an easy diatribe on the sins of the fathers. The priests are in a no-win situation where they deny the natural sex urges of the body by considering them unnatural.

★★★★

D and W: Fred Schepisi; Ph: Ian Baker; M: Bruce Smeaton.
Cast: Arthur Dignam, Nick Tate, Simon Burke.

THE DEVIL'S RAIN. (1975) Falls mainly on the inane. The devil worshipers are eyeless; you should be so lucky. A spirit-dampener with Ernest Borgnine trying to work his way into Satan's favor by hunting down the decendants of a colonial family that betrayed him in a previous life. A good cast, including William Shatner and Tom Skerritt, is humiliated and today wishes this rain would go away.
PG. ★
D: Robert Fuest; W: Gabe Essoe, James Ashton and Gerald Hopman; Ph: Alex Phillips; M: Al de Lory.
Cast: Ernest Borgnine, Ida Lupino, Eddie Albert, William Shatner.

DIAL M FOR MURDER. (1954) The pivotal phone number is a Mayfair exchange and the stiffly acted (except for Ray Milland and John Williams), theatrical mystery is only middling-fair Hitchcock. It covers several themes that interested him but he explored them with more depth elsewhere. Milland, an ominous smoothie, arranges the murder of his wife by blackmailing a criminal. He plans to be out for the evening at a stag dinner. His carefully laid plan is cut to pieces by a convenient pair of scissors.

★★★

D: Alfred Hitchcock; W: Frederick Knott; Ph: Robert Burks; M: Dmitri Tiomkin.
Cast: Ray Milland, Grace Kelly, Robert Cummings, John Williams.

DIAMONDS. (1975) Doesn't last forever. It just seems that way. Robert Shaw, in one of his more lamentable hack movies, leads a multi-gadgeted robbery of a burglar-proof vault in Tel Aiv. Shelley Winters keeps popping up as a Jewish widow and an indication of the quality of the film is that her appearances are a welcome diversion. Dated even when it was released.
PG. ★★

D: Menahem Golan; W: Golan and David Paulsen; Ph: Adam Greenberg; M: Roy Budd.
Cast: Robert Shaw, Richard Roundtree, Barbara Seagull, Shelley Winters.

DIAMONDS ARE FOREVER. (1971) Sean Connery returned to the role of James Bond with a timely reminder that 007 is a very rough diamond. He ends up in a Las Vegas crematorium in a coffin that is about to be incinerated, but Connery put life back in the character. The stunts include a chase through Las Vegas and an attack by homicidal lesbians as Bond thwarts yet another world conquest by Blofeld. This one involves a thinly veiled pastiche of Howard Hughes.

★★★

D: Guy Hamilton; W: Richard Maibaum and Tom Mankiewicz; Ph: Ted Moore; M: John Barry.
Cast: Sean Connery, Jill St. John, Charles Gray, Lana Wood.

THE DIARY OF ANNE FRANK. (1959) Perhaps the most famous instance of the "personalization" of the Holocaust, a catastrophe of such horrible dimensions that many feel that reduction to a comprehensible scale leads to trivialization. Nonetheless, there is a certain poignance in Millie Perkins' Anne. She is a 13-year-old Jewish girl hiding from the Gestapo for two years in an Amsterdam attic with her family. Perkins is at her best conveying Anne's sense of yearning for what life might have been. Shelley Winters won a supporting actress Oscar for her belligerent histrionics.

★★★

D: George Stevens; W: Frances Goodrich and Albert Hackett; Ph: William C. Mellor; M: Alfred Newman.
Cast: Millie Perkins, Shelley Winters, Joseph Schildkraut, Richard Beymer.

A DIFFERENT STORY. (1978) A homosexual and a lesbian get married and have a baby. Fine when it celebrates their difference, but the movie collapses in trying to come to terms with it. Heterosexuals will find their change of heart improbable and gays will think it outrageous. Two very skilled leads are wasted.
R. ★★
D: Paul Aaron; W: Henry Olek; Ph: Philip Lathrop; M: David Frank.
Cast: Perry King, Meg Foster, Peter Donat, Valerie Curtin.

THE D.I. (1957) A slog through bootcamp with Jack Webb doing the yelling and an explanation of why the Marines are so few in number. The film is nothing to be proud of in its march through the usual training film boys-into-men banalities. Webb, in fact, directs with all the elan of an army training film on dismantling weapons.

★★

D: Jack Webb; W: James Lee Barrett; Ph: Edward Colman; M: David Buttolph.
Cast: Jack Webb, Don Dubbins, Jackie Loughery, Lin McCarthy.

DILLINGER. (1973) John Milius was later to invest his passion for bloodily staged violence with philosophical overtones in *Conan the Barbarian*. In his directing debut, there are no such airs to the mayhem, although this is not a view of a notorious hood that J. Edgar Hoover would sanction. Warren Oates, an often under-rated talent, is excellent in the lead. Dillinger's wild career through the headlines is traced to the point where he was gunned down outside the Biograph theater in Chicago in 1934.
R. ★★★
D and W: John Milius; Ph: Jules Brenner; M: Barry Devorzon.
Cast: Warren Oates, Ben Johnson, Michelle Philips, Cloris Leachman.

DIMPLES. (1936) Shirley Temple on the New York Bowery before the Civil War, but this outing belongs in the high rent area of her movies. Frank Morgan is delightful as her thieving grandfather who uses his moppet to distract his victims. Of course, an angelic society type takes her off the Bowery and puts her on the stage.

★★★

D: William A. Seither; W: Arthur Sheekman and Nat Perrin; Ph: Bert Glennon; M: Louis Silvers.
Cast: Shirley Temple, Frank Morgan, Helen Westley, Robert Kent.

DINER. (1982) That rarity in American movies, a grown-up film about growing up. Its tone is that of an adult looking ruefully back on the rites of passage into manhood rather than of a young person still struggling through them. Incisive and often hilarious, *Diner* evokes Baltimore in the fifties and tells the story of five friends who have reached their twenties but can't abandon the habits of adolescence. Their haunt is an all night diner where they are safe to rehash sports and rock and roll away from the mysteries of sex and women.

R. ★★★★
D and W: Barry Levinson; Ph: Peter Sova.
Cast: Steve Guttenberg, Daniel Stern, Kevin Bacon, Mickey Rourke.

DINNER AT EIGHT. (1933) An all-star feast hosted by George Cukor at his most gracious. Despite the artificial device—a hostess with ambitions tosses a dinner party and we get to know the guests through anecdotes—the casting is faultless, as is the direction. The revelations go beyond character to comment on the distance between public posture and reality.

★★★★
D: George Cukor; W: Francis Marion and Herman J. Mankiewicz; Ph: William Daniels.
Cast: Marie Dressler, John Barrymore, Lionel Barrymore, Jean Harlow.

DIPLOMATIC COURIER. (1952) Lukewarm Cold War thriller. Tyrone Power pursues Patricia Neal and the Russian plans to invade Yugoslavia. Both targets seem to be of equal importance.

★★
D: Henry Hathaway; W: Casey Robinson and Liam O'Brien; Ph: Lucien Ballard; M: Sol Kaplan.
Cast: Tyrone Power, Patricia Neal, Stephen McNally, Hildegarde Neff.

THE DIRTY DOZEN. (1967) Lee Marvin orders his convict commandos to shoot the officers when they make a suicidal raid on German headquarters. "Theirs or ours?" is the response and it's typical of the anti-authoritarian humor that sets Robert Aldrich's film apart from other macho war adventures. The men choose an almost certain suicide over capital punishment and their training is more amusing than the actual raid. Quite violent.

★★★
D: Robert Aldrich; W: Nunnally Johnson and Lukas Heller; Ph: Edward Scaife; M: Frank de Vol.
Cast: Lee Marvin, Ernest Borgnine, Robert Ryan, Charles Bronson.

DIRTY HARRY. (1971) A crude but very effective appeal to the most primal emotions of vengeance that introduced Detective Harry Callahan to a world-wide audience. His turf is the liberal and sophisticated city of San Francisco and his moral territory the familiar ground between law and justice.

Harry contrives to administer the latter in pursuit of a sniper. The film, shrewdly directed by veteran Don Siegel, allowed Eastwood an easy and weirdly logical transition from spaghetti westerns to tough urban cop dramas.

★★
D: Don Siegel; W: Hary Julian Fink, Rita Fink and Dean Reisner; Ph: Bruce Surtees; M: Lalo Schifrin.
Cast: Clint Eastwood, Harry Guardino, Reni Santoni, John Vernon.

DIRTY MARY, CRAZY LARRY. (1974) Exclusively for rubberneckers who slow down to ogle accidents and, in its way, a precursor of the *Smokey and the Bandit* series. The car crashes are welcome since they interrupt the dialogue. Peter Fonda holds up a supermarket to finance his dream of becoming a stock-car racer and the rest is stock footage. Vic Morrow is the irate sheriff in pursuit.

PG. ★
D: John Hough; W: Leigh Chapman and Antonio Santean; Ph: Mike Margulies; M: Jimmy Haskell.
Cast: Peter Fonda, Vic Morrow, Susan George, Adam Roarke.

THE DISCREET CHARM OF THE BOURGEOISIE. (1972) In one of Luis Bunuel's most savagely conceived and riotously executed works, a group of upper middle class types arrive at a house for dinner. It's the wrong night and what ensues is a wild collage of surreal dreams and interruptions by soldiers, terrorists and policemen. A typical moment in the inspired satire has a bishop murdering the man who killed his parents—after giving the victim absolution.

★★★★
D: Luis Bunuel; W: Bunuel and Jean-Claude Carriere; Ph: Edmond Richard.
Cast: Fernando Rey, Delphine Seyrig, Stephane Audran, Bulle Ogier.

DIVA. (1981) A flashy, winning and totally unpredictable proof that a French connection can exist between the opera stage and the underworld. Part police thriller, part offbeat love story—between a diva and a smitten young postal worker—it keeps the viewer off balance with its dash and surprises. *Diva* is a tale of two tapes—one records the voice of the prima donna and the other the last words of a murdered prostitute which will incriminate several powerful figures. It is one for the record books itself.

★★★★

D: Jean-Jacques Beineix; W: Beineix and Jean Van Hamme; Ph: Philippe Rousselot; M: Vladimir Cosma.
Cast: Wilhelmenia Fernandez, Frederic Andrei, Richard Bohringer, Thuy An Luu.

THE DIVINE NYMPH. (1980) One of the films Laura Antonelli made in the seventies that turned a promising career into a high-class centerfold. It is set in the twenties in Italy but plays like a third-rate nineteenth century opera. She becomes the mistress of a nobleman who takes revenge on the cousin who raped her when she was fifteen.

★★

D: Giuseppe Patroni Griffi; W: Griffi and A. Valdarnini; Ph: Giuseppe Rotunno; M: Ennio Morricone.
Cast: Laura Antonelli, Terence Stamp, Marcello Mastroianni, Ettore Manni.

DIVORCE AMERICAN STYLE. (1967) A pungent and often amusing look at suburban marriage that is full of wry observation and blessed with Jason Robards. In spite of its years, *Divorce American Style* remains timely since much of its humor is built around the fact that divorce can produce great economic hardship. Dick Van Dyke and Debbie Reynolds are the central couple.

★★★

D: Bud Yorkin; W: Norman Lear; Ph: Conrad Hall; M: David Grusin.
Cast: Dick Van Dyke, Debbie Reynolds, Jason Robards, Jean Simmons.

DOCTOR IN THE HOUSE. (1954) The droll misadventures—both medical and amorous—of the students at St. Swithin's hospital. Based on the popular books by Richard Gordon, it was the first of a series of enormously popular "Doctor" movies, which use essentially the same humor and framework. With James Robertson Justice at his crustiest as the head surgeon and Dirk Bogarde leading the students, this is by far the best of the series.

★★★

D: Ralph Thomas; W: Nicholas Phipps; Ph: Ernest Steward; M: Bruce Montgomery.
Cast: Dirk Bogarde, Kenneth More, Donald Sinden, James Robertson Justice.

DOCTOR ZHIVAGO. (1965) In length (197 minutes) and dimension, David Lean's rendering of Boris Pasternak's novel has the epic dimension it demands. Robert Bolt's screenplay is articulate but its structure leans too heavily on an episodic style that can be confusing. Tumultuous events are represented by tumult on the screen. One does not often find memorable acting in such massive productions, but Julie Christie's Lara and Tom Courtenay's revolutionary stand out. The action follows the suffering of a doctor before and during the Russian revolution.

★★★

D: David Lean; W: Robert Bolt; Ph: Frederick Young; M: Maurice Jarre.
Cast: Omar Sharif, Julie Christie, Rod Steiger, Alec Guinness.

DODGE CITY. (1939) Errol Flynn's accent is explained by making him an Irish adventurer in his first western. Michael Curtiz never quite found the handle of the six-shooter in his long and illustrious career and his costume collaborations with Flynn are much better. Flynn cleans up the corrupt town and engages in one of the more admired saloon punch-ups in the genre.

★★★

D: Michael Curtiz; W: Robert Buckner; Ph: Ray Rennahan; M: Max Steiner.
Cast: Errol Flynn, Bruce Cabot, Olivia De Havilland, Ann Sheridan.

DOG DAY AFTERNOON. (1975) Al Pacino has a special flair for attracting sympathy for complex and morally compromised men. Sal, a homosexual, enlists the aid of a fundamentalist psychopath to rob a Brooklyn bank and is forced to take hostages. He becomes the orchestrator and the victim of a media event. A lacerating, gritty film that is both funny and moving and it remains one of the best in the Sidney Lumet canon. The dialogue is right off the sidewalks of New York and it makes a real difference to the impact of the picture.

R.   ★★★★★

D: Sidney Lumet; W: Frank Pierson; Ph: Victor J. Kemper.
Cast: Al Pacino, John Cazale, Chris Sarandon, Charles Durning.

THE DOGS OF WAR. (1981) John Irvin lets Frederick Forsyth's novel slip through his fingers by being too faithful to it. Forsyth documented the mercenary life and the details of organizing a coup at great length and in reflecting this emphasis, Irvin slows the story to a painstaking tempo. The hows of the trade take precedence over the whys as Christopher Walken mounts a *coup d'etat* in an African state. The work is more deserving of a *coup de grace*.

R. ★★
D: John Irvin; W: Gary DeVore and George Malko; Ph: Jack Cardiff; M: Geoffrey Burgon. Cast: Christopher Walken, Tom Berenger, Colin Blakely, Hugh Millais.

THE DOMINO PRINCIPLE. (1977) Gene Hackman is a convicted murderer who will be given his freedom in return for killing an unidentified politician, presumably the President. No one involved in the film feels at liberty to confide in the audience. It brims with references to "them." "They are never anything you can identify," says one protagonist. In this reading, they are absurdly close to Hackman the hit-man as the plans for the killing go ahead. Cryptically paranoid to the end.

R. ★★
D: Stanley Kramer; W: Adam Kennedy; Ph: Fred Koenekamp, Ernest Laszlo; M: Billy Goldenberg.
Cast: Gene Hackman, Eddie Albert, Candice Bergen, Richard Widmark.

DONA FLOR AND HER TWO HUS-BANDS. (1978) An erotic and amusing Brazilian ghost story with some arch observations on marriage, this is the film *Kiss Me Goodbye* was meant to be. The heroine's sexy heel of a husband dies and comes back to do more than haunt her when she remarries a boring druggist. Told in a droll, deadpan manner that is highly effective.

★★★
D and W: Bruno Barreto; Ph: Maurilo Salles; M: Chico Buarque.
Cast: Sonia Braga, Jose Wilker, Mauro Mendonca, Dinorah Brilanti.

DON GIOVANNI. (1979) Joseph Losey moved the setting from Seville to Venice and made an honorable effort to rethink the ways in which opera can be filmed. His version of Mozart's masterpiece is an interesting failure that, in opening up the work with the camera, exposes its theatricality. Thus Don Ottavio gives us "Il Mio Tesoro" while being rowed through a marsh and it looks silly. Losey also tried to politicize some events in the plot. Forgive these idiosyncrasies and enjoy the excellent singing.

★★★
D: Joseph Losey; Ph: Gerry Fisher; M: Mozart (Lorin Maazel conducting the Paris Opera Orchestra).
Cast: Ruggero Raimondi, Kiri Te Kanawa, John Macurdy, Edda Moser.

DON'S PARTY. (1982) Bruce Beresford, whose films include *Tender Mercies*, shows little compassion for his fellow Australians in a savage attack on posturing masculinity. An election night party becomes an evening of unmitigated nastiness among friends with the focus on the ruinous impact a certain kind of machismo can have on relationships. Misery doesn't love company here. Misery *is* company.

★★★
D: Bruce Beresford; W: David Williamson; Ph: Don McAlpine; M: Leon Jan.
Cast: John Hargreaves, Jeanie Drynan, Graeme Blundell, Veronica Lang.

DOUBLE INDEMNITY. (1944) A dream-team collaboration produced one man's nightmare and what is generally regarded as one of the best exercises in *film-noir* from the forties. Raymond Chandler wrote the terse dialogue from James M. Cain's story and the film looks at its characters from a viewpoint of a spider in the web. Fred MacMurray is Walter Neff, a defiantly ordinary soul who is so smitten with Barbara Stanwyck that he agrees to kill her husband so that they can collect the insurance. Edward G. Robinson is in terrific form as the the investigator who becomes suspicious.

★★★★★
D: Billy Wilder; W: Wilder and Raymond Chandler; Ph: John Seitz; M: Miklos Rozsa.
Cast: Fred MacMurray, Barbara Stanwyck, Edward G. Robinson, Porter Hall.

THE DOVE. (1974) Robin Lee Graham became the youngest man to sail alone around the world in 1970 and his feat is dutifully recreated. An attempt to relieve the inevitable monotony is made with a desultory romance and snippets of travelogue. Sven Nykvist's sea vistas are very handsome.

PG. ★★
D: Charles Jarrott; W: Peter Beagle and Adam Kennedy; Ph: Sven Nykvist; M: John Barry.
Cast: Joseph Bottoms, Deborah Raffin, John McLiam, Dabney Coleman.

DOWN ARGENTINE WAY. (1940) More a postcard than a movie with every cliche about South America imaginable. Betty Grable goes to Argentina and falls for the charms of a racehorse owner. Splashy, colorful and defiantly air-headed.

★★

D: Irving Cummings; W: Darrell Ware and Karl Tunberg; Ph: Leon Shamroy; M: Emil Newman.
Cast: Betty Grable, Don Ameche, Carmen Miranda, Charlotte Greenwood.

DOWNHILL RACER. (1969) One of the more incisive sports films that dispenses with the cheerleading Rocky motif to examine what it takes to excel at the highest level. Robert Redford is understated and low-key which is what the role of a self-centered loner requires and his coach (Gene Hackman) is a complementary balance. Michael Ritchie is fascinated with the drive to win and he expressed it here in a sport that lends itself to the camera. The ski sequences are first-class, but you don't have to like or even know the sport to enjoy the film.

★★★

D: Michael Ritchie; W: James Salter; Ph: Brian Probyn; M: Kenyon Hopkins.
Cast: Robert Redford, Gene Hackman, Camilla Sparv, Joe Jay Jalbert.

DRACULA. (1931) For audiences it was love at first bite and Bela Lugosi's count was the one that started the almost countless variations and repetitions that culminated in the so aptly named *Dracula's Dog*. He had played the role on stage and was well prepared to protest "I never drink...wine" when the cameras rolled. However, unlike James Whales superb Frankenstein films, *Dracula* has not worn that well and there is not much more than Lugosi to the first appearance of Dracula. It begins very well but the life slips away when Dracula reaches England.

★★★

D: Tod Browning; W: Garrett Fort and Dudley Murphy; Ph: Karl Freund.
Cast: Bela Lugosi, David Manners, Helen Chandler, John Balderston.

DRACULA. (1979) The damp wind from the grave bears the scent of cologne in Frank Langella's unique interpretation of Bram Stoker's Count. He does Dracula as a figure of languid eroticism and inconsolable loneliness, but the freshness and style of his reading is wasted. John Badham has surrounded it with the usual bag of horror tricks and generous gore that stomps all over the subtlety of Langella, who became a Broadway star in the role.
R.

★★★

D: John Badham; W: W.D. Richter; Ph: Gilbert Taylor; M: John Williams.
Cast: Frank Langella, Laurence Olivier, Kate Nelligan, Donald Pleasence.

DRACULA—PRINCE OF DARKNESS. (1966) One of the more anemic Hammer films about Transylvania's favorite son. Although Christopher Lee is back as the allnight sucker, this sequel to *Horror of Dracula* deserves a quiet burial, if not a stake through the heart. Two couples are lured to the castle by the butler. He didn't do what happens thereafter.

★★

D: Terence Fisher; W: John Sansom; Ph: Michael Reed; M: James Bernard.
Cast: Christopher Lee, Barbara Shelley, Andre Keir, Francis Matthes.

DRAGNET. (1954) A drag unless you are a diehard fan of the old television show. Sgt. Friday—he of the polite address and expressionless face—and his partner look into the murder of a convict with mob ties. No discernible difference from the series, just longer.

★★

D: Jack Webb; W: Richard Breen; Ph: Edward Colman.
Cast: Jack Webb, Ben Alexander, Richard Boone, Stacy Harris.

DRAGONSLAYER. (1981) A worthy quest done in by its screenplay long before the hero takes on the dragon. It leans to such idiotic assertions as "Horsrik has misspoke himself", which sounds like a terrible accident with a wheel. The actual dragon confrontation, courtesy of George Lucas' wizards, is very impressive, but the pre-fight show is a worn collage of fairy tale themes. Parents might want to bear in mind that the monster at the end is pretty alarming for younger children.
PG.

★★

D: Matthew Robbins; W: Hal Barwood; Ph: Derek Vanlint; M: Alex North.
Cast: Peter MacNicol, Caitlin Clarke, Ralph Richardson, Chloe Salaman.

DR. DOLITTLE. (1967) In terms of entertainment, this woeful musical could not have a more accurate title. Based on the Hugh Lofting stories, which the scriptwriter read and totally misunderstood. Rex Harrison, the vet who talks to his charges, is accused of lunacy. He is certainly open to the indictment for taking the part. Bereft of charm and decent music, the film's only claim to fame is that it nearly bankrupted Twentieth Century-Fox.

★

D: Richard Fleischer; W: Leslie Bricusse; Ph: Robert Surtees; M: Lionel Newman.
Cast: Rex Harrison, Samantha Eggar, Anthony Newley, Richard Attenborough.

DREAMER. (1979) Hollywood bowling. If there is one thing more boring than bowling itself, it is surely watching other people bowl. This is what happens when you make a movie which ignores the obvious and it is a bowling movie without a single worthwhile frame. Tim Matheson agonizes over leaving his job as a club pro to go bowling for dollars on the tour. Jack Warden is in his usual athletic supporter role as the coach.
PG. ★
D: Noel Nosseck; W: James Proctor and Larry Bishop; Ph: Bruce Surtees; M: Bill Conti.
Cast: Tim Matheson, Jack Warden, Susan Blakely, Richard B. Shull.

DREAMSCAPE. (1984) There are probably millions of people who wake up in a cold sweat after a nightmare about seeing a movie in whcih Eddie Albert plays the President of the United States. Dreams come true in a very poor second cousin to Douglas Trumbull's *Brainstorm*. Psychics are able to enter the dreams of others and there is an attempt to kill the nightmare-troubled President while he sleeps. Much nonsense is spoken about dream linkage, which sounds like an option on a General Motors engine. A subnormal venture into the paranormal.
PG-13. ★
D: Joseph Ruben; W: Ruben, David Loughery and Chuck Russell; Ph: Brian Tufano; M: Maurice Jarre.
Cast: Dennis Quaid, Kate Capshaw, Max Von Sydow, Christopher Plummer.

DR. EHRLICH'S MAGIC BULLET. (1940) A stirring and absorbing biography of Paul Ehrlich, the man who discovered the way to treat syphillis.

★★★

D: William Dieterle; W: John Huston, Heinz Herald and Norman Burnside; Ph: James Wong Howe; M: Max Steiner.
Cast: Edward G. Robinson, Ruth Gordon, Albert Bassermann, Otto Kruger.

DRESSED TO KILL. (1980) A triumph of style and technique over substance from Brian De Palma. In a story of a transexual murderer in Manhattan, he contrives to be both glossily erotic and to pander to latent puritanism. Women who stray are murdered with all the slick flair at his command. He is so indifferent to the credibility of his characters that one pursued victim leaves the safety of a friendly taxi to run into a dark subway station. Such clumsy artifice unravels *Dressed to Kill*.
R. ★★
D and W: Brian De Palma; Ph: Ralf Bode.
Cast: Michael Caine, Nancy Allen, Angie Dickinson, Keith Gordon.

THE DRESSER. (1983) Cinema for people who love the theater. Peter Yates' love of the theater borders on reverence and we come to share his homage through two awesome performances from Albert Finney and Tom Courtenay. Finney is mesmerizing as Sir, a lion of the stage, trying to keep his company together in wartime England and trying to hold on to his sanity. The use of *King Lear* allows judicious parallels between the on-stage play-within-a-play and the backstage action.
PG. ★★★★
D: Peter Yates; W: Ronald Harwood; Ph: Kevin Pike; M: James Horner.
Cast: Albert Finney, Tom Courtenay, Edward Fox, Eileen Atkins.

THE DRIVER. (1978) A getaway flick that got away from director Walter Hill, who invested the story of a crook who drives with nerveless skill and the cop pursuing him with a brooding laconic tone. *The Driver* fails the test through miscasting. Ryan O'Neal is as gripping as a stop sign at a quiet interesction. Where a touch of obsession would be enough for the detective, Bruce Dern goes overboard. It makes the well-executed chases loud and meaningless.
R. ★★
D and W: Walter Hill; Ph: Philip Lathrop; M: Michael Small.
Cast: Ryan O'Neal, Bruce Dern, Isabelle Adjani, Ronee Blakley.

DR. JEKYLL AND MR. HYDE. (1932) For its time a surprisingly sexy version of Stevenson's classic story that went on to earn classic status of its own as one of the great horror films of the thirties. Subsequent stabs at the timeless tale of the balance of good and evil in the soul of man have never mustered the hypnotic force on display here. Part of that stems from atmosphere, but most of it can be attributed to Frederic March's moving performance.

★★★★★

D: Rouben Mamoulian; W: Samuel Hoffenstein and Percy Heath; Ph: Karl Struss.
Cast: Frederic March, Miriam Hopkins, Rose Hobart, Holmes Herbert.

DR. JEKYLL AND MR. HYDE. (1941) Victor Fleming, faced with the stiff competition of the Mamoulian film, slipped in a Freudian dream sequence. Ingrid Bergman managed to get herself cast as Ivy and Fleming tried to explore the psychological implications of Stevenson's brilliant premise. But Spencer Tracy's game try has a schizoid and indecisive air to it and he is miscast.

★★★

D: Victor Fleming; W: John Lee Mahin; Ph: Joseph Ruttenberg; M: Franz Waxman.
Cast: Spencer Tracy, Ingrid Bergman, Lana Turner, Ian Hunter.

DR. NO. (1963) Sean Connery began the James Bond series with an adventure that pitted him against Joseph Wiseman, one of the nastier villains to cross the path of 007. Many fans of Bond rightly place *Dr. No* near the top of the list. Apart from Connery's nice balance of suavity and menace and the excellent pacing of the various scrapes, *Dr. No* is much closer to the Ian Fleming spirit than later entries. Dr. No tries to sabotage the American space program from his West Indies base but Bond plans some sabotage of his own.

★★★★

D: Terence Young; W: Richard Maibaum, Johanna Harwood and Berkely Mather; Ph: Ted Moore; M: Monty Norman.
Cast: Sean Connery, Joseph Wiseman, Ursula Andress, Jack Lord.

THE DROWNING POOL. (1975) Paul Newman's second outing as Lew Archer is paced at the tempo of a slowly dripping tap. Ross MacDonald's California novel is transplanted to Louisiana and, like a good wine, it does not travel well. Nor does his convoluted plotting translate effectively on the screen. Archer goes to the aid of an old flame who must deal with a bizarre family and a blackmailer. The film is partly a sea of red herrings and partly a quagmire.
PG. ★★
D: Stuart Rosenberg; W: Tracy Keenan Wynn, Lorenzo Semple, Jr., and Walter Hill; Ph: Gordon Willis; M: Michael Small.
Cast: Paul Newman, Joanne Woodward, Tony Franciosa, Murray Hamilton.

DR. PHIBES RISES AGAIN. (1972) And it's not bad medicine. Vincent Price, tossing in enough camp to accomodate a boyscout jamboree, returns as Dr. Phibes whose quest for the elixir of life is made more urgent by the need to revive his wife. Lots of inventive murders and a must for those who like their horror mixed with hilarity.

★★★

D: Robert Fuest; W: Fuest and Robert Blees; Ph: Alex Thomson; M: John Gale.
Cast: Vincent Price, Robert Quarry, Fiona Lewis, Valli Kemp.

DR. STRANGELOVE OR HOW I LEARNED TO STOP WORRYING AND LOVE THE BOMB. (1963) Stanley Kubrick is alone among directors in his ability to produce a masterpiece or something close to it in just about every genre he attempts. Actually, *Dr. Strangelove* defies any category as much as it disdains mere praise. It is a black comedy about nuclear madness that has never lost its bite or urgency and no film has approached its uncanny ability to be simultaneously funny and terrifying. The satire of the military and political assumptions under which we live has a devastation of nuclear proportions. A mad general decides to attack the Soviet Union and one of the B-52s actually gets through. Peter Sellers, playing the roles of U.S. President, British officer and manic Strangelove, leads a virtuoso cast.

★★★★★

D: Stanley Kubrick; W: Terry Southern and Peter George; Ph: Gilbert Taylor; M: Laurie Johnson.
Cast: Peter Sellers, Sterling Hayden, George C. Scott, Peter Bull.

DRUM. (1976) It would be hard to name a movie more revolting than *Mandingo*, but this sequel managed it. Apart from the sex and blood, it contrives to show slavery in a way that panders to the very instincts that made the practice possible in the first place. Ken Norton was boiled alive in *Mandingo*, but he's back for more. Everyone concerned deserves the same fate.
R.
D: Steve Carver; W: Norman Wexler; Ph: Lucien Ballard; M: Charlie Smalls.
Cast: Ken Norton, Warren Oates, Isela Vega, Yaphet Kotto.

DRUMS ALONG THE MOHAWK. (1939) The young Henry Fonda is the epitome of true grit in John Ford's splendid and unrivalled evocation of life on the frontier in pre-Revolutionary America. The film is a meticulous history, which makes it a genuine exception, and a rousing adventure orchestrated by Ford. The director loves the characters but never romanticizes the harsh realities of their existence. Fonda takes Claudette Colbert to the wilderness and they are burned out by Indians.

★★★★

D: John Ford; W: Lamar Trotti and Sonya Levien; Ph: Bert Glennon; M: Alfred Newman.
Cast: Henry Fonda, Claudette Colbert, Edna May Oliver, John Carradine.

THE DUCHESS AND THE DIRTWATER FOX. (1976) An answer to a question no one asked. What would you get if you took all the humor out of *Blazing Saddles* and left in all the vulgarity? A smutfest that wastes both George Segal and Goldie Hawn. He steals the loot from a bank robbery, leaving the bandits with a boxful of manure. The viewer soon knows how the robbers feel.
PG ★

D: Melvin Frank; W: Barry Sandler, Jack Rose and Frank; Ph: Joseph Biroc; M: Charles Fox.
Cast: George Segal, Goldie Hawn, Conrad Janis, Thayer David.

DUCK SOUP. (1933) The Marx Brothers versus fascism and they take no prisoners in what is generally regarded as their best movie, a rating that puts it in a class by itself. Groucho, alias Rufus Firefly, becomes President of Freedonia and has to cope with spies and other mayhem. It is strewn with brilliant one-liners and sight gags, including a shelling of the president's office that stops when Groucho pulls down the shades. It also features Parliamentarians dancing to the tune of "All God's Chillun Got Guns."

★★★★★

D: Leo McCarey; W: Bert Kalmar, Harry Ruby, Arthur Sheekman, Nat Perrin; Ph: Henry Sharp; M: Bert Kalmar and Harry Ruby.
Cast: The Marx Brothers, Margaret Dumont, Louis Calhern, Edgar Kennedy.

DUEL. (1971) Steven Spielberg has few rivals in the orchestration of tension and here is early proof. Made for television, it became a theatrical hit in Europe and Universal re-

leased it to cinemas in 1983. Dennis Weaver is driving along minding his own business when he finds himself being pursued by an oil tanker. Spielberg makes this a terrifying experience that will be familiar to any turnpike driver who has dodged malicious trucks.

★★★★

D: Steven Spielberg; W: Richard Matheson.

DUEL IN THE SUN. (1946) David Selznick tried and failed to make a western *Gone With the Wind*, but, frankly, my dear, nobody gave much of a damn. His dream turned into a nightmare of expense and revolving door direction before King Vidor took over and it's a case of fascinating failure. Jennifer Jones, a half-breed Indian girl, causes upheaval in a cattle tycoon's household when both brothers come under her spell. Cynics of the time called it *Lust in the Dust*, but it's an instructive failure.

★★

D: King Vidor; W: Oliver H.P. Garrett and David O. Selznick; Ph: Lee Garmes; M: Dmitri Tiomkin.
Cast: Gregory Peck, Jennifer Jones, Joseph Cotten, Lionel Barrymore.

THE DUELLISTS. (1977) Ridley Scott's film has the beauty of a Gainsborough painting and it is rather like a walk through a gallery instead of a visit to the cinema. The movie becomes so obsessed with how it looks that it loses contact with what it is trying to say. Two officers in the Napoleonic wars begin duelling over a small slight and keep trying to kill each other. The theme of honor overcoming sanity tends to get lost in the static and glossy elegance.
PG. ★★★

D: Ridley Scott; W: Gerald Vaughn-Hughes; Ph: Frank Tidy; M: Howard Blake.
Cast: Keith Carradine, Harvey Keitel, Albert Finney, Edward Fox.

DUMBO. (1941) There are more famous Disney productions, but his treatment of the story of an elephant who learns to fly and joins Timothy Mouse in his adventures takes a back seat to none of them. It is one of the most endearing pieces ever created at the studio.

★★★★

D: Ben Sharpsteen; M: Frank Churchill and Oliver Wallace.

E

EACH DAWN I DIE. (1939) A devious prosecutor has a crusading reporter framed and sent to the slammer. In prison with James Cagney is George Raft, but the absurdities tossed into the later going only prove that Warner Brothers should have thrown away the key and forgotten about the prison genre. It combines a lack of originality with artifice, but the leads are fun to watch.

★★

D: William Keighley; W: Norman Reilly Raine, Warren Duff and Charles Perry; Ph: Arthur Edeson; M: Max Steiner.
Cast: James Cagney, George Raft, George Bancroft, Jane Bryan.

THE EAGLE HAS LANDED. (1976) Comes down with a whimper rather than a bang, courtesy of John Sturges and a cast of that mythic army of "good" Germans. They are bent on kidnapping Churchill in 1943 and the film lands it labors mightily to establish the moral credentials of the worthy Teutons. A hilarious cacophony of Anglo-German accents, led by Michael Caine's Bavarian cockney. Sutherland appears to be doing a Barry Fitzgerald impression as an IRA agent.

PG. ★★

D: John Sturges; W: Tom Mankiewicz; Ph: Anthony Richmond; M: Lalo Schifrin.
Cast: Donald Sutherland, Michael Caine, Robert Duvall, Jenny Agutter.

THE EARTHLING. (1980) Not horror or sci-fi, as the title might suggest, but a family film that says some unexceptional things well. William Holden looks painfully convincing as a dying man who is returning to the secluded valley of his childhood to spend his last days. An orphaned boy insists on tagging along and he reluctantly accepts him and teaches him the ways of the land. Fine Australian scenery.

PG. ★★★

D: Peter Collinson; W: Lanny Cotler; Ph: Don McAlpine; M: Dick De Benedictis.
Cast: William Holden, Ricky Schroder, Jack Thompson, Olivia Hamnett.

EARTHQUAKE. (1974) The destruction of Los Angeles does not seem such a bad idea when films like this are produced there. The usual clutch of marquee names disappear in the gaping holes in the plot. Ava Gardner, 52 at the time, plays the daughter of Lorne Greene, then 64. She also hisses, "Don't you dare lower your voice to me" at Charlton Heston. The story is loosely gathered around Heston, a civil engineer, and his extra-marital affair. The movie is not helped by the fact that its climactic disaster takes place in the middle of the proceedings.

PG. ★

D: Mark Robson; W: George Fox and Mario Puzo; Ph: Philip Lathrop; M: John Williams.
Cast: Charlton Heston, Ava Gardner, Lorne Greene, Marjoe Gortner.

EASTER PARADE. (1948) Fred Astaire and Judy Garland do "A Couple of Swells" and there's no denying that's what they are. A frothy show business plot about a song and dance man changing partners and an endearing Irving Berlin score add to the entertainment and make you wish this particular partnership would go on to other musicals.

★★★

D: Charles Walters; W: Sidney Sheldon, Frances Goodrich and Albert Hackett; Ph: Harry Stradling; M: Irving Berlin.
Cast: Fred Astaire, Judy Garland, Ann Miller, Peter Lawford.

EAST OF EDEN. (1954) Elia Kazan's adventurous and overboiled version of John Steinbeck's story is now enshrined as the vehicle that made James Dean a star. In fact, the role of Cal made him a rallying point for the frustrations of the young in the midst of a grey and conformist decade in American life. One of the unanswerable speculations in movies is what course his career would have taken if he had lived. The film is a rather tendentious reworking of Cain and Abel in rural California and there is much that is interesting and exasperating in it besides Dean's stunning arrival on the screen.

★★★

D: Elia Kazan; W: Paul Osborn; Ph: Ted McCord; M: Leonard Rosenman.
Cast: James Dean, Raymond Massey, Dick Davalos, Jo Van Fleet.

EASY MONEY. (1983) The longest mother-in-law gag ever commited to film and the joke is on the son-in-law. Your enjoyment of this easy-going piece will be in direct proportion to your respect for Rodney Dangerfield. He brings his night-club personality to the tale of a slob who has to straighten out in order to qualify for an inheritance. Some lines are on the money and some are awful, but Dangerfield has a kinetic energy that keeps things moving.

R. ★★
D: James Signori; W: Rodney Dangerfield, P.J. O'Rourke, Dennis Blair, Michael Endler; Ph: Fred Schuler; M: Laurence Rosenthal.
Cast: Rodney Dangerfield, Joe Pesci, Candy Dazzar, Geraldine Fitzgerald.

EASY RIDER. (1969) Rolling Stoned. Dennis Hopper's odyssey is generally credited with creating a largely disastrous counter-cultural revolution in Hollywood. Studios, desperate to touch the fickle youth movement, hurled money at anyone in blue jeans. The pall of pot-smoke hangs over the film responsible for the boomlet. Peter Fonda and Hopper ride their bikes from California to New Orleans and it turns into a celebrated trip. It has an ease of its own, but the real reason to see it is Jack Nicholson's turn as a drunken lawyer.

★★★
D: Dennis Hopper; W: Peter Fonda, Terry Southern and Hopper; Ph: Laszlo Kovacs; M: Various artists.
Cast: Dennis Hopper, Peter Fonda, Jack Nicholson.

EATING RAOUL. (1982) A tongue-in-cheek black comedy that lends a new meaning to the notion of having a friend over for dinner. In a round-house swing at sexual hedonism, a straightforward and down-at-the-heels couple realize their dream of opening a country restaurant by knocking off swingers. Outrageously clever in manipulating our sympathies, but Paul Bartel doesn't really have a viewpoint on the issues he raises with such arch cunning.

R. ★★★
D: Paul Bartel; W: Bartel and Richard Blackburn; Ph: Gary Theitges; M: Arion Ober.
Cast: Paul Bartel, Mary Woronov, Robert Beltran, Ed Begley, Jr.

EAT MY DUST. (1976) From the Roger Corman factory and the absolute pits, even by the low standards of the car-smash movie. Ron Howard took a break from *Happy Days* to make a movie about a kid who steals a hot-rod to impress his girl-friend. The rest is just chases and smashes and invites rubber-necking rather than viewing.

PG. ★

D and W: Charles Griffith; Ph: Eric Saarinen; M: David Grisman.
Cast: Ron Howard, Christopher Norris, Dave Madden, Warren Kemmerling.

EDDIE AND THE CRUISERS. (1983) Whatever happened to Eddie Wilson, a rock star who vanished after a meteoric rise to the top? Almost twenty years after the disappearance a TV reporter cares enough to find out although there is nothing on hand to make us share her concern or curiosity. Brooding tone and silly dialogue.

PG. ★★
D: Martin Davidson; W: Martin and Arlene Davidson; Ph: Fred Murphey; M: Jack Cafferty.
Cast: Michael Pare, Tom Berenger, Helen Schneider, Matthew Lawrence.

EDUCATING RITA. (1983) A good deal of Lewis Gilbert's charmer takes place in the classroom of a British university, but the real subject is class. The British are far more fascinated with their own system than the rest of the world. Thus what seems obvious to us—that a woman should aspire to more than a life of domestic drudgery—is treated with great wonder. For all that, Michael Caine's boozy professor, reluctantly stuck with feisty Julie Walters, makes you forget the rather weak assumptions of the film's plot.

PG. ★★★
D: Lewis Gilbert; W: Willy Russell; Ph: Frank Watts; M: David Hentschel.
Cast: Michael Caine, Julie Walters, Michael Williams, Maureen Lipman.

THE EDUCATION OF SONNY CARSON. (1974) Sonny Carson, a Brooklyn community leader, wrote an angry autobiography of his troubled times as a ghetto kid who became a convict and later an activist. The film is meandering, but it is propelled by the sheer fury of its vision of the hopelessness of the slums. The street scenes, where Sonny gradually turns from honor student to gang member, have a raw power and the film is unusual in that it does not go in for the cheap exploitation common to black movies in the early seventies.

R. ★★★
D: Michael Campus; W: Campus and Fred Hudson; Ph: Ed Brown; M: Coleridge-Taylor Perkinson.
Cast: Ronny Clanton, Don Gordon, Joyce Walker, Paul Benjamin.

EDVARD MUNCH. (1976) A portrait of the great Norwegian artist as a young and spiritually ravaged man. British documentary maker Peter Watkins' most ambitious project mixes fact and drama to explore Munch's suffering and connect it to his painting. An inventive approach to film biography. ★★★★
D and W: Peter Watkins; Ph: Odd Geir Saether.
Cast: Geir Westby, Gro Fraas, Kerstii Allum .

THE EGYPTIAN. (1954) The construction of the pyramids went faster than Michael Curtiz's turgid epic. Marlon Brando, with rare judgement, passed on the lead and chose to play Napoleon in *Desiree* instead. Edmund Purdom subs as a doctor in ancient Egypt who develops a prescient faith in a single deity. The single spark of vitality came from Peter Ustinov as Purdom's servant. Ustinov considers *The Egyptian* one of the debacles of his career. ★★
D: Michael Curtiz; W: Philip Dunne and Casey Robinson; Ph: Leon Shamroy; M: Alfred Newman.
Cast: Edmond Purdom, Jean Simmons, Victor Mature, Gene Tierney.

THE EIGER SANCTION. (1975) An uphill climb that gets sillier as it nears the top. Based on the Trevanian novel about the art professor who finances his collecting by killing people for the government. Clint Eastwood sets out to avenge the death of an American intelligence agent and winds up on the famous mountain with the suspect. The only reason to see the film is because it's there and the climbing sequences are very good.
R. ★★
D: Clint Eastwood; W: Warren B. Murphy, Hal Dresner and Rod Whitaker; Ph: Frank Stanley; M: John Williams.
Cast: Clint Eastwood, George Kennedy, Vonetta McGee, Jack Cassidy.

EL CID. (1961) Anthony Mann's gorgeously mounted epic chronicles the legend of Rodrigo Diaz, a nobleman who became known as El Cid and who led Spaniards in their struggle against the Moors. His ardor for Chimene interrupts the battle action, which is so well staged that the pageantry element of the movie seems slow. In its climax, Charlton Heston played one of his most enduring scenes as a corpse who can inspire his followers even in death. Among epic spectacles, *El Cid* stands as one of the finest. ★★★★
D: Anthony Mann; W: Frederick Frank and Philip Yordan; Ph: Robert Krasker; M: Miklos Rozsa.
Cast: Charlton Heston, Sophia Loren, Raf Vallone, Geraldine Page.

EL DORADO. (1967) Drawn from a novel by Harry Brown called "The Stars in Their Courses", Howard Hawks' western offers stars in their near dotage. The real inspiration is Hawks' *Rio Bravo*, an infinitely better movie, and why he wanted to do it again is a puzzle. John Wayne looks decidedly over-the-Boot-hill. He has to sober up Robert Mitchum, whose drinking can be attributed to the script, to cope with the bad element in town. Only fool's gold in this El Dorado. ★★
D: Howard Hawks; W: Leigh Brackett; Ph: Harold Rosson; M: Nelson Riddle.
Cast: John Wayne, Robert Mitchum, James Caan, Charlene Holt.

THE ELECTRIC HORSEMAN. (1979) Robert Redford rides into the movie lit up by booze and the lights on his cowboy suit. The points the film makes are illuminated with the same subtlety, but it's an amusing attack on conglomerates and the cynicism of business and the media. Redford is Sonny Steele, a broken down rodeo star who would rather push breakfast cereal than break any more bones. Fonda is a self-assured network correspondent trying to get her story.
PG. ★★★
D: Sydney Pollack; W: Robert Garland; Ph: Owen Roizman; M: Dave Grusin.
Cast: Robert Redford, Jane Fonda, Willie Nelson, John Saxon.

THE ELEPHANT MAN. (1980) A *tour de force* from John Hurt as the hopelessly deformed John Merrick. Trapped inside the hideous growths inflicted by his disease, Merrick escaped life as a carnival freak to win acceptance in Victorian society before his death at the age of 27. David Lynch concentrates on Merrick's relationship with his physician and a beautiful actress and makes judicious use of black and white to tone down the monstrous aspects of Merrick's condition. He makes the wrenching story a pliable metaphor of the outsider.
PG. ★★★★

D: David Lynch; W: Christopher De Vore and Eric Bergren; Ph: Freddie Francis; M: John Morris.
Cast: John Hurt, Anthony Hopkins, Anne Bancroft, John Gielgud.

11 HARROWHOUSE. (1974) A diamond heist in a London jewelry center in which nothing arresting happens and the few ideas on hand are borrowed from other movies like *Topkapi*. Charles Grodin, a diamond house underling who hates his boss, cooks up the scheme, but the director is intent on making things as limp as possible and his apathy undermines a spunky cast.

PG ★★
D: Aram Avakian; W: Jeffrey Bloom; Ph: Arthur Ibbetson; M: Michael J. Lewis.
Cast: Charles Grodin, James Mason, Candice Bergen, Trevor Howard.

ELMER GANTRY. (1960) The old time religion embodied in a two-timing hypocrite who is played with enormous vitality by Burt Lancaster. He won an Oscar and his energy flows through *Elmer Gantry*, which is adapted from Sinclair Lewis' novel about how much lying lay behind the preachers of the truth in the Midwest in the 1920s.

★★★★
D and W: Richard Brooks; Ph: John Alton; M: Andre Previn.
Cast: Burt Lancaster, Jean Simmons, Arthur Kennedy, Shirley Jones.

EMBRYO. (1976) With the possibilities of possessed children exhausted, Ralph Nelson tried going back to the womb. In order to prevent the aging process Barbara Carrera needs the secretion of a baby's pituitary gland. Rock Hudson trudges through the film looking somewhat miffed, as well he might.

R. ★
D: Ralph Nelson; W: Anita Doohan and Jack W. Thomas; Ph: Fred Koenekamp; M: Gil Melle.
Cast: Rock Hudson, Barbara Carrera, Diane Ladd, Roddy McDowall.

THE EMIGRANTS. (1972) A superior and sincere attempt to surmount cliche in chronicling the experience of leaving a cherished homeland and settling in the New World. Jan Troell, the talented Swedish director, traces a group of his countrymen who are forced to leave because of famine. They make their way to Minnesota despite many setbacks. Beautifully photographed—Troell is a brilliant cinematographer—in a way that shows a foreigner's awe of the American landscape. That becomes an important ingredient in the film. The characters are sober, but the players—especially Liv Ullmann—bring them to vivid life. The story was continued in Troell's *The New Land*.

★★★★
D: Jan Troell; W: Troell and Bengt Forslund; Ph: Jan Troell; M: Erik Nordgren.
Cast: Max Von Sydow, Liv Ullmann, Eddie Axberg, Svenolof Bern.

EMMANUELLE. (1974) Soft core pornography from France that has survived because of its glossiness and production values. These may be superior to the domestic motel variety prevalent at the time, but the film is remarkably empty-headed and chauvinistic. There is absolutely no male nudity. A young Frenchwoman seeks and finds sexual experiences in Thailand.

X. ★
D: Just Jaeckin; W: Jean-Louis Richard; Ph: Richard Suzuki and Marie Saunier; M: Pierre Bachelet.
Cast: Sylvia Kristel, Marika Green, Daniel Sarky, Alain Cuny.

THE EMPEROR OF THE NORTH POLE. (1973) The monarch in question is the king of the road among the bums who ride the railroads in the Pacific Northwest during the Depression. Robert Aldrich's gratuitously violent movie is certainly depressing. Lee Marvin must rise to the challenge and win the imperial title by taking on a train guard who likes to kill hoboes.

★★
D: Robert Aldrich; W: Christopher Knopf; Ph: Joseph Biroc; M: Frank de Vol.
Cast: Lee Marvin, Keith Carradine, Ernest Borgnine, Charles Tyner.

THE EMPIRE STRIKES BACK. (1980) *Star Wars* grew up in the second installment with Luke Skywalker's maturity and his further initiation into the ways of the Jedi knights under the tutelage of Yoda. There is more attention to character and a more sober tone with the flip exchanges between Leia and Han Solo providing some needed humorous breaks. The set-piece spectacles —the battle on the ice planet, Hoth, and the flight through an asteroid belt—top those in *Star Wars*. But it is Lucas' uncanny grasp of what children want from a story and his ability to deliver that puts this series in a galaxy all by itself.

PG. ★★★★★

D: Irvin Kershner; W: Lawrence Kasdan and Leigh Brackett; Ph: Peter Suschitzsky; M: John Williams.
Cast: Mark Hamill, Carrie Fisher, Harrison Ford, Billy Dee Williams.

THE END. (1978) Sophomoric gallows humor about a real estate man who learns of his imminent death—from a blood disease—and decides to commit suicide. He succeeds, at least artistically. The jokes lean toward vulgar jabs at doctors, hospitals and urine tests. Burt Reynolds can direct himself, but he can't control his friends and you are in no danger of dying from laughter.
R. ★★
D: Burt Reynolds; W: Jerry Belson; Ph: Bobby Byrne; M: Paul Williams.
Cast: Burt Reynolds, Dom DeLuise, Sally Field, Strother Martin.

ENDANGERED SPECIES. (1982) A little paranoid, very provocative and well-managed suspense from Alan Rudolph. A New York cop and a lady sheriff in Colorado investigate the strange mutilation of cattle and find more than they bargained for.
R. ★★★
D: Alan Rudolph; W: Rudolph and John Binder; Ph: Paul Lohman; M: Gary Wright.
Cast: Robert Urich, Jobeth Williams, Paul Dooley, Hoyt Axton.

ENDLESS LOVE. (1981) If you're still awake at the end of Franco Zeffirelli's paean to puppy love, congratulations. He addressed the obsessive love of a 17-year-old youth with a solemnity more befitting the last rites instead of the first ones of sexual initiation. Nowhere does he try to scrutinize it and long stretches are spent watching the lovers writhing in soft light. A soft head helps in making it through to the conclusion.
R. ★
D: Franco Zeffirelli; W: Judith Rascoe; Ph: David Watkin; M: Lionel Richie.
Cast: Brooke Shields, Martin Hewitt, Shirley Knight, Don Murray.

THE END OF THE GAME. (1976) Can a perfect crime—a murder—be committed in the very presence of the law? Maximilian Schell, adapting Friedrich Durrenmatt's novel *The Judge and His Hangman* furnishes a tantalizing, if rather preachy answer. The killing of an undercover agent involves four characters in ways that they are unwilling to admit to each other.
R. ★★★

D: Maximilian Schell; W: Schell and Freidrich Durrenmatt; Ph: Ennio Guarnieri .
Cast: Jon Voight, Robert Shaw, Martin Ritt, Jacqueline Bisset.

THE ENEMY BELOW. (1957) A superior submarine film that owes its considerable appeal to the attention paid to the enemy. The standard destroyer-stalking-the-U-boat idea is fleshed out with an ample look at both parties and a grudging respect develops between the two antagonists. The Germans are shown as merely obeying their orders in launching wholesale slaughter and it is the film's only misjudgement. The special effects do not show their age.
★★★
D: Dick Powell; W: Wendell Mayes; Ph: Harold Rosson; M: Leigh Harline.
Cast: Robert Mitchum, Curt Jurgens, Al Hedison, Theodore Bikel.

AN ENEMY OF THE PEOPLE. (1981) Steve McQueen, in a decision that was more admirable than wise, used his influence to get Ibsen's play on film. He took the role of Thomas Stockmann, the rural doctor who discovers a tannery is polluting the environment. The film was never released theatrically, for reasons that will be obvious. McQueen, shrouded in a Woodstock beard and granny glasses, turns in a performance that is more game than germane to Ibsen's work.
G. ★★
D: George Schaefer; W: Alexander Jacobs(adaptor); Ph: Paul Lohmann; M: Leonard Rosenman.
Cast: Steve McQueen, Bibi Andersson, Charles Durning, Michael Higgins.

THE ENFORCER. (1976) Dirty Harry Callahan, the thinking caveman's detective, takes on such subversive documents as the U.S. Constitution in pursuit of urban terrorists who have devised the new crime of "mayornapping." The terrorists are absurdly homicidal, murdering innocent people for no other reason than to increase viewer hostility and justify the actions of Eastwood's macho cop. Third in the hugely successful series.
R. ★★
D: James Fargo; W: Stirling Silliphant; Ph: Charles W. Short; M: Jerry Fielding.
Cast: Clint Eastwood, Tyne Daley, Harry Guardino, Bradford Dillman.

ENSIGN PULVER. (1964) Joshua Logan, having scored such a success with *Mr.*

Roberts, tried to continue the voyage with the further adventures of Pulver. However, two people who would logically be pivotal to such an enterprise—Jack Lemmon and Henry Fonda—are AWOL. A navy comedy with very little salt in its humor resulted.

★★

D: Joshua Logan; W: Logan and Peter Feibleman; Ph: Charles Lawton; M: George Duning.
Cast: Robert Walker, Burl Ives, Walter Matthau, Tommy Sands.

THE ENTERTAINER. (1960) A glum grey seaside resort in England in the fifties is the setting for a demonstration of acting from Laurence Olivier that is overwhelming in its virtuosity and volcanic in its anger. John Osborne's play gave Olivier one of his most splendid modern roles as Archie Rice, a failed resort entertainer whose bitterness at life and desperate appearances on stage mask a personality of considerable complexity. Olivier explores all of them.

★★★★

D: Tony Richardson; W: John Osborne and Nigel Kneale; Ph: Oswald Morris; M: John Addison.
Cast: Laurence Olivier, Joan Plowright, Brenda de Banzie, Roger Livesey.

ENTER THE DRAGON. (1973) The last film by martial arts king Bruce Lee before his premature death and the last word on the subject. Lee takes on arch villain Han, who runs a slave business from an impregnable fortress, with the help of Jim Kelly and John Saxon. Very violent, but not as dumb as the many imitations. If you're wondering why Lee still has millions of fans, his last genuine work is the first place to start.

R. ★★★

D: Robert Clouse; W: Michael Allin; Ph: Gilbert Hubbs; M: Lalo Schifrin.
Cast: Bruce Lee, John Saxon, Jim Kelly, Shih Kien.

ENTRE NOUS. (1983) Diane Kurys' exquisite dissection of two marriages and the lasting friendship between the two wives does not turn the men into ogres. They are callous, coarse and most of all lacking in self-awareness. It is set in provincial France in the fifties, which was not a period for rethinking sex roles. The changes happen anyway and the husbands don't realize it. Kurys is on the side of the women—and so is the audience—but there is compassion for everyone involved in the broken relationships.

PG. ★★★★

D: Diane Kurys; W: Kurys and Alain Le Henry; Ph: Bernard Lutic; M: Luis Bacalov.
Cast: Isabelle Huppert, Miou-Miou, Guy Marchand, Jean-Pierre Bacri.

EQUUS. (1977) Sidney Lumet, showing the courage to make a film instead of merely film a play, exploits the medium to the fullest. His sequences that show us the visions of a mad youth illuminate what was only suggested in the theater without imposing themselves on the flow of a rich drama. Richard Burton is a magnet that holds the play together as a psychiatrist engaged in a secular exorcism of a youth who has blinded six horses. Only the psychiatrist's narrative reminiscences impede the pace of the film.

R. ★★★★

D: Sidney Lumet; W: Peter Shaffer; Ph: Oswald Morris; M: Richard Rodney Bennett.
Cast: Richard Burton, Peter Firth, Harry Andrews, Colin Blakely.

THE ESCAPE ARTIST. (1983) An intriguing and bewildering directing debut from the great cinematographer Caleb Deschanel. Whether the results are what he intended is equally vague since the film was re-edited. As it stands, *The Escape Artist* is a blend of dream and reality in which two sons cope with the sins of their fathers. Griffin O'Neal, Ryan's son, is a kid to watch in the future. Here he is the son of a Houdini-style escape artist who has learned his father's trade.

PG. ★★★

D: Caleb Deschanel; W: Melissa Mathison and Stephen Zito; Ph: Stephen H. Burum; M: Georges Delerue.
Cast: Griffin O'Neal, Raul Julia, Teri Garr, Joan Hackett.

ESCAPE FROM ALCATRAZ. (1979) Top-notch prison movie fueled by Clint Eastwood's laconic anger. In one of his best roles, he plays Frank Morris, the mastermind of the last escape from the notorious island prison before it was closed in 1963. The despair and boredom are cogently rendered and the preparation and execution of the escape have an excruciating tension.

R. ★★★★

D: Don Siegel; W: Richard Tuggle; Ph: Bruce Surtees; M: Jerry Fielding.
Cast: Clint Eastwood, Patrick McGoohan, Roberts Blossom, Jack Thibeau.

ESCAPE FROM ATHENA. (1979) Any credits that include "and Elliott Gould as Charlie" amount to fair warning. George Cosmatos, who himself is a one-man warning to beware of Greeks bearing cameras, offers a grab-bag of plot ideas from a dozen behind-the-lines war movies and Roger Moore as a German prison commandant for bad measure. Mostly, it has to do with the theft of ancient Greek treasures.
PG. ★★
D: George Cosmatos; W: Edward Anhalt and Richard Lochte; Ph: Gil Taylor; M: Lalo Schifrin.
Cast: Roger Moore, Telly Savalas, Elliott Gould, David Niven.

ESCAPE FROM FORT BRAVO. (1953) An articulate western that survives a slow beginning and profits from William Holden's weary cynicism as a frontier cavalry officer charged with keeping Confederate prisoners inside an army stockade. He becomes involved with a woman who is secretly trying to organize the escape attempt of her confederate lover. Rousing action once the escape starts and handsome Death Valley locations.
★★★
D: John Sturges; W: Frank Fenton; Ph: Robert Surtees; M: Jeff Alexander.
Cast: William Holden, Eleanor Parker, John Forsythe, William Demarest.

ESCAPE FROM NEW YORK. (1981) Manhattan strewn with garbage and teeming with vicious criminals. Only this time it's in the future and the island has been turned into a maximum security prison. John Carpenter could have worked harder on setting up his premise before plunging into an implausible adventure. Kurt Russell has to rescue the president of the United States from the Big Apple.
R. ★★★
D: John Carpenter; W: Carpenter and Nick Castle; M: John Carpenter.
Cast: Kurt Russell, Donald Pleasence, Lee Van Cleef, Ernest Borgnine.

ESCAPE FROM THE PLANET OF THE APES. (1971) Roddy McDowall and Kim Hunter use the astronaut's ship to escape and land in Los Angeles in the seventies. Even laid-back California with its generous share of freaks isn't prepared for articulate apes and the third film in the series has some fun with what amounts to a double inversion

of the idea for the original *Planet of the Apes.*
★★★
D: Don Taylor; W: Paul Dehn; Ph: Joseph Biroc; M: Jerry Goldsmith.
Cast: Roddy McDowall, Kim Hunter, Bradford Dillman, Eric Braeden.

ESCAPE TO WITCH MOUNTAIN. (1975) A refreshing change from the slew of possessed children in occult movies. The Disney production features most of the studio's merits and few of its faults. Two children from another planet have various psychic powers. Ray Milland, a millionaire who wishes to use their skills for his own dastardly end, and the cops chase them all over the countryside. Told from the kids' point of view.
G. ★★★
D: John Hough; W: Robert Malcolm Young; Ph: Frank Phillips; M: Johnny Mandel.
Cast: Ray Milland, Donald Pleasence, Eddie Albert, Kim Richards.

ESCAPE 2000. (1983) The future—an Orwellian world moved up to 1995—served up as violent escapism and nothing more. In a society that frowns on oringinality and being different, Steve Railsback is a deviate and must be hunted down. The film frowns on the same things and is exceptionally bloody in its action sequences.
R. ★
D: Brian Tenchard-Smith; W: Jon George and Neil Hicks; Ph: John McClean; M: Brian May.
Cast: Steve Railsback, Olivia Hussey, Michael Craig, Carmen Duncan.

E.T.—THE EXTRA-TERRESTRIAL. (1982) Steven Spielberg finally found a story whose content approached his tremendous technical and visual skills and the result is a masterpiece that ranks with *The Wizard of Oz* as the best gift the movies have bestowed on children. Spielberg touches adults as well by reminding them what childhood was like—something he has never forgotten. A boy befriends and protects a stranded alien from curious authorities and their communion is one of the most touching love stories in film. The action is seen from the perspective of the boy and E.T. so that we too are drawn into their relationship. A technically flawless work that deploys light to dazzling emotional effect, *E.T.* quite understandably became the all-time box office champion.

PG. ★★★★★
D: Steven Spielberg; W: Melissa Mathison;
Ph: Allen Daviau; M: John Williams.
Cast: Henry Thomas, Dee Wallace, Peter
Coyote, Drew Barrymore.

THE EUROPEANS. (1979) Beautiful to look
at and—a rarity in film these days—beautiful to listen to. The adaptation of Henry James
novel about the arrival of two sophisticated
European relatives in the household of a
Boston family finds more than friction between old and new worlds. It becomes a
graceful argument on the purpose of life and
how it is to be lived as the daughter comes
under the influence of the Europeans.
★★★★
D: James Ivory; W: Ruth Prawer Jhabvala;
Ph: Larry Pizer; M: Richard Robbins.
Cast: Lee Remick, Robin Ellis, Lisa Eichhorn,
Wesley Addy.

EVERGREEN. (1934) An apt title for a
British musical comedy that has held up
well. The suitably silly story has a young
woman impersonating her mother with many
complications and the whole production is
significantly improved by the Rodgers and
Hart score.
★★★
D: Victor Saville; W: Emlyn Williams and
Marjorie Gaffney; M: Rodgers and Hart.
Cast: Jessie Matthews, Sonnie Hale, Betty
Balfour, Barry Mackay.

EVERYTHING HAPPENS AT NIGHT.
(1939) Even though there is a little skating,
the studio tried to take Sonja Henie off the
ice to broaden her appeal. Two journalists
track down her father but forget their by-
lines and lose their hearts to Henie.
★★
D: Irving Cummings; W: Art Arthur and
Robert Harari; Ph: Edward Cronjager; M:
Cyril J. Mockridge.
Cast: Sonja Henie, Ray Milland, Robert
Cummings, Maurice Moscovich.

**EVERYTHING YOU ALWAYS WANTED
TO KNOW ABOUT SEX.** (1972) Woody
Allen's spirited and occasionally raunchy
riposte to Dr. David Reuben, the reigning sex
guru at the time. The instruction takes the
form of seven episodes illustrating various
points and most of the time Woody hits the

money. Who can resist Woody as a sperm
nervous about his destination or Gene Wil-
der as a doctor in love with a sheep? It con-
tains some of the most inventive visual
humor in the Allen canon.
R ★★★★
D and W: Woody Allen; Ph: David Walsh; M:
Mundell Lowe.
Cast: Woody Allen, Gene Wilder, Lynn
Redgrave, Anthony Quayle.

EVERY WHICH WAY BUT LOOSE.
(1978) Monkey business with, of all people,
Clint Eastwood. For some reason, moviegoers lapped it up. Philo Bedoe (Eastwood) is
a guy who gets in brawls so he can bet on
himself and whose companion is an orang-
utang named Clyde. A loose string of adventures involving Hell's Angels and a country singer who likes one-night stands on and
off the stage. A riot for anyone who likes jokes
about apes breaking wind.
R. ★★
D: James Fargo; W: Jeremy Joe Kronsberg;
Ph: Rexford Metz; M: Steve Dorff.
Cast: Clint Eastwood, Sondra Locke, Geoffrey Lewis, Beverly D'Angelo.

THE EVIL. (1978) An agnostic psychologist and his friends are trapped in a haunted
house by a ghost and a know-nothing director. They die off graphically every five minutes or so. Hear no evil and certainly see no
evil.
R. ★
D: Gus Trikonis; W: Donald G. Thompson;
Ph: Mario Di Leo; M: John Harris.
Cast: Richard Crenna, Joanna Pettet, Cassie
Yates, Victor Buono.

THE EVIL DEAD. (1983) Someone called
Samuel M. Raimi, one of the evil living who
churn out such rubbish, was 22 when he
directed this invitation to revulsion. An IQ
below that figure is required to sit through it
An amateur homage to some movies, like
Friday the 13th, that are terrible in their own
right. The usual bunch of young people get
theirs in gory detail when they decide to take
a camping trip.
D and W: Samuel M. Raimi; Ph: Tim Philo; M:
Joe LoDuca.
Cast: Bruce Campbell, Ellen Sandweiss,
Betsy Baker.

THE EVIL OF FRANKENSTEIN. (1964)
When the baron gets back to the castle the
monster's literally on ice and the movie has
nothing new to add when it melts. The third

Hammer Frankenstein film with Peter Cushing is both routine and redundant.

★★

D: Freddie Francis; W: John Elder; Ph: John Wilcox; M: Don Banks.
Cast: Peter Cushing, Peter Woodthorpe, Sandor Eles, Kiwi Kingston .

EVIL UNDER THE SUN. (1982) A whodunit that reaches its conclusion with the audience yawning "who cares?" is in trouble. Peter Ustinov's second outing as Agatha Christie's sleuth Hercule Poirot finds the great detective unraveling the murder of a hated stage star at a Mediterranean resort hotel. The usual assembly of eccentrics provide a rather plodding mystery. Anthony Shaffer, who wrote the witty *Sleuth*, is ill at ease in translating Christie and there is no consistency to the acting.

PG. ★★

D: Guy Hamilton; W: Anthony Shaffer; Ph: Christopher Challis; M: Music of Cole Porter.
Cast: Peter Ustinov, Colin Blakely, Jane Birkin, Nicholas Clay.

EXCALIBUR. (1981) John Boorman's mournful and rhapsodic evocation of Camelot and dashed hopes is one that keys on the central myths in the legend of King Arthur. Boorman created what he called a "Middle Earth" look and alternated between dreamlike beauty and nightmares of lust, rage and death. There is a slight stiffness to the dialogue and a tendency to see the characters as figures on a great tapestry, but Boorman's retelling has no rivals in the Camelot stakes.

R. ★★★★★

D: John Boorman; W: Boorman and Rospo Pallenberg; Ph: Alex Thomson; M: Trevor Jones.
Cast: Nicol Williamson, Helen Mirren, Nigel Terry, Nicholas Clay.

EXECUTIVE SUITE. (1954) An intelligent foray into the corporate board-room and its politics and one of the first American movies to take a serious tack with business life. The president of a furniture company dies and a struggle for control ensues among the executives.

★★★

D: Robert Wise; W: Ernest Lehman; Ph: George Folsey .
Cast: William Holden, June Allyson, Frederic March, Walter Pidgeon.

EXHIBITION. (1975) What happens when a French porn star is invited to hold forth on her philosophy as well as put out on the screen? The star, Claudine Beccarie, emerges from a foreign entanglement of bodies to discuss life and love. The picture enjoyed the same cult popularity in France that *Deep Throat* won here. Beccarie says she is trying to encourage bisexuality in her humanitarian work. This is the kind of movie that does wonders for celibacy. Sexually explicit.

★

D: Jean-Francois Davy; Ph: Roger Fellou.
Cast: Claudine Beccarie, Benoit Archenoul, Frederique Barral, Michel Dauba.

EXODUS. (1960) The politics and hypocrisy surrounding the beginnings of the modern state of Israel are the strong suit of Otto Preminger's massive and heavy-handed version of the Leon Uris novel. It shows the consequence in human suffering of cynical statecraft as Newman leads his people in migrating from Cyprus to the blockaded new land. The relationships that are supposed to sustain interest in the movie, notably Newman as a resistance leader and Eva Marie Saint as an American nurse, aren't especially gripping. The length (220 minutes) also becomes wearing. Fittingly, this tale of freedom was the first script that the blacklisted Dalton Trumbo was able to write under his own name after his political exile.

★★★

D: Otto Preminger; W: Dalton Trumbo; Ph: Sam Leavitt; M: Ernest Gold.
Cast: Paul Newman, Eva Marie Saint, Ralph Richardson, Lee J. Cobb.

THE EXORCIST. (1973) The infernal spellbinder that unleashed a decade of shabby imitations. Linda Blair vomiting bile and spewing the foulest language (actually the voice of Mercedes McCambridge) is transformed from happy innocence into a vehicle for the devil himself. Friedkin took a lot of chances with excess, but he moved the film with a speed that establishes an illusion of credibility and Blatty's screenplay helped. The fact that one of the priests has to contend with his own doubts heightens the slickly done drama. Physically graphic and not for kids.

R. ★★★★

D: William Friedkin; W: William Peter Blatty; Ph: Owen Roizman; M: George Crumb.
Cast: Linda Blair, Jason Miller, Ellen Burstyn, Max Von Sydow.

EXORCIST II—THE HERETIC. (1977) Richard Burton would doubtless cross the River Lethe to forget the indelible blight on his career. He lurches through the film as an obsessed priest and with the look of the man in the grip of a profound, if not terminal hangover. The film finds Linda Blair older but no wiser and is filled with theological mumbo-jumbo. It was released in two versions, both of which bombed. James Earl Jones leads the African contingent and wears a silly hat and an understandably sheepish expression.
R.   ★
D: John Boorman; W: William Goodhart; Ph: William A. Fraker; M: Ennio Morricone.
Cast: Richard Burton, Linda Blair, Louise Fletcher, James Earl Jones.

EXPERIENCE PREFERRED...BUT NOT NECESSARY. (1983) No one involved in the charming piece from Britain had much experience, but their work is to be preferred to many more celebrated coming-of-age films for its winning, low-key approach. A young student earns tuition money working for a summer at a Welsh resort hotel and director Peter Duffell emphasizes friendship over sex as she graduates to full adulthood.
R.   ★★★
D: Peter Duffell; W: June Roberts; Ph: Phil Meheux; M: John Scott.
Cast: Elizabeth Edmonds, Sue Wallace, Geraldine Griffith, Karen Meagher.

EXPOSED. (1983) An essay on modern terrorism that's as subtle as a pipe bomb. Rudolf Nureyev is cruelly exposed by the need to speak lines of dialogue. They creak with pretension and that makes things even worse. The central relationship—a Midwesterner who becomes an international model and a violin virtuoso out to avenge himself on a Carlos-style terrorist—is ludicrous. The two stories have nothing to do with each other and James Toback's perversely macho attitude to women is an added drawback.
R.   ★★
D and W: James Toback; Ph: Henri Decase; M: Georges Delerue.
Cast: Rudolf Nureyev, Nastassja Kinski, Harvey Keitel, Ian McShane.

EXPRESSO BONGO. (1959) A satirical look at the beginnings of the sixties British rock scene with Laurence Harvey as an agent pushing Cliff Richard toward the big-time.

His cut may be ten percent, but Harvey's slick and funny performance is 90 percent of the movie's claim to attention. It has an accurate period flavor.
                                                        ★★★
D: Val Guest; W: Wolf Mankowitz; Ph: John Wilcox; M: Monty Norman and David Heneker.
Cast: Laurence Harvey, Cliff Richard, Sylvia Syms, Yolande Donlan.

AN EYE FOR AN EYE. (1981) Look for the eyebrow. It belongs to Christopher Lee and arches quizzically over what it sees. He is a television station owner and drug dealer who turns into the quarry for Chuck Norris. The martial arts champion's acting is as crude as a hand splitting a brick, but no one who likes chop-socky will be disappointed. He's a detective avenging his partner's death. The ayes don't have it for a film as poorly done as *An Eye for an Eye*.
R.   ★★
D: Steve Carver; W: Willaam Gray and James Bruner; Ph: Roger Shearman; M: William Goldstein.
Cast: Chuck Norris, Christopher Lee, Richard Roundtree, Mako.

EYE OF THE NEEDLE. (1981) Even though we know the invasion of Normandy was not disrupted by a German agent and went off as planned, the "what if?" premise of Ken Follett's thriller is the most absorbing of the books of "faction" about World War II. In this crisp adaptation, Donald Sutherland is the agent trying to spirit vital information to his bosses and Kate Nelligan the woman who must put aside her feelings and stop him. The film makes the wise choice of concentrating on their relationship rather than the police manhunt.
R.   ★★★
D: Richard Marquand; W: Stanley Mann; Ph: Alan Hume; M: Miklos Rozsa.
Cast: Donald Sutherland, Kate Nelligan, Philip Martin Brown, Stephen Mackenna.

EYES OF LAURA MARS. (1978) A flashy variation on the slasher film motif that gives the audience the killer's perspective. A high fashion photographer who likes to pose her models in murder situations begins seeing visions of the real thing. We never find out how or why. Some adroit direction from Irvin Kershner, but he can't manoever around the barrelful of red herrings in the screenplay.
R.   ★★

D: Irvin Kershner; W: John Carpenter and David Zelag Goodman; Ph: Victor J. Kemper; M: Artie Kane.
Cast: Faye Dunaway, Tommy Lee Jones, Brad Dourif, Rene Auberjonois.

EYEWITNESS. (1981) A suave and engaging thriller for anyone who believes that ice goddesses of television news fall in love with apartment building janitors. William Hurt is the self-contained Vietnam veteran —neither insane nor even mad at anyone for a change. A murder in his building brings the object of his obsession in to cover the case. The characters are brightly done by the *Breaking Away* team, but *Eyewitness* can't see its way past the central implausibility.
R. ★★★
D: Peter Yates; W: Steve Tesich; Ph: Matthew Leonetti; M: Stanley Silverman.
Cast: William Hurt, Sigourney Weaver, Christopher Plummer, James Woods.

F

A FACE IN THE CROWD. (1957) A searing indictment of the powers and manipulative capacity of the mass media that is all the more extraordinary for its prescience. Long before it became fashionable to question the way we make celebrities, Budd Schulberg wrote this study of a yokel who is turned into a crackerbarrel philospher of the air. Andy Griffiths never again came near his performance here, which mixes cornpone and cynicism in just the right amounts.

★★★★

D: Elia Kazan; W: Budd Schulberg; Ph: Harry Stradling; M: Tom Glazer.
Cast: Andy Griffiths, Lee Remick, Walter Matthau, Patricia Neal.

THE FACE OF FU MANCHU. (1965) Is as inscrutable as ever in the first and best of Christopher Lee's ventures into Fulery. Nayland Smith has to nail Fu before he can unleash a fiendish plot to conquer the world with poison gas. Stylish production values and a nice sense of humor.

★★★

D: Don Sharp; W: Harry Alan Towers; Ph: Ernest Steward; M: Chris Whelan.
Cast: Christopher Lee, Nigel Green, Tsai Chin, Howard Marion Crawford.

FACE TO FACE. (1976) Ingmar Bergman's continuing essay on desolation and anguish reached an excruciating degree of proximity, as the title suggests. Liv Ullmann, as a psychiatrist who suffers a nervous breakdown, does much to lessen the didactic quality of one of Bergman's more lugubrious films. It comes from a time in his life that he says was filled with anxieties. "We can't really cure anyone," declares a shrink. "Some get well in spite of us'." The movie perhaps more therapeutic for Bergman than his audience.

R. ★★★

D and W: Ingmar Bergman; Ph: Sven Nykvist.
Cast: Liv Ullmann, Erland Josephson, Aino Taube, Kristina Adolphson.

FADE TO BLACK. (1980) An ingenious but ambiguously rendered premise about the consequences of living in a reel world. Dennis Christopher is a film buff with a bad case of "bijouitis". His head is crammed with trivia and his sex life consists of masturbating while pondering Mariyln Monroe stills.

Naturally, he decides to take out his enemies by re-enacting famous murders in movies. However, these are done as camp set-pieces that ruin the suspense.

R. ★★★

D and W: Vernon Zimmerman; Ph: Ed Barger; M: Craig Safan.
Cast: Dennis Christopher, Linda Kerridge, Eve Brent Ashe, Tim Thomerson.

FAHRENHEIT 451. (1967) Paranoid futurism isn't the idiom that springs to mind when you think of Francois Truffaut and the heat of genuinely felt passion is missing from a well-crafted adaptation of Ray Bradbury's speculation. Oskar Werner is equally reticent as the future fireman whose tasks include burning books that might encourage independent thought in fascist society. He eventually goes over to the book people.

★★★

D and W: Francois Truffaut; Ph: Nicholas Roeg; M: Bernard Herrmann.
Cast: Oskar Werner, Julie Christie, Cyril Cusack, Anton Diffring.

THE FALLEN IDOL. (1948) A thriller of high ingenuity form Carol Reed that puts the viewer in the place of an eight-year-old boy. He is the son of a diplomat and he idolizes the family's butler whom he comes to believe is involved in a murder. Reed imparted a strong sense of the fears of childhood and played upon a communal memory to exemplary effect.

★★★★

D: Carol Reed; W: Graham Greene; Ph: Georges Perinal; M: William Alwyn.
Cast: Ralph Richardson, Michele Morgan, Bobby Henrey, Sonia Dresdel.

FAME. (1980) Alan Parker's exuberant celebration of the joys and sorrows of life at New York's High School of the Performing Arts has more energy than sense of direction. He swings between the view of the school as a metaphor for the city and those who come to it with high ambitions, bouts of high voltage *Hair*-style choreography and maudlin realism. He cuts between the characters so much that watching the film is like listening to several conversations at once at an interesting party.

R. ★★★

D: Alan Parker; W: Christopher Gore; Ph: Michael Seresin; M: Michael Gore.

Cast: Eddie Barth, Irene Cara, Lee Curreri, Laura Dean.

FAMILY PLOT. (1976) Alfred Hitchcock ranked his 53rd and last film among his best. Not quite, but it is still a deliciously complex mystery that draws on the master's sly wit and the mellower side of his nature. The plot is geometrically precise and involves a chauffeur, a medium and a pair of kidnappers. Although the script is no more than serviceable there are a couple of vintage Hitchcock scenes to cherish, especially a graveyard sequence with two characters tracing the parallel lines of the story among the tombs.
PG. ★★★
D: Alfred Hitchcock; W: Ernest Lehman; Ph: Leonard J. South; M: John Williams.
Cast: Bruce Dern, Barbara Harris, Karen Black, William Devane.

THE FAN. (1949) Oscar Wilde and Otto Preminger are an unlikely couple on paper. And on film. A lot of Wilde's epigrammatic wit is lost in a lumbering story based on his play, *Lady Windermere's Fan*. Scandal rears its ugly head when a lady leaves her fan in her lover's apartment. Strictly for the loyal Preminger fan.
★★
D: Otto Preminger; W: Walter Reisch, Dorothy Parker and Ross Evans; Ph: Joseph La Shelle; M: Daniel Amfitheatrof.
Cast: Jeanne Crain, Madeleine Carroll, Richard Greene, George Sanders.

THE FAN. (1981) A pointless piece of exploitation that aroused some controversy because of the murder of John Lennon. A psychotic fan, obsessed with a Broadway star, feels compelled to kill the object of his adoration. The film-makers have nothing to add to our understanding of the subject and spend the time with murders and in demeaning Lauren Bacall's star quality.
R. ★
D: Edward Bianchi; W: Priscilla Chapman and John Hartwell; Ph: Dick Bush; M: Pino Donaggio.
Cast: Lauren Bacall, James Garner, Maureen Stapleton, Hector Elizondo.

FANNY AND ALEXANDER. (1983) Ingmar Bergman called it "a declaration of love for life" and "the sum total of my life as a film-maker." In pondering the several generations of a Swedish provincial family at the turn of the century, Bergman shines a benevolent light on the dark corners of the soul. Most of the familiar concerns are raised and discussed and the central theme is that the child is father to the man. The story unfolds through the eyes of Alexander and through his perspective we see adults who too often behave like children. The family runs a theater, which allows Bergman many parallels between life and art.
R. ★★★★★
D and W: Ingmar Bergman; Ph: Sven Nykvist; M: Daniel Bell.
Cast: Bertil Guve, Pernilla Allwin, Gunn Wallgren, Erland Josephson.

FANTASIA. (1940) At its best, Disney's fusion of sound and image fashioned animation of quite extraordinary imagination. At worst, it reduces great art to syrupy cuteness with the vision of Beethoven's Pastoral Symphony as a fantasy about centaurs. But the Night on Bald Mountain sequences, the opening Bach toccata and Mickey Mouse doubling as the Sorcerer's Apprentice represent the summit of the animator's art.
★★★★★
D: Walt Disney; M: Various composers(The Philadelphia Orchestra conducted by Leopold Stokowski).

FANTASTIC VOYAGE. (1966) In one of the more bizarre propositions you will find in science fiction movies, a submarine containing a team of doctors is reduced to the size of a microbe and injected into the body of a dying man in an effort to reach a clot in his brain. A device for shrinking the viewer's brain might help and the movie does not do much with its loony premise. The special effects do little for its credibility. The movie also forces the actors into being mere reactors to various emergencies.
★★
D: Richard Fleischer; W: Harry Kleiner; Ph: Ernest Laszlo; M: Leonard Rosenman.
Cast: Stephen Boyd, Raquel Welch, Edmond O'Brien, Donald Pleasence.

FAREWELL MY LOVELY. (1975) Third version of the Raymond Chandler private eye classic (the others were *The Falcon Takes Over* (1942) and *Murder, My Sweet* in 1944). There is no better Marlowe than Robert Mitchum's laconic and weary account of the detective trudging through the sleazy dives of Los Angeles in the forties. Marlowe is looking for the girl-friend of an ex-convict.
R. ★★★★

D: Dick Richards; W: David Zelag Goodman; Ph: John A. Alonzo; M: David Shire.
Cast: Robert Mitchum, Charlotte Rampling, John Ireland, Sylvia Miles.

A FAREWELL TO ARMS. (1957) A failure that induced David Selznick to say goodbye to the movie business. In the remake of the Gary Cooper 1932 original, Rock Hudson is the wounded ambulance driver and Jennifer Jones is his nurse. Hemingway's slight story of doomed love is hopelessly inflated.
★★
D: Charles Vidor; W: Ben Hecht; Ph: Oswald Morris; M: Mario Nascimbene.
Cast: Rock Hudson, Jennifer Jones, Vittorio de Sica, Alberto Sordi.

FAST BREAK. (1978) Although the plot has the inevitability of a free throw, the basketball comedy is one of the better post-Rocky sports exercises. Gabe Kaplan, the coach of a ramshackle Nevada school, recruits a motley group to take on a Top Ten team. The dialogue leans to one liners over natural speech, but *Fast Break* has a refreshing candor about underhanded recruiting in college athletics.
PG. ★★★
D: Jack Smight; W: Sandor Stern; Ph: Charles Correll; M: David Shire.
Cast: Gabe Kaplan, Harold Sylvester, Michael Warren, Bernard King.

THE FASTEST GUN ALIVE. (1956) A surprise hit in its day, perhaps because there is an element of fantasy behind a slightly silly plot. It casts Glenn Ford as a mild-mannered storekeeper whose rumored—and then proven—speed on the draw and marksmanship makes him the target of reputation seekers. The gunplay is ballistically, if not historically accurate. The movie is as far removed as one can get from the way real gunfights were contested on the frontier. Broderick Crawford looks as if he would have trouble drawing a check, but both he and Ford enter into the hokey spirit of the picture.
★★★
D: Russell Rouse; W: Rouse and Frank Gilroy; Ph: George Folsey; M: Andre Previn.
Cast: Glenn Ford, Broderick Crawford, Jeanne Crain, Russ Tamblyn.

FAST TIMES AT RIDGEMONT HIGH. (1982) Cameron Crowe's book becomes a routine piece of teen comedy and he has no one to blame but himself since he wrote the script. Other than Sean Penn's amusing turn as a likeable dope, Amy Heckerling's directing debut transforms a diverting array of young actors into a cast of caricatures and stereotypes.
R. ★★
D: Amy Heckerling; W: Cameron Crowe; Ph: Matthew Leonetti; M: Bob Destocki.
Cast: Sean Penn, Jennifer Jason Leigh, Phoebe Cates, Robert Romanus.

FATE IS THE HUNTER. (1964) Glenn Ford leads the painstaking investigation of a plane crash that took the lives of 53 people and ruined the reputation of the pilot, a wartime buddy. The detailed approach to the legwork rather than the peripheral drama makes it interesting.
★★★
D: Ralph Nelson; W: Harold Medford; Ph: Milton Krasner; M: Jerry Goldsmith.
Cast: Glenn Ford, Nancy Kwan, Rod Taylor, Suzanne Pleshette.

FATHER GOOSE. (1964) Cary Grant lends his customary grace to the proceedings even if he's out of uniform and neither tuxedo nor tie is in sight. He's an easygoing drifter working as a spotter for the Australians on a remote South Sea island in World War II. His life becomes an adventurous farce when Leslie Caron and a bunch of schoolkids show up.
★★
D: Ralph Nelson; W: Peter Stone and Frank Tarloff; Ph: Charles Lang, Jr.; M: Cy Coleman.
Cast: Cary Grant, Leslie Caron, Trevor Howard.

FATSO. (1980) Anne Bancroft made her directing debut and also wrote the roles of fat in a distinctly unappetizing foray into obesity. She can't make up her mind whether fatness is funny or pathetic. Dom DeLuise is relatively restrained (for him) as a card shop owner fighting a losing battle of the bulge. The concluding assertion is that it's what's inside that counts and it's pretty empty in there.
PG. ★★
D and W: Anne Bancroft; Ph: Brianne Murphy; M: Joe Renzetti.
Cast: Dom DeLuise, Anne Bancroft, Ron Carey, Candice Azzara.

THE F.B.I. STORY. (1959) Subsequent revelations about the nastier side of J. Edgar

Hoover's paranoia have done much to undermine the slavish and effusive praise for the achievements of the bureau. James Stewart reflects on a career that knew more than its share of political extremists and gangsters. Apart from him, there is little to distinguish it in sentiment or perception from the long-running television series.

★★

D: Mervin LeRoy; W: Richard Breen and John Twist; Ph: Joseph Biroc; M: Max Steiner.
Cast: James Stewart, Vera Miles, Larry Pennell, Nick Adams.

THE FEARLESS VAMPIRE KILLERS. (1967) Not a rare stake. Roman Polanski plays a vampire hunter's assistant but his send-up of Dracula films is in sore need of a transfusion of wit. There are some clever jokes such as a Jewish vampire who can't be double crossed into eternity, but the invention is weak. Many of the so-called serious Hammer films are funnier. Incredibly, the same writing team produced *Tess*.

★★

D: Roman Polanski; W: Polanski and Gerard Brach; Ph: Krzystof Komeda; M: Wilfred Shingleton.
Cast: Jack McGowran, Roman Polanski, Sharon Tate, Alfie Bass.

FEAR STRIKES OUT. (1957) The coiled tension that is part of Anthony Perkins' armory found an ideal outlet in a blunt but effective re-creation of the emotional and mental problems of Jimmy Piersall, the baseball player who suffered a nervous breakdown.

★★★

D: Robert Mulligan; W: Ted Berkman; Ph: Haskell Boggs; M: Elmer Bernstein.
Cast: Anthony Perkins, Karl Malden, Norma Moore, Perry Wilson.

F FOR FAKE. (1975) A flamboyant film about forgery from Orson Welles that is true to its content: it is a cheap bauble masquerading as a gem. The man who pulled off one of the great media hoaxes in history—the fake Martian invasion announced on radio—ponders Elmyr de Hory, a brilliant art forger. Lots of trickery and some pomposity.

★★★

D and W: Orson Welles; Ph: Christian Odasso and Gary Graver; M: Michel Legrand.
Cast: Orson Welles, Elmyr de Hory, Clifford Irving, Edith Irving.

FIDDLER ON THE ROOF. (1971) If you wonder why he sounds so good, it's because Isaac Stern played for the soundtrack. The lavish translation of an immensely likeable hit musical to the screen is done with similar professionalism throughout. Topol's Tevye is suitably larger than life. It's a life lived under the threat of pogroms and the plot deals with his eventual migration to America in 1905. The musical is based on Sholem Aleichem's stories and the rousing score keeps it moving. It was originally a full three hours long, but several shorter versions exist.

★★★

D: Norman Jewison; W: Joseph Stein; Ph: Oswald Morris; M: Jerry Bock.
Cast: Topol, Norma Crane, Leonard Frey, Molly Picon.

THE FIENDISH PLOT OF FU MANCHU. (1980) If the mark of genius is to make something out of desperately inferior material, Peter Sellers proved himself in his final picture. He is both Fu, who is 168 and can only keep going by giving himself an electric shock with the nearest appliance, and Inspector Nayland of Scotland Yard. He is also surrounded by a shambles that resulted from trouble on the set and much misguided editing.
PG. ★★
D: Piers Haggard; W: Jim Maloney and Rudy Dochtermann; Ph: Jean Tournier; M: Marc Wilkinson.
Cast: Peter Sellers, Sid Caesar, Helen Mirren, David Tomlinson.

THE FIEND WHO WALKED THE WEST. (1958) A sagebrush remake of *Kiss of Death*. The kiss is administered by Robert Evans in an overwrought and ludicrous extension of the famous Richard Widmark role. Evans, who went on to greener pastures as the producer of *The Godfather*, and Hugh O'Brian are cellmates. When the killer is released, O'Brian is offered a pardon if he can help capture him.

★★

D: Gordon Douglas; W: Philip Yordan and Harry Brown; Ph: Joe MacDonald; M: Leon Klatzkin.
Cast: Hugh O'Brian, Robert Evans, Dolores Michaels, Linda Cristal.

THE FIFTH MUSKETEER. (1978) One musketeer too many and not to be confused with Richard Lester's lively entries in the Dumas stakes. An international cast spouts international, easily dubbed dialogue in a

remake of Dumas' *The Man in the Iron Mask*. A great deal of arthritic, Saturday matinee swordplay. Beau Bridges takes the role of Louis XIV and his twin brother in the familiar tale of intrigue around the throne.
PG. ★★
D: Ken Annakin; W: David Ambrose; Ph: Jack Cardiff; M: Riz Ortolani.
Cast: Beau Bridges, Sylvia Kristel, Ursula Andress, Cornel Wilde.

THE FIGHTING SEABEES. (1944) In wartime, everyone's efforts have to be duly noted and that's why John Wayne is in a celebration of the hardhats' contribution to the struggle. He and Dennis O'Keefe organize construction workers under the noses of the Japanese and spend a good portion of the film fighting over Susan Hayward.
★★
D: Edward Ludwig; W: Borden Chase and Aeneas Mackenzie; Ph: William Bradford; M: Walter Scharf and Roy Webb.
Cast: John Wayne, Dennis O'Keefe, Susan Hayward, William Frawley.

THE FINAL CONFLICT. (1981) Round Three of *The Omen* series completes the unblessed trinity and turns out to be as much fun as spending Lent with a bunch of flagellants. It contains the timeless question and answer: "You're not a practicing Christian?" "No, I'm a practicing journalist!" Nauseating claptrap filled with mad monks, dog Latin, dogs that do the Devil's bidding and a heavenly chorus announcing the second coming of Christ. Believe it or not, it is actually charted by scientists at an observatory.
R. ★
D: Graham Baker; W: Anthony Birkin; Ph: Robert Paynter; M: Jerry Goldsmith.
Cast: Sam Neill, Rossano Brazzi, Don Gordon, Lisa Harrow.

THE FINAL COUNTDOWN. (1980) A ludicrous, nuclear-powered shaggy dog story. The U.S.S. Nimitz goes through a time warp and shows up at Pearl Harbor on the infamous day with atomic weaponry that can change history. But, as President Roosevelt predicted, no one has forgotten Pearl Harbor. We know nothing happened and so do the officers and men aboard the nuclear carrier. In effect, they spend the running time discussing doing something they know they didn't do. Katharine Ross shows up with a

real shaggy dog on a pleasure boat as fair warning.
PG. ★★
D: Don Taylor; W: David Ambrose, Gerry Davis, Thomas Hunter and Peter Powell; Ph: Victor J. Kemper; M: John Scott.
Cast: Kirk Douglas, Martin Sheen, Katharine Ross, James Farentino.

THE FINAL OPTION. (1983) Released in Europe under the title *Who Dares Wins*, which is the motto of the SAS, the crack British commando unit. Based on the true incident in which the commandos liberated hostages being held in a London embassy by terrorists. The action, when it finally arrives, is vividly staged. But the plot surrounding a woman terrorist, an infiltrator and the arrival of the American Secretary of State is flimsy and the dialogue verbose.
R. ★★
D: Ian Sharp; W: Reginald Rose; Ph: Phil Meheux.
Cast: Judy Davis, Lewis Collins, Richard Widmark, Robert Webber.

THE FINAL TERROR. (1983) A bunch of young hikers are led by a Vietnam veteran on drugs into a California forest. They behave as dumbly as only characters in this kind of film can manage. Very gory.
R. ★
D: Andrew Davis; W: Ronald Shusett, Jon George and Neill Hicks.
Cast: Daryl Hannah, Rachel Ward, John Friedrich, Adrian Zmed.

FINDERS KEEPERS. (1984) There's $5 million stashed in a coffin aboard a train and everybody's after it. But Richard Lester has a hard time breathing life into the proceedings and his solution is to propel it at express train speed. His gift is for this kind of madcap, sight gag humor but there are more hits than misses along the track.
R. ★★
D: Richard Lester; W: Ronnie Graham, Terence Marsh and Charles Dennis; M: Ken Thorne.
Cast: Michael O'Keefe, Beverly D'Angelo, David Wayne, Ed Lauter.

FINGERS. (1978) If James Toback's debut has the seamy look of *Taxi Driver*, it's because Michael Chapman did the photography for both. But the contained rage of the Scorsese film is missing in a rambling and often pretentious piece that shows Toback's obsession with obsessions. A concert pianist makes the rounds as a gangland debt collector for his father in an improbable situation that Toback uses for much vivid sex and violence.

R. ★★

D and W: James Toback; Ph: Michael Chapman.

Cast: Harvey Keitel, Tisa Farrow, Jim Brown, Michael V. Gazzo.

FIRE AND ICE. (1983) The commercial failure of Ralph Bakshi's interesting collaboration with the popular illustrator Frank Frazetta proved how difficult it is for serious animation to find an audience. The technique on display is very impressive, but the story is the usual melange of sword and sorcery with dashing heroes opposed by someone called Nekron. The dialogue is also ponderous and the appeal is totally visual.

PG. ★★★

D: Ralph Bakshi; W: Roy Thomas and Gerry Conway; M: William Kraft.

Cast: (Voices) Susan Tyrrell, Maggie Rosswell, William Ostrander, Stephen Mandel.

FIREFOX. (1982) A jet-propelled Clint Eastwood vehicle that takes too long to leave the ground. The adaptation of Craig Thomas' thriller is really two movies in one with two hours of leaden espionage surrounding the plan to hijack an advanced Russian fighter and 30 minutes of spectacular escape footage. The slow going would have been relieved by Eastwood's laconic contempt for authority, but he is very restrained here as the pilot chosen for the suicide mission.

PG ★★

D: Clint Eastwood; W: Alex Lasker and Wendell Wellmann; Ph: Bruce Surtees; M: Maurice Jarre.

Cast: Clint Eastwood, Freddie Jones, David Huffman, Warren Clarke.

FIRE OVER ENGLAND. (1936) Like *Alexander Nevsky* in its attempt to stir patriotic fires against a looming threat by celebrating an historical triumph. In terms of quality, the similarity ends there. Flora Robson is suitably regal as Elizabeth I, who is beset by traitors in her own court and Spanish belligerence in 1588. Laurence Olivier dashes off to Spain to sort things out and save England. Historically, it's rubbish and the Armada seems to be crossing a duck pond, but the cast is superior. Watch closely and you'll see an uncredited James Mason.

★★★

D: William K. Howard; W: Clemence Dane and Sergei Nolbandov; Ph: James Wong Howe; M: Richard Addinsell.

Cast: Laurence Olivier, Flora Robson, Vivien Leigh, Leslie Banks.

FIRE SALE. (1977) Almost everyone in the antic garment business family offered here is insane and its feeble wit depends on how amusing you find mental derangement. The patriarch of the demented Jewish brood arranges to burn down his own clothing store and collect the insurance by conning his crazy brother into committing the crime. The humor is strictly from the bargain basement.

PG. ★★

D: Alan Arkin; W: Robert Klane; Ph: Ralph Woolsey; M: Dave Grusin.

Cast: Alan Arkin, Rob Reiner, Sid Caesar, Vincent Gardenia.

FIRST BLOOD. (1982) In his fifth non-*Rocky* film, Sylvester Stallone caught on with a routine piece of exploitation that is directed with more flair than sense by Ted Kotcheff. Stallone is a Medal of Honor winner numbed into psychosis by Vietnam and pushed over the edge by a small-town sheriff. Mostly a noisy manhunt that rushes over some gaping plot-holes.

R. ★★

D: Ted Kotcheff; W: Michael Kozoll, O. Moonblood(Stallone) and William Sackheim; Ph: Andrew Laszlo.

Cast: Sylvester Stallone, Richard Crenna, Brian Dennehy, David Caruso.

THE FIRST DEADLY SIN. (1980) The main sin is one of omission. Frank Sinatra stalks a Manhattan killer who likes to knock off male pedestrians with an ice pick, but there is no attempt to amplify the murderer's motives. Otherwise, a very routine police procedural with Sinatra bucking the bureaucracy and reading children's stories to his dying wife. Whether she is succumbing to these readings or a kidney infection is never clear.

R. ★★

D: Brian G. Hutton; W: Manny Rubin; Ph: Jack Priestley; M: Gordon Jenkins.

Cast: Frank Sinatra, Faye Dunaway, Brenda Vaccaro, James Whitmore.

FIRST LOVE. (1977) A *menage a trois* involving a college student, a beautiful older woman and a married lawyer. The student is an idealist who shuns the hearty promiscuity

of the campus and puts the woman on a pedestal—a perch she finds precarious. With a woman director in charge, one would reasonably expect the film to focus on the most interesting conflict—the woman's. Instead, the student's almost medieval notions of love dominate and his idealism comes across as callousness. His plight is remote and the woman's unexplored.
R. ★
D: Joan Darling; W: Jane Stanton Hitchcock, David Freeman; Ph: Bobby Byrne; M: Joe Sill.
Cast: William Katt, Susan Dey, John Heard, Beverly D'Angelo.

FIRST MEN IN THE MOON. (1964) American astronauts land and discover they are not the first but the second exploring party. The honor goes to a Victorian eccentric played to the hilt by Lionel Jeffries in a cheerful rendering of the H.G. Wells fantasy. The early going with the revelations about Jeffries anti-gravity paint have more spirit than the silliness on the moon and its population of monsters.
★★
D: Nathan Juran; W: Jan Read and Nigel Kneale; Ph: Wilkie Cooper; M: Laurie Johnson.
Cast: Lionel Jeffries, Edward Judd, Martha Hyer.

FIRST MONDAY IN OCTOBER. (1981) President Reagan nominated Sandra Day O'Connor just before this fiction about the first woman Supreme Court Justice came out. There is a courtroom collision of commerce and sense in the casting of Jill Clayburgh, who is decades younger than a woman who would plausibly receive such an appointment. She is a conservative ranged against Walter Matthau's crusty liberal and the film would have surmounted its built-in problems as a straightforward comedy. It is bogged down—like our court system—with redundant debates.
R. ★★
D: Ronald Neame; W: Jerome Lawrence and Robert E. Lee; Ph: Fred Koenekamp; M: Ian Fraser.
Cast: Jill Clayburgh, Walter Matthau, Barnard Hughes, Jan Sterling.

THE FIRST NUDIE MUSICAL. (1976) A rancid, cheaply executed concoction that grafts mild porn to old musicals. On paper, this seems ridiculous. On film, it's even worse.

The sleaziness of today's 42nd Street and its boisterous perversions is introduced to the world of *42nd Street* and other cherished musicals. Someone called Sammy Can't must have written lyrics like "Gotta sing, Gotta dance/While I'm taking off my pants."
R.
D: Mark Haggard and Bruce Kimmel; W: Bruce Kimmel; Ph: Douglas H. Knapp; M: Bruce Kimmel.
Cast: Stephen Nathan, Cindy Williams, Bruce Kimmel, Leslie Ackerman.

THE FIRST TIME. (1978) A charming, wittily observed foray into virgin territory with a 17-year-old on the brink of manhood and one that a lot of American hack directors could profitably study. Four French teens are obsessed with losing their virginity and the film has a gentle humor that puts it far above the trash Hollywood churns out on the subject.
★★★
D and W: Claude Berri; Ph: Jean-Caesar Chiabaut; M: Rene Urteger.
Cast: Alain Cohen, Charles Denner, Zorica Lozic, Claude Lubicki.

FISH HAWK. (1980) At the turn of the century, an Osage Indian lives in a white settlement and drinks a lot. One reason is that his only company consists of a dog and the village idiot. Another may be the drunken Indian stereotyping that weighs heavily on an otherwise innocuous family entertainment from Canada. Most of it is taken up with the Indian's friendship with a farm boy.
G. ★★
D: Donald Shebib; W: Blanche Hanalis; Ph: Rene Verzier; M: Samuel Matlovsky.
Cast: Will Sampson, Charlie Fields, Geoffrey Bowes, Mary Pirle.

F.I.S.T. (1978) An effective earthy performance from Sylvester Stallone as a union leader in a saga that begins in the thirties on a Cleveland loading dock. Clearly based on Jimmy Hoffa and the Teamsters, *F.I.S.T.* suffers from a tendency to reduce complex economic and social issues in an effort to make them accessible. It remains an absorbing study of the compromises involved in success and the supporting cast is excellent.
PG. ★★★
D: Norman Jewison; W: Joe Eszterhaus and Sylvester Stallone; Ph: Laszlo Kovacs; M: Bill Conti.

Cast: Sylvester Stallone, Rod Steiger, Peter Boyle, Melinda Dillon.

A FISTFUL OF DOLLARS. (1966) A film full of rancid violence that did two things which cannot be construed as major advances for the screen. Clint Eastwood became a star whose mean stare through cheroot smoke and habit of mowing down anyone who affronted him found a vast, global following. Secondly, it was the first strand in the spaghetti western cult. It is based on Kurosawa's *Yojimbo* and puts Eastwood in a Mexican town where his behavior makes Dirty Harry look like a liberal.

★

D: Sergio Leone; W: Leone and Duccio Tessari; Ph: Massimo Dallamano; M: Ennio Morricone.
Cast: Clint Eastwood, Marianne Koch, John Welles, Wolfgang Lukschy.

FITZCARRALDO. (1982) Werner Herzog continued his exploration of what is allegedly civilized and what is innocently primitive in an epic and highly successful account of a failed dream. A mad rubber planter, who is actually saner than his greedy colleagues, becomes obsessed with erecting an opera house in the middle of the jungle. Rarely has the device of the madman as a measure of society's failures been more eloquently used and the film —shot in Peru—has a mesmerizing visual beauty.
PG.   ★★★★★
D and W: Werner Herzog; Ph: Thomas Mauch; M: Popol Vuh.
Cast: Klaus Kinski, Jose Lewgoy, Miguel Angel Fuentes, Paul Hittscher.

FIVE EASY PIECES. (1970) Jack Nicholson drifting around the country in a film whose mood and style owe a debt to *Easy Rider*. It is, under Bob Rafelson's observant direction, far superior because it defers to Nicholson's extraordinary talent and a very able supporting cast. With this performance he began the succession of movies that made him a dominant actor in the seventies. He disdains conventional life and finds work on oil rigs and it was no easy piece of work to give the film its strong focus.

★★★★
D: Bob Rafelson; W: Adrien Joyce; Ph: Laszlo Kovacs .
Cast: Jack Nicholson, Karen Black, Susan Anspach, Lois Smith.

FIVE FINGERS. (1952) A stylish espionage thriller elevated by James Mason. It is based on the *Operation Cicero,* the account of L. C. Moyzisch's spying activities in Turkey. Mason is a humble valet in the British Embassy in Ankara who sells secrets to the Germans.

★★★
D: Joseph L. Mankiewicz; W: Michael Wilson; Ph: Norbert Brodine; M: Bernard Herrmann.
Cast: James Mason, Danielle Darrieux, Michael Rennie, Walter Hampden.

FIVE MILLION MILES TO EARTH. (1968) When a science fiction production lacks the money to put on a spectacle it sometimes forces the director and writer to go a little deeper into character and ideas. Such was the case with this tale of the discovery during an archeological dig in London of a buried ship with dead aliens aboard. Its original inspiration was the excellent old Quatermass series on British television and it is also known as *Quatermass and the Pit.*

★★★
D: Roy Ward baker; W: Nigel Knewale; Ph: Arthur Grant; M: Tristram Cary.
Cast: Andrew Keir, Barbara Shelley, James Donald, Maurice Good.

FIVE STAR FINAL. (1931) The last word in newspaper movies of the period and a still absorbing if rather simplistic discussion of journalistic ethics. A tabloid editor pursues a circulation-building murder story even though it threatens to ruin innocent lives. Edward G. Robinson, as the tough editor, holds the film even in its lapses into sentimentality.

★★★★
D: Mervyn LeRoy; W: Robert Lord and Byron Morgan; Ph: Sol Polito; M: Leo Forbstein.
Cast: Edward G. Robinson, Boris Karloff, H. B. Warner, Marian Marsh.

FIVE WEEKS IN A BALLOON. (1962) An overblown comedy adventure that makes the movie seem that long. It fails to capture the Jules Verne spirit, which depends on Victorian eccentricity dealing with moments of great peril. The British government dispatches the balloon to lay claim to yet more of Africa.

★★
D: Irwin Allen; W: Allen, Charles Bennett and Albert Gail; Ph: Winton Hoch; M: Paul Sawtell.
Cast: Red Buttons, Fabian, Barbara Eden, Cedric Hardwicke.

FIXED BAYONETS. (1951) Sam Fuller's high standing as an admired director of B movies is explained by this kind of work. The story of an American platoon fighting a rear-guard action in freezing Korea may be run-of-the-trench, but Fuller gives it a gritty reality and Richard Basehart is very impressive as a corporal who doesn't like killing. Fuller's heart was with the grunts in the front line and it improves the production.

★★★

D and W: Sam Fuller; Ph: Lucien Ballard; M: Roy Webb.
Cast: Richard Basehart, Gene Evans, Michael O'Shea, Richard Hylton.

THE FLAME AND THE ARROW. (1950) Robin Hood, Italian style. Burt Lancaster and Nick Cravat, who later made *The Crimson Pirate*, swing across the screen in an equally vital costume adventure that is played for fun and makes as much room as possible for their dazzling acrobatics. Lancaster leads a revolution against medieval tyranny and Jacques Tourneur's direction is far above the hack-work that so often comes with screen swordplay.

★★★

D: Jacques Tourneur; W: Waldo Salt; Ph: Ernest Haller; M: Max Steiner.
Cast: Burt Lancaster, Virginia Mayo, Robert Douglas, Nick Cravat.

FLAMING STAR. (1960) One of the brighter lights in Elvis Presley's career and arguably his best dramatic part. He proved he could ruin a western in *Charro*, but here, under Don Siegel's veteran hand and with dialogue that is not hostile to his limited compass, Elvis is presentable. He is a half-breed trying to pacify whites and Kiowas.

★★★

D: Don Siegel; W: Clair Huffaker and Nunnally Johnson; Ph: Charles Clarke; M: Cyril Mockridge.
Cast: Elvis Presley, Dolores del Rio, Steve Forrest, Barbara Eden.

FLASHDANCE. (1983) The title suggests a musical about dirty old men in raincoats, but the truth is even worse. A young girl is a welder by day and a dancer in a seedy bar by night. What she really wants to be is a ballerina and the film has a frenzied dumbness that makes you want to pull a leg-warmer over your head. Only in Hollywood would they ask you to believe that Pittsburgh steelworkers drive around in Porsches and live in mock-tudor mansions. The movie is all flash and dance with little character and plot and bad enough to be beyond mockery.

R.

D: Adrian Lyne; W: Tom Hedley, Joe Eszterhaus; Ph: Don Peterman; M: Giorgio Moroder.
Cast: Jennifer Beals, Michael Nouri, Lilia Skala, Sunny Johnson.

FLASH GORDON. (1980) In a $20-million reincarnation Flash is the quarterback of the New York Jets. He is thus accustomed to standing behind bad and offensive lines and they abound in the script. Flash is delivered into the clutches of Ming, which becomes an excuse for assorted pea-brained escapes. The sets look like a Chinese restaurant and the kiddie plot is souped up with raunchy *double entendres* that one hopes are above the heads of children.

PG.   ★

D: Michael Hodges; W: Lorenzo Semple, Jr.; Ph: Gil Taylor; M: Queen.
Cast: Max Von Sydow, Sam Jones, Melody Anderson, Topol.

THE FLIGHT OF THE EAGLE. (1983) The incredible voyage of three Swedish explorers who set out for the North Pole in a hot-air balloon in 1897. Jan Troell, who is best known here for *The Emigrants*, elevates the survival motif by making the journey a voyage of self-discovery. The balloon crashes and the three men endure unimaginable privations. This is not an adventure movie of suspense, but a gradual revelation of character under stress.

★★★★

D: Jan Troell; W: Troell, George Oddner, and Klaus Rifberg; Ph: Jan Troell; M: Olaf Sundman.
Cast: Max Von Sydow, Goran Strangertz, Sverre Anker Ousdal, Lotta Larson.

FLIGHT OF THE PHOENIX. (1965) The downed passengers and crew of a cargo plane rise from the sands instead of the ashes. Serviceable if rather measured adventure in the Sahara that blames the drunken English navigator responsible for the crash. An ingenious German finds a way of rebuilding the plane before they die of thirst.

★★★

D: Robert Aldrich; W: Lucas Heller; Ph: Joseph Biroc; M: Frank de Vol.
Cast: James Stewart, Richard Attenborough, Peter Finch, Hardy Kruger.

THE FLIM FLAM MAN. (1967) The flimsiness of the comic idea is artfully disguised by George C. Scott, who dominates this modest movie as a charming rogue. No scam is beneath him at the card table or in life as a con man and he recruits a young army deserter to help him out. Irvin Kershner, who later directed *The Empire Strikes Back*, showed an early flair for action in a riotous car chase.

★★★

D: Irvin Kershner; W: William Rose; Ph: Charles Lang; M: Jerry Goldsmith.
Cast: George C. Scott, Michael Sarrazin, Sue Lyon, Harry Morgan.

FLOWER DRUM SONG. (1961) Time has not been kind to a musical marred by an occidental view of Oriental life that is best described as patronizing. A Chinese girl comes to San Francisco's Chinatown as a contract bride and the plodding development and dull script make the enterprise seem longer than the Golden Gate bridge. Not one of the more signal Rodgers and Hammerstein collaborations.

★★

D: Henry Koster; W: Joseph Fields; Ph: Russell Metty; M: Richard Rodgers and Oscar Hammerstein.
Cast: Nancy Kwan, James Shigeta, Juanita Hall, Myoshi Umeki.

THE FLY. (1958) A scientist fooling around with mother nature—breaking down molecules—sets a job for the swat team when he accidentally changes heads with a fly. Not nearly as silly as it sounds and well written by James Clavell.

★★

D: Kurt Neumann; W: James Clavell; Ph: Karl Struss; M: Paul Sawtell.
Cast: Al Hedison, Patricia Owens, Vincent Price, Herbert Marshall.

FLYING DOWN TO RIO. (1933) The chorus girls dance on airplane wings, but this charming piece of fluff is now celebrated as the take-off point of two pretty good dancers named Astaire and Rogers. They teamed up here for the first time and the rest is history. The top billing went to others, but Astaire and Rogers made an impression that launched them into orbit.

★★★

D: Thornton Freeland; W: Cyril Hume, H.W. Hannemann and Erwin Gelsey; Ph: Roy Hunt; M: Vincent Youmans.
Cast: Dolores Del Rio, Gene Raymond, Fred Astaire, Ginger Rogers.

FLYING LEATHERNECKS. (1951) It's possible to allow for all the ineptly spliced battle footage between shots of heroic Marine pilots in their cockpits, but there's no excuse for the screenplay. It trots out the one about the feud between the tough-for-their-own-good father figure (John Wayne) and his liberal deputy (Robert Ryan). Ryan is actually forced to recite Donne in defense of his position. The action is the South Pacific with the fliers trying out new ground-to-air communication strategies.

★★

D: Nicholas Ray; W: James Edward Grant; Ph: William Snyder; M: Roy Webb.
Cast: John Wayne, Robert Ryan, Janis Carter, Don Taylor.

FM. (1978) It says here that an FM station out there has disc jockeys who rebel against management for scheduling too many commercials. Poorly done youth vs. establishment with amusing turns from Martin Mull and Alex Karras. Linda Ronstadt, in concert, gives *FM* a momentary upbeat. The rest is dead-beat.

PG. ★★

D: John A. Alonzo; W: Ezra Sacks; Ph: David Myers.
Cast: Michael Brandon, Eileen Brennan, Alex Karras, Martin Mull.

THE FOG. (1980) John Carpenter's post-*Halloween* outing assumes the meteorological qualities of a fogbank, rolling inshore with some purpose and then spreading out aimlessly. More a ghost story than a horror film, *The Fog* has ancient mariners coming out of the mist in search of vengeance against a small coastal town. The usual trapped woman, rescued child and booze-sodden priest are on hand. "Stay away from the fog," shouts Adrienne Barbeau and, for all the flashy technique, she's right.

R. ★★

D: John Carpenter; W: Carpenter and Debra Hill; Ph: Dean Cundey; M: John Carpenter.
Cast: Adrienne Barbeau, Hal Holbrook, Janet Leigh, Jamie Lee Curtis.

FOLIES—BERGERE. (1935) Throughout his life Maurice Chevalier suffered through all manner of impersonations of himself. In a thoroughly delightful musical, he is a nobleman who hires an entertainer who does an impersonation of him. It's a double role that sets up some comic situations in his domestic life and the light story is housed in a lavish production.

★★★

D: Roy del Ruth; W: Hal Long and Bess Meredyth; Ph: Barney McGill; M: Alfred Newman.
Cast: Maurice Chevalier, Merle Oberon, Ann Sothern, Eric Blore.

FOLLOW THE FLEET. (1936) Instead, follow the feet of Fred Astaire and Ginger Rogers who are in top form. The musical is otherwise enjoyable whimsy about two sailors on leave and two sisters. The Irving Berlin songs include "Let Yourself Go." Take his advice.

★★★

D: Mark Sandrich; W: Dwight Taylor; Ph: David Abel; M: Irving Berlin.
Cast: Fred Astaire, Ginger Rogers, Randolph Scott, Harriet Hilliard.

FOOD OF THE GODS. (1976) Unfit for human consumption. Loosely based on parts of the H.G. Wells novel with a substance oozing out of the ground to change rats, mice, rabbits and chickens into monsters. Some of it oozed into the feed of the scriptwriter. There is no other explanation for what he wrote. The effects suggest the last ad your local exterminator ran on UHF. The action takes place at a remote farm house that is not remote enough.
PG.

D and W: Bert I. Gordon; Ph: Reginald Morris; M: Elliot Kaplan.
Cast: Marjoe Gortner, Pamela Franklin, Ralph Meeker, Ida Lupino.

FOOTLIGHT PARADE. (1933) The enormous success of *42nd Street* encouraged many musicals in the same vein and the team responsible for the archetypal backstage movie got together again. In almost every way it's better than *42nd Street*. James Cagney is the fast-talking producer whose theater presentations are jeopardized by the advent of the talkies. The script is snappy and smart and Busby Berkeley's farfetched choreography is the icing on the cake.

★★★★

D: Lloyd Bacon; W: Manuel Seff and James Seymour; Ph: George Barnes; M: Harry Warren, Al Dubin, Sammy Fain and Irving Fahal.

Cast: James Cagney, Joan Blondell, Ruby Keeler, Dick Powell.

FOOTLOOSE. (1984) Free up your fantasies and try believing the following. The kids in a small town who have sophisticated discussions about types of marijuana don't dance. The local firebrand preacher thinks it's lewd and for reasons never clear, they go along. Kevin Bacon arrives to shake things up. A fifties rock and roll movie plot lost and forlorn in the eighties. Manic choreography and a soundtack in search of some celluloid to wrap the album in.
PG. ★

D: Herbert Ross; W: Dean Pitchford; Ph: Ric Waite; M: Various artists.
Cast: Kevin Bacon, John Lithgow, Lori Singer, Christopher Penn.

FOOTSTEPS IN THE DARK. (1941) Errol Flynn gropes for the right style as a crime novelist who becomes involved in the solution of a real murder. He needed a howdunit course in whodunit detection and never seems comfortable in what amounted to a pause between his costume adventures. The lightness he brought to those is very strained here.

★★

D: Lloyd Bacon; W: Lester Cole and John Wexley; Ph: Ernest Haller; M: Fredrick Hollander.
Cast: Errol Flynn, Brenda Marshall, Ralph Bellamy, Alan Hale.

FOR A FEW DOLLARS MORE. (1967) Sergio Leone churned out the second Clint Eastwood spaghetti western in the sure and certain hope of making a few dollars more than *A Fistful of Dollars*. The amoral tone and passion for posed and often interminable shots were now entrenched. You get the impression that it's not so much a style as a matter of meeting fan expectations. Eastwood and Lee Van Cleef are bounty hunters with a problem—they're both after the same reward. Another violent bore.

★

D and W: Sergio Leone; Ph: Massimo Dallamano; M: Ennio Morricone.
Cast: Clint Eastwood, Lee Van Cleef, Gian Maria Volante, Klaus Kinski.

FORBIDDEN PLANET. (1956) One of the finest science fiction films of the fifties borrowed its plot from a very unlikely source —Shakespeare's *The Tempest*. Prospero becomes a stranded explorer named Morbius, who lives on Altair IV with his comely daughter. Also present is a literally electrifying Caliban, a monster who draws its strength from an intriguing source. With the exception of Walter Pidgeon the acting is lifeless, but the script teems with fascinating ideas and *Forbidden Planet* is still admired for its striking effects. They were, like the film, far ahead of their time.

★★★★

D: Fred Wilcox; W: Cyril Hume; Ph: George Folsey; M: Louis and Bebe Barron.
Cast: Walter Pidgeon, Anne Francis, Leslie Nielsen, Warren Stevens.

FORCE OF ONE. (1980) The one in question is Chuck Norris, a devotee of the Bronsonian school of utterly impassive acting. Although in the hands of a capable director and joined by a competent cast of professionals, Norris cannot carry a movie. He goes after a bad-apple karate champion and a California drug ring.
PG. ★
D: Paul Aaron; W: Ernest Tidyman; Ph: Roger Shearman; M: Dick Halligan.
Cast: Chuck Norris, Clu Gulager, Ron O'Neal, James Whitmore.

FORCE TEN FROM NAVARONE. (1978) The famous destruction of the guns at the end of *The Guns of Navarone* opens the sequel in an attempt to establish its antecedents. It merely invites unfavorable comparisons and forces actors of the caliber of Robert Shaw to say things like "The place is crawling with krauts." A diffuse, episodic effort with Shaw (this was his last film) and Edward Fox joining a behind-the-lines American mission inside occupied Yugoslavia.
PG. ★★
D: Guy Hamilton; W: Robin Chapman and George MacDonald Fraser; Ph: Chris Challis; M: Ron Goodwin.
Cast: Robert Shaw, Harrison Ford, Edward Fox, Barbara Bach.

FOREIGN CORRESPONDENT. (1940) Alfred Hitchcock's personal contribution to the war effort exposes a Nazi espionage ring. A workman-like plot finds an American journalist on the tail of Nazi kidnappers. It takes him to Holland where Hitchcock staged a celebrated sequence with a windmill turning in the wrong direction and another with a hair-raising plane crash.
★★★

D: Alfred Hitchcock; W: Joan Harrison and Charles Bennett; Ph: Rudolph Mate; M: Alfred Newman.
Cast: Joel McCrea, Laraine Day, Herbert Marshall, George Sanders.

FOREVER AMBER. (1947). With Otto Preminger at the helm and the raunchy (by forties standards) ingredients of the titillating novel banished in the name of decency, the costume epic seems to take an eternity. Linda Darnell is the courtesan who bed-hops her way to the top in the court of Charles II but loses her man and child as the price.
★★

D: Otto Preminger; W: Philip Dunne and Ring Lardner; Ph: Leon Shamroy; M: David Raksin.
Cast: Linda Darnell, Cornel Wilde, Richard Greene, George Sanders.

FOR ME AND MY GAL. (1942) Gene Kelly's debut in movies has Judy Garland, some gorgeous songs and impeccable and imaginative direction from Busby Berkeley. It also has a surprisingly serious theme in casting him as an entertainer who is willing to injure himself to get out of the draft in World War 1. Since this was hardly the kind of behavior countenanced in World War II, he learns the error of his ways.
★★★

D: Busby Berkeley; W: Richard Sherman and Sid Silvers; Ph: William Daniels; M: Georgie Stoll and Roger Edens.
Cast: Gene Kelly, Judy Garland, George Murphy, Marta Eggerth.

THE FORMULA. (1980) John Avildsen aroused the same emotions one felt in an energy crisis gas line—anger, confusion and boredom. A Los Angeles cop, who actually has dialogue like "I must resent this implication," investigates a murder and uncovers a long suppressed Nazi formula for synthetic fuel. Troubled by much infighting during production and chopped to pieces in the editing room, what remains is confusing and almost impossible to follow.
R ★
D: John Avildsen; W: Steve Shagan; Ph: James Crabe; M: Bill Conti.
Cast: George C. Scott, Marlon Brando, Marthe Keller, John Gielgud.

FORT APACHE, THE BRONX. (1981) Paul Newman's weathered grittiness anchors a portrait of America's toughest precinct that tries to cover too much of the depressing territory. His John Murphy, who has patrolled these mean, rubbled streets for 14 years, is a mixture of vast cynicism and rough compassion for the victims of slum life. Heywood Gould's screenplay has an irritating habit of raising situations and then forgetting about them but its heart is in the right place.

R. ★★★
D: Daniel Petrie; W: Heywood Gould; Ph: John Alcott; M: Jonathan Tunick.
Cast: Paul Newman, Ken Wahl, Ed Asner, Danny Aiello.

FOR THE LOVE OF BENJI. (1977) Successor to the popular *Benji*, but by this time the original mutt was 17 and retired. His replacement has the same remorseless cuteness. The plot of the film, which finds Benji being chased by villains and spies in Athens, is a little complex for the younger children at which it is aimed.

G. ★★
D and W: Joe Camp; Ph: Don Reddy; M: Eull Box;
Cast: Patsy Garrett, Cynthia Smith, Allen Fiuzat.

THE FORTUNE. (1975) Like a visit to a supermarket in that you come away with less than you expected for the money. Despite the stellar talent, a very limp script undermines the efforts of Jack Nicholson and Warren Beatty, two twenties con-men trying to knock off an heiress. They are hopelessly inept killers. Where there should be wit, there is only aggressive bonhomie.

R. ★★
D: Mike Nichols; W: Adrien Joyce; Ph: John A. Alonzo; M: David Shire.
Cast: Jack Nicholson, Warren Beatty, Stockard Channing, Florence Stanley.

THE FORTUNE COOKIE. (1966) Not one of the more fortunate pairings of Walter Matthau and Jack Lemmon. Lemmon is a television cameraman injured while covering a Cleveland Browns game and Matthau is his conniving lawyer and brother-in-law who cooks up a scheme to make a bundle out of the accident. Matthau's characterization is consistently funny and on the mark and it was recognized with an Oscar.

★★
D: Billy Wilder; W: Wilder and I.A.L. Diamond; Ph: Joseph La Shelle; M: André Previn.
Cast: Jack Lemmon, Walter Matthau, Ron Rich, Cliff Osmond.

48 HRS. (1982) A racial male bonding comedy that tries to find room for both a routine police procedural and Eddie Murphy. The movie lies down and plays dead so that Murphy, a horny street hustler out on a pass to help catch a murderer, can do his stand-up routines. They're very funny, especially in his rousting of a redneck bar and his attempts make up for years of enforced celibacy.

R. ★★
D: Walter Hill; W: Roger Spottiswoode, Hill, Larry Gross and Steven E. de Souza; Ph: Ric Waite; M: James Horner.
Cast: Eddie Murphy, Nick Nolte, Annette O'Toole, Frank McRae.

THE 49TH PARALLEL. (1941) Six German submariners in Canada and the U.S.A. are bent on sabotage. The propaganda element, which questioned North American neutrality, is strong but does not overwhelm the inherent excitement of the film. It is brilliantly scored by Vaughan Williams.

★★★
D: Michael Powell; W: Rodney Ackland and Emeric Pressburger; Ph: Frederick Young; M: Ralph Vaughan Williams.
Cast: Richard George, Eric Portman, Raymond Lovell, Peter Moore.

42ND STREET. (1933) "You're going out a youngster, but you've got to come back a star!" And, guess what, she did. Countless imitations of an already hackneyed plot can't dull the exuberance of a landmark musical, which continued to thrive on the stage even in the eighties. Ruby Keeler goes on after the star breaks a leg, presumably by tripping over a backstage cliche. Enhanced by some famous Busby Berkeley numbers.

★★★
D: Lloyd Bacon; W: James Seymour and Rian James; Ph: Sol Polito; M: Al Dubin and Harry Warren.
Cast: Warner Baxter, Ruby Keeler, Bebe Daniels, George Brent.

FOR YOUR EYES ONLY. (1981) The twelfth James Bond film saw the second unit director, John Glen, promoted to full charge of the proceedings. It was fitting because by this time the series was little more than the sum of its stunts. Less gadgetry than *Moonraker* and one has to admit the stunts are very well done. Bond tries to recover a device vital to Britain's nuclear deterrent.

PG. ★★★
D: John Glen; W: Richard Maibaum and

Michael Wilson; Ph: Alan Hume; M: Bill Conti.
Cast: Roger Moore, Carole Bouquet, Topol, Lynn-Holly Johnson.

FOUL PLAY. (1978) Colin Higgins' inept Hitchcock spoof is for people who find the sight of old ladies spelling out obscenities on a scrabble board amusing. Goldie Hawn's daffy charm is not enough to keep this heavily padded romp going. She is a librarian who becomes unwittingly involved with a detective and in a plot to assassinate the Pope.
PG.   ★★
D and W: Colin Higgins; Ph: David Walsh; M: Charles Fox.
Cast: Chevy Chase, Goldie Hawn, Burgess Meredith, Dudley Moore.

FOUR CLOWNS. (1970) Another first class anthology from Robert Youngson. This one features clips from the work of Laurel and Hardy, Buster Keaton and Charley Chase.
                                                     ★★★

FOUR FOR TEXAS. (1963) But zero for effort. Frank Sinatra and Dean Martin argue over the gambling rights to Galveston in a losing bet from Robert Aldrich. Understandably disinterested in the plot, Aldrich spends a great deal of camera time traversing the startling breasts of Anita Ekberg and Ursula Andress. Piggy and stupid.
                                                     ★
D: Robert Aldrich; W: Aldrich and Teddi Sherman; Ph: Ernest Laszlo; M: Nelson Riddle.
Cast: Frank Sinatra, Dean Martin, Anita Ekberg, Ursula Andress.

FOUR FRIENDS. (1981) Steve Tesich, the talented writer of *Breaking Away*, bit off more than he could chew. He tries to sandwich the tumult of the sixties into two hours and he does not offer the perspective of hindsight. Rather, he simulates the tumult and the film has all the order of the 1968 Democratic convention. The years are reflected in the experiences of four friends.
R.   ★★
D: Arthur Penn; W: Steve Tesich; Ph: Ghislain Cloquet; M: Elizabeth Swados.
Cast: Jodi Theen, Craig Wasson, Jim Metzer, Michael Huddleston.

FOUR MEN AND A PRAYER. (1938) The sons of a British army officer who lost both

his life and his reputation seek vengeance against the businessmen who murdered him. A well-told adventure that reaffirms John Ford's gifts as a story-teller without touching appreciably on his deeper qualities.
                                                     ★★★
D: John Ford; W: Richard Sherman and Sonya Levien; Ph: Ernest Palmer; M: Louis Silvers.
Cast: David Niven, Richard Greene, Loretta Young, George Sanders.

THE FOUR MUSKETEERS. (1975) One more is not too many in an engaging sequel—shot at the same time—to *The Three Musketeers*. Michael York returns as the naive klutz D'Artagnan embroiling his companions in dastardly plots and narrow escapes. It doesn't quite have the spontaneous combustion of the first film, but left-overs should always be this good.
PG.   ★★★
D: Richard Lester; W: George MacDonald Fraser; Ph: David Watkin; M: Lalo Schifrin.
Cast: Oliver Reed, Michael York, Frank Finlay, Richard Chamberlain.

THE FOUR SEASONS. (1981) Like the Vivaldi concertos from which it takes its title, Alan Alda's serious comedy boasts elegance of writing and precision of structure. It makes you wish it would go on for years. The subject is marriage and friendship and a critical time of life when there is more behind you than ahead. The lives and anxieties of three couples are scrutinized through the course of a pivotal year. One of the signal American films about mid-life.
PG.   ★★★★★
D and W: Alan Alda; Ph: Victor Kemper; M: Music of Vivaldi.
Cast: Alan Alda, Carol Burnett, Jack Weston, Sandy Dennis.

THE FOX AND THE HOUND. (1981) The first full-length (83 mins.) feature from the new generation of animators who took over from the storied creators of *Snow White* and *Fantasia*. Their work is technically accomplished, especially at the end when the fox takes on a ferocious bear at a waterfall. But kids tend to find the story, which emphasizes a test of friendship, unduly somber and it's hard to disagree with them. The story of the fox and the hound plays like an Aesop fable with some slapstick thrown in.
G.   ★★★
D: Art Stevens, Ted Berman and Richard Rich; M: Buddy Baker.

Cast: (voices) Mickey Rooney, Kurt Russell, Pearl Bailey, Jack Albertson.

FOXES. (1980) Down in the Valley (San Fernando, that is) with four teenaged girls and the usual problems. Adrian Lyne is more honest than most in his approach, which displays a refreshing sense that the real problem is that kids aren't allowed to grow up in their own good time. There is too much peer and media pressure. Jodie Foster is exceptional and Sally Kellerman even better as her divorced mother. The acting is superior to the ideas in the script.

R. ★★★
D: Adrian Lyne; W: Gerald Ayres; Ph: Leon Bijou; M: Giorgio Moroder.
Cast: Jodie Foster, Sally Kellerman, Scott Baio, Randy Quaid.

THE FOXES OF HARROW. (1947) In New Orleans in the 1820s a man who has left Ireland because of his illegitimacy turns into a real bastard. Rex Harrison isn't a very convincing swine and the film wallows in cheap emotion when he and the society lass he marries fall upon hard times.

★★
D: John Stahl; W: Wanda Tuchock; Ph: Joseph La Shelle; M: David Buttolph.
Cast: Rex Harrison, Maureen O'Hara, Richard Haydn, Victor McLaglen.

FRAMED. (1975) Early on, the heroine is struck on the head by a pigeon dropping. The bird is a good film critic. Joe Don Baker allies himself with the Mafia when he emerges from prison to wreak vengeance on the people who framed him for murder. The high point is Baker's monolgue on surviving delivered to a roach in his cell. The roach had nothing to add to the pigeon's opinion. Very violent

R. ★
D: Phil Karlson; W: Mort Briskin; Ph: Jack A. Marta; M: Pat Williams.
Cast: Joe Don Baker, Conny Van Dyke, Brock Peters, John Marley.

FRANCES. (1982) A biography of Frances Farmer, the thirties star who wound up in a succession of mental institutions, that sheds more heat than light on the subject. Was Farmer really ill or was she a victim of cruel circumstances? The film settles for the usual Hollywood banalities to explain her condition and then indulges in Dickensian scenes of abuse in an asylum. Farmer scorned the studio system and longed to get back to the legitimate theater and that may have been part of her problem. In spite of these weaknesses, *Frances* is worth a viewing for Jessica Lange's sympathetic work as the actress.

R. ★★★
D: Graeme Clifford; W: Eric Bergren, Christopher Devore and Nicholas Kazan; Ph: Laszlo Kovacs; M: John Barry.
Cast: Jessica Lange, Kim Stanley, Jeffrey DeMunn, Sam Shepard.

FRANCIS OF ASSISI. (1961) A life of the saint that martyrs the viewer with its lumbering piety. Bradford Dillman is the son of a wealthy 13th century merchant who befriends animals and takes up a life of poverty, which includes the very poor script.

★★
D: Michael Curtiz; W: Eugene Vale, James Forsyth and Jack Thomas; Ph: Piero Portalupi; M: Mario Nascimbene.
Cast: Bradford Dillman, Dolores Hart, Stuart Whitman, Pedro Armendariz.

FRANKENSTEIN. (1931) For half a century other directors have tried to re-create the chemistry that yielded a horror film of vast influence and one that deserves every bit of praise and analysis heaped upon it. Boris Karloff's career was defined by his ominous playing of the monster who is brought to life with the brain of a criminal. Astonishingly, James Whale actually capped his work here with the even better *Bride of Frankenstein*

★★★★★
D: James Whale; W: Francis Farragoh, John Balderston and Garrett Ford; Ph: Arthur Edeson; M: David Broekman.
Cast: Boris Karloff, Colin Clive, Mae Clarke, John Boles.

FRANKENSTEIN CREATED WOMAN. (1967) Another Peter Cushing effort that should never have left the body shop. The baron resurrects a beautiful woman with a beef against the men who had her executed.

★
D: Terence Fisher; W: John Elder; Ph: Arthur Grant; M: James Bernard.
Cast: Peter Cushing, Susan Denberg, Thorley Walters, Robert Morris.

FREAKY FRIDAY. (1976) One of the better entries in the erratic efforts of the Disney studio to accomodate the rapidly changing family film market in the seventies. Barbara Harris and Jodie Foster, as her daughter, learn much from changing places magically. Runs out of steam.

G. ★★★
D: Gary Nelson; W: Mary Rodgers; Ph: Charles F. Wheeler; M: Johnny Mandel.
Cast: Barbara Harris, Jodie Foster, John Astin.

FREEBIE AND THE BEAN. (1974) Freestyle, off-beat and not especially funny cop comedy. James Caan and Alan Arkin are two plainclothes San Francisco cops stalking a numbers racketeer and the film begins as a spoof of police movies. As the cars and bodies pile up, it gets nastier and indulges in the sins it criticizes. Richard Rush directs in a frenzied style that is occasionally amusing in the first half.

R. ★★
D: Richard Rush; W: Robert Kaufman; Ph: Laszlo Kovacs; M: Dominic Frontiere.
Cast: James Caan, Alan Arkin, Loretta Swit, Jack Kruschen.

THE FRENCH CONNECTION. (1971) The two detectives who actually made a huge heroin bust get to play small roles but the gutsy police thriller belongs to Gene Hackman who, belatedly, became a star as Popeye Doyle. Popeye and his partner track the heroin consignment from Marseilles when it arrives in New York. The long waits in grubby New York neighborhoods and a keen sense of the business of drugs enhance the film, but it is the action sequences—including a famous car chase under an elevated railroad—that won *The French Connection* its popularity.

★★★★
D: William Friedkin; W: Ernest Tidyman; Ph: Owen Roizman; M: Don Ellis.
Cast: Gene Hackman, Roy Scheider, Fernando Rey, Tony LoBianco.

THE FRENCH CONNECTION II. (1975) The sequel has none of the punch or tautness of its illustrious predecessor and is of interest only for the dimension Gene Hackman added to the role of Popeye Doyle, the determined New York narc. Doyle goes to Marseilles to pursue his heroin smuggling investigation and heap insults on everything French. Like a good wine, he does not travel well and Popeye belongs in New York.

R. ★★
D: John Frankenheimer ; W: Robert Dillon, Laurie Dillon and Alexander Jacobs; Ph: Claude Renoir; M: Don Ellis.

Cast: Gene Hackman, Fernando Rey, Bernard Fresson, Jean-Pierre Castaldi.

THE FRENCH DETECTIVE. (1979) Within the confines of tautly done police procedural, Pierre Granier-Deferre and Lino Ventura explore the uses of power and corruption and the point in disputing the system. Ventura and a jaded young partner investigate a murder during a provincial election campaign and the trail takes them to a powerful political figure.

★★★★
D: Pierre Granier-Deferre; W: Francis Veber; Ph: Jean Collomb.
Cast: Lino Ventura, Patrick Dewaere, Victor Lanoux.

THE FRENCH LIEUTENANT'S WOMAN. (1981) Harold Pinter tried to resolve the problems inherent in John Fowles' novel, which is built on a contemporary commentary on a nineteenth century affair, by positing a film-within-a-film. Jeremy Irons and Meryl Streep are making a movie about the Victorian lovers and having an affair themselves. It's an ingenious notion, but the nineteenth century sequences throb with such passion that the contemporary scenes are a flimsy interruption. It is a noble and intriguing failure that gave the remarkable Streep her first starring role. She did not waste the opportunity.

R. ★★★
D: Karel Reisz; W: Harold Pinter; Ph: Freddie Francis; M: Carl Davis.
Cast: Meryl Streep, Jeremy Irons, Hilton McRae, Emily Morgan.

FRENZY. (1972) The detective in Alfred Hitchcock's British thriller is saddled with a wife who keeps cooking gourmet meals he doesn't want. But Hitchcock sets out a feast for the viewer in taking up one of his most familiar themes—the unjustly accused man. In this case, Jon Finch is suspected of being a notorious murderer after his wife is killed and he is literally tied to the crime by an incriminating necktie.

R. ★★★★
D: Alfred Hitchcock; W: Anthony Shaffer; Ph: Gilbert Taylor; M: Ron Goodwin.
Cast: Jon Finch, Alec McCowen, Barry Foster, Vivien Merchant.

FRIDAY FOSTER. (1975) Black but not comic. Pam Grier stars in a movie rendering of the comic strip heroine photojournalist. It did not make much of a picture with one ludicrous episode succeeding another as Friday investigates a plot against black politicians. Silly, but at least no one involved took it very seriously.

R.   ★
D: Arthur Marks; W: Orville Hampton; Ph: Harry May; M: Luchi De Jesus.
Cast: Pam Grier, Yaphet Kotto, Godfrey Cambridge, Thalmus Rasulala.

FRIDAY THE 13TH. (1980) Why Sean Cunningham's abominable horror film caught on with kids is a mystery greater than anything in the plot. Although its debt to *Halloween* is undeniable, its success greatly encouraged legions of imitations in which a movie exists for the depiction of killing and nothing else. Cunningham's take place in a summer camp and are as disgusting as he can make them.

R.   ★
D: Sean Cunningham; W: Victor Miller; Ph: Barry Abrams;
Cast: Betsy Palmer, Adrienne King, Jeannine Taylor, Robbi Morgan.

FRIDAY THE 13TH, PART THREE. (1982) A young woman who has endured the trauma of seeing her friends butchered goes —you guessed it—back to the scene of the crime for a summer vacaton. Idiotic, gruesome and consistently offensive, it opens with a vagrant tossing an eyeball around. More than three parts of the body follow.

R.   ★
D: Steve Miner; W: Martin Kitrosser; Ph: Gerald Feil; M: Harry Manfredini.
Cast: Dana Kimmell, Paul Kratka, Tracie Savage, Jeffrey Rogers.

FRIDAY THE 13TH—THE FINAL CHAPTER. (1984) The only reason for the existence of this appendix (the only organ not dismembered by the killer) is that the third installment grossed $36 million. There's an impalement, a decapitation, a garroting and a couple of other killings. Then the credits roll. Virtually plotlesss and more a dramatized autopsy than a movie. A young man goes back to the lake to seek revenge against the mass murderer, who miraculously returns to life despite being whacked in the head with an axe.

R.   ★
D: Joseph Zito; W: Barney Cohen; Ph: Joao Fernandes; M: Harry Manfredini.
Cast: Kimberly Beck, Corey Feldman, E. Erich Anderson, Peter Barton.

FRIENDLY PERSUASION. (1956) Pat Boone's singing of the title song is enough to make anyone hostile, but this is a quietly worthwhile and unaffected piece. A family of Indiana Quakers faces some harsh decisions when the Civil War breaks out and the son (an excellent Anthony Perkins) believes his duty to fight over-rides his religious principles. There is a good deal of humor to prevent the argument from becoming tendentious and Gary Cooper is in premium form as the father.

    ★★★
D: William Wyler; W: Michael Wilson; Ph: Ellsworth Fredericks; M: Dmitri Tiomkin.
Cast: Gary Cooper, Dorothy McGuire, Anthony Perkins, Marjorie Main.

THE FRIENDS OF EDDIE COYLE. (1973) With friends such as these, enemies are a superfluous commodity. George Higgins rejuvenated the street hustler crime novel with his terrific ear for dialogue and that is the strong suit of Peter Yates' film version. Robert Mitchum at his world-weariest is a small-time Boston crook caught between his colleagues and the cops.

R.   ★★★
D: Peter Yates; W: Paul Monash; Ph: Vernon J. Kemper; M: Dave Grusin.
Cast: Robert Mitchum, Peter Boyle, Richard Jordan, Steven Keats.

FRIGHTMARE. (1983) A horror film star dies and becomes one of the ungrateful dead. The idea may owe something to the shenanigans that went on with John Barrymore's body. Fans of the star steal the body from a high-tech mausoleum, thereby prompting the usual slew of slayings of youthful stereotypes.

R.   ★
D and W: Norman Thaddeus Vane; Ph: Joel King; M: Jerry Mosley.
Cast: Ferdinand Mayne, Jennifer Starret, Nita Talbot, Luca Bercovici.

THE FRISCO KID. (1979) A feeble comedy western. A rabbi trekking toward San Francisco declares, "In the Talmud it says find thyself a teacher." Or, better yet, a writer. Gene Wilder spends most of his time with eyes raised heavenward and averted from the script. He is partnered with sharp-shooting Harrison Ford in a dim parody of the buddy film. *Torah, Torah, Torah* would be a better title.

PG.   ★★
D: Robert Aldrich; W: Michael Elias and

Frank Shaw; Ph: Robert B. Hauser; M: Frank DeVol.
Cast: Gene Wilder, Harrison Ford, Ramon Bieri, Leo Fuchs.

THE FROGMEN. (1951) The stroke chosen is, unfortunately, the crawl and the story of the underwater demolition teams that blew up Japanese targets is awash with war movie cliches. For all that, it's still a fascinating look at an unusual and incredibly dangerous form of combat. Richard Widmark is the by-the-book commander who has to prove himself to his men before leading an excitingly shot attack on a submarine base. ★★★
D: Lloyd Bacon; W: John Tucker Battle; Ph: Norbert Brodine; M: Lionel Newman.
Cast: Richard Widmark, Dana Andrews, Gary Merrill, Jeffrey Hunter.

FROM BEYOND THE GRAVE. (1976) A British horror film that is demonstrably at death's door in four separate tales of he supernatural. The presence of Peter Cushing, as the proprietor of a sinister London shop that dispenses merchandise with occult properties, serves as a glum reminder of the great days of Hammer Films. A lot of familiar English faces, but what is even a good actor supposed to do with lines like "Let's have a seance."? The episode involving Ian Bannen and Diana Dors is the best of a sorry lot.
PG. ★★
D: Kevin Connor; W: Robin Clarke and Raymond Christodoulou; Ph: Alan Hume.
Cast: Peter Cushing, Ian Bannen, Donald Pleasence, Ian Carmichael.

FROM HERE TO ETERNITY. (1953) The adaptation of James Jones' sprawling novel of army life in Honolulu before the attack on Pearl Harbor is full of what were for Hollywood quite daring questions. The underlying assumptions of the army and its values are scrutinized and the attitude makes for a richly rewarding movie. The casting is unerring with Montgomery Clift as the sensitive Prewitt, a soldier who won't fight—in the ring. The action is built around his conflicts with the sadistic Sergeant Fatso Judson and various romantic relationships. The film was the hit of its year and won eight Oscars. ★★★★
D: Fred Zinnemann; W: Daniel Taradash; Ph: Burnett Guffey; M: George Duning.
Cast: Montgomery Clift, Burt Lancaster, Deborah Kerr, Frank Sinatra.

FROM MAO TO MOZART. (1981) The Chinese government invited violin virtuoso Isaac Stern to undertake a teaching visit and concert tour. Much Chinese is spoken but the exhilirating and often moving documentary only goes to show that the language of music needs no translation.
PG. ★★★★
D and W: Murray Lerner.

FROM NOON TILL THREE. (1976) This odd and ineffectual western takes up the disparagement of the heroic archetype, a worn theme that was done much better elsewhere in the seventies. Bronson tries to escape his own stereotype in a role that requires more than his menacing presence. As a bank robber forced into a dalliance with a beautiful widow (Jill Ireland), he lacks a sense of irony and self-deprecation the film demands.
PG. ★★
D and W: Frank Gilroy; Ph: Lucien Ballard; M: Elmer Bernstein.
Cast: Charles Bronson, Jill Ireland, Douglas Fowley, Stan Haze.

FROM RUSSIA WITH LOVE. (1963) Robert Shaw dyed his hair and Sean Connery still had his in the second and, by most sensible estimates, the best of the James Bond films. The locations are exotic and the women are as ravishing—and as ravished—as ever. But what sets From Russia With Love apart is its quality as a genuine and convincing thriller. Bond is lured into a trap by SPECTRE and one hair-breadth escape is plied another. Shaw does the psycho killer with tremendous authority and his efforts to murder Bond on the Orient Express produced one of the best fights in the whole series. ★★★★
D: Terence Young; W: Richard Maibaum and Johanna Harwood; Ph: Ted Moore; M: John Barry.
Cast: Sean Connery, Robert Shaw, Daniela Bianchi, Pedro Armendariz.

FROM THE EARTH TO THE MOON. (1958) Munitions tycoon Joseph Cotten develops an energy source that he calls Power X. The script for this insult to Jules Verne is strictly Brand X and makes a game cast of actors look very foolish. The tycoon commissions a moon rocket after the Civil War. The interior looks like a flying Victorian parlor and the dialogue is hilarious. ★★

D: Byron Haskin; W: Robert Blees and James Leicester; Ph: Edwin DuPar; M: Louis Forbes.
Cast: Joseph Cotten, George Sanders, Don Dubbins, Debra Paget.

FROM THE TERRACE. (1960) You may feel like jumping from the balcony rather than lasting all the way through a labored version of John O'Hara's novel. Paul Newman tries to win the love of his father in a routine tale of what the idle rich do with all that time on their hands. Myrna Loy drinks and the urge to join her is overwhelming ★★
D: Mark Robson; W: Ernest Lehman; Ph: Leo Tover; M: Elmer Bernstein.
Cast: Paul Newman, Joanne Woodward, Myrna Loy, Ina Balin.

THE FRONT. (1976) Surely the first movie to conclude with a role of "discredits" for participants like Martin Ritt and Zero Mostel, who were blacklisted in the fifties. What stands between the movie and lasting credit is a matter of focus. It concentrates on the front man—a cashier played by Woody Allen—who is hired to pass off the work of blacklisted writers as his own and becomes a success. The movie puts Woody in a richly comic situation and then makes him shun the writers. Our curiosity about them and the government is not satisfied and the film raises far more questions than it answers. It remains a sobering effort.
PG. ★★★
D: Martin Ritt; W: Walter Bernstein; Ph: Michael Chapman; M: Dave Grusin.
Cast: Woody Allen, Michael Murphy, Zero Mostel, Herschel Bernardi.

FRONTIER MARSHAL. (1939) Randolph Scott in a more or less faithful account of Wyatt Earp and the events leading up to the celebrated shoot-out at the O.K. Corral. One of the westerns that revived the genre that year but not up to *Gunfight at the O.K. Corral.* ★★★
D: Allan Dwan; W: Sam Hellman; Ph: Charles Clarke; M: Samuel Kaylin.
Cast: Randolph Scott, Cesar Romero, Nancy Kelly. John Carradine.

THE FRONT PAGE. (1974) Billy Wilder, in this third remake of the play, chose to retain its staginess and it proved a wise decision. Jack Lemmon is the reporter in Chicago in the twenties and Walter Matthau the cantankerous editor who won't let him quit and go to Philadelphia. The expletives have been undeleted and the story is played as a breezy farce. Not vintage Wilder, but well worth it for the consummate comic timing of the two stars.
PG. ★★★
D: Billy Wilder; W: I.A.L. Diamond and Wilder; Ph: Jordan S. Croneweth; M: Billy May.
Cast: Walter Matthau, Jack Lemmon, Carol Burnett, Susan Sarandon.

FUNERAL IN BERLIN. (1966) The middle slows down to the pace of a cortege and you have to stay awake to keep track of the convolutions in the plot that twist around the devious characters. The second Harry Palmer adventure (after *The Ipcress File*) takes Michael Caine to an atmospherically rendered Berlin to mastermind a defection. This one is based on Len Deighton's *The Berlin Memorandum.* ★★★
D: Guy Hamilton; W: Evan Jones; Ph: Otto Heller; M: Konrad Elfrers.
Cast: Michael Caine, Oscar Homolka, Eva Renzi, Paul Hubschmid.

THE FUNHOUSE. (1981) Tobe Hooper, of *The Texas Chainsaw Massacre* fame, does some more, if less gruesome hack work. A bunch of teenagers wind up in a carnival funhouse and there is a booby prize for anyone who can't guess what happens. Hooper could't do much with a trite premise.
R. ★★
D: Tobe Hooper; W: Larry Block; Ph: Andrew Laszlo; M: John Beal.
Cast: Elizabeth Berridge, Cooper Huckabee, Kevin Conway, Sylvia Miles.

FUN IN ACAPULCO. (1963) But only if you passionately admire Elvis Presley. For those who don't there's not much beyond the handsome Mexican locations and scenic Ursula Andress. Elvis is a lifeguard at a resort who is saving himself for either Andress or Elsa Cardenas. ★★
D: Richard Thorpe; W: Alan Weiss; Ph: Daniel Fapp; M: Joseph Lilley.
Cast: Elvis Presely, Ursula Andress, Paul Lukas, Alejandro Rey.

FUNNY LADY. (1975) Barbra Streisand returns as Fanny Brice, the role that made her a star in *Funny Girl.* She is in good form

in a part that is tailored for her, but the reason for seeing the sequel is, surprisingly enough, James Caan. His Billy Rose, a truculent showman in the thirties and forties who marries Fanny, is a tour de force. Herbert Ross, who choreographed *Funny Girl*, directs this time. It opens with real style but succumbs to verbosity in the second half.
PG. ★★★
D: Herbert Ross; W: Jay Presson Allen and Arnold Schulman; Ph: James Wong Howe; M: Peter Matz (musical director).
Cast: Barbra Streisand, James Caan, Ben Vereen, Omar Sharif.

FUN WITH DICK AND JANE. (1976) George Segal and Jane Fonda are a couple living beyond their means and, unfortunately, beyond the resources of the scriptwriters. They take to a life of crime when he loses his job, a course justified by the fact that everyone else in the movie is a thief of one sort of another. The film settles for situation comedy, which is not a format conducive to the satirical bite it needs.
PG. ★★★
D: Ted Kotcheff; W: Jerry Belson, David Giler, Mordecai Richler; Ph: Fred J. Koenekamp; M: Ernest Gold.
Cast: George Segal, Jane Fonda, Ed McMahon, Dick Gautier.

THE FURTHER PERILS OF LAUREL AND HARDY. (1968) Robert Youngson selected some hilarious clips from the early days— mostly silents made between 1927 and 1929— for a winning anthology.
★★★

FURY. (1936) Fritz Lang's first film in America is a study of mob psycholgoy and the capacity of outwardly decent, law-abiding citizens to seek mindless vengeance. Lang goes beyond the obvious and tells the story from two sides that proves that good and evil is an arbitrary distinction. A man is wrongly accused of kidnapping, fakes his own death and thus puts the mob on trial. He is placed in the position of being the judge and jury of the people who tried to lynch him. A work rich in moral ambiguities.
★★★★★

D: Fritz Lang; W: Lang and Bartlett Cormack; Ph: Joseph Ruttenberg; M: Franz Waxman.
Cast: Spencer Tracy, Sylvia Sidney, Walter Abel, Bruce Cabot.

THE FURY. (1978) Another chance to be furious with Brian De Palma for wasting his time. Two young people with advanced psychic powers attract the unwelcome attention of sinister government agents. Kirk Douglas joins the many Hollywood luminaries who have done a fatherly turn in horror films. De Palma is far more interested in technique than simple story-telling and much too fond of detailed killings.
R. ★★
D: Brian De Palma; W: John Farris; Ph: 'Richard H. Kline; M: John Williams.
Cast: Kirk Douglas, Amy Irving, Andrew Stevens, John Cassavetes.

FURY AT SMUGGLER'S BAY. (1961) Actually they were known as wreckers and their method was to lure unwary merchant ships onto the rocky English coast and plunder them. Peter Cushing is the squire and Bernard Lee the leader of the gang in a passable 19th century adventure.
★★
D and W: John Gilling; Ph: Harry Waxman; M: Harold Geller.
Cast: Peter Cushing, Bernard Lee, William Franklyn, John Fraser .

FUTUREWORLD. (1976) Sequel to the 1973 fantasy *Westworld* with a premise that no voter could dispute. The political leaders of the world will become brainwashed robots and the secret is housed inside a Disneyland for the depraved called Futureworld. The film gives itself away shortly after the credits, but it does have an amusing pastiche of the Barbara Walters school of reporting from Blythe Danner.
PG. ★★
D: Richard T. Heffron; W: Mayo Simon, George Schenck; Ph: Howard Schwarz; M: Fred Karlin.
Cast: Peter Fonda, Blythe Danner, Arthur Hill, Yul Brynner.

G

GABLE AND LOMBARD. (1976) Lombard finds Gable on the set of *Gone with the Wind*, prompting him to demand, "You really think I enjoy kissing that English broad?" And that's one of the wittier lines in a factually inaccurate and consistently fatuous account of the romance of Clark Gable and Carol Lombard. The script plays like something lifted from a fan magazine and James Brolin does an act that comes across as a poor imitation of Rich Little impersonating Gable.
R. ★
D: Sidney J. Furie; W: Barry Sandler; Ph: Jordan S. Cronenweth; M: Michel Legrand.
Cast: James Brolin, Jill Clayburgh, Red Buttons, Alan Garfield.

GALILEO. (1975) An American Film Theater production of the didactic and sometimes tedious Brecht play. What it needs above all is an actor of real fire and strength to carry it past Brecht's homilies. Topol's account of the great 17th century astronomer is more unctuous than anything else. The film traces Galileo's career from 1609, when he improved on the telescope, to the later development of the theories that outraged the inquisitors of the church.
PG. ★★★
D: Joseph Losey; W: Losey and Barbara Bray; Ph: Michael Reed; M: Hanns Eisler.
Cast: Topol, Edward Fox, Michel Lonsdale, Tom Conti.

THE GALLANT HOURS. (1959) Admiral William F. "Bull" Halsey and the strain of command in the Pacific in World War II. James Cagney did his best, but the conception of the film works against him.
★★
D: Robert Montgomery; W: Beirne Lay, Jr. and Frank Gilroy; Ph: Joe MacDonald; M: Roger Wagner.
Cast: James Cagney, Dennis Weaver, Richard Jaeckel, Ward Costello.

GALLIPOLI. (1981) An infamous World War I debacle where English stupidity and Turkish bullets cost thousands of Australian lives is movingly reconstructed by Peter Weir. He follows the conventions of the war film —the boys training and maturing into men—but his execution is original. Weir's movie has an almost lyric sense of lost innocence and the conclusion in the trenches is heart-rending. Mel Gibson and Mark Lee are two athletes who respond to the lure of adventure and join up. Weir celebrates the lives of these men and mourns the tragic waste.
PG. ★★★★
D: Peter Weir; W: David Williamson; Ph: Russell Boyd; M: Brian May.
Cast: Mark Lee, Mel Gibson, Bill Hunter, Robert Grubb.

GAMBIT. (1966) The opening gambit is to offer Shirley MacLaine as a Eurasian. Her alliance with Michael Caine, a cockney rogue who wants to steal some priceless art from a millionaire, has the right chemistry and *Gambit* is one of the best light-hearted caper movies of the sixties.
★★★
D: Ronald Neame; W: Jack Davies and Alvin Sargent; Ph: Clifford Stine; M: Maurice Jarre.
Cast: Michael Caine, Shirley MacLaine, Herbert Lom, John Abbott.

THE GAMBLER. (1974) James Caan's Axel Freed is a compulsive gambler and a college professor whose relationships are ruined by his obsession. He borrows money from his mother to pay off his debts and then wagers it on three basketball games. Despite James Toback's sometimes pompous screenplay, Caan is absorbing in a study of a man who gambles not for the joy of winning but for the almost sexual pleasure of taking risks.
R. ★★★
D: Karel Reisz; W: James Toback; Ph: Victor J. Kemper; M: Mahler (Symphony No. 1, conducted by Jerry Fielding).
Cast: James Caan, Paul Sorvino, Lauren Hutton, Morris Carnovsky.

THE GAME OF DEATH. (1979) The death that matters took place five years before the release. Bruce Lee died then, but that did not stop producer Raymond Chow from cobbling together about ten minutes of film the martial arts star had shot before his passing. For the rest a stand-in is used. Two heavies try to muscle in on Lee's show business earnings. There is a quite diverting fight using Kareem Abdul-Jabbar.
R. ★
D: Robert Clouse; W: Jan Speers; Ph: Geoffrey Godar; M: John Barry.

Cast: Bruce Lee, Gig Young, Dean Jagger, Hugh O'Brian.

GANDHI. (1982) Einstein said that future generations would find it difficult to believe a man of such saintliness ever walked the earth. Richard Attenborough's enthralling, Oscar-laden biography does not canonize one of the century's pivotal figures. It is scrupulously honest and makes Gandhi accessible and human. It opens with the assassination of the father of non-violence and closes with the same event. In coming full circle, it traces Gandhi from his early days as an idealistic lawyer to his eventual triumph in ousting the British from India. Ben Kingsley is magnificent as Gandhi and film-making on this epic scale has rarely been so intelligent and moving.
PG. ★★★★★
D: Richard Attenborough; W: John Briley; Ph: Billy Williams and Ronnie Taylor; M: Ravi Shankar.
Cast: Ben Kingsley, Candice Bergen, Edward Fox, John Gielgud.

GARDE A VUE. (1982) The title means "Preventive Detention". A suspect in the murder of two girls is interrogated on New Year's Eve in a cat and mouse game where the roles keep reversing. Tense, clever and as interested in the cop as much as the supposed murderer. No one comes close to Lino Ventura in playing cops who manage to hold on to their decency in a world of corruption and compromise.
★★★★
D: Claude Miller; W: Miller and Jean Herman; Ph: Bruno Nuytten; M: Georges Delerue.
Cast: Lino Ventura, Michel Serrault, Romy Schneider, Guy Marchand.

GASLIGHT. (1944) Ingrid Bergman's luminous portrait of a wife whose husband is trying to drive her mad won her the best actress Oscar and is the main point of interest. George Cukor's vision of Victorian London is broodingly atmospheric. Bergman is the niece of a murdered woman and lives with her mysterious husband in the house where the crime took place. Cukor's is a remake of a British version directed by Thorold Dickinson.
★★★
D: George Cukor; W: John Van Druten, Walter Reisch and John Balderston; Ph: Joseph Ruttenberg; M: Bronislau Kaperrg.
Cast: Ingrid Bergman, Charles Boyer, Joseph Cotten, Angela Lansbury.

GATOR . (1976) Burt Reynolds revives the moonshiner character from *White Lightning*, but it does not strike twice. Gator McCloskey emerges from jail and helps the feds nail a boyhood pal who has turned into a Southern gangster. A walk-through of machismo and mayhem.
PG. ★★
D: Burt Reynolds; W: William Norton; Ph: William A. Fraker; M: Charles Bernstein.
Cast: Burt Reynolds, Jerry Reed, Jack Weston, Lauren Hutton.

THE GAUNTLET. (1978) Clint Eastwood's cop is more mellowed and merciful than Dirty Harry Callahan and he directs himself with a manic energy that does little to obscure the silliness. He is assigned to bring back a minor witness from Las Vegas and finds that he has been set up by a corrupt police commissioner. More objects, including a bus and a house, are riddled with bullets than people. A pleasant change in that regard.
R. ★★
D: Clint Eastwood; W: Michael Butler and Dennis Shryack; Ph: Rexford Metz; M: Jerry Fielding.
Cast: Clint Eastwood, Sondra Locke, Pat Hingle, William Prince.

THE GAY DIVORCEE. (1934) Fred Astaire and Ginger Rogers do "the Continental" and dance to Cole Porter's *Night and Day*. It was their first starring vehicle and while the years have shown up the creaky comedy, the dance numbers are among the finest in their movies.
★★★★
D: Mark Sandrich; W: Dorothy Yost, George Marion, Jr., and Edward Kaufman; Ph: David Abel; M: Max Steiner (musical director).
Cast: Fred Astaire, Ginger Rogers, Edward Everett Horton, Alice Brady.

THE GENERAL. (1926) Buster Keaton, impassive in the face of imminent catastrophe and winning out in the end. The comedy was inspired by a true story involving a Civil War trainman named Andrews. His girl was kidnapped and his train taken by damn Yankees and he got them back. Keaton turned this into a brilliant succession of gags and it is one of the classic comedies of the silent era.
★★★★★
D: Buster Keaton and Clyde Bruckman; W: Al Boasberg and Charles Smith; Ph: J. Devereux Jennings

Cast: Buster Keaton, Marion Mack, Glen Cavander, Jim Farley.

GENTLEMAN JIM. (1942) A biography of Jim Corbett, the heavyweight champion of the world, that is played for lightweight laughs by Errol Flynn and an enjoyable cast. It begins in San Francisco in 1887 with Corbett toiling as a clerk in the Comstock bank and looking for his opportunity and its best scenes trace his entry into the then illegal world of prize-fighting. Flynn does Corbett as a combination of a prototype Rocky and Muhammad Ali's brash self-confidence.

★★★

D: Raoul Walsh; W: Vincent Lawrence and Horace McCoy; Ph: Sid Hickox; M: Heinz Roemheld.
Cast: Errol Flynn, Alexis Smith, Alan Hale, John Loder.

GENTLEMAN'S AGREEMENT. (1947) The impact of Elia Kazan's immensely artificial assault on anti-Semitism has inevitably been eroded by massive upheavals in race relations since it was made. In order to discover how Jews are treated, Gregory Peck pretends to be one in the course of a magazine assignment. Kazan's honest effort suffers because the existence of prejudice is greeted with a sense of discovery. In its own day, the film caused much controversy and disagreement.

★★★

D: Elia Kazan; W: Moss Hart ; Ph: Arthur Miller; M: Alfred Newman .
Cast: Gregory Peck, Dorothy McGuire, John Garfield, Celeste Holm.

THE GENTLEMAN TRAMP. (1978) Eighty minutes is left from the original 150 minutes of a documentary on the life of Charlie Chaplin. That is, of course, not enough time and the film is cursory in treating Chaplin's heyday. There is still generous footage from his great works mixed in with newsreel clips and the documentary covers most of his celebrated troubles.
G.   ★★★
D: Richard Patterson; M: Charles Chaplin.
Cast: Walter Matthau (narrator).

GENTLEMEN PREFER BLONDES. (1953) The two girls from Little Rock who are only interested in one sort of stone—diamonds. There is something almost poignant about Marilyn Monroe belting out "Diamonds are a Girl's Best Friend" in view of what happened later. Howard Hawks' approach to the journey of the two gold-diggers to Paris is frenzied with a whimsical anti-male touch that adds to the girls' charms and justifies their attitude to romance.

★★★

D: Howard Hawks; W: Charles Lederer ; Ph: Harry J. Wild; M: Jules Styne and Leo Robin.
Cast: Marilyn Monroe, Jane Russell, Charles Coburn, Elliott Reed.

THE GEORGE RAFT STORY. (1961) Whether it really is the true story of George Raft is open to much debate, but Ray Danton is a smooth lead. The film traces Raft's gangster-ridden life as an unhappy hoofer in New York to Hollywood and points out that it was tough not to know hoods in Hell's Kitchen. Neville Brand contributes his guttural reading of Al Capone.

★★

D: Joseph Newman; W: Crane Wilbur; Ph: Carl Guthrie; M: Jeff Alexander.
Cast: Ray Danton, Julie London, Jayne Mansfield, Frank Gorshin.

GEORGY GIRL. (1966) James Mason said the success of the film stemmed from "the right people in the right jobs" and how right he was. He is an aging, paternal figure whose fatherly affection for a dowdy young woman changes to something else. Lynn Redgrave invested Georgy with a rare and moving poignance and this very polished film is an incisive discussion of morals and obligations.

★★★★

D: Silvio Narizzano; W: Margaret Forster and Peter Nichols; Ph: Ken Higgins; M: Alexander Faris.
Cast: Lynn Redgrave, James Mason, Charlotte Rampling, Alan Bates.

THE GETAWAY. (1972) The memorable metaphor finds Steve McQueen and Ali McGraw buried under the trash in a garbage truck. It reflects Sam Peckinpah's view of the world. A thirties style gangster film set in contemporary West Texas. McQueen and McGraw are married bank robbers who get involved in a botched hold-up and spend the rest of the movie trying to get away from double-crossing crooks and the law. Peckinpah tosses in his usual copyrighted violence.
PG.   ★★
D: Sam Peckinpah; W: Walter Hill; Ph: Lucien Ballard; M: Quincy Jones.
Cast: Steve McQueen, Ali McGraw, Ben Johnson, Sally Struthers.

GET CRAZY. (1983) Allan Arkush, director of the cult film *Rock 'n Roll High School*, used to be an usher at New York's Filmore East rock emporium. His memories and energy do something to elevate a combination of backstage concert intrigues and retarded masturbation and make-out jokes for teenagers. Malcolm McDowell does a passable pastiche of Mick Jagger in a cheerful shambles about a promoter who wants to knock down the the theater and build a skyscraper on the site.

R. ★★
D: Allan Arkush; W: Danny Opatoshu, David Taylor and Henry Rosenbaum; Ph: Thomas Del Ruth; M: Michael Boddicker.
Cast: Malcolm McDowell, Allen Goorwitz, Daniel Stern, Ed Begley, Jr.

THE GHOST AND MRS. MUIR. (1947) A spirited romance later pillaged for a dumb television series. Rex Harrison's light comic gift is used to advantage in the role of the ghost of an old salt who haunts and comes to love and aid a beautiful widow after she rents a New England cottage. Among the most charming of all ghost-written movies.

★★★
D: Joseph Mankiewicz; W: Philip Dunne; Ph: Charles Lang; M: Bernard Herrmann.
Cast: Rex Harrison, Gene Tierney, George Sanders, Edna Best.

GHOSTBUSTERS. (1984) You don't generally find special effects of this calibre in comedy nor a performance as perfectly calibrated as Bill Murray's. It is the latter element that makes the broad, off-beat humor so effective and surely contributed to the enormous popularity of the film. After a sluggish start, Ivan Reitman establshed the balance between humor and fear and the tone is endearingly loony. Murray, Dan Aykroyd and Harold Ramis take on the next world by making ghostbusting a capitalist enterprise. Ramis' part was originally slated for John Belushi.

PG. ★★★
D: Ivan Reitman; W: Dan Aykroyd and Harold Ramis; Ph: Laszlo Kovacs; M: Elmer Bernstein.
Cast: Bill Murray, Dan Aykroyd, Harold Ramis, Sigourney Weaver.

GHOST STORY. (1981) Four of Hollywood's grand old men stranded in a grinding and manipulative horror story. They call themselves the Chowder Club and meet over brandy to tell ghost stories—all of which are more frightening than the subject of the movie. Their past holds a supposedly dreadful secret, but it turns out to be one that a good lawyer could pass off as an accident and a bad one as manslaughter. Consequently the action is as lively as a graveyard at midnight.

R. ★★
D: John Irvin; W: Lawrence D. Cohen; Ph: Jack Cardiff; M: Philippe Sarde.
Cast: Fred Astaire, John Houseman, Melvyn Douglas, Douglas Fairbanks, Jr.

GIANT. (1956) A huge (201 minutes) and sprawling consideration of the economic convulsions brought on by the passing of old money (cattle) in deference to new money (oil) in Texas. George Stevens won an Oscar for imposing some kind of order on his Texas-sized undertaking and James Dean surely deserved more than a nomination for the brooding intensity of his Jett Rink. It was his last movie and a testimony to the fact that the world lost more than a teen icon in his premature death.

★★★
D: George Stevens; W: Fred Guiol and Ivan Moffat; Ph: William Mellor; M: Dmitri Tiomkin.
Cast: Rock Hudson, James Dean, Elizabeth Taylor, Mercedes McCambridge.

G.I. BLUES. (1960) Actually, Elvis Presley wasn't that blue since the most publicized peacetime army stint in history was over. In the service in West Germany, Elvis romances a night-club singer and part of the movie was shot while he was still in the army. Nobody had the temerity to shoot at Elvis during his hitch. Passable Presleyana.

★★
D: Norman Taurog; W: Edmund Beloin and Henry Garson; Ph: Loyal Griggs; M: Joseph Lilley.
Cast: Elvis Presley, Juliet Prowse, Robert Ivers, Leticia Roman.

GIDGET. (1959) The film that is probably most responsible for the tidal wave of sun and surf beach movies during the sixties. Sandra Dee pines for James Darren in the least mindless of the Gidget trips and this is strictly for those who yearn nostalgically for simpler times.

★★
D: Paul Wendkos; W: Gabrielle Upton; Ph: Burnet Guffey; M: George Duning.

Cast: Sandra Dee, Cliff Robertson, James Darren, Arthur O'Connell.

GIGI. (1958) Colette's story of virtue's triumph decked out with Lerner and Loewe tunes and decorated by the ever-alluring Leslie Caron. It won the Academy Award and gave Maurice Chevalier another trademark with "Thank Heaven for Little Girls". Gigi is in training for a life in the dubious family business, but matters turn out otherwise.

★★★★
D: Vincente Minnelli; W: Alan Jay Lerner; Ph: Joseph Ruttenberg; M: Frederick Loewe.
Cast: Leslie Caron, Louis Jourdan, Maurice Chevalier, Hermione Gingold.

THE GIRL CAN'T HELP IT. (1956) A lot of dumb blonde jokes at Jayne Mansfield's expense and breast-stroking camera-work. Put up with that and you get a fun fifties comedy with the added bonus of such acts as Fats Domino, Little Richard, The Platters, Gene Vincent and Eddie Cochran in full voice. Edmond O'Brien is a thug who hires a press agent to make his moll a star. It can't help being a valuable rock and roll archive today.

★★★
D: Frank Tashlin; W: Tashlin and Herbert Baker; Ph: Leon Shamroy; M: Lionel Newman.
Cast: Jayne Mansfield, Tom Ewell, Edmond O'Brien, Henry Jones.

GIRLFRIENDS. (1978) A piquant and affecting study of female friendship from Claudia Weill. Susan Weinblatt is an aspiring photographer who is trying to rise above the bar mitzvah circuit and come to terms with the departure of her room-mate for marriage. Weill, a documentary-maker in her feature film debut, has a keen feel for New York and its idioms and *Girlfriends* brims with sharp observations.

★★★
D: Claudia Weill; W: Vicki Polon; Ph: Fred Murphy; M: Michael Small.
Cast: Melanie Mayron, Anita Skinner, Eli Wallach, Christopher Guest.

THE GIRL FROM PETROVKA. (1974) Goldie Hawn schlepping plants and a Russian accent around Moscow. The Russians threw the production company out of Moscow (it moved to Vienna) and you can hardly blame them. Hawn is Oktyabrina, a flighty Muscovite, who has an affair with Hal Holbrook, Soviet bureau chief of the Chicago Herald. The film isn't longer than the SALT talks; it only seems that way.
PG   ★★
D: Robert Ellis Miller; W: Allan Scott and Chris Bryant; Ph: Vilmos Zsigmond; M: Herny Mancini.
Cast: Goldie Hawn, Hal Holbrook, Anthony Hopkins, Gregoire Aslan.

GIRL HAPPY. (1965) Elvis Presley's romantic bliss is complicated by the fact that one of the girls is a gangster's daughter. He's a night-club entertainer working in Fort Lauderdale during the notorious spring break.

★★
D: Boris Sagal; W: Harvey Bullock and R.S. Allen; Ph: Philip Lathrop; M: George Stoll.
Cast: Elvis Presley, Harold Stone, Shelley Fabares, Gary Crosby.

GIRLS, GIRLS, GIRLS. (1962) And all of them want Elvis Presley, a humble tuna fisherman by day and a singer of songs like "Return to Sender" by night. Froth for the fans.

★★
D: Norman Taurog; W: Edward Anhalt and Allan Weiss; Ph: Loyal Griggs; M: Joseph Lilley.
Cast: Elvis Presley, Stella Stevens, Laurel Goodwin, Jeremy Slate.

GIVE 'EM HELL, HARRY!. (1975) James Whitmore's masterly re-creation of the wit and wisdom of President Harry Truman is filmed straightforwardly with only a few close-ups to suggest a movie rather than a theatrical experience. "If you laid all those economists end to end," opines Harry, "they'd point in all directions." The obvious highlights —such as the firing of General MacArthur—are included in an enjoyable one-man show from a gifted actor.

★★★★
D: Steve Binder; W: Samuel Gallu; Ph: Ken Palius.
Cast: James Whitmore.

THE GLENN MILLER STORY. (1954) A straightforward and occasionally mawkish biography of the bandleader and his quest for the distinctive sound. James Stewart is refreshingly direct and the threat of monotony is held off by the loving re-creation of Miller's music and the special sound of his arrangements. Gene Krupa and Louis Armstrong are on hand for good measure.

★★★

D: Anthony Mann; W: Valentine Davies and Oscar Brodney; Ph: William Daniels; M: Henry Mancini (musical director).
Cast: James Stewart, June Allyson, Harry Morgan, Charles Drake.

GLORIA. (1980) John Cassavetes stood the gangster convention on its ear in a sobering variation on *Little Miss Marker.* Gena Rowlands is scintillating as a retired mob moll stuck with a newly orphaned boy and some incriminating evidence against her former associates. Cassavetes found the right combination of the spontaneity of his more experimental work and a disciplined format.
PG. ★★★★
D and W: John Cassavetes; Ph: Fred Schuler; M: Bill Conti.
Cast: Gena Rowlands, Buck Henry, Julie Carmen, John Adames.

G-MEN. (1935) With growing outcry over the glorification of gangsters, James Cagney switched sides and *the* public enemy became the public's friend. He is as kinetic and mesmerizing as ever in the story of a lawyer who joins the Justice Department to seek vengeance for the death of a friend.

★★★

D: William Keighley; W: Seton Miller; Ph: Sol Polito; M: Leo Forbstein.
Cast: James Cagney, Ann Dvorak, Margaret Lindsay, Robert Armstrong.

THE GO-BETWEEN. (1970) An old man recalls his boyhood and a time when he served as an intermediary between two lovers separated by class. Joseph Losey, in one of his finest pictures, conjures up the workings of memory and constructs a complex world beneath this simple premise. Beyond the love story is the boy's fate and a summer that ended his innocence.

★★★★

D: Joseph Losey; W: Harold Pinter; Ph: Geoffrey Fisher; M: Michel Legrand.
Cast: Alan Bates, Julie Christie, Dominic Guard, Michael Redgrave.

THE GODFATHER. (1971) The guilty admiration the movies have always shown the gangster culminated in Francis Ford Coppola's epic about a Mafia dynasty. He took Mario Puzo's trashy novel and fashioned a brilliant film that shrewdly played on our feelings that there is a vast gap between

real justice and the legal system. The life of the family, anchored by Marlon Brando's incomparable account of Don Vito Corleone, is so involving that its sins seem somehow acceptable. The more so when the police are seen as corrupt. The saga covers the succession question of who will lead the family after the Godfather's death. The casting and every other aspect of the production contributed to its standing as one of the enduring popular classics.

★★★★★

D: Francis Ford Coppola; W: Coppola and Mario Puzo; Ph: Gordon Willis; M: Nino Rota.
Cast: Marlon Brando, Al Pacino, James Caan, Robert Duvall.

THE GODFATHER, PART II. (1974) An odd and only partly successful resumption of the story. The Corleone family may be related but the two segments that make up the sequel are not. The family has moved west to Nevada where Michael Corleone jousts with a Jewish mobster and offers Sicilian defenses to Senate committees investigating the rackets in the late fifties. Spliced into this dull material is a superb account of the early life of Vito Corleone (Robert De Niro) that really belongs in the first film.
R. ★★★
D: Francis Ford Coppola; W: Coppola and Mario Puzo; Ph: Gordon Willis; M: Nino Rota.
Cast: Al Pacino, Robert Duvall, Diane Keaton, Robert De Niro.

GOING APE. (1981) Scrapings from the monkey house floor slapped on celluloid. The theory is that if a primate could sit at a keyboard to infinity he would eventually reproduce the works of Shakespeare. This would represent his first effort at the typewriter. To keep an inheritance a man has to look after three orangutans. Any one of the latter could have written a funnier movie.
PG. ★
D and W: Jeremy Joe Kronsberg; Ph: Frank V. Phillips; M: Elmer Bernstein.
Cast: Tony Danza, Jessica Walter, Stacey Nelkin, Danny De Vito.

GOING IN STYLE. (1980) A charming comedy based on some hard truths. It has some tear-jerking scenes but the tears are at least honestly jerked. Three old men with meager pensions and nothing to fend off boredom decide to alleviate their plight by holding up a bank. They have nothing to lose since prison will treat them a lot better than the outside world. Martin Brest, who wrote and directed, is not sure what to do or say after the amusingly staged hold-up.

PG. ★★★
D and W: Martin Brest; Ph: Billy Williams; M: Michael Small.
Cast: George Burns, Lee Strasberg, Art Carney, Charles Hallahan.

GOING MY WAY. (1944) A rosy picture of the priesthood that might have started a stampede to the nearest seminary. Leo McCarey's script and direction won Oscars that were merited for his uncanny ability to keep the picture from being entirely engulfed in sentimentality. Bing Crosby is the young priest assigned to a tough New York parish and Barry Fitzgerald the curmudgeonly padre.

★★★
D: Leo McCarey; W: McCarey, Frank Cavett and Frank Butler; Ph: Lionel Lindon; M: James Van Heusen, *et. al.*
Cast: Bing Crosby, Barry Fitzgerald, Rise Stevens, Frank McHugh.

GOIN' SOUTH. (1978) Jack Nicholson directed and starred in a western without airs at a time when the genre was gasping for life. His Henry Moon is a rogue destined for the gallows unless one of the town's many widows will marry him. One does and if the rest is predictable—she forces him to work a gold claim—the acting is a constant pleasure.

PG. ★★★
D: Jack Nicholson; W: John Herman Shaner, *et al.*; Ph: Nestor Almendros and Percy Botkin.
Cast: Jack Nicholson, Mary Steenburgen, Christopher Lloyd, John Belushi.

GOLD. (1974) Standard, but professionally done adventure set mostly in a cavernous South African mine. The gnomes of Zurich, led by an irrepressible John Gielgud, want to raise the world price of gold by flooding a major mine. Roger Moore is the mine manager and the film's underground sequences are well done. It falters when he surfaces for an idle romance with Susannah York.

PG. ★★
D: Peter Hunt; W: Wilbur Smith; Ph: Ousama Rawi; M: Elmer Bernstein.
Cast: Roger Moore, Susannah York, John Gielgud, Ray Milland.

GOLDEN BOY. (1939) Clifford Odets' play

got punched around but is still recognizable in the screen version which gave the young William Holden his first star vehicle. He is torn between the lure of the ring and becoming a violinist.

★★★
D: Rouben Mamoulian; W: Lewis Meltzer, Daniel Taradash and Sarah Y. Mason; Ph: Nicholas Musuraca; M: Victor Young.
Cast: William Holden, Barbara Stanwyck, Lee J. Cobb, Sam Levene.

GOLDEN NEEDLES. (1974) The prize is an ancient Chinese statue that holds acupunctural secrets to the renewal of youth. The film is no prize with Joe Don Baker beating up Orientals and people saying things like "I guess I'm just a Hong Kong whore." Quite violent and not for those who are squeamish about injections.

R. ★
D: Robert Clouse; W: S. Lee Pogostin and Sylvia Schneble; Ph: Gilbert Hubbs; M: Lalo Schifrin.
Cast: Joe Don Baker, Elizabeth Ashley, Jim Kelly, Burgess Meredith.

THE GOLDEN SEAL. (1983) A boy befriends an exotic creature stranded in a hostile environment and protects it from adults. Sound familiar? Call it *Sea T.* The creature is a mythic golden seal, prized by eskimos and whites and thus in danger from both. Conscientious family entertainment in the *Wilderness Family* vein, it misses several opportunities to go up a notch or two.

PG. ★★
D: Frank Zuniga; W: John Groves; Ph: Eric Saarinen; M: John Barry.
Cast: Steve Railsback, Michael Beck, Penelope Milford, Torquil Campbell.

THE GOLDEN VOYAGE OF SINBAD. (1973) Sinbad is not so bad this time out, courtesy of Ray Harryhausen's monsters and other trickery and the ride on the carpet is diverting if not magical. For some reason they work better here than in *Clash of the Titans* and they are smoothly integrated into a story kids will relish. Sinbad sets off in search of a golden crown and does battle with an evil magician.

★★★
D: Gordon Hessler; W: Brian Clemens and Ray Harryhausen; Ph: Ted Moore; M: Miklos Rozsa .
Cast: John Phillip Law, Caroline Munro, Tom Baker, Douglas Wilmer.

GOLDFINGER. (1964) Untarnished by the years and surely the wittiest Bond movie. Number three in the series pits Sean Connery against Gert Frobe, who has a very unstandard way of using gold on beautiful women. He is out to contaminate the supply at Fort Knox with radiation. Bond's weapons include a gadget-laden Aston-Martin, one of the most celebrated cars in films. The opposition counters with Oddjob, a lethal hat check man.

★★★★

D: Guy Hamilton; W: Richard Maibaum and Paul Dehn; Ph: Ted Moore; M: John Barry.
Cast: Sean Connery, Gert Frobe, Honor Blackman, Harold Sakata.

G'OLE. (1983) Sean Connery narrates a documentary that endeavors to cram as much action as possible from the 1982 World Cup soccer championship in Madrid. There were 24 teams and the movie picks among the preliminary matches as well as the finals. Noisy soundtrack and lots of flashy camera-work should delight most soccer buffs. The film exists in several edited versions to reflect the national interest of the fans in the countries where it was released.

★★★

D: Tom Clegg; W: Stan Hey; Ph: Harvey Harrison; M: Rick Wakeman.
Cast: Narrated by Sean Connery.

GONE WITH THE WIND. (1939) Victor Fleming took the directing credit but half the Directors Guild pitched in before being fired by David Selznick. This shrewd mixture of massive spectacle and touching romance is virtually unique in that its popularity has survived several generations of changing tastes and times and it still pulls in hefty ratings when it is shown on television. It cost $4.5 million and that paid for such famous set pieces as the burning of Atlanta, but it is surely the cast that has kept it in such favor. Vivien Leigh's Scarlett O'Hara endures a succession of personal tragedies during the Civil War.

★★★★

D: Victor Fleming; W: Sidney Howard; Ph: Ernest Haller; M: Max Steiner.
Cast: Vivien Leigh, Clark Gable, Olivia de Haviland, Leslie Howard.

THE GOODBYE GIRL. (1977) One of the best films from the prolific pen of Neil Simon. A touching comedy about an actor trying to survive in New York and a dancer trying to survive without actors in her life. Elliot (Richard Dreyfuss), chanting mantras and worrying about his diet, is one of Simon's more inspired creations. The humor stems from three people—the third is the dancer's daughter—who can't acknowledge their vulnerability to the world or each other. Suavely directed by veteran film Simonizer Herbert Ross.

PG. ★★★★

D: Herbert Ross; W: Neil Simon; Ph: David M. Walsh; M: Dave Grusin.
Cast: Richard Dreyfuss, Marsha Mason, Quinn Cummings, Paul Benedict.

THE GOOD, THE BAD AND THE UGLY. (1968) By the time Clint Eastwood made his third spaghetti western, the pasta had become cold and unappetizing. The acting ranges from terminally laconic (Eastwood) to hopelessly hammy (Eli Wallach). The plot is a wet noodle about three men, all of them demonstrably bad, trying to find a cache of gold buried in a cemetery. The film is insufferably long because of the director's passion for having his actors strike macho poses and squint into the sun.

★★

D: Sergio Leone; W: Leone, Age Scarpelli and Luciano Vincenzoni; Ph: Tonino delli Colli; M: Ennio Morricone.
Cast: Clint Eastwood, Eli Wallach, Lee Van Cleef.

GORDON'S WAR. (1973) Hollywood may have ignored Vietnam, but returning veterans were another matter. They were plausible vengence figures and they could handle exotic weaponry. In one of the earlier forays, Paul Winfield is a black veteran who rounds up his buddies to avenge the death of his wife by practically razing Harlem.

R. ★★

D: Ossie Davis; W: Howard Friedlander and Ed Spielman; Ph: Victor J. Kemper; M: Andy Badale.
Cast: Paul Winfield, Carl Lee, David Downing, Tony King.

THE GORGON. (1964) It says here that the Medusa, the mythical creature with the serpentine hair-do, wasn't killed by Perseus. Instead it lives in a 19th century castle and villagers coming in sight of it get literally stoned. Terence Fisher is a veteran at making this kind of hokum work and Peter Cushing and Christopher Lee take it very gravely.

★★

D: Terence Fisher; W: John Gilling; Ph: Mi-

chael Reed; M: James Bernard.
Cast: Peter Cushing, Christopher Lee, Barbara Shelley, Richard Pasco.

GORKY PARK. (1983) The core of the mystery is the identity of three corpses found in Moscow's famous park. Their faces have been removed and the achievement of Michael Apted lay in removing a lot of flesh from the novel without defacing it. He keeps the central theme of a Russian cop as the hero chasing an American villain who is involved in smuggling. Filmed in Helsinki, it still has an authentic feel of a people who live under an inert bureaucracy. William Hurt and Lee Marvin make sharp antagonists.
R. ★★★
D: Michael Apted; W: Dennis Potter; Ph: Ralph D. Bode; M: James Horner.
Cast: William Hurt, Lee Marvin, Joanna Pacula, Brian Dennehy.

GORP. (1980) An exceptionally revolting teen comedy set in a summer camp. It opens with barnyard animals relieving themselves in the camp director's bedroom and spends the rest of the time in the toilet.
R. ★
D: Joseph Ruben; W: Jeffrey Konvitz.
Cast: Michael Lembeck, David Huddleston, Dennis Quaid, Fran Drescher.

GOSPEL. (1983) An unpretentious and straightforward documentary that offers a record of a concert in Oakland. Calif. Beginning with the Mighty Clouds of Joy and "Ride the Mighty High," it features a series of gospel acts, some of whose songs have found a wider following.
G. ★★★
D: David Leivich and Fred Ritzenberg; Ph: David Meyers.
Cast: The Mighty Clouds of Joy, the Clark Sisters, Shirley Caesar, Edwin Hawkins.

THE GRADUATE. (1967) In one of the many hilarious scenes strewn through Mike Nichols' influential comedy, Dustin Hoffman is soberly advised to get into plastics. He wants something less fabricated out of life and certainly there is not an ounce of artifice in Hoffman's first starring role. The mordant sexual humor stems from his involvement with his best friend's mother which complicates life when he falls for her daughter. Nichols caught the look of people groping around in the fog of the new liberalism perfectly.
★★★★

D: Mike Nichols; W: Buck Henry and Calder Willingham; Ph: Robert Surtees; M: Dave Grusin (Songs by Simon and Garfunkel).
Cast: Dustin Hoffman, Anne Bancroft, Katharine Ross, Murray Hamilton.

GRAND HOTEL. (1932) The idea of a public place as a convenient narrative focus for airing the private lives of the characters brought together was to become a trusted formula. In a glittering early example, the real reason to see this Oscar winner is the list of names on the guest register. Garbo is the ballerina past her prime and Lionel Barrymore is terminally ill and determined to go in style. In our dull Holiday Inn era, it's fun to watch acting of the flamboyance that abounds in *Grand Hotel*.
★★★
D: Edmund Goulding; W: William A. Drake; Ph: William Daniels; M: Cedric Gibbons.
Cast: Greta Garbo, John Barrymore, Lionel Barrymore, Joan Crawford.

GRAND PRIX. (1966) John Frankenheimer's tour of the European racing circuit is on the fast track when he's busy with the fast cars but the plot is strictly a stop for the pits of narrative invention. Away from the racing, the drivers and their assorted lovers are in more danger from the dialogue than a collision on the track. They give it a sporting try and the racing footage, which made rather excessive use of split screen techniques, is admirable.
★★
D: John Frankenheimer; W: Robert Alan Arthur; Ph: Lionel Lindon; M: Maurice Jarre.
Cast: James Garner, Eva Marie Saint, Brian Bedford, Yves Montand.

GRANDVIEW U.S.A. (1984) The view from Grandview, an archetypal small Midwestern town, is limited for some of its inhabitants. Randal Kleiser, who specializes in the emotional quandaries of young people, doesn't have much to add to the familiar refrain. A young man wants to escape to college and independence. His father wants him to stay and come into his real estate business.
R. ★★
D: Randal Kleiser; W: Ken Hixon; Ph: Reynaldo Villalobos; M: Thomas Newman.
Cast: Patrick Swayze, Jamie Lee Curtis, C. Thomas Howell, Troy Donahue.

THE GRAPES OF WRATH. (1940) Surely part of the power of John Ford's masterpiece arises from the fact that it was made when the Depression and the Dust Bowl were a painful and recent memory rather than dimly recalled history. In perhaps his greatest screen role, Henry Fonda made Steinbeck's Tom Joad a figure of quintessential American heroism. The Joads are forced westward to the labor camps of California and an existence that barely ranks as survival. As a chronicle of ordinary courage and a vision of the convulsion of a society, Ford's achievement has never been matched.

★★★★★

D: John Ford; W: Nunally Johnson; Ph: Gregg Toland; M: Alfred Newman.
Cast: Henry Fonda, Jane Darwell, John Carradine, Charles Grapewin.

GRAY LADY DOWN. (1978) A nuclear submarine collides with a freighter and sinks to the bottom under the weight of a ponderous screenplay. The boat is crammed with stereotypes—noble captain, trusty sidekick etc.—and the conflicts are very routine. A skin deep treatment. Take *Das Boot* instead.
PG. ★★
D: David Greene; W: Howard Sackler and James Whittaker; Ph: Stevan Larner; M: Jerry Fielding.
Cast: Charlton Heston, David Carradine, Stacy Keach, Ned Beatty.

GREASE. (1978) The production numbers have all the effervescence of a glass of champagne left standing in the sun for a couple of days and no one who endured the fifties as an adolescent will find anything recognizable. The scene is Rydell High School and the single conflict—should the girl hang out with the greasers or a more respectable faction—has been flattened out. Memorable only for some of the dance numbers and the sight of Stockard Channing trying to pass for a high school senior.
PG. ★★
D: Randal Kleiser; W: Bronte Woodward; Ph: Bill Butler; M: Jim Jacobs and Warren Casey.
Cast: John Travolta, Olivia Newton-John, Stockard Channing, Jeff Conaway.

GREASE 2. (1982) John Travolta and Olivia Newton-John proved to be two of the smartest truants in scholastic history when they refused to sign up for another semester at Rydell High. Someone named Maxwell Caulfield, who could neither sing nor dance, thus found himself starring in a musical. The action deals with a talent show staged by the seniors.
PG. ★
D: Patricia Birch; W: Ken Finkleman; Ph: Frank Stanley; M: Louis St. Louis.
Cast: Maxwell Caulfield, Michelle Pfeiffer, Lorna Luft, Adrian Zmed.

GREASED LIGHTNING. (1977) Michael Schultz, after the awful *Car Wash*, did something to clean up his record with this account of Wendell Scott, a black moonshiner and the first to break the color barrier on the stock-car racing circuit. Slow-moving for such a fast subject, this is one of Pryor's quieter performances as a driver who got his break after the local sheriff locked him up. Clumsily emphatic on the subject of Southern prejudice.
PG. ★★
D: Michael Schultz; W: Kenneth Vose, Melvyn Van Peebles and Lawrence DuKore; Ph: George Bouillet; M: Fred Karlin.
Cast: Richard Pryor, Beau Bridges, Pam Grier, Cleavon Little.

THE GREAT AMERICAN BROADCAST. (1941) Deserves some static for its rewriting of the early days of radio, but it's a musical with a pleasant plot and some insights into an industry in its infancy. It culminates in the first coast-to-coast broadcast.
★★
D: Archie Mayo; W: Don Ettlinger; Ph: Leon Shamroy; M: Alfred Newman.
Cast: Alice Faye, Jack Oakie, John Payne, Cesar Romero.

THE GREAT CARUSO. (1950) One of the fascinating speculations in music is what sort of career in opera Mario Lanza would have enjoyed if he had not gone into movies. Certainly, he would never have been another Caruso, but that does not stop him from singing the great man's more noted arias exceptionally. The acting is another story, but in these circumstances, it's not important. Lanza's best film.
★★★
D: Richard Thorpe; W: Sonya Levien and William Ludwig; Ph: Joseph Ruttenberg; M: Johnny Green(musical director).
Cast: Mario Lanza, Ann Blyth, Dorothy Kirsten, Jarmila Novotna.

THE GREAT DICTATOR. (1940) Charlie Chaplin had much to say when he finally opened his mouth in his first all talking picture. Like Lubitsch's *To Be or Not to Be*,

The Great Dictator is a prime example of the deflating power of humor. Chaplin appears (silently) as a poor Jewish barber who happens to look like Hynkel, the barbaric dictator of Tomania. Escaping from a concentration camp, the barber is mistaken for the dictator with hilarious results.

★★★★★

D and W: Charles Chaplin; Ph: Karl Struss and Rollie Totheroh; M: Meredith Wilson.
Cast: Charles Chaplin, Paulette Godard, Jack Oakie, Reginald Gardiner.

THE GREAT ESCAPE. (1963) Well-mounted, escapist fun and inspired by the real-life mass breakout by a group of allied prisoners from a German P.O.W. camp. Steve McQueen, tossing his baseball around the solitary confinement cell and making a spectacular bid for freedom on a motor-bike leads a strong international cast.

★★★

D: John Sturges; W: James Clavell and W.R. Burnett; Ph: Daniel Fapp; M: Elmer Bernstein.
Cast: James Garner, Steve McQueen, Richard Attenborough, Charles Bronson.

THE GREATEST. (1977) Muhammad Ali made this film in the serio-comic twilight of a great career when the opponents he chose —like the immortal Alfredo Evangelista— were a boxing version of *Send in the Clowns*. The biography is subjective and partisan with Ali playing himself, an act he had refined to the last *bon mot* by this time. The points are made with the subtlety of a haymaker, but the movie serves as a timely and needed reminder of his once brilliant skills and the outrageous way he was treated for refusing to be drafted.
PG. ★★★
D: Tom Gries; W: Ring Lardner, Jr.; Ph: Harry Stradling, Jr.; M: Michael Masser.
Cast: Muhammad Ali; Ernest Borgnine, John Marley, Lloyd Haynes.

THE GREATEST STORY EVER TOLD. (1965) But certainly not the greatest way of telling it. You could read half the Bible in the time it takes to reach the end and the whole enterprise seems bent on encouraging atheism. The story of Jesus is given as an excuse for big name cameos and the one reason for making it all the way through the movie is to hear John Wayne, as a centurion, declaim, "Truly, this was the son of God."

★★

D: George Stevens; W: Stevens and James

Lee Barrett; Ph: William Mellor and Loyal Griggs; M: Alfred Newman.
Cast: Max Von Sydow, Dorothy McGuire, Claude Rains, Jose Ferrer.

GREAT EXPECTATIONS. (1945) David Lean's film exceeded the great expectations the names on both sides of the camera encourage. Dickens' sprawling novel and its memorable gallery of characters is brought to order and given a strong focus. From the startling opening of Pip's encounter with an ecaped convict to his subsequent adventures and changes of fortune, there is tremendous vitality and dramatic impetus. Lean's work is rightly regarded as one of the signal achievements in British film-making after the war.

★★★★★

D: David Lean; W: Lean and Ronald Neame; Ph: Guy Green; M: Walter Goehr.
Cast: John Mills, Valerie Hobson, Bernard Miles, Francis Sullivan.

THE GREAT GATSBY. (1974) Like a prototypical F. Scott Fitzgerald character —beautiful and afflicted with ennui. Jack Clayton's direction and the lavish production design concentrate on what the film looks like instead of what it ought to say. Robert Redford's Jay Gatsby is reticent and remote and the picture gawks at the rich instead of scrutinizing them with some degree of insight. Sam Waterston narrates the doomed tale of Gatsby and his shady dealings and love for Daisy, trapped in a miserable blue-blood marriage.
PG. ★★
D: Jack Clayton; W: Francis Ford Coppola; Ph: Douglas Slocombe; M: Nelson Riddle.
Cast: Robert Redford, Mia Farrow, Bruce Dern, Karen Black.

THE GREAT LOCOMOTIVE CHASE. (1956) Prime live-action Disney with Fess Parker in the true story of James J. Andrews, a union officer who led a motley crew of volunteers on a dangerous mission into Confederate territory. The kidnapping of a train sets up some neatly turned chase scenes that are good enough to make the finale—the capture and escape of the northerners— a bit of a let-down.

★★★

D: Francis D. Lyon; W: Lawrence E. Watkin; Ph: Charles Boyle; M: Paul J. Smith.
Cast: Fess Parker, Jeffrey Hunter, Jeff York, John Lupton.

THE GREAT MUPPET CAPER. (1981)

The Muppets do better in televised snippets, but there is still considerable diversion in their second effort. Jim Henson has a firm grasp on what amuses kids and there's enough whimsy—John Cleese as an English twit eating dinner while a pig climbs a drainpipe—to hold adults. Kermit and company are the worst journalists this side of the National Enquirer and the big story is a missing baseball diamond.

G. ★★★
D: Jim Henson; W: Jay Tarses, Jack Rose, Tom Patchett and Jerry Juhl; Ph: Oswald Morris; M: Joe Raposo.
Cast: Diana Rigg, Charles Grodin, John Cleese, Robert Morley.

THE GREAT NORTHFIELD MINNESOTA RAID. (1972) The oft-told tale of the last and bloody hurrah of the James-Younger gang and their ill-fated attempt to rob the Northfield bank. Walter Hill did it straightforwardly and with a social conscience in *The Long Riders*. Philip Kaufman is more self-conscious than anything else and his film teems with sly asides and even a primitive baseball game. Robert Duvall renders Jesse James as a nut, which certainly runs counter to the outlaw hero tradition.

★★★
D and W: Philip Kaufman; Ph: Bruce Surtees; M: Dave Grusin.
Cast: Robert Duvall, Cliff Robertson, Luke Askew, Elisha Cook, Jr.

THE GREAT PROFILE. (1940) If you have tears, prepare to shed them for a curious comedy that is genuinely sad. John Barrymore, gamely intending some fun at his own expense, is a once formidable actor living off his legend and drowning in an ocean of booze. Since this closely reflects what happened to Barrymore, the laughter has a very hollow ring.

★★
D: Walter Lang; W: Milton Sperling and Hilary Lynn; Ph: Ernest Palmer; M: Cyril J. Mockridge.
Cast: John Barrymore, Mary Beth Hughes, Gregory Ratoff, John Payne.

THE GREAT RACE. (1965) Blake Edwards was later to raise slapstick to an exalted comic level in the company of Peter Sellers in the Inspector Clouseau movies. Here is a chance to see a training film in which he tosses in every sight gag known to man and then some. The race is by car from New York to Paris and the antagonists include Tony Curtis and Jack Lemmon. This race does not belong to the swift at an original running time of 163 minutes.

★★★
D: Blake Edwards; W: Arthur Ross; Ph: Russell Harlan; M: Henry Mancini.
Cast: Tony Curtis, Jack Lemmon, Natalie Wood, Peter Falk.

THE GREAT SANTINI. (1980) Robert Duvall's Bull Meechum, a "gung-ho dinosaur" Marine flier, is a mass of contradictions made totally plausible. In the peacetime corps of 1962 at his station in Beaufort, S.C., Meechum turns his household into a battleground with the best of intentions. He is, in Duvall's inspired reading, a man who provokes hostility in attempting to love and Lewis John Carlino makes that the basis of a superior study of family tensions.

PG. ★★★★
D and W: Lewis John Carlino; Ph: Ralph Woolsey; M: Elmer Bernstein.
Cast: Robert Duvall, Blythe Danner, Michael O'Keefe, Lisa Jane Persky.

THE GREAT SCOUT AND CATHOUSE THURSDAY. (1976) Oliver Reed as an Indian trying to spread venereal disease among the white population, thus turning a dose of clap into a round of applause. A weak and witless western that tries to be bawdy, vulgar and funny. Two out of three is bad in this case. Reed and Lee Marvin trying to recover money owed them by a rail baron in a film as silly as its title.

PG. ★★
D: Don Taylor; W: Richard Shapiro; Ph: Alex Phillips, Jr.; M: John Cameron.
Cast: Lee Marvin, Kay Lenz, Oliver Reed, Robert Culp.

THE GREAT TRAIN ROBBERY. (1978) Michael Crichton is so preoccupied with Victorian hypocrisy and discussing things like child prostitution that his film occasionally moves like a commuter local instead of an express. The first robbery of a moving train loaded with gold bullion for British troops in the Crimea is still gripping. But Crichton devotes so much time to the preparations that the crime is a bit of an anti-climax. Sean Connery is in top form as the anti-establishment hero.

PG. ★★★
D and W: Michael Crichton; Ph: Geoffrey Unsworth; M: Jerry Goldsmith.
Cast: Sean Connery, Donald Sutherland, Lesley-Anne Down, Alan Webb.

THE GREAT WALDO PEPPER. (1975) Great fun for anyone whose fear of flying doesn't begin in the cab on the way to the airport. Robert Redford lends an easy charm to Waldo, a barnstorming pilot in the twenties in Nebraska , who fantasizes about duelling with the Red Baron. He gets his wish in Hollywood. The real star is Frank Tallman, who orchestrated the fantastic aerial stunts. **PG.** ★★★
D: George Roy Hill; W: William Goldman; Ph: Robert Surtees; M: Henry Mancini.
Cast: Robert Redford, Bo Svenson, Bo Brundin, Susan Sarandon.

THE GREAT WHITE HOPE. (1970) The sleaziness, racketeering and racism that taint today's boxing world are nothing new and the indictment was never more eloquently handled than in James Earl Jones' spellbinding account of Jack Johnson. Johnson, the first black heavyweight champion and here renamed Jefferson, punched his way through social barriers as well as opponents. His passion for his white mistress (Jane Alexander) was his undoing in the early years of the century. Jones repeated his admired Broadway performance and Martin Ritt made the most of the play's cinematic possibilities.
★★★★
D: Martin Ritt; W: Howard Sackler; Ph: Burnett Guffey; M: Lionel Newman.
Cast: James Earl Jones, Jane Alexander, Lou Gilbert, Joel Fluellen.

THE GREEK TYCOON. (1978) Batty fiction based on the romance of Jackie Kennedy and Aristotle Onassis. The latter was an intriguing man in both senses of the word, but no effort is made to examine him. "I am a peasant. A vulgar peasant," shouts Anthony Quinn and proves it in postcard settings in the Aegean and New York. Watching it unfold is like thumbing through the pages of Vogue.
PG. ★
D: J. Lee Thompson; W: Mort Fine; Ph: Tony Richmond; M: Stanley Myers.
Cast: Anthony Quinn, Jacqueline Bisset, Raf Vallone, Edward Albert.

THE GREEN BERETS. (1968) John Wayne placed his cinematic myth in the service of a political argument in the only major film made about Vietnam while the war was in progress. The movie makes one understand Hollywood's reluctance. Written with a trenching tool, it follows a bunch of Special Forces types in their holy cause and even has David Janssen as a pinko reporter. They don't come in any other color in this kind of movie and he is eventually persuaded that the sword, or at least the machine gun, is mightier than the pen.
★
D: John Wayne, Ray Kellogg; W: James Lee Barrett; Ph: Winton C. Hoch; M: Miklos Rosza.
Cast: John Wayne, David Janssen, Aldo Ray.

THE GREEN ROOM. (1979) Francois Truffaut directs himself in a work set at the extremities of grief. A man has lost his young wife and has been traumatized by the carnage he witnessed in World War I. He deals with death by keeping memories alive in a carefully constructed limbo. Truffaut is a prophet of unrelieved gloom on the subject.
PG. ★★★
D and W: Francois Truffaut; Ph: Nestor Almendros; M: Maurice Jaubert.
Cast: Nathalie Baye, Francois Truffaut, Jean Daste, Jean-Pierre Ducos.

GREMLINS. (1984) Joe Dante's inferno features creatures who are more impish than satanic and his off-beat sense of humor keeps *Gremlins* from becoming another shabby screamer. It falls somewhere between *E.T.* and *Alien* and has a lot of fun with fifties sci-fi situations in a small town suddenly overwhelmed with mischievous and sometimes nasty gremlins. It's hard to keep them rolling in the aisles when they're hidng under the seats, but Dante does it better than most. The creatures are very convincing and may be a little much for younger kids, despite the rating.
PG. ★★★
D: Joe Dante; W: Chris Columbus; Ph: John Hora; M: Jerry Goldsmith.
Cast: Hoyt Axton, Zach Gilligan, Phoebe Cates, Frances Lee McCain.

THE GREY FOX. (1983) A touching and wistful portrait of growing old. Bill Miner is an outlaw who emerges from a 30-year stretch in San Quentin and confronts the twentieth century. In this western, which stresses character above action, character actor Richard Farnsworth gave a star performance. As he resumes the only trade he knows—holding up trains instead of stages—the gorgeous photography offers many striking contrasts between natural splendor and encroaching industry.
PG. ★★★★

D: Philip Borsos; W: John Hunter; Ph: Frank Tidy; M: Michael Conway Baker.
Cast: Richard Farnsworth, Jackie Burroughs, Wayne Robson, Ken Pogue.

GREYSTOKE— THE LEGEND OF TARZAN, LORD OF THE APES. (1984) Hugh Hudson's version of the legend is an act of restoration. After years of confinement in deepest camp, Tarzan becomes the subject of a provocative essay of the conflict between the rational and the animal in man and his place in the scheme of things. The first half recounts his raising by apes and is film-making of raw and primal power. The second returns him to England where Greystoke's place among the nobility and his responses constantly bring into question our notions of what is civilized. There is considerable but justified violence in the jungle scenes.
PG.   ★★★★★
D: Hugh Hudson; W: P.H. Vazak (Robert Towne) and Michael Austin; Ph: John Alcott; M: John Scott.
Cast: Christopher Lambert, Ralph Richardson, Andie MacDowell, Ian Holm.

GRIZZLY. (1976) We all had teddy bears as kids. Who ever had a great white shark doll? That's the problem with yet another *Jaws* rip-off. We are invited to sympathize with people shooting at a giant bear from a helicopter and take an interest in a plot bodily lifted from *Jaws.* "That's all we need," says a forest ranger, "a killer bear on the loose." Necessity is not the mother of invention.
PG.   ★
D: William Girdler; W: David Sheldon and Harvey Flaxman; Ph: William Asman; M: Robert O. Ragland.
Cast: Christopher George, Andrew Prine, Richard Jaeckel, Joan McCall.

THE GROOVE TUBE. (1974) Ken Shapiro and Lane Sarasohn originally did these vulgar and occasionally on-target lampoons of television on videotape and showed them on campuses. They refilmed the sketches for the big screen, but many of them are too long for their premise—like a clown reading dirty books on a children's show. In subsequent years, the same subject has been handled with more finesse—mostly on television itself.
X.   ★★
D: Ken Shapiro; W: Shapiro and Lane Sarasohn; Ph: Bob Bailin; M: Buzzy Linhart.
Cast: Chevy Chase, Ken Shapiro, Richard Belzer, Christine Nazareth.

GUADALCANAL DIARY. (1943) One of the better war films made during the hostilities. The situations and the characters were to be made thrice familiar by constant repetition, but there is fine ensemble playing as the Marines storm the beaches in the Pacific. It is based on Richard Tregaskis' book.
                          ★★★
D: Lewis Seiler; W: Lamar Trotti; Ph: Charles Clarke; M: David Buttolph.
Cast: Preston Foster, Lloyd Nolan, William Bendix, Richard Conte.

GULLIVER'S TRAVELS. (1939) The global success of *Snow White* encouraged Max and David Fleischer to have a go at full length animation instead of Betty Boop cartoons, their most popular creation. Swift would have satirized the results and they gave Disney little to worry about. Still a good diversion for the kids.
                          ★★★
D: Dave Fleischer; W: Dan Gordon, Cal Howard and Ted Pierce; Ph: Charles Schettler; M: Ralph Rainer and Leo Robin.

THE GUMBALL RALLY. (1976) Deserving of a speeding ticket more than a review. A crash-laden celebration of a transcontinental race in defiance of the speed limit and anyone with an IQ over 55 is going to find this a very wearing exercise. The stunt driving for stunted minds is at least preferable to *The Cannonball Run,* which managed to put proctology jokes between the exit ramps a few years later.
PG.   ★
D: Chuck Bail; W: Leon Capetanos; Ph: Richard Glouner; M: Dominic Frontiere .
Cast: Michael Sarrazin, Normann Burton, Gary Busey, John Durren.

GUNFIGHT AT THE O.K. CORRAL. (1957) A western that earns a place in one's affections in spite of itself. Despite the justified criticism of the lameness of the script and the diffuseness of the story before the climactic fight between the Earp brothers and the Clanton faction, it has always had its admirers. I'm one of them because of the depth Burt Lancaster brought to Wyatt Earp and Kirk Douglas to the consumptive Doc Holliday. The most interesting relationship in the movie, between Holliday and his girlfriend Kate, is short-changed.
                          ★★★
D: John Sturges; W: Leon Uris; Ph: Charles B. Lang; M: Dmitri Tiomkin.
Cast: Burt Lancaster, Kirk Douglas, Jo Van Fleet, Rhonda Fleming.

THE GUNFIGHTER. (1950) Although the theme of Henry King's terrific western has been endlessly repeated, it has rarely been done with the skill and authority displayed here. It is an economically told tragedy of an aging gunman who wishes to abandon his way of life for some domestic peace. His reputation tempts younger gunfighters to challenge him and he is ultimately the victim of his own legend. Gregory Peck, quite rightly, counts this among his best performances.

★★★★

D: Henry King; W: William Bowers and William Sellers; Ph: Arthur Miller; M: Alfred Newman.
Cast: Gregory Peck, Helen Westcott, Millard Mitchell, Jean Parker.

GUNGA DIN. (1939) What Rudyard Kipling would have thought of Hollywood's treatment of his story is anyone's guess. What everyone else thought was immediately apparent and *Gunga Din*, the saga of the water boy who saved the regiment in India, occupies an entrenched place among high adventures. Its strongest point is the threesome of sergeants played by Cary Grant, Douglas Fairbanks, Jr., and Victor McLaglen and its fine sense of humor.

★★★★★

D: George Stevens; W: Joel Sayre, Fred Guiol, Ben Hecht and Charles MacArthur; Ph: Joseph August; M: Alfred Newman.
Cast: Cary Grant, Douglas Fairbanks, Jr., Victor McLaglen, Sam Jaffe.

GUNS AT BATASI. (1964) Richard Attenborough was an actor before he became a world class director and this is a reminder of the calibre of his work. He is a regimental sergeant major, hidebound by the traditions of the service, who is forced to improvise when his colonial outpost is threatened by rebels. The first-rate drama addresses the difficulty such men have when they are deprived of habitual rules and the larger topic of military involvement in politics.

★★★★

D: John Guillermin; W: Robert Holles; Ph: Douglas Slocombe; M: John Addison.
Cast: Richard Attenborough, Flora Robson, Jack Hawkins, John Leyton.

THE GUNS OF NAVARONE. (1961) Visual spectacle, high suspense and some thoughtful points about taking responsibility place this among the finest World War II mov-

ies. Gregory Peck leads a motley crew of commandos in scaling a terrifying cliff, avoiding German patrols and finally in attacking a fortress whose giant guns control a strategically vital strait. Superbly scored by Dimitri Tiomkin.

★★★★

D: J. Lee Thompson; W: Carl Foreman; Ph: Oswald Morris; M: Dimitri Tiomkin.
Cast: Gregory Peck, David Niven, Stanley Baker, Anthony Quinn.

GUYANA. (1980) An exploitative reliving of the mass suicide at Jonestown that appalled the world. Stuart Whitman plays the Rev. Jim Johnson—a renaming of the mad Rev. Jim Jones—and the film dramatizes the events that led to the attack on a visiting congressman and his entourage and the subsequent suicides.

R.   ★

D: Rene Cardona; W: Cardona and Carlos Valdemar; Ph: Leopoldo Villasenor; M: Nelson Riddle.
Cast: Stuart Whitman, Gene Barry, John Ireland, Joseph Cotten.

GUYS AND DOLLS. (1955) Damon Runyon's gallery of gangsters and street hustlers comes to rather stilted life in the screen version of the Broadway hit. Marlon Brando takes on a bet that his charms can disarm Jean Simmons, a Salvation Army lady. His casting was a gamble that did not pay off. However, the score is so infectious that it doesn't matter that much.

★★★

D and W: Joseph L. Mankiewicz; Ph: Harry Stradling; M: Frank Loesser.
Cast: Marlon Brando, Frank Sinatra, Jean Simmons, Vivian Blaine.

GYPSY. (1962) One of the tunes is "All I Need is a Girl." Hollywood decided it needed Rosalind Russell instead of Ethel Merman, who scored a great success as the overbearing and slightly insufferable stage mother in the Broadway show. It's still fashionable to bemoan the switch, but the truth is Russell does a very creditable job in an enjoyable musical about the mother living out her dreams through her daughters.

★★★

D: Mervin LeRoy; W: Leonard Spiegelgass; Ph: Harry Stradling; M: Stephen Sondheim and Jules Styne.
Cast: Rosalind Russell, Natalie Wood, Karl Malden, James Milhollin.

H

HAIL THE CONQUERING HERO. (1944) At a time when it was certainly not fashionable to do so, Preston Sturges produced this riotously funny spoof of American hero worship and what it does to heroes. The ingenious device is a young man whose hay fever is so bad that he is discharged from the Marines. Somehow this is perceived as jungle fever back home in his small town and he is suddenly a hero and a candidate for mayor. Sturges has some mordant things to say about politics as well.

★★★★

D and W: Preston Sturges; Ph: John Seitzmann; M: Werner Heymann.
Cast: Eddie Bracken, Ella Raines, Bill Edwards, Raymond Walburn.

HAIR. (1979) The stage musical was a wilted flower child left over from the sixties when Milos Forman came to direct the film. He worked wonders, chiefly by making it a vehicle for mordant observation of the decade and some of its pivotal issues. Treat Williams leads the band of New York hippies who undertake the liberation of a country boy on his way to join the Army. The songs and choreography are done with high voltage energy.
PG. ★★★★

D: Milos Forman; W: Michael Weller; Ph: Mroslav Ondricek; M: Galt MacDermot.
Cast: Treat Williams, John Savage, Beverly D'Angelo, Annie Golden.

THE HALLELUJAH TRAIL. (1965) No hymn of praise is earned. Burt Lancaster escorts a wagon train laden with whisky past thirsty Indians, Brian Keith and early prohibitionists. Although Lancaster and Keith have elsewhere displayed a keen feel for light comedy, the direction does them in and the cast would have been better off drinking the supplies and forgetting the whole endeavor.
★★

D: John Sturges; W: John Gay; Ph: Robert Surtees; M: Elmer Bernstein.
Cast: Burt Lancaster, Brian Keith, Lee Remick, Jim Hutton.

HALLOWEEN. (1978) John Carpenter's technically agile horror movie has much to answer for since it encouraged many clones. The most sickening aspect of this kind of film-making is to place the viewer in the perspective of the killer as he goes about his business. It is the lowest imaginable voyeurism and it became almost mandatory after *Halloween.*
R. ★★

D: John Carpenter; W: Carpenter and Debra Hill; Ph: Dean Cundy; M: John Carpenter.
Cast: Donald Pleasence, Jamie Lee Curtis, Nancy Loomis, P.J. Soles.

HALLOWEEN II. (1981) More corpses, courtesy of a murder in a whirlpool bath, pile up in a lifeless sequel that is little more than a crude reprise of the techniques that made the original so popular. There were some of the ever popular "creative differences" over—you should forgive the expression—the final cut. It is still a very ordinary slasher film and it wasn't worth the argument. The action moves to a hospital where the killer shows up to continue his sick rampage.
R. ★

D: Rick Rosenthal; W: John Carpenter and Debra Hill; Ph: Dean Cundey; M: John Carpenter and Alan Howarth.
Cast: Jamie Lee Curtis, Donald Pleasence, Charles Cyphers, Pamela Shoop.

HALLOWEEN III: SEASON OF THE WITCH. (1982) While you try to figure out what on earth this has to do with its two predecessors, a toymaker plans to ruin the minds of the nation's children with a device implanted in Halloween masks. The fact that Saturday morning television has already done the job didn't occur to anyone here. A dreadful hodgepodge of cliches and the trick is on the viewer.
R. ★

D and W: Tommy Lee Wallace; Ph: Dean Cundey; M: John Carpenter.
Cast: Dan O'Herlihy, Stacey Nelkin, Tom Atkins, Ralph Strait.

HALLS OF MONTEZUMA. (1951) The Marines fighting their way across the South Pacific, swarming up beaches and leaping over war film stereotypes. An unabashedly patriotic hymn to the leathernecks, but Richard Widmark, a teacher who must learn the military craft, surmounts the obstacles in his performance. The main action involves finding hidden rocket sites on an island to be attacked.
★★

D: Lewis Milestone; W: Michael Blankfort; Ph: Winton C. Hoch; M: Lionel Newman.

Cast: Richard Widmark, Jack Palance, Reginald Gardiner, Robert Wagner.

HAMLET. (1948) Laurence Olivier's second Shakespearean film is an opinionated triumph. It is surely the most difficult of the tragedies in the problems it poses a film director. Olivier cut here and there and even ejected Fortinbras and sought out the psychological tensions of the drama. His active and very agile camera follows that view and his Hamlet is no breast-beating man of inaction. Besides the glorious ensemble acting, this *Hamlet* is a document to treasure of what the century's leading actor had to say about the role when he had absolute charge of the proceedings.

★★★★★

D: Laurence Olivier; W: Olivier and Alan Dent(Adaptors); Ph: Desmond Dickinson; M: William Walton.
Cast: Laurence Olivier, Eileen Herlie, Basil Sydney, Norman Wooland.

HAMMETT. (1982) The seminal detective story writer Dashiel Hammett gets involved in a real-life mystery involving the murder of a Chinese girl and the corrupt rich in San Francsco in the twenties. Hammett would have tossed this mystery in the waste basket and Wim Wenders, the German director making his American film debut, goes for stylized atmosphere in which the events of the lame story are marooned.
PG. ★★
D: Wim Wenders; W: Ross Thomas and Dennis O'Flaherty; Ph: Joseph Biroc; M: John Barry.
Cast: Frederic Forrest, Peter Boyle, Marilou Henner, Roy Kinnear.

THE HAND. (1981) No round of applause merited, but it is light on the gore and bloodletting. Michael Caine goes slumming as a cartoonist who loses his hand in an auto accident. The disembodied member has a life of its own, which means death for an assortment of people.
R. ★★
D and W: Oliver Stone; Ph: King Baggot; M: James Horner.
Cast: Michael Caine, Andrea Marcovicci, Annie McEnroe, Bruce McGill.

THE HANDS OF ORLAC. (1961) A surgeon lends a hand to a concert pianist who has lost his in an accident. They belong to a dead murderer who has ideas of his own on their use. The story comes from a silent film

and the dialogue in the remake should be under a similar restriction. Christopher Lee hams it up as a magician who blackmails the musician.

★★

D: Edmond Greville; W: Greville and John Baines; Ph: Desmond Dickinson; M: Claude Bolling.
Cast: Mel Ferrer, Christopher Lee, Donald Wolfit, Dany Carrel.

HANDS OF THE RIPPER. (1971) More than just another Jack the Ripper rip-off and a lot more thoughtful than the loud title might suggest. The clever idea is to have Jack the Ripper's daughter seek the help of a psychiatrist who is an early disciple of Freud. Her ancestry has done grave psychological damage and she believes that she is a murderess. Backed up by solid Hammer films craftsmanship.

★★★

D: Peter Sasdy; W: L.W. Davidson; Ph: Kenneth Talbot; M: Christopher Gunning.
Cast: Eric Porter, Angharad Rees, Dora Bryan, Jane Merrow.

HANG 'EM HIGH. (1968) Hollywood, quite correctly, thought there were a few dollars more in the man with no name and less expression. Clint Eastwood survives a lynching and returns to dispense his inimitable brand of justice to those responsible.

★★

D: Ted Post; W: Leonard Freeman and Mel Goldberg; Ph: Leonard South; M: Dominic Frontiere.
Cast: Clint Eastwood, Pat Hingle, Inger Stevens, Ed Begley.

HANKY PANKY. (1982) The first outing of Gene Wilder and Gilda Radner as a comedy team and the joke is on them. Wilder is an architect who becomes entangled in a Hitchcockian mystery involving murder, computer tapes and espionage. Everyone chases him and he is easy to find because he shouts his dialogue and the situation is a direct steal from *North by Northwest*.
PG. ★
D: Sidney Poitier; W: David Taylor and Henry Rosenbaum; Ph: Arthur Ornitz; M: Tom Scott.
Cast: Gene Wilder, Gilda Radner, Richard Widmark, Kathleen Quinlan.

HANNAH K. (1983) An American woman lawyer tries to sort out her affections for three lovers and make a new life for herself

in modern Israel. Neither Jill Clayburgh nor the great Costa-Gavras find the setting or the idea amenable to arresting development.
R. ★★
D: Cost-Gavras; W: Franco Solinas; Ph: Ricardo Arnovich; M: Gabriel Yared.
Cast: Jill Clayburgh, Jean Yanne, Gabriel Byrne, Muhammad Bakri.

HANOVER STREET. (1979) Peter Hyams' bomb about romance during the London blitz. It forces Harrison Ford to say to his English beloved, "Think of me when you drink tea." Their love—he's a pilot and she's a volunteer nurse—is set against an incredibly precious view of London during the war and Lesley-Anne Down makes it through the hostilities with hair and make-up perfectly intact.
PG. ★★
D and W: Peter Hyams; Ph: David Watkin; M: John Barry.
Cast: Harrison Ford, Lesley-Anne Down, Christopher Plummer, Alec McCowen.

THE HAPPY HOOKER. (1975) A "biography" of Xaviera Hollander, a call-girl from Holland who grew rich and famous by dispensing Dutch treats in the U.S.A. She is played, in a mercurial piece of miscasting by Lynn Redgrave. The kinks in the amours of Hollander and the girls she assembled in her New York brothel are referred to rather than re-enacted, which has much distressed the raincoat set. The movie would be stupidly harmless if it weren't for its recurring insistence that prostitution is terrific fun.
R. ★
D: Nicholas Sgarro; W: William Richert; Ph: Dick Kratina; M: Don Elliott.
Cast: Lynn Redgrave, Jean-Pierre Aumont, Lovelady Powell, Nicholas Pryor.

HARDCORE. (1978) Paul Schrader's second film is a muddled plunge into the world of Los Angeles pornography and prostitution. A strict Calvinist tries to find his runaway daughter and Schrader tries to make it different by having him set up in business as a sex merchant. A potentially interesting conflict is lost in the tortured religious view: the girl is a tainted virgin symbol and the father a figure enduring Christ-like temptation to redeem his daughter. This doesn't mix too well with the familiar *Death Wish* elements.
R. ★★
D and W: Paul Schrader; Ph: Michael Chapman; M: Jack Nitzsche.

Cast: George C. Scott, Peter Boyle, Season Hubley, Dick Sargent.

A HARD DAY'S NIGHT. (1964) The first Beatles film resists any labels in its freshness, puckish humor and the originality of its invention. The group could have cashed in on their global popularity by having a hack bash out a star vehicle to carry their songs. Instead they collaborated with Richard Lester, who had already shown his mastery of zany sight gags in *The Running, Jumping, Standing-Still Film.* What resulted was an hilarious comic documentary that showed what it was like to be a Beatle and captured the blithe spirit the Beatles embodied in the early sixties. The group prepares for a TV show interrupted by flights of fancy and the machinations of Paul's grandad.
★★★★★
D: Richard Lester; W: Alun Owen; Ph: Gilbert Taylor; M: The Beatles.
Cast: The Beatles, Wilfred Brambell, Norman Rossington, Victor Spinetti.

HARDLY WORKING. (1981) Jerry Lewis returned to the screen after a 10-year absence and the mystery is why he bothered. He is a clown in a third-rate circus, a situation that aptly describes the film. When the show folds he seeks other jobs and reprises gags from his old movies. They weren't funny then and unless you're from France, where they think Lewis is a genius, they're not funny now.
PG. ★★
D: Jerry Lewis; W: Lewis and Michael Janover; Ph: James Pergola; M: Morton Stevens.
Cast: Jerry Lewis, Susan Oliver, Deanna Lund, Harold Stone.

HARD TIMES. (1975) Charles Bronson knocks a lot of people down and leaves the viewer punch-drunk. In New Orleans during the Depression, a fighter and his manager go through a series of tiresome bouts so that Bronson can raise money for a goal the movie never deigns to tell us. A racy turn from James Coburn as the manager, but more a fight card than a movie. Not especially bloody despite the material.
PG. ★★
D: Walter Hill; W: Bryan Gindorff, Bruce Henstell and Hill; Ph: Philip Lathrop; M: Barry DeVorzon.
Cast: James Coburn, Charles Bronson, Jill Ireland, Strother Martin.

HARD TO HOLD. (1984) And also hard to believe that Rick Springfield would choose such a boring and unsuitable piece. He is cast as a rock singer who falls for a child psychologist but everything is grimly contrived and the view of his milieu is so dishonest that you wonder why Springfield allowed it.

PG. ★★
D: Larry Peerce; W: Tom Hedley; Ph: Richard Kline; M: Tom Scott.
Cast: Rick Springfield, Janet Eilber, Patti Hansen, Albert Salmi.

HARLAN COUNTY, U.S.A. (1977) An absorbing and moving documentary about a 13-month old coal strike in eastern Kentucky that is fervently anti-capitalist. Whenever some left-wing assertion seems too belabored, a representative of the coal company pops up to say something incredibly foolish or callous. An Academy Award winner (Best Documentary). The film concentrates on the miners' wives, a remarkable group of women, and gives flesh and blood to an essentially polemical work.

PG. ★★★★
D: Barbara Kopple; Ph: Hart Perry; M: Hazel Dickens.

HARPER. (1966) A first-rate version of Ross MacDonald's *The Moving Target* with Paul Newman showing a suitable blend of ennui and jaded gallantry. Lauren Bacall hires him to find her missing husband and if there's nothing especially original about the mystery or the Los Angeles milieu, it is rarely done as well as this.

★★★★
D: Jack Smight; W: William Goldman; Ph: Conrad Hall; M: Johnny Mandel.
Cast: Paul Newman, Lauren Bacall, Shelley Winters, Arthur Hill.

HARRY AND TONTO. (1974) Harry is too young to be doddering and senile and too old to find a useful role in society, a condition that besets growing millions of Americans. Paul Mazursky and Art Carney combined to give a vivid and touching portrait of a common dilemma and there are many astute comments on our attitudes to aging. Carney won the Oscar for his work.

PG. ★★★★
D and W: Paul Mazursky; Ph: Michael Butler; M: Bill Conti.
Cast: Art Carney, Ellen Burstyn, Chief Dan George, Geraldine Fitzgerald.

HARRY AND WALTER GO TO NEW YORK. (1976) The comedy involves bank robbery, but the real crime here is mugging —acting division. A strained farce about two vaudevillians in which every joke is milked until it curdles. Caan and Gould become involved with a populist newspaper in New York in the 1880s and a suave safe-cracker. An air of desperation hangs over the whole tedious venture.

PG. ★★
D: Mark Rydell; W: John Byrum, Robert Kaufman; Ph: Laszlo Kovacs; M: David Shire.
Cast: James Caan, Elliott Gould, Carol Kane, Michael Caine.

HARRY BLACK AND THE TIGER. (1958) Great White Hunter Stewart Granger starts drinking after a coward nearly gets him killed by a tiger. Get a head start on Granger if you want to make it all the way through. The characters in the triangular romance are boring enough to add to one's natural prejudice on behalf of the tiger. Ignore them and watch the Indian scenery.

★★
D: Hugo Fregonese; W: Sydney Boehm; Ph: John Wilcox; M: Clifton Parker.
Cast: Stewart Granger, Barbara Rush, Anthony Steel, Kamala Devi.

A HATFUL OF RAIN. (1957) Among the first Hollywood efforts to examine the problem of drug addiction and of far more than historic interest. Despite the burden of being a pioneer, *A Hatful of Rain* is still a powerful study of self destruction and the wreckage it leaves in the lives of those close to the addict. Don Murray is wonderfully accurate in exploring the junkie's emotions and his unwillingness to face the truth and his support is front rank.

★★★★★
D: Fred Zinnemann; W: Michael V. Gazzo and Alfred Hayes; Ph: Joe MacDonald; M: Bernard Herrmann.
Cast: Don Murray, Eva Marie Saint, Anthony Franciosa, Lloyd Nolan.

HAWMPS. (1976) Boorish family entertainment from Joe Camp, creator of the *Benji* films. The U.S. Cavalry experiments with camels, producing a lot of *F Troop* slapstick and D minus entertainment. The Israelis say a camel is a horse assembled by a committee. Camp's film echoes that maxim.

G. ★★
D: Joe Camp; W: William Bickley and Michael Warren; Ph: Don Reddy; M: Euel Box.
Cast: James Hampton, Christopher Connelly, Slim Pickens, Denver Pyle.

HEAD OVER HEELS. (1979) Also known as *Chilly Scenes of Winter*. Joan Micklin Silver's arch and off-beat look at the loves of ordinary people is forcefully acted but tinged with the dullness of the characters. A civil servant becomes infatuated with a woman in the office who has left her husband. "She has a choice between an oversized dull guy and a medium-sized dull guy. Poor Laura," he says. Poor viewer, too.

PG. ★★
D and W: Joan Micklin Silver; Ph: Bobby Byrne; M: Ken Lauber.
Cast: John Heard, Mary Beth Hurt, Peter Riegert, Gloria Grahame.

HEART BEAT. (1979) John Byrum's attempt to find the pulse of the Beat Generation. Jack Kerouac, a novelist whose influence exceeded his own talent, is the subject, but the events that formed him as a prophet of his generation are not here. Instead he is already a legend and that is not conducive to satisfying biography.

R. ★★★
D and W: John Byrum.
Cast: Nick Nolte, John Heard, Sissy Spacek, Ray Sharkey.

HEARTBEEPS. (1981) There is a documented case of an industrial robot killing a worker in Japan. If the androids in this singularly daft comedy had turned on the producer and director we would all be better off. In 1995, two robots fall in love—that's right—and escape from the factory. A police tank pursues them and the fact that movies like this are ever made is profoundly disheartening.

PG. ★
D: Alan Arkush; W: John Hill; Ph: Charles Rosher; M: John Williams.
Cast: Andy Kaufman, Bernadette Peters, Kenneth McMillan, Randy Quaid.

THE HEARTBREAK KID. (1972) The dream team of Elaine May, director, and Neil Simon, screenwriter, should have produced a better comedy. There is an ugly mean streak in the way *The Heartbreak Kid* treats its characters and it gets worse as the film progresses. Charles Grodin is a sporting goods salesman who marries his Jewish sweetheart only to discover he loathes some of her personal habits, such as eating candy bars in bed. He is drawn to a WASP girl during their Miami honeymoon.

PG. ★★
D: Elaine May; W: Neil Simon; Ph: Owen

Roizman; M: Garry Sherman.
Cast: Charles Grodin, Cybill Shepherd, Jeannie Berlin, Eddie Albert

HEARTLAND. (1981) The view of the west in Richard Pearce's touching film is neither romanticized nor revisionist. Like the best historical films, it captures the rhythm and pace of life in another time when a 10-mile trip looms as an insurmountable and life-threatening distance to a woman in labor. *Heartland* is strongly reminiscent of *Days of Heaven* but it prefers social and personal detail to political statement. A woman and her young daughter struggle for existence in Wyoming in 1910. The still underrated Rip Torn is especially good as the man she grudgingly marries.

★★★★
D: Richard Pearce; W: Beth Ferris; Ph: Fred Murphy; M: Charles Gross.
Cast: Rip Torn, Conchata Ferrell, Barry Primus, Megan Folson.

HEARTLAND REGGAE. (1978) A serviceable introduction to the unique Jamaican music with some decent concert footage most notable for the contributions of Bob Marley, the reggae superstar who died in 1981.

★★★
D: Jim Lewis; Ph: John Swaby.

HEARTS & MINDS. (1975) A superbly edited and savagely effective Oscar-winning documentary about the American intervention in Vietnam. Its title comes from Lyndon Johnson's famous quote about winning the war through the hearts and minds of the people. The documentary, consisting chiefly of cunningly edited news footage covering 20 years, is mostly about the appalling consequences of the win-at-any-cost attitude.

R. ★★★★
D: Peter Davis; Ph: Richard Pearce.

HEARTS OF THE WEST. (1975) An antidote to the movies that dwell on the darker side of Hollywood. Howard Zieff made an affectionate and likable comedy about the back-lots on Gower Street in Los Angeles in the thirties where westerns were churned out at an assembly line pace. Jeff Bridges, as a farm boy who becomes a cowboy star by accident, leads an adroit cast. Made with love—probably too much of it—for the period.

PG. ★★★
D: Howard Zieff; W: Rob Thompson; Ph:

Mario Tosi; M: Ken Lauber.
Cast: Jeff Bridges, Andy Griffith, Alan Arkin, Blythe Danner.

HEAT AND DUST. (1983) Two parallel illicit love stories separated by sixty years in India. Julie Christie, in modern India, probes the scandalous affair six decades before when her great aunt succumbed to a native, albeit a noble one. The team of James Ivory and Ruth Prawer Jhabvala do better with more restrained material than the uncontrollable passion on display here.
R. ★★★
D: James Ivory; W: Ruth Prawer Jhabvala; Ph: Walter Lassally; M: Richard Robbins.
Cast: Julie Christie, Gretchen Scacchi, Christopher Cazenove, Shashi Kapoor.

HEAVEN CAN WAIT. (1943) Ernst Lubitsch's flair for blending mordant observation with gossamer fantasy serves this delightful consideration of the human condition. Don Ameche ends his rake's progress at the door to Hell, but the Devil considers his sins unworthy of membership.
★★★★
D: Ernst Lubitsch; W: Samuel Raphaelson; Ph: Edward Cronjager; M: Alfred Newman.
Cast: Don Ameche, Gene Tierney, Charles Coburn, Marjorie Main.

HEAVEN CAN WAIT. (1978) A divine comedy that updates *Here Comes Mr. Jordan* and, for once, gives remakes a good name. A pro quarterback dies prematurely and is sent back to inhabit the body of a nasty millionaire. A flawlessly judged way with the ironies inherent in the situation and an undercurrent of warm humanity distinguish one of the signal comic achievements of the seventies. Gossamer fantasy becomes an argument for the spiritual survival of love.
PG. ★★★★★
D: Warren Beatty and Buck Henry; W: Beatty and Elaine May; Ph: William A. Fraker; M: Dave Grusin.
Cast: Warren Beatty, Julie Christie, James Mason, Jack Warden.

HEAVEN KNOWS, MR. ALLISON. (1957) An innocuous celebration of platonic love from, of all people, John Huston. Robert Mitchum, a hard-boiled Marine, and Deborah Kerr, a Roman Catholic nun, find themselves dodging Japanese troops on a South Pacific island. Their ideas of what constitutes a heavenly time are radically different.
★★★

D: John Huston; W: Huston and John Lee Mahin; Ph: Oswald Morris; M: Georges Auric.
Cast: Robert Mitchum, Deborah Kerr.

HEAVEN'S GATE. (1980) Michael Cimino's western, greeted with hysterical animosity and derision when it opened, was withdrawn and drastically cut from its initial 3 hours, 47 minutes running time. At either length it is a work that boasts a consistent felicity of expression from a director who has nothing much to say—at least in this film. The moving imagery of *The Deer Hunter* gives way to mere window dressing. It is a style that certainly doesn't suit a discursive and rambling account of the Johnson County Wars. The action and motivation one expects are absent.
PG. ★★
D and W: Michael Cimino; Ph: Vilmos Zsigmond; M: David Mansfield.
Cast: Kris Kristofferson, Isabelle Huppert, Christopher Walken, John Hurt.

HEAVY METAL. (1981) An awful mix of pretension and naivete that tries to be gold and turns out to be kitchen foil. Pounding rock music and an idiotic fantasy of good and evil that is as crude in execution as it is in conception.
R. ★
D: Gerald Potterton; W: Dan Goldberg and Len Blum; M: Elmer Bernstein.

HEDDA. (1976) Adaptation of the Royal Shakespeare Company's stage production that was much praised for Glenda Jackson's work as Hedda Gabler. Ibsen's play makes a decent transition to the screen with Hedda declaring, "For once in my life I want to finally have power over someone's fate." It turns into a ruinous ambition as she becomes pregnant by a husband she abhors and tries to take revenge on an old lover.
PG. ★★★
D: Trevor Nunn; W: Henrik Ibsen (adapted by Nunn); Ph: Douglas Slocombe; M: Laurie Johnson.
Cast: Glenda Jackson, Peter Eyre, Timothy West, Jennie Linden.

HEIDI. (1937) An inevitable combination: Shirley Temple and the beloved children's story. Heidi is a little Swiss girl who lives with her grandfather and faces mountainous obstacles when a wicked aunt takes her away and sells her into servitude. Done with some patented Temple songs.
★★★

D: Allan Dwan; W: Walter Ferris and Julien Josephson; Ph: Arthur Miller; M: Louis Silvers.
Cast: Shirley Temple, Jean Hersholt, Arthur Treacher, Helen Westley.

HEIDI'S SONG. (1982) A retelling of the classic children's story that sounds a lot better than it looks. The music and lyrics are rather overbearing for the circumstances and the voices will be familiar. The animation is very simplistic and only younger kids will be held by the film.
G. ★★
D: Robert Taylor; W: Joseph Barbera and Jameson Brewer; M: Hoyt Curtin.
Cast: (Voices) Lorne Greene, Sammy Davis, Jr., Margery Gray, Michael Bell.

THE HEIRESS. (1949) From Henry James' novel *Washington Square*. Olivia De Havilland won the Oscar for her Catherine Sloper, a woman forced to weigh the sincerity of her suitors against their greed. She and her father have different views because they have different needs.
★★★
D: William Wyler; W: Ruth and Augustus Goetz; Ph: Leo Tover; M: Aaron Copland.
Cast: Olivia De Havilland, Montgomery Clift, Ralph Richardson, Miriam Hopkins.

HE KNOWS YOU'RE ALONE. (1980) Armand Mastroianni is Marcello's cousin and here are grounds for deportation. This time the mad killer was jilted on his wedding night and takes it out on brides-to-be. Filmed on Staten Island, the location of Brian De Palma's *Sisters*. Don't feed the head in the fish tank.
R. ★
D: Armand Mastroianni; W: Scott Parker; Ph: Gerald Fell; M: Alexander and Mark Peskanov.
Cast: Don Scardino, Caitlin O'Heaney, Elizabeth Kemp, Tom Rolfing.

HELLO, DOLLY. (1969) The musical is based on Thornton Wilder's *The Matchmaker* and the colorful film had to overcome a mismatch of its own. Barbra Streisand, then only in her mid-twenties, was, of course, much too young to play matchmaker Dolly Levi. When she's singing in the overstaged production numbers, it doesn't matter, but elsewhere it does.The title number with Louis Armstrong is a winner.
★★★
D: Gene Kelly; W: Ernest Lehman; Ph: Harry Stradling; M: Jerry Herman.

Cast: Barbra Streisand, Walter Matthau, Michael Crawford, Louis Armstrong.

HELL ON FRISCO BAY. (1956) Edward G. Robinson is fun to watch and hell on Alan Ladd in their scenes together. Ladd is a cop who was framed and comes back to the waterfront to settle the score with the gangster responsible. Routine beyond Robinson's performance.
★★
D: Frank Tuttle; W: Sidney Boehm and Martin Rackin; Ph: John Seitz; M: Max Steiner.
Cast: Alan Ladd, Edward G. Robinson, Joanne Dru, Paul Stewart.

HELP! (1965) Richard Lester and the Beatles, a proven dream team in *A Hard Day's Night*, found it hard work capping the brilliant first effort. The music is, of course, wonderful, but the comic zest flags too often. Buffoons led by Leo McKern chase the fab four because Ringo has a coveted ring.
★★★
D: Richard Lester; W: Charles Wood and Marc Behm; Ph: David Watkin; M: The Beatles.
Cast: The Beatles, Leo McKern, Victor Spinetti, Roy Kinnear.

HENNESSY. (1975) A fine and unsung performance from Rod Steiger, as an Irishman who loses his family and turns himself into a human bomb in an attempt on the life of Queen Elizabeth. Crisply directed and understated, the film is an updating of the famous Gunpowder Plot of 1605 when Guy Fawkes tried to blow up Parliament. Documentary footage of the Royal Family heightens the realism.
PG. ★★★
D: Don Sharp; W: John Gay; Ph: Ernest Steward; M: John Scott.
Cast: Rod Steiger, Lee Remick, Richard Johnson, Trevor Howard.

HENRY V. (1944) The play is by no means the best of Shakespeare's histories and it is ironic that it should become so successful on film. Laurence Olivier's acting is everything you would expect and his direction is a revelation with some strokes of genius. One of these is to begin as a play in the Globe Theater and then open out into the possibilities of film, culminating in an excitingly mounted Battle of Agincourt. It was a great popular success and not only because the play's patriotic sentiments were timely.
★★★★★

D: Laurence Olivier; W: Alan Dent(Adaptor); Ph: Robert Krasker; M: William Walton.
Cast: Laurence Olivier, Felix Aylmer, Robert Newton, Esmond Knight.

HERBIE GOES TO MONTE CARLO.
(1977) The actors take a back seat to the mechanized stars in an assembly line Disney comedy. The Volkswagen with a mind of its own falls for a female sports car, thereby expanding our definition of auto-eroticism. Set amid the clamor of the Monte Carlo rally and a reasonable diversion for younger children.
G. ★★
D: Vincent McEveety; W: Arthur Alsberg, Don Nelson; Ph: Leonard South; M: Frank de Vol.
Cast: Dean Jones, Don Knotts, Julie Sommars.

HERBIE RIDES AGAIN.
(1974) Sequel to the popular *The Love Bug* puts the talking Volkswagen in a renovated San Francisco firehouse that is the target of a developer who wants to build a skyscraper on the site. A suitably silly plot allows the maximum number of chases and pratfalls as Herbie saves the firehouse and its owner (Helen Hayes) from the capitalists. Kids will like it.
G. ★★
D: Robert Stevenson; W: Bill Walsh; Ph: Frank Phillips.
Cast: Helen Hayes, Keenan Wynn, Ken Barry, Stefanie Powers.

HERCULES.
(1957) The spaghetti epic that started the curious craze for watching Steve Reeves—and later other hulks—act with their biceps. Reeves, a former Mr. Universe but an actor of painfully parochial limitations, helps Jason retrieve the Golden Fleece. The only ones really fleeced were the paying customers.
★
D: Pietro Francisci; W: Francisci and Ennio de Concini; Ph: Mario Brava; M: Enzo Masetti.
Cast: Steve Reeves, Sylva Koscina, Gianna Maria Canale, Fabrizio Mione.

HERCULES.
(1983) Incredible junk. Lou Ferrigno, the musclebound pillar of *The Incredible Hulk*, as the strong man of myth. Lewis Coates, who cooked up the weird melange of outer space and older legend, is so scrupulously faithful to the time-honored tale of Hercules that the Gods live on the Moon instead of Mount Olympus. The film opens with the creation of the Universe and the stupidty of what ensues seems to last seven days.
PG.
D and W: Lewis Coates; Ph: Alberto Spagnoli; M: Paul Donaggio.
Cast: Lou Ferrigno, Sybil Danning, Ingrid Anderson, William Berger.

HERE COMES MR. JORDAN.
(1941) One of the very few instances where a remake is better than the original. Warren Beatty's splendid *Heaven Can Wait* was derived from this pleasing fantasy. Robert Montgomery is a boxer abruptly and prematurely sent upstairs. He can't return to his old body because it's been cremated. Claude Rains' Mr. Jordan has to sort it out.
★★★
D: Alexander Hall; W: Sidney Buchman and Seton Miller; Ph: Joseph Walker; M: Fredrick Hollander.
Cast: Claude Rains, Robert Montgomery, Evelyn Keyes, Rita Johnson.

A HERO AIN'T NOTHING BUT A SANDWICH.
(1978) An honorably sincere but dramatically unprepossessing essay on the blight of drugs. A 13-year-old Watts boy becomes a heroin addict, largely, one infers, because of ambivalent feelings about his stepfather. Didactic but warmly acted.
PG. ★★
D: Ralph Nelson; W: Alice Childress; Ph: Frank Stanley; M: Tom McIntosh.
Cast: Paul Winfield, Cicely Tyson, Larry B. Scott, Helen Martin.

HERO AT LARGE.
(1980) A pea-brained comedy about a New York actor who dons a Captain Adventure suit for a movie promotion and then begins to take himself seriously. There is no reason why you should. He starts intervening in New York's crime wave in a way that would ordinarily land him in a padded room in Bellevue Hospital. That's where the idea for the film arguably comes from.
PG. ★
D: Martin Davidson; W: A.J. Carothers; Ph: David M. Walsh; M: Patrick Williams.
Cast: John Ritter, Anne Archer, Bert Convy, Kevin McCarthy.

HEROES.
(1977) The title is an ironic reference to the greeting that awaited Vietnam war veterans when they came home. Henry Winkler gives a good account of himself as an unhinged veteran who becomes obsessed with crossing the country to start a

worm farm in the Northwest. The structure is looser than it has to be, but Winkler and Sally Field are low-key in a way that suits the movie. Watch out for a splendid cameo by Harrison Ford as another traumatized vet.
PG. ★★★
D: Jeremy Paul Kagan; W: James Carabatsos; Ph: Frank Stanley; M: Jack Nitzsche.
Cast: Henry Winkler, Sally Field, Harrison Ford, Val Avery.

THE HEROES OF TELEMARK. (1965) The Germans want to move 10,000 pounds of heavy water from a Norwegian factory to the fatherland to build an atomic bomb. The World War II adventure is even heavier going. It raises arresting moral dilemmas—should the few die to save millions later?—and then ignores them. In its place, Norwegian resistance fighters argue incessantly among themselves. Handsome locations and journeyman action sequences.
★★
D: Anthony Mann; W: Ivan Moffat and Ben-Barzman; Ph: Robert Krasker; M: Malcolm Arnold.
Cast: Kirk Douglas, Richard Harris, Ulla Jacobsson, Anton Diffring.

HESTER STREET. (1974) In the not so gay eighteen nineties on Manhattan's Lower East Side, Jewish immigrants try to deal with the conflict between New World realities and the values they have brought from Russia. Their world and its tumult, where a man's proudest boast to a woman is "I have a bed of my own," is marvelously evoked. At the center, we watch Carol Kane progress from naivete to American shrewdness. Afflicted with a touch of feminist hindsight, but still a richly satisfying film.
PG. ★★★★
D and W: Joan Micklin Silver; Ph: Kenneth Van Sickle; M: William Bolcom.
Cast: Carol Kane, Steven Keats, Mel Howard, Doris Roberts.

HEY, GOOD LOOKIN'. (1982) Made in 1975 and then shelved by Warner Brothers, who were nervous about the content of Ralph Bakshi's raunchy animation. It's a funny and spirited celebration of street life in Brooklyn in the fifties, complete with every low-life you can think of and it has some highly accomplished moments of animation.
R. ★★★
D and W: Ralph Bakshi; M: John Madara and Rich Sandler.
Cast: (Voices) Richard Romanus, David Proval, Jessie Welles, Tina Bowman.

THE HIDING PLACE. (1975) Based on the autobiography of a Dutch Bible teacher who, with her family, hid Jews from the Nazis. She then smuggled them out of Holland in what became known as "God's Underground." Produced under the auspices of Billy Graham's organization, the movie's inherent drama is vitiated by the piety it wishes to encourage. Given that drawback, it still manages to hold the viewer with the emotional power of the story.
PG. ★★
D: James F. Collier; W: Allan Sloane and Lawrence Holben; Ph: Michael Reed; M: Tedd Smith.
Cast: Julie Harris, Eileen Heckart, Arthur O'Connell, Jeannette Clift.

THE HIGH AND THE MIGHTY. (1954) One of the films that led eventually to the *Airport* series and therefore a picture that has much to answer for. On a flight across the Pacific, a engine loses and gains the opportunity to have an assortment of boring passengers air their problems. Many of the banalities later enshrined in *Airport* and other disaster flicks and trashed in *Airplane* can be found here. John Wayne and Robert Stack are in the cockpit.
★★
D: William Wellman; W: Ernest K. Gann; Ph: William Clothier; M: Dmitri Tiomkin.
Cast: John Wayne, Robert Stack, Robert Newton, Claire Trevor.

HIGH ANXIETY. (1978) Some of the highest jinks master parodist Mel Brooks ever mustered went into an hilarious homage to Hitchcock. Because this is a parody of one director rather than a genre, it becomes a send-up of specific films instead of cliches and conventions. Hysteria, not manly courage, is the order of the day when a psychiatrist discovers strange goings-on in the Institute for the Very Very Nervous after he takes over.
PG. ★★★★
D: Mel Brooks; W: Brooks, Ron Clark, Rudy DeLuca and Barry Levinson; Ph: Paul Lohmann; M: John Morris.
Cast: Mel Brooks, Madeline Kahn, Cloris Leachman, Harvey Korman.

HIGH NOON. (1952) Fred Zinnemann's classic western endures as a viscerally exciting film that manages to include a provocative discussion of both notions of personal honor and the meaning of justice and responsibility. And all in the space of 85 incredibly tense minutes. The pared simplicity of the premise finds a marshall forced to decide between confronting a vengeful killer or leaving with his new bride. In a reading of quite awesome presence, Gary Cooper makes the lawman's dilemma agonizing. His decision is compounded by pressure from his Quaker fiancee and the contagious cowardice that overwhelms the townspeople. The man who has the most to lose defends those with the most to gain.

★★★★★

D: Fred Zinnemann; W: Carl Foreman; Ph: Floyd Crosby; M: Dmitri Tiomkin.
Cast: Gary Cooper, Grace Kelly, Thomas Mitchell, Lloyd Bridges.

HIGH PLAINS DRIFTER. (1973) Clint Eastwood directs himself toward opposite directions. His tale of a stranger taking over a town and then being asked to defend it by the inhabitants can be taken as a serious exercise with surreal overtones or a tongue-in-holster put-on. On either count, it doesn't work very well and the appeal is for those who mistake this kind of moody posturing for acting.
R. ★★
D: Clint Eastwood; W: Ernest Tidyman; Ph: Dee Barton; M: Henry Bumstead.
Cast: Clint Eastwood, Verna Bloom, Marianna Hill, Mitch Ryan.

HIGH ROAD TO CHINA. (1983) A barefaced raid on the lost ark that houses Steven Spielberg's treasure. The makers throw in the same ingredients but forget that you need a chef. Tom Selleck's first feature film is a tired vehicle that sends him roaring around the unfriendly skies in an attempt to find a young woman's father. He is personable enough but he makes you appreciate how good Harrison Ford is in this kind of movie. That is ironic because Selleck was the first choice for the role of Indiana Jones. He had to bow out because of commitments to his *Magnum P.I.* television series.
PG. ★★
D: Brian G. Hutton; W: Sandra Weintraub and S. Lee Pogostin; Ph: Ronnie Taylor; M: John Barry.
Cast: Tom Selleck, Bess Armstrong, Jack Weston, Wilford Brimley.

HIGH SIERRA. (1941) George Raft, probably after flipping a coin, turned down the role of Roy Earle, a killer on the lam from the law. It was given to Humphrey Bogart, who went to great and successful lengths to make the gangster a sympathetic figure. As westerns were later to attempt in films like *The Shootist*, Bogart is drawn as an aging figure with no place in a changing world. It's an effective ploy and with his tough-mindedness it overwhelms the soppier elements involving a crippled girl.

★★★★

D: Raoul Walsh; W: John Huston and W.R. Burnett; Ph: Tony Gaudio; M: Adolph Deutsch.
Cast: Humphrey Bogart, Ida Lupino, Joan Leslie, Alan Curtis.

HIGH SOCIETY. (1956) A matter of addition and subtraction. The addition of Cole Porter songs like "True Love" is an undeniable plus, but putting Grace Kelly in the Katharine Hepburn role in this musical remake of *The Philadelphia Story* is a definite detraction. The spirit of the original is missing and anyone with a true love of *The Philadelphia Story* is likely to be disappointed.

★★★

D: Charles Walters; W: John Patrick; Ph: Paul C. Vogel; M: Cole Porter.
Cast: Grace Kelly, Bing Crosby, Frank Sinatra, Celeste Holm.

A HIGH WIND IN JAMAICA. (1965) There is a hint of *Lord of the Flies* in an off-beat adventure story based on Richard Hughes' book. Pirates led by Anthony Quinn capture a group of children, whose presence on board poses a series of problems. Spirited and well-written, although its concluding ultimate sacrifice by Quinn is a little hard to believe.

★★★

D: Alexander Mackendrick; W: Ronald Harwood, Denis Canon and Stanley Mann; Ph: Douglas Slocombe; M: Larry Adler.
Cast: Anthony Quinn, James Coburn, Dennis Price, Gert Frobe.

THE HILLS HAVE EYES. (1977) Maybe they do, but whether you can retain what's in your stomach while sitting through this putrid little cult film is more debatable. It consists of blood interrupted occasionally by guts as a mob of cannibals attacks a family on vacation. The diversions include a crucifixion and disembowelments. Wes Craven even throws in a canary getting its head bitten off. He should see a shrink, or perhaps more appropriately, a veterinarian.
R. ★
D and W: Wes Craven.
Cast: John Steadman, Janus Blythe, Arthur King, Russ Grieve.

THE HINDENBURG. (1975) A very trying balloon. Robert Wise made a yoeman's effort to give us something more than a leaden zeppelin, but the screenplay —a speculation on sabotage causing the celebrated 1937 disaster—does him in. The giant dirigible crosses the Atlantic with George C. Scott, as a "good" German, hunting for saboteurs. The technical work conveys what a voyage on such an alien craft would have been like, but that doesn't stop the film from imitating the doomed balloon. It's vast, inflated and more than a little ponderous.
PG.　　　　　　　　　　　★★
D: Robert Wise; W: Nelson Gidding; Ph: Robert Surtees; M: David Shire.
Cast: George C. Scott, Anne Bancroft, Burgess Meredith, William Atherton.

HIS GIRL FRIDAY. (1939) It is an insult to a superb comedy—certainly one of the finest yielded by the thirties—to call it a remake of *The Front Page*. The plot is the same but now Hildy Johnson is a woman and the former wife of her tyrannical editor Walter Burns. The flashy dialogue is a constant joy and almost makes you forget the poor fellow—Earl Williams—about to be executed.
　　　　　　　　　　★★★★★
D: Howard Hawks; W: Charles Lederer; Ph: Joseph Walker; M: Morris W. Stoloff.
Cast: Cary Grant, Rosalind Russell, Ralph Bellamy, Gene Lockhart.

HISTORY OF THE WORLD—PART 1. (1981) Was Judas rude to the waiter at the Last Supper? Was Torquemada his century's leading song and dance man? Mel Brooks has some funny questions to raise, but the answers are mostly pretty terrible. A riotous dance sequence about the Spanish Inquisition is the only part worthy of Brooks.
R.　　　　　　　　　　　★★
D and W: Mel Brooks; Ph: Woody Owens; M: John Morris.
Cast: Mel Brooks, Dom DeLuise, Madeleine Kahn, Harvey Korman.

HOLIDAY. (1938) A sophisticated and elegant piece that exploits the chemistry between Katharine Hepburn and Cary Grant to the hilt. George Cukor, proving what a knowing director of prime actresses he was, moves it flawlessly. Grant is Johnny Case, who falls in love with his fiancee's sister Linda (Hepburn). Adapted from Philip Barry's play.
　　　　　　　　　　　★★★★

D: George Cukor; W: Sidney Buckman and Donald Ogden Stewart; Ph: Franz Planer; M: Sidney Cutner.
Cast: Katharine Hepburn, Cary Grant, Doris Nolan, Edward Everett Horton.

HOLLYWOOD CAVALCADE. (1939) An exceptionally dumb musical that will still delight film buffs with its subject—the early days of movies. Don Ameche takes Alice Faye west in 1913 and there is some fascinating footage from the silent era and appearances by Buster Keaton, Mack Sennett, Ben Turpin and the Keystone Kops.
　　　　　　　　　　　★★
D: Irving Cummings; W: Irving Pascal; Ph: Ernest Palmer; M: Louis Silvers.
Cast: Don Ameche, Alice Faye, J. Edward Bromberg, Alan Curtis.

THE HOLLYWOOD KNIGHTS. (1980) If you took all the humor and skill out of *American Graffiti* and substituted jokes about urinating in punch bowls, mooning buttocks and toilet jokes, you end up with Floyd Mutrux's unspeakable comedy. The knights are a Beverly Hills car club enjoying themselves before Vietnam and the film is about as funny as the war.
R　　　　　　　　　　　★
D and W: Floyd Mutrux; Ph: William A. Fraker; M: Rick Eaker (coordinator).
Cast: Tony Danza, Robert Wuhl, Gary Graham, Richard Schaal.

HOMAGE TO CHAGALL. (1977) Reverent Canadian documentary that is at its best when it allows the work of one of the century's leading painters to speak for itself. The film invites Chagall, seated in the garden of his French country home, to discuss the connection between his life and paintings. The pivotal points—his childhood in Russia and his arrival in Paris—are especially well illustrated. James Mason gives an adoring narration, which is more than justified by the level of Chagall's art in the film.
G.　　　　　　　　　　★★★★
D and W: Harry Rasky; Ph: Kenneth W. Gregg; M: Lou Appelbaum.

HOMBRE. (1967) A thinking man's western marred only by the artifice of its ending. Paul Newman, a white raised by Apaches and a misfit in two worlds, encounters bigotry aboard a stagecoach. When outlaws attack, it is the outcast who rises to the occasion. There are some obvious borrowings from *Stagecoach*, but the script is more in-

clined to pursue moral implications. ★★★
D: Martin Ritt; W: Irving Ravetch and Harriet Frank, Jr.; Ph: James Wong Howe; M: David Rose.
Cast: Paul Newman, Frederic March, Richard Boone, Diane Cilento.

HONDO. (1953) John Wayne's Hondo Lane, an army scout who takes an interest in a widow and her young son on their isolated homestead, deserves a higher place in the assessment of his work and of westerns in general. As in the later *The Searchers*, this is essentially a character study that brings together a family and a man who stands apart from normal bonds and relationships. In this case, the widow and son—left by the man of the homestead—are threatened by marauding Apaches. The film has a just eye for both sides of each issue it raises. ★★★★
D: John Farrow; W: James Edward Grant; Ph: Robert Burks; M: Emil Newman.
Cast: John Wayne, Geraldine Page, Ward Bond, Michael Pate.

HONEYSUCKLE ROSE. (1980) An entire film built on the characters you might find in a third-rate country and western song—the liquored-up cowboy cheating on his wife with a younger woman. Jerry Schatzberg, in playing this eternal triangle amidst the fiddles and guitars, can't decide if this is a Willie Nelson concert film interrupted by some backstage action or a character study laced with a few songs.. Nelson is not far from his real-life persona as he tries to cope with the various temptations of the road.
PG. ★★★★
D: Jerry Schatzberg; W: William D. Witliff and John Binder; Ph: Robby Muller; M: Richard Baskin.
Cast: Willie Nelson, Dyan Cannon, Amy Irving, Slim Pickens.

HONKY TONK FREEWAY. (1981) An off-the-road movie about a Florida town that is put off the map when it is bypassed by a new superhighway. John Schlesinger made his criticism of the corrupting power of the American dream in *Midnight Cowboy* and it was far more eloquent. The humor and style here suggest the highway to Robert Altman's *Nashville* and the results are a traffic jam of competing comic views.
PG. ★★
D: John Schlesinger; W: Edward Clinton; Ph: John Bailey; M: Elmer Bernstein.

Cast: William Devane, Beau Bridges, Hume Cronyn, Beverly D'Angelo.

HONKYTONK MAN. (1982) The doctor examines Clint Eastwood, cast as a tubercular, chain-smoking country singer, and declares, "That man shouldn't be singing in the shower." After listening to Eastwood croak through a few numbers, one fervently agrees with the diagnosis. Give Eastwood credit for taking a chance—he's one of the few major stars who will—but the movie depends on our believing that he's a major singing talent. Set in Dust Bowl Oklahoma, but the farmers are not *Grapes of Wrath* types. They hardly seem upset even when Clint sings.
PG. ★★
D: Clint Eastwood; W: Clancy Carlisle; Ph: Bruce Surtees; M: Snuff Garrett and Steve Dorff.
Cast: Clint Eastwood, Kyle Eastwood, John McIntire, Alexa Kenin.

HOOPER. (1978) A boisterous film-within-a-film that explains the price stuntmen pay in the name of fantasy. The light-hearted machismo prevents *Hooper* from getting to the heart of a pretty serious subject, but it is fun on its own terms and by far the best of the Burt Reynolds/Hal Needham collaborations. Reynolds is a battered stuntman gearing up for one last "gag." Robert Klein steals the film as his vain director.
PG. ★★★
D: Hal Needham; W: Thomas Rickman and Bill Kerby; Ph: Bobby Byrne; M: Bill Justis.
Cast: Burt Reynolds, Jan-Michael Vincent, Sally Field, Brian Keith.

HOPSCOTCH. (1980) A frenzied globe-trotter about a hunted CIA agent that is redeemed by the fact that Walter Matthau and Glenda Jackson are along for the ride. Matthau threatens to publish a tell-all memoir about CIA plots, including one to send Castro some poisoned cigars. The agency responds with its usual intelligence by trying to kill him. The pair make the most of the limited material.
R. ★★★
D: Ronald Neame; W: Bryan Forbes and Brian Garfield; Ph: Arthur Ibbetson; M: Ian Fraser.
Cast: Walter Matthau, Glenda Jackson, Ned Beatty, Sam Waterston.

HORROR OF DRACULA. (1958) Christopher Lee makes you feel a lot more than horror in his debut as Dracula and a reading that stands with those of Lugosi and Langella. He went on to make a slew of vampire movies for Hammer Films, but this stands as the best of his stops at the Transylvania Station. Its inspiration is the Bram Stoker novel rather than a sequel-monger's invention and the supporting cast and production values represent this under-rated studio's finest achievement. Also distributed under the title *Dracula*.

★★★★

D: Terence Fisher; W: Jimmy Sangster; Ph: Jack Asher; M: James Bernard.
Cast: Christopher Lee, Peter Cushing, Michael Gough, Melissa Stribling.

HORSE FEATHERS. (1932) Groucho grouches in song that whatever it is, he's against it and the number of targets lampooned by the Marx Brothers bears him out. He is Professor Wagstaff, the kind of president Huxley College doesn't need, and Chico and Harpo are jocks for the football team. Non-stop gags, almost all of them on the mark.

★★★★

D: Norman McLeod; W: S.J. Perelman, Bert Kalmar, Harry Ruby and Will B. Johnstone; Ph: Ray June; M: Bert Kalmar.
Cast: Groucho, Chico, Harpo and Zeppo Marx, Thelma Todd.

THE HORSE SOLDIERS. (1959) A twist on the conflict central to so many John Wayne films that pits him against a subordinate who questions his harsh methods. And not a very interesting twist at that, even though Wayne and William Holden give it a manful try. They lead the men of a Union Army outfit on operations behind the Confederate lines. While they refrained from making Holden a drunk, the screenwriters gave him little else to use.

★★

D: John Ford; W: John Lee Mahin and Martin Rackin; Ph: William Clothier; M: David Buttolph.
Cast: John Wayne, William Holden, Constance Towers, Hoot Gibson.

HOT DOG. (1984) Baloney for the teen market. The customary mix of sex and come-uppance for the arrogant is set against a free style championship for skiers. Peter Markle, who impressed some people with *The Personals*, only added to the mountain of trash the genre has become.

R. ★

D: Peter Markle; W: Mike Marvin; Ph: Paul Ryan; M: Peter Bernstein.
Cast: David Naughton, Patrick Houser, Tracy Smith, John Patrick Reger.

HOT LEAD AND COLD FEET. (1978) Innocuous Disney western humor enhanced by Jim Dale. The English comedian plays three roles, including twin brothers who are presented with an endurance test by the will of their father. Handsome Oregon backdrops and passable slapstick.

G. ★★

D: Robert Butler; W: Joe McEveety, Arthur Alsberg and Don Nelson; Ph: Frank Phillips; M: Buddy Baker.
Cast: Jim Dale, Karen Valentine, Don Knotts, Jack Elam.

THE HOT ROCK. (1972) When Robert Redford emerges from the slammer he risks a swift return trip by agreeing to heist a jewel from the Brooklyn Museum. He and George Segal made a delightful pair of inept crooks who steal the gem but then lose it. Peter Yates keeps it moving at a fast clip.

PG. ★★★

D: Peter Yates; W: William Goldman; Ph: Ed Brown; M: Quincy Jones.
Cast: Robert Redford, George Segal, Ron Leibman, Paul Sand.

HOT STUFF. (1979) The appalling directing debut of Dom DeLuise, whose acting skill runs the gamut from frenzied to hysterical. A Miami police squad catches thieves by setting up a store to buy the stolen goods. The film is a fence that needs mending with one absurdity piled upon another and a screenplay that consists largely of jokes about excrement. In the end, the local Mafia sends a traditional greeting—a dead fish wrapped in a newspaper. It sums up the movie.

PG. ★

D: Dom DeLuise; W: Michael Kane and Donald Westlake; Ph: James Pergola; M: Patrick Williams.
Cast: Dom DeLuise, Jerry Reed, Suzanne Pleshette, Ossie Davis.

THE HOUND OF THE BASKERVILLES. (1938) The first and one of the best Sherlock Holmes stories pairing the accomplished team of Basil Rathbone and Nigel Bruce as Holmes and Watson. Sir Henry Baskerville's life is threatened when he takes over the family estate and the murder weapon has four legs and a bite that is far worse than its bark.

★★★

D: Sidney Lanfield; W: Ernest Pascal; Ph: Peverell Marley; M: Cyril J. Mockridge.
Cast: Basil Rathbone, Nigel Bruce, Richard Greene, Wendy Barrie.

THE HOUND OF THE BASKERVILLES. (1959) Peter Cushing and Andre Morell did very well by Holmes and Watson in a remake of the much admired Rathbone/Bruce version. As you might expect from a Hammer film, there is more emphasis on sex and violence when Holmes unravels the mystery of the moor, but it does not measurably intrude on his cerebral deductions and our enjoyment of them. Christopher Lee does well by Sir Henry.

★★★

D: Terence Fisher; W: Peter Bryan; Ph: Jack Asher; M: James Bernard.
Cast: Peter Cushing, Christopher Lee, Andre Morell, Marla Landi.

HOUR OF THE GUN. (1967) John Sturges' sequel to *Gunfight at the OK Corral* is minus the services of Burt Lancaster and Kirk Douglas, who were the chief assets of the original. He chose his replacements by going deliberately against type and cast James Garner as Earp and Jason Robards as Holliday. They are both excellent and different from their predecessors and the comparisons make fascinating viewing for western fans. Earp and Holliday have to face legal maneuvering as well as bullets when they resume their pursuit of Ike Clanton.

★★★

D: John Sturges; W: Edward Anhalt; Ph: Lucien Ballard; M: Jerry Goldsmith.
Cast: James Garner, Jason Robards, Robert Ryan, Steve Ihnat.

THE HOUSE BY THE LAKE. (1977) Typical of the precipitous decline of the Canadian film industry during the late seventies. Sleazy exploitation with a voyeuristic dentist conning his girlfriend into spending a weekend at a lakeside mansion. There, four rapists lurk and you will not find such an extreme view of men and libido outside a convention of lesbians. Vaccaro's vengeance on her tormentors is like a *Death Wish* for women and panders to the same base instincts.

R. ★

D and W: William Fruet.
Cast: Brenda Vaccaro, Don Stroud, Richard Ayres, Kyle Edwards.

HOUSE CALLS. (1978) Badly in need of a script doctor, Howard Zieff's movie took on modern medicine and the plight of the newly single, but still middle-aged. Logic suggests they have little to do with each other and *House Calls* confirms the suspicion. Walter Matthau, in one of his bluffer outings, is a first-rate surgeon in a fourth rate hospital. He has been widowed and plays the field until he meets a feisty English divorcee.

PG. ★★

D: Howard Zieff; W: Max Shulman, Julius Epstein, Alan Mandel and Charles Shyer; Ph: David M. Walsh; M: Henry Mancini.
Cast: Walter Matthau, Glenda Jackson, Art Carney, Richard Benjamin.

HOUSE OF FRANKENSTEIN. (1945) A monstrous overkill for the diehard horror aficionado. Universal got the dubious notion of cramming its popular misfits into one movie. Thus Boris Karloff, as the baron instead of the monster, resurrects Wolfman and John Carradine does an amusing turn as Dracula. Pretty pointless otherwise.

★★

D: Erle C. Kenton; W: Curt Siodmak and Edward Lowe; Ph: George Robinson; M: Hans Salter.
Cast: Boris Karloff, Lon Chaney, Jr., John Carradine, J. Carrol Naish.

HOW FUNNY CAN SEX BE?. (1976) Not very. Eight sketches about lust with Giancarlo Giannini and the luscious Laura Antonelli taking eight roles apiece. The playlets deal with Italian sexual mores, which lends the film a quaint flavor, and there are frequent lapses of taste.

R. ★★

D: Dino Risi; W: Risi and Ruggero Maccari; Ph: Alfio Contini; M: Armando Travaioli.
Cast: Giancarlo Giannini, Laura Antonelli, Carla Mancini.

HOW GREEN WAS MY VALLEY. (1941) Four Oscars went to John Ford's compassionate and affecting study of a Welsh mining family caught in the economic upheavals of their industry at the beginning of this century. A crusty father and five of his sons endure the filth of the pits and hope the youngest boy will make something better of himself. An eloquently told and beautifully filmed piece that does not scale the heights Ford had reached in a similar vein in *The Grapes of Wrath*. It remains one of his most popular movies.

★★★★

D: John Ford; W: Philip Dunne; Ph: Arthur Miller; M: Alfred Newman.

Cast: Walter Pidgeon, Maureen O'Hara, Donald Crisp, Roddy McDowall.

THE HOWLING. (1981) Joe Dante gets caught between trying to induce howls of laughter and screams of terror, but his arch good humor saves the day. His lair of werewolves skulks around a California rural retreat. Patrick Macnee is the senior werewolf and has to contend with various factions who have differing opinions of the direction of werewolvery in the eighties. Both an homage and a satire enhanced by Rob Bottins' brilliant special effects work.
R. ★★★
D: Joe Dante; W: John Sayles and Terence H. Winkless; Ph: John Hora; M: Pino Donaggio.
Cast: Patrick Macnee, Dee Wallace, Dennis Dugan, Christopher Stone.

HOW THE WEST WAS WON. (1962) As the title suggests, the film was a little too big for its britches. It began life as a then fashionable Cinerama spectacle and the three directors went for sweeping scope. The winning of the west is viewed through several generations of a family and specifically through the life of a frontier girl as she ages into matriarchy. Parts of it work quite well and some of the all-star cast come off presentably, but it's too conscious of the need to be big. And bigger isn't always better.
★★★
D: John Ford, Henry Hathaway and George Marshall; W: James R. Webb; Ph: William Daniels; M: Alfred Newman.
Cast: Debbie Reynolds, James Stewart, John Wayne, Henry Fonda.

HOW TO BEAT THE HIGH COST OF LIVING. (1980) People who have to step over a pile of bills at the front door on their way to the supermarket are unlikely to find Hollywood's view of the recession even faintly amusing. The women have economic problems like an antique store that is losing money. They rob a shopping mall to rectify matters, a crime the script passes off as an act of defiant feminism. Hopeless inflation of an unpromising comic idea.
PG. ★★
D: Robert Scheerer; W: Robert Kaufman; Ph: Jim Crabe.
Cast: Jane Curtin, Susan Saint James, Jessica Lange, Richard Benjamin.

HOW TO MARRY A MILLIONAIRE. (1953) A comedy about three gold-diggers that fails to hit pay dirt. But the trio consists of Lauren Bacall, Marilyn Monroe and Betty Grable and their energy does something to disguise Nunnally Johnson's inability to add anything new to a worn theme. The threesome rent a Manhattan penthouse and try to land the big one.
★★
D: Jean Negulesco; W: Nunnally Johnson; Ph: Joe MacDonald; M: Cyril Mockridge and Alfred Newman.
Cast: Betty Grable, Marilyn Monroe, Lauren Bacall, William Powell.

HOW TO MURDER YOUR WIFE. (1964) Jack Lemmon is a swinging single who wakes up married one morning. He's also a cartoonist and that allows an initially clever comedy to toy with the real and the imagined in his efforts to get rid of her. Terry-Thomas contributes some needed wit and hauteur as Lemmon's valet, but the movie goes on long after the idea has expired.
★★★
D: Richard Quine; W: George Axelrod; Ph: Harry Stradling; M: Neil Hefti.
Cast: Jack Lemmon, Terry-Thomas, Virna Lisi, Eddie Mayehoff.

HOW TO STEAL A MILLION. (1966) An object lesson in how to make off with a movie from Hugh Griffith. The Welsh actor is an art forger who has to retrieve one of his creations from a Paris museum or the gig is up. Audrey Hepburn, his daughter, and Peter O'Toole make an engaging pair of thieves and the robbery is quite ingenious.
★★★
D: William Wyler; W: Harry Kurnitz; Ph: Charles Lang; M: Johnny Williams.
Cast: Audrey Hepburn, Peter O'Toole, Hugh Griffith, Charles Boyer.

HUCKLEBERRY FINN. (1974) The team responsible for this drastically sanitized children's version of Twain's classic also made *Tom Sawyer* for kids in 1973. *The Adventures of Huckleberry Finn* does not lend itself to the kiddie city treatment—it's too dark and complex. The songs are lifeless and the movie only works effectively when it mines Twain's book for humor. The tougher stuff—like Huck dealing with his father—has been toned down.
G. ★★
D: J. Lee Thompson; W: Richard M. Sherman and Robert B. Sherman; Ph: Laszlo Kovacs; M: The Sherman Brothers.
Cast: Jeff East, Paul Winfield, David Wayne, Harvey Korman.

HUDSON'S BAY. (1940) A romanticized and inaccurate account of the formation of the Hudson's Bay Company and its role in deciding that—for the most part—Canadians would speak English. Paul Muni's Pierre Radison is a trapper who survives various crises, including the sight of Vincent Price playing Charles II, to found the company.

★★★

D: Irving Pichel; W: Lamar Trotti; Ph: Peverell Marley; M: Alfred Newman.
Cast: Paul Muni, Gene Tierney, Laird Cregar, John Sutton.

THE HUMAN FACTOR. (1975) Watching George Kennedy in this kind of role is like being garroted by an incompetent Spaniard. The standard vengeance fare—he is a NATO expert whose family is massacred by terrorists—is embellished with the use of computers for the hunt. They are far less mechanical than the actors and allow a NATO general to sound excited and say, "Run his whole profile through the event probability mode."

R.   ★★
D: Edward Dmytryk; W: Peter Powell and Thomas Hunter; M: Ennio Morricone.
Cast: George Kennedy, John Mills, Raf Vallone, Barry Sullivan.

THE HUMAN FACTOR. (1980) Otto Preminger took out the human element in Graham Greene's absorbing novel and churned out a ponderous discussion of treason. Should a man's loyalty be to his country or to his immediate family? A good question flimsily answered in a surprisingly superficial screenplay by Tom Stoppard. A mid-level British secret service agent becomes a mole for the Russians and another man is killed for his treason.

PG.   ★★
D: Otto Preminger; W: Tom Stoppard; Ph: Mike Malloy; M: Richard and Gary Logan.
Cast: Nicol Williamson, Richard Attenborough, Derek Jacobi, Robert Morley.

THE HUNCHBACK OF NOTRE DAME. (1939) It took an actor of Charles Laughton's capacity to stand out against the sheer opulence of the production in Hollywood's second and finest telling of Victor Hugo's story. His Quasimodo is no shrinking cripple but a fascinating and poignant creation. Laughton towers over the proceedings just as Quasimodo looks down on Paris from his perch in the belfry. Moved by love, he rescues Maureen O'Hara from her executioners.

★★★★

D: William Dieterle; W: Sonya Levien and Bruno Frank; Ph: Jospeh H. August; M: Alfred Newman.
Cast: Charles Laughton, Cedric Hardwicke, Maureen O'Hara, Edmond O'Brien.

THE HUNCHBACK OF NOTRE DAME. (1957) In the Quasimodish sweepstakes, Anthony Quinn is little more than a pimple on the hunchback. Going up against Lon Chaney and Charles Laughton is rash enough and Quinn makes it worse by generally chewing the bell-ropes. This is an international production that was dubbed and the bell tolls for it early and often .

★★

D: Jean Delannoy; W: Jean Aurenche and Jacques Prevert; Ph: Michel Kelber; M: Georges Auric.
Cast: Anthony Quinn, Gina Lollobrigida, Alain Cluny, Jean Danet.

THE HUNCHBACK OF NOTRE DAME. (1978) and (1982). Two further readings of the oft-told story that you are likely to encounter. Both were made for television in England and both are presentable. In the 1978 version Warren Clarke does Quasimodo and Anthony Hopkins does it better in the later production.

THE HUNGER. (1983) Shrewdly constructed to deaden one's appetite for movies with its glossy and unrelenting pretension. In an atmosphere of decadence which is really rotten, vampires live off regular transfusions in contemporary New York. Their idea of ridding the world of New Wave punks is wholly admirable, but Tony Scott has his brother Ridley's name without any signs of the talent. Lots of lesbianism, languor and sultry ambience and not much else.

R.   ★
D: Tony Scott; W: Ivan Davis and Michael Thomas; Ph: Stephen Goldblatt; M: Michel Rubin and Denny Jaeger.
Cast: David Bowie, Catherine Deneuve, Susan Sarandon, Cliff De Young.

THE HUNTER. (1980) Steve McQueen rose to stardom as a bounty hunter in the old TV series *Wanted Dead or Alive*. Visibly ill from the cancer that would kill him, he resumed the profession and, sadly, it still plays like a superficial TV series. Supposedly based on the exploits of Ralph Thorson, a real-life

hunter of bail jumpers, McQueen is stuck with an action role that alternates with very weak comedy about his girl-friends Lamaze classes. He deserved a better farewell.
PG. ★★
D: Buzz Kulik; W: Ted Leighton and Peter Hyams; Ph: Fred J. Koenekamp; M: Michel Legrand.
Cast: Steve McQueen, Eli Wallach, Kathryn Harrold, LeVar Burton.

THE HUNTERS. (1958) American fliers in the Korean war are grounded by an unusually contrived script. A genuinely schizoid war film that is quite good in the air and when it has some action and very flat in trying to flesh out the private lives of the pilots. Robert Mitchum is the crusty commander who has to cope with an incipient coward in the squadron and eventually rescue him from behind enemy lines. The jet combat footage against Russian MIGs is quite striking.
★★
D: Dick Powell; W: Wendell Hayes; Ph: Charles Clarke; M: Paul Sawtell.
Cast: Robert Mitchum, Robert Wagner, Richard Egan, May Britt.

HUSTLE. (1975) An incoherent, often incomprehensible film whose title belies an overwhelming inertia. Burt Reynolds is stranded in the part of an L.A. detective who lives with a call girl. The movie has something to do with the case of a girl who died of a drug overdose, but it constantly strays into superfluous vignettes about various perverts roaming the streets of Los Angeles.
R. ★
D: Robert Aldrich; W: Steve Shagan; Ph: Joseph Biroc; M: Frank de Vol.
Cast: Burt Reynolds, Catherine Deneuve, Ben Johnson, Paul Winfield.

THE HUSTLER. (1961) The pooling of three actors in roles tailored to ther special gifts produced a movie of volcanic power. Paul Newman's Fast Eddie, a pool shark of compulsive ambition, Jackie Gleason's worldly champ and George C. Scott's jaded gambler combined for one of the enduring screen essays on winning and the American dream. The pool sequences have a gritty intensity that puts other "big game" movies behind the eightball.
★★★★★.
D: Robert Rossen; W: Rossen and Sidney Carroll; Ph: Eugene Shuftan; M: Kenyon Hopkins.
Cast: Paul Newman, George C. Scott, Jackie Gleason, Piper Laurie.

I

I AM A FUGITIVE FROM A CHAIN GANG.
(1932) Paul Muni won the Oscar for his moving performance as an innocent man who is changed—and very much for the worse—by his brutal experiences in a Georgia prison. Audiences of the time were shocked by the unsparing depiction of routine cruelty on the chain gang. The film went further in showing how such treatment could corrupt a decent man and condemn him to a life of outlawry.

★★★★
D: Mervyn LeRoy; W: Sheridan Gibney, Brown Holmes and Robert E. Burns; Ph: Sol Polito.
Cast: Paul Muni, Glenda Farrell, Helen Vinson, Preston Foster.

ICE CASTLES. (1979) Shameless tearjerker that makes *You Light Up My Life* seem like the work of an unrepentant cynic. A talented figure skater loses her sight in an accident and that is the least of the movie's handicaps. Under the tutelage of her boyfriend, she picks herself up and skates on to the sound of Marvin Hamlisch's score for a large orchestra of clumsily plucked heartstrings.
PG. ★
D: Donald Wrye; W: Wrye and Gary L. Baim; Ph: Bill Butler; M: Marvin Hamlisch.
Cast: Robby Benson, Lynn-Holly Johnson, Colleen Dewhurst, Tom Skerritt.

ICE COLD IN ALEX. (1958) The 132 minute version of J. Lee Thompson's taut war film was hacked down to 80 minutes and called *Desert Attack*. The original is well worth seeking out. John Mills is a boozed-up, battle-weary officer who finds himself charged with escorting two nurses to Alexandria. They pick up a German spy along the way.

★★★
D: J. Lee Thompson; W: T.J. Morrison and Christopher Landon; Ph: Gilbert Taylor; M: Leighton Lucas.
Cast: John Mills, Sylvia Sims, Anthony Quayle, Harry Andrews.

ICEMAN. (1984) Fred Schepisi, the very talented Australian director, is stuck with a script that ruins a good idea by making position papers out of people. The discovery of a 40,000-year-old man in the polar ice and his revival is handsomely done, but he becomes the object of a predictable debate between the scientists and the humanists. It's capped off with some far-fetched mysticism. The neanderthal, eloquently played by John Lone, is by far the most human character.
PG. ★★
D: Fred Schepisi; W: Chip Proser and John Drimmer; Ph: Ian Baker; M: Bruce Smeaton.
Cast: Tim Hutton, Lindsay Crouse, John Lone, Josef Sommer.

THE ICE PIRATES. (1981) The adventurers storm aboard a rival spaceship via the toilet, surprising a creature relieving itself. There is no relief from the relentless vulgarity as the buccaneers fight over water, the most precious commodity in the galaxy. Taste is in another universe and the recurring joke involves a slug whose bite imparts space herpes.
PG ★
D: Stewart Raffill; W: Rafill and Stanford Sherman; Ph: Matthew Leonetti; M: Bruce Broughton.
Cast: Robert Urich, Mary Crosby, Michael Adams, Anjelica Huston.

I CONFESS. (1953) No less an authority than Alfred Hitchcock confesed to being less than totally satisfied with the thriller he shot in Quebec. The technique is there but the irony and dark humor are absent and Hitchcock could not find much to do with a premise that is both trite and contrived. Montgomery Clift is a priest with a past who is bound to silence when a murderer tells all in the privileged sanctity of the confessional booth.

★★★
D: Alfred Hitchcock; W: George Tabori and William Archibald; Ph: Robert Burks; M: Dmitri Tiomkin.
Cast: Montgomery Clift, Anne Baxter, Brian Aherne, Karl Malden.

I DISMEMBER MAMA. (1972) More dreary than gory, despite the title. Originally released under the tamer title of *Poor Albert and Little Annie*. The psychotic killer runs away from the asylum because they won't let him watch pornographic movies, any of which would be preferable to this drivel. He is outraged at his mother for having him committed, a fate the director deserves more than the hero.
R. ★
D: Paul Leder; W: William Norton; Ph: Wil-

liam Swenning; M: Herschel Burke Gilbert.
Cast: Zooey Hall, Geri Reischl, Joanne Moore Jordan, Greg Mullavey.

IF... (1968) Lindsay Anderson later attacked British society as a whole with a meat cleaver in *Britannia Hospital*. In a heavily symbolist trial of the same approach, a public school and its repressions serve as the microcosm of a stultifying way of life in the world at large. The boys are provoked beyond endurance and there is a visceral anger and power to Anderson's vision.

★★★★

D: Lindsay Anderson; W: David Sherwin; Ph: Miroslav Ondricek; M: Marc Wilkinson.
Cast: Malcolm McDowell, David Wood, Richard Warwick, Robert Swann.

IF EVER I SEE YOU AGAIN. (1978) A repeat viewing is the last thing anyone would wish. Former commercial jingle writer Joe Brooks, the perpetrator of *You Light Up My Life*, went one worse with the story of a jingle writer trying to resume a romance with his college sweetheart. They even frolic in the snow.
PG.   ★
D and W: Joe Brooks; Ph: Adam Holender; M: Joe Brooks.
Cast: Joe Brooks, Shelley Hack, Jimmy Breslin, Jerry Kellen.

I'M ALL RIGHT, JACK. (1960) A savagely funny grilling of British industry, which then as now was hardly industrious. Ian Carmichael is a twit whose enthusiasm for work at a factory disrupts the sedate pace preferred by the union and the corrupt schemers in management. He provokes a strike and various farcical developments. Peter Sellers, proving himself as an actor as well as comedian, does a brilliant send-up of a pompous shop steward.

★★★★

D: John Boulting; W: Boulting and Frank Harvey; Ph: Max Greene; M: Ken Hare.
Cast: Ian Carmichael, Peter Sellers, Terry-Thomas, Irene Handl.

I MARRIED A MONSTER FROM OUTER SPACE. (1958) And marriage counseling can't help her predicament. A great title that doesn't deliver. The young wife gets the surprise of her life on the honeymoon when the guy in bed turns out to be a cunning clone created by aliens in a nearby flying saucer.

★★

D: Gene Fowler; W: Louis Vittes; Ph: Haskell Boggs; M: John Fulton.
Cast: Tom Tryon, Gloria Talbot, Robert Ivers, Ken Lynch.

I MARRIED A WITCH. (1942) A gossamer ghost fantasy typical of the times that is blessed with Veronica Lake and the adroit direction of Rene Clair. She is a witch still burning over the man who sent her to the stake in the seventeenth century and now charged with carrying out a curse on his descendants.

★★★

D: Rene Clair; W: Robert Pirosh and Marc Connelly; Ph: Ted Tezlaff ; M: Roy Webb.
Cast: Veronica Lake, Frederic March, Susan Hayward, Robert Benchley.

I'M DANCING AS FAST AS I CAN. (1982) A game effort from Jill Clayburgh in a losing cause. Based on Barbara Gordon's book about her fight against addiction to valium, the film takes the strange tack of linking a television producer's struggle against the drug with her efforts to complete a movie about someone dying of cancer. The tactic rearranges one's sympathies and makes Clayburgh's tantrums somehow trivial.
R.   ★★
D: Jack Hofsiss; W: David Rabe; Ph: Jan De Bont.
Cast: Jill Clayburgh, Nicol Williamson, Geraldine Page, Dianne West.

I'M NO ANGEL. (1933) In the case of Mae West, the title amounts to a highly redundant admission and it's a minor wonder how she got away with some of the lines in what is perhaps her best movie. The single entendres flow thick and fast with Mae as a lion tamer and a line tosser in a carnival and Cary Grant as her quarry.

★★★★

D: Wesley Ruggles; W: Mae West; Ph: Leo Tover.
Cast: Mae West, Cary Grant, Edward Arnold, Gregory Ratoff.

I, MOBSTER. (1958) Steve Cochran rises to the occasion as a gangster in an otherwise routine rise-and-fall story. For the rest, a predictable trajectory from punk to boss, courtesy of B movie king Roger Corman.

★★

D: Roger Corman; W: Steve Fisher; Ph: Floyd Crosby ; M: Gerald Fried.
Cast: Steve Cochran, Lita Milan, Robert Strauss, Celia Lovsky.

INCHON. (1982) Produced for the staggering sum of $48 million by the Unification Church, it should have been called *Shoot the Moonie*. General Douglas MacArthur is portrayed as a soldier of Christ even though he thought of God as a junior aide on his staff. Laurence Olivier finds the script a cross to bear. It covers the preliminaries and the pivotal battle of the Korean War and is no more than smug, anti-communist propaganda.
PG. ★
D: Terence Young; W: Robin Moore and Laird Koenig; Ph: Bruce Surtees; M: Jerry Goldsmith.
Cast: Laurence Oliver, Jacqueline Bisset, Ben Gazzara, Toshiro Mifune.

IN COLD BLOOD. (1967) The anatomy of a murder done with a scrupulous eye for detail and a sometimes annoying penchant for psychological exposition. Richard Brooks adapted Truman Capote's harrowing book and the two cold killers who wiped out an entire rural family are meticulously done by Robert Blake and Scott Wilson.
★★★
D and W: Richard Brooks; Ph: Conrad Hall; M: Quincy Jones.
Cast: Robert Blake, Scott Wilson, John Forsythe, Paul Stewart.

THE INCREDIBLE JOURNEY. (1963) An odd, but quite satisfying cross-breeding of a typical Disney family outing with his True-Life nature series. A labrador, a terrier and a cat try to make it across 250 miles of Canadian countryside to be reunited with their owners. The purely animal sequences, predictably, are the best part of the film.
★★★
D: Fletcher Markle; W: James Algar; Ph: Kenneth Peach; M: Oliver Wallace.
Cast: Emile Genest, John Drainie, Tommy Tweed, Sandra Scott.

THE INCREDIBLE SARAH. (1976) The incredible Glenda Jackson props up the absurd theater of this frenzied account of the great actress' early years on the boards. It plays like a series of curtain calls interrupted by scenes of high melodrama from Berhardt's life. Off-stage she copes with a layabout husband and theatrical rivalries. It is interesting to see Jackson do roles as she thinks Bernhardt would have tackled them. The rest of the film is simply incredible.
PG. ★★
D: Richard Fleischer; W: Ruth Wolff; Ph:

Christopher Challis; M: Elmer Bernstein.
Cast: Glenda Jackson, Daniel Massey, Yvonne Mitchell, Douglas Wilmer.

THE INCREDIBLE SHRINKING MAN. (1957) The years have not diminished one of the signal science fiction achievements of the fifties. Richard Matheson's script takes the same old premise—a man is subjected to radiation and changes—and does something provocative with it. The victim begins to shrink and the movie works as an exciting piece of suspense and an intelligent discussion of how we perceive our place in the world and how size can change emotional dimension. It's a genuinely affecting little film.
★★★
D: Jack Arnold; W: Richard Matheson; Ph: Ellis W. Carter; M: Joseph Gershenson.
Cast: Grant Williams, Randy Stuart, April Kent, Paul Langton.

THE INCREDIBLE SHRINKING WOMAN. (1980) Jane Wagner's habit of writing career-threatening roles for Lily Tomlin reached a point of diminishing returns. Tomlin's gradual shrinkage is an excuse for much obtuseness and an argument that she is a symbol of the way American housewives are belittled. Little things don't always mean a lot.
PG. ★
D: Joel Schumacher; W: Jane Wagner; Ph: Bruce Logan; M: Suzanne Ciani.
Cast: Lily Tomlin, Charles Grodin, Ned Beatty, Henry Gibson.

THE INCUBUS. (1982) The Middle Ages believed the incubus was a demon who visited people in their sleep. He found plenty of victims in the audience for this hack horror outing. The usual mad slasher fare with John Cassavetes as a a doctor counting spermatozoa—perhaps he was trying to get to sleep too. Rape and mutilation interrupted by autopsies.
R. ★
D: John Hough; W: George Franklin; Ph: Albert Dunk; M: Stan Myers.
Cast: John Cassavetes, John Ireland, Kerrie Keane, Helen Hughes.

INDIANA JONES AND THE TEMPLE OF DOOM. (1984) Steven Spielberg's "prequel" pits Indy against a malevoient Far East cult and its violence put him on the wrong side of many upset parents. Once more, the technical brilliance is there in force, but the story and dialogue are far weaker in the second adventure. Instead of Nazis, Indy confronts high priests who are too reminiscent of the camp figures in *Help* and Saturday matinees to provide the requisite menace. Spielberg, noting such scenes as a man having his heart ripped out, said it wasn't for younger kids. He's right.

PG. ★★★
D: Steven Spielberg; W: Willard Huyck and Gloria Katz; Ph: Douglas Slocombe; M: John Williams.
Cast: Harrison Ford, Kate Capshaw, Amrish Puri, Roshan Seth.

INDISCREET. (1958) Stanley Donen quite rightly approached the filming of the Broadway comedy *Kind Sir* as a jeweler setting two gems—Cary Grant and Ingrid Bergman. Grant is a diplomat who lies about his marital history to Ingrid Bergman, who is typecast as a beautiful actress. The settings in London's ritzy Mayfair are self-consciously urbane, but the stars atone for the whimsy .

★★★
D: Stanley Donen; W: Norman Krasna; Ph: Frederick A. Young; M: Richard Bennett.
Cast: Cary Grant, Ingrid Bergman, Cecil Parker, Phyllis Calvert.

I NEVER PROMISED YOU A ROSE GARDEN. (1977) Madness is at the center of this adaptation of the novel rather than a means of instigating the action—its usual function in film. This places an unfair burden on Kathleen Quinlan and she carries it very well as Deborah Blake, a schizophrenic in a mental institution. The hospital scenes are unsparing, but the movie is weakened by its attempt to depict the girl's fantasies.

R. ★★★
D: Anthony Page; W: Lewis John Carlino and Gavin Lambert; Ph: Bruce Logan; M: Paul Chihara.
Cast:Kathleen Quinlan, Bibi Andersson, Sylvia Sidney.

THE INFORMER. (1935) Thirty pieces of silver become twenty pounds in John Ford's somber study of the Ireland he later celebrated in a happier vein in *The Quiet Man*. Victor McLaglen's Gypo Nolan is the Judas figure in Dublin during the twenties and twenty pounds will take two people to America and freedom. His betrayal of his best friend is an act of higher treason and the wake scene in which the dead man's family and allies sense the truth is vintage early Ford. The symbolism—especially the re-

deeming Christ at the end—now seems overbearing, but *The Informer* is still a forceful tragedy tailored to McLaglen's rough presence.

★★★★★
D: John Ford; W: Dudley Nichols; Ph: Joseph H. August; M: Max Steiner.
Cast: Victor McLaglen, Margot Grahame, Preston Foster, Heather Angel.

INHERIT THE WIND. (1960) Since the creationists still doggedly argue their case, there's relevance as well as intense drama in Stanley Kramer's re-staging of the celebrated Monkey trial of the twenties. In Tennessee, John Scopes, a young school teacher is charged with defying a state law that banned Darwin's theories from the classroom. He is defended by Clarence Darrow and prosecuted by William Jennings Bryan. First class acting, including a very good account of H.L. Mencken from Gene Kelly, and some overstated moralizing that one expects from Kramer.

★★★★
D: Stanley Kramer; W: Nathan Douglas and Harold Jacob; Ph: Ernest Laszlo; M: Ernest Gold.
Cast: Spencer Tracy, Frederic March, Gene Kelly, Florence Eldridge.

THE IN-LAWS. (1979) Alan Arkin and Peter Falk might seem an odd couple but the pairing works very well. Arkin is a neurotic dentist who becomes embroiled in the international intrigues of Falk, who is either a CIA man or a lunatic. Or both. Arthur Hiller's lackadaisical direction is often annoying but the friction between Arkin's hysteria and Falk's benign earthiness produces some very funny scenes.

PG. ★★★
D: Arthur Hiller; W: Andrew Bergman; Ph: David M. Walsh; M: John Morris.
Cast: Peter Falk, Alan Arkin, Richard Libertini, Nancy Dussault.

IN LIKE FLINT. (1967) Beautiful women plot to take over the world, but nobody gave much thought to the plot of the film. A lifeless sequel to the already weak *Our Man Flint* that reduces James Coburn to a preening, egocentric performance that is more irritating than amusing.

★
D: Gordon Douglas; W: Hal Fimberg; Ph: William Daniels; M: Jerry Goldsmith.
Cast: James Coburn, Lee J. Cobb, Jean Hale, Andrew Duggan.

THE INNOCENT. (1976) Luchino Visconti's last film is a fitting epitaph in its visual splendor but it strays from the sardonic dissection of a marriage into Verdian melodrama. Giancarlo Giannini, liberated from political point-scoring in Wertmuller diatribes, is an Italian aristocrat who cheats on his beautiful wife. When she retaliates with an affair of her own there are tragic consequences. The compassion Visconti extends to the aristocrat is misplaced.

R.   ★★★
D: Luchino Visconti; W: Visconti, Susso Cecchi D'Amico and Enrico Medioli; Ph: Pasqualino De Santis; M: Franco Mannino.
Cast: Giancarlo Giannini, Laura Antonelli, Jennifer O'Neill, Rina Morelli.

THE INNOCENTS. (1961) Inspired by Henry James' *The Turn of the Screw* and Jack Clayton tightens the screws with a flair that puts the possession movies of the seventies to shame. Deborah Kerr, a new governess in an old mansion, has to cope with two sweet children who are in the thrall of two dead lovers. One of the very best ghost stories in movies.

★★★★
D: Jack Clayton; W: William Archibald and Truman Capote; Ph: Freddie Francis; M: Georges Auric.
Cast: Deborah Kerr, Peter Wyngarde, Megs Jenkins, Pamela Franklin.

THE INN OF THE SIXTH HAPPINESS.
(1958) Robert Donat as a mandarin and Curt Jurgens as a Chinese officer and North Wales masquerading as China. Despite these improbabilities, the recounting of the life of Gladys Aylward makes an appealing drama. Ingrid Bergman carries the film as the missionary leading some Chinese children to safety in the turbulence before World War II. It was Donat's last movie.

★★★
D: Mark Robson; W: Isobel Lennart; Ph: F.A. Young; M: Malcolm Arnold.
Cast: Robert Donat, Ingrid Bergman, Curt Jurgens, Michael David.

IN OLD CHICAGO. (1938) *The Towering Inferno* of its day. Henry King recreates the great fire of Chicago and Mrs. O'Leary's notorious cow who started it all by kicking over a lantern. Before the bovine arson, there is a rather moralizing tale involving Mrs. O'Leary's two ambitious sons.

★★★
D: Henry King; W: Lamar Trotti and Sonya Levien; Ph: Peverell Marley; M: Louis Silvers.

Cast: Alice Brady, Tyrone Power, Don Ameche, Alice Faye.

IN SEARCH OF NOAH'S ARK. (1977) Pseudo-documentary that is many cubits too long for its content and makes Noah look like a forlorn wino. Produced at a cost of several dollars by the pious scholars of Sun International, the schlokumentary purports to show that Noah gathered unto himself a zoo and beached his ark on Mount Ararat. Full of leaky arguments, lousy photography and pompous narration that only a diehard fundamentalist could ignore.

G.
D: James Conway; W: James Conway and Charles Sellier; Ph: George Stapleford; Cast: Brad Crandall.

IN SEARCH OF THE CASTAWAYS.
(1962) A look for the point of the plot would be in order in the adaptation of the Jules Verne story. Two children and some adults set out for South America in search of their father only to discover that he's in Australia and the movie turns into a rambling Cook's tour. The set-piece escapes don't blend with the story.

★★
D: Robert Stevenson; W: Lowell S. Harley; Ph: Paul Beeson; M: William Alwyn.
Cast: Hayley Mills, Maurice Chevalier, George Sanders, Wilfrid Hyde White.

INSERTS. (1976) A controversial film in its day, because the sex earned an X. It turned out to be a storm in a C-cup and all this glum endeavor earns now is an inarguable place as Richard Dreyfuss' most degrading film. He is a director in thirties Hollywood who is reduced to making stag films and uttering John Byrum's inert dialogue. A self-conscious and pretentious effort in the boulevard-of-broken-dreams vein.

X.   ★
D and W: John Byrum; Ph: Denys Coop.
Cast: Richard Dreyfuss, Jessica Harper, Bob Hoskins, Veronica Cartwright.

INTERIORS. (1978) Woody Allen left the security of humor—and a good portion of his fans—in a Bergmanesque and sober study of the kind of characters he had previously used for laughs. At his level, whether something is funny or serious is a matter of perspective, but there is a stilted quality and stretches of unWoody-like verbosity here. A seemingly controlled mother endures a trial separation that touches her three daughters in different ways. The ideas and anxieties are the same ones that inspire Allen in overtly lighter moments and he has expressed them more pungently elsewhere.

★★★

D and W: Woody Allen; Ph: Gordon Willis. Cast: Geraldine Page, Diane Keaton, E.G. Marshall, Kristin Griffith.

INTERMEZZO. (1939) The sweeping strains of the music of the great romantic composers accompany the romance of a concert violinist and the young student who becomes his mistress. Ingrid Bergman did the protege during her Swedish film-making career and this was her bow in English.

★★★

D: Gregory Ratoff; W: George O'Neil; Ph: Gregg Toland. Cast: Leslie Howard, Ingrid Bergman, John Halliday, Edna Best.

INTERNATIONAL VELVET. (1978) Pompous sequel to the Elizabeth Taylor evergreen that looks like a calendar photograph of the English countryside and keeps pausing for brief homilies on the price of winning. Tatum O'Neal, an orphan who falls under the spell of a horse and occasionally off him, turns into a lady and it's not her cup of tea as she makes a try for the Olympic equestrian team. A literal sermon on the mount.
PG. ★★
D and W: Bryan Forbes; Ph: Tony Imi; M: Francis Lai. Cast: Tatum O'Neal, Anthony Hopkins, Christopher Plummer, Nanette Newman.

THE INTERNECINE PROJECT. (1974) The Watergate era lent credibility to a slick speculation on what a man might do to assure his appointment as a presidential advisor. James Coburn is a Harvard academic with a shady past who comes up with the idea of persuading four people who know about him to kill each other. Harry Andrews, as a British army major, is the one to watch.
PG. ★★★
D: Ken Hughes; W: Barry Levinson and Jonathan Lynn; Ph: Geoffrey Unsworth; M: Roy Budd. Cast: James Coburn, Lee Remick, Harry Andrews, Ian Hendry.

IN THE HEAT OF THE NIGHT. (1969) It is not the temperature that is reddening the already red neck of Rod Steiger, but the presence of a black Philadelphia detective in his southern bailiwick. In a perfectly judged mix of humor, tension and observation, Steiger and Poitier embark on the investigation of a murder which is almost secondary to what is revealed about the two men.

★★★★

D: Norman Jewison; W: Stirling Silliphant; Ph: Haskell Wexler; M: Quincy Jones. Cast: Rod Steiger, Sidney Poitier, Warren Oates, Quentin Dean.

IN THE REALM OF THE SENSES. (1977) A minor cause in its day because it was impounded by U.S. Customs on obscentity charges. Nagisa Oshima's film is based on a true story, but it rarely strays into the realm of sense. It is of interest to see what a director of real skill can do in a milieu best known for non-acting and motel interiors. This becomes gorenography as a woman kills the man she loves after a couple of hours of graphically presented copulation.

★★

INTRUDER IN THE DUST. (1949) William Faulkner's novel about a black man of vast dignity who refuses to play the part prejudice has allotted him in Mississippi becomes a movie that refuses to bow to Hollywood racial convention. The old man, confronted by the prospect of being lynched after an accusation of murder, is not some condescending liberal stereotype. Faulkner's world—it was shot in Oxford, Miss.—forms a rich background.

★★★★

D: Clarence Brown; W: Ben Maddow; Ph: Robert Surtees; M: Adolph Deutsch. Cast: David Brian, Claude Jarman, Juano Hernandez, Porter Hall .

INVADERS FROM MARS. (1953) A little boy comes into contact with aliens and he's the only one who knows. Sound familiar? This is a sort of hostile *E.T.*, as befits fifties sci-fi. No one believes the kid and people keep disappearing until the army comes along to have it out with the space ship. Dime store effects and a garbled viewpoint. It was directed by the famous production designer William Cameron Menzies.

★★

D: William Cameron Menzies; W: Richard Blake; Ph: John Seitz; M: Raoul Kraushaar. Cast: Helena Carter, Arthur Franz, Jimmy Hunt, Leif Erickson.

INVASION OF THE BODY SNATCHERS. (1956) Don Siegel's shrewd and impeccably made science fiction classic is both an exciting film and an indictment of conformity and political attitudes that encouraged everyone to toe the line and frowned on independence of mind and spirit. These were very pertinent matters in the McCarthy era and they are just as valid today. Siegel's excellent work would survive without such relevance as a tense thriller. A psychiatrist has to cope with the fact that only he and his girlfriend are seemingly a small town's only surviving humans when alien "pods" take over. Kevin McCarthy, who plays the doctor, appeared briefly in Philip Kaufman's sequel.

★★★★

D: Don Siegel; W: Daniel Mainwaring and Sam Peckinpah; Ph: Ellsworth Fredericks; M: Carmen Dragon.
Cast: Kevin McCarthy, Dana Wynter, Larry Gates, King Donovan.

INVASION OF THE BODY SNATCHERS. (1978) One of the best remakes ever made, Philip Kaufman's riveting version of the 1956 sci-fi classic rethinks rather than merely updates the original. In San Francisco, alien organisms arrive via flowers and the leader of the new order is a pop psychiatrist who spouts suave claptrap. The populace succumbs, because the new arrivals are just one more pollutant. Donald Sutherland, a health inspector, finds the awful truth and his worst fears are justified. Lively acting and a honed screenplay full of macabre wit.
PG. ★★★★
D: Philip Kaufman; W: W.D. Richter; Ph: Michael Chapman; M: Denny Zetlin.
Cast: Donald Sutherland, Leonard Nimoy, Jeff Goldblum, Brooke Adams.

THE INVISIBLE MAN. (1933) In the normal Hollywood process, an audience sees someone it likes in a film it adores and a star is born. Claude Rains reversed the tradition and became a box office draw because movie goers liked what they didn't see. James Whale's version of the H.G. Wells story is a nice concoction of thrills and the humor possible when a man becomes invisible. Inevitably, he is a mad scientist who wishes to put his discovery to corrupt use.

★★★★

D: James Whale; W: R.C. Sheriff and Philp Wylie; Ph: Arthur Edeson.
Cast: Claude Rains, William Harrigan, Gloria Stuart, Henry Travers.

THE INVISIBLE MAN RETURNS. (1940) The sequel is worth seeing. It has Vincent Price, the brother of the original no-show, wrongly accused of murder. With the help of

the formula he makes himself invisible and finds the real killer.

★★★

D: Joe May; W: Curt Siodmak, Lester Cole and Cedric Belfrage; Ph: Milton Krasner; M: Hans Salter.
Cast: Vincent Price, John Sutton, Cedric Hardwicke, Nan Grey.

INVITATION TO THE DANCE. (1956) Since the invitation was issued by no less than Gene Kelly, the response should be affirmative. Unfortunately, the three ballet episodes that make up the feature are not the kind of choreography identified with Kelly and the film ran afoul of its studio. It was a major disappointment for Kelly, but it's worth watching for what he would do in such a milieu.

★★

D and W: Gene Kelly; Ph: Frederick Young; M: Various composers.
Cast: Gene Kelly, Claire Sombert, David Paltenghi, Daphne Dale.

IN WHICH WE SERVE. (1941) Noel Coward, the urbane observer of upper class foibles, expanded his horizons for this celebration of the pluck of Englishmen of all classes serving during the war. The posture, understandably, is propagandistic with a disparate group of men aboard the British destroyer Torrin. It is not the kind of thing you would expect Coward to do well, but he is patriotic without being patronizing to what he thought of as the lower orders.

★★★★

D: Noel Coward and David Lean; W: Noel Coward; Ph: Ronald Neame; M: Noel Coward.
Cast: Noel Coward, John Mills, Michael Wilding, Celia Johnson.

I OUGHT TO BE IN PICTURES. (1982) Another formulaic piece that raised the question of what Neil Simon ought to be doing in films. This is a junior edition of one of Simon's favorite movie motifs—the woman who finds herself after considerable struggle. She goes to live with a father she hasn't seen in years and tries to make it in Hollywood.
PG. ★★
D: Herbert Ross; W: Neil Simon; Ph: David Walsh; M: Marvin Hamlisch.
Cast: Walter Matthau, Dinah Manoff, Ann-Margret, Lance Guest.

THE IPCRESS FILE. (1965) Michael Caine made a stong impression in his debut as

Harry Palmer, the lower class spy with upper crust appetites, because he ran so counter to the intelligence agent epitomized by Sean Connery. That advantage has long since disappeared in an avalanche of disillusioned espionage fiction, but Caine's work holds up very well. Palmer is blackmailed and otherwise abused by both sides in his efforts to stop a brain drain of scientists. ★★★

D: Sidney J. Furie; W: James Doran and Bill Cannaway; Ph: Otto Heller; M: John Barry.
Cast: Michael Caine, Nigel Green, Sue Lloyd, Guy Doleman.

I SENT A LETTER TO MY LOVE. (1981) If it is vain to cling to one's youth, Simone Signoret is the world's most modest actress. She was 60 when she added this portrait of a lonely spinster to the gallery of memorable old women she has created. The spinster tends to a crippled brother and, in fear of even greater loneliness after his death, puts a lonely hearts ad in the paper. The brother's is the only reply and the film almost collapses under the weight of its contrivance. Signoret makes it worthwhile.
★★★

D: Moshe Mizrahi; W: Mizrahi and Gerard Brach; Ph: Ghislain Cloquet; M: Philippe Sarde.
Cast: Simone Signoret, Jean Rochefort, Delphine Seyrig.

THE ISLAND. (1980) Disastrous version of Peter Benchley's novel about seventeenth century pirates who have survived into our time to prey on boats in the Bermuda Triangle. They sound like Robert Newton's Long John Silver doing an imitation of Yoda. A father goes in search of his lost son. The whole dismal endeavor belongs in the Bermuda Triangle.
R. ★
D: Michael Ritchie; W: Peter Benchley; Ph: Henri Decae; M: Ennio Morricone.
Cast: Michael Caine, David Warner, Angela Punch McGregor, Frank Middlemass.

THE ISLAND AT THE TOP OF THE WORLD. (1974) Not based on a Jules Verne inspiration and, not surprisingly, one of the weaker Disney films in the fantasy/adventure vein. In 1907, two explorers set out to find a lost Viking civilization near the North Pole and a son who disappeared while searching for it. Silly mishmash of Viking histrionics and killer whales, but a passable story for kids.
G. ★★

D: Robert Stevenson; W: John Whedon; Ph: Frank Phillips; M: Maurice Jarre.
Cast: Donald Sinden, David Hartman, Jacques Marin, David Gwillim.

ISLAND IN THE SUN. (1957) Sexual and political turmoil in the British West Indies rendered hopelessly self-conscious by the introduction of the then volatile subject of interracial relationships. But the subject is introduced instead of addressed and director Robert Rossen treads warily around it. There is nothing else of any note or merit.
★★

D: Robert Rossen; W: Alfred Hayes; Ph: F.A. Young; M: Malcolm Arnold.
Cast: James Mason, Joan Fontaine, Dorothy Dandridge, Harry Belafonte.

THE ISLAND OF DR. MOREAU. (1977) The H.G. Wells story is grafted onto the DNA controversy with hybrid results. Burt Lancaster, as a scientist designing genes so that animals are altered into man-beasts, plays Moreau as if the part amused rather than engaged him. Michael York is washed ashore on the mysterious island and tries to intervene, causing Lancaster to attempt a retailoring of his genes. The film never exudes the air of menace it needs.
PG. ★★
D: Don Taylor; W: John Herman Shaner and Al Ramrus; Ph: Gary Fisher; M: Laurence Rosenthal.
Cast: Burt Lancaster, Michael York, Barbara Carrera, Nigel Davenport.

ISLAND OF THE BURNING DOOMED. (1967) Also known as *Island of the Burning Damned*. A heat wave strikes an island off the British coast, allowing the natives to indulge the English national pastime of discussing the weather. Hammer Films stalwarts keep a modest fantasy of alien invasion reasonably alive, but this is not hot stuff.
★★

D: Terence Fisher; W: Ron Liles; Ph: Reg Wyer; M: Malcolm Lockyer.
Cast: Peter Cushing, Christopher, Lee, Patrick Allen, Sarah Lawson.

ISLANDS IN THE STREAM. (1976) An earnest, almost religious offering of Hemingway's ideas on masculinity that swam bravely against the commercial currents of its day. Based on a posthumous Hemingway novel, the script confirms the contention that minor Hemingway represents a great prose style trapped in a 14-year-old's brain. Scott plays a marlin-bashing, gun-fondling artist living in

the Bahamas and trying to re-establish a relationship with his three sons. The burden of machismo is crushing toward the end.
PG. ★★
D: Franklin Schaffner; W: Denne Bart Petticlerc; Ph: Fred J. Koenekamp; M: Jerry Goldsmith.
Cast: George C. Scott, Claire Bloom, David Hemmings, Gilbert Roland.

IT CAME FROM BENEATH THE SEA. (1955) A bargain basement giant octopus does what all those homophobic television evangelists dream of doing and rips half of San Francisco apart. The creature goes berserk because of atomic testing radiation and gets its comeuppance from a submarine torpedo. Cheerfully ludicrous.
★★
D: Robert Gordon; W: George Worthing Yates and Hal Smith; Ph: Henry Freulich; M: Mischa Bakaleinikoff.
Cast: Kenneth Tobey, Faith Domergue, Donald Curtis, Ian Keith.

IT CAME FROM HOLLYWOOD. (1982) It should never have left. An anthology of the awful from Tinseltown's past that tries to do for schlock what *That's Entertainment* did for musicals. The choosers don't know the difference between a good bad movie and a purely bad movie. The samples range from *The Creature from the Black Lagoon*, which doesn't deserve to be here, to *The Man with Two Heads*, which Ray Milland would dearly love to burn.
PG. ★★
D: Malcolm Leo and Andrew Solt; W: Dana Olsen.
Cast: Dan Aykroyd, John Candy, Thomas Chong, Richard Marin (presenters).

IT HAPPENED ONE NIGHT. (1934) It happens to be one of the best comedies of the thirties and strong competition for the finest in other decades. Clark Gable emerged as a star in the part of the hard-nosed reporter eventually softened by a rich heiress during their sundry and still funny adventures between Miami and New York. It established both Gable and Frank Capra and made off with a bunch of deserved Oscars.
★★★★★
D: Frank Capra; W: Robert Riskin; Ph: Joseph Walker; M: Louis Silvers.
Cast: Clark Gable, Claudette Colbert, Walter Connolly, Roscoe Karns.

IT HAPPENED TOMORROW. (1944) There is, the saying goes, nothing older than yesterday's newspaper. But what would happen if a reporter started receiving tomorrow's newspaper? Rene Clair had a special way with these light fantasies and he has a lot of fun as the journalist exploits his good fortune. One day he opens the paper and finds some alarming tidings in the obituary column.
★★★
D: Rene Clair ; W: Dudley Nichols and Clair; Ph: Archie Stout; M: Robert Stoltz.
Cast: Dick Powell, Linda Darnell, Jack Oakie, Edgar Kennedy.

I, THE JURY. (1982) Guilty of handing out cruel and unusual punishment to both the cast and anyone who can sit through its non-stop sadism and sexism. It is not hard to see why it dropped dead commercially and quickly went to tape and cable. Armand Assante, a talented performer, can do nothing with the brutish writing and awful one-liners as Mickey Spillane's Mike Hammer. In an updated setting, he seems a neanderthal and shameless shamus.
R. ★
D: Richard Heffron; W: Larry Cohen; Ph: Andrew Laszlo; M: Bill Conti.
Cast: Armand Assante, Barbara Carrera, Alan King, Laurene Landon.

IT LIVES AGAIN. (1978) Son of *It's Alive* and even sicker. Someone must have dropped Larry Cohen on his head during infancy. Unfortunately he survived to make films about killer babies being hounded down by the government. As much fun as a baby with colic at 3 A.M.
R. ★
D and W: Larry Cohen; Ph: Fenton Hamilton; M: Laurie Johnson.
Cast: Frederic Forrest, Kathleen Lloyd, John P. Ryan, John Marley.

IT'S A MAD, MAD, MAD, MAD WORLD. (1963) Stanley Kramer's gigantic comedy is about some stashed money but the string of inflatable jokes is no buried treasure. With the galaxy of comic players assembled for the Cinemascope production, it would be amazing if the film did not deliver its share of laughs. And as the hectic pursuit of the money gets under way, it does occasionally come through. Most of the jests, however, would be a lot more effective if they were not blown out of proportion to their content. This is especially true of the slapstick humor.
★★

D: Stanley Kramer; W: William and Tania Rose; Ph: Ernest Laszlo; M: Ernest Gold.
Cast: Spencer Tracy, Jimmy Durante, Milton Berle, Sid Caesar.

IT'S A WONDERFUL LIFE. (1946) James Stewart is brought to the contemplation of suicide by setbacks to his small-town business. Through heavenly intervention he is shown the value of his existence and only Frank Capra could bring off such potentially syrupy material.

★★★

D: Frank Capra; W: Capra, Albert Hackett and Frances Goodrich; Ph: Joseph Walker; M: Dmitri Tiomkin.
Cast: James Stewart, Henry Travers, Donna Reed, Lionel Barrymore.

IT'S MY TURN. (1980) Another upscale anxiety attack from a Jill Clayburgh torn between her architect lover in Chicago and a baseball player in New York whose career has been wrecked by an injury. Wrecked by dialogue that is penned in California-speak with much talk of nurturing and having too much or too little space.

R. ★★

D: Claudia Weill; W: Eleanor Bergstein; Ph: Bill Butler; M: Patrick Williams.
Cast: Jill Clayburgh, Michael Douglas, Charles Grodin, Beverly Garland.

IVANHOE. (1953) The young Elizabeth Taylor was at her most ravishing as Rebecca and that is vital to the credibility of Walter Scott's classic tale of Saxon honor and Norman villainy. Ivanhoe, torn between the honorable Rowena and the tempting, but off-limits Jewess Rebecca, fights to bring King Richard back to England. It is, of course, big budget, Hollywood medieval, but it's done with conviction and flair and Robert Taylor is a virile hero.

★★★

D: Richard Thorpe; W: Aeneas Mackenzie and Noel Langley; Ph: F.A. Young; M: Miklos Rozsa.
Cast: Robert Taylor, Elizabeth Taylor, Joan Fontaine, Emlyn Williams.

IVAN THE TERRIBLE—PARTS ONE AND TWO. (1944/1946) Sergei Eisenstein planned a trilogy about the nobleman who became the first ruler of the Russians in the sixteenth century. He finished two parts and died of a heart attack while planning the third. What is left constitutes film-making on a scale that is no longer possible because (a) nobody has the resources and (b) no one approaches Eisenstein's gift for visual composition. That gift tends to overwhelm the study of character and motive. The action covers the coronation of the young Ivan and the revolt of the Boyars and its unfolding is often and rightly compared to grand opera.

★★★★★

D and W: Sergei Eisenstein; Ph: Andrei Moskvin; M: Sergei Prokofiev.
Cast: Nikolai Cherkasov, Serafima Birman, Ludmila Tselikovskaya, Mikhail Mazvanov.

I WANNA HOLD YOUR HAND. (1978) A genuine charmer that deserves to be better known (it was kissed off by its studio and never released nationally.) A bunch of kids from New Jersey make it to New York and all the frenzy that greeted the arrival of the Beatles in 1964. The zany exuberance of the event is lovingly captured and everything moves at a romp.

PG. ★★★

D: Bob Zemeckis; W: Zemeckis and Bob Gale; Ph: Donald M. Morgan; M: Songs of the Beatles.
Cast: Nancy Allen, Bobby DiCicco, Marc McClure, Susan Kendall Newman.

I WANT TO LIVE. (1958) An emotionally charged attack on capital punishment. Susan Hayward won the Oscar for her portrayal of Barbara Graham, a woman convicted of a murder and executed even though there were grounds for questioning her guilt. The film is based on the newspaper stories written by Ed Montgomery, who led a losing crusade to save Graham. None of the arguments about capital punishment have measurably changed and the execution scene is extremely tough viewing.

★★★

D: Robert Wise; W: Nelson Gidding and Don Mankiewicz; Ph: Lionel Lindon; M: John Mandel.
Cast: Susan Hayward, Simon Oakland, Virginia Vincent, Theodore Bikel.

I WAS A TEENAGE WEREWOLF. (1957) The little house on the prairie never had to put up with a teenager like Michael Landon. Under hypnosis, he becomes the kind of kid who goes beyond wolf whistling at the girls. Landon touched some kind of yearning and the film became a substantial hit.

★★

D: Gene Fowler; W: Ralph Thornton; Ph: Joseph La Shelle; M: Paul Dunlap.
Cast: Michael Landon, Whit Bissell, Yvonne Lime, Guy Williams.

J

JABBERWOCKY. (1977) As Lewis Carroll warned, "Beware the Jabberwock, my son." Glumly vulgar English lavatory humor mired in the Middle Ages and occasionally enlivened by a decent sight gag. Two of the Monty Python troupe were behind it and two is not enough. A barrel-maker (Michael Palin) makes his way to the big city to earn the money to marry the fat Griselda and eventually meets the monstrous jabberwock. Most of the comedy is best described as "slapstuck" with a lot of milling around and shouting.
★★
D: Terry Gilliam; W: Gilliam and Charles Alverson; Ph: Terry Bedford; M: De Wolfe.
Cast: Michael Palin, Max Wall, Deborah Fallender, John Le Mesurier.

THE JACKPOT. (1950) One of Jimmy Stewart's unsung comic achievements that is well worth a look. He is very funny as a man who wins a radio quiz show and is showered with prizes like revolting furniture and a Shetland pony that are of absolutely no use to him.
★★★
D: Walter Lang; W: Phoebe and Henry Ephron; Ph: Joseph La Shelle; M: Lionel Newman.
Cast: James Stewart, Barbara Hale, James Gleason, Fred Clark.

JACKSON COUNTY JAIL. (1976) The inspiration, to use the word loosely, is presumably the Joan Little case—a young black woman who killed the jailer who raped her. Here an upper-middle class New Yorker has the same experience in a Southern slammer. The real issue of there being one law for the poor and another for the affluent is lost in various idiocies surrounding her revenge.
R.
★
D: Michael Miller; W: Donald Stewart; Ph: Bruce Logan; M: Loren Newkirk.
Cast: Yvette Mimieux, Tommy Lee Jones, Robert Carradine, Frederic Cook.

JACQUES BREL IS ALIVE AND WELL AND LIVING IN PARIS. (1975) But his vital signs are weak in the American Film Theater production. Unlike others in the series, this version of the popular revue with its sentimental art songs doesn't just point the camera at the stage. Director Denis Heroux inflated every image suggested by the lyrics with disastrous, overblown results. There are 26 songs overwhelmed by Heroux's style, but nonetheless quite well performed.
PG. ★★
D: Denis Heroux; W: Eric Blau; Ph: Rene Verzier; M: Francois Rauber(conductor).
Cast: Elly Stone, Mort Shuman, Joe Masiell, Jacques Brel.

JAGUAR LIVES. (1979) Bruce Lee Lewis, a martial arts champion, should have stayed in the gym. The film has something to do with a secret agent and international heroin traffic.
R.
★
D: Ernest Pintoff.
Cast: Donald Pleasence, Christopher Lee, Joe Lewis, Capucine.

JAILHOUSE ROCK. (1957) Elvis Presley's best musical starts him off in jail—with a raucously choreographed title number—and sends him off on a trajectory as a rock star who forgets his rough beginnings and his friends. Nothing original, but at least the role suited Elvis.
★★
D: Richard Thorpe; W: Guy Trosper; Ph: Robert Bronner; M: Jeff Alexander(md).
Cast: Elvis Presley, Judy Tyler, Mickey Shaughnessy, Dean Jones.

JANE EYRE. (1944) The most memorable aspect of a respectful and well-cast rendering of Charlotte Bronte's novel is Bernard Herrmann's eerie score. It's among his best and Orson Welles also made a suitably brooding Rochester to Joan Fontaine's governess. The mood, if not the subtext of Bronte's work, is captured.
★★★
D: Robert Stevenson; W: Stevenson, Aldous Huxley and John Houseman; Ph: George Barnes; M: Bernard Herrmann.
Cast: Orson Welles, Joan Fontaine, Margaret O'Brien, Peggy Ann Garner.

JANIS. (1975) Shallow look at a potentially fascinating subject—the life and death of Janis Joplin. The great blues singer died of a drug overdose in 1970, ending a meteoric career in pop music. This collage of concert footage and her answers to bland questions from interviewers hardly deserves its biographical label.

R. ★★
D: Howard Alk; Ph: Ron Haines; M: Janis Joplin, Big Brother and the Holding Company, and others.

JASON AND THE ARGONAUTS. (1963) Skeletons that rise from the ground to fight Jason and his men and monsters of every persuasion add up to an inspired outing for special effects wizard Ray Harryhausen. The acting is a Greek miss, particularly from Nancy Kovack and Todd Armstrong, and that tends to dilute the impact of Harryhausen's hard work. Jason has to endure all manner of perils before the fleece is his.
★★
D: Don Chaffey; W: Jan Read and Beverly Cross; Ph: Wilkie Cooper; M: Bernard Herrmann.
Cast: Todd Armstrong, Honor Blackman, Andrew Faulds, Niall McGinnis.

JAWS. (1975) Steven Spielberg's unrivaled gift for creating tension and manipulating the fear of the audience found a perfect outlet in Peter Benchley's novel about a great white shark that terrorizes an East Coast resort. His principal and very simple device is to keep the shark off the screen and let the viewer use his imagination. Somewhat labored on land, but the seagoing sequences have a visceral force, underlined by John Williams' edgy score. Robert Shaw is especially memorable as the professional shark-hunter. One of the most popular movies ever made and rightly so.
PG ★★★★★
D: Steven Spielberg; W: Peter Benchley and Carl Gottlieb; Ph: Bill Butler; M: John Williams.
Cast: Roy Scheider, Richard Dreyfuss, Robert Shaw, Lorraine Gary.

JAWS 2. (1978) The script for an inane sequel passed through more hands than a marijuana joint at a rock concert. No one solved the problem of finding some way to continue a story that ended with such a cathartic bang in *Jaws*. Roy Scheider reprised his police chief role with visible reluctance. A friend of Bruce returns to haunt Amity, but Scheider can't convince the greedy local brass of the danger.
PG. ★★
D: Jeannot Szwarc ; W: Carl Gottlieb and Howard Sackler; Ph: Michael Butler; M: John Williams.

Cast: Roy Scheider, Lorraine Gary, Murray Hamilton, Joseph Mascolo.

JAWS 3-D. (1983) Being asked to direct the third outing is the movie equivalent of receiving a dead fish wrapped in a newspaper by the Mafia. Joe Alves tosses it into a marine park in Florida along with assorted chunks of human anatomy. The shark is unconvincing and inept, a quality the cast soon comes to share. The tension and the play on what you don't see in Steven Spielberg's untoppable original gives way to an ebb tide of gore. Bruce is loose in the underwater park and has an appetite for waterskiers.
PG. ★
D: Joe Alves; W: Richard Matheson and Carl Gottlieb; Ph: James A. Contner; M: Alan Parker.
Cast: Dennis Quaid, Lou Gossett, Jr., Bess Armstrong, Simon MacCorkindale.

THE JAZZ SINGER. (1953) In the first remake of the film that ushered in the talkies, you get Peggy Lee in some standard songs but you have to put up with Danny Thomas. Unwilling to settle down in Philadelphia after a hitch in Korea, he chooses show-biz over synagogue. Shamelessly sentimental, but at least without the obscene wallowing of the 1980 version.
★★
D: Michael Curtiz; W: Frank Davis, Lewis Meltzer and Leonard Stern; Ph: Carl Guthrie; M: Max Steinerf.
Cast: Danny Thomas, Peggy Lee, Mildred Dunnock, Eduard Franz.

THE JAZZ SINGER. (1980) A Hall of Fame trash movie that no connoisseur should miss. Laurence Olivier is the whining cantor in one of his most demeaning roles. When he asks Neil Diamond why he doesn't want a career in the synagogue, the singer retorts, "God doesn't pay so good, pop." The producers paid Olivier enough to abase himself. Diamond goes to L.A. and makes it, giving rich movie people another chance to tell the rest of the country how miserable success can make you.
PG. ★
D: Richard Fleischer; W: Herbert Baker; Ph: Isidore Manofsky; M: Leonard Rosenman.
Cast: Laurence Olivier, Neil Diamond, Lucie Arnaz, Catlin Adams.

JEKYLL & HYDE...TOGETHER AGAIN. (1982) Jekyll snorts cocaine to turn into

Hyde and you might try No-Doze for what is easily the dreariest trashing of Stevenson's schizoid classic. In the mercifully brief 87 minutes there is not a single funny line and there are whole scenes that make one cringe in disbelief.
R. ★
D: Jerry Belson; W: Monica Johnson, Harvey Miller, Michael Leeson and Belson; Ph: Philip Lathrop; M: Barry DeVorzon.
Cast: Mark Blankenfield, Bess Armstrong, Krista Errickson, Michael McGuire.

JENNIFER. (1978) A *Carrie-on* movie that flagrantly plagiarizes the Brian De Palma hit. Tormented by snobbish schoolmates, a country girl takes her revenge through her power over snakes. "The sad thing about this is that everybody loses," says friendly teacher Bert Convy about a cheating scandal. It applies to the film too.
PG. ★
D: Brice Mack; W: Kay Cousins Johnson.
Cast: Lisa Pelikan, Bert Convy, Nina Foch, Amy Johnston.

THE JERK. (1979) A grueling ninety minutes of inane crudity. Steve Martin, a white lad raised by black sharecroppers, goes from rags to riches to rags in an exceedingly ragged outing when he invents a device that prevents a person's glasses from sliding down the nose. Navin(Martin) is a simple jerk and not a wild and crazy guy and the jokes are pounded to death.
R. ★★
D: Carl Reiner; W: Steve Martin, Carl Gottlieb and Michael Elias; Ph: Victor J. Kemper; M: Jack Elliott.
Cast: Steve Martin, Bernadette Peters, Catlin Adams, Bill Macy.

JEREMIAH JOHNSON. (1972) Robert Redford excels in putting meaning in his looks and since there are many moments of silence, it helps a great deal. He is a mountain man trying to escape a former life as a soldier, but his skill against the Indians turns him into a legend. The film was shot in Utah and the scenery is a co-star in a leisurely, well-told story.
PG. ★★★
D: Sydney Pollack; W: John Milius and Edward Anhalt; Ph: Duke Callaghan; M: John Rubinstein and Tim McIntire.
Cast: Robert Redford, Will Geer, Stefan Gierasch, Allyn Ann McLerie.

JESSE JAMES. (1939) A vigorous apologia for the notorious outlaw with Henry Fonda stealing the picture as Frank James. The career of the brothers is presented faithfully and explained as a response to their brutalizing war experiences and to the capitalists preying on their homestead. It is a view that put the movie ahead of its time. One of only three westerns made by Henry King.
★★★★
D: Henry King; W: Nunnally Johnson; Ph: W. Howard Greene; M: Louis Silvers.
Cast: Tyrone Power, Henry Fonda, Nancy Kelly, Randolph Scott.

JESUS. (1979) Hollywood has never been comfortable with the Messiah and this biography is at least free of heavenly choirs, over-abiding shepherds and John Wayne (*The Greatest Story Ever Told*) intoning, "Truly, this was the son of God." Instead, it's a blandly pious and stagnant picture that sticks closely to the Gospel accounding to St. Luke. The dialogue, unfortunately, comes from the modern rather than the King James version with its exalted prose.
G. ★★
D: Peter Sykes and John Kirsh; W: Barnet Fishbein.
Cast: Brian Deacon, Niko Mitai, Alexander Scourby, Eli Danker.

JET PILOT. (1957) John Wayne, an American agent, in a typical Cold War exercise of unusual ineptitude that puts him in a hot and thoroughly implausible romance with a Russian spy. Utterly forgettable, or so the participants should hope.
★
D: Josef Von Sternberg; W: Jules Furthman; Ph: Winton C. Hoch; M. Bronislau Kaper.
Cast: John Wayne, Janet Leigh, Jay C. Flippen, Paul Fix.

JEZEBEL. (1938) To console Bette Davis for the fact that the part of Scarlett O'Hara had gone with the wind, Warner Brothers came up with what amounts to a rival star vehicle. Davis responded to the part of Julie Marston, a Southern belle who takes a dreadful toll on men's hearts, with a performance that won her the Oscar. The plot is a silly confection about Julie's efforts to make her fiance jealous.
★★★
D: William Wyler; W: Clements Ripley, John Huston and Abem Finkel; Ph: Ernest Haller; M: Max Steiner.

Cast: Bette Davis, Henry Fonda, George Brent, Margaret Lindsay.

JIM THORPE—ALL AMERICAN. (1951) There is a cruel irony to the title since Thorpe was deprived of his Olympic medals because of a professional football contract. They were only recently restored to his family. A pretty good athlete named Burt Lancaster plays an incredible one in Thorpe, an Indian who overcame poverty and prejudice to become the star of the 1912 Olympics. The biography forces Lancaster to hurdle some lame dialogue and the structure is standard. For all that, it's a winning performance.

★★★

D: Michael Curtiz; W: Everett Freeman and Douglas Morrow; Ph: Ernest Haller; M: Max Steiner.
Cast: Burt Lancaster, Charles Bickford, Steve Cochran, Phyllis Thaxter.

JINXED. (1982) Made amid much rancor between the star and a director who did not find the material congenial to his talent for action. You can hardly blame him since it forces Bette Midler to rely on her night club mannerisms and contrived tackiness. She is a lounge singer trying to make it to the big room and ditch a boorish gambler. Siegel visibly loses interest in the proceedings.
R.   ★
D: Don Siegel; W: Bert Blessing and David Newman; Ph: Vilmos Zsigmond; M: Bruce Roberts and Miles Goodman.
Cast: Bette Midler, Rip Torn, Ken Wahl, Val Avery.

JOHN AND MARY. (1969) Peter Yates is a director who can normally turn his hand to anything and make it interesting. His skills were not enough to make much of a one-night stand in the singles scene whose new morality—or rather lack of it—posed so many problems. Dustin Hoffman and Mia Farrow don't even exchange names until the morning after. The screenplay shares the characters' befuddlement over the new rules.

★★

D: Peter Yates; W: John Mortimer; Ph: Gayen Rescher; M: Quincy Jones.
Cast: Dustin Hoffman, Mia Farrow, Michael Tolan, Sunny Griffin.

JOHNNY APOLLO. (1940) A son is estranged from his father, who is jailed for embezzlement. In a somewhat contrived reaction, the young man becomes a gangster and winds up in the same jail as his father. Melodramatic, especially toward the end, but quite polished and Dorothy Lamour makes a good moll.

★★

D: Henry Hathaway; W: Philip Dunne and Rowland Brown; Ph: Arthur Miller; M: Cyril J. Mockridge.
Cast: Tyrone Power, Dorothy Lamour, Edward Arnold, Lloyd Nolan.

JOHNNY GUITAR.(1953) A western that is off the beaten trail in placing women at the center of the action. A woman who has built up a gambling establishment has to defend it from a posse of outraged townsfolk. She does so with the aid of a gunman.

★★★

D: Nicholas Ray; W: Philip Yordan; Ph: Harry Stradling; M: Victor Young.
Cast: Sterling Hayden, Joan Crawford, Scott Brady, Mercedes McCambridge.

JOHNNY TREMAIN. (1956) A boy's-eye-view of some of the pivotal events of the American revolution that is as educational as it is entertaining. The Disney studio assembled the film from two television shows recounting the adventures of a youth in Boston in 1773 and with the Sons of Liberty two years later. Quite sophisticated in its treatment of the time and the issues.

★★★

D: Robert Stevenson; W: Tom Blackburn; Ph: Charles Boyle; M: George Bruns.
Cast: Hal Stalmaster, Luana Patten, Jeff York, Sebastian Cabot.

THE JOKER IS WILD. (1957) Frank Sinatra as Joe E. Lewis, the comedian who was forced into that line of work when gangsters messed up his singing voice. Sinatra's in fine form and sings the standard "All the Way."

★★★

D: Charles Vidor; W: Oscar Saul; Ph: Daniel Fapp; M: Walter Scharf.
Cast: Frank Sinatra, Mitzi Gaynor, Eddie Albert, Jeanne Crain.

JONAH WHO WILL BE 25 IN THE YEAR 2000. (1976) A Swiss film that brings together eight refugees from the turbulence of the sixties some seven years later. They all took part in the student dissent and now struggle for ways to live in more placid and selfish times. The characters tend to be podiums for the

director's views as much as people, but this is a fresh treatment of a theme that is popular in American movies.
★★★
D: Alain Tanner; W: John Berger and Tanner; Ph: Renato Berta; M: Jean-Marie Senia.
Cast: Jean-Luc Bideau, Myriam Meziere, Roger Jendly.

JOSEPH ANDREWS. (1977) There is a great deal of difference between the literary quality of *Tom Jones* and *Joseph Andrews*, Henry Fielding's first picaresque novel. The film maintains the distance even though some of the same ingredients are here. Peter Firth is the naive hero who survives comic misadventures in eighteenth century England without learning much from them. The three-way irony of Tom Jones, the people who abuse him and the narrator is missing and the joy of the earlier film seems a little forced here.
R.
★★★
D: Tony Richardson; W: Alan Scott and Chris Bryant; Ph: David Watkin; M: John Addison.
Cast: Peter Firth, Ann-Margret, Michael Hordern, Beryl Reid.

JOURNEY BACK TO OZ. (1972) Liza Minnelli recreates her mother's celebrated role in *The Wizard of Oz* by lending her voice to the story of the wicked witch's scheme to practice urban renewal on Emerald City.
G.
★★★
D: Hal Sutherland; M: Sammy Cahn and James Van Heusen.

JOURNEY TO THE CENTER OF THE EARTH. (1959) The directions are in a pet rock that Pat Boone shows to scientist James Mason. In a hokey and good-natured rendering of Jules Verne's fantasy, things get shallower as the ensuing expedition goes deeper. The journey is interrupted by monsters, floods and even mushrooms. There is also a goose who easily out-acts Boone. So, for that matter, does his pet rock.
★★
D: Henry Levin; W: Walter Reisch and Charles Brackett; Ph: Leo Tover; M: Bernard Herrmann.
Cast: James Mason, Pat Boone, Arlene Dahl, Diane Baker.

JUAREZ. (1939) Another in the series of inspirational biographies from Paul Muni. As the Mexican revolutionary leader bent on ousting the Emperor Maximilian, Muni leads an able cast in a spectacular production that falls prey to its lofty aspirations. John Huston, a man who loves Mexico, wrote an accurate but strangely undramatic script. The picture is handsome but curiously uninvolving.
★★★
D: William Dieterle; W: John Huston; Ph: Tony Gaudio; M: Erich Wolfgang Korngold.
Cast: Bette Davis, Paul Muni, Claude Rains, Brian Aherne.

JUDGMENT AT NUREMBERG. (1961) For all the decency and humanity that Spencer Tracy imparts to the central figure of the American judge, the verdict has to be that Stanley Kramer and his passion for pontification should not have been let loose on such a juicy subject. The trials of the Nazi war criminals cry out for an ability to organize as well as moralize.
★★
D: Stanley Kramer; W: Abby Mann; Ph: Ernest Laszlo; M: Ernest Gold.
Cast: Spencer Tracy, Marlene Dietrich, Burt Lancaster, Richard Widmark.

JUGGERNAUT. (1974) Made during the height of the disaster movie fad, Richard Lester's tale of the hijacking of the luxury liner *Britannic* proved that class can do wonders for cliches. Richard Harris is charged with defusing a cache of bombs aboard the ship whose passengers cannot leave because of high seas. Deftly directed and blessed with an enjoyable supporting cast.
PG.
★★★
D: Richard Lester; W: Richard Alan Simmons; Ph: Gerry Fisher; M: Ken Thorne.
Cast: Richard Harris, Omar Sharif, David Hemmings, Anthony Hopkins.

JULIA. (1977) Fred Zinnemann takes a wrenching memoir and transforms it into a superlative film about the workings of memory. The movie, based on Lillian Hellman's *Pentimento*, recounts her friendship with Julia, a woman from a wealthy European family who takes up socialism and pays for it with her life in Nazi Germany. This is a relationship of commanding emotion set against a tapestry of Europe in 1939 and a world on the brink of barbarism. The seamlessly edited flashbacks of the friendship create a filmed image of the way memory functions and past motives influence present

conduct. The acting is just as memorable.
PG. ★★★★★
D: Fred Zinnemann; W: Alvin Sargent; Ph: Douglas Slocombe; M: George Delerue.
Cast: Jane Fonda, Vanessa Redgrave, Jason Robards, Maximilian Schell.

JULIUS CAESAR. (1953) The attention and publicity went to Marlon Brando's excellent Mark Antony, but the laurel crowns belong to James Mason's very moving Brutus and John Gielgud's aptly-judged Cassius. Otherwise, a well conceived and consistently high-minded view of Shakespeare that is attentive to the moral and political choices in the text.
★★★★
D and Adapted: Joseph L. Mankiewicz; Ph: Joseph Ruttenberg; M: Miklos Rozsa.
Cast: Marlon Brando, James Mason, John Gielgud, Greer Garson.

THE JUNGLE BOOK. (1967) An unfaithful but entertaining animated version of the Kipling tales from Walt Disney. Mowgli, an Indian boy, is left to fend for himself, is raised by the denizens of the jungle and likes it so much that he never wants to leave. Told at the leisurely pace of a camp-fire story.
★★★

D: Wolfgang Reithermann; M: George Bruns.
Cast: (Voices) Phil Harris, Sebastian Cabot, George Sanders, Louis Prima.

JUNGLE CAT. (1960) The last but certainly not the least of the True-Life series made by the Disney studio is a fascinating study of the South American jaguar. It was shot and edited with the care that was a hallmark of these documentaries and shows the jaguar's ingenuity in pursuing intransigent prey like alligators and boa constrictors.
★★★
D and W; James Algar; Ph: James R. Simon, *et. al.*; M: Oliver Wallace.
Cast: Winston Hibler(narrator).

JUST TELL ME WHAT YOU WANT. (1980) Alan King gives us a flamboyant and diverting answer to the question: What would a Jewish Howard Hughes be like? He gobbles up companies and collects mistresses. Ali McGraw, a television producer, is what he wants and the victim of his vengeance when she runs off with a young playwright.
R. ★★★
D: Sidney Lumet; W: Jay Presson Allen; Ph: Oswald Morris; M: Charles Strouse.
Cast: Alan King, Ali McGraw, Myrna Loy, Keenan Wynn.

K

KAGEMUSHA. (1980) In a magnificent elegy that amounts to a twilight masterpiece from Akira Kurosawa, a great artist contemplates delusion and reality. Kurosawa, with his incomparable gift for visual composition and keen sense of historic irony, takes a samurai fable about a thief who is forced to assume the identity of a dead warlord. Hence the title, which means "Shadow Warrior." The warlord knows his clan cannot survive his death because he has so many enemies. In the end, Kurosawa makes this an examination of how we are impelled not by the truth but by what we believe to be the truth.

★★★★★
D: Akira Kurosawa; W: Kurosawa and Masato Ide; Ph: Kazuo Mayagawa; M: Shinichiro Ikebe.
Cast: Tatsuro Nakadai, Tsutomu Yamazaki, Kenichi Hagiwara.

THE KEEP. (1983) Michael Mann, director of the excellent *Thief*, proved that one man's castle is another's debacle. In 1941, Nazi troops move into an ominous castle keep in Yugoslavia and unleash an evil that metaphorically reflects their own barbarism. The film itself shows no signs of reflection and matches its pretensions with a level of acting that deserves a stretch in the dungeon.
R. ★
D and W: Michael Mann; Ph: Alex Thomson; M: Tangerine Dream.
Cast: Scott Glenn, Alberta Watson, Juergen Prochnow, Robert Prosky.

THE KENTUCKIAN. (1955) A good-humored trip to the American frontier in the early nineteeth century that has two notable firsts: Burt Lancaster's bow as a director and Walter Matthau's debut in movies. Lancaster directs himself as a roustabout pioneer and wisely tosses in a lot of physical action with Nick Cravat. Matthau uses a bullwhip as the heavy in the kind of villainy he eventually escaped.
★★★
D: Burt Lancaster; W: A.B. Guthrie, Jr.; Ph: Ernest Laszlo; M: Bernard Herrmann.
Cast: Burt Lancaster, Diane Foster, Diana Lynn, Walter Matthau.

KENTUCKY. (1938) Lovers kept apart by a long-standing feud that goes back to an old Civil War grudge between two families.

Horse lovers may find the stables and racing sequences attractive. Walter Brennan won an Oscar as best supporting actor as the curmudgeon who keeps the feud going.
★★
D: David Butler; W: Lamar Trotti and John Taintor Foote; Ph: Ernest Palmer; M: Louis Silvers.
Cast: Richard Greene, Loretta Young, Walter Brennan, Douglas Dumbrille.

KENTUCKY FRIED MOVIE. (1977) Vulgar spoofs of movies, television and commercials that are as low as the bad taste they satirize. An occasional amusing moment, such as Henry Gibson demolishing celebrity telethons in a United Appeal for the Dead. But most of it is weak and some of the skits were out of date—like the disaster movie take-off—even when the film came out. The three writers went on to do the much funnier *Airplane*.
R. ★★
D: John Landis; W: David Zucker, Jerry Zucker, Jim Abrahams.

KEY LARGO. (1948) You can take Bogart's battles with a bunch of hoods in a Florida hotel as a metaphor for standing up to evil before it takes over everything. And with Hitler still a very fresh and unpleasant memory, some people did. Whether one of them was John Huston is open to debate. Or you can take it as no more than a rousing melodrama that pits Bogart against Edward G. Robinson. Bogie is a veteran who has lost his faith in causes until he returns to find Lauren Bacall, the widow of one of his men.
★★★
D: John Huston; W: Huston and Richard Brooks; Ph: Karl Freund; M: Max Steiner.
Cast: Humphrey Bogart, Lauren Bacall, Edward G. Robinson, Claire Trevor.

THE KEYS OF THE KINGDOM. (1944) The role that unlocked the door to stardom for Gregory Peck. In a pious, sincere and somewhat cumbersome version of A.J. Cronin's novel, Peck is an orphan who finds his place as a priest and his life's work as a missionary in China. The film traces his life from boyhood to reluctant retirement.
★★★
D: John M. Stahl; W: Joseph Mankiewicz and Nunnally Johnston; Ph: Arthur Miller; M: Alfred Newman.

Cast: Gregory Peck, Thomas Mitchell, Vincent Price, Rose Stradner.

KHARTOUM. (1966) The recurring complaint against Hollywood's long and dubious relationship with history is that the facts are never allowed to get in the way of a good story. Or even a bad one. This account of the conflict between General Gordon and Mahdi is far more faithful to the truth than most and Charlton Heston and Laurence Olivier generate considerable friction. The action takes place in the heat of the Sudan in the last century and the battles and sieges are handsomely staged.

★★★

D: Basil Dearden; W: Robert Ardrey; Ph: Edward Scaife and Harry Waxman; M: Frank Cordell.
Cast: Charlton Heston, Laurence Olivier, Ralph Richardson, Richard Johnson.

KID GALAHAD. (1937) A knockout boxing classic. Edward G. Robinson is a fight manager who turns a bell-hop into a boxer. Humphrey Bogart appears as a promoter and he remade the film four years later in *The Wagons Roll at Night*. It was done again and woefully as an Elvis Presley musical in 1962.

★★★★

D: Michael Curtiz; W: Seton Miller; Ph: Tony Gaudio; M: Max Steiner.
Cast: Edward G. Robinson, Bette Davis, Wayne Morris, Jane Bryan.

KIDNAPPED. (1938) Twentieth Century-Fox kidnapped Stevenson's title, but any connection with the book ends there. Freddie Bartholomew is a youngster whose kidnap is arranged by a greedy uncle after his inheritance. An adventurer helps him out. The background is Hollywood's notion of eighteenth century Scotland. Still a passable adventure.

★★

D: Alfred Werker; W: Sonya Levien and Eleanor Harris; Ph: Gregg Toland; M: Arthur Lange.
Cast: Warner Baxter, Freddie Bartholomew, Arleen Whelan, C. Aubrey Smith.

KIDNAPPED. (1960) Robert Stevenson, directing the children's classic by Robert Louis Stevenson, did not do enough editing. The faithful version of the book has some excellent scenes, but a lot of it is confusing and kids will have a hard time following who

did what to whom. A boy is kidnapped and becomes involved with a Scottish adventurer after an evil uncle disinherits him.

★★

D and W: Robert Stevenson; Ph: Paul Beeson; M: Cedric Thorpe Davie.
Cast: Peter Finch, James MacArthur, Bernard Lee, Niall MacGinnis.

THE KIDNAPPING OF THE PRESIDENT. (1980) The snatch takes place in Toronto and Hal Holbrook brings some class to an otherwise routine thriller as the President fo the U.S. The terrorists are cardboard cutouts of fanaticism and they want $100 million in diamonds for the President's release. Poor writing saps the tension.

R. ★★

D: George Mendeluk; W: Richard Murphy; Ph: Michael Malloy; M: Paul J. Zaza.
Cast: Hal Holbrook, William Shatner, Van Johnson, Ava Gardner.

THE KILLER ELITE. (1975) A lot of the movie is devoted to the searing orthopedic saga of James Caan recovering from a bullet in the knee. The rest of it, like Caan, proceeds with a pronounced limp. A private force undertakes assignments that are too dirty for the C.I.A. Yes, there are some. An Asian politician must be protected from Japanese terrorists. Part action film, which Peckinpah excels at, and part an obtuse essay of duplicity in high places. The second half, as a result, makes very little sense. Not violent by Peckinpah's standards.

PG. ★★

D: Sam Peckinpah; W: Marc Norman and Stirling Silliphant; Ph: Philip Lathrop; M: Jerry Fielding.
Cast: James Caan, Robert Duvall, Arthur Hill, Gig Young.

KILLER FORCE. (1976) A band of mercenaries tries to rob a South African diamond mine guarded by rejects from the Afrika Korps. As the raid starts, Peter Fonda announces flintily, "From here on in, we crawl" and the film does. It boasts such sallies as "Where were you when they handed out the feelings?" and has absolutely nothing to say about its political setting.

R. ★

D: Val Guest; W: Michael Winder, Gerald Sanford and Guest; Ph: David Millin; M: George Garvarentz.
Cast: Peter Fonda, Telly Savalas, Christopher Lee, Hugh O'Brian.

THE KILLERS. (1946) From Ernest Hemingway's story that posited the idea of a man who does not run from people trying to murder him. After the killing, an insurance investigator becomes obsessed with resolving this conumdrum. A first class thriller that marked the debut of Burt Lancaster in the part of the victim. There is a considerably more violent version directed by Don Siegel and released in 1964 with Lee Marvin, Ronald Reagan and John Cassavetes.

★★★★

D: Robert Siodmak; W: Anthony Veiller; Ph: Woody Bredell; M: Miklos Rozsa.
Cast: Edmond O'Brien, Ava Gardner, Burt Lancaster, Albert Dekker.

THE KILLING OF A CHINESE BOOKIE. (1976) Uncompromising, even by John Cassavetes' standards. He occasionally takes a part in a bad movie to raise the money for his own defiantly individualistic films. He has had his successes, but this is not one of them. Sprawling and exasperating study of a seedy Los Angeles night club owner who is ordered to kill a Chinese bookie to settle a debt. Atmospheric but empty.
R. ★★
D and W: John Cassavetes; M: Bo Harwood.
Cast: Ben Gazzara, Timothy Carey, Seymour Cassel, Morgan Woodward.

KIND HEARTS AND CORONETS. (1949) A delicious and macabre comedy with Alec Guinness doing no less than eight parts in a display of multiple virtuosity that Peter Sellers was later to make a specialty. Dennis Price, denied what he feels is his rightful claim to the title of the Duke of Chalfont, trims the family tree with eight ingenious murders. The victims are all played by Guinness and the ending is in keeping with the film's wry view of justice and social climbing.

★★★★

D: Robert Hamer; W: Hamer and John Dighton; Ph: Douglas Slocombe.
Cast: Alec Guinness, Dennis Price, Valerie Hobson, Joan Greenwood.

THE KING AND I. (1956) Yul Brynner played the king more than 4000 times on stage in two runs separated by 25 years. He liked to say that time and the women's movement made the musical more relevant. Age has not withered the charms of the musical nor dulled the magical score of the Rodgers and Hammerstein version of *Anna and the King of Siam*. The English governess eventually tames the barbarian king. Brynner

won the Oscar for his petulant monarch.

★★★★

D: Walter Lang; W: Ernest Lehman; Ph: Leon Shamroy; M: Richard Rodgers.
Cast: Yul Brynner, Deborah Kerr, Rita Moreno, Martin Benson.

KING KONG. (1933) The world's favorite ape scaled the Empire State building and in a half century no film has come along to challenge his postition at the top. The monarch of all monsters, Kong is brought from Skull Island to Manhattan Island where he develops a fit of pique. The film is, of course, a re-telling of beauty and the beast and one that succeeds because the audience is made to feel for the predicament of both. Despite the many advances in movie technology since the release of *King Kong*, the technical work is still amazingly good. Even though so many scenes from the classic have entered the screen hall of fame, they never lose their freshness and invention. The stature of *King Kong* is best measured against the supposedly high-tech remake (see below).

★★★★★

D: Merian Cooper and Ernest Schoedsack; W: James Creelam and Ruth Rose; Ph: Edward Linden, Verne Walker and J. O. Taylor; M: Max Steiner.
Cast: Fay Wray, Burce Cabot, Robert Armstrong, Frank Reicher.

KING KONG. (1976) "When Jaws die, nobody cry. When monkey die everybody cry," predicted producer Dino De Laurentiis in his bizarre English. If you have tears, prepare to shed them for this limp remake which revived the world's favorite ape after 43 years. The movie laughs at itself in all the wrong places and then tries for poignance and tension at the disappointing climax on top of the World Trade Center. It even passes off Kong as a symbol of Third World purity.
PG. ★★
D: John Guillermin; W: Lorenzo Semple, Jr.; Ph: Richard H. Kline; M: John Barry.
Cast: Jeff Bridges, Charles Grodin, Jessica Lange.

KING OF BURLESQUE. (1935) Behind the scenes on Broadway. Warner Baxter goes legit as a producer and gets into trouble when he marries a woman to match his new station in life. The usual morals and hoary cliches, but a pleasant enough score.

★★

D: Sidney Lanfield; W: Gene Markey and

Harry Tugend; Ph: Peverell Marley; M: Victor Baravelle.
Cast: Warner Baxter, Alice Faye, Jack Oakie, Arline Judge.

THE KING OF COMEDY. (1983) Another riveting portrait of contemporary derangement from Robert De Niro and Martin Scorsese. This time the madness is pathetic rather than criminal and the film is a sardonic study of our obsession with fame and stardom. Rupert Pupkin is an atrocious comedian who kidnaps a celebrated talk show host (a very good Jerry Lewis) in his desperation to make it. Scorsese's work is a black explanation of the kind of yearning that produces a Mark Chapman or a John Hinckley.
PG.   ★★★★
D: Martin Scorsese; W: Paul Zimmerman; Ph: Fred Schuler; M: Robbie Robertson.
Cast: Robert De Niro, Jerry Lewis, Sandra Bernhard, Diahnne Abbott.

KING OF KINGS. (1961) When Jeffrey Hunter was chosen to play Jesus there was much snide humor. In fact, the completed production is a far more commendable foray into religious terrain that has encouraged all kinds of excess. It's an unadorned and straightforward dramatization of Christ's life with acting that is persuasive instead of the arthritic and solemn utterance common to such undertakings.
                                       ★★★
D: Nicholas Ray; W: Philip Yordan; Ph: Franz Planer; M: Miklos Rozsa.
Cast: Jeffrey Hunter, Robert Ryan, Siobhan McKenna, Frank Thring.

KING OF THE GYPSIES. (1978) A meandering and entertaining melodrama that deals with a young man who would not be king and the inevitable conflict that arises between tribal loyalties and a desire for a life of his own. The struggle of the gypsies to retain their way of life in a shopping-malled America is more arresting than the personal frictions.
R.   ★★★
D and W: Frank Pierson; Ph: Sven Nykvist; M: David Grisman.
Cast: Eric Roberts, Sterling Hayden, Susan Sarandon, Shelley Winters.

KING OF THE KHYBER RIFLES. (1953) Tyrone Power is an officer but his colleagues are not sure he's a gentleman. When a chap's a half-caste he has to prove the stiffness of his upper lip by slaughtering as many of the natives as possible, thereby winning a place in the mess and the love of the commander's comely daughter. A remake of John Ford's *The Black Watch*.
                                       ★★
D: Henry King; W: Ivan Goff and Ben Roberts; Ph: Leon Shamroy; M: Bernard Herrmann.
Cast: Tyrone Power, Terry Moore, Michael Rennie, John Justin.

KING OF THE MOUNTAIN. (1981) Young L.A. daredevils race against each other on Mulholland Drive. One of them allows, "I could drive that course blindfolded." You might try the same tack with the film. Any hopes for that are dashed when you realize that the director and writer take the racers with absolute seriousness. Incidentally, they do all their high speed antics without ever encountering civilian traffic. In Los Angeles?
PG.   ★
D: Noel Nosseck; W: H.R. Christian; Ph: Donald Peterman; M: Michael Melvoin.
Cast: Harry Hamlin, Dennis Hopper, Joseph Bottoms, Deborah Van Valkenburgh.

KING RICHARD AND THE CRUSADERS. (1954) The alleged inspiration of a truly dopey historical film is Sir Walter Scott's *The Talisman*. It is utterly without charm and its connection with the book is barely recognizable. For that, at least, Scott lovers can be grateful. The actors certainly needed their armor to deflect criticism. George Sanders essays Richard the Lion-Heart with a visibly faint heart. Saladin is done by Rex Harrison, who dyed his skin brown probably so he could later claim he was never in the wretched epic.
                                       ★
D: David Butler; W: John Twist; Ph: Peverell Marley; M: Max Steiner.
Cast: Rex Harrison, George Sanders, Virginia Mayo, Laurence Harvey.

KING'S ROW. (1942) The royalty among movie soap operas and an instance of what can be done with first-rate talent and commitment on both sides of the camera. And that includes Ronald Reagan, who has a right to be proud of his work in a dissection of the seamy underside of life in a small American town before World War I. It is often called a precursor to *Peyton Place*, but it is far better and the Korngold score underpins the dark emotions in the film.
                                       ★★★★
D: Sam Wood; W: Casey Robinson; Ph:

James Wong Howe; M: Erich Wolfgang Korngold.
Cast: Anne Sheridan, Ronald Reagan, Robert Cummings, Claude Rains.

KISSIN' COUSINS. (1964) A double helping of Elvis Presley—as an Air Force public relations officer and a mountain yokel—but only half as good as his better musicals. Elvis the officer has to persuade the rubes that there's really nothing wrong with having a missile installation in their community. ★★
D: Gene Nelson; W: Nelson and Gerald Drayson Adams; Ph: Ellis Carter; M: Fred Karger.
Cast: Elvis Presley, Arthur O'Connell, Glenda Farrell, Jack Albertson.

KISS ME DEADLY. (1955) The French, especially Francois Truffaut, have a great deal of admiration for Robert Aldrich's elevation of Mickey Spillane's novel. It is a stylized and moody treatment of a pulp story about a ring of spies and a cache of valuable radioactive material. Mike Hammer, Spillane's hero, foils the spies, but it's really a case of style overwhelming substance. Aldrich ranked it with his best work. ★★★
D: Robert Aldrich; W: A.I. Bezzerides; Ph: Ernest Laszlo; M: Frank de Vol.
Cast: Ralph Meeker, Albert Dekker, Maxine Cooper, Paul Stewart.

KISS ME GOODBYE. (1982) Robert Mulligan's ghost story has geniality in its favor and little else. One member of its eternal triangle has gone to his eternal reward, but the payoff on earth is a lot more temporary. It depends on the single comic irony of a widow talking to the ghost while others find her behavior strange. He returns to try to disrupt her remarriage.
PG. ★★
D: Robert Mulligan; W: Charles Peters; Ph: Donald Peterman; M: Ralph Burns.
Cast: James Caan, Sally Field, Jeff Bridges, Paul Dooley.

KISS OF DEATH. (1947) The famous scene in which a cackling Richard Widmark made his mark as a psycho killer by pushing Mildred Dunnock and her wheelchair down the stairs has long since obscured the other merits of Henry Hathaway's gritty melodrama. These include a fine Victor Mature portrait of a petty hood driven to rat on his accomplices and an authentic New York locale. ★★★
D: Henry Hathaway; W: Ben Hecht and Charles Lederer; Ph: Norbert Brodine; M: David Buttolph.
Cast: Victor Mature, Brian Donlevy, Richard Widmark, Taylor Holmes.

THE KLANSMAN. (1974) Local necks get redder by the minute as civil rights activists in Alabama keep "botherin' our nigras." The thick-headed plot tries to encompass racial attitudes from the plantation days to the present and klansmen mingle with unswatted superflies. Richard Burton essays a Southern accent with hilarious results as the owner of a mountain outside town and a liberal bias. Lee Marvin is the sheriff trying to keep the lid on things.
R. ★
D: Terence Young; W: Millard Kaufman and Samuel Fuller; Ph: Lloyd Ahern and Aldo Tonti; M: Dale Warren and Stu Gardner.
Cast: Richard Burton, Lee Marvin, O.J. Simpson, Cameron Mitchell.

KLUTE. (1971) Within the constrictions of a mature thriller whose somewhat predictable developments didn't allow a great deal of room, Jane Fonda found the space to fashion an astonishlingly detailed and engrossing portrait of a high-level call girl. It is a study that shows the penalties and rewards that a certain kind of personality can find. The surrounding action is grown-up and finely constructed by Alan Pakula. Donald Sutherland is a cop who becomes involved with her while investigating a disappearance. A deserved Academy Award went to Fonda.
R. ★★★★
D: Alan Pakula; W: Andy Lewis and Dave Lewis; Ph: Gordon Willis; M: Michael Small.
Cast: Jane Fonda, Donald Sutherland, Roy Scheider, Charles Cioffi.

KNOCK ON ANY DOOR. (1949) Nicolas Ray's feeling for the plight of youth got the better of him. John Derek is on trial and the social forces that turned him into a criminal are outlined in flashback. Humphrey Bogart makes his plea as the defense attorney. The issues raised are still very much with us but they are clumsily aired here. ★★
D: Nicholas Ray; W: Daniel Taradash and John Monks, Jr.; Ph: Burnett Guffey; M: George Anthell.

Cast: Humphrey Bogart, John Derek, George Macready, Ellene Roberts.

KNIGHTRIDERS. (1981) Cult horror director George Romero (*Night of the Living Dead* etc.) stepped out of the bloodbath to make a curiosity—Camelot on wheels. A group of men tour the country, put on motor-bike jousts and live by the code of the Knights of the Round Table. The parallels don't work and the sword stays stuck in the stone in spite of Romero's game effort to pull it out.
R. ★★
D and W: George Romero; Ph: Michael Gornick; M: Donald Rubinstein.
Cast: Ed Harris, Gary Lahti, Tom Savini, Amy Ingersoll.

KNIGHTS OF THE ROUND TABLE. (1954) There is more vitality in the figures in a medieval tapestry than in the actors in this routine run-through of the story of Camelot's triangle of Arthur, Lancelot and Guinevere. Lack-luster action and a score far better than the movie deserves. Robert Taylor did better in armor in *Ivanhoe*.
★★
D: Richard Thorpe; W: Talbot Jennings, Jan Lustig and Noel Langley; Ph: Frederick Young; M: Miklos Rozsa.
Cast: Robert Taylor, Mel Ferrer, Ava Gardner, Anne Crawford.

KNUTE ROCKNE, ALL AMERICAN. (1940) "Win it for the Gipper" was later to take on an ominous Republican meaning when Ronald Reagan ran for the White House. In a biography of the celebrated football coach, he does the running for Notre Dame as George Gipp. Unashamed and emotional in its treatment of the subject.
★★
D: Lloyd Bacon; W: Robert Buckner; Ph: Tony Gaudio.
Cast: Pat O'Brien, Ronald Reagan, Gale Page, Donald Crisp.

KOYAANISQATSI. (1983) A fabulous fusion of sound and image which argues convincingly that a picture is worth a thousand words. There are none here, just Godfrey Reggio's images of natural splendor and industrial squalor and Philip Glass' mesmerizing score. The film is built on contrasts to support the meaning of its title, which is Hopi Indian for "life out of balance." A highly original production that took seven years to create.
★★★★
D: Godfrey Reggio; W: Reggio and Ron Fricke; Ph: Ron Fricke; M: Philip Glass.

KRAMER VS. KRAMER. (1979) Some women complained about a mysogynist streak in Robert Benton's superb study of the intolerable dilemma created by an unhappy marriage and the presence of a child. Meryl Streep leaves Dustin Hoffman to fume, "Daddy's gotta bring home the bacon *and* cook it" and raise their son. Hoffman, in one of his great roles, emerges from the confusion of sexual love to find the unadulterated kind offered by his son. Sensitively written, memorably acted and justly honored with Oscars.
PG. ★★★★★
D and W: Robert Benton; Ph: Nestor Almendros; M: Erma E. Levin.
Cast: Dustin Hoffman, Meryl Streep, Justin Henry, Jane Alexander.

KRONOS. (1957) A giant metal monster from outer space with an Arabic mentality tries to steal the earth's energy. Jeff Morrow makes the world safe for man and auto.
★★
D: Kurt Neumann; W: Lawrence Lewis Goldman; Ph: Kurt Struss; M: Paul Sawtell.
Cast: Jeff Morrow, Barbara Lawrence, John Emery, George O'Hanlon.

KRULL. (1983) A $27 million equivalent of a Chinese menu with one from Column A (*Excalibur*), one from Column B (*Flash Gordon, Star Wars*) and a selection of appetizers from other movies. Peter Yates brings no magic to an overblown piece of sword and sorcery featuring the familiar quest of a young king to rescue his bride from Slayers who turn into reptiles when they are zapped. You'll be hungry for something else an hour after *Krull* is mercifully over.
PG. ★
D: Peter Yates; W: Stanford Sherman; Ph: Peter Suchitsky; M: James Horner.
Cast: Ken Marshall, Lysette Anthony, Freddie Jones, Francesca Annis.

L

LA BALANCE. (1983) Bob Swaim, an American who has lived in Paris for many years, struck a wonderful balance between traditional gangster film ingredients and the strengths of French cinema. He added a pinch of gallic to the tale of cops and thieves in Paris' tough Belleville section. He created a swiftly-paced and forcefully acted movie that ponders the ancient issue of the difference between what is right and what is legal. A special police squad blackmails a pimp into becoming an informer.
R. ★★★★
D: Bob Swaim; W: Swaim and M. Fabiani; Ph: Bernard Zitzermann; M: Roland Bocquet.
Cast: Philippe Leotard, Nathalie Baye, Richard Berry, Christophe Malavoy.

LA CAGE AUX FOLLES. (1979) Far superior to the Broadway musical it inspired, this sophisticated French farce has a lot of fun at the expense of sexual bigots. Two middle-aged homosexuals who have lived together for years over a risque transvestite nightclub face a domestic crisis. The son of one them decides to marry the daughter of a moral majority-style politician. Ugo Tognazzi and Michel Serrault, as the lovers, bring a great deal of humanity to their characters and that enriches a basically broad comedy.
R. ★★★
D: Edouard Molinaro; W: Francis Veber; Ph: Armando Mannuzzi; M: Ennio Morricone.
Cast: Ugo Tognazzi, Michel Serrault, Michel Galabru, Remy Laurent.

LA CAGE AUX FOLLES II. (1981) *La Cage aux Folles* was an enormous crossover success with both straights and gays and surely one reason was the hard slap it took at common assumptions about homosexuality. The sequel was fashioned with a limp wrist. This time, the butt of the jokes is not heterosexual bigotry, but the twittering queen done so well by Michel Serrault. The movie makes fun of the night club owner and his lover and then tries to present their relationship as noble at the end. The plot is a weak spy spoof with many changes of dress and scenery.
R. ★★
D: Edouard Molinaro; W: Francis Veber; Ph: Armando Nannuzzi; M: Ennio Morricone.
Cast: Ugo Tognazzi, Michel Serrault, Marcel Bozzuffi, Michel Galabru.

THE LACEMAKER. (1977) A movie that is, like a piece of Chantilly lace, exquisitely crafted with an infinite care for detail. Isabelle Huppert is marvelous as a naive working girl drawn to an affair with the sort of student churned out by French universities—a somber and self-important bore. The film deals with the cost of a special kind of arrogance and snobbery and has a measured contempt for men who try to remake women to their own specifications.
★★★★
D: Claude Goretta; W: Goretta and Pascal Laine; Ph: Jean Boffety; M: Pierre Jansen.
Cast: Isabelle Huppert, Yves Beneyton, Florence Giorgetti, Anne Marie.

LA CHIENNE. (1931) The title means "the bitch" and refers to the wife of a downtrodden cashier. The film is Jean Renoir's first venture into sound and is of far more than historical interest. Renoir replenishes a familiar triangle involving the cashier, the whore he loves and the pimp she adores by injecting dark humor into what could be merely a routine melodrama.
★★★★
D: Jean Renoir; W: Renoir and Pierre Schwab; Ph: Theodore Sparkhul.
Cast: Michel Simon, Janie Mareze, Georges Flamant, Magdeleine Berubet.

LACOMBE, LUCIEN. (1974) An oafish youth, Lucien Lacombe, spurned by the Resistance in World War II France, joins the Vichy police as an informer. He becomes involved with a Jewish tailor and his daughter and is alternately crude in the use of his powers and clumsy in his displays of affection. Louis Malle sees him as just as much a victim as his prey in one of the most sophisticated French films about the touchy subject of collaboration.
R. ★★★★
D: Louis Malle; W: Malle and Patrick Modiano; Ph: Tonino Delli Colli; M: Django Reinhardt.
Cast: Pierre Blaise, Aurore Clement, Holger Lowenadier, Therese Gieshe.

LADY AND THE TRAMP. (1955) A lighthearted Disney romance in the dog-eat-dog world. Walt said the story gave him some freedom to create because it was not a beloved classic. The results are middling animation and several servings of syrup. A snobbish dog enjoys a canine romance and several hair-raising adventures with mutt from the wrong side of the track.

★★★

D: Hamilton Luske, Clyde Geronimi, Wilfred Jackson; W: Erdman Penner, Joe Rinaldi, Ralph Wright and Donald Da Gradi; M: Oliver Wallace.
Cast: (Voices) Peggy Lee, Barbara Luddy, Larry Roberts, Bill Thompson.

THE LADY EVE. (1941) Henry Fonda is a millionaire who has a passion for herpetology, but who can't recognize a snake in the grass when Barbara Stanwyck appears. A romantic farce set aboard a liner crossing the Atlantic, it combines two effortless and effervescent stars with the light touch and sure pacing of Preston Sturges. It's one of the director's funniest films.

★★★★

D and W: Preston Sturges; Ph: Victor Milner; M: Leo Shuken.
Cast: Henry Fonda, Barbara Stanwyck, Charles Coburn, Eugene Pallette.

THE LADY FROM SHANGHAI. (1947) Orson Welles' bizarre thriller has a climax that is literally all done by mirrors and a world-weary observation that "Everybody is somebody's fool sometime." His Michael O'Hara is a young Irishman who joins a rich man's yacht and is asked to fake a disappearance that becomes an actual murder. The ending in the hall of mirrors pits Welles against Rita Hayworth, who was soon to become the former Mrs. Welles. That may explain the way the movie treats the heroine.

★★★

D and W: Orson Welles; Ph: Charles Lawton, Jr.; M: Heinz Roemhld.
Cast: Orson Welles, Rita Hayworth, Everett Sloane, Glenn Anders.

LADY IN CEMENT. (1968) Frank Sinatra in his second Tony Rome private eye flick. Somebody has dropped a concrete-shod woman into Biscayne Bay and the film proceeds in the same direction when Rome asks why.

★★

D: Gordon Douglas; W: Marvin H. Albert and Jack Guss; Ph: Joseph Biroc; M: Hugo Montenegro.
Cast: Frank Sinatra, Raquel Welch, Richard Conte, Martin Gabel.

LADY IN THE LAKE. (1947) Robert Montgomery's idea was to use the camera to make the viewer see the world and the case at hand through the eyes of the detective. It becomes an almost frivolous and wearing gimmick that really adds nothing to perception or understanding. The Raymond Chandler story, as was his custom, is full of hairpin turns and dead-ends and the trickery gets in the way. Philip Marlowe is on the trail of a missing wife.

★★

D: Robert Montgomery; W: Steve Fisher; Ph: Paul Vogel; M: David Snell.
Cast: Robert Montgomery, Lloyd Nolan, Audrey Totter, Tom Tully.

THE LADYKILLERS. (1955) A *Kind Hearts and Coronets* among the lower classes and an equally splendid black comedy. A gang of amiable rogues plans a robbery in a boarding house while pretending to practice a Boccherini quintet. After the crime, their sweet old landlady finds out and their efforts to kill her keep backfiring. Cheerfully nasty with Alec Guinness leading the thieves and Peter Sellers making an early mark in movies.

★★★★

D: Alexander Mackendrick; W: William Rose; Ph: Otto Heller; M: Tristram Cary.
Cast: Alec Guinness, Cecil Parker, Herbert Lom, Peter Sellers.

LADY SINGS THE BLUES. (1972) A powerhouse account of Billie Holliday's losing battle with drugs from Diana Ross, who is nothing short of supreme. Unfortunately, the movie surrounding her is addicted to the cost-of-success and downfall-through-drugs cliches. Holliday's life from her days as a maid in a Baltimore brothel to her travails with heroin is offered with some factual liberties. To her credit, Ross doesn't try to imitate a voice that is unique in American music, but creates a special blues sound that has its own validity and impact.

R. ★★★

D: Sidney J. Furie; W: Terence McCloy, Chris Clark and Suzanne De Passe; Ph: John Alonzo; M: Michel Legrand.
Cast: Diana Ross, Billy Dee Williams, Richard Pryor, James Callahan.

THE LADY VANISHES. (1938) No director handled strangeness on a train—or anywhere else for that matter—with the aplomb of Alfred Hitchcock. A tantalizing blend of humor and suspense built around the disappearance of an old lady on a transcontinental express. A girl who met her and a musician search and uncover a nasty spy ring.

★★★★

D: Alfred Hitchcock; W: Sidney Gilliat and Frank Launder; Ph: Jack Cox; M: Louis Levy. Cast: Michael Redgrave, Margaret Lockwood, Paul Lukas, Dame May Whitty.

LA GRANDE BOURGEOISIE. (1977) An elaborate retelling of a sensational murder in 1897 Bologna that describes how the investigation escalated into a major political issue. A brother plots the killing of his sister's violent husband, thus putting an end to "this life sentence blessed by the Holy Roman Church." There are incestuous undertones to the act of brotherly love. Bolgnini, besides giving us a visually ravishing film, furnishes an intimate view of the principals and their motives. It allows us to measure them against the public consequences of their acts.

★★★★

D: Mauro Bolognini; W: Sergio Bazzini and Bolognini; Ph: Ennio Guarnieri; M: Ennio Morricone.
Cast: Giancarlo Giannini, Catherine Deneuve, Fernando Rey, Marcel Bazzuffi.

LA LUNA. (1979) Bertolucci said that incest is a fantasy that lurks in all of us and that only in consummation is it perversion. His vacuous work is merely perverse. An American opera singer and her 15-year-old son are the protagonists but the psychological exploration necessary is missing. The mother is unbelievable and the son is a whining bore. So is the movie.
R.   ★
D: Bernardo Bertolucci; W: Giuseppe and Bernardo Bertolucci and Clare Peploe; Ph: Vittorio Storaro; M: Various opera composers.
Cast: Jill Clayburgh, Matthew Barry, Laura Betti, Renato Salvatori.

LANCELOT OF THE LAKE. (1975) A French re-telling of the Arthurian legend and one of the most striking and original ever filmed. Robert Bresson sees Lancelot's dilemma over Guinevere as conflict between religious scruples and lust rather than one dividing his loyalties between King Arthur and his Queen. The view of medieval life is unsparing and this account has only been bested by *Excalibur*.

★★★★

D and W: Robert Bresson; Ph: Pasqualino de Santis; M: Philippe Sarde.

Cast: Luc Simon, Laura Duke Condominas, Humbert Balsan, Patrick Bernard.

LARCENY INC. (1942) An ingratiatingly done if not original farce that plays off the old adage about crime and payment. The performances, especially the harried Edward G. Robinson, are smoothly professional. He is an ex-con who buys a luggage shop next to a bank and finds his plans to burrow through to the vault disrupted when business starts booming.

★★★

D: Lloyd Bacon; W: Everett Freeman and Edwin Gilbert; Ph: Tony Gaudio.
Cast: Edward G. Robinson, Jane Wyman, Broderick Crawford, Anthony Quinn.

LASSITER. (1984) Tom Selleck's second attempt to translate his huge television popularity to the big screen is less than a Magnum opus. He is a jewel thief in 1939 London who is blackmailed by the cops into stealing a fortune in diamonds from the German embassy. For a caper movie it is remarkably weak in the vital areas of plot and pace and Selleck is stiff and uncomfortable.
R.   ★★
D: Roger Young; W: David Taylor; Ph: Gil Taylor; M: Ken Thorne.
Cast: Tom Selleck, Jane Seymour, Lauren Hutton, Bob Hoskins.

THE LAST DAYS OF POMPEII. (1935) Only the volcano remains from the book. The scenarists forged a story about a blacksmith who comes to realize the vanity of wealth before the set is engulfed in lava. The spectacle isn't worth the melodrama.

★★★

D: Ernest Schoedsack; W: Ruth Rose and Boris Ingster; Ph: Eddie Linden, Jr; M: Roy Webb.
Cast: Basil Rathbone, Preston Foster, Alan Hale, Dorothy Cooper.

THE LAST DETAIL. (1974) A young sailor who knows nothing about life is sentenced to eight years in the brig for petty theft. The dubious honor of escorting him from Virginia to New Hampshire falls to Jack Nicholson, a foul-mouthed veteran, and Otis Young. Hal Ashby takes a serio-comic view of their escapades and *The Last Detail* is both funny and touching. Nicholson's enormously energetic performance propels the film.
R.   ★★★★

D: Hal Ashby; W: Robert Towne; Ph: Michael Chapman; M: Johnny Mandel.
Cast: Jack Nicholson, Randy Quaid, Otis Young, Clifton James.

THE LAST EMBRACE. (1979) There are really two movies competing for limited space in a frequently flashy Hitchcock tribute. One finds espionage agent Roy Scheider convinced that someone is trying to kill him, possibly his superior in a nebulous intelligence agency. The other is a bizarre character (Janet Margolin) with a genuinely odd reason for killing people. The two elements pull the movie in different directions and it winds up in aimless circles. A scintillating gunfight in a belfry and a climax at Niagara Falls make it worth a look.
R.   ★★
D: Jonathan Demme; W: David Shaber; Ph: Tak Fujimoto; M: Miklos Rozsa.
Cast: Roy Scheider, Janet Margolin, Sam Levene, John Glover.

THE LAST HARD MEN. (1976) Andrew McLaglen sowed a wild oater in this attempt to film another elegy to the passing of the west and its heroes. "A man who has to think twice ain't no man," observes James Coburn and no one connected with the film loses his manhood. Charlton Heston is a lawman on the trail of Coburn, a fugitive who blames him for the death of his wife. Their confrontation has all the interest of two scorpions duelling under a rock.
R.   ★★
D: Andrew V. McLaglen; W: Guerdon Trueblood; Ph: Duke Callaghan; M: Jerry Goldsmith.
Cast: Charlton Heston, James Coburn, Barbara Hershey.

THE LAST HURRAH. (1958) John Ford, who gave a lyric humor to *The Quiet Man* and a hard touch to *the Informer*, takes up the Irish on this side of the water. Spencer Tracy's Frank Skeffington is a wily old pro on his final campaign and life on the hustings is enlivened by an assortment of well-drawn characters and a rich sense of humor.
★★★
D: John Ford; W: Frank Nugent; Ph: Charles Lawton, Jr.
Cast: Spencer Tracy, Jeffrey Hunter, Dianne Foster, Pat O'Brien.

THE LAST MARRIED COUPLE IN AMERICA. (1980) It is not marriage but wit that is the endangered species in Gilbert Cates'

film, which amounts to little more than sex and a single joke. George Segal and Natalie Wood are the couple trying to stay together in the midst of epidemic divorce. The film veers between satire and sermon and features several boring upscale Californians. Its humor sputters like a malfunctioning jacuzzi.
R.   ★★
D: Gilbert Cates; W: John Herman Shaner; Ph: Ralph Woolsey; M: Charles Fox.
Cast: Natalie Wood, George Segal, Richard Benjamin, Valerie Curtin.

THE LAST METRO. (1981) Francois Truffaut did not try to have the last word on collaboration and anti-Semitism during the German occupation of France. He is more taken by the intricate drama and responses of men and women under pressure in a wartime theater in Paris. Catherine Deneuve tries to run the company and cope with actors who accept the way things are or decide to resist. Courage rather than cowardice holds center stage and some of the larger issues get lost in the glare of the footlights. Nonetheless, *The Last Metro* is a deeply affecting film on its own terms.
R.   ★★★★
D: Francois Truffaut; W: Truffaut, Suzanne Schiffman and Jean-Claude Grumberg; Ph: Nestor Almendros; M: Georges Delerue.
Cast: Catherine Deneuve, Gerard Depardieu, Jean Poiret, Andrea Ferreol.

THE LAST PICTURE SHOW. (1971) Peter Bogdanovich's subsequent career proved highly erratic, but he would deserve a place in film history anyway for his second feature. It should be required viewing for those who know him only through later mistakes and for the legions of hacks churning out rites of passage movies for the teen market today. It is one of the most sensitive, exquisitely detailed and touching portraits of growing pains in movies. The action is set in the fifties in a small Texas town and the nostalgic tone never weighs down the movie.
★★★★★
D: Peter Bogdanovich; W: Bogdanovich and Larry McMurty; Ph: Robert Surtees.
Cast: Timothy Bottoms, Jeff Bridges, Cloris Leachman, Ben Johnson.

THE LAST REMAKE OF BEAU GESTE. (1977) The late Marty Feldman's first effort as a director is like one of those forced marches in the Foreign Legion movies it spoofs. It begins in good spirits, flags under the merciless dictates of its length and picks

itself up for a panting finish. Feldman's debt as a parodist to his mentor, Mel Brooks, is obvious, but he brought a decidedly zany English note to the lampooning. An enjoyable English cast led by Michael York and Feldman as "identical" twins.
PG. ★★★
D: Marty Feldman; W: Feldman and Chris J. Allen ; Ph: Gerry Fisher; M: John Morris.
Cast: Marty Feldman, Michael York, Ann-Margret, Peter Ustinov.

THE LAST STARFIGHTER. (1984) Nick Castle owes a lot to Spielberg and Lucas, but while his grab-bag teen fantasy is derivative, its sense of humor is original. A video whiz kid gets whisked away to outer space to fight real battles as the last hope of the universe. Hokey fun and blessed with some old pros like Robert Preston and Dan O'Herlihy (He's the one underneath all that lizard make-up). The special effects are almost entirely computer-generated.
PG. ★★★
D: Nick Castle; W: Jonathan Betuel; Ph: King Baggot; M: Craig Safan.
Cast: Lance Guest, Robert Preston, Dan O'Herlihy, Catherine Mary Stewart.

LAST TANGO IN PARIS. (1972) In its day, a *cause celebre* in which more attention was paid to Marlon Bando's sexual prowess than the remarkable quality of his performance. The sex is simulated and the language strong and, apart from Brando, *Last Tango* is as dull as as the last dance at an overlong ball. He is Paul, an American widower recovering from his loss in a purely physical relationship. Paul believes that sex makes life tolerable. Maybe, but this movie needs something more to support the weight of its pretensions.
★★
D: Bernardo Bertolucci; W: Bertolucci and Franco Arcalli; Ph: Vittorio Storaro; M: Gato Barbieri.
Cast: Marlon Brando, Maria Schneider, Darling Legitimus, Jean Pierre Leaud.

THE LAST TYCOON. (1976) Harold Pinter—he of the spoken enigma and the pregnant pause—cannot accommodate his brilliant style to Fitzgerald's twilight visions. And Elia Kazan cannot accomodate himself to Pinter. But De Niro's Monroe Stahr, the young Hollywood mogul obsessed with a girl who reminds him of his dead wife, is riveting. It includes a speech on the hold movies exercise on the popular imagination that is

destined for the anthologies. Not up to what the credits would lead one to hope.
PG. ★★★
D: Elia Kazan; W: Harold Pinter; Ph: Victor Kemper; M: Maurice Jarre.
Cast: Robert De Niro, Robert Mitchum, Tony Curtis, Jeanne Moreau.

THE LAST UNICORN. (1982) The last word in tacky animation and not even kids whose standards have been set by Saturday morning cartoons are likely to find anything to enjoy in it. That work of this woeful calibre was passed of as a feature film is a piece of arrant cynicism. The story of the adventures of a unicorn is less than enchanting too.
G. ★
D: Arthur Rankin and Jules Bass; W: Peter S. Beagle; Ph: Hiroyasu Omoto; M: Jimmy Webb.
Cast: (voices) Alan Arkin, Jeff Bridges, Mia Farrow, Tammy Grimes.

THE LAST WALTZ. (1978) The final concert of the Band afer sixteen years together produced a superlative rock film. Martin Scorsese disdained the standard procedures and moved around the event to give it a sense of occasion. The Band is joined by a Who's Who of friends including Joni Mitchell, Bob Dylan, Eric Clapton and Neil Diamond.
PG. ★★★★
D: Martin Scorsese; Ph: Michael Chapman, Laszlo Kovacs et. al.

THE LAST WAVE. (1978) A daring and highly effective Australian thriller that fuses suspense and the supernatural. A Sydney lawyer (Richard Chamberlain) defends some aborigines in a murder case and begins having nightmares and visions that he does not understand. The film builds to a chilling, apocalyptic climax with Chamberlain caught between the familiar and the incredible.
PG. ★★★★
D: Peter Weir; W: Weir, Tony Morphett and Petru Popescu; Ph: Russell Boyd; M: Charles Wain.
Cast: Richard Chamberlain, Olivia Hamnet, Frederick Parslow, Vivean Gray.

THE LATE SHOW. (1977) Robert Benton takes every time-honored cliche of the private eye movie and casts them adrift in contemporary Los Angeles, and there is nothing more adrift than contemporary L.A. Art Carney, who excels in portraits of aging, is an over-the-hill detective whose spirit is still willing but whose flesh is all too weak. Lily

Tomlin offers effective counterpoint as a small-time drug dealer. But Benton invested all his inspiration in the two characters and the Chandlerian plot becomes confusion and sloppiness masquerading as complexity.
PG. ★★★
D and W: Robert Benton; Ph:Chuck Rosher; M: Ken Wannberg.
Cast: Art Carney, Lily Tomlin, Bill Macy, Ruth Nelson.

LA TRAVIATA. (1983) Most directors, faced with the incandescent passions in Verdi's tragic vision, would bank the fires. Franco Zeffirelli keeps everything at white heat in this gorgeously mounted rendering of the opera. The doomed love of Violetta and Alfredo is told in flashbacks, a daring and highly effective approach that gives inexorable weight to the drama. Teresa Stratas, as Violetta, is both an accomplished actress and a splendid singer. This production ranks with Bergman's *The Magic Flute* as the best opera film ever made.
PG. ★★★★★
D and W:: Franco Zeffirelli; ; Ph: Ennio Guarnieri; M: James Levine (conducting the Metropolitan Opera Orchestra).
Cast: Teresa Stratas, Placido Domingo, Cornell MacNeil, Alan Monk.

THE LAUGHING POLICEMAN. (1973) The crime is no laughing matter—a killer opens fire on a bus filled with passengers. One of them is a cop and Walter Matthau and Bruce Dern team to track down the murderer. San Francisco substitutes for Stockholm in what was originally a Martin Beck thriller. Matthau and Dern make an entertaining and contrasting pair. Gays will not be happy with the rationale for the murders.
★★★
D: Stuart Rosenberg; W: Thomas Rickman; Ph: David Walsh; M: Charles Fox.
Cast: Walter Matthau, Bruce Dern, Lou Gossett, Albert Paulsen.

LAURA. (1944) Rouben Mamoulian directed some of the sequences in one of the most riveting mysteries of the forties or any other decade and then stepped down. Otto Preminger took over and imposed a lean narrative style that was to prove very influential in the genre. Clifton Webb is accused of murdering his girl-friend out of jealousy. But there is no face left on the corpse. Is it she? Dana Andrews investigates and falls prey to his own obsession. A startling and still dis-

turbing movie topped off by David Raksin's evocative score.
★★★★★
D: Otto Preminger; W: Jay Dratler, Samuel Hoffenstein and Betty Reinhardt; Ph: Joseph La Shelle; M: David Raksin.
Cast: Gene Tierney, Dana Andrews, Clifton Webb, Vincent Price.

THE LAVENDER HILL MOB. (1951) One the classics of English screen comedy that presents bank robbery as a blow against conformity and monotony by a symbol of the faceless workers of the world. Alec Guinness' arch, low-key playing is perfect as the obscure bank clerk who masterminds the theft of gold bullion. Stanley Holloway is an apt complement as a dreamer of a different sort who joins him.
★★★★★
D: Charles Crichton; W: T.E.B. Clarke; Ph: Douglas Slocombe; M: Georges Auric.
Cast: Alec Guinness, Stanley Holloway, Alfie Bass, Sid James.

LA VIE CONTINUE. (1982) The title means "Life goes on" and it's one of those platitudes a widow hears repeatedly. Annie Girardot is a woman unsuited by age or dispostion to widowhood and the director, who also made *Madame Rosa*, ponders her plight in scenes which alternate observation with heavy sentimentailty. Girardot makes the point that the woman is mourning for a lost routine as much as a man and she is the only reason for watching the film.
★★
D: Moshe Mizrahi; W: Mizrahi and Rachel Fabien; Ph: Yves Lafaye; M: Georges Delerue.
Cast: Annie Girardot, Jean-Pierre Cassel, Pierre Dux, Michel Aumont.

LAW AND DISORDER. (1974) Foreign directors often bring a fresh perspective on American life to films. Ivan Passer, a gifted Czech, takes a familiar story—two middle aged New Yorkers deciding to do something about crime in their neighborhood—and gives us a new angle. Paced at a leisurely tempo that allows Carroll O'Connor, in his screen debut, and Ernest Borgnine to develop their characters fully.
R. ★★★
D: Ivan Passer; W: Passer, William Richert and Kenneth Harris Fishman; Ph: Arthur J. Ornitz; M: Andy Badale.
Cast: Carroll O'Connor, Ernest Borgnine, Karen Black, Ann Wedgeworth.

LAWRENCE OF ARABIA. (1962) In the vastness of the desert and the scope of an epic of this scale there ought to be room to explore the complex figure of T.E. Lawrence. But he was a mystic and mystifying figure as well as a hero to his generation and Robert Bolt's intelligent decision is to maintain the veil of mystery. Peter O'Toole was the ideal choice to support this view. Thus the canvas is huge and the action, which traces the adventures of an Englishman who became a leader of the Arabs in the first World War, has a huge sweep. But the central figure is a tantalizing enigma showing different facets of his personality as the work progresses.

★★★★★

D: David Lean; W: Robert Bolt; Ph: Frederick Young; M: Maurice Jarre.
Cast: Peter O'Toole, Jack Hawkins, Omar Sharif, Arthur Kennedy.

LEADBELLY. (1976) The great black folksinger sits in a jail cell dictating his memoirs and the biography unfolds in flashbacks. And a superior one it is in tracing the life and hard times of Huddie Ledbetter, known as Leadbelly to everyone who loves the blues. The film knows the trouble he went through and pulls no punches. Robert Mosley is terrific in the title role and the soundtrack is a winner.

PG. ★★★

D: Gordon Parks; W: Ernest Kinoy; Ph: Bruce Surtees; M: Fred Karlin (vocals by HiTide Harris).
Cast: Robert E. Mosley, Paul Benjamin, Madge Sinclair, Alan Manson.

LE BEAU MARIAGE. (1982) A young woman decides to get married and the object of her affections, as they say in a baseball trade, is a player to be named later. Eric Rohmer sees the contemporary mating ritual as a courtly dance to which nobody knows the steps. A wry and serious comedy about a woman who is in love with the idea of marriage rather than a specific man.

PG. ★★★

D and W: Eric Rohmer; Ph: Bernard Lutic; M: Ronan Girre.
Cast: Beatrice Romand, Andre Dusollier, Arielle Dombasle, Feodor Atkine.

LE CHAT. (1975) Between frequent drinks, Simone Signoret says, "There ought to a law against two people living together who don't love each other." What makes the film very unusual is the fact that the two people are old and the movie is one of the most rancid and depressing views of aging ever put on film. Signoret and Jean Gabin spar in an apartment house that awaits the wrecker's ball. The stray cat adopted by Gabin becomes the focal point of their mutual hatred.

★★★

D: Pierre Granier-Deferre; W: Pascal Jardin and Granier-Deferre; Ph: Walter Wottitz; M: Philippe Sarde.
Cast: Jean Gabin, Simone Signoret, Annie Cordy, Jacques Rispal.

THE LEFT-HANDED GUN. (1958) A western from left field that holds the viewer despite—or perhaps one should say—because of its flaws. Years later, Paul Newman made a fascinating dissection of Buffalo Bill with Robert Altman. His Billy the Kid is another consideration of what happens to already unbalanced men when they have to live with their own legends in an entirely different reality. His Bill is a sniveling psycho done with many Method mannerisms. This is Arthur Penn's directing debut.

★★★

D: Arthur Penn; W: Leslie Stevens; Ph: Peverell Marley; M: Alexander Courage.
Cast: Paul Newman, John Dehner, Lita Milan, Hurd Hatfield.

THE LEFT HAND OF GOD. (1955) Humphrey Bogart bit the bullet and took the cloth as an American pilot who gets caught up in the affairs of a Chinese warlord and escapes by pretending to be a Catholic priest. From then on things get progressively dumber, but Bogart and Lee J. Cobb, the bellicose bandit, liven it up.

★★

D: Edward Dmytryk; W: Alfred Hayes; Ph: Franz Planer; M: Victor Young.
Cast: Humphrey Bogart, Lee J. Cobb, Gene Tierney, Agnes Moorehead.

THE LEGACY. (1979) A strong will and stomach are prerequisites for lasting through a mixture of black magic and murder. An architect and her boyfriend wind up in the ever popular sinister mansion where business associates of the owner find an unsavory agenda. Fans of the Who's Roger Daltrey may relish his turn as a man choking on a chicken bone and undergoing a tracheotomy. The rest of the film sticks in the craw.

R. ★

D: Richard Marquand; W: Jimmy Sangster, Patrick Tilley and Paul Wheeler; Ph: Dick Bush; M: Michael J. Lewis.

Cast: Katharine Ross, Sam Elliot, John Standing, Ian Hogg.

THE LEGEND OF HELL HOUSE. (1973) Don't be put off by the exploitative title. The script is the work of the accomplished horror and fantasy writer Richard Matheson and while the ideas are formulaic, the acting and writing are superior to the strident norm. A wealthy man brings four people to a house that has claimed the lives of the curious. ★★★
D: John Hough; W: Richard Matheson; Ph: Alan Hume; M: Brian Hodges and Delia Derbyshire.
Cast: Pamela Franklin, Roddy McDowall, Clive Revill, Gayle Hunnicutt.

THE LEGEND OF THE LONE RANGER. (1981) The masked man's horse is far and away the best actor and the stunningly inept film turns out to be a dark cloud with a Silver lining. Someone called Klinton Spilsbury dons the mask and he is so bad that the urge to make him wear a hood is overwhelming. The re-telling of the original story of the Lone Ranger's beginnings veers between camp and sobriety. An expensive shambles.
PG. ★
D: William Fraker; W: William Roberts, Michael Kane, Ivan Goff and Ben Roberts; Ph: Laszlo Kovacs; M: John Barry.
Cast: Klinton Spilsbury, Michael Horse, Jason Robards, Christopher Lloyd.

LE MAGNIFIQUE. (1972) Weak satire of secret agentry and the Bond market. Jean-Paul Belmondo is a hack thriller writer with a fantasy life as a spy enjoying fast cars and faster women. The film is not especially effective since there is so much self-deprecation in the movies it spoofs.
★★
D: Philippe De Broca.
Cast: Jean-Paul Belmondo, Jacqueline Bisset, Vittorio Capriolo, Mario David.

LENNY. (1974) The style of Bob Fosse's searing biography of comedian Lenny Bruce is semi-documentary and it's also only half the truth. In this reading Lenny is a martyr and known facts about his lifelong attachment to hard drugs and details of his family life are elided. Dustin Hoffman gives us a superbly rounded Lenny instead of settling for just an impression. The film tracks his career from the Catskills club circuit to his storied battles with the law on obscenity as a national satirist. Valerie Perrine did her best work in movies as Lenny's wife.
R. ★★★★★
D: Bob Fosse; W: Julian Barry; Ph: Bruce Surtees; .
Cast: Dustin Hoffman, Valerie Perrine, Jan Miner, Stanley Beck.

LENNY BRUCE WITHOUT TEARS. (1975) A companion to Dustin Hoffman's portrait, which rendered Lenny without warts. Fred Baker began collecting material for the documentary when the comedian died in 1966. The high points—perhaps low would be more accurate—are an interview with Bruce, visibly the worse for drugs, conducted by Nat Hentoff and some performance footage. The overall view however, is rather simplistic.
★★★
D and W: Fred Baker.

THE LEOPARD. (1963) Visconti's masterly historical film is only now coming into its own. The problem has always been atrocious dubbing and editing worthy of an ax murderer in the versions usually seen in this country. In its full majesty, it is a gorgeous piece with Burt Lancaster giving a haunting account of a Sicilian aristocrat clinging to the old ways in a world of change and turbulence—Italy in the 1860s.
★★★★★
D: Luchino Visconti; W: Visconti and others; Ph: Giuseppe Rotunno; M: Nino Rota.
Cast: Burt Lancaster, Claudia Cardinale, Alain Delon, Rina Morelli.

LEPKE. (1975) Louis Lepke Buchalter, head of Murder Inc., was not a nice Jewish boy. Tony Curtis is hilarious, storming the screen and shouting "Where's it going to get us? To the top of the heap—miles above those Italian goniffs?" Riddled with gangster cliches, the film is very defensive about Lepke. It sees him as a family man in an odd business—the Kosher Nostra?—as he rises from the Lower East Side to the top.
R. ★
D: Menahem Golan; W: Wesley Hau and Tamor Hoffs; Ph: Andrew Davis; M: Ken Wannberg.
Cast: Tony Curtis, Anjanette Comer, Michael Callan, Warren Berlinger.

LES MISERABLES. (1952) Victor Hugo's perennial, in the fourth Hollywood attempt, is a decently produced and solidly acted version. Michael Rennie is Jean Valjean, the man who pays an incredible price for stealing a crust of bread, and Robert Newton is in fine fettle as Javert, the obsessed policeman who hounds him through the years. The novel's more profound points about the uses of justice and the law are superficial in this reading.

★★★
D: Lewis Milestone; W: Richard Murphy; Ph: Joseph La Shelle; M: Alex North.
Cast: Robert Newton, Michael Rennie, Debra Paget, Edmund Gwenn.

LES VIOLONS DU BAL. (1974) A film within a film that seeks to draw parallels between perceived police oppression in modern France and the savagery of the German occupation in World War II. Such comparisons were politically popular in France at the time, but they do not work well cinematically. Michel Drach's work concentrates on a Jewish director trying to make a picture about what happens to him in Paris as a boy. The WW II scenes are both tense and touching as a mother tries to keep her family together and one step ahead of Les Boches.

★★★
D and W: Michel Drach; Ph: Yann Le Masson; M: Jean Manuel de Scarano and Jacques Monty.
Cast: Jean-Louis Trintignant, Marie-Josee Nat, Michel Drach, David Drach.

L'ETOILE DU NORD. (1983) The title means the North Star and refers to a train that runs between Brussels and Paris. The real stars, Philippe Noiret as a murderer, and Simone Signoret, as a landlady who boards him, are worth the price of the ticket. It begins as film noir suspense and gives way to a study of lives of quiet desperation. The murderer charms the other tenants with his stories as the police close in.
PG. ★★★
D: Pierre Granier-Deferre; W: Granier-Deferre, Jean Aurenche and Michel Grisolia; Ph: Pierre William Glenn; M: Philippe Sarde.
Cast: Philippe Noiret, Simone Signoret, Fanny Cottencon, Julie Jezequel.

LET'S DO IT AGAIN. (1975) Reunion of Sidney Poitier and Bill Cosby, who made *Uptown Saturday Night*, in a breezy and amiable farce. Directed at black audiences, but shunning the usual exploitation, the movie's cast is only weakened by Jimmy Walker. Cosby and Poitier are lodge brothers who become involved with the underworld in their efforts to raise $50,000 for a new building.

PG. ★★★
D: Sidney Poitier; W: Richard Wesley; Ph: Donald M. Morgan; M: Curtis Mayfield.
Cast: Sidney Poitier, Bill Cosby, John Amos, Ossie Davis.

LET'S MAKE LOVE. (1960) George Cukor and a roster of this order create great expectations. The comedy falls short, but it's an amusing bauble. Yves Montand is a millionaire spoofed in a Broadway revue starring Marilyn Monroe. He passes himself off as an actor and takes lessons from Bing Crosby and Gene Kelly before joining the show.

★★★
D: George Cukor; W: Norman Krasna; Ph: Daniel L. Fapp; M: Lionel Newman.
Cast: Yves Montand, Marilyn Monroe, Gene Kelly, Bing Crosby.

LET'S SCARE JESSICA TO DEATH. (1971) Everybody's got to start somewhere and a lot of young directors who later distinguished themselves began in the low rent horror market. John Hancock bowed with the story of a woman mental patient who is released to go and live with her husband at a New England farm. The lady who shows up as a guest has strange appetites. Hancock did not find this congenial material but Zohra Lampert is effective.

★★
D: John Hancock; W: Norman Jonas and Ralph Rose; Ph: Bob Baldwin; M: Orville Stoeber.
Cast: Zohra Lampert, Barton Heyman, Gretchen Corbett.

LETTER FROM AN UNKNOWN WOMAN. (1948) A pianist who remembers his concert scores but has less than total recall of his conquests in love faces a ghost from the past. The woman and her son are dying of typhus when she confesses her unrequited love in a letter. Max Ophuls brought the film off without pandering and with a flair for the idiom.

★★★
D: Max Ophuls; W: Howard Koch; Ph: Franz Planer; M: Daniele Amfitheatrof.
Cast: Joan Fontaine, Louis Jourdan, Mady Christians, Marcel Journet.

LIANNA. (1983) John Sayles' thoughtful and compassionate study of a woman acknowledging her lesbianism and facing the consequent break-up of her marriage to a New Jersey college professor is everything *Making Love* could and should have been. Unburdened by the usual Hollywood commercial considerations and blessed with both insight and and a wonderful ear for dialogue, Sayles writes a moving and realistic film. The low budget actually helps in the latter regard. His women are far more vivid than the men, but that is the consequence of the film's emotional stance. There are very few good movies about homosexuality; this is one of them.

R.   ★★★★
D and W: John Sayles; Ph: Austin de Besche; M: Mason Daring.
Cast: Linda Griffiths, Jane Hallaren, Jon DeVries, Jo Henderson.

LIES MY FATHER TOLD ME. (1975) Unctuous and idyllic memoir of a Jewish childhood in Montreal that provokes the question, "Do I Hear a Schmaltz?" A grandfather is adored by the movie and his grandson. He is a rag-and-bone man who reads one book (guess which) and tells kids it rains because the earth tells God it's thirsty. Strong drink is required to absorb the overbearing sentimentality and the crude juxtaposition of the old and new worlds of immigrants.

PG.   ★★
D: Jan Kadar; W: Ted Allan; Ph: Paul Van der Linden; M: Sol Kaplan.
Cast: Yossi Yadin, Len Birman, Marilyn Lightstone, Jeffrey Lynas.

THE LIFE AND TIMES OF JUDGE ROY BEAN. (1972) The judge (Paul Newman) "knows the law since I spent my entire life in its flagrant disregard." Newman sets himself up as judge and jury in a misbegotten town in the Southwest and one expects John Huston to make something of the satiric possibilities. Instead, the western is amiable and rather aimless, but several of the secondary characters are done with off-beat verve by a well-chosen cast.

PG.   ★★★
D: John Huston; W: John Milius; Ph: Richard Moore; M: Maurice Jarre.
Cast: Paul Newman, Ava Gardner, Jacqueline Bisset, Anthony Perkins.

LIFEBOAT. (1944) Alfred Hitchcock brought his protean technical skills to bear on the challenge of filming an entire drama on a single set—a lifeboat adrift in the Atlantic with eight survivors. They pick up the U-boat captain who torpedoed their ship and he is the only one who can navigate. Hitchcock was confined more by the propaganda aspects of the picture than the space, but his craftsmanship shines through.

                                       ★★★

D: Alfred Hitchcock; W: Jo Swerling; Ph: Glen MacWilliams; M: Hugo Friedhofer.
Cast: Tallulah Bankhead, William Bendix, Walter Slezak, John Hodiak.

LIFEGUARD. (1976) The lifeguard is 32, which is senile by California standards. Girls come up to him and say, "I want to make love to you. I thought about it ever since you bandaged my finger." Should Rick continue to do the breast-stroke on his appointed beach or sell cars? All the elan and fascination of a Mark Spitz commercial.

PG.   ★
D: Daniel Petrie; W: Ron Koslow; M: Paul Williams.
Cast: Sam Elliott, Kathleen Quinlan, Stephen Young, Parker Stevenson.

LIFE OF BRIAN. (1979) The Gospel according to St. John (Cleese) and his Monty Python cohorts. Three Magi go to the wrong stable to worship Brian, who grows up to become Judea's leading twit. Dozens of crucified victims belting out "The Bright Side of Life" and other religious humor caused much pulpit fulmination. But most of the humor here is political and devastating.

R.   ★★★
D: Terry Jones; W: Jones, Michael Palin, John Cleese, Graham Chapman, Terry Gilliam, Eric Idle; Ph: Peter Biziou; M: Geoffrey Burgon.
Cast: Terry Jones, Graham Chapman, John Cleese, Michael Palin.

THE LIFE OF EMILE ZOLA. (1937) A noble, Academy Award-winning biography of the writer which centers on his intervention in the Dreyfus case. Paul Muni, as he demonstrated in his portrait of Pasteur, had a special flair for bringing great men to life and he is surrounded here by a very handsome production.

                                       ★★★★
D: William Dieterle; W: Norman Reilly Raine; Ph: Tony Gaudio; M: Max Steiner.
Cast: Paul Muni, Joseph Schildkraut, Gale Sondergaard, Gloria Holden.

LILI MARLEEN. (1981) In Rainer Werner Fassbinder's foray into Nazism—itself a rare enough trip for a German film-maker—one waits expectantly for a great director's observations on his country's darkest hour. He has the ingredients —a woman, brilliantly realized by Hanna Schygulla, who is both an adornment of Hitler's regime and the lover of a subversive. But Fassbinder is more taken with creating atmosphere and his flamboyance becomes an irritating disappointment. It is almost a corrupt pastiche of the show business success story and, given the assembled talent, it becomes exasperating.

★★★

D: Rainer Werner Fassbinder; W: Manfred Purzer; Ph: Eaver Schwartzenberger; M: Peer Raben.

Cast: Hanna Schygulla, Giancarlo Giannini, Mel Ferrer, Karl Heinz Von Hassel.

LILLIAN RUSSELL. (1940) An elaborate and somewhat sanitized reading of the life of one of the great entertainers of the late nineteenth century. Thirty years are covered— from her discovery in 1880 to her marriage to a journalist (Henry Fonda), but the movie does not do her justice.

★★

D: Irving Cummings; W: William Anthony McGuire; Ph: Leon Shamroy; M: Alfred Newman.

Cast: Alice Faye, Don Ameche, Henry Fonda, Edward Arnold .

LIMELIGHT. (1952) Charlie Chaplin in a posture of occasionally sentimental reflection on his own life with Calvero the clown serving as his vehicle. The resonance between Chaplin's life and Calvero enriches the film greatly and it unfolds as a tragedy of a man who renews the life of another and goes to his own death. Parts of it are over-written, but the overall impact is undeniable.

★★★★

D and W: Charles Chaplin; Ph: Karl Strauss; M: Charles Chaplin.

Cast: Charles Chaplin, Claire Bloom, Buster Keaton, Nigel Bruce.

THE LION IN WINTER. (1968) Katharine Hepburn's Oscar-winning Eleanor of Aquitaine is complemented by Peter O'Toole's equally skilled Henry II. The middle ages, usually a cinematic excuse for pageantry and battle, are here presented as a family feud and a time of good talk. James Goldman's play has wit, but the dialogue often sounds contrived even with performers of this caliber uttering it. As a solution to the perennial problem of how people are to speak in historical drama, it has validity.

★★★

D: Anthony Harvey; W: James Goldman; Ph: Douglas Slocombe; M: John Barry.

Cast: Peter O'Toole, Katharine Hepburn, Jane Merrow, John Castle.

LION OF THE DESERT. (1981) Libyan oil money paid the $30 million for an epic about the country's Bedouin resistance to Mussolini after World War I. It has the scale such money can buy, but it is as empty as a desert landscape. The film is strongly reminiscent of *Lawrence of Arabia* in look and scope but it lacks involving characters. Anthony Quinn is the implacable leader of the rebels.

PG. ★★

D: Moustapha Akkad; W: H.L. Craig; Ph: Jack Hildyard; M: Maurice Jarre.

Cast: Anthony Quinn, Oliver Reed, Irene Papas, Rod Steiger.

LIPSTICK. (1976) A distaff *Death Wish* with Margaux Hemingway's acting reducing the viewer's will to live. The complexities of rape and the way its victims are treated by the judicial system take a back seat to crude mass appeal. Hemingway is a cover girl who exacts the maximum vengeance on the rapist, a deranged composer. Anne Bancroft is the most striking presence in the film as the prosecutor.

R. ★

D: Lamont Johnson; W: David Rayfiel; Ph: William A. Fraker; M: Michael Polnareff.

Cast: Margaux Hemingway, Chris Sarandon, Anne Bancroft, Mariel Hemingway.

LISZTSOMANIA. (1975) Ken Russell's continuing grudge against the great composers reached an all-time low. Liszt is a prototype rock star and Wagner the precursor of Hitler. Roger Daltrey, the vacuous British singer, is Liszt making love in a piano shaped bed. This gives way to an image of a phallus being mutilated by a guillotine. Had enough? Ludicrous, even by Russell's standards and a misreading of history that is matched only by its mishearing of the music of Liszt and Wagner.

R.

D and W: Ken Russell; Ph: Peter Suchitsky; M: John Forsyth(musical director).

Cast: Roger Daltrey, Sara Kestelman, Ringo Starr, Paul Nicholas .

LITTLE BIG MAN. (1970) Virtuoso work from Dustin Hoffman as Jack Crabb, who— at the ripe old age of 121—has much to tell us about how the west really was. In recounting experiences that took Crabb all over the map, Arthur Penn's film is broadly satiric before becoming overtly serious. The points it makes about the slaughter of Indians are inarguable but the attempt to draw parallels between those massacres and the American presence in Vietnam is very forced and out of synch with the earlier part of the picture.

★★★

D: Arthur Penn; W: Calder Willingham; Ph: Harry Stradling; M: John Hammond.
Cast: Dustin Hoffman, Martin Balsam, Faye Dunaway, Jeff Corey.

LITTLE CAESAR. (1931) For the remainder of his long and distinguished career, Edward G. Robinson was indelibly identified with Rico, the murderous gangster who is modeled on Al Capone. Generations of impressionists have embellished his powerhouse performance in a movie which prompted a whole school of crime pictures that moralized over the supposedly paltry wages of sin. Very few of them were on a level with *Little Caesar*, which belongs among the royal ranks of gangster films.

★★★★

D: Mervyn Le Roy; W: Francis Farragoh and Robert E. Lee; Ph: Tony Gaudio.
Cast: Edward G. Robinson, Douglas Fairbanks, Jr., Glenda Farrell, William Collier.

THE LITTLE FOXES. (1941) Bette Davis and one of the nastiest families in movies hold the screen in an accomplished adaptation of Lillian Hellman's stage hit. Davis gives a bravura account of Regina, a woman of all-encompassing greed. Her brothers need money to buy a cotton mill in the South at the turn of the century. Her husband finds out about the missing money and dies of a heart attack. She watches him die after telling him she has always hated him in a scene that Davis makes memorably chilling.

★★★★

D: William Wyler; W: Lillian Hellman; Ph: Gregg Toland; M: Meredith Wilson.
Cast: Bette Davis, Herbert Marshall, Teresa Wright, Richard Carlson.

LITTLE MISS MARKER. (1980) The pleasure of this remake lies in savoring Walter Matthau's uncanny knack of sharing the screen with children and making it seem child's play. As Sorrowful Jones, the bookie who inherits a kid, he wears an ill-fitting suit, but the part is tailor-made for him. Wisely, the story was kept in the thirties where its Runyonesque events can still be believed.
PG. ★★★
D and W: Walter Bernstein; Ph: Philip Lathrop; M: Henry Mancini.
Cast: Walter Matthau, Julie Andrews, Tony Curtis, Bob Newhart.

A LITTLE NIGHT MUSIC. (1978) Like a vintage wine that doesn't travel well, Stephen Sondheim's musical did not survive the transition from the stage. The gossamer texture becomes synthetic fabric with Elizabeth Taylor heaving herself through an awful rendering of "Send in the Clowns." In Vienna in 1905 a middle-aged lawyer and his still virgin wife are at the center of adulterous goings-on. The songs somehow survive but there are some deletions.
PG. ★★
D: Harold Prince; W: Hugh Wheeler; Ph: Arthur Ibbetson; M: Stephen Sondheim.
Cast: Elizabeth Taylor, Len Cariou, Diana Rigg, Lesley-Anne Down.

THE LITTLE PRINCE. (1974) A lot of talent, including Lerner and Loewe's first collaboration since *Camelot*, fizzles in an adaptation of Antoine De Saint-Exupery's beloved children's story. A little boy stops in our world on a galactic journey in search of truth. Lots of gimmicky special effects tend to overwhelm the simplicity of the tale and Donen makes too much of the boy as a symbol of lost innocence.
G. ★★
D: Stanley Donen; W: Alan Jay Lerner; Ph: Christopher Challis; M: Alan Jay Lerner and Frederick Loewe.
Cast: Richard Kiley, Steven Warner, Gene Wilder, Bob Fosse.

THE LITTLE PRINCESS. (1939) Temple in technicolor for the first time and a rather Dickensian setting and story. The ogre this time is a boarding school headmistress who turns Shirley into a domestic servant after her father is reportedly killed in the Boer War. The highlight is a Cockney song and dance routine with Arthur Treacher. *The Little Princess* is generally numbered among her best pictures.

★★★

D: Walter Lang; W: Ethel Hill and Walter Ferris; Ph: Arthur Miller; M: Louis Silvers.
Cast: Shirley Temple, Richard Greene, Anita Louise, Arthur Treacher.

A LITTLE ROMANCE. (1979) George Roy Hill's hymn to sexual awakening with two young lovers, who are hardly into their teens, strolling the streets of Paris. He gets around the fact that the sweet nothings of puppy love would bore an audience silly by having his lovers occupy a rarefied intellectual atmosphere. Their musings contrast with the dumbness of the adult world. They depart from character and from Paris to reach Venice and the film falls apart. Laurence Olivier, as an aging boulevadier, is in a situation that brings out the least in him.

PG. ★★
D: George Roy Hill; W: Allan Burns; Ph: Pierre William Glenn; M: George Delerue.
Cast: Diane Lane, Thelonious Bernard, Laurence Olivier, Arthur Hill.

A LITTLE SEX. (1982) A man accustomed to a lot of sex tries fidelity and is, naturally, subjected to an unending stream of offers from empty-headed beauties. Remorselessly consciousness-lowering.

R. ★★
D: Bruce Paltrow; W: Robert DeLaurentis; Ph: Bill Butler .
Cast: Tim Matheson, Wallace Shawn, Kate Capshaw, Edward Herrmann.

THE LITTLEST OUTLAW. (1955) A pleasant cautionary tale from Disney that rails against cruelty to animals. A ten-year-old Mexican boy saves a horse from torture and they escape to various adventures involving bandits and gypsies.

★★
D: Roberto Gavaldon; W: Bill Walsh; Ph: Alex Phillips.
Cast: Pedro Armendariz, Joseph Calleia, Rodolfo Acosta, Andres Velasquez.

THE LITTLEST REBEL. (1935) A sentimental journey even by Shirley Temple standards. Her mother is dying and her father is off fighting for the Confederacy in the Civil War. She has to make a personal appeal for his life to Abe Lincoln when he is captured and convicted of spying.

★★
D: David Butler; W: Edwin Burke; Ph: John Seitz; M: Cyril Mockridge.
Cast: Shirley Temple, John Boles, Jack Holt, Karen Morley.

THE LITTLE THEATER OF JEAN RENOIR. (1974) There is nothing small about the humanity that infuses these three playlets that Renoir originally made for French television in his 80th year. The first is a fable about two beggars who are given a Lucullan Christmas feast. The second is a sharp satire on a woman obsessed with clean floors. The third and best is called *The King of Yvetot* is an engrossing story of tolerance in which a sea captain takes in a young man and is cuckolded by him.

★★★★

D: Jean Renoir .
Cast: Jeanne Moreau, Fernand Sardou, Francoise Arnoul, Jean Carmet.

LITTLE WOMEN. (1933) George Cukor's storied gift for directing women was little known before this charming rendition of Louisa May Alcott's much loved account of a New England family during the Civil War. Katharine Hepburn leads an immaculate cast and Cukor manages to frame their work in a nostlagic atmosphere that never becomes cloyingly sentimental.

★★★★
D: George Cukor; W: Sarah Y. Mason and Victor Heerman; Ph: Henry Gerrard; M: Max Steiner.
Cast: Katharine Hepburn, Paul Lukas, Joan Bennett, Frances Dee.

LIVE AND LET DIE. (1973) After George Lazenby had reduced 007 to about an 002 on the espionage Richter scale in his one James Bond film, Roger Moore took over the license to kill and renewed the fortunes of the series. The gadgeteering that would ultimately reduce him to a cipher was not yet in full swing and the pace is zippy. Bond goes up against a cast of black villains led by Yaphet Kotto who has some new ideas on the uses of heroin.

★★★
D: Guy Hamilton; W: Tom Mankiewicz; Ph: Ted Moore ; M: George Martin.
Cast: Roger Moore, Jane Seymour, Yaphet Kotto, Geoffrey Holder.

THE LIVING DESERT. (1953) The sugar-coating of real life and the propensity for investing animals with cute human qualities are what you have to put up with in the first of the Disney True-Life adventures. In return for your patience, the marvelous photography, which itself took immense patience to shoot, brings the North American desert to life.

★★★
D: James Algar; W: Algar and Winston Hibler; Ph: Paul Kenworthy, Jr., et. al.; M: Paul J. Smith.

LLOYD'S OF LONDON. (1936) "Members of the syndicate have deserted me. I can't go on," moans Tyrone Power. No, it's not another Mafia epic, but a slightly pompous and historically fanciful account of the rise of a messenger boy to the top of the legendary insurance firm in the 18th century. Every decision made along the way—even about love—has a mercenary tinge and there is an unsavory belief that the goals of patriotism and capitalism are inseparable.

★★★

D: Henry King; W: Ernest Pascal and Walter Ferris; Ph: Bert Glennon; M: Louis Silvers.
Cast: Tyrone Power, Madeleine Carroll, George Sanders, Freddie Bartholemew.

LOCAL HERO. (1983) Bill Forsyth reaffirmed his unique comic gift in this ingenious inversion that keeps us constantly off-balance. An American oil company wants to buy up a Scottish village, but it's the natives who prove to be the greedy capitalists. Forsyth has a wonderful eye and ear and the basic story is enriched with all manner of whimsical vignettes and blithely funny characters.

PG. ★★★★★

D and W: Bill Forsyth; Ph: Chris Menges; M: Mark Knopler.
Cast: Burt Lancaster, Peter Riegert, Fulton Mackay, Norman Chancer.

THE LODGER. (1944) A clear-headed look at Jack the Ripper in fog-shrouded London and what turned out to be one of Laird Cregar's last films. In a fitting valedictory, he is the enigmatic lodger who takes rooms in a Whitechapel boarding house in the 1880s and goes about his business. Since he *is* Jack the Ripper, *The Lodger* uses the opportunity to explore his murderous impulses. Based on Marie Belloc-Lowndes' novel.

★★★

D: John Brahm; W: Barre Lyndon; Ph: Lucien Ballard; M: Hugo Friedhofer.
Cast: Merle Oberon, Laird Cregar, Cedric Hardwicke, George Sanders.

LOGAN'S RUN. (1976) A slow walk through the 23d century where anyone over 30 has outlived his usefulness and is bumped off by the government. Might be a prescient look at the future of Social Security, but it never tries to explain or discuss the society that produced this policy. Michael York and Jenny Agutter attempt an escape, only to find Peter Ustinov in an undergrowth-covered city, doing his number three American accent. Presentable special effects in the first half.

PG. ★★

D: Michael Anderson; W: David Zelag Goodman; Ph: Ernest Laszlo; M: Jerry Goldsmith.
Cast: Michael York, Jenny Aguttter, Peter Ustinov, Richard Jordan.

LOLITA. (1962) Believe it or not, Stanley Kubrick originally wanted Noel Coward to take the part of Humbert Humbert, the middle-aged academic who falls for a 14-year-old girl. (She is younger in the Nabokov novel). Common sense prevailed and James Mason played Humbert, who marries a woman he despises to be near her daughter. His rendering of Humbert's obsession is the most convincing aspect of the film, but Kubrick's direction is dispassionate.

★★★

D: Stanley Kubrick; W: Vladimir Nabokov; Ph: Oswald Morris; M: Nelson Riddle.
Cast: James Mason, Shelley Winters, Sue Lyon, Peter Sellers.

LONELY ARE THE BRAVE. (1962) A quite extraordinary picture that deserves to be better known. The cowboy or gunslinger out of step with encroaching civilization was a familiar recourse of western writers. Here it is updated with the last cowboy and his horse fleeing a modern posse and its technology. The lead performances by Kirk Douglas and Walter Matthau (the pursuing sheriff) are superb and the story is allowed to speak for itself. It is rich in contrasting images of frontier freedom and the constrictions of contemporary life.

★★★★★

D: David Miller; W: Dalton Trumbo; Ph: Philip Lathrop; M: Jerry Goldsmith.
Cast: Kirk Douglas, Walter Matthau, Gena Rowlands, Carroll O'Connor.

THE LONELY GUY. (1984) May well be defined as anyone who finds Steve Martin's fifth outing in a leading role funny. A weak mixture of TV sitcom and black humor about a semi-jerk who is constantly rebuffed by women and writes a best-selling guide for lonely men. Baby boom women who complain about the drastic man shortage will be bemused by this premise. Nothing else is remotely amusing and Martin is stalled in another bad vehicle.

R. ★★

D: Arthur Hiller; W: Ed Weinberger and Stan Daniels; Ph: Victor J. Kemper; M: Jerry Goldsmith.
Cast: Steve Martin, Judith Ivey, Charles Grodin, Steve Lawrence.

THE LONELY LADY. (1983) After being raped with a garden hose, a young woman named Jerilee decides to become a screenwriter. The incomparable Pia Zadora, looking at the camera like a baby seal blinking in

strong sunlight, struggles to the top in a shamelessly dishonest view of Hollywood. She gets there by marrying a top screenwriter who is, of course, impotent and given to making jealous remarks about the hose.
R.   ★
D: Peter Sasdy; W: John Kershaw; Ph: Brian West; M: Charles Calelo.
Cast: Pia Zadora, Lloyd Bochner, Jared Martin, Bibi Besch.

THE LONGEST DAY. (1962) Hollywood invades Omaha beach for a star-strewn re-telling of D-Day. The theory was that having a familiar face in each military cameo would help the audience to grasp what was going on. In fact, none of them have enough time to enlist the sympathy of the viewer. But they can't afford to make films like this any more and even though it's more elephantine than epic, *The Longest Day* is still a stirring, old-school war effort. Another plus is that the Germans speak subtitled German instead of the usual Nazified English.
                                                       ★★★
D: Andrew Marton, Ken Annakin and Bernhard Wicki; W: Cornelius Ryan, Romain Gary, James Jones, David Pursall and Jack Seddon; Ph: Henri Persin, Walter Wottitz, Pierre Levent, Jean Bourgoin; M: Maurice Jarre and Paul Anka.
Cast: John Wayne, Robert Mitchum, Henry Fonda, Robert Ryan.

THE LONG GOOD FRIDAY. (1982) Bob Hoskins brings an animal power to Harold Shand, a London mobster who gradually discovers that his power and influence are an illusion. The British gangster flick is a first rate thriller, an arresting character study and a feast of clever puns on the stock figures in old crime pictures. The cockney dialogue is occasionally hard to follow, but it's worth the effort. Shand finds his grand scheme to build a casino disrupted by a group that doesn't play by any rules.
R.   ★★★★
D: John Mackenzie; W: Barry Keefe; Ph: Phil Meheux.
Cast: Bob Hoskins, Helen Mirren, Eddie Constantine, Dave King.

THE LONG HOT SUMMER. (1958) It finally caves in under the heat, but the forced marriage of several William Faulkner stories holds up for most of the going because the cast is so winning. Orson Welles is a Mississippi tyrant and Paul Newman the young drifter who disrupts the delicate balance in a contentious family. Alex North's score increases the temperature.
                                                       ★★★
D: Martin Ritt; W: Irving Ravetch and Harriet Frank, Jr.; Ph: Joseph La Shelle; M: Alex North.
Cast: Orson Welles, Paul Newman, Joanne Woodward, Anthony Franciosa.

THE LONG RIDERS. (1980) Brothers in arms are played by by real-life brothers in Walter Hill's spirited and biased account of the James-Younger gang after the Civil War. There are too many brothers for any of them to emerge as fully realized characters and the film is episodic and indifferent to explaining the social and political climate that allowed the gang to operate so successfully. It builds fitfully to the debacle at Northfield, Minn. Very handsome, full of balletic violence and blessed with a terrific Ry Cooder score.
R.   ★★★
D: Walter Hill; W: Bill Bryden; Ph: Ric Waite; M: Ry Cooder.
Cast: David, Keith and Robert Carradine, James and Stacy Keach, Dennis and Randy Quaid.

LOOK BACK IN ANGER. (1959) In 1956, John Osborne's play burst upon the London theater scene and transformed it with the volcanic rage of its working class protagonist. In retrospect, it can still be savored for Richard Burton's searing account of Jimmy Porter, whose rage is such that it almost defies articulate focus. The trend in plays and films Osborne initiated does very little to blunt the force of Burton's anger.
                                                       ★★★
D: Tony Richardson; W: Nigel Kneale; Ph: Oswald Morris; M: Chris Barber.
Cast: Richard Burton, Mary Ure, Claire Bloom, Edith Evans.

LOOKER. (1981) Michael Crichton's macabre speculation on the possible uses of television commercials succumbs to its own brand of commercialism. He has a flair for making abstruse technology intelligible. Here a Beverly Hills surgeon—an improbably cast Albert Finney with an accent somewhere between Yorkshire and California mellowspeak—tries to find out why his beautiful women patients are disappearing. The idea of the film is superior to what Crichton makes of it.
PG.   ★★★
D and W: Michael Crichton; Ph: Paul Loh-

mann; M: Barry DeVorzon.
Cast: Albert Finney, Susan Dey, James Coburn, Leigh Taylor-Young.

LOOKING FOR MR. GOODBAR. (1977) The Theresa Dunn who steps from the pages of the popular Judith Rossner novel into the film does so without a limp. The crippled teacher is changed to a more universal emblem of a woman who is frank in her sexual needs and the aggressor in gratifying them. Keaton gives a remarkable portrait of a woman who teaches deaf children by day and prowls singles bars in Manhattan by night and finds that no one will listen to her. The men are overdrawn and Brooks treats the story as a thriller. Several erotic scenes.
R.   ★★★
D and W: Richard Brooks; Ph: William A. Fraker; M: Artie Kane.
Cast: Diane Keaton, Tuesday Weld, Richard Kiley, William Atherton.

LOOKING TO GET OUT. (1982) Hal Ashby's look at gambling is messier than the ashtrays after an all-night poker game. Jon Voight and Burt Young escape from New York ahead of their bookie creditors on their way to Las Vegas, where they hope to right themselves in a big game. An unrelieved shambles.
R.   ★
D: Hal Ashby; W: Jon Voight and Al Schwartz; Ph: Haskell Wexler; M: Johnny Mandel.
Cast: Jon Voight, Ann-Margret, Burt Young, Bert Remsen.

THE LORD OF THE RINGS. (1978) An epochal feat of animation that was overwhelmed by the size of the undertaking. Ralph Bakshi's version of the J.R.R. Tolkien vision of Middle Earth and its denizens is full of stunning work —the ring wraiths, the fight between Gandalf and Balrog—and the first half sweeps the viewer along. But the film becomes a victim of compression and the second half can only be understood by people who have read the book. Tolkienphiles were mad about what was left out and the uninitiated had to puzzle over what was left in.
PG.   ★★★
D: Ralph Bakshi; W: Chris Conkling and Peter Beagle; Ph: Timothy Galfas; M: Leonard Rosenman.

THE LORDS OF DISCIPLINE. (1983) A military school drama that takes its place at the end of the long grey line. It evinces the same attitude toward the audience that such schools show toward cadets. If you enjoy being yelled at and treated as a moron, you may like the proceedings. In a Charleston military academy, circa 1965, some cadets discover the code they live by is fraudulent. As subtle as a parade ground bellow.
R.   ★★
D: Franc Roddam; W: Lloyd Fonvielle and Thomas Pope; Ph: Brian Tufano; M: Howard Blake.
Cast: David Keith, Robert Prosky, G. D. Spradlin, Mark Breland.

THE LORDS OF FLATBUSH. (1974) A picture more celebrated for the later success of three of its stars than for any intrinsic reason. It's piece of nostalgia for the fifties that has a nice sense of the period and its sexual mores and music but with little to add in the way of fresh ideas or approaches. The lords are the usual high school layabouts getting into predictable scrapes. Sylvester Stallone showed signs of his popular appeal as Rocky in the part of Stanley the greaser.
PG.   ★★★
D: Stephen F. Verona and Martin Davidson; W: Verona, Gayle Gleckler and Martin Davidson; Ph: Joseph Mangine and Edward Lachman; M: Joe Brooks.
Cast: Sylvester Stallone, Henry Winkler, Perry King, Paul Mace.

LOST AND FOUND. (1979) A candid title in that Glenda Jackson and George Segal were found for a reunion, but the wit that made *A Touch of Class* so delightful was lost. Segal, a college professor with aspirations for making the Harvard faculty, is a widower who literally collides with Jackson on a ski slope. Any hope that their subsequent marriage and jousting would yield the same incisive results as the discussion of adultery in *A Touch of Class* is quickly dashed.
PG.   ★★
D: Melvin Frank; W: Frank and Jack Rose; Ph: Douglas Slocombe; M: John Cameron.
Cast: G!enda Jackson, George Segal, Maureen Stapleton, Hollis McClaren.

THE LOST CITY OF ATLANTIS. (1977) Hilarious documentary, featuring kindergarten scholarship and demanding, "Were the Atlantians natives or alien refugees?" So cheaply assembled and addle-brained that it ought to be called *Close Discounters of the Third Kind.* Atlantis, according to the film-makers, went under because of meddling with the psychic force. "Were they red-skinned Giants?" the narrator asks. Were they the New York Giants? Look elsewhere for answers.

PG. ★

D: Richard Martin; W: Sara Nickerson; Ph: Steve Shuttack; M: Armidav Aloni.

THE LOST HONOR OF KATHERINA BLUM. (1975) Volker Schlondorff's study of the conflicting claims of news reporting and the right to privacy is one of the best films ever made about journalism. A young girl's life is radically altered when she unwittingly becomes involved with a bank robber. One reporter justifies making up quotes by saying, "We must help simple people express themselves." The film is a thoughtful essay on a complex issue and a moving character study.

★★★★★

D: Volker Schlondorff ; W: Schlondorff and Magarethe Von Trotta Ph: Jost Vancano; M: Hans Werner Henze.
Cast: Angela Winkler, Mario Adorf, Dieter Laser, Heinz Bennet.

THE LOST HORIZON. (1937) Frank Capra found a perfect film for his touch in bringing James Hilton's novel to the screen. It is a story that required very precise taste and judgement to work and Capra had an abundance of both. The resulting fantasy is quite affecting. Four refugees from a revolution find themselves in an idyllic civilization where the best and noblest instincts of mankind prevail.

★★★★

D: Frank Capra; W: Robert Riskin; Ph: Joseph Walker; M: Dmitri Tiomkin.
Cast: Ronald Colman, Sam Jaffe, H.B. Warner, Thomas Mitchell.

THE LOST PATROL. (1934) The many imitations and remixing of the basic characters and ingredients have done very little to defuse the impact of John Ford's consideration of a group of men under unrelenting pressure. The patrol is British and it is lost in both senses of the word in the deserts of Mesopotamia. Hostile Arabs pick the soldiers off one by one. A tense, gripping film.

★★★★

D: John Ford; W: Dudley Nichols; Ph: Harold Wenstrom; M: Max Steiner.
Cast: Boris Karloff, Victor McLaglen, Reginald Denny, Wallace Ford.

THE LOST WEEKEND. (1945) Billy Wilder took on alcohol, a subject that was not quite taboo but certainly box office poison. Ray Milland's Don Birnam is one of the most memorable drunks in screen history and the film follows him through a binge that begins when his brother leaves for the weekend. The edgy desperation of the addict—Milland is a failed author reduced to trying to hock his typewriter—is superbly caught. The ending in which he forsakes demon rum has more to do with the times than the thrust of the picture.

★★★★

D: Billy Widler; W: Wilder and Charles Brackett; Ph: John Seitz; M: Miklos Rozsa.
Cast: Ray Milland, Jane Wyman, Howard Da Silva, Philip Terry.

THE LOST WORLD. (1960) The second version of the Conan Doyle fantasy about an expedition to the Amazon in search of pre-historic life. The first was a noteworthy silent film in 1925. Here Claude Rains leads a grab-bag party into the presence of some unvconvincing creatures.

★★

D: Irwin Allen; W: Allen and Charles Bennett; Ph: Winton Hoch; M: Paul Sawtell.
Cast: Claude Rains, Michael Rennie, Jill St. John, David Hedison.

LOVE AND DEATH. (1975) If Christ was a carpenter, what did he charge for book-shelves? The answer to this and many other burning questions surfaces in Woody Allen's hilarious slaughter of the sacred cows of Russian literature. A superb fusion of everything from mordant satire to hilarious slapstick. Boris Grushenko (Woody) is Russia's leading coward on a mission to assassinate Napoleon while romping inadequately through various bedrooms. Allen does his trademark character but *Love and Death* is a landmark film in his development from comedian to director.

PG ★★★★★

D and W: Woody Allen; Ph: Ghislain Cloquet; M: Sergei Prokofiev.
Cast: Woody Allen, Diane Keaton, Georges Adel, Frank Adu .

LOVE AT FIRST BITE. (1979) Frightful rather than frightening and a compelling argument for closed casket Dracula movies. Dracula is 700 years old and so are the jokes in a witless parody of vampire conventions. Ousted by the communists, the count moves to New York and the disco scene. George

Hamilton taints an honorable horror tradition by playing Dracula as a cross between a vaudeville buffoon and an incorrigible romantic. Lots of racial jokes, none of them funny.

PG. ★

D: Stan Dragoti; W: Robert Kaufman; Ph: Edward Rosson; M: Charles Bernstein.
Cast: George Hamilton, Susan St. James, Richard Benjamin, Arte Johnson.

LOVE CHILD. (1983) Given the sorry history of women-in-prison movies and the fact that such a film is usually an excuse for male sex fantasies, this is an honest and sincere piece of work. It is based on the story of Terry Jean Moore, who became pregnant by a prison guard and then fought to keep the baby. Larry Peerce's direction tends to be overemotional about matters that speak eloquently for themselves.

R. ★★★

D: Larry Peerce; W: Katherine Specktor and Anne Girard; Ph: Jim Pergola; M: Charles Fox.
Cast: Amy Madigan, Beau Bridges, Mackenzie Phillips, Albert Salmi.

LOVE IN THE AFTERNOON. (1957) If Gary Cooper looks more than a little weary, you will soon understand why. He is stuck with the role of an American playboy in Paris who becomes involved with the daughter of a private detective. Audrey Hepburn adds her effervescent presence, but it's a flat effort for everyone else.

★★

D: Billy Wilder; W: Wilder and I.A.L. Diamond; Ph: William Mellor; M: Franz Waxman.
Cast: Audrey Hepburn, Gary Cooper, Maurice Chevalier, Van Doude.

LOVE IS A MANY-SPLENDORED THING. (1955) Henry King kept the mawkishness in check, at least until the end, and brought off a soap opera of both taste and class. The last two ingredients are contributed by William Holden and Jennifer Jones. An American newsman and a Eurasian doctor fall in love in Hong Kong. The doomed affair is played out with operatic fervor.

★★★

D: Henry King; W: John Patrick; Ph: Leon Shamroy; M: Alfred Newman.
Cast: William Holden, Jennifer Jones, Torin Thatcher, Murray Matheson.

LOVE ME TENDER. (1956) Elvis Presley died in more ways than one in his movie debut. It was an inimical choice that put the singer in a western instead of a format that could exploit his music a little more. Presley is one of four brothers from the Confederate army who have their own civil war over some stolen money. In the end—and in an apt image—Elvis appears as a ghost.

★★

D: Robert D. Webb; W: Robert Buckner; Ph: Leo Tover; M: Lionel Newman.
Cast: Richard Egan, Elvis Presley, Debra Paget, Robert Middleton.

LOVE OF LIFE. (1969) A French documentary that portrays an artist who is an old man in years only. Artur Rubinstein was 82 when the film was made and it celebrates his unique personality, his rich store of anecdotes culled from a long life as a virtuoso pianist. He also has some profound observations to offer about music. Through family albums and memoirs, it traces Rubinstein from childhood to international fame.

★★★

D and W: Francois Reichenbach and S.G. Patris.

LOVE ON THE RUN. (1978) The fifth installment of Francois Truffaut's continuing chronicle of the growth—if not the maturing— of his screen alter ego, Antoine Doinel. It is one of the weaker entries in the series and argues that Truffaut is better in a more objective vein, as in *Small Change*, than in autobiography. Antoine has just divorced and published his first novel. "Writing to settle old scores isn't art," he is told. Truffaut proves that the same adage applies to filmmaking.

★★★

D and W: Francois Truffaut.
Cast: Jean-Plerre Leaud, Marie-France Pisier.

THE LOVES OF EDGAR ALLEN POE. (1942) Deserving of premature burial. Any connection between the dark genius of Poe and this biography is accidental and it proves, once again, how difficult it is to dramatize the creative process of writing. Poe's tragic life is here a cheap melodrama that does not even yield a superficial understanding of the author.

★★

D: Harry Lachman; W: Tom Reed and Samual Hoffenstein; Ph: Lucien Andriot; M: Emil Newman.
Cast: Linda Darnell, John Shepperd, Virginia Gilmore, Jane Darwell.

LOVING COUPLES. (1980) If *Shampoo* was made as an utterly serious look at the Beverly Hills lifestyle, it would probably emerge as this lame stab at a comedy of contemporary morals. Two doctors, married to each other, split, taking his and her Mercedes for the departure. Shirley MacLaine tries to inject some vivacity as the ex-wife coping with new sexual rules, but she is done in by the totally uncritical attitude Jack Smight takes toward his characters.
R. ★★
D: Jack Smight; W: Martin Donovan; Ph: Philip Lathrop.
Cast: Shirley MacLaine, James Coburn, Susan Sarandon, Stephen Collins.

LOVING YOU. (1957) Elvis Presley's second movie casts him as a gas station attendant who winds up pumping life into the music business with his style of singing. Discovered by a press agent, he livens up a country band and goes on to fame and fortune.Fine if you love Elvis and the songs include "Teddy Bear" and "Mean Woman Blues."
★★
D: Hal Kanter; W: Kanter and Herbert Baker; Ph: Charles Lang, Jr. .
Cast: Elvis Presley, Wendell Corey, Lizabeth Scott, Dolores Hart.

LT. ROBINSON CRUSOE. (1966) The ebullient Dick Van Dyke stranded in a lame-brained update of the Defoe story. He's a downed navy pilot who washes up on a desert island where he spends a great deal of time falling down and avoiding the native girls who eventually show up.
★★
D: Byron Paul; W: Bill Walsh and Donald Da Gradi; Ph: William Snyder; M: Bob Brunner.
Cast: Dick Van Dyke, Nancy Kwan, Akim Tamiroff, Arthur Malet.

LUCKY LADY. (1975) Stanley Donen's comic adventure of rum-running during Prohibition is about as palatable as bath-tub gin. Liza Minnelli is at the center of the movie and often—physically—between Burt Reynolds and Gene Hackman. The film, which pits this odd *menage-a-trois* against a crime boss and the Coast Guard, tries to be cynical, sentimental and boisterously funny—often in the same scene. An expensive dud.
PG. ★★
D: Stanley Donen; W: William Huyck and Gloria Katz; Ph: Geoffrey Unsworth; M: Ralph Burns.
Cast: Gene Hackman, Burt Reynolds, Liza Minnelli, Michael Hordern.

LUMIERE. (1976) Jeanne Moreau's debut as a director is an auspicious one that does not cost us the presence of a great actress since she casts herself as one of the four women in the film. An episodic and thoughtful account of four actresses. The choices of the first three illuminate the options, both past and present, of the fourth—played by Moreau. Some of the secondary relationships in the film seem to exist only for the light they shed on Moreau's predicament. Still a crisply written, honest movie.
R. ★★★★
D and W: Jeanne Moreau; Ph: Richard Aronovitch; M: Astor Piazzola.
Cast: Jeanne Moreau, Francine Racette, Lucia Bose, Caroline Cartier.

LUST FOR LIFE. (1956) Colorful, in the best sense of the word. Vincente Minnelli's adaptation of Irving Stone's biographical novel of the painful life of Vincent Van Gogh and his difficult relationship with fellow artist Paul Gaugin is both exciting and accurate. And those are adjectives rarely used in conjunction with movies about painters. Anthony Quinn won an Oscar for his Gaugin, but the laurels here belong to Kirk Douglas for his genuinely tortured Van Gogh.
★★★★
D: Vincente Minnelli; W: Norman Corwin; Ph: F.A. Young; M: Miklos Rozsa.
Cast: Kirk Douglas, Anthony Quinn, James Donald, Pamela Brown.

THE LUSTY MEN. (1952) In Nicholas Ray's rodeo drama the brand at hand is a triangle of the romantic kind. The action sequences are well done and the arena atmosphere is so authentic you can almost smell the ring. An old champion teaches a young rancher the ropes.
★★★
D: Nicholas Ray; W: Horace McCoy and David Dortort; Ph: Lee Garmes; M: Roy Webb.
Cast: Robert Mitchum, Arthur Kennedy, Susan Hayward, Arthur Hunnicutt.

M

M. (1931) Fritz Lang's brilliant and archetypal study of a psychotic killer is immeasurably enhanced by the man he chose to play the part. Peter Lorre, whistling snatches of Grieg when he goes about his gruesome business as a child killer, is one of the most memorable murderers to ever haunt the screen. In the starkly evoked Berlin underworld, both the police and the flotsam of the criminal community stalk Lorre.
★★★★★
D: Fritz Lang; W: Thea Von Harbou and Lang; Ph: Fritz Arno Wagner; M: Adolf Jansen.
Cast: Peter Lorre, Otto Wernicke, Gustav Grundgens.

MACARTHUR. (1977) A screenplay that consists of long grey lines and succeeds in making General Douglas MacArthur dull. His worst enemy would not have called him that. An even-handed biography that would be better off with a point of view, the film generates sympathy for the general without increasing our understanding of him. MacArthur's career from 1942 to his ouster in the Korean war is dutifully traced. Worth it for Gregory Peck's work in the title role.
PG.　　　　　　　　　　　　★★
D: Joseph Sargent; W: Hal Barwood, Matthew Robbins; Ph: Mario Tosi; M: Jerry Goldsmith.
Cast: Gregory Peck, Dan O'Herlihy, Ed Flanders, Ward Costello.

MACBETH. (1948) There is something in this play that tempts directors to excess. Even though he had little in the way of money and made his version in an incredible three weeks of shooting, Orson Welles succumbed. Despite the tacky sets, there are one or two striking moments, but stretches of speech are not intelligible.
★★
D: Orson Welles; Ph: John Russell; M: Jacques Ibert .
Cast: Orson Welles, Jeannette Nolan, Dan O'Herlihy, Roddy McDowall.

MACBETH. (1971) Not all the perfumes of Arabia can disguise the stench of spilled blood in Roman Polanski's extremist view of the tragedy. The most that can be said for his reading is that it has a crude originality. In seeking to make the play more graphic, he certainly succeeded even to the point of a beheading. However, what also got lopped off was a good deal of Shakespeare's poetry and that is rank impertinence. Sensible discussion of the film when it was released proved impossible since it was Polanski's first since the murder of his wife by the Manson cult. It seems to have tainted his view of Shakespeare's bloody drama.
★★
D: Roman Polanksi; Ph: Gilbert Taylor; M: The Third Ear Band.
Cast: John Finch, Francesca Annis, Martin Shaw, Nicholas Selby.

MACHINE GUN KELLY. (1958) And then came Bronson holding a Thompson. In his first starring role Bronson revealed to an anxious world the single expression that would see him through just about everything else he essayed on the screen. It suits a gangster well enough. Kelly takes up a life of crime even though he has a severe drawback—he's very scared of dying. Much noise from the Thompson machine gun.
★★
D: Roger Corman.
Cast: Charles Bronson, Susan Cabot, Jack Lambert, Wally Campo.

MACON COUNTY LINE. (1974) Two brothers drifting through the South on their way to enlist run into a case of mistaken identity and a script that sorely needs selective servicing. A sheriff who is enough of a caricature to turn any Southerners neck red with anger believes they have murdered his wife. Nasty, brutish and, being set in 1954, anachronistic on the subject of race relations.
R.　　　　　　　　　　　　　　★
D: Richard Compton; W: Compton and Max Baer; Ph: Daniel Lacambre; M: Stu Phillips.
Cast: Alan Vint, Jesse Vint, Cheryl Waters, Geoffrey Lewis.

MADAME ROSA. (1978) Another instance of the way that Simone Signoret has turned the clock to her advantage. She deepens a standard screen figure—the good-hearted whore—as a woman of compassion who takes care of the children of other prostitutes. Her portrait is one that conveys the burden of the years with dignity in the face of death and the film is refreshingly unsentimental.
PG.　　　　　　　　　　　★★★★

D and W: Moshe Mizrahi.
Cast: Simone Signoret, Claude Dauphin, Sammy Ben Youb.

THE MAD ADVENTURES OF RABBI JACOB. (1974) Elaborate French farce that combines slapstick with a brickbat satire of pride and prejudice in the person of the wonderful Louis de Funes. The comedian is a colossal bigot whose anti-Semitism is equalled only by his hatred of foreign drivers. Bizarre circumstances force him to pretend to be a rabbi and learn the error of his ways.
G.   ★★★
D: Gerard Oury; W: Oury, Daniele Thompson and Josy Eisenberg; Ph: Henri Decae; .
Cast: Louis de Funes, Suzy Delair, Marcel Dalio, Claude Giraud.

MADHOUSE. (1974) Vincent Price, as a faded horror movie star, looks at a gathering of vampires at a costume party and sneers, "In my days in Hollywood, the monsters didn't need make-up." Price is making a comeback on television and people keep getting slaughtered in the studio. He plays it to the campy hilt and clips from his old Roger Corman flicks are spliced into the modern story. One for the Price-conscious and those who like a little macabre wit with their horror.
PG.   ★★★
D: Jim Clark; W: Greg Morrison; Ph: Roy Parslow; M: Douglas Gamley.
Cast: Vincent Price, Peter Cushing, Robert Quarry, Adrienne Corri.

MAD MAX. (1979) A huge international hit that George Miller followed up with *The Road Warrior* (also known in some parts as *Mad Max II*). A high class and very well directed Australian *Death Wish*, it offers Mel Gibson as a cop in the not too distant and none too appetizing future. He leaves the force to go after the motor cycle gang that murdered his family. Nothing new in that, but the execution is scintillating and in the staging of a chase Miller is up there with Spielberg.
R.   ★★★
D: George Miller; W: Miller and James McCausland.
Cast: Mel Gibson, Joanne Samuel, Hugh Keays-Byrne, Tim Burns.

MADO. (1977) Claude Sautet, the director of the moving *Vincent, Francois, Paul and the Others*, chose the right actors but the wrong material. His leisurely style is not suit-ed to the pacing of a story about corrupt real estate speculators. Mado is a high-class prostitute whose clients include an honest property dealer. Sautet is more interested in their relationship, which would be fine if it were not entangled in such a complex plot.
                                         ★★
D: Claude Sautet; W: Sautet and Claude Neron; Ph: Jean Boffety; M: Philippe Sarde.
Cast: Michel Piccoli, Ottavia Piccolo, Jacques Dutronc, Charles Denner.

MAGIC. (1978) A ventriloquist falls prey to schizoid impulses emanating from his doll and the viewer is treated like a dummy. The worn Jekyll and Hyde theme has to draw us into the magician/ventriloquist's anguish to have any chance of success, but the bulk of the *Magic* takes place after the event when the conjurer has become a national celebrity. He flees to a motel where predictable murders ensue. One of the few blots on Richard Attenborough's distinguished copy book.
R.   ★★
D: Richard Attenborough; W: William Goldman; Ph: Victor J. Kemper; M: Jerry Goldsmith.
Cast: Anthony Hopkins, Ann-Margret, Burgess Meredith, Ed Lauter.

THE MAGIC FLUTE. (1975) Only the most diehard operaphobe could resist Ingmar Bergman's magical fusion of music and image. Mozart's opera is sung in Swedish and translated in almost doggerel subtitles. Bergman cut the opera and stressed the acting over the singing, but he captured the gaiety and exuberance of the masterpiece. Filming opera is never easy and this is one of the most successful efforts.
G.   ★★★★★
D and W: Ingmar Bergman; Ph: Sven Nykvist; M: Swedish State Broadcasting Network Symphony(Conducted by Eric Ericson).
Cast: Ulrik Cold, Josef Kostlinger, Erik Saeden, Birgit Nordin.

THE MAGIC OF LASSIE. (1978) Comeback of moviedom's favorite mutt for the first time since 1951. Two kids run away from home to recover the collie, who has been claimed by a mean new owner. Harmless songs from the Sherman brothers and a decent cast make for workmanlike family entertainment
G.   ★★
D: Don Chaffey; W: Jean Holloway, Robert and Richard Sherman; M: Robert and Richard Sherman.

Cast: James Stewart, Alice Faye, Mickey Rooney, Pernell Roberts.

THE MAGNIFICENT AMBERSONS. (1942) Orson Welles' second film, following the awesome triumph of *Citizen Kane*, was hacked down to 88 minutes by the studio. What is left is often magnificent in execution. It is set at the point in modern history where those who owned land faced the rising class which possessed industrial skills and capacities, a transition that is reflected in the emotional collisions in the movie. Welles also had to suffer an ending being added to the film, whose treatment remains an outstanding example of studio boorishness.

★★★★★

D and W: Orson Welles; Ph: Stanley Cortez; M: Bernard Herrmann.
Cast: Joseph Cotten, Dolores Costello, Anne Baxter, Tim Holt.

THE MAGNIFICENT DOPE. (1942) A modestly successful comedy about an all-American failure. Don Ameche runs a self-help program and it is his claim that anyone can make it under his tutelage. To prove it he picks a slovenly hick (Henry Fonda). The old city vs. country joke is refreshed by Fonda's easy charm as the rube.

★★★

D: Walter Lang; W: George Seaton; Ph: Peverell Marley; M: Emil Newman.
Cast: Henry Fonda, Lynn Bari, Don Ameche, Edward Everett Horton.

THE MAGNIFICENT SEVEN. (1960) Any director would be crazy to try to remake Kurosawa's stunning *The Seven Samurai*. So John Sturges transplanted it to the west with richly satisfying results. The lordless samurai become gunmen who have run out of range wars to fight. For differing reasons they agree to defend a Mexican village against a band of brigands. The bandits are led by Eli Wallach whose hamminess is more lethal than his gun. A great adventure with intelligent underpinnings as well as brightly executed action. The casting is perfect and—in the case of Yul Brynner—daring.

★★★★

D: John Sturges; W: William S. Roberts; Ph: Charles Lang, Jr.; M: Elmer Bernstein.
Cast: Yul Brynner, Steve McQueen, James Coburn, Robert Vaughn.

MAGNUM FORCE. (1973) One way to make Dirty Harry Callahan seem more mainstream politically is to suggest that there are cops more right-wing than he is. This may sound preposterous, but there is Harry stalking a death-squad in his own department. The second Clint Eastwood outing as Harry is amoral rather than immoral and extremely violent.

R. ★★

D: Ted Post; W: John Milius; Ph: Frank Stanley; M: Lalo Schifrin.
Cast: Clint Eastwood, Hal Holbrook, Mitch Ryan, Felton Perry.

MAHOGANY. (1975) An unintended black comedy that finds Diana Ross scrambling from the ghetto to the top of the fashion world as a model and designer. Standing on the balcony of her luxurious Roman villa, she declares, "It's a long way from 41st and Ellis." Sure is and this one is a long way from even mediocrity. Billy Dee Williams as an activist and Tony Perkins, as a professional decadent, compete for her favors. Try *Lady Sings the Blues* instead.

PG. ★

D: Berry Gordy; W: John Byrum; Ph: David Watkin; M: Michael Masser.
Cast: Diana Ross, Anthony Perkins, Billy Dee Williams, Jean-Pierre Aumont.

THE MAIDS. (1975) One of the worst of the American Film Theater productions. Jean Genet's play, first performed in Paris in 1947, argues the need to release hostility through fantasy. Two maids who hate their mistress act out her murder. Among its other sins, the film makes little of the opportunity to flesh out fantasy and reality on the screen and wastes three very good actresses.

PG. ★★

D: Christoper Miles; W: Miles and Robert Enders; Ph: Douglas Slocombe; M: Laurie Johnson.
Cast: Glenda Jackson, Susannah York, Vivien Merchant, Mark Burns.

THE MAIN EVENT. (1979) "There is an orgy going on inside my nose," declares Barbra Streisand and what follows is an adulatory tour of the rest of her body at exercise classes and elsewhere. Supposedly, *The Main Event* ponders the role inversion when Streisand finds her company's only remaining asset is the contract of an inept boxer. There is no room in or out of the ring for anyone except Streisand and the film is knocked out by its egocentricity.

PG. ★★

D: Howard Zieff; W: Gail Parent and Andrew Smith; Ph: Mario Tosi; M: Paul Jabara.

Cast: Barbra Streisand, Ryan O'Neal, Paul Sand, Whitman Mayo.

MAJOR BARBARA. (1940) *Pygmalion* proved so popular as a movie that another George Bernard Shaw stage hit seemed like a good idea to the same team. At times, it is verbose, but the cast has an infectious enthusiasm. The daugher of an armaments manufacturer is a Salvation Army major who becomes involved with an intellectual.

★★★

D: Gabriel Pascal; W: George Bernard Shaw; Ph: Ronald Neame; M: William Walton.
Cast: Wendy Hiller, Rex Harrison, Robert Morley, Robert Newton.

MAJOR DUNDEE. (1965) If the story of a Union officer leading a motley bunch of confederate prisoners in pursuit of Indian renegades seems muddled, don't blame Sam Peckinpah. The generous 134 minute running-time represents, by all accounts, substantial studio cutting to get it down to a commercial length. Charlton Heston did very well by the major and there's lots of Peckinpah action. The Indians have kidnapped some children and the hunt takes the unlikely posse across the border to Mexico.

★★★

D: Sam Peckinpah; W: Peckinpah, Harry Fink and Oscar Saul; Ph: Sam Leavitt; M: Daniele Amphitheatrof.
Cast: Charlton Heston, Richard Harris, Senta Berger, James Coburn.

MAKING LOVE. (1982) A sanitized and —by Hollywood standards—sympathetic account of a young doctor's emergence from the closet. His marriage is so blissful that it undermines his eventual acknowledgement of his homosexuality when he falls for a writer. As films about gay life go, this is one of the better mainstream efforts. But that's not saying much.
R. ★★★
D: Arthur Hiller; W: Barry Sandler; Ph: David M. Walsh; M: Leonard Rosenman.
Cast: Michael Ontkean, Kate Jackson, Harry Hamlin, Wendy Hiller.

MAKING THE GRADE. (1984) A definite misnomer that would not amuse a first-grader. A millionaire sends a street-smart surrogate to school in his place and havoc that is supposed to be hilarious results. Stolen from *Trading Places*, which itself took from *the Prince and the Pauper*.
R. ★

D: Dorian Walker; W: Gene Quintano; Ph: Jacques Haitkin; M: Basil Poledouris.
Cast: Judd Nelson, Joanna Lee, Gordon Jump, Ronald Lacey.

THE MALTESE FALCON. (1941) The brilliance of John Huston's debut as a director made it easy to forget that his was the third version of Dashiel Hammett's story. In it he found the theme of the corrosive power of greed that recurs so often in his film-making. *The Maltese Falcon* is a superb entertainment in which the grasping amorality of the characters is almost as comic as it is suspenseful. They are such piranhas that Bogart's Sam Spade, for all his faults, is by contrast heroic. Huston persuades us to that view by placing the movie in Spade's perspective. Spade, doggedly trying to unravel the intrigue surrounding an ancient statue, is one of Bogart's great creations and the climax is full of mordant ironies. In one film, he, Huston and a splendid cast took the gumshoe off street level to the high-rent district and redefined what a private eye film could be.

★★★★★

D and W: John Huston; Ph: Arthur Edeson; M: Adolph Deutsch.
Cast: Humphrey Bogart, Mary Astor, Sydney Greenstreet, Peter Lorre.

MAME. (1974) Bloated and dispirited rendering of the muscial about the lovable aunt introducing her nephew to the joys of life during the Depression. Those who like the stage version will resent its reduction to little more than a score and the lack of exuberance. Those who don't know it can safely pass an over-produced and dated effort.
PG. ★★
D: Gene Saks; W: Paul Zandel; Ph: Philip Lathrop; M: Jerry Herman.
Cast: Lucille Ball, Beatrice Arthur, Bruce Davison, Robert Preston.

A MAN CALLED HORSE. (1969) A profile in courage that has its partisans. Richard Harris is in his element in the part of an English nobleman whose hunting party is wiped out by Indians. He not only survives, but prospers by proving his manhood and tolerance for pain through gruesome ordeals. This becomes an excuse for a great deal of bloody-minded violence served up with a good helping of pretension. However, its sincere interest in Indian customs is commendable and its popularity prompted two sequels.

★★

D: Elliot Silverstein; W: Jack di Witt; Ph: Robert Hauser; M: Leonard Rosenman.
Cast: Richard Harris, Judith Anderson, Corinna Tsopei, Jean Gascon.

MANDINGO. (1975) James Mason tells his son and heir to stop mounting black wenches on the plantation in Louisiana in 1840. "You need a white lady to give you a son with human blood," he explains. He does and finds out she's not a virgin. Sex, gore galore and a horrible fight between two black slaves. One of the most depraved films of the seventies.
R.
D: Richard Fleischer; W: Norman Wexler; Ph: Richard H. Kline; M: Maurice Jarre.
Cast: James Mason, Susan George, Perry King, Ken Norton.

A MAN FOR ALL SEASONS. (1966) Four Oscars went to Fred Zinnemann's respectful treatment of Robert Bolt's drama of the clash of wills and conscience between Henry VIII and Sir Thomas More. It led to the execution of the latter and there is real fire in the playing of Robert Shaw (the king) and Paul Scofield's complex More. The situation between them was unique and Bolt managed to bring it to life without compromising historical accuracy.
★★★★
D: Fred Zinnemann; W: Robert Bolt; Ph: Ted Moore; M: Georges Delerue.
Cast: Paul Scofield, Robert Shaw, Wendy Hiller, Susannah York.

MAN FRIDAY. (1976) Robinson Crusoe, observes Friday, "talks gibberish most of the time." So does the screenwriter in a muddle-headed retelling of Defoe's satirical classic from Friday's perspective. In this reading, Crusoe is a slightly daft ascetic, who says things like, "That's not God. It's a banana." Friday is a black flower child whose dialogue sounds like a third-rate Jamaican calypso. Deserves to be left on the nearest desert island.
PG. ★
D: Jack Gold; W: Adrian Mitchell; Ph: Alex Phillips; M: Carl Davis.
Cast: Peter O'Toole, Richard Roundtree.

THE MAN FROM LARAMIE. (1955) A very well mounted western and one of James Stewart's more memorable contributions to the genre. His laconic presence is ideal as a cowboy who is after the men who are selling guns to Indians. His search is made more urgent by the fact that they killed his brother.
★★★★
D: Anthony Mann ; W: Frank Burt and Philip Yordan; Ph: Charles Lang, Jr.; M: George Duning.
Cast: James Stewart, Arthur Kennedy, Donald Crisp, Cathy O'Donnell.

THE MAN FROM SNOWY RIVER. (1983) An Australian youth who has lost his father in the high country must come of age on a cattle ranch whose restrictions represent a dim view of civilization. The wild horses, not surprisingly, are metaphors for freedom. The idea of the boy coping with the loss of his father through a quest is nothing new, but the Down Under setting and characters give it a fresh look.
PG. ★★★
D: George Miller; W: John Dixon; Ph: Keith Wagstaff; M: Bruce Rowland.
Cast: Kirk Douglas, Tom Burlinson, Jack Thompson, Sigrid Thornton.

MANHATTAN. (1979) Woody Allen returned to the familiar milieu peopled by neurotic New Yorkers who lead examined lives in which there are more questions than answers. He treats them as objects of sardonic sympathy as well as targets of satire, a very fragile balance that *Manhattan* sustains brilliantly. It is built on two contiguous triangles with Allen as a television writer involved with a teenager and Diane Keaton as a walking anxiety attack.
R. ★★★★★
D ann W: Woody Allen; Ph: Gordon Willis; M: Music of George Gershwin.
Cast: Woody Allen, Diane Keaton, Michael Murphy, Mariel Hemingway.

MAN HUNT. (1941) Fritz Lang's absorbing thriller is based on the novel *Rogue Male* by Geoffrey Household and he makes a somewhat bizarre premise believable. Walter Pidgeon, a hunter on holdiay in Germany, has a chance to shoot Hitler. He is beaten senseless by the Gestapo and left for dead. Back in London, German agents pursue him and Lang's direction of the chase is masterly.
★★★★
D: Fritz Lang; W: Dudley Nichols; Ph: Arthur Miller; M: Alfred Newman.
Cast: Walter Pidgeon, Joan Bennett. George Sanders, John Carradine.

MANIAC. (1981) Some movies make you want to throw up your hands in despair.

Maniac makes you want to throw up. The epitome of the new horror pornography that thrives on violence against women, it offers a throat-cutting, a garroting, a scalping and a shotgun blast to the head in loving detail. And that's while the credits are rolling. It belongs in an abbatoir.

D: William Lustig; W: Joe Spinell; Ph: Robert Lindsay; M: Jay Chataway.
Cast: Joe Spinell, Caroline Munro, Gail Lawrence, Kelly Piper.

MAN IN THE ATTIC. (1954) Bargain basement and redundant remake of *The Lodger*. Jack Palance is suitably menacing as the mystery guest whose tenure at a boarding house coincides with the Jack the Ripper killings in fog-bound London.
★★
D: Hugo Fregonese; W: Robert Presnell, Jr., and Barre Lyndon; Ph: Leo Tover; M: Lionel Newman.
Cast: Jack Palance, Constance Smith, Byron Palmer, Frances Bavier.

THE MAN IN THE GLASS BOOTH. (1975) Pedestrian transfer of Robert Shaw's play. He had his name removed from the film's credits in protest over the changes. Arthur Goldman is either a wealthy Jew still haunted by his experiences in a concentration camp or a Nazi war criminal. The movie took out Shaw's ironic tone and substituted an ending of courtroom melodrama that effectively ruined the work.
PG. ★★
D: Arthur Hiller; W: Edward Anhalt; Ph: Sam Leavitt.
Cast: Maximilian Schell, Lawrence Pressman, Lois Nettleton, Luther Adler.

THE MAN IN THE GRAY FLANNEL SUIT. (1956) The version of the Sloan Wilson novel has a certain historic interest in showing how the fifties viewed a conflict that was to acquire increasing urgency and controversy. The question is whether business success is worth the sacrifice of personal satisfaction. It wasn't asked that often in the fifties and it's a pity the answer is so pat.
★★
D and W: Nunnally Johnson; Ph: Charles Clarke; M: Bernard Herrmann.
Cast: Gregory Peck, Jennifer Jones, Frederic March, Marisa Pavan.

THE MAN IN THE IRON MASK. (1939) James Whale's excellent version of the immortal Alexander Dumas story prefers action over anything else. Whale, now revered for his horror films, enjoyed himself hugely and so, obviously, did the cast. The story involves King Louis XIV's dastardly treatment of his twin brother, whom he has locked away in a dungeon until the three musketeers come along to stir things up.
★★★★
D: James Whale; W: George Bruce; Ph: Robert Planck; M: Lucien Moraweck.
Cast: Louis Hayward, Warren Williams, Alan Hale, Bert Roach.

THE MANITOU. (1978) A 400-year-old bad medicine man, who looks like a cigar store Indian dipped in chocolate, tries to make his way into the world over the opposition of Tony Curtis. Curtis' method is to chant impenetrable Brooklynese while a good witch doctor (Michael Ansara) actually says things like, "I normally wait three risings of the sun before taking on a job."
PG. ★
D: William Girdler; W: Girdler, Tom Pope and Jon Cedar; Ph: Michel Hugo; M: Lalo Schifrin.
Cast: Tony Curtis, Michael Ansara, Susan Strasberg, Stella Stevens.

THE MAN OF A THOUSAND FACES. (1957) The face that counts belongs to James Cagney who does wonders in a biography of Lon Chaney, the master of make-up and disguise, that suffers because Hollywood made up parts of it. Despite the sentimentality involving Chaney's deaf-mute parents, Cagney achieves the most difficult feat for an actor—playing a part as another actor would do it.
★★★
D: Joseph Pevney; W: R. Wright Campbell, Ivan Goff and Ben Roberts; Ph: Russell Metty; M: Frank Skinner.
Cast: James Cagney, Dorothy Malone, Roger Smith, Robert Evans.

MAN OF LA MANCHA. (1972) Solemn, up-close and personal version of the stage musical. Peter O'Toole's Don Quixote is no impossible dreamer. He's a certifiable lunatic. James Coco's Sancho Panza is so realistic that you wonder why he spends his time trudging after the madman. The film moves between Cervantes in prison and scenes of his immortal fantasy about the eccentric knight. Arthur Hiller's direction amounts to tilting at windmills.
G. ★★

D: Arthur Hiller; W: Dale Wasserman; Ph: Goffredo Rotunno; M: Mitch Leigh.
Cast: Peter O'Toole, James Coco, Sophia Loren, Harry Andrews.

MAN OF MARBLE. (1977) Andrzej Wajda traces the impact of Stalinism and its aftermath on Poland, a country whose religious and social traditions were totally at odds with such a system. His means is the life of a model worker whose honesty causes him suffering, imprisonment and the loss of his wife. Wajda is even-handed and compassionate, but he has no mercy for political hypocrisy, which abounds in *Man of Marble*.
★★★★
D: Andrzej Wajda; W: Aleksander Scibor-Rylski; Ph: Edward Klozinski; M: Andrzej Korzynski.
Cast: Krystyna Janda, Jerzy Radziwilowicz, Jacek Lomnicki.

MAN ON A TIGHTROPE. (1953) Elia Kazan filmed one of his lesser works in Bavaria with Frederic March as the leader of a Czech circus troupe who chafes under communist restrictions and wishes to flee to the west with his company.
★★
D: Elia Kazan; W: Robert E. Sherwood; Ph: Georg Kraus; M: Franz Waxman.
Cast: Frederic March, Terry Moore, Cameron Mitchell, Gloria Grahame.

MAN ON THE ROOF. (1977) A superbly done police thriller from Sweden that is based on one of the popular Martin Beck mysteries. Beck was transplanted to the United States by Walter Matthau in *The Laughing Policeman*, but he belongs at home. Beck and his partner on the track of a cop-hating sniper. Hair-raising action, but mostly enjoyable for the depth of character of the detectives and the ennui of Sweden's cradle-to-grave welfare society.
R.   ★★★★★
D and W:: Bo Widerberg; Ph: Odd Geir Safther; M: Bjorn Jason Lindh.
Cast: Carl-Gustav Lindstedt, Hakan Serner, Sven Wolter, Thomas Helberg.

THE MAN WHO FELL TO EARTH. (1976) Good-looking science-fiction that begins with promise and then plummets quickly. David Bowie is quite effective as an alien who amasses a fortune in the electronics industry while yearning to go home. He is neither hostile nor a figure who shows up the flaws of humanity. Nor is he much else and it all ends in a sprawl of unanswered questions and tangled metaphors.
R.   ★★
D: Nicholas Roeg; W: Paul Mayersburg; Ph: Anthony Richmond; M: John Phillips.
Cast: David Bowie, Candy Clark, Buck Henry, Rip Torn.

THE MAN WHO KNEW TOO MUCH. (1934) When a film-maker of Alfred Hitchcock's genius is allowed to give us two versions of the same story, you are guaranteed an argument among buffs over the superiority of one or the other. This is a witty, darker treatment that now seems more theatrical. A family's silence about an impending political assassination is purchased through the kidnapping of the son. This marked Peter Lorre's debut in English language films.
★★★★
D: Alfred Hitchcock; W: A.R. Rawlinson, D.B. Wyndham Lewis, Edwin Greenwood, Emlyn Williams and Charles Bennett; Ph: Curt Courant; M: Arthur Benjamin.
Cast: Leslie Banks, Edna Best, Peter Lorre, Nova Pilbeam.

THE MAN WHO KNEW TOO MUCH. (1955) Alfred Hitchcock's remake of the story brings out its deeper side. Against the random blows of fate, the threatened family must look to its inner resources and is made stronger by the ordeal. Nothing is what it seems, not even a simple accident aboard a bus that sets in motion the chain of events which leads to the kidnapping of the family's only son by terrorists. The sequence in which an assassin stalks his prey during a concert at the Albert Hall is Hitchcock at his very finest.
★★★★★
D: Alfred Hitchcock; W: John Michael Hayes; Ph: Robert Burks; M: Bernard Herrmann.
Cast: James Stewart, Doris Day, Christopher Olsen, Daniel Gelin.

THE MAN WHO LOVED WOMEN. (1977) "We can't make love from dawn to dusk—that's why they invented work," cautions a tireless Lothario's doctor. In this effortless and witty film, Francois Truffaut studies a man who lives in defiance of that dictum. Bertrand Morance is an obsessive who will crash his car into a woman's just to meet her. Full of wisdom and irony and a funny discussion of how far persistence and flattery will take a man.
★★★★

D: Francois Truffaut; W: Truffaut, Michel Fermaud and Suzanne Schifmann; Ph: Nestor Almendros; M: Maurice Jaubert.
Cast: Charles Denner, Brigitte Fossey, Genevieve Fontanel.

THE MAN WHO LOVED WOMEN. (1983) Blake Edward's calamitous version of the Truffaut film finds Burt Reynolds as the tireless Lothario. Reynolds is a successful sculptor and the film jumps around various sexual episodes in his life. Its view of the proceedings is as aimless as his bed-hopping. Edwards, a believer in group therapy, then burdened the screenplay with a couch-load of psychological jargon that is offered with utter seriousness. The co-athors of the script are his son and a psychologist, which explains some of its failings.
R. ★★
D: Blake Edwards; W: Edwards, Milton Wexler and Geoffrey Edwards; Ph: Haskell Wexler; M: Henry Mancini.
Cast: Burt Reynolds, Julie Andrews, Kim Basinger, Marilu Henner.

THE MAN WHO NEVER WAS. (1956) The corpse of a drowned man is transformed into an ingenious red herring by Allied intelligence in a well-mounted World War II espionage thriller. The Nazis smell something fishy. The body carries phoney plans to persuade the Germans that the next invasion target is Greece rather than Turkey. Ronald Neame lets the movie drift with the tide a little when Stephen Boyd, a German agent, tries to check on the truth.
★★★
D: Ronald Neame; W: Nigel Balchin; Ph: Oswald Morris; M: Alan Rawsthorne.
Cast: Clifton Webb, Gloria Grahame, Stephen Boyd, Robert Fleming.

THE MAN WHO SHOT LIBERTY VALANCE. (1962) It is not liberty, but justice and the law that is at the heart of John Ford's moving western. A senator, whose political career was launched by his shooting of a gunslinger, returns to the town of Shinbone years later. As his reminiscences unfold, we come to know what really happened and to think about the occasional impotence of the law and a rougher justice meted out by John Wayne. The flashback structure allows Ford's film a measure of calm consideration of the issue as Jimmy Stewart tells the story of his youth. The film's studio look has been criticized, but it actually adds to the impact.
★★★★

D: John Ford; W: James Warner Bellah and Willis Goldbeck; Ph: William Clothier; M: Cyril Mockridge.
Cast: James Stewart, John Wayne, Lee Marvin, Vera Miles.

THE MAN WHO WASN'T THERE. (1983) Wit does a disappearing act in a comedy shot in 3-D whose reason for existence is completely invisible and whose script is strictly one-dimensional. Bruce Malmuth takes the estimable *The Invisible Man* series and turns the idea into a session for diehard voyeurs. Agents of various powers chase the invisble man and his formula when the film isn't busy being offensively leering.
R. ★
D: Bruce Malmuth; W: Stanford Sherman; Ph: Eric Haren.
Cast: Steve Guttenberg, Art Hindle, Lisa Langlois, Jeffrey Tambor.

THE MAN WHO WOULD BE KING. (1975) In one of Kipling's finest tales, John Huston found an exotic and effective vehicle for expounding on his favorite theme of the corrupting power of greed. The India of the 1880s comes to us without Hollywood tinsel and for once we can feel the seductive power it exercised over generations of Englishmen. Michael Caine and Sean Connery complement each other as two soldier-adventurers who rise to an improbable monarchy over a primitive tribe and pay the price.
PG. ★★★★★
D: John Huston; W: Huston and Gladys Hill; Ph: Oswald Morris; M: Maurice Jarre.
Cast: Sean Connery, Michael Caine, Christopher Plummer, Saeed Jaffrey.

THE MAN WITH THE GOLDEN ARM. (1955) Otto Preminger wasn't interested in the roots of addiction so much as its horrible consequences. For that reason he was criticized when the film was released, instead of for the luridness of the plot and its pat production code ending. For all that, Frank Sinatra's Frankie Machine—sometime drummer and poker player and full time heroin addict—has endured.
★★★★
D: Otto Preminger; W: Walter Newman and Lewis Meltzer; Ph: Sam Leavitt; M: Elmer Bernstein.
Cast: Frank Sinatra, Eleanor Parker, Kim Novak, Arnold Stang.

THE MAN WITH THE GOLDEN GUN. (1974) A misfire. The ninth film in the James

Bond series confirms the view that an 007 flick is only as good as the villain in it. This time its Scaramanga, which is not a rash you can pick up in Mexico but an international assassin who lives on a Far East island with a dwarf. Bond's vendetta against him is interspersed with a tired plot about a solar energy device. Leaden script with one good line when Bond snarls, "I've never killed a midget before, but..."

PG. ★★
D: Guy Hamilton; W: Richard Maibaum and Tom Mankiewicz; Ph: Ted Moore and Oswald Morris; M: John Barry.
Cast: Roger Moore, Maud Adams, Christopher Lee, Britt Ekland.

THE MAN WITH TWO BRAINS. (1983) A comedy for half-wits that's as funny as a frontal lobotomy. Steve Martin spends long stretches conversing with pickled brains, which is not to imply that the dialogue was written with any thought. Martin is a brain surgeon accidentally involved in a murder mystery. He trusts his cheating wife in Vienna and all *The Man With Two Brains* induces is a splitting headache.

R. ★
D: Carl Reiner; W: Reiner, Steve Martin and George Gips; Ph: Michael Chapman; M: Jerry Goldsmith.
Cast: Steve Martin, Kathleen Turner, David Warner.

MAN, WOMAN AND CHILD. (1983) Erich Segal, the classical scholar best known for his slushy romances, actually exceeds the fatuity of *Love Story* and *Oliver's Story*. This is Bob's story. A fling in the French surf produces a son he never knew about and when the mother dies, the kid washes up in California. Sheen and Danner are orphaned by the sentimental idiocies of the screenplay and the ignorance the film shows toward the realities of family life is almost touching.

PG ★
D: Dick Richards; W: Erich Segal and David Goodman; Ph: Richard H. Kline; M: George Delerue.
Cast: Martin Sheen, Blythe Danner, Sebastian Dungan, Arlene McIntyre.

MARATHON MAN. (1976) A suave, atmospheric thriller that blends the themes of resurgent Nazism with distrust of government. The imagery is occasionally obvious and the plot is sometimes exasperating as Laurence Olivier, in a haunting portrait of rank evil, pursues Dustin Hoffman and a cache of war loot. A now celebrated scene finds Olivier making the whine of a dental drill more terrifying than the throat-slashings that punctuate the rest of the movie.

R. ★★★★
D: John Schlesinger; W: William Goldman; Ph: Conrad Hall; M: Mel Small.
Cast: Laurence Olivier, Dustin Hoffman, William Devane, Roy Scheider.

MARCH OR DIE. (1977) The new generation of Hollywood directors that came to power in the seventies have a passion for the films of their youth. Dick Richards throws good money after a bad movie in this lavish celebration of every banality ever found in a Foreign Legion film. Hackman, like the other characters in the film, has a past and no future as he reluctantly leads a party of archaeologists to pillage a tomb revered by the Arabs. The kind of thing that has been parodied endlessly is here treated with the utmost seriousness.

PG. ★★
D: Dick Richards; W: David Zelag Goodman; Ph: John Alcott; M: Maurice Jarre.
Cast: Gene Hackman, Terence Hill, Catherine Deneuve, Max Von Sydow.

MARILYN. (1963) Marilyn Monroe's career in clips from 15 films, ranging from *A Ticket to Tomahawk* to *Something's Got to Give*, the production she was working on when she died. Rock Hudson narrates the documentary, which doesn't aspire to be anything more than skin-deep.

★★
W: Don Medford.

THE MARK OF ZORRO. (1940) Top marks in the masked man sweepstakes go to the stylish remake of the version by Douglas Fairbanks, Sr. Although not a natural swashbuckler, Tyrone Power did Zorro with great zest and the production is very stylish. Films in this genre are made by their villains as much as the heroes and there was none better than Basil Rathbone as Zorro's nemesis.

★★★★
D: Rouben Mamoulian; W: John Taintor Foote; Ph: Arthur Miller; M: Alfred Newman.
Cast: Tyrone Power, Basil Rathbone, Linda Darnell, Gale Sondergaard.

MAROONED. (1969) Three astronauts are stranded in space where the chief advantage is that they won't have to sit through John Sturges' handsomely mounted drama, which unfolds in a bigger vacuum. Gregory Peck is the man in charge on the ground as the crew's oxygen supply runs out. So do Sturges' ideas on making what is a potential edge-of-the-seat movie exciting. There is much labored worrying over the waiting wives and the dialogue has all the pep of a NASA training manual.

★★

D: John Sturges; W: Mayo Simon; Ph: Daniel Fapp.
Cast: Gregory Peck, Gene Hackman, Richard Crenna, James Franciscus.

THE MARQUISE OF O. (1976) A ravishingly beautiful film about the consequences of a rape. Rohmer takes the simple story of a noblewoman dishonored and impregnated in Italy in 1798 and fashions an ironically observed discussion of the gap between social principles and human passions. The Russian count who takes advantage of the marquise wants to marry her out of love and a need to salvage his honor, but she becomes an outcast. Elegantly acted by a German cast.
PG. ★★★★
D and W: Erich Rohmer; Ph: Nestor Almendros.
Cast: Edith Clever, Bruno Ganz, Peter Luhr, Edda Seippel.

THE MARRIAGE OF MARIA BRAUN. (1979) Among the finest works of the brilliant, if erratic Rainer Werner Fassbinder. Through the figure of a woman who progresses from naivete to ultra-confidence and success, Fassbinder offers an ironic study of German society rising from the ashes after World War II. Maria Braun marries a soldier who is then sent to the front. Her commitment to him lasts through a variety of affairs and other tests and Hanna Schygulla is in superb form as Maria.
R. ★★★★
D: Rainer Werner Fassbinder; W: Peter Marthescheimer and Pea Frohlich; Ph: Michael Balhaus; M: Peer Raben.
Cast: Hanna Schygulla, Klaus Lowitsch, Ivan Gottfried John, Gisela Uhlen.

MARY OF SCOTLAND. (1936) Although the conflict between Elizabeth I and Mary, Queen of Scots, seems made for the screen the complexity of the underlying issues and the length of the story conspire against the director. In this case, it's John Ford and his work is uncharacteristically stiff and ponderous and suggests that he did not find the material to his taste. His aloofness proved contagious and this is not among Hepburn's better efforts.

★★

D: John Ford; W: Dudley Nichols; Ph: Joseph H. August; M: Nathaniel Shilkret.
Cast: Katharine Hepburn, Frederic March, Donald Crisp, Florence Eldridge.

MARY POPPINS. (1964) Walt Disney crammed everything he knew about captivating kids and their elders into an enchanting fantasy that made a star of Julie Andrews. She sweeps into the movie as the "practically perfect" nanny and her rivals for the job of overseeing the Banks children are blown away by a magical gust of wind. She is able to transport the children and the audience on a series of adventures that have lost none of their appeal. Charming performances and scintillating technical execution.
★★★★★
D: Robert Stevenson; W: Bill Walsh and Donald Da Gradi; Ph: Edward Colman; M: Richard and Robert Sherman.
Cast: Julie Andrews, Dick Van Dyke, David Tomlinson, Glynis Johns.

M*A*S*H. (1970) When satire reaches the level of sustained ferocity to be found in Robert Altman's black comedy, it is generally hard to find room for compassion. The achievement of Altman's most accessible—and successful—film is that it functions as a very funny black comedy, a powerful anti-war and anti-military statement and a deeply felt portrait of how decent men and women respond to unrelenting and pointless carnage. At a mobile army hospital, two surgeons try to save the wounded and keep their sanity amidst the mud and madness. The film inspired a long-running television series that was worthy of the original and that was certainly a first.
★★★★★
D: Robert Altman; W: Ring Lardner, Jr.; Ph: Harold Stine; M: Johnny Mandel.
Cast: Elliott Gould, Donald Sutherland, Tom Skerritt, Sally Kellerman.

THE MASK OF DIMITRIOS. (1944) A reunion of Sidney Greenstreet and Peter Lorre and a bird of a slightly different feather from *The Maltese Falcon*. Lorre is a a Dutch mystery writer who is in Istanbul to satisfy his curiosity about Zachary Scott, an unsavory victim of murder. A splendid cast, a brooding atmosphere reeking of back-stabbing intrigue and double-crosses. It's based on Eric Ambler's *A Coffin for Dimitrios*.

★★★

D: Jean Negulesco; W: Frank Gruber; Ph: Arthur Edeson; M: Adolph Deutsch.
Cast: Peter Lorre, Sidney Greenstreet, Zachary Scott, Faye Emerson.

THE MASK OF FU MANCHU. (1932) Behind it is no less than Boris Karloff, brandishing fingernails that are almost as long as the sword of Genghis Khan—the prize he seeks. This is the definitive Fu Manchu movie because it takes the right approach and refuses to allow the humor to become campy. Fu, of course, wants to take over the world by wiping out whites and he has a nasty bag of tricks awaiting people who bother him.

★★★

D: Charles Brabin; W: John Willard, Irene Kuhn and Edgar Allan Woolf; Ph: Tony Gaudio.
Cast: Boris Karloff, Myrna Loy, Lewis Stone, Karen Morley.

THE MASQUE OF THE RED DEATH. (1964) Roger Corman's reputation rests on his low-budget quickies. This very stylish and gloomy horror film is therefore untypical, even though it was made at the same frenzied pace. It combines the Poe story of the title with another one from the master and sets the action in a terrifying castle dominated by Prince Prospero(Vincent Price). While plague ravages 12th century Italy, Prospero lives out his own ideas of home entertainment. Price was rarely so menacing and the striking photography is by Nicholas Roeg, who went on to loftier movies.

★★★

D: Roger Corman; W: Charles Beaumont; Ph: Nicholas Roeg; M: David Lee.
Cast: Vincent Price, Jane Asher, Hazel Court, Patrick Magee.

THE MASTER GUNFIGHTER. (1974) In style and craftsmanship, Tom Laughlin's preposterous western is reminscent of a military training film on ominous social diseases. Japanese sword fights among nineteenth century Californians are among the absurdities strewn through the addled tale of a hero who kills innocent people to hang on to his hacienda. Ron "Superfly" O'Neal is transformed into Spanish Fly for the proceedings.
PG. ★
D: Tom Laughlin; W: Harold Lapland.
Cast: Tom Laughlin, Ron O'Neal, Lincoln Kilpatrick, Barbara Carrera .

THE MASTER OF BALLANTRAE. (1953)

Far short of a masterpiece even though the locations are handsome and Errol Flynn gave the swordplay his best cut. A toned-down version of Robert Louis Stevenson's beloved novel in which two brothers take different sides when Bonnie Prince Charles makes his ill-fated attempt to seize the throne from the incumbent Hanover monarchy. Where Stevenson introduced a considerable degree of ambiguity, the film turns the tale into a Cain and Abel saga.

★★★

D: William Keighley; W: Herb Meadow; Ph: Jack Cardiff; M: William Alwyn.
Cast: Errol Flynn, Anthony Steel, Roger Livesey, Beatrice Campbell.

MASTER OF THE WORLD. (1961) The airborne *Nautilus* is called the *Albatross* and it hangs around the neck of William Witney in his efforts to emulate *20,000 Leagues Under the Sea*. Vincent Price, like Captain Nemo, is a belligerent pacifist who believes the good end justifies the very mean means. Richard Matheson tried to write some sense into the idea, but the fantasy is a shoddy production that never rises to the level of its underwater inspiration.

★★

D: William Witney; W: Richard Matheson; Ph: Gil Warrenton; M: Les Baxter.
Cast: Vincent Price, Charles Bronson, Henry Hull, Mary Webster.

A MATTER OF TIME. (1976) A richness of embarrassments for all concerned with the senior Minnelli seemingly intent on photographing his daughter's nose from every conceivable angle. Adapted from the novel *A Film of Memory*—they at least had the good sense not to use that title. Bergman is an impoverished countess given to many lapses of sense and stretches of boring incoherence. So is the film, in which she takes a hotel maid under her wing.
PG. ★
D: Vincent Minnelli; W: John Gay; Ph: Geoffrey Unsworth; M: Nino Oliviero.
Cast: Ingrid Bergman, Liza Minnelli, Charles Boyer, Tina Aumont.

McCABE AND MRS. MILLER. (1971) A far more salutary trip to the west for Robert Altman than *Buffalo Bill and the Indians* turned out to be. This gossamer creation brings Warren Beatty to a mining town at the turn of the century. He is a gambler and perhaps a gunslinger who establishes a brothel and falls for the madam. Upon this flimsy foundation Altman builds a western that wittily disparages Hollywood's packaging of the west. At the same time, Altman's trademark devices give the film a gritty realism to go along with the lyric beauty he uncovers in the scenery and the ramshackle town.

★★★★

D: Robert Altman; W: Altman and Brian Mackay; Ph: Vilmos Zsigmond; M: Leon Ericksen.
Cast: Warren Beatty, Julie Christie, Rene Auberjonois, Shelley Duvall.

McKENNA'S GOLD. (1969) As the credits roll, vultures wheel overhead and down below is a lifeless, large scale western. It was mutilated by the studio when it was released and the plot consequently makes little sense. Gregory Peck finds an old Indian and a map to the ultimate gold-mine and he accumulates a motley assortment of adventurers when he looks for it. Omar Sharif's idea of playing a bad Mexican is to act with his teeth. J. Lee Thompson is no alchemist and the movie remains pure dross.

★★

D: J. Lee Thompson; W: Carl Foreman; Ph: Joseph MacDonald, Harold Wellman; M: Quincy Jones.
Cast: Gregory Peck, Omar Sharif, Telly Savalas, Keenan Wynn.

MCLINTOCK!(1963) The ungreening of *The Quiet Man*. John Wayne and Maureen O'Hara go at it again and he's a lot louder than he was in Ford's film. Wayne is a cattleman trying to convince his wife to forgive and forget and come home. A few amusing scenes but you're better off in Ireland.

★★

D: Andrew McLaglen; W: James Edward Grant; Ph: William Clothier; M: Frank de Vol.
Cast: John Wayne, Maureen O'Hara, Patrick Wayne, Yvonne de Carlo.

MEAN STREETS. (1973) Martin Scorsese brings you the sidewalks of New York. He grew up in Little Italy in lower Manhattan and he opens up a world of petty thieves and hustlers who ply their trade on streets that are as mean as they come. Robert De Niro's Johnny Boy is a haunting portrait and Harvey Keitel, a low level Mafia soldier inhibited by scruples, is equally impressive. Scorsese went on to more famous New York movies like *Taxi Driver*, but this one has the power of discovery to propel it.

R.   ★★★★

D: Martin Scorsese; W: Scorsese and Mardik Martin; Ph: Norman Gerard.
Cast: Robert De Niro, Harvey Keitel, Amy Robinson, David Proval.

MEATBALLS. (1979) *Animal House* goes to summer camp with predictable results. Camp North Star is next to a rich kids' camp and you can guess what happens. The meatballs are the counselors and the only reason to catch the film is Bill Murray, who, happily, went on to better things.

PG.   ★★

D: Ivan Reitman; W: Len Blum, Harold Ramis, Dan Goldberg and Janis Allen; Ph: Don Wilder.
Cast: Bill Murray, Harvey Atkin, Kate Lynch, Russ Banham.

MEATBALLS—PART II. (1984) A return to summer camp that has a great deal of trouble making up its mind about its audience, which is not to imply that a brain was present at any stage of the production. Part teen sex and anti-authority humor and, for the younger set, a defiantly witless sub-plot about an alien taken in by the kids. He stays in the camp outhouse, which is where the film belongs.

PG.   ★

D: Ken Widerhorn; W: Bruce Singer; Ph: Donald Morgan; M: Ken Harrison.
Cast: Richard Mulligan, John Mengatti, Hamilton Camp, Kim Richards.

THE MECHANIC. (1972) Michael Winner, who later directed Charles Bronson in *Death Wish*, tries to make something out of the story of a hired killer. The assassin disguises his murders by inducing heart attacks and gas main explosions, but nothing can mask Bronson's limitations. In his hands, the super-cool killer is a clod. Jan-Michael Vincent eats a sandwich and watches his girl-friend bleed to death and thus earns a place as Bronson's apprentice. And you're actually supposed to care about what happens to them.

PG.   ★

D: Michael Winner; W: Lewis John Carlino; Ph: Richard Kline; M: Jerrry Fielding.
Cast: Charles Bronson, Jan-Michael Vincent, Jill Ireland, Keenan Wynn.

MEGAFORCE. (1982) The kind of atrocity that should be banned under the Geneva Convention. A strike team that makes the *A-Team* look and sound like the Royal Shakespeare Company, use armored motorcycles

to go after a mercenary terrorist. Mr. T could write better dialogue.
PG. ★
D: Hal Needham; W: James Whittaker, Albert Ruddy, Andre Morgan and Needham; Ph: Michael Butler; M: Jerry Immel.
Cast: Barry Bostwick, Persis Khambatta, Edward Mulhare, Henry Silva.

MELVIN AND HOWARD. (1980) On a lonely desert road, Melvin Dummar, a lowly gas station attendant, picks up an old man. Later, when Howard Hughes dies, Dummar produces the celebrated Mormon will under which he inherits the billionaire's fortune. Quite rightly, the focus of mordantly observed piece of modern Americana is Melvin rather than Howard. Jonathan Demme made a flawlessly acted essay on greed in its many guises.
R. ★★★★
D: Jonathan Demme; W: Bo Goldman; Ph: Tak Fujimoto; M: Bruce Langhorne.
Cast: Jason Robards, Paul Le Mat, Mary Steenburgen, Jack Kehoe.

THE MEMORY OF JUSTICE. (1976) Marcel Ophuls, best known for *The Sorrow and the Pity*, complied a massive documentary of the Nuremberg war crimes trials. There is little that is excessive or repetitious in the four-hour running time and Ophuls opens the issue up to the larger questions of justice and responsibility. He brings Vietnam and Algeria into the argument. Ophuls is a sharp and informed interviewer with a knack for eliciting revealing answers from his subjects.
★★★★
D: Marcel Ophuls; Ph: Mike Davis.

THE MEPHISTO WALTZ. (1971) A sophisticated and subtly played possession movie. Alan Alda is a journalist who wins an interview with a reclusive, world-famous concert pianist. The musician is dying of leukemia and strange things begin happening to the reporter. He finds he is in danger of exchanging his body and soul for a by-line and about to discover a new meaning for deadlines. A good cast and no hysterics.
★★★
D: Paul Wendkos; W: Ben Maddow; Ph: William Spencer; M: Jerry Goldsmith.
Cast: Alan Alda, Curt Jurgens, Jacqueline Bisset, Bradford Dillman.

MERRILL'S MARAUDERS. (1962) There is an emotional resonance to Jeff Chandler's stirring portrait of Gen. Merrill, a dying leader who ignores his own suffering to goad his men. It was Chandler's last film. It's also among his best because the direction is in the hands of Sam Fuller, who has few equals in mixing war action with a first-hand knowledge of the more mundane details of life among the grunts. They fight their way across Burma.
★★★
D: Sam Fuller; W: Fuller and Milton Sperling; Ph: William Clothier; M: Howard Jackson.
Cast: Jeff Chandler, Ty Hardin, Andrew Duggan, Peter Brown.

MERRY CHRISTMAS, MR. LAWRENCE. (1983) Take a cult Japanese director, a Japanese pop star and David Bowie and place them in a prison camp in 1942. A predictably strange brew results with a commandant trying to break Bowie through a dense layer of homoeroticism and sadism. The struggle for power within the camp is reflected in a futile struggle for meaning in the film. "In truth," intones Tom Conti, the captured colonel. "No one is right." Not here anyway.
R. ★★
D: Nagisa Oshima; W: Oshima and Paul Mayersberg; Ph: Toichiro Nauroshima; M: Ryuichi Sakamoto.
Cast: David Bowie, Tom Conti, Ryuichi Sakamoto, Jack Thompson.

METALSTORM. (1983) Someone called Jared Syn wears an art deco outfit that makes him look like Manhattan's Chrysler building and a hairpiece suggestive of a dead otter. On an unnamed world his sin is cryptically explained as "inciting the nomads." The action traces efforts to find him and flagrantly rips off *The Road Warrior.*
PG. ★
D: Charles Band; W: Ian Adler; Ph: Chris Condon; M: Richard Band.
Cast: Jeffrey Byron, Mike Preston, Kelly Palzis, Richard Moll.

METEOR. (1979) In what amounts to fair warning, the narrator says meteors used to be taken as signs of impending doom. The glum prophecy is fulfilled quickly. A five mile wide meteor that looks as menacing as a pet rock is on a collision course with earth and only a joint Soviet-American effort to blow it up stands in the way. Traditional fifties sci-fi plotting.
PG. ★
D: Ronald Neame; W: Stanley Mann and

Edmund H. North; Ph: Paul Lohmann; M: Laurence Rosenthal.
Cast: Sean Connery, Natalie Wood, Karl Malden, Brian Keith.

METROPOLIS. (1926) The version of Fritz Lang's vision of the future —circa 2026— that you are most likely to encounter is the one released in 1984 with a score by Giorgio Moroder. Lunatics throw acid on great oil paintings, so why not acid rock at Lang's classic? In committing first degree Moroder on *Metropolis*, color was added to compound the felony and the music from various hard rockers is pounding and monotonous. Lang's film is a still imposing spectacle that shows a ruling class enslaving the rest of humanity.
★★★★
D: Fritz Lang; W: Thea Von Harbou; Ph: Karl Freund.
Cast: Brigitte Helm, Alfred Abel, Gustav Frohlich, Fritz Rasp.

MICKEY'S CHRISTMAS CAROL. (1983) The first Mickey Mouse cartoon in thirty years offered a chance to compare the work of the new Disney animators with the storied older crew. Their effort is presentable but without the flair or imaginative spark of the studio's animated classics. The 24-minute feature casts the familiar Dickens characters with Donald Duck as Scrooge and Mickey as his hapless clerk.
G. ★★★

MIDDLE AGE CRAZY. (1980) Bruce Dern's Bobby Lee Burnett is a man who has everything, including a wife who cries "Bingo!" every time she has an orgasm. His complaint is male menopause, which makes him buy a Porsche and run off with a cheerleader when he turns 40. My complaint is that a serious condition of men in middle life is reduced to a phase that's over by the end of the picture.
R. ★★
D: John Trent; W: Carl Kleinschmitt; Ph: Reginald H. Morris; M: Matthew McCauley.
Cast: Bruce Dern, Ann-Margret, Graham Jarvis, Eric Christmas.

MIDNIGHT EXPRESS. (1978) An embellished account of Billy Hays, who was tossed into a Turkish jail for smuggling hashish. In order to present him as a martyr, the Turks are shown as unspeakable barbarians. Alan Parker's violent film also suggests that the kind of treatment dished out in the prison is an outrage for foreigners but acceptable for Turkish inmates. Parker tries to make Hays far more than the figure of pathos he actually is.
R. ★★
D: Alan Parker; W: Oliver Stone; Ph: Michael Seresin; M: Giorgio Moroder.
Cast: Brad Davis, Randy Quaid, John Hurt, Irene Miracle.

MIDNIGHT MADNESS. (1980) The city of Los Angeles becomes a giant game board with competing teams of college students in a movie that hasn't a clue about comedy or much of anything else. It's the work of two film school graduates who should go back to the first grade. Crammed with the usual stereotypes of college life.
PG. ★
D and W: David Wechter and Michael Nankin; Ph: Frank Phillips; M: Julius Wechter.
Cast: David Naughton, Debra Clinger, Eddie Deezen, Brad Wilkin.

A MIDSUMMER NIGHT'S SEX COMEDY. (1982) A paean to the joys of nature becomes the counterpoint for the pain of six characters on a country weekend at the turn of the century. With Woody Allen in charge there is, of course, a dark clound inside the sylvan lining. Three men in differing stages of life and emotional commitment and their women play out a tale of the price one pays for seizing or not seizing the moment. A romantically wistful and genial work that found Allen emerging from the bitterness of *Stardust Memories*.
PG. ★★★★
D and W: Woody Allen; Ph: Gordon Willis; M: Music of Mendelssohn.
Cast: Woody Allen, Mia Farrow, Tony Roberts, Jose Ferrer.

MIDWAY. (1976) The country was still soured by the Vietnam experience, so Hollywood turned to a sincere and deafening account of one of the pivotal sea battles in history. The opportunity to present unblemished heroism and clear-cut moral choices is seized unabashedly. More big-name stars than admirals, a silly sub-plot involving Charlton Heston and a son he keeps addressing as "Tiger" and awful Richard Loo-speak on the Japanese side. Still, the film captures the scope of the Pacific battle and the part luck played in the outcome.
PG. ★★★
D: Jack Smight ; W: Donald Sanford; Ph: Harry Stradling, Jr.; M: John Williams.

Cast: Charlton Heston, Henry Fonda, Robert Mitchum, Glenn Ford.

MIGHTY JOE YOUNG. (1949) The commoner's *King Kong*. Members of the same team that produced the monarch of monster movies settled for a plebian twist with an ape going Hollywood. The gifted special effects are present, but there is nothing especially viable about the underlying idea. It belongs in the basement of the Empire State building.

★★

D: Ernest Schoedsack; W: Ruth Rose; Ph: Roy Hunt; M: Roy Webb.
Cast: Terry Moore, Ben Johnson, Frank McHugh, Robert Armstrong.

MIKEY AND NICKY. (1976) Elaine May shot 1.5 million feet of film in Philadelphia and then got in a fight with Paramount over the editing. For once the studio was right. This incredibly prolix and rambling film has something to do with a hit man, the bookie who is his target and the friend he should not trust. The dialogue is of the free-form spontaneity more appropriate to a Cassavetes film and few signs of May's considerable talent ever peep through.

R. ★★
D and W: Elaine May; Ph: Victor J. Kemper; M: John Strauss.
Cast: John Cassavetes, Ned Beatty, Peter Falk, Rose Arrick.

MILDRED PIERCE. (1945) In the passionate and melodramatic account of a woman's relationship with her incredibly nasty daughter, some critics suggest that Joan Crawford was drawing on her own experiences. It's a conjecture that Christine Crawford, author of *Mommy Dearest*, would certainly dispute. Crawford rises from waiting tables to success in the restaurant business in a bravura, old-fashioned performance that stops just this side of affectation.

★★★

D: Michael Curtiz; W: Ranald MacDougall and Catherine Turney; Ph: Ernest Haller; M: Max Steiner.
Cast: Joan Crawford, Ann Blyth, Jack Carson, Zachary Scott.

THE MILLIONAIRESS. (1960) A mere shaving from the original play by George Bernard Shaw. The world's richest woman finds her money meaningless when she falls for a socialist Hindu doctor who tends the sick in London's East End. The comic and political points are dropped like anvils, but Sellers does a charming Indian and Sophia Loren was never more breathtakingly beautiful.

★★

D: Anthony Asquith; W: Wolf Mankowitz; Ph: Jack Hildyard; M: Georges Van Parys.
Cast: Sophia Loren, Peter Sellers, Alistair Sim, Vittorio de Sica.

THE MIRACLE ON 34TH STREET. (1947) Yes, Virginia, there may be a Santa Claus and Edmund Gwenn, who won the Oscar for his work, is the one to convince you. A Christmas evergreen that has lost none of its guileless charm, it features Gwenn as a department store Santa who claims he's the real thing. The subsequent trial contends he might not be in error.

★★★

D and W: George Seaton; Ph: Charles Clarke; M: Cyril Mockridge.
Cast: Edmund Gwenn, Maureen O'Hara, John Payne, Gene Lockhart.

THE MIRROR CRACK'D. (1980) A placid Agatha Christie Miss Marple mystery where the turns by the stars outshine those in the plot. Kim Novak and Elizabeth Taylor are two aging screen sirens who hate each other and someone is trying to poison the latter. Their catty exchanges and Tony Curtis' Hollywood sleaze liven up a film that is as slow as life in the English village where murder takes place.

PG. ★★
D: Guy Hamilton ; W: Jonathan Hales and Barry Sandler; Ph: Christopher Challis; M: John Cameron.
Cast: Angela Lansbury, Elizabeth Taylor, Kim Novak, Tony Curtis.

MISSING. (1982) Charles Horman, a Harvard graduate, is a child of the sixties who writes left wing articles in Santiago, Chile. Costa-Gavras, who has no peers in the depiction of fascism, recounts the true story of his disappearance and the agonizing search mounted by his wife and father. The acting is splendid in its restrained eloquence and the Greek director has framed it with a reticence of his own. He lets a few images— bodies laid out in a mortuary, a soldier slashing at a woman's slacks with a bayonet—say everything.

R. ★★★★
D: Costa-Gavras; W: Costa-Gavras and Donald Stewart; Ph: Ricardo Aronovich; M: Vangelis.

Cast: Jack Lemmon, Sissy Spacek, Melanie Mayron, John Shea.

THE MISSIONARY. (1982) A missionary comes home from Africa and is plunged into an elegant black comedy. His bishop assigns him to the recovery of fallen women in London's East End and he soon falls in with them. The wit is charming, the class jokes agreeably mean and on the mark and Michael Palin, one of the Monty Pythons, gives an arch charm to the minister.
R.   ★★★★
D: Richard Loncraine; W: Michael Palin; Ph: Peter Hannan; M: Mike Moran.
Cast: Michael Palin, Maggie Smith, Trevor Howard, Denholm Elliott.

THE MISSOURI BREAKS. (1976) A highly anticipated pairing of two of our most fascinating actors that was justly scorned when people finally got to see it. Marlon Brando's sexually indeterminate hired gun is one of the strangest things he's ever done. Jack Nicholson, as his quarry in a Montana cattle rustling saga, looks on in bemusement. Pompous, violent and muddled, the film put the western several steps closer to Boot Hill.
PG.   ★★
D: Arthur Penn; W: Tom McGuane; Ph: Michael Butler; M: John Williams.
Cast: Marlon Brando, Jack Nicholson, Randy Quaid, Kathleen Lloyd.

MISTER ROBERTS. (1955) Jack Lemmon may have the Oscar for his hilarious Ensign Pulver, but the acting one eventually savors in this sobering comedy aboard a rustbucket in World War II comes from Henry Fonda and James Cagney. Fonda repeated his stage role as a man of gentle instincts who yearns to be in a war that is passing him by and the outcome is genuinely affecting. Cagney is the captain making life miserable for everyone except his audience. The film has many things to say about what boredom and ambition do to men in a particular environment and its humor has never lost its pungency. John Ford withdrew from the direction and handed over to Mervin LeRoy.
                                          ★★★★★
D: Mervin LeRoy; W: Frank Nugent and Joshua Logan; Ph: Winton Hoch; M: Franz Waxman .
Cast: Jack Lemmon, Henry Fonda, James Cagney, William Powell.

MITCHELL. (1975) You're a Los Angeles mobster who wants to eliminate a trouble-some cop. Naturally, you do it discreetly by chasing him all over the landscape with two dune buggies. Exceptionally dumb police movie that has something to do with a heroin shipment. It consists mostly of car chases or getting in and out of cars. Several scenes feature Joe Don Baker simply sitting in his car and there is more entertainment to be had at your local garage.
R.   ★
D: Anrdew V. McLaglen; W: Ian Kennedy Martin; Ph: Harry Stradling; M: Larry Brown and Jerry Styner.
Cast: Joe Don Baker, Linda Evans, John Saxon, Martin Balsam.

MIXED COMPANY. (1974) A sort of multiracial edition of *My Three Sons*. A basketball coach, rendered impotent by mumps and down on his team, decides to adopt a black, a Vietnamese and an Indian girl. Disney with ethnic jokes.
PG.   ★
D: Mel Shavelson; W: Shavelson and Mort Lachman; Ph: Stan Lazan; M: Fred Karlin.
Cast: Joe Bologna, Barbara Harris, Lisa Gerritson, Arianne Heller.

MOBY DICK. (1956) Credit John Huston with making a genuine effort to convey the moral underpinnings, the symbolism and the mysticism of Melville's novel instead of settling for a superficial sea-going adventure. If all the elements do not quite meld they are at least there for the attentive viewer. This has led some to criticize the film as slow and disjointed and certainly Gregory Peck's Ahab is at times as wooden as his leg. Huston's is the third and easily the best film of Ahab's obsessive pursuit of the white whale that maimed him. The whaling sequences were done with great difficulty at sea and they remain very impressive.
                                          ★★★
D: John Huston; W: Huston and Ray Bradbury; Ph: Oswald Morris; M: Philip Stainton.
Cast: Gregory Peck, Richard Basehart, Leo Genn, Orson Welles.

MODERN PROBLEMS. (1981) Many of the problems that plague contemporary comedy are displayed in one of Chevy Chase's sappier endeavors. An air-traffic controller who trudges through life and suffers various humiliations acquires telekinetic powers. He is the kind of nerd who makes you side with his tormentors and all he does with his new skill is extract petty vengeance.
PG.   ★★

D: Ken Shapiro; W: Shapiro, Tom Sheroh-
man and Arthur Sellers; Ph: Edmond Koons;
M: Dominic Frontiere.
Cast: Chevy Chase, Dabney Coleman, Patti
D'Arbanville, Mary Kay Place.

MODERN TIMES. (1936) As timely now as
when Charlie Chaplin made his grudging
concession to the sound era. If you discount
a patter song, the only use of sound is the
noise of modern life. Its essential theme is
the collision between man and machine and
those who exploit labor. Its many brilliant
sequences are highlighted by the hilarious
and devastating look at the assembly line
worker who beccomes the victim of an automatic feeding machine. It was Chaplin's last
"silent" and it ranks high on the list of his
achievements.
★★★★★
D and W: Charles Chaplin; Ph: Rollie Totheroh and Ira Morgan; M: Charles Chaplin.
Cast: Charles Chaplin, Paulette Goddard,
Henry Bergman, Chester Conklin.

MOHAMMAD, MESSENGER OF GOD.
(1976) Moustapha Akkad said he wished to
make his religion more intelligible with this
plodding epic in which the face of the prophet is never revealed. He merely proves that it
is impossible to make a good film on one's
knees. The prophet's absence, because of
Islamic injunctions, means that the central
figure in the film is missing and there is nothing to fill the gap. Throughout the three
hours, piety pre-empts dramatic interest.
PG. ★★
D: Moustapha Akkad; W: H.A.L. Craig; Ph:
Jack Hildyard; M: Maurice Jarre.
Cast: Anthony Quinn, Irene Papas, Michael
Ansara.

MOMENT BY MOMENT. (1978) A debacle spoken in Californiese ("You've had your
desirability reaffirmed") and proof that women
directors can be just as bad as men when
it comes to making a vacuous love story. John
Travolta is a drifter called Strip, and he takes
his name literally. Between dressing and un-
dressing he has an affair with a bored upper
class woman. Jane Wagner's idea of conveying that ennui is to force us to share it.
R. ★
D and W: Jane Wagner; Ph: Philip Lathrop;
M: Lee Holdrige.
Cast: John Travolta, Lily Tomlin, Andra
Akers, Bert Kramer.

MOMMIE DEAREST. (1981) Hollywood
has made a lot of cliff-hangers over the
years, but the supposed inside story on Joan
Crawford and motherhood is a literal coat-
hanger. Finding a wire one in her daugher
Christine's closet, she flies into a rage. In a
let-it-all hang-out version of Christine's best
seller, Crawford is the star of her own monster movie. The best—or the worst—thing
you can say about *Mommie Dearest* is that
it's the Joan Crawford film Joan Crawford
never made.
PG. ★★
D: Frank Perry; W: Perry, Frank Yablans,
Tracy Hotchner and Bob Getchell; Ph: Paul
Lohmann; M: Henry Mancini.
Cast: Faye Dunaway, Diana Scarwid, Steve
Forrest, Howard Da Silva.

MONKEY BUSINESS. (1952) It seems
entirely apt that Cary Grant should star in a
comedy about the accidental discovery of a
serum that retards aging and literally knocks
years off one's appearance and behavior.
He obviously kept some after the shooting.
The humor is heightened by the fact that a
chimp makes the scientific breakthrough.
The results for Grant, his wife and boss are
predictable and amusing.
★★★
D: Howard Hawks; W: Ben Hecht, Charles
Lederer and I.A.L. Diamond; Ph: Milton
Krasner; M: Leigh Harline.
Cast: Cary Grant, Ginger Rogers, Charles
Coburn, Marilyn Monroe.

MONSIEUR HULOT'S HOLIDAY. (1952)
Jacques Tati's delightful creation has something of Mr. Magoo in his make-up through
an endless capacity to cause disaster without noticing. Hulot wants only to please the
other holiday-makers at a French seaside
resort but fate is forever getting in the way of
good intentions.
★★★
D: Jacques Tati; W: Tati and Henri Marquet;
Ph: Jacques Mercanton; M: Alain Romans.
Cast: Jacques Tati, Nathalie Pascaud, Michele Rolla, Louis Perrault.

MONSIGNOR. (1982) The Vatican signals
the election of a new pope by burning the
final ballots and sending up a smoke signal.
Next time the cardinals can use the script for
what should be called *My Brilliant Curia*. An
American priest struggles through the dense
intrigues of church politics and boredom
becomes the eighth deadly sin. A debacle,
but one that can be savored for its spectacular awfulness.
R. ★

D: Frank Perry; W: Abraham Polonsky and Wendell Mayes; Ph: Billy Williams; M: John Williams.
Cast: Genevieve Bujold, Christopher Reeve, Fernando Rey, Jason Miller.

MONTY PYTHON AND THE HOLY GRAIL. (1975) The British comedy troupe puts the round table on a square screen in a riotously funny romp through Arthurian myth . When the king cites the legend of the Lady of the Lake, a peasant retorts, "Some strange woman lying in a pond? Just because some watery tart threw a sword at you...." Sketches and silliness loosely tied to Arthur's search for the legendary chalice.
★★★★
D: Terry Gilliam; W: Graham Chapman, John Cleese, Eric Idle and Michael Palin; Ph: Terry Bedford; M: Neil Innes.
Cast: Graham Chapman, John Cleese, Terry Gilliam, Eric Idle .

MONTY PYTHON'S THE MEANING OF LIFE. (1983) It adds little more than hilarity to our understanding of existence, but what's wrong with that? A series of riotously funny episodes loosely strung together around a seven ages of man theme. They gamble a lot, but their batting average is higher than anyone else in screen comedy. The humor is vitriolic toward everything from Catholic attitudes to birth control to English school teachers
R. ★★★★
D: Terry Jones; W: The Monty Pythons; Ph: Peter Hannan.
Cast: Graham Chapman, Terry Jones, John Cleese, Eric Idle, Michael Palin.

MOONFLEET. (1955) A boy embroiled with smugglers on the Dorset coast in the 1770s. Familiar terrain, but Fritz Lang didn't find it especiallly congenial. He is more interested in atmosphere than pertinent details of plot and motive. The boys's guardian turns out to be the leader of the smugglers and an inheritance is at stake.
★★
D: Fritz Lang; W: Margaret Fitts and Jan Lustig; Ph: Robert Planck; M: Miklos Rozsa.
Cast: Stewart Granger, George Sanders, Joan Greenwood, Viveca Lindfors.

THE MOON IN THE GUTTER. (1983) Jean-Jacques Beineix followed up the briliant *Diva* with a work that defied the laws of physics by placing an atmosphere inside a vacuum. It is an odd and empty attempt to fuse nineteenth century romanticism with existentialism and Beineix is completely indifferent to developing or trying to explain his characters. Gerard Depardieu is obsessed with finding the murderer of his sister.
R. ★★
D: Jean-Jacques Beineix; W: Beineix and Oliver Megault; Ph: Philippe Rousselot; M: Gabriel Yared.
Cast: Gerard Depardieu, Nastassja Kinski, Vittorio Mezzogiorno, Victoria Abril.

MOONLIGHTING. (1982) Jeremy Irons, moonlighting from his usual patrician roles, fashions a haunting portrait of a compromised man that is also a precise political statement. He is the leader of a gang of Polish workers who come to London illegally to renovate a house. Back home, the Solidarity crisis erupts and Irons tries to keep it from the others. The film was made in only five months and that belies the craftsmanship and exactitude of its imagery.
PG. ★★★★
D and W: Jerzy Skolimowski; Ph: Tony Pierce Roberts; M: Stanley Myers.
Cast: Jeremy Irons, Eugene Lipinski, Jiri Stanislaw, Eugeniusz Haczkiewicz.

MOON OVER MIAMI. (1941) In the precondominium era, the Condos Brothers do the dancing and Betty Grable and Carol Landis migrate from Texas to Florida in search of Mr. Right, who must be Mr. Rich. A forgettable score, which tends to be fatal to such enterprises, but *Moon Over Miami* undeniably established Grable's musical stardom in the forties.
★★
D: Walter Lang; W: Brown Holmes and Vincent Lawrence; Ph: Peverell Marley; M: Alfred Newman.
Cast: Betty Grable, Carol Landis, Don Ameche, Robert Cummings.

MOONRAKER. (1979) The gadgeteers are in the driver's seat in the eleventh James Bond adventure. It has nothing to do with the Ian Fleming novel, which was hopelessly outdated, and less with his skill as a storyteller. Lewis Gilbert regards the plot as an interference with the stunts and the display of hardware. The villain, played straightforwardly by Michel Lonsdale, plans a worldwide plague while he watches from the safety of a space station.
PG. ★★★
D: Lewis Gilbert; W: Christopher Wood; Ph: Jean Tournier; M: John Barry.

Cast: Roger Moore, Michel Lonsdale, Lois Chiles, Richard Kiel.

THE MOON-SPINNERS. (1964) Jewel thievery and intrigue on the island of Crete with some tale-spinning that takes a few cretinous turns. Haley Mills, by then 18 and evincing an interest in men, and the return of Pola Negri to the screen after a 20-year absence are of interest. Mainly, the production fell through the gap between the adult audience and the younger viewer.
★★
D: James Neilson; W: Michael Dyne; Ph: Paul Beeson; M: Ron Grainer.
Cast: Hayley Mills, Pola Negri, Eli Wallach, Peter McEnery.

MORE AMERICAN GRAFFITI. (1979) An update on the characters rather than a lame sequel. The happy innocents of George Lucas' reminiscence of his California youth grow up and collide with the turbulent sixties. Sock hops surrender to napalm and Vietnam and other issues. Lovers of the original may be annoyed, but this is a striking if not wholly successful approach.
PG. ★★★
D and W: B.W.L. Norton; Ph: Caleb Deschanel .
Cast: Candy Clark, Ron Howard, Bo Hopkins, Paul Le Mat.

THE MORE THE MERRIER. (1942) The home front instead of the real front gets some attention in George Stevens'· well-turned if rather syrupy comedy. Jean Arthur is a Washigton, D.C., office worker who does her bit for the housing shortage by taking in two lodgers and romance makes a quick entry soon afterwards.
★★★
D: George Stevens; W: Robert Russell, Frank Ross, Richard Flournoy and Lewis Soter; Ph: Ted Tetzlaff; M: Leigh Harline.
Cast: Jean Arthur, Joel McCrea, Charles Coburn, Richard Gaines.

MORGAN. (1966) A wonderfully subversive comedy that mixes sixties zaniness with blacker humor. Through bad luck or misjudgement, David Warner never fulfilled the great promise of his work in Karel Reisz' piquant film. He is overwhelming as a London painter whose wife wants a divorce and whose fanciful obsession with gorillas plays a part in his rebuttal. Off the wall of the cage and still extremely funny.
★★★★
D: Karel Reisz; W: David Mercer; Ph: Gerry

Trupin and Larry Pizer; M: John Dankworth.
Cast: David Warner, Vanessa Redgrave, Robert Stephens, Irene Handl.

MORNING GLORY. (1933) Katharine Hepburn in the glorious spring of her career brings a marvelous freshness and vivacity to a standard making-it-in-show-business theme. It's all about Eva Lovelace, a young actress from New England who gets her big break when the star holds out for more money. Familiar stuff, but Hepburn was enchanting and won her first Oscar.
★★★
D: Lowell Sherman; W: Howard J. Green; Ph: Bert Glennon.
Cast: Katharine Hepburn, C. Aubrey Smith, Adolphe Menjou, Douglas Fairbanks, Jr.

MOSCOW DOES NOT BELIEVE IN TEARS. (1980) Nor, with a 150 minute running time, does it believe in brevity. In one of the most incredible votes in Oscar history, this modest Russian tale of three women coming of age in the capital managed to beat out *Kagemusha* and *The Last Metro* as the best foreign film. The tone is mildly satirical, which one supposes is daring given the country of origin.
★★
D: Vladimir Menshov; W: Valentin Chiornykh; Ph: Igor Slabnevitch.
Cast: Vera Alentova, Irina Moravyova, Natalia Vavlivova, Raisa Ryazanova.

MOSCOW ON THE HUDSON. (1984) Touching, whimsically funny and patriotic in the best sense of the word, Paul Mazursky's plunge into the American melting pot concentrates on some people who really can't go home again. Russian emigres in New York cope with a bewildering new world and try to sever the ties to the old one. Robin Williams gives a marvelously restrained account of a circus musician who defects and the film tries and succeeds in being something more than satirical.
PG ★★★★
D: Paul Mazursky; W: Mazursky and Leon Capetanos; Ph: Donald McAlpine; M: David McHugh.
Cast: Robin Williams, Maria Conchita Alonso, Alejandro Rey, Cleavant Derricks.

THE MOST DANGEROUS GAME. (1932) The year before they made *King Kong*, the same team of film-makers collaborated on a picture that argues that men can be a lot less civilized than apes. The much-imitated idea is that people who like to hunt and kill animals for sport are only a step removed from doing the same thing to their fellow man. Leslie Banks is a nobleman whose diversion consists of luring innocent people to his island where they become targets of his marksmanship.

★★★

D: Ernest Schoedsack and Irving Pichel; W: James Creelman; Ph: Henry Gerrard; M: Max Steiner.
Cast: Leslie Banks, Joel McCrea, Fay Wray, Robert Armstrong.

MOTEL HELL. (1980) A tedious attempt to do to horror movies what *Airplane* did to the disaster genre. The specific object of derision is *The Texas Chainsaw Massacre,* a picture that is as far beyond satire as it is beneath contempt. One of the things amputated here is wit. Rory Calhoun is a motel owner who makes sausages out of guess what?
R. ★
D: Kevin Connor; W: Steven-Charles Jaffe and Robert Jaffe; Ph: Thomas DelRuth; M: Lance Rubin.
Cast: Rory Calhoun, Nina Parsons, Paul Linke, Elaine Joyce.

MOTHER, JUGS AND SPEED. (1976) Life aboard a private ambulance in Los Angeles that is full of sick jokes and definitely not worth chasing. Raquel Welch wants to be a woman ambulance driver and the test seems to be how many breast jokes she can survive —including the "jugs" of the title. An attempt at humor in the M*A*S*H vein that ends up on a stretcher.
R. ★
D: Peter Yates; W: Tom Mankiewicz; Ph: Ralph Woolsey; M: Joel Sill.
Cast: Bill Cosby, Harvey Keitel, Raquel Welch, Larry Hagman.

MOTHER KUSTERS GOES TO HEAVEN. (1977) The prolific and short-lived Rainer Werner Fassbinder opens with an undeniable truth—a murder-suicide. Then he asks what becomes of the same truth in different perspectives. A diatribe against the callousness and manipulation of journalism and the impotence of left-wing politics. The widow of the suicide, marvelously played by Brigitte Mira, has to cope with reporters and activists trying to exploit the death of her husband, a factory worker. A shrewd and subtly observant movie.

★★★★

D: Rainer Werner Fassbinder; W: Fassbinder,

Kurt Raab; Ph: Michael Balhaus; M: Peer Raben.
Cast: Brigitte Mira, Ingrid Caven, Armen Meier, John Karlheinz.

MOTHER LODE. (1983) Actually more of a father's burden with Charlton Heston taking the parts of twin brothers and his son directing. Heston goes in for a bizarre Scottish accent as a gold prospector in the Canadian wilds whose quest is interrupted by a couple looking for a lost friend. Everyone catches gold fever and there are few surprises. The scenery and photography are handsome.
PG. ★★
D and W: Fraser Heston; Ph: Richard Leiterman; M: Kenn Wannberg.
Cast: Charlton Heston, Nick Mancuso, Kim Basinger, John Marley.

MOTHER'S DAY. (1980) The victims —three college friends—get to attack their tormentors—a crazy mother and her two demented sons. This none too original turn allows *Mother's Day* a double helping of especially gruesome scenes of torture. Not even the director's mother could love it.

D: Charles Kaufman; W: Kaufman and Warren D. Leight; Ph: Joe Mangine; M: Phil Gallo and Clem Vicari.
Cast: Nancy Hendrickson, Deborah Luce, Tiana Pierce, Holden McGuire.

MOUNTAIN FAMILY ROBINSON. (1980) The kind of family movie that has people called Boomer in it. The third outing for the Wilderness family with the usual adventures involving animals and the threat of eviction. Not bad for younger children. For some reason, the London Symphony Orchestra was hired to play the score.
G. ★★
D: John Cotter; W: Arthur R. Dubs; Ph: James Roberson; M: Robert O. Ragland.
Cast: Robert Logan, Susan Damante Shaw, Heather Rattray, Ham Larsen.

THE MOUSE THAT ROARED. (1959) International terrorism and the other unsavory aspects of current Cold War politics lend a quaint charm to the Peter Sellers diversion. The Duchy of Grand Fenwick, casting about desperately for funds, declares war on the United States with the sole purpose of losing and living prosperously on the ensuing foreign aid. Sellers plays three roles.

★★★

D: Jack Arnold; W: Roger Macdougall and Stanley Mann; Ph: John Wilcox; M: Edwin Astley.
Cast: Peter Sellers, Jean Seberg, David Kossoff, William Hartnell.

MOVE OVER, DARLING. (1963) *My Favorite Wife* remains the favored version of the story. The remake has Doris Day returning from her presumed death in an air-crash to discover that there's now another wife in the way. Somewhat strained, but the leads make it work.

★★

D: Michael Gordon; W: Hal Kanter and Jack Sher; Ph: Daniel Fapp; M: Lionel Newman.
Cast: Doris Day, James Garner, Polly Bergen, Chuck Connors.

MOVIE MOVIE. (1978) Most film spoofs turn into parodies lost and this is not one but two of the great exceptions. Larry Gelbart (of *Tootsie* fame) said at the time that he wrote two parodies because he did not believe one could be stretched across feature length. It amounts to a double helping. *Dynamite Hands* is a ring full of every boxing movie cliche you've ever dreamed of. Even better is *Baxter's Beauties of 1933*, an exuberant and affectionate skewering of thirties musicals.
PG. ★★★★
D: Stanley Donen; W: Larry Gelbart and Sheldon Keller; Ph: Charles Rosher, Jr.; M: Ralph Burns.
Cast: George C. Scott, Harry Hamlin, Eli Wallach, Red Buttons.

MR. BILLION. (1977) European heart-throb Terence Hill in a hopelessly inflated comedy about an Italian mechanic who inherits a billion dollars from a rich American uncle. Jackie Gleason is in charge of the effort to prevent him from reaching San Francisco to collect. The reputations of several good character actors take a drubbing and Kaplan resorts to much desperate action to flesh out the empty and often crass script.

★

D: Jonathan Kaplan; W: Kaplan and Ken Friedman; Ph: Matthew F. Leonetti; M: Dave Grusin.
Cast: Terence Hill, Valerie Perrine, Jackie Gleason, Slim Pickens.

MR. DEEDS GOES TO TOWN. (1936) City vs. country has rarely been exploited with such good nature and faith in the decency of man. Gary Cooper is a rube given to playing the tuba and the twist is that he makes his fortune before going to New York. The Big Apple beckons after he inherits $20 million. He is used by all and sundry and has to fight off rapacious relatives in a famous courtroom defense.

★★★★
D: Frank Capra; W: Robert Riskin; Ph: Joseph Walker; M: Howard Jackson.
Cast: Gary Cooper, Jean Arthur, Lionel Stander, George Bancroft.

MR. KLEIN. (1977) One of the group of films produced in France in the seventies that addressed the painful subject of anti-Semitism and collaboration in World War II. A wealthy Catholic finds himself mistaken for a Jew. Losey is more preoccupied with the metaphors suggested by this predicament than the possibilities of subtle drama. Alain Delon is equally cool and withdrawn in the title role.

★★★
D: Joseph Losey; W: Franco Solinas; Ph: Gerry Fisher; M: Egisto Macchi.
Cast: Alain Delon, Jeanne Moreau, Michel Lonsdale, Juliet Berto.

MR. MAJESTYK. (1974) A genuine curiosity that offers something unique in movies: "meloncholia." Charles Bronson, a watermelon grower in Colorado, earns the enmity of the Mafia for bizarre reasons. This allows a scene in which his crop is machine-gunned to shreds by hoods. The fact that Bronson acts like a vegetable doesn't help in an otherwise routine action film.
PG. ★
D: Richard Fleischer; W: Elmore Leonard; Ph: Richard Kline; M: Charles Bernstein.
Cast: Charles Bronson, Al Lettieri, Linda Cristal, Lee Purcell.

MR. MOM. (1983) The role reversal in which a husband stays home with the kids and the wife goes off to work has been trotted out before. What makes the diffference is Michael Keaton's engaging performance as the father whose affection far exceeds his ability to cope. He breaks out of the stereotype and it's not surprisng that the movie caught on. Good family entertainment.
PG. ★★★
D: Stan Dragoti; W: John Hughes; Ph: Victor J. Kemper; M: Lee Holdridge.
Cast: Michael Keaton, Teri Garr, Frederick Koehler, Taliesin Jaffe.

MR. QUILP. (1975) What the Dickens are they doing making a musical out of *The Old*

Curiosity Shop? The question lingers after the final credits. Dickens' novel is not an obvious candidate for light children's fare and the attempted solution is to make the villains so grotesque that they are ridiculous. Harmless enough until the end, when the film waxes serious. Anthony Newley is in charge of making this convincing in the title role. The wretched songs he wrote don't help.
G. ★★
D: Michael Tuchner; W: Louis Kamp and Irene Kamp; Ph: Christopher Challis; M: Elmer Bernstein.
Cast: Anthony Newley, Michael Hordern, David Hemmings, David Warner.

MR. RICCO. (1975) Dean Martin ambles in without his walking schtick—a glass of booze and a raised eyebrow. But in their absence, fatigue soon overwhelms both him and the viewer. A defense attorney takes on the case of a black militant accused of killing two San Francisco cops and survives several attempts on his life. The plot is a muddle that is never sorted out to anyone's satisfaction.
PG. ★★
D: Paul Bogart; W: Robert Hoban; Ph: Frank Stanley; M: Chico Hamilton.
Cast: Dean Martin. Eugene Roche, Thalmus Rasulala, Denise Nicholas.

MRS. MINIVER. (1942) World War II from a woman's point of view and the best thing about it is Greer Garson's noble Englishwoman confronting privations and emotional damage as her country fights for survival. It's very much a Hollywood view of England at the time, but its value transcends the obvious preaching.
★★★
D: William Wyler; W: Arthur Wimperis and George Froeschel; Ph: Joseph Ruttenberg; M: Herbert Stothart.
Cast: Greer Garson, Walter Pidgeon, Teresa Wright, Dame May Whitty.

MR. SMITH GOES TO WASHINGTON. (1939) James Stewart had a peerless ability to convey an innate decency on the screen without seeming in the slightest way priggish. Frank Capra capitalized on it by sending him to the capital as a young senator who discovers the grubby realities of politics. The corniness of the story—and the faith in the system that borders on wishful thinking—is lightening by Capra's marvelous sense of humor and the presence of Jean Arthur, as Stewart's secretary.
★★★★

D: Frank Capra; W: Sidney Buchman; Ph: Joseph Walker; M: Dmitri Tiomkin.
Cast: James Stewart, Claude Rains, Jean Arthur, Thomas Mitchell.

THE MUMMY. (1932) The mother of them all and the mummy dearest to the hearts of fans. It is best watched with an effort to forget or at least ignore the later accretions and excess bandages that made mummyribilia an object of derision—even to Abbott and Costello. Boris Karloff swathes himself as an Egyptian notable revived afer a very big sleep and much taken with a girl he sees as a reincarnation of an old love.
★★★
D: Karl Freund; W: John Balderston; Ph: Charles Stumar.
Cast: Boris Karloff, Zita Johann, David Manners, Arthur Byron.

THE MUMMY. (1959) "You must not continue digging here," warns the fanatical Egyptian as the pith-helmeted British prepare to violate the sanctity of a mummy's tomb. Hammer films ignored the warning and got away with it. The potential for the ridiculous is high, but it is suavely avoided. A straight-faced, slightly ponderous tale of an exhumed mummy taking it out on the graverobbers in Victorian England.
★★★
D: Terence Fisher; W: Jimmy Sangster; Ph: Jack Asher; M: Frank Reizenstein.
Cast: Peter Cushing, Christopher Lee, Yvonne Furneaux, Eddie Byrne.

THE MUPPET MOVIE. (1979) Kermit and the gang made a terrific debut. The world's favorite frog goes from Georgia to Hollywood, collecting muppets along the way. It's strongly reminiscent of *The Wizard of Oz* done up with contemporary humor and, like that classic, should not be dismissed as just a kids' film. A marvelously blended movie.
G. ★★★★
D: James Frawley; W: Jerry Juhl and Jack Burns; Ph: Isidore Mankofsky; M: Paul Williams and Kenny Ascher.
Cast: Charles Durning, Bob Hope, Milton Berle, Mel Brooks.

THE MUPPETS TAKE MANHATTAN. (1984) Kermit, Miss Piggy and the gang try to make it on the Great White Way. Along the way they encounter everyone from the mayor to muggers as the world's favorite frog seeks his destiny as a playwright. The third muppet movie restored the series to the quality of the first one.
G. ★★★

D: Frank Oz; W: Oz, Jay Tarses and Tom Patchett; Ph: Robert Paynter; M: Ralph Burns.
Cast: (voices) Jim Henson, Frank Oz, Dave Goelz.

MURDER BY DEATH. (1976) A lame tribute to the conventions of the whodunit, but the only mystery is how so much talent could produce so little diversion. A millionaire invites five of the world's greatest detectives to dinner and a murder with a reward going to the sleuth who can solve it. Neil Simon wrote a play called *Only When I Laugh*. Not much danger of that here.
PG. ★★
D: Robert Moore; W: Neil Simon; Ph: David M. Walsh; M: Dave Grusin.
Cast: Peter Sellers, Peter Falk, James Coco, Alec Guinness.

MURDER BY DECREE. (1978) Bob Clark has a better eye for the Victorian period than for his story. Christopher Plummer, the 27th actor to don the deerstalker as Sherlock Holmes, gives a traditional and very diverting account of the great detective. The mystery centers around the identity of Jack the Ripper and the theory that he could have been a member of the royal family. Things are telegraphed early and the fun lies in watching Holmes and Watson put the pieces of the puzzle together.
PG. ★★★
D: Bob Clark; W: John Hopkins; Ph: Reg Morris; M: Carl Zittrer.
Cast: Christopher Plummer, James Mason, Donald Sutherland, Genevieve Bujold.

MURDERER'S ROW. (1966) Dean Martin's fondness for the grape may be explained by the recurring appearance of this Matt Helm adventure on the Late Show. He acts like a man groggy from a recent fall off a barstool, but what's Karl Malden's excuse for showing up? Malden's the villain who kidnaps Ann-Margret. To round out the vanity production, Martin's son, Dino is in the cast.
★
D: Henry Levin; W: Henry Baker; Ph: Sam Leavitt; M: Lalo Schifrin.
Cast: Dean Martin, Karl Malden, Ann-Margret, Camilla Sparv.

MURDER INC. (1960) A run-of-the-mill, factually based gangster story distinguished by Peter Falk's slimy characterization of Abe Reles, a hood who turned on his colleagues. Stuart Whitman and May Britt are a young couple who become involved with the syndicate's plans to operate murder as a capitalist enterprise in the thirties.
★★
D: Burt Balaban and Stuart Rosenberg; W: Irv Tunick and Mel Barr ; Ph: Gayne Rescher; M: Frank de Vol.
Cast: Peter Falk, Stuart Whitman, May Britt, Henry Morgan.

MURDER ON THE ORIENT EXPRESS. (1974) A cerebral thriller and a stylish paean to the thirties from Sidney Lumet. The celebrated train is trapped in a snowdrift and Hercule Poirot, masterfully done by Albert Finney, must find the murderer of an American millionaire. This being Agatha Christie, everyone has a motive. A witty script with Sean Connery rounding on Poirot and demanding, "I want your solemn oath as a foreigner." The passengers on board are not strangers on a train and this remains the the best of the Agatha Christie-inspired films.
PG. ★★★★
D: Sidney Lumet; W: Paul Dehn; Ph: Geoffrey Unsworth; M: Richard Rodney Bennett.
Cast: Albert Finney, Ingrid Bergman, Sean Connery, Lauren Bacall.

MURDERS IN THE RUE MORGUE. (1932) Bela Lugosi is a still chilling Dr. Mirakle who kidnaps women to further his experiments with a gorilla. Based on the Edgar Allen Poe story and roundly chastised for violence and perversion in its day.
★★★
D: Robert Florey; W: Tom Reed, John Huston and Dale Avery; Ph: Karl Freund .
Cast: Bela Lugosi, Sidney Fox, Leon Ames, Bert Roach.

MURDERS IN THE RUE MORGUE. (1971) Poe's story takes the stage in the fourth film version. The action is switched to a Paris theater where the actors and others tend to make bloody exits.
★★
D: Gordon Hessler; W: Charles Wicking and Henry Slesar; Ph: Manuel Berengier; M: Waldo de Los Rios.
Cast: Jason Robards, Herbert Lom, Lili Palmer, Adolfo Celi.

THE MUSIC MAN. (1962) River City in Iowa is never quite the same after a roguish and charming Pied Piper shows up to suggest the organization of a boys band. Robert Preston's Harold Hill is a commanding and enormously vital figure in an adaptation of the stage show that Hollywood had the good sense not to change appreciably. The songs include "76 Trombones" and "Till There Was You"

★★★★
D: Morton Da Costa; W: Marion Hargrove; Ph: Robert Burks; M: (songs) Meredith Wilson.
Cast: Robert Preston, Shirley Jones, Buddy Hackett, Hermione Gingold.

MUSTANG COUNTRY. (1976) Passable children's entertainment about the pursuit of a black stallion, but why bother when you can see The Black Stallion? Joel McCrea came out of retirement at the age of 70 to play a rancher who undertakes the capture of the mustang. His help includes an orphaned Indian boy and a dog whose ability to fetch sticks is repeated tediously.
G.   ★★
D and W: John Champion ; Ph: J. Barry Herron; M: Lee Holdridge.
Cast: Joel McCrea, Nika Mina, Robert Fuller, Patrick Wayne.

MY BLOODY VALENTINE. (1981) Some of it was shot in a coal mine and, unfortunately, there was no cave-in. In the town of Valentine Bluffs, the bodies pile up when the mad killer returns. The excuse this time is that he was trapped in a mine accident and survived by eating his co-workers. His diet should have included the movie.
R.   ★
D: George Mihalka; W: John Beaird ; Ph: Rodney Gibbons; M: Paul Zaza.
Cast: Paul Kelman, Lori Hallier, Neil Affleck, Keith Knight.

MY BODYGUARD. (1980) A genuine and touching look at the pangs of growing up that suffers only from taking the setbacks of adolescence as seriously as kids do. Tony Bill picked a universal experience—coping with the bigger kids and bullies in high school—and made a very impressive directing debut. Clifford, a sharp-witted teen, tries to enlist a large and morose kid as his protection. A charming antidote to the usual teen fare.
PG.   ★★★★
D: Tony Bill; W: Alan Ormsby; Ph: Michael D. Margulies; M: Dave Grusin.
Cast: Chris Makepeace, Adam Baldwin, Matt Dillon, Ruth Gordon.

MY BRILLIANT CAREER. (1980) A wry and high spirited Australian essay on the enduring dilemma of a woman who has to choose between marriage and a career. Set at the turn of the century, it is occasionally given to feminist hindsight that rings hollow. Judy Davis is wonderful as Sybylla, a woman who knows what she doesn't want out of life but who only has a vague notion of what alternatives she might pursue. Two men try to make up her mind.
G.   ★★★
D: Gillian Armstrong; W: Eleanor Witcombe; Ph: Don McAlpine; M: Nathan Waks.
Cast: Judy Davis, Wendy Hughes, Sam Neill, Robert Grubb.

MY DARLING CLEMENTINE. (1946) One of John Ford's major achievements in the genre and Henry Fonda's towering account of Wyatt Earp, this western deals in myths and legends rather than precise history. Ford even scorned Tombstone, the site of the epic gunfight between the Earps and the Clantons, in favor of his beloved Monument Valley. The photography and composition are as exquisite as anything he did and Victor Mature surprised many of his detractors with his account of Doc Holliday.
★★★★★
D: John Ford; W: Winston Miller and Samuel Engel; Ph: Joseph MacDonald; M: Cyr Mockridge.
Cast: Henry Fonda, Victor Mature, Linda Darnell, Walter Brennan.

MY DINNER WITH ANDRE. (1981) A meal you never want to end and a feast for those who thought the art of conversation had been killed by talk shows and creeping gumbyism. Louis Malle invites us to take a seat at the table and decide if there is any middle ground between Andre Gregory, the avant-garde director, and Wallace Shawn, the New York actor and playwright. First Andre recounts his mystical experiences in some of the world's weirder communes and then, in a subtle shift, Malle makes us feel the contrasts between the two men. All dinners should be this entertaining.
PG.   ★★★★
D: Louis Malle; Ph: Jeri Sopanen ; M: James Bruce.
Cast: Wallace Shawn, Andre Gregory, Roy Butler, Jean Lenauer.

MY FAIR LADY. (1964) A fair list of the best post-war Hollywood musicals would have to find room for My Fair Lady although George Cukor's version is not without its flaws. It is generally agreed that Audrey

Hepburn, who was chosen over Julie Andrews, is a liablity in the early going and an asset to the later scenes. Rex Harrison's Higgins took the Oscar and dominates the movie in a way that helps it through some lesser moments. Everything else reflects the care and craftsmanship the Lerner and Loewe reworking of *Pygmalion* deserved.

★★★★

D: George Cukor; W: Alan Jay Lerner; Ph: Harry Stradling; M: Frederick Loewe.
Cast: Rex Harrison, Audrey Hepburn, Stanley Holloway, Gladys Cooper.

MY FAVORITE YEAR. (1982) Peter O'Toole takes a sketchily written and unoriginal character and turns him into an uproarious figure that sweeps Richard Benjamin's tribute to the infancy of television past its more sentimental moments. He is Alan Swann, a debauched movie star who has to appear on a Sid Caesar-style comedy show to thwart deportation. The frenzied and spontaneous world of the Caesar era is affectionately caught.

PG. **★★★★**

D: Richard Benjamin; W: Norman Steinberg and Dennis Palumbo; Ph: Gerald Hirschfield; M: Ralph Burns.
Cast: Peter O'Toole, Mark Linn-Baker, Jessica Harper, Joseph Bologna.

MY MAN GODFREY. (1936) The ultimate Depression comedy is anything but depressing. Its sublimely funny premise sends wealthy Carole Lombard on a scavenger hunt. She comes up with a scavenger at a garbage dump—a man down on his luck whom she takes home to work as a butler. What Lombard really found was a part rich in opportunities that she seized gleefully and, in William Powell, an exquisite foil. The picture had a pungent relevance in the thirties that made it very popular. June Allyson and David Niven remade it in the fifties and succeeded in reminding us how good the first version really is.

★★★★

D: Gregory La Cava; W: La Cava, Morris Ryskind and Eric Hatch; Ph: Ted Tetzlaff.
Cast: Carole Lombard, William Powell, Alice Brady, Mischa Auer.

MYRA BRECKENRIDGE. (1970) Rex Reed undergoes a sex change operation and turns into Raquel Welch. Gore Vidal's novel turns into a tasteless shambles.

★

D: Michael Sarne; W: Sarne and David Giler; Ph: Richard Moore; M: Lionel Newman.
Cast: Mae West, John Huston, Raquel Welch, Rex Reed.

MYSTERIOUS ISLAND. (1961) Jules Verne would be more than a little mystified at what was done to his story, but it emerges as a stand-out children's adventure. Civil war prisoners escape from a jail in a balloon and are blown far off course to a remote and uncharted island. In the company of some conveniently shipwrecked women they take on the best Ray Harryhausen has to offer in the monster department and fall in with Captain Nemo. Bernard Herrmann's score is a bonus.

★★★

D: Cy Endfield; W: John Prebble, Daniel Ullman and Crane Wilbur; Ph: Wilkie Cooper; M: Bernard Herrmann.
Cast: Gary Merrill, Michael Craig, Joan Greenwood, Herbert Lom.

THE MYSTERIOUS ISLAND OF CAPTAIN NEMO. (1974) A remake of the much better *Mysterious Island* with the fugitive balloonists landing on an island populated by machines rather than monsters. Omar Sharif, as Nemo, is hardly on the screen at all and looks bored when he is. Under the circumstances you can hardly blame him.

PG. **★**

D: Juan Antonio Bardem and Henri Colpi; W: Bardem and Jacques Champreux; Ph: Enzo Serafin; M: Gianni Ferrio.
Cast: Omar Sharif, Philippe Nicaud, Gerald Tichy, Jess Hahn.

THE MYSTERY OF EDWIN DROOD. (1935) Charles Dickens' unfinished final novel is given a quite polished treatment by Stuart Walker. Claude Rains is at the center as the man of outward probity who teaches the choir but who is not above a little opium and romantic envy when the sun goes down.

★★★

D: Stuart Walker; W: John Balderston.
Cast: Claude Rains, David Manners, Heather Angel, Valerie Hobson.

THE MYSTERY OF THE WAX MUSEUM. (1933) Michael Curtiz' harrowing tale of a sculptor who is hideously deformed and takes to redefining our notion of live sculpture is still pretty frightening. The special effects involving melting wax are prime for their time and add to the suspense as the sculptor makes Fay Wray the next victim on his list.

★★★★

D: Michael Curtiz; W: Don Mullally and Carl Erickson; Ph: Ray Rennahan.
Cast: Lionel Atwill, Fay Wray, Glenda Farrell, Frank McHugh.

MY TUTOR. (1983) Yet another boy-meets-older-woman for the teen fantasy market. He needs French lessons and learns more than grammar in the arms of Caren Kaye. At the ripe old age of thirty, she qualifies as ancient in this market. The sex is also a little more explicit than is usual.

R.   ★

D: George Bowers; W: Joe Roberts; Ph: Marc Ahlberg; M: Webster Lewis.
Cast: Caren Kaye, Matt Lattanzi, Kevin McCarthy, Clark Brandon.

N

THE NAKED AND THE DEAD. (1958) Norman Mailer's novel about a squad of American soldiers in the Pacific did much to cut through the impression of the war left by a vast accumulation of movies made to further the cause. Hollywood did some cutting of its own and the book that made Mailer's reputation was castrated. The conspicuous absentee is the four-letter language and raunchiness that banished the book to the top shelf of public libraries. Another casualty is the insight into the way men react to extreme peril. It ends up being a very cowardly combat film.
★★

D: Raoul Walsh; W: Denis and Terry Sanders; Ph: Joseph La Shelle; M: Bernard Herrmann.
Cast: Aldo Ray, Cliff Robertson, Raymond Massey, William Campbell.

THE NAKED CITY. (1948) The television series later inspired by Jules Dassin's slice-of-life thriller had the famous tag-line, "There are eight million stories in the naked city. This has been one of them." There are doubtless many better than the one Dassin chose, but what elevates his work is the way New York and the pulse of its streets is captured. Two homicide detectives seach for a girl's killer, but that is almost incidental to the film's style and atmosphere.
★★★★

D: Jules Dassin; W: Malvin Wald and Albert Maltz; Ph: William Daniels; M: Miklos Rozsa.
Cast: Barry Fitzgerald, Howard Duff, Dorothy Hart, Don Taylor.

NAPOLEON. (1927) Archivists restored one of the legendary achievements of the silent era. Abel Gance's film runs four magnificent hours (the original was six hours). Epic in scale, startling in technique and visual impact, it covers only the first half of Napoleon's life. Gance was a believer in Napoleon and his legacy and his film is a celebration of Bonaparte's life. However, he finds room for puckish humor and some shrewd observations on politics. Mostly, this is a masterpiece to be enjoyed for its astounding virtuosity.
★★★★★

D and W: Abel Gance; Ph: Jules Kruger; M: Carmine Coppola.
Cast: Vladimir Roudenko, Albert Dieudonne, Gina Manes, Nicolas Koline.

NASHVILLE. (1975) Robert Altman, in one of his best films, transformed the mecca of country music into a metaphor of American life. A panorama of vignettes with a host of characters loosely associated with the music and a concert for a presidential candidate. The glimpses into private lives that are tortured, hopeful, phoney or just defeated are masterly and compassionate. Altman's vision shuns satire and his work is both sprawling and intimate. The picture remains one of the definitive examinations of the American dream.
R. ★★★★★
D: Robert Altman; W: Joan Tewkesbury ; Ph: Paul Lohmann; M: Richard Baskin (musical director).
Cast: Henry Gibson, Lily Tomlin, Keith Carradine, Karen Black.

NASTY HABITS. (1976) Of all the responses one could make to the Watergate scandal, "Get thee to a nunnery!" seems the least likely. Based on Muriel Spark's *The Abbess of Crewe*, the film parodies the central characters in the political scandal in an election in a Philadelphia convent. A 10-minute sketch idea perhaps, but longer than Lent when stretched to a feature movie. And just as much fun.
PG. ★★
D: Michael Lindsay-Hogg; W: Robert Enders; Ph: Douglas Slocombe; M: John Cameron.
Cast: Glenda Jackson, Melina Mercouri, Sandy Dennis.

NATE AND HAYES. (1983) A pirate voyage that offers something less than high spirits on the high seas. It commits a cardinal error for an adventure film of telling its story in a flashback that drains the suspense. Tommy Lee Jones and Michael O'Keefe act as if they are in different films in their pursuit of a girl they both love. She is kidnapped by a slaver (a very scary Max Phipps) and there is a mean and unwarranted streak of violence throughout.
PG. ★★
D: Ferdinand Fairfax; W: John Hughes and David Odell; Ph: Tony Imi; M: Trevor Jones.
Cast: Tommy Lee Jones, Michael O'Keefe, Jenny Seagrove, Max Phipps.

NATIONAL LAMPOON'S CLASS REUNION. (1982) Class, of course, is a conspicuous absentee from any aspect of a

wretched comedy from some of the *Animal House* crowd. An assortment of zanies is stalked by a transvestite seeking vengeance for some ancient high school wrong.
R.   ★
D: Michael Miller; W: John Hughes; M: Peter Bernstein.
Cast: Gerrit Graham, Miriam Flynn, Fred McCarren, Stephen Furst.

NATIONAL LAMPOON'S VACATION. (1983) *Animal House* on holiday. The idea is to make a movie about a vacation in which everything goes wrong. That description applies to the film which is a bad trip through jokes about mental retardation, masturbation and hemmorhoids. Chevy Chase continued to wear out his welcome on the big screen, but the real fault lies with John Hughes, a writer who adopts the form of satire without having anything to criticize.
R.   ★
D: Harold Ramis; W: John Hughes; Ph: Victor J. Kemper; M: Ralph Burns.
Cast: Chevy Chase, Beverly D'Angelo, Randy Quaid, Imogene Coca.

THE NATURAL. (1984) Devotees of Bernard Malamud's novel are likely to feel shortchanged because its sophistication has given way to a direct Hollywood approach. But on its own terms, Barry Levinson's view of Roy Hobbs, the baseball legend who appears as an over-the-hill veteran and becomes a star with a mysterious past, has much to commend it. Levinson, who proved himself so sensitive to American pop culture in *Diner*, sees Hobbs' story as an argument for the possibility of redemption, whatever the odds. Redford is exemplary and the supporting cast matches him.
PG.   ★★★★
D: Barry Levinson; W: Roger Towne and Phil Dusenberry; Ph: Caleb Deschanel; M: Randy Newman.
Cast: Robert Redford, Robert Duvall, Glenn Close, Kim Basinger.

NATURAL ENEMIES. (1980) A tedious consideration of the ultimately unnatural act. Hal Holbrook is a magazine executive who conceives the idea of murdering his wife and three children and spends the film asking questions about it. The director made his name in trailers and short features, but you would never know it from the unrelieved tedium he serves up.
R.   ★★
D and W: Jeff Kanew; Ph: Richard E. Brooks; M: Don Ellis.

Cast: Hal Holbrook, Louise Fletcher, Peter Armstrong, Beth Berridge.

NEA. (1978) Piquant and ingenious black comedy that inverts the young-girl-coming-of-age motif by having a sixteen-year-old write a best-selling pornographic novel called *Nea*. Since she has no experience, this is entirely a work of steamy imagination. A good skewering of pornography that runs out of steam in the last laps when it gets serious about the girl's relationships.
                                                   ★★★
D: Nelly Kaplan; W: Kaplan and Jean Chapot; Ph: Andreas Winding.
Cast: Sammy Frey, Ann Zacharias, Micheline Presle, Francoise Brion.

NED KELLY. (1970) It's hard to imagine even the most rabid Mick Jagger fan deriving much pleasure from this sadistic piece of miscasting. He plays the outlaw honored in poem and song by Australians as a Down Under Robin Hood. Jagger and his band wore armor which came in handy when the critics offered their opinions. Tony Richardson's direction is uncharacteristic and depressing.
                                                    ★★
D: Tony Richardson; W: Richardson and Ian Jones; Ph: Gerry Fisher; M: Shel Silverstein.
Cast: Mick Jagger, Allen Bickford, Geoff Gilmour, Mark McManus.

THE NEPTUNE FACTOR. (1973) A minor disaster flick that ought to be impaled on a trident. Daniel Petrie's direction has all the excitement of watching guppies feeding in an aquarium. An underwater laboratory is damaged by an earthquake and a rescue mission is attempted. The fish who attack the rescue vessel are far more expressive than the actors.
PG   ★
D: Daniel Petrie; W: Jack DeWitt; Ph: Harry Makin; M: William McCauley.
Cast: Ben Gazzara, Yvette Mimieux, Walter Pidgeon, Ernest Borgnine.

THE NESTING. (1981) A nondescript horror film about a gothic novelist whose problems come home to roost when she rents a Victorian mansion. She suffers from agoraphobia (the fear of open places) and this one is bad enough to induce cinemaphobia even in the undiscerning.
R.   ★
D: Armand Weston; W: Weston and Daria Price; Ph: J. Ferades; M: Jack Malken.

Cast: John Carradine, Gloria Grahame, Robin Groves, Christopher Loomis.

NETWORK. (1976) Paddy Chayefsky's savagely funny demolition of television, an industry that pursues profit without honor, is half satire and half a jeremiad full of mythic symbols. Peter Finch gave a brilliant valedictory performance as the anchorman whose show is locked in a ratings half-Nielsen and who decides to blow his brains out on network television. The effect is not unlike witnessing a typhoon and then being led through the wreckage by Chayefsky and Sidney Lumet.
R. ★★★★★
D: Sidney Lumet; W: Paddy Chayefsky; Ph: Owen Roizman; M: Elliot Lawrence.
Cast: Peter Finch, William Holden, Faye Dunaway, Ned Beatty.

NEVADA SMITH. (1966) In this otherwise standard revenge western, Steve McQueen showed signs of defining his screen persona. Here he is a half-breed and illiterate young man bent on killing the three men who murdered his parents. The interest of the film, apart from the splendid photography and suave direction, lies in the way it divides time between the youth's efforts to find himself as he searches for the men.
★★★
D: Henry Hathaway; W: John Michael Hayes; Ph: Lucien Ballard; M: Alfred Newman.
Cast: Steve McQueen, Karl Malden, Brian Keith, Suzanne Pleshette.

NEVER CRY WOLF. (1983) A Walt Disney production, but as soon as a lonely Arctic biologist starts eating field mice, you know it's going to be different. Carroll Ballard's film, drawn from Farley Mowat's book about his expriences living with wolves in the Canadian Arctic, is a gorgeous adventure that is flawlessly executed. It is also a provocative essay on what man does to his world in the name of progress. Charles Martin Smith adds some fine touches of humor to the sumptuous production, which was shot in the Yukon and Alaska.
PG. ★★★★
D: Carroll Ballard; W: Curtis Hanson, Sam Hamm and Richard Kletter; Ph: Hiro Narita; M: Mark Isham.
Cast: Charles Martin Smith, Brian Dennehy, Samson Jorah.

THE NEVERENDING STORY. (1984) A sophisticated challenge for children that goes beyond fantasy to make them under-stand the role of the imagination in our lives. Wolfgang Petersen took Michael Ende's popular book and lavished $27 million to bring the vision of Fantasia to life. With an obvious debt to *The Wizard of Oz*, the film transports an emotionally troubled boy to Fantasia, a world menaced by a force called the Nothing. Fantasia is sustained by the dreams of humanity.
PG. ★★★★
D: Wolfgang Petersen; W: Petersen and Herman Weigel; Ph: Jost Vacano; M: Giorgio Moroder.
Cast: Noah Hathaway, Barret Oliver, Tarni Stronach, Moses Gunn.

NEVER GIVE A SUCKER AN EVEN BREAK. (1941) The story is by that inimitable raconteur Otis Criblecoblis, better known as W.C. Fields. It has Fields diving out of an airplane and into a mythical country where he has a field day with humorous possibilities. Very original, including a Fields cure for insomnia—"Get plenty of sleep"— a song about chickens in Kansas and all capped off with a zany chase.
★★★
D: Edward Cline; W: John T. Neville and Prescott Chaplin; Ph: Charles Van Enger; M: Frank Skinner.
Cast: W.C. Fields, Gloria Jean, Leon Errol, Franklin Pangborn.

NEVER ON SUNDAY. (1960) Some movies are better heard than seen and that's certainly the case with Jules Dassin's reworking of the ever-popular Pygmalion theme. A scholarly type tries to reform a Greek hooker, played with effusive energy by Melina Mercouri, who became irreversibly identified with the part and the wonderful music.
★★
D and W: Jules Dassin; Ph: Jacques Natteau; M: Manos Hadjidakis.
Cast: Melina Mercouri, Jules Dassin, Georges Foundas, Tito Vandis.

NEVER SAY NEVER AGAIN. (1983) Sean Connery returned as James Bond and wasted little time in proving that Roger Moore is less when it comes to playing 007. He did not restore the series to its pristine sixties level, but there is both humor and toughness in this middle-aged Bond. And, appropriately, the movie's a little flabby in the middle. This is down-to-earth, hard-nosed Bond and a welcome change from the cartoon gadgetry of the later Moore films.
PG. ★★★

D: Irvin Kershner; W: Lorenzo Semple, Jr.;
Ph: Douglas Slocombe; M: Michel Legrand.
Cast: Sean Connery, Klaus Maria Brandauer,
Barbara Carrera, Max Von Sydow.

THE NEW CENTURIONS. (1972) "Put your
twenty [years] in and take the forty percent,"
advises the police veteran and the film is
equally half-hearted. The first to be adapted
from Joseph Wambaugh's Los Angeles cop
novels, it is too episodic to really establish its
characters. This is a shame because it
emphasizes the emotional strain of police
work. Television series in the same vein,
most notably *Hill Street Blues*, have undermined its impact and originality.
PG. ★★
D: Richard Fleischer; W: Stirling Silliphant;
Ph: Ralph Woolsey; M: Quincy Jones.
Cast: George C. Scott, Stacy Keach, Scott
Wilson, Jane Alexander.

THE NEW LAND. (1973) Jan Troell's
rewarding study of the immigrant experience—one that got beneath the surface of the
cliches of pioneering—resumed the story of
The Emigrants. The leisurely three hours
cover the dozen years that follow the settlement of a group of Swedes, who have fled
famine in their old land, in Minnesota. Together, the two films make an imposing
document. For credits, see *the Emigrants*.
★★★

NEW YORK, NEW YORK. (1977) Martin
Scorsese made two excellent films here and
then tried to shoehorn them into one movie.
There isn't quite enough room. One element
is a splendidly done pastiche of the forties
musical, complete with Liza Minnelli belting
out the big production numbers. The mood
and tempo turns from waltz to blues in considering Minnelli's tortured relationship with
a sax player (De Niro) in the waning days of
the big band era. Not a total success, but
still entertaining.
PG. ★★★
D: Martin Scorsese; W: Earl Mac Rauch; Ph:
Laszlo Kovacs; M: Ralph Burns.
Cast: Robert De Niro, Liza Minnelli, Barry
Primus, Lionel Stander.

THE NEXT MAN. (1976) Sean Connery as
a laird of Arabia in a film that combines aggressive dumbness with a kindergarten view
of world politics. He is a Saudi Arabian diplomat with a Scottish accent and a dream of
peace to be achieved by pulling his country
out of OPEC and into an alliance with Egypt.

It makes him a target for assassination in a
film naive enough to believe that you can kill
policy if you erase its chief advocate.
PG. ★★
D: Richard Sarafian; W: Mort Fine, Alan
Trustman, David M. Wolf; Ph: Michael Chapman; M: Michael Kamen.
Cast: Sean Connery, Cornelia Sharpe, Adolfo Celi.

NEXT STOP GREENWICH VILLAGE.
(1976) A pause that refreshes. Paul Mazursky relied on memories of his early days as an
actor in the early fifties when the Village was
in its pristine Bohemian state. The time and
place are lovingly conjured and the sense of
liberation from the surrounding greyness of
the decade is amusingly argued. Larry La-
pinksy is the quasi-autobiographical hero
and the film recounts his efforts to escape
Brooklyn and a blubbering mother for the
freedom of the Village.
R. ★★★★
D and W: Paul Mazursky; Ph: Arthur Ornitz;
M: Bill Conti.
Cast: Lenny Baker, Shelley Winters, Ellen
Greene, Lois Smith.

NICKELODEON. (1976) Peter Bogdano-
vich went back to the days of the first picture
show in this tedious piece of self-indulgence.
By his account, the pioneers of the movie
business spent most of their time falling
down—both on and off camera. Ryan
O'Neal is a director by accident and Burt
Reynolds a prototype movie star, but the
film's pratfalls become pitfalls. Hollywood
should not be entrusted with its own history.
PG. ★★
D: Peter Bogdanovich; W: W.D. Richter; Ph:
Laszlo Kovacs; M: Richard Hazard.
Cast: Burt Reynolds, Ryan O'Neal. Tatum
O'Neal, Brian Keith.

A NIGHT AT THE OPERA. (1935) The
work in which the Marx Brothers answered
the question: how many people can fit in a
stateroom on a transatlantic liner? This
sequence belongs with the all-time moments
in movie comedy. Otherwise, they leave
havoc in their wake on the ship and at an
opera house in an outing that is second only
to *Duck Soup*.
★★★★★
D: Sam Wood ; W: George S. Kaufman and
Morris Ryskind; Ph: Merritt Gerstad; M:
Herbert Stothart (musical director).
Cast: Groucho, Chico and Harpo Marx,
Margaret Dumont.

NIGHT CROSSING. (1982) In a period when the Disney studio was floating a lot of trial balloons in its releases they even tried launching a real one. The results were equally disappointing. Two East German families plot their daring air escape —it's based on a true story—but Disney pieties about domestic life keep the natural tensions and conflicts at a gentle simmer. The cast labors mightily to inflate the proceedings, but the performers are done in by a terminally innocuous script.
PG. ★★
D: Delbert Mann; W: John McGreevey; Ph: Tony Imi; M: Jerry Goldsmith.
Cast: John Hurt, Beau Bridges, Jane Alexander, Ian Bannen.

NIGHTHAWKS. (1978) A bland and honest portrait of a homosexual London schoolteacher. The director adopts a documentary style that leads to repetitive scenes of promiscuity, which may satisfy the teacher but makes for a dull movie. The best moment finds the teacher explaining his condition to the boys in his class.
★★
D and W: Ron Peck and Paul Hallam.
Cast: Ken Robertson.

NIGHTHAWKS. (1981) If international terrorism really operated in the manner suggested this would be a much safer place. The chief hostage taken is the viewer's intelligence with Sylvester Stallone, a New York cop, stalking a Carlos-style terrorist. It has all the order of the aftermath of a department store bombing.
R. ★★
D: Bruce Malmuth; W: David Shaber; Ph: James Contner; M: Keith Emerson.
Cast: Sylvester Stallone, Rutger Hauer, Billy Dee Williams, Lindsay Wagner.

A NIGHT IN HEAVEN. (1983) There is cockeyed optimism in the title and a fairer name would be *Classdance*. It ineptly takes the older woman/younger man theme of *Class* and marries it to *Flashdance*. *A Night in Heaven* turns out to be a hellishly bad and embarrassing union with a college teacher ogling a male stripper. Christopher Atkins brings the same expression to parking a car that he does to the heights of sexual passion.
R. ★
D: John Avildsen; W: Joan Tewkesbury; Ph: David Quaid; M: Jan Hammer.
Cast: Christopher Atkins, Lesley Ann Warren, Robert Logan, Deborah Rush.

NIGHTMARE ALLEY. (1947) Tyrone Power, with good reason, thought Stan Carlisle his best role. Carlisle is an ambitious carnival barker who maneuvers his way to fame in Chicago as a spiritualist. Before his downfall, he makes a fortune preying on the hopes of rich clients. The screenplay is cynical to the point of nihilism and although *Nightmare Alley* is set out like a typical Hollywood parable, it's something much darker and richer. In the end, a carnie type asks, "How can a man get so low?" "He reached too high," replies another philosophically.
★★★★
D: Edmund Goulding; W: Jules Furthman; Ph: Lee Garmes; M: Cyril Mockridge.
Cast: Tyrone Power, Coleen Gray, Joan Blondell, Taylor Holmes.

NIGHTMARES. (1983) Poor man's *Twilight Zone* that plunges the anthology horror film into total darkness. Four variations, the most repellent involving a ferocious rat chasing a suburban family, on very familiar and here extremely boring themes. The best of a weak litter rips off *Tron* in a story about a kid desperate to play his favorite video game.
R. ★
D: Joseph Sargent; W: Christopher Crowe and Jeffrey Bloom; Ph: Mario DiLeo and Gerald Perry Finnerman; M: Craig Safan.
Cast: Richard Masur, Veronica Cartwright, Cristina Raines, Emilio Estevez.

NIGHT OF THE HUNTER. (1955) There are few more sinister figures in movies than Robert Mitchum's Preacher Powell, a psychopath whose religious fervor permits him to knock off wealthy ladies. Charles Laughton's only effort as a director is a nightmare that stems from the contradictions that exist in all of us and which are best summed up by the fact that the preacher has love and hate tattooed on his hands. Adults are taken in by his act but kids are not fooled. He pursues two children who know the whereabouts of some hidden money.
★★★★★
D: Charles Laughton; W: James Agee; Ph: Stanley Cortez; M: Walter Schumann.
Cast: Robert Mitchum, Shelley Winters, Billy Chapin, Sally Jane Bruce.

NIGHT OF THE LIVING DEAD. (1968) George Romero's cult flick has the dead clambering out of their graves to eat the intestines of their victims. The gore is so specific that you may well lose your dinner watching it. As in the follow-up, *Dawn of the Dead*, Romero partisans claim there is pointed satire buried somewhere. You'll need a pick and shovel to find it. ★★

D: George Romero; W: John russo; .
Cast: Judith O'Dea, Duane Jones, Karl Hardman, Keith Wayne.

THE NIGHT OF THE SHOOTING STARS. (1983) War rarely seems more insane than when it is over and the fighting and barbarity continue. Paolo and Vittorio Taviani acknowledge this without belaboring it in their brilliant picture of Italy at the point of liberation with the Americans advancing, the Germans retreating and the people caught in the middle. There is a quality of wonder amid the terror and the movie's most ingenious stroke is to tell the story through the eyes of a child. It is a recollection given to her own child three decades later and stresses that life and the human spirit somehow prosper.
R. ★★★★★
D: Paolo and Vittorio Taviani; W: The Tavianis and Giuliani De Negri; Ph: Franco di Giacomo; M: Nicola Piovani.
Cast: Omero Antonutti, Margarita Lozano, Claudio Bigagli, Massimo Bonetti.

THE NIGHT PORTER. (1973) The love that dares not speak its name is sado-masochism and the reason can be traced to the broken glass Dirk Bogarde shoves into Charlotte Rampling's mouth. A genuinely depraved movie that argues that there are good and bad Nazis. Bogarde is an SS concentration camp officer hiding out as a porter in a grand hotel for perverts and Rampling is a wartime victim drawn to resume their cruel dalliance.
R.
D: Liliana Cavana; W: Cavana and Italo Moscati; Ph: Alfio Contini; M: Daniele Paris.
Cast: Dirk Bogarde, Charlotte Rampling, Philippe Leroy, Gabriele Ferzetti.

NIGHT SHIFT. (1982) Another attempt to pass off prostitution as fun. It is based on a true story about two Manhattan morgue attendants who ran a call-girl service on the side. Only in New York. It wasn't, one hastens to add, for necrophiliacs. Nor was it funny. Ron Howard thinks it's hilarious. It's hard to keep the laughs coming when the central idea is peddling women. Michael Keaton, who like Howard, went on to better things gives the film some energy.
R. ★
D: Ron Howard; W: Lowell Ganz and Baba-

loo Mandell; Ph: Jack Crabe; M: Burt Bacharach.
Cast: Henry Winkler, Michael Keaton, Gina Hecht, Shelley Long.

THE NIGHT THE LIGHTS WENT OUT IN GEORGIA. (1981) A one-watt bulb in a coal mine casts more light on life and its problems than this filmed country and western song. In a world flushed with rednecks, Dennis Quaid sings in bars and his sister jealously disrupts his attempted sexual conquests. It plays like a country song with too much melodrama and too many verses.
PG. ★★
D: Ronald Maxwell; W: Bob Bonney; Ph: Bill Butler; M: David Shire.
Cast: Dennis Quaid, Kristy McNichol, Mark Hamill, Sunny Johnson.

A NIGHT TO REMEMBER. (1958) British *sang-froid* collides with iceberg in a fastidious recreation of the unthinkable fate of the supposedly unsinkable liner *Titanic* in 1912. Based on Walter Lord's book, the film is more crowded than one of the ship's lifeboats. It displays a keen sense of class differences among the passengers without offering an opinion on what that meant to their eventual fate. The emotional climax is ruined by special effects that seem to have been shot in somebody's bathtub.
★★★
D: Roy Baker; W: Eric Ambler; Ph: Geoffrey Unsworth; M: William Alwyn.
Cast: Kenneth More, Honor Blackman, David McCallum, George Rose.

NIGHT TRAIN. (1940) Also known as *Night Train to Munich* and a winner by any name. Carol Reed's spicy thriller is a shrewd mixture of laughs and suspense with the daughter of a Czech industrialist being used by the Gestapo. Rex Harrison is the British agent who comes to the rescue.
★★★
D: Carol Reed; W: Sydney Gilliat and Frank Launder; Ph: Otto Kanturek; M: Louis Levy.
Cast: Margaret Lockwood, Rex Harrison, Paul Henreid, Basil Radford.

NIGHTWING. (1979) "It just doesn't seem natural," says an Indian with reservations, "for a man to spend his life—his entire life —killing bats." Or an entire movie. Vampire bats loose on an Indian reservation, a terrain full of opportunities for mumbled jumbo. Partly an old-fashioned fifties-style horror flick and partly a garbled look at tribal rivalries and Indian mysticism. The bats look like the ones that flap around the Count on *Sesame Street*. Too incoherent to generate any tension.

PG. ★
D: Arthur Hiller; W: Steve Shagan, Bud Shrake and Martin Cruz Smith; Ph: Charles Rosher; M: Henry Mancini.
Cast: Nick Mancuso, David Warner, Kathryn Harrold, Strother Martin .

NIJINSKY. (1980) One of the great artistic upheavals of the century in which Sergei Diaghilev and Stravinsky thrust ballet into the modern era is explained in terms of sexual jealousies. Two dancers play Nijinsky and Romola, who tries to break up his homosexual relationship with Diaghilev. They can't act and they don't do enough dancing to establish the genius of Nijinsky. The script also distorts some of the facts as the dancer tries to fend off encroaching madness.

R. ★★
D: Herbert Ross; W: Hugh Wheeler; Ph: Douglas Slocombe; M: John Lanchberry-(cond.).
Cast: George de la Pena, Leslie Browne, Alan Bates, Carla Fracci.

NINE HOURS TO RAMA. (1963) Richard Attenborough's *Gandhi* has mercifully supplanted the plodding depiction of the hours leading to the assassination of the great man. Although Mark Robson filmed in India, he fails to catch the intricate religious and political issues surrounding the murder. Horst Buchholz is out of his depth as the killer, even allowing for the superficiality of the screenplay.

★★
D: Mark Robson; W: Nelson Gidding; Ph: Arthur Ibbetson; M: Malcolm Arnold.
Cast: Horst Buchholz, Jose Ferrer, J. S. Casshyap, Robert Morley .

NINE MEN. (1942) The recruits think there is such a thing as too much training. The sergeant teaches them otherwise by recounting his experiences in desert warfare when he and his squad lost their commanding officer. The film re-enacts what happened to the squad and preaches to the converted both among the recruits and in the audience.

★★★
D and W: Harry Watt; Ph: Roy Kellino; M: John Greenwood.
Cast: Jack Lambert, Richard Wilkinson, Gordon Jackson, Frederick Piper.

1984. (1956) George Orwell arrived at the year by reversing the last two numbers of 1948, the date of the book's creation. The movie version was made when 1984 was a long way off and it is a rather stilted and distant evocation of Oceania, the fascist state. Winston Smith bridles at the crushing conditions in a totalitarian world. The script, quite properly, is issue-oriented instead of dramatic and thus quite faithful to Orwell until the ending.

★★★
D: Michael Anderson; W: Ralph Bettinson and William Templeton; Ph: C. Pennington Richards; M: Malcolm Arnold.
Cast: Edmond O'Brien, Michael Redgrave, Jan Sterling, David Kossoff.

1941. (1980) A classic instance of more being less and the one blot on Steven Spielberg's exemplary career. Panic breaks out in California after Pearl Harbor, causing people to behave like idiots and tempting Spielberg to set-piece stunts that do nothing to mask the feeble script. The Japanese are thought to be intent on destroying Hollywood in *1941*. Hollywood proved it needed no help here.

PG. ★★
D: Steven Spielberg; W: Robert Zemeckis and Bob Gale; Ph: William A. Fraker; M: John Williams.
Cast: John Belushi, Dan Aykroyd, Ned Beatty, Lorraine Gary.

1990: THE BRONX WARRIORS. (1983) A Bronx cheer would be a compliment. The one about the corporate heiress who gets bored at business meetings and runs away to a gang-infested and lawless borough that the police have given up on. Plagiarism of *Escape From New York* is the inescapable conclusion. Abysmal dialogue with the quality of the film conveyed by the name of its hero: Trash.

R.
D: Enzio Castellari; W: Dardanno Sachetti; Ph: Sergio Salvati; M: Walter Rizzati.
Cast: Vic Morrow, Mark Gregory, Fred Williamson, Christopher Connelly.

NINE TO FIVE. (1980) A good notion that runs out of steam before the morning coffee break, a syndrome that will be familiar to office workers. Colin Higgins bludgeons home the many inequities that face working women and satire of stereotypes descends into broad caricature. Dabney Coleman represents the pigs of America as the boss and he is such a swine that it undermines *Nine to Five*. The best sequence allows the women to air their vengeance fantasies against him.

R. ★★★
D: Colin Higgins; W: Higgins and Patricia Resnick; Ph: Reynaldo Villalobos; M: Charles Fox.
Cast: Jane Fonda, Dolly Parton, Lily Tomlin, Dabney Coleman.

NINOTCHKA. (1939) What Ernst Lubitsch did to the Nazis a little later in *To Be or Not to Be* he did to the communists in a graceful and sophisticated dig at Stalinism. Garbo is a revelation as the girl dispatched to Paris to save some over-indulgent Russians from their sins. She too defects and there is a running contrast between the gaiety of Paris and the glum dullness of communism. Nothing had changed when Paul Mazursky took up the same theme in *Moscow on the Hudson*.

★★★★
D: Ernst Lubitsch; W: Billy Wilder, Charles Brackett and Walter Reisch; Ph: William Daniels; M: Werner Heymann.
Cast: Greta Garbo, Melvyn Douglas, Ina Claire, Bela Lugosi.

92 IN THE SHADE. (1975) Authors are always moaning about the movies ruining their books. Thom McGuane didn't help their cause when he directed the version of his off-beat novel. Slow mixture of comedy and drama with Peter Fonda and Warren Oates as rival fishing guides. A pity celluloid doesn't melt at this temperature.

R. ★
D and W: Thom McGuane; Ph: Michael C. Butler; M: Michael J. Lewis.
Cast: Peter Fonda, Warren Oates, Elizabeth Ashley, Burgess Meredith.

NOBODY'S PERFECT. (1981) Only the candor of the title, which is borne out by an extraordinarily stupid and ineptly done comedy, commend the directing debut of Peter Bonerz. Three men lose their car in a Miami pothole and find they can't sue the city. Their response is to stage a caper and we would all have been better off if everyone had stayed in the hole until it was paved over.

PG. ★★
D: Peter Bonerz; W: Tony Kenrick; Ph: James Pergola; M: David McHugh.

Cast: Gabe Kaplan, Robert Klein, Alex Karras, Susan Clark.

NO NUKES. (1980) An eclectically chosen selection of rock stars do their numbers at a filmed concert in Madison Square Garden on behalf of the anti-nuclear movement. Fluently filmed, the concert is interrupted by footage of an anti-nuclear rally and a sobering talk from a leukemia victim who witnessed an atomic test.

PG. ★★★

NORMAN...IS THAT YOU?. (1976) Adaptation of a dinner theater perennial and very poor fare. George Schlatter, who created television's *Laugh-In*, tries not to be limp-wristed in presenting a black couple who discover their son is homosexual. But the movie is consistently limp-minded and filled with hollow one-liners that make nonsense of its message of tolerance at the end. Wayland Flowers makes an uninhibited contribution.

PG. ★★
D: George Schlatter; W: Ron Clark, Sam Bobrick and Schlatter; Ph: Gayne Rescher; M: William Goldstein.
Cast: Pearl Bailey, Redd Foxx, Dennis Dugan, Michael Warren.

NORMA RAE. (1979) A woman's film set in the economic trenches where most Americans live. Sally Field won an Oscar for her portrait of a union worker trying to organize a southern textile mill. Martin Ritt directs and resists his usual urge to climb on a soapbox and the story strikes a fine balance between labor and love. It is enriched by the parallel themes of a woman awakening to her potential in the context of the larger struggle.

PG. ★★★★
D: Martin Ritt; W: Irving Ravetch and Harriet Frank, Jr.; Ph: John A. Alonzo; M: David Shire.
Cast: Sally Field, Ron Leibman, Beau Bridges, Pat Hingle.

THE NORSEMAN. (1978) Through scholarship and research much is now known about the voyages of the Vikings—none of it by Charles Pierce, the author and director. He is bent on turning Lee Majors into a Bionic Beowulf whose speaks with a Kentucky drawl. Every time he tries to say "Norseman" it comes out as "Oarsman." He crosses the Atlantic to find his father. Pierce depicts this feat by throwing some water in front of the camera and having Cornel Wilde yell "Row!" a couple of times.

PG. ★

D and W: Charles Pierce; Ph: Robert Bethard; M: Jaime Mendoza-Nava.

Cast: Lee Majors, Cornel Wilde, Mel Ferrer, Jack Elam.

THE NORTH AVENUE IRREGULARS.

(1978) So-so Disney fare from the studio's period of uncertainty over what constituted family entertainment. Edward Herrmann strikes the right mixture of callowness and determination in the part of a minister who takes over a run-down parish and recruiting the church ladies for a war on the syndicate. Lots of chases and slapstick, but some of the modest points about the spread of corruption will be lost on the kids.

G. ★★

D: Bruce Bilson; W: Don Tait; Ph: Leonard J. South; M: Robert F. Brunner.

Cast: Edward Herrmann, Cloris Leachman, Barbara Harris, Karen Valentine.

NORTH BY NORTHWEST. (1959) Alfred

Hitchcock never had more fun with one of his favorite motifs —a man caught between the authorities and villains through no fault of his own. Cary Grant is the advertising executive who finds himself between a rock (the famous climax at Mount Rushmore) and a hard place (harried across a cornfield by a crop-dusting plane). If *North by Northwest* is celebrated for such moments of episodic brilliance, it's because the plot does not stand strong scrutiny. And it doesn't matter at all.

★★★★

D: Alfred Hitchcock; W: Ernest Lehman; Ph: Robert Burks; M: Bernard Herrmann.

Cast: Cary Grant, Eva Marie Saint, James Mason, Jessie Royce Landis.

NORTH DALLAS FORTY. (1979) A look

at the pro game that the National Football League would rather kick than receive. Nick Nolte's Phil Elliott is an over-the-hill pass catcher who can't let go of the game and *North Dallas Forty* is a first-rate examination of what goes on in the locker room and on the field from the drug-taking to the cattle auction attitude to the players. It weakens measurably with Elliott's two romances, but it remains among the best American sports films and subsequent drug scandals have proved it far ahead of its time.

R. ★★★★

D: Ted Kotcheff; W: Kotcheff, Frank Yablans and Peter Gent; Ph: Paul Lohmann; M: John Scott.

Cast: Nick Nolte, Mac Davis, Charles Durning, Bo Svenson.

NORTH TO ALASKA. (1960) The colder

air refreshed John Wayne and he entered into the exuberant spirit of a carefree and exuberant western that desires only to leave you punch-drunk. This is achieved with a fistfight every five minutes including one of the all-time saloon punch-ups. Wayne and Stewart Granger look for gold and quarrel over girls and Ernie Kovacs steals the picture as a con man.

★★★

D: Henry Hathaway; W: John Lee Mahin, Martin Rackin and Claude Binyon; Ph: Leon Shamroy; M: Lionel Newman.

Cast: John Wayne, Stewart Granger, Ernie Kovacs, Capucine.

NORTHWEST MOUNTED POLICE. (1940)

If nothing else, Cecil B. de Mille was a showman and why he chose to deprive himself of a show here is a bit of a puzzle. The outdoor Canadian scenery is obviously done indoors and the sense of scale is missing from an otherwise humdrum piece of indomitability against the odds. Gary Cooper, a Texas ranger, chases his man into Canada.

★★

D: Cecil B. de Mille; W: Jessy Lasky, Alan LeMay and C. Gardner Sullivan; Ph: Victor Milner; M: Victor Young.

Cast: Gary Cooper, Paulette Goddard, Madeleine Carroll, Preston Foster.

NOT A LOVE STORY. (1982) A team of

Canadian women got a government grant to put together a documentary about what pornography does to the women exploited by it. Their work was so graphic and hardhitting that several provinces banned it and the film became a liberal cause celebre. Apart from its notoriety, it is a cold and sobering look at a sleazy world and the awful facts speak for themselves.

★★★

D: Bonnie Sherr Klein; W: Pierre Letarte.

NOTHING PERSONAL. (1980) Nothing

special. With Suzanne Somers, another television star coming a cropper as a Washington lawyer fighting an environmental case. Feminists will be thrilled with the way she uses her body for legal research. Donald Sutherland sleepwalks through a ridiculous

223

role of a professor who is given school funds to fight the location of a new military base.
PG. ★
D: George Bloomfield; W: Robert Kaufman.
Cast: Suzanne Somers, Donald Sutherland, Laurence Dane, Roscoe Lee Browne.

NO TIME FOR SERGEANTS. (1958) Andy Griffith's best known film is not his best film—the honor belongs to his excellent lead in *A Face in the Crowd*. In this barrack room comedy he is once again a hick, whose monumental naivete threatens the throne of Sergeant King. Both Griffith and Myron McCormick had the roles down pat after a long Broadway run.
★★★
D: Mervin Le Roy; W: John Lee Mahin; Ph: Harold Rosson; M: Ray Heindorf.
Cast: Andy Griffith, Myron McCormick, Murray Hamilton, William Fawcett.

NOT NOW DARLING. (1972) A further indication that the British relish farces with raunchy puns as a defense against the realities of sex itself. Transferred to the screen with no attempt to change the door-slamming theatricality, it offers a furrier who is trying to bribe a potential mistress with a mink.
PG. ★
D: Ray Cooney and David Croft; W: John Chapman.
Cast: Leslie Phillips, Barbara Windsor, Ray Cooney, Moira Lister.

NOTORIOUS. (1945) Ingrid Bergman does Alicia Huberman with a sensuous flair that is attentively caught by Alfred Hitchcock. He extracts the maximum tension from what is really a situation of moderate promise. Note, for instance, what he can do with a coffee cup that contains poison. Alicia marries the leader of a Nazi spy ring in South America despite her love for an American agent (Cary Grant).
★★★★
D: Alfred Hitchcock; W: Ben Hecht; Ph: Ted Tetzlaff; M: Roy Webb.
Cast: Ingrid Bergman, Cary Grant, Claude Rains, Louis Calhern.

NOW VOYAGER. (1942) "Let's not ask for the moon... We have the stars" is one of the all-time closing lines in movies and *Now Voyager* is a triumph of its stars over the shameless tear-jerking in the script. Bette Davis carries off the fantasy—a repressed woman who emerges from her shell and enters into an ill-fated relationship. The movie is beloved to the Tobacco Institute for its celebrated scene in which Paul Henreid lights two cigarettes before giving one to Davis.
★★★
D: Irving Rapper; W: Casey Robinson; Ph: Sol Polito; M: Max Steiner.
Cast: Bette Davis, Claude Rains, Paul Henreid, Gladys Cooper.

THE NUDE BOMB. (1980) The networks were smart enough to bid farewell to the *Get Smart* series in the early seventies. Would you believe Don Adams made a dumb attempt to revive it in what plays like three episodes strung together? Smart tries to expose the people behind a weapon that removes clothes. Agent 86 is as amusing as Agent Orange and only the film's title is accurate.
PG. ★
D: Clive Donner; W: Arne Soltan, Bill Dana and Leonard B. Stern; M: Lalo Schifrin.
Cast: Don Adams, Vittorio Gassman, Sylvia Kristel, Andrea Howard.

NUDO DI DONNA (PORTRAIT OF A WOMAN NUDE). (1983) Nino Manfredi, the estimable Italian actor, directed and starred in a study of sexual illusions and delusions. Unfortunately, he is torn between a sex farce and something a lot more pointed and the film loses its way in the second half. Shot against the incomparable backdrop of Venice, it casts Manfredi as a man who has become impotent with his wife and takes up with a mistress. Could she be the same woman?
★★★
D: Nino Manfredi; W: Manfredi, Ruggero Maccari and Furio Scarpelli; Ph: Danilo Desideri; M: Maurizio Giammarco.
Cast: Nino Manfredi, Eleonora Giorgi, Jean-Pierre Cassel, George Wilson.

THE NUN'S STORY. (1959) A hymn of praise is not unwarranted for Fred Zinnemann and his excellent cast for avoiding the many perils posed by the story of a nun's travails from novice to eventual nay-sayer. Audrey Hepburn, in an appealing and exquisitely calibrated performance, goes from convent to the Congo. There a worldly physician forces her to re-examine her commitment to the order. The reticence in the face of much temptation to excess makes that conflict one that we share.

★★★

D: Fred Zinnemann; W: Robert Anderson; Ph: Franz Planer; M: Franz Waxman.
Cast: Audrey Hepburn, Peter Finch, Edith Evans, Peggy Ashcroft.

THE NUTTY PROFESSOR. (1963) In France, where, for some unfathomable reason, he is revered as a cinematic genius, this is regarded as the summit of Jerry Lewis' comic art. Since rational assessment says that puts *The Nutty Professor* on top of a molehill, we can agree with the French. He plays a bumbling scientist who finds a formula that turns him into a smooth Romeo in what is easily the worst of the many variations on *Dr. Jekyll and Mr. Hyde.*

★

D: Jerry Lewis; W: Lewis and Bill Richmond; Ph: W. Wallace Kelley; M: Walter Scharf.
Cast: Jerry Lewis, Stella Stevens, Howard Morris, Kathleen Freeman.

O

OBJECTIVE BURMA. (1945) The British, who fought long and hard in Burma, certainly objected to the notion that Americans, led by Errol Flynn, won the campaign. There are few other grounds for carping in an expertly made and exciting war film that follows American paratroopers in their attack on a Japanese radar installation. The film doesn't shrink away from the grim realities of combat in the jungle and, despite the miffed feelings of the British, Flynn gave a fine performance that dispensed with his mannerisms. ★★★
D: Raoul Walsh; W: Lester Cole and Randy MacDougall; Ph: James Wong Howe; M: Franz Waxman.
Cast: Errol Flynn, James Brown, William Prince, George Tobias.

OBLOMOV. (1981) From the director best known for *Slave of Love*, this long and rewarding film is based on the the 19th century novel by Ivan Gonchorov. It is a classic study of depression masquerading as laziness and inertia. Oblomov can see no point in getting out of bed and loses himself in guilty dreams. Even when he falls in love, he is a prisoner of his dreams. The period is beautifully evoked. ★★★★
D: Nikit Mikhalkov; W: Aleksandr Ababashyan and Mikhalkov; Ph: Pavel Lebeshev ; M: E. Artemiev.
Cast: Oleg Tabakov, Elena Solevey, Andrei Popov, Yuri Bogatyryev.

OBSESSION. (1976) There is more than a vestige of *Vertigo* in Brian De Palma's stylish mystery. Cliff Robertson is splendid as a husband who believes himself responsible for the death of his wife. Sixteen years later, her double shows up. The film is full of Hitchcock references and themes and only falters in the pat incredibility of its ending. It remains a fine homage rather than a slavish imitation of the master.
PG. ★★★
D: Brian De Palma; W: Paul Schrader; Ph: Vilmos Zsigmond; M: Bernard Herrmann.
Cast: Cliff Robertson, Genevieve Bujold, John Lithgow, Sylvia Williams.

OCEAN'S ELEVEN. (1960) The pictures made by Frank Sinatra's "Rat Pack" have the air of party to which the viewer is invited as a grudging afterthought and excluded from some of the jokes. It's not the kind of party you would want to attend anyway. Sinatra and Company plan to rob five Las Vegas casinos. Not without irony since the gambling palace lounges have sustained them in later years. It did well enough to encourage a vogue for crime caper movies. ★★
D: Lewis Milestone; W: Charles Lederer and Harry Brown; Ph: William Daniels; M: Nelson Riddle.
Cast: Frank Sinatra, Peter Lawford, Sammy Davis, Jr., Dean Martin.

THE OCTAGON. (1980) Over-plotted with two many angles for a martial arts movie. Chuck Norris is as wooden as ever in reprising the part of Scott James, the retired martial arts champion. Much kung-foolery results when he takes on a mean ninja cadre of assassins. There is one good fight when he takes on a hooded chap armed with more blades than a Swiss army knife.
R. ★
D: Eric Karson; W: Leigh Champman; Ph: Michel Hugo; M: Dick Halligan.
Cast: Chuck Norris, Lee Van Cleef, Karen Carlson, Tadashi Yamashita.

OCTOPUSSY. (1983) Sean Connery turned Roger Moore into Agent 003.5 by offering *Never Say Never Again* in the same year. Moore's sixth Bond film delivers the merchandise with the usual helpings of cars, chauvinism and comic-strip villainy. It's what the global Bond market expects and you can hardly blame Moore. The stunts, especially an opening escape by jet plane, are as accomplished as ever. Bond gets involved with jewel smuggling and rival factions in the Kremlin.
PG. ★★★
D: John Glen; W: Ricaard Maibaum, Michael Wilson and George MacDoanld Fraser; Ph: Alan Hume; M: John Barry.
Cast: Roger Moore, Maude Adams, Louis Jourdan, Kristina Wayborn.

THE ODD COUPLE. (1968) One of the most effective collaborations of Jack Lemmon and Walter Matthau. Two divorced men condemned to live as a couple by fate and circumstances. Some of Neil Simon's wittiest writing illuminates the grating contrast between Matthau's slob and Lemmon's squeaky clean neurotic. They have come to wear these characters like a favorite old suit, but Simon's ideas are tailor-made this time. ★★★

D: Gene Saks; W: Neil Simon; Ph: Robert B. Hauser; M: Neal Hefti.
Cast: Jack Lemmon, Walter Matthau, John Fiedler, Herb Edelman.

ODD MAN OUT. (1946) James Mason has only a few lines throughout this astonishing suspense film, but by the end we are on intimate terms with his character. He is a fugitive in Belfast after being wounded in a politically motivated bank robbery and Carol Reed directs the pursuit with incredible skill. Mason roams the city, beset by delirious bouts and treachery at every turn. There are few bleaker views of the human spirit than the one so brilliantly offered in *Odd Man Out*.
★★★★★
D: Carol Reed; W: F. L. Green and R.C. Sheriff; Ph: Robert Krasker; M: William Alwyn.
Cast: James Mason, Robert Newton, Robert Beatty, Fay Compton.

THE ODESSA FILE. (1974) An intelligent adaptation of Frederick Forsyth's best-selling novel about a young German journalist on the trail of some unrepentant SS officers. It has some scenes of individual excellence, but suspense is sacrificed to wordiness. Even with this room, the discussion of German attitudes to Nazism after the fact is not particularly enlightening. The reporter stumbles across a plot to unleash a plague on Israel. Well-acted but with few surprises.
PG. ★★★
D: Ronald Neame; W: Kenneth Ross and George Markstein; Ph: Oswald Morris; M: Andrew Lloyd Webber.
Cast: Jon Voight, Maximilian Schell, Maria Schell, Maria Tamm.

ODE TO BILLY JOE. (1976) Halfway through this relentles dirge the urge to throw yourself off the Tallahachee bridge is overwhelming. Bobby Gentry's hit song about doomed love and suicide had been around for nine years when the lame and ill-written attempt to dramatize the hit surfaced. Set in Mississippi in 1953 and written by Herman Raucher, who penned *The Summer of '42*. The intervening years did not improve his skills.
PG. ★
D: Max Baer; W: Herman Raucher; Ph: Michael Hugo; M: Michel Legrand.
Cast: Robby Benson, Glynnis O'Connor, Joan Hotchkis, Sandy McPeak.

AN OFFICER AND A GENTLEMAN. (1982) Taylor Hackford's suave refashioning of Hollywood's military school cliches ignored basic changes in our attitude toward such training. That's probably why it became a huge hit. It is a nostalgic, early sixties look at love and perseverance and it takes place in a social and political vacuum. The scenarist went to officer candidate school in the early sixties and it shows. The women scheme to catch a husband and the men struggle against a tough instructor and other obstacles. Lou Gossett, Jr., and Richard Gere are excellent as the main antagonists.
R. ★★★
D: Taylor Hackford; W: Douglas Day Stewart; Ph: Donald Thorin; M: Jack Nitzsche.
Cast: Richard Gere, Debra Winger, Lou Gossett, Jr., Lisa Blount.

OF MICE AND MEN. (1939) Lewis Milestone's moving and sparely told rendering of John Steinbeck's story doesn't reach the heights achieved in another Steinbeck-inspired film, *The Grapes of Wrath*. But then very few movies do. Burgess Meredith and Lon Chaney, Jr., are excellent as George and Lennie—one full of cunning and the other a hulking brute. The latter's strength is his ultimate ruin.
★★★★
D: Lewis Milestone; W: Eugene Solow; Ph: Norbert Brodine; M: Aaron Copland.
Cast: Burgess Meredith, Lon Chaney, Jr., Charles Bickford, Roman Bohnen.

OF UNKNOWN ORIGIN. (1983) And also of no redeeming value. George Cosmatos, who made the plague film *The Cassandra Crossing*, turns to the creatures who so often carry it. A man finds a large rat in his house and becomes obsessed with trapping it and finding out about the ways of the rodent. As appetizing as rat poison.
R. ★
D: George Cosmatos; W: Brian Taggert; Ph: Rene Verzier; M: Ken Wannberg.
Cast: Peter Weller, Jennifer Dale, Lawrence Dane, Kenneth Welsh.

OH, GOD. (1977) Carl Reiner tries hard enough to test the patience of a saint in this innocuous and surprisingly popular comedy. Denver is a California supermarket manager who cannot make the world believe God has singled him out. Burns, as the cigar-chomping deity, lends the film some charm.
PG. ★★★
D: Carl Reiner; W: Larry Gelbart; Ph: Victor Kemper; M: Jack Elliot.

Cast: John Denver, George Burns, Ralph Bellamy, Donald Pleasence.

OH, GOD! BOOK II. (1980) George Burns, who may be as old as God and who is certainly funnier, returns as the deity to tell a little girl, "Sometimes you have to believe in things you can't see." One thing you can see and not believe is this sequel for those who wish to be bored again. God enlists the girl in starting a campaign to revive interest in Him. Her slogan is "Think God." I think not. **PG.** ★
D: Gilbert Cates; W: Josh Greenfeld, *et al.*; Ph: Ralph Woolsey; M: Charles Fox.
Cast: George Burns, Louanne, Suzanne Pleshette, Howard Duff.

THE OKLAHOMA KID. (1939) Somebody had the none too bright idea of telling a young James Cagney to go west. He did and brought along many of his trademark mannerisms, most of them as out of place as a rocket ship in a western. The novelty is increased by a black-clad Humphrey Bogart as a villain and Cagney's singing. Cagney takes it out on the people who lynched his father. ★★
D: Lloyd Bacon; W: Warren Duff, Robert Buckner and Edward Parmore; Ph: James Wong Howe; M: Max Steiner.
Cast: James Cagney, Humphrey Bogart, Rosemary Lane, Donald Crisp.

OLD BOYFRIENDS. (1979) A clinical psychologist emerging from a messy divorce decides to delve into her past relationships to come to some terms with her present malaise. Although the premise holds much promise, her odyssey becomes an act of revenge against her old lovers for real and imagined wrongs. *Old Boyfriends* cannot resolve the basic contradiction between Talia Shire's sympathetic account of the heroine and some of the appalling things she does. **R.** ★★
D: Joan Tewkesbury; W: Paul and Leonard Schrader; Ph: William A. Fraker; M: David Shire.
Cast: Talia Shire, John Belushi, Richard Jordan, Keith Carradine.

THE OLD MAN AND THE SEA. (1958) A conscientious translation of the Hemingway story that leaves the rowing to Spencer Tracy. His struggle is not so much against the forces of nature (he's a Cuban fisherman) as the intractability of Hemingway's narrative in film terms—a problem the author himself could not solve. Nobody, with the exception of James Wong Howe, gave Tracy much help and the enterprise drowns under the weight of its own inertia. ★★
D: John Sturges; W: Ernest Hemingway; Ph: James Wong Howe; M: Dmitri Tiomkin.
Cast: Spencer Tracy, Felipe Pazos, Harry Bellaver.

OLD YELLER. (1957) Countless other Disney boy-and-his-dog movies and imitations by others do not weaken the appeal of a children's film that has retained its charm. Beneath the simple tale of two Texas boys coping with the absence of their father and sharing some adventures with a stray dog they adopt, there is some guidance on handling life's harder lessons. It was so successful that it led Disney to emphasize live-action over animation. ★★★★
D: Robert Stevenson; W: Fred Gipson; Ph: Charles Boyle; M: Oliver Wallace.
Cast: Fess Parker, Dorothy McGuire, Tommy Kirk, Kevin Corcoran.

OLIVER! (1968) A truly exceptional musical from Carol Reed that will have you pleading for more—as Oliver does in the workhouse food line. Handsomely choreographed and inventively scored, *Oliver!* tells Dickens' most familiar story—the adventures of Oliver Twist in the London underworld—without sidestepping the harsh realities. The songs include standards like "As Long as He Needs Me". ★★★★
D: Carol Reed; W: Vernon Harris; Ph: Oswald Morris; M: Lionel Bart.
Cast: Mark Lester, Ron Moody, Oliver Reed, Harry Secombe.

OLIVER'S STORY. (1978) Sequel to the five-hanky mega-tearjerker *Love Story*. Inconsolable after the death of his wife, Oliver Barrett tries to find himself, despite mounting evidence that there's nothing worth looking for. After the funeral he buries himself in his law practice and it's up to Candice Bergen to exhume his interest in life. Grief is an introspective emotion that does not yield to screen treatment and the trouble with *Oliver's Story* is that it has no story. **PG.** ★
D: John Korty; W: Erich Segal; Ph: Arthur Ornitz; M: Francis Lai.

Cast: Ryan O'Neal, Candice Bergen, Nicola Pagett, Edward Binns.

OLIVER TWIST. (1948) The irony is that a stronger and more compact story produced a weaker film than David Lean's earlier *Great Expectations*. The abject squalor of Victorian London, where the orphan Oliver takes up with a gang of thieves led by Fagin, is presented unsparingly and a couple of the scenes with Bill Sikes are still scary. Alec Guinness' Fagin was condemned as anti-Semitic in this country and the film was censored.

★★★
D: David Lean; W: Lean and Stanly Haynes; Ph: Guy Green; M: Arnold Bax.
Cast: Alec Guinness, Robert Newton, John Howard Davies, Henry Stephenson.

THE OMEGA MAN. (1971) Richard Matheson's celebrated novel *I Am Legend* is the source of a film for the second time (the other being *The Last Man on Earth*). The vampire lore and the elaborate physiological speculation on the condition of vampirism are missing. Instead a plague has swept across the earth and Charlton Heston has to hold the fort against a horde of mutants. There are several striking scenes and Heston's stalwart presence is right for the role.

★★★
D: Boris Sagal; W: John and Joyce Corrington; Ph: Russell Metty; M: Ron Grainger.
Cast: Charlton Heston, Anthony Zerbe, Rosalind Cash.

THE OMEN. (1976) A devilishly good exercise in a genre saturated with drivel, this macabre tale of a U.S. ambassador's son with satanic tendencies is brought off with great techical virtuosity by Richard Donner. The acting is commendably understated, which is not customary in this kind of movie, and the pace and tension good enough to sweep the viewer along in an adroit variation on *The Exorcist* theme. Sired two devil's children in awful sequels.

R. ★★★★
D: Richard Donner; W: David Seltzer; Ph: Gil Taylor; M: Jerry Goldsmith.
Cast: Gregory Peck, Lee Remick, David Warner.

JACQUELINE SUSANN'S ONCE IS NOT ENOUGH. (1975) Hair-dryer fiction that over-heats the brain. Closet lesbians, daddy-haunted virgins, impotent writers and even an astronaut who allows, "We didn't get along when we flew to the moon and it was no different when I got back." Silly soap opera that connoisseurs of trash will enjoy. Deborah Raffin searches the world's ritzier addresses for the man who can measure up to her father.

R. ★
D: Guy Green; W: Julius Epstein; Ph: John A. Alonzo; M: Henry Mancini.
Cast: Kirk Douglas, Alexis Smith, Deborah Raffin, David Janssen.

ONCE UPON A TIME IN AMERICA. (1984) Sergio Leone's attempt at a gangster epic was drastically cut for its American release and it's a pathetic spaghetti eastern. Seeing the film at full-length doesn't make much difference, except for two genuinely disgusting rape scenes that betray a neanderthal attitude to women. Otherwise, Leone's work is a good-looking shambles about Jewish boys who come to no good. They are so unsavory that it is hard to take any interest in what happens to them. A sad waste of a great actor's time.

R. ★
D: Sergio Leone; W: Leone, Leonardo Benvenuti, Piero de Bernardo and Enrico Medioli; Ph: Tonino delli Colli; M: Ennio Morricone.
Cast: Robert de Niro, James Woods, Elizabeth McGovern, Tuesday Weld.

ONCE UPON A TIME IN THE WEST. (1969) Hollywood gave Sergio Leone, the head pasta maker of the spaghetti western school, the money to make a movie in the real west. No less than Monument Valley, where John Ford filmed so memorably. The change of scenery did not do much for Leone's movie-making and once again we have his idea of how the west was. Charles Bronson substitutes for Clint Eastwood and is indistinguishable from the famous pillars of stone in the valley. Henry Fonda goes against type as the heavy.

★★
D: Sergio Leone; W: Leone and Sergio Donati ; Ph: Tonino Delli Colli; M: Ennio Morricone.
Cast: Charles Bronson, Henry Fonda, Jason Robards, Claudia Cardinale.

THE ONE AND ONLY. (1978) The De-Fonzification of Henry Winkler fell into an unhappy daze. The usual struggle for showbiz success is couched in the aspirations of one Andy Schmidt and his efforts to make it to Broadway. Carl Reiner finds those efforts alternately touching and amusing and everything falls apart when Schmidt becomes a professional wrestler.

PG. ★

D: Carl Reiner; W: Steve Gordon; Ph: Victor J. Kemper; M: Patrick Williams.
Cast: Henry Winkler, Kim Darby, Gene Saks, William Daniels.

ONE-EYED JACKS. (1960) It's not easy to keep both eyes open during long stretches of Marlon Brando's lesson in why some actors should not be allowed to direct themselves. There is certain fascination to seeing what a performer of his calibre would do in a western, but it soon evaporates. He pursues Karl Malden down through the years and catches up with him in Monterey. The movie is very good-looking and cries out for an unsparing editor to remove the flab.

★★

D: Marlon Brando; W: Guy Trosper and Calder Willingham; Ph: Charles Lang, Jr.; M: Hugo Friedhofer.
Cast: Marlon Brando, Karl Malden, Pina Pellicer, Katy Jurado.

ONE FLEW OVER THE CUCKOO'S NEST. (1975) Milos Forman, the Czech director who views America with such a clear eye, added considerable ambiguity to his adaptation of Ken Kesey's 1963 novel.The two antagonists, a free-spirited convict, who may or may not be crazy and Nurse Ratched have been toned down. The atmosphere is grey, not black and white. Jack Nicholson's convict is a *tour de force* and remains one of his great roles. He cons his way into the asylum to avoid work and attempts to organize resistance among the patients. The film leaves us unsure of Nicholson's sanity and even less certain of what constitutes madness. It won all five major Oscars.

R. ★★★★★

D: Milos Forman; W: Laurence Hauben and Bo Goldman; Ph: Haskell Wexler; M: Jack Nitzche.
Cast: Jack Nicholson, Louise Fletcher, William Redfield, Will Sampson.

ONE FROM THE HEART. (1982) The narrative heart is missing from a $27 million extravaganza that contributed to Francis Ford Coppola's financial troubles. If looks were everything it would be a triumph, but there is very little to it beyond style and its commercial failure is understandable. In a dream-like Las Vegas, a bored couple seek out new lovers and the viewer remains a detached and uninvolved observer.

R. ★★

D: Francis Ford Coppola; W: Coppola and Armyan Bernstein; Ph: Ronald V. Garcia; M: Tom Walts.
Cast: Frederic Forrest, Teri Garr, Raul Julia, Lainie Kazan.

101 DALMATIANS. (1961) Dogs and their owners trip over each other and fall in love. The dogs, Pongo and Perdita, get picked on for littering to the tune of fifteen pups by two Cockney crooks. The animation, especially of the villains, is extraordinarily convincing and the movie has some pertinent things to say about the relationship of man and animals.

★★★★

D: Wolfgang Reitherman, Hamilton Luske, Clyde Geronimi; W: Bill Peet; M: George Bruns.
Cast: (Voices) Rod Taylor, Lisa Davis, Cate Bauer, Ben Wright.

ONE HUNDRED RIFLES. (1969) Tom Gries directed this western at a machine-gun clip that does much to obscure the rudimentary acting. Burt Reynolds, a bank robber, and Jim Brown, a sheriff pursuing him, go to Mexico where they become involved in a guerilla war against the army. There is no pretense at offering anything more than loud action.

★★

D: Tom Gries; W: Gries and Clair Huffaker; Ph: Cecilio Paniagua; M: Jerry Goldsmith.
Cast: Burt Reynolds, Raquel Welch, Jim Brown, Fernando Lamas.

ONE IN A MILLION. (1936) Sonja Henie proved herself a good skate. That skill, along with some astute career management by Daryl Zanuck, made her a star. Adolphe Menjou discovers her in Switzerland and brings her to Madison Square Garden. Quite harmless and very popular in its day.

★★

D: Sidney Lanfield; W: Leo Praskins and Mark Kelly; Ph: Edward Cronjager; M: Louis Silvers.
Cast: Sonja Henie, Adolphe Menjou, Don Ameche, Ned Sparks.

ONE MILLION YEARS B.C. (1967) Raquel Welch, in a designer pelt, answers the burning question: Did prehistoric women shave their legs? Done with all the sophistication of a cave drawing, the view of life back then finds mankind separated into Rock People and Shell People, who are slightly more mod. Ray Harryhausen dusted off his monsters for the occasion.

★

D: Don Chaffey; W: Michael Carreras; Ph: Wilkie Cooper.
Cast: Raquel Welch, John Richardson, Percy Herbert, Martine Beswick.

ONE OF OUR DINOSAURS IS MISSING.
(1975) The family film on the endangered species list in a very weak Disney effort. The time is London in the twenties and a microfilm is hidden among a dinosaur's bones in a museum. Peter Ustinov is wasted as a Chinese agent trying to recover it from some competing nannies. Even the production values are below par for a Disney film.
G. ★★
D: Robert Stevenson; W: Bill Walsh; Ph: Paul Beeson; M: Ron Goodwin.
Cast: Peter Ustinov, Helen Hayes, Derek Nimmo, Clive Revill.

ONE SINGS, THE OTHER DOESN'T.
(1977) The friendship of two women, spanning decades and a multitude of emotions. The film survives its own feminist rhetoric. The relationship begins in their teens and follows them through assorted crises in what director Varda called, "a quiet, imaginary dialogue punctuated with postcards." The film moves between the two lives with clumsy commentary. It is more a celebration of womanhood than a tirade against its unjust penalties.
★★★
D and W: Agnes Varda; Ph: Charlie Van-Damme; M: Francois Wertheimer.
Cast: Valerie Mairesse, Therese Liotard, Ali Raffi, Robert Daides.

ONE TRICK PONY.
(1980) Paul Simon gathered together everything he had seen and suffered in the ephemeral world of pop music. Jonah Levin, one-time folk superstar, is approaching 40 in life and not on the Billboard chart. Simon flails away at the hucksters and moguls and has much to say about what music means to the performer and listener. At home, there is domestic crisis that is banally rendered, but *One Trick Pony* takes off on the road when Levin attempts a final comeback.
R. ★★★
D: Robert Young; W: Paul Simon; Ph: Dick Bush; M: Paul Simon.
Cast: Paul Simon, Blair Brown, Rip Torn, Joan Hackett.

ON GOLDEN POND.
(1981) The line between art and life is very blurred. A frail Henry Fonda plays a curmudgeonly, dying old man who comes to terms with his daughter after years of bickering and hostility. Since the latter is done by Jane Fonda, the adaptation of Ernest Thompson's play has a great deal of resonance. Fonda Senior enlists a great deal of sympathy for a character who doesn't really deserve it. It became his valedictory and no farewell could have made us fonder of him. The Fondas and Katharine Hepburn transcend an often inane screenplay whose lines would do in lesser talent.
PG. ★★★
D: Mark Rydell; W: Ernest Thompson; Ph: Billy Williams; M: Dave Grusin.
Cast: Henry Fonda, Jane Fonda, Katharine Hepburn, Doug McKeon.

ON HER MAJESTY'S SECRET SERVICE.
(1969) To this day the biggest secret is the reasoning of the producers who picked George Lazenby to take over from Sean Connery. The action takes place in the Alps and the mountains have more mobility than Lazenby's face. He is so stiff that there is a vacuum in what is otherwise a quite flamboyant Bond film with some noteworthy chases and Diana Rigg as a bonus. Bond goes after Blofeld, whose latest nasty scheme is to blight the world with disease. Mercifully, Lazenby's license to kill was withdrawn afterwards.
★★
D: Peter Hunt; W: Richard Maibaum; Ph: Michael Reed; M: John Barry.
Cast: George Lazenby, Diana Rigg, Telly Savalas, Ilse Steppat.

THE ONION FIELD.
(1979) The classiest of the films inspired by Joseph Wambaugh's knowledgeable police books is a work of "faction." Two nondescript thugs kidnap two Los Angeles police officers, killing one. The other escapes and lives with his guilt as the case drags through the courts. Wambaugh and director Harold Becker went beyond the policeman as soldier-martyr to an incisive psychological study that never makes compromises for the sake of melodrama.
R. ★★★★
D: Harold Becker; W: Joseph Wambaugh; Ph: Charles Rosher; M: Eumir Depdato .
Cast: John Savage, James Woods, Franklyn Seales, Ted Danson.

ONLY WHEN I LAUGH.
(1981) Not for those who are content with only laughter in a Neil Simon film. He reworked an old play, *The Gingerbread Lady*, into a vehicle for Marsha Mason. It's hard to play a drunk who

attracts nothing but sympathy but Mason brings it off. The theme is the healing power of friendship in coping with the crises of life. She's an actress trying to stay off the bottle and deal with a justly alienated daughter.

R ★★★

D: Glenn Jordan; W: Neil Simon; Ph: David Walsh; M: David Shire.
Cast: Marsha Mason, Kristy McNichol, James Coco, Joan Hackett.

ON THE AVENUE. (1937) Consistently on the mark and bouyed by Irving Berlin's songs. Dick Powell gets more than he bargained for when he produces a revue that skewers a wealthy family. They complicate a romance when they sue him.

★★★

D: Roy Del Ruth; W: Gene Markey and William Counselman; Ph: Lucien Andriot; M: Irving Berlin.
Cast: Dick Powell, Madeleine Carroll, Alice Faye, George Barbier.

ON THE BEACH. (1959) Stanley Kramer and the opportunities for moralizing presented by Nevil Shute's excellent novel about the last survivors of an atomic war are a dangerous combination. He is relatively muted in that regard and the subject matter is such that it would be pretty hard not to make an arresting film. After World War III, an American submarine heads toward Australia to await the inevitable. Too much that is too obvious is said, but it's still a powerful movie.

★★★

D: Stanley Kramer; W: John Paxton; Ph: Daniel Fapp and Giuseppe Rotunno; M: Ernest Gold.
Cast: Gregory Peck, Fred Astaire, Ava Gardner, Anthony Perkins.

ON THE NICKEL. (1980) The nickel in question is Fifth Street in Los Angeles, the heart of the city's Skid Row. Ralph Waite plunged in where more commercial filmmakers feared to tread, but his discussion of life among hopeless alcoholics succumbs to the same maudlin self-pity you often hear from drunks. Waite (the father in *The Waltons*) heads a good cast in an odd story of winos trying to recover the ashes of a departed alcoholic.

★★

D and W: Ralph Waite; Ph: Ric Waite; M: Fredric Myrow.
Cast: Ralph Waite, Donald Moffat, Penelope Allen, Hal Williams.

ON THE TOWN. (1949) Three sailors take shore leave in New York in search of girls and fun and it's an unalloyed pleasure to go along for the ride. The Leonard Bernstein score sets the pace as Frank Sinatra chases a woman cabbie and Gene Kelly looks for a girl he has only seen in a picture.

★★★★

D: Stanley Donen and Gene Kelly; W: Adolph Green and Betty Comden; Ph: Harold Rosson; M: Leonard Bernstein.
Cast: Frank Sinatra, Gene Kelly, Jules Munshin, Betty Garrett.

ON THE WATERFRONT. (1954) Generations of impressionists should be paying royalties to Marlon Brando for his endlessly imitated scene with Rod Steiger in the back of a car. We should merely pay tribute to an indelible portrait of a man whose fists are quicker than his brain. The unabashed melodrama calls attention to corruption on the docks and in its time it was regarded as anti-union. It is more about the circumstances under which an unlikely man would stand up for the right thing. Should Malloy, the keeper of pigeons on the roof, become a stool pigeon? The force of the acting transcends the melodrama.

★★★★

D: Elia Kazan; W: Budd Schulberg; Ph: Boris Kaufman; M: Leonard Bernstein.
Cast: Marlon Brando, Rod Steiger, Karl Malden, Eva Marie Saint.

ON THE YARD. (1979) Malcolm Braly spent twenty years in prison and it shows in his screenplay. Life in the slammer is portrayed with clear-eyed sobriety. The deadening routine is interrupted by eruptions of violence and most of it deals with a conflict between a lone wolf and the convict who controls the yard. Filmed in Pennsylvania's Rockview Penitentiary.

R. ★★★

D: Raphael D. Silver; W: Malcolm Braly; Ph: Alan Metzger; M: Charles Gross.
Cast: John Heard, Thomas Waites, Mike Kellin, Richard Bright.

OPEN SEASON. (1974) Set in Michigan, but actually shot in Spain and directed at the pace of a long siesta. Three Vietnam veterans kidnap a couple every year and then hunt them down. This movie hides behind a sermon on the coarsening influence of war, but it's really a very shabby and violent piece of exploitation.

R. ★

D: Peter Collinson; W: David Osborn and Liz Charles-Williams; Ph: Fernando Arribas; M: Ruggero Cini.
Cast: Peter Fonda, Cornelia Sharpe, John Phillip Law, Richard Lynch.

ORCA. (1977) A killer whale lunches on a shark just to remind us of the cinematic antecedents of one of the worst of the *Jaws* imitations. The movie never surmounts the problem of our sympathies. They lie with the whale, a beautiful creature routinely slaughtered by man, rather than Richard Harris, who looks profoundly hungover throughout the proceedings. Charlotte Rampling is on hand as the mandatory marine biologist offering such ineffable advice as "We know very little about the killer whale except that it exists." Oh, really?
PG. ★
D: Michael Anderson; W: Luciano Vincenzoni, Sergio Donati; Ph: Ted Moore, J. Barry Herron; M: Ennio Morricone.
Cast: Richard Harris, Charlotte Rampling, Will Sampson, Keenan Wynn.

ORCHESTRA WIVES. (1942) A trumpeter marries a nice girl but will he fall for the strumpet singer? While you scratch your brains over this burning question, tap your toes to the incomparable Glenn Miller band and such hits as *Serenade in Blue*. It was Miller's last film.
★★
D: Archie Mayo; W: Karl Tunberg and Darrell Ware; Ph: Lucien Ballard; M: Alfred Newman.
Cast: George Montgomery, Ann Rutherford, Cesar Romero, Glenn Miller.

ORDINARY PEOPLE. (1980) The quality that sets Robert Redford's film apart is his ability to fashion eloquent scenes about an inhibited family, whose members do not believe in making scenes at any price. Articulate people unable to articulate what they feel live in claustrophobic politeness until the suicidal depression of the son brings on a crisis. The only real weakness is the rather pat approach to despair and nihilism. Nobly acted with Mary Tyler Moore managing to overcome the contempt-tinged pity extended to her character by the otherwise exemplary and even-handed screenplay.
R. ★★★★
D: Robert Redford; W: Alvin Sargent; Ph: John Bailey; M: Marvin Hamlisch.
Cast: Donald Sutherland, Mary Tyler Moore, Tim Hutton, Judd Hirsch.

THE OSTERMAN WEEKEND. (1983) Sam Peckinpah returned to directing after a five-year layoff and promptly got lost in a single weekend. Robert Ludlum's densely plotted novel becomes a dense movie that has a paranoid cryptogram instead of a plot. The actors, understandably, show no clear grasp of their characters. A television personality hosts a weekend for some college chums who are suspected of being part of a Soviet espionage ring.
R. ★★
D: Sam Peckinpah; W: Alan Sharp ; Ph: John Coquillon; M: Lalo Schifrin.
Cast: Rutger Hauer, John Hurt, Craig T. Nelson, Burt Lancaster.

OTHELLO. (1966) If Laurence Olivier's *Hamlet* is more cinematic, it's because he set out to make a film instead of film a play. Within the familiar strictures, this invaluable movie records one of Olivier's greatest interpretations and we should hold it in the same regard as the *King Lear* he made for television in 1983.
★★★★
D: Stuart Burge; W: William Shakespeare; Ph: Geoffrey Unsworth; M: Richard Hampton.
Cast: Laurence Olivier, Frank Finlay, Joyce Redman, Maggie Smith.

THE OTHER. (1972) Movies about possessed children promise more of the same, but Tom Tryon's adaptation of his own novel is quite a respectable, if not very original entry. In New England in the thirties, good and evil reside in twin boys and strange goings on result.
★★★
D: Robert Mulligan; W: Tom Tryon; Ph: Robert Surtees; M: Jerry Goldsmith.
Cast: Uta Hagen, Diana Muldaur, Victor French, Chris Connelly.

THE OTHER SIDE OF MIDNIGHT. (1977) Some films are dull enough to have you sneaking a glance at your watch. This vulgar epic has you checking the calendar. A vengeance fantasy for women based on Sidney Sheldon's best-seller, it recounts the rise to stardom of a French actress and her obsession with the man who rejected her.
R. ★
D: Charles Jarrott; W: Herman Raucher, Daniel Taradash; Ph: Fred J. Koenekamp; M: Michel Legrand.
Cast: Marie-France Pisier, Raf Vallone, John Beck, Susan Sarandon.

THE OTHER SIDE OF THE MOUNTAIN.
(1975) A soap opera that does not hold back the suds and sentimentality. The true and very sad story of Jill Kinmont, who suffered a paralyzing accident while training for the U.S. Olympic ski team in 1956. Other tragedies follow until a tough ski coach (Beau Bridges) falls in love with her. There is so much genuine courage on hand, it does not need or deserve the treatment given here.
PG   ★★
D: Larry Peerce; W: David Seltzer; Ph: David M. Walsh; M: Charles Fox.
Cast: Marilyn Hassett, Beau Bridges, Belinda Montgomery, Nan Martin.

THE OTHER SIDE OF THE MOUNTAIN— PART 2. (1978) The resumption of Jill Kinmont's story slides downhill in an avalanche of contrived sentimentality. Her genuine courage—the skier who befriended her after her accident was killed in a plane crash—is obscured in a precious, softly focused view of her handicap. She goes to California for a vacation with her mother and marries the truck driver who rents them his summer house.
PG.   ★★
D: Larry Peerce; W: Douglas Day Stewart; Ph: Ric Waite; M: Lee Holdridge.
Cast: Marilyn Hassett, Timothy Bottoms, Nan Martin, Gretchen Corbett.

OUR MAN FLINT. (1966) Even in the sixties, with Sean Connery in the role, the James Bond movies had a self-deprecating humor that make parody difficult. James Coburn's super-agent is one of the funnier attempts, although it runs out of things to poke fun at long before the final credits. Flint is an American Bond trying to stop a world take-over between orgasms.
                                         ★★
D: Daniel Mann; W: Hal Fimberg and Ben Starr; Ph: Daniel Fapp; M: Jerry Goldsmith.
Cast: James Coburn, Lee J. Cobb, Gila Golan, Edward Mulhare.

THE OUTFIT. (1974) Lurid, brutal and rather old-fashioned gangster fare elevated by Robert Duvall. He is a convict who emerges from jail seeking the inevitable vengeance against the mob through a series of heists. Colorful characters and some pungently written scenes put the picture a cut above the norm for the genre.
PG.   ★★★

D and W: John Flynn; Ph: Bruce Surtees; M: Jerry Fielding.
Cast: Robert Duvall, Joe Don Baker, Karen Black, Robert Ryan.

OUTLAND. (1981) Peter Hyams borrowed western themes to a degree that deserved retitling as *High Moon*. On a starkly realized mining operation on one of Jupiter's moons, Hyams pitted a new marshal against shady corporate forces. What raises his work to the top level of science-fiction is the shrewd blending of contemporary doubt and cynicism, western heroism and technology that makes space a threatening place. It is no backdrop as in *Star Wars*. The cast has far more character than is commonly found in the genre,
R.   ★★★★
D and W: Peter Hyams ; Ph: Stephen Goldblatt; M: Jerry Goldsmith.
Cast: Sean Connery, Peter Boyle, Frances Sternhagen, James B. Sikking.

THE OUTLAW. (1943) Howard Hughes liked to do things in a big way and when he saw the size of Jane Russell's bosom he made the cleavage one of the stars of the film. The now innocent shots kept the film in notice. Supporting the bra that Hughes designed for Russell is a good cast in an inferior plot dealing with Billy the Kid.
                                         ★★
D: Howard Hughes; W: Jules Furthman; Ph: Gregg Toland; M: Victor Young.
Cast: Walter Huston, Jane Russell, Jack Beutel, Thomas Mitchell.

OUTLAW BLUES. (1977) Peter Fonda is a convict whose hit song is ripped off by a country and western star. He comes out to pursue (a) his rights (b) Susan Saint James and (c) stardom. His singing is about as attractive as a life sentence. The movie at least goes easy on the car smashes and dumb southern lawmen yelling "sumbitch" and gesticulating.
PG.   ★★
D: Richard T. Heffron; W: B.W.L. Norton; Ph: Jules Brenner; M: Charles Bernstein.
Cast: Peter Fonda, Susan Saint James, John Crawford, James Callahan.

THE OUTLAW JOSEY WALES. (1976) Clint Eastwood's fourth outing as a director casts him as an outlaw after a band of guerillas who killed his wife and son. This act is supposed to confer absolution for the vio-

lence that follows as Eastwood makes his way south after the end of the Civil War. Technically an advance on his spaghetti westerns, but more of the same old thing in pursuit of a few dollars more.
PG.   ★★
D: Clint Eastwood; W: Phil Kaufman, Sonia Chernus; Ph: Bruce Surtees; M: Jerry Fielding.
Cast: Clint Eastwood, Chief Dan George, Sondra Locke.

THE OUTSIDERS. (1983) Francis Ford Coppola, after many financial headaches and the failure of *One From the Heart*, returned to the small movie with this elegantly made version of the S.E. Hinton novel. Her book deals with gangs on both sides of the tracks and Coppola's film is almost derailed by the perspective he brings to the story. Rather than the wise reflections of a man looking back on adolescent passions, there is a celebration of them without any special insight. Two boys flee after a murder of a rival gang member in Tulsa in the mid sixties. Kids should respond to its shrewd viewpoint and the way the film shares the extremities of teenage emotions.
PG.   ★★
D: Francis Ford Coppola; W: Kathleen Knutsen Rowell; Ph: Stephen H. Burum; M: Carmine Coppola.
Cast: Matt Dillon, C. Thomas Howell, Ralph Macchio, Diane Lane.

OVER THE EDGE. (1979) It is not hard to see why Jonathan Kaplan's uncompromising and ultimately depressing look at today's suburban kids is a cult favorite. The kids of New Granada see nothing inviting in their future and thus make the present an act of protest and destruction. Kaplan and his shrewd writers make you feel their point of view and that gives *Over the Edge* a very hard-edged quality.
PG.   ★★★
D: Jonathan Kaplan; W: Tim Hunter and Charlie Haas; Ph: Andrew Davis; M: Sol Kaplan.
Cast: Michael Kramer, Matt Dillon, Pamela Ludwig, Vincent Spano.

THE OX-BOW INCIDENT. (1943) A classic western and one of the definitive movie examinations of mob psychology. Although it is much admired, *The Ox-bow Incident* has never been popular because it is very hard to take and there is an absence of the conventional heroism audiences expect in the genre. The film uses that expectation brilliantly. Three men are accused and hung for cattle rustling and the people responsible have to live with the later discovery of their innocence.
                                                    ★★★★★
D: William Wellman; W: Lamar Trotti; Ph: Arthur Miller; M: Cyril J. Mockridge.
Cast: Henry Fonda, Dana Andrews, Mary Beth Hughes, Anthony Quinn.

P

THE PACK. (1977) One of the herd of animals sent in the wake of *Jaws* and in search of similar earnings. Dogs left by tourists on an island over the years turn nasty and start treating humans like Alpo. They actually look rather cute and you're soon on their side. Especially with Joe Don Baker, the game warden, looking on with the expression of a caveman trying to understand the stock market.

R. ★

D and W: Robert Clouse.
Cast: Joe Don Baker, Hope Alexander Willis, Richard Shull, R.G. Armstrong.

THE PAJAMA GAME. (1957) A musical that made more than 7½ cents, which is the hourly raise the workers in a pajama factory want from the boss. From this unlikely material, Stanley Donen shaped a scintillating movie that even non-admirers of Doris Day have to like. She's the union leader and, of course, the singer of the strong contingent of songs.

★★★

D: Stanley Donen; W: George Abbott and Richard Bissell; Ph: Harry Stradling; M: Richard Adler and Jerry Ross.
Cast: Doris Day, John Raitt, Eddie Foy, Jr., Reta Shaw.

PANIC IN NEEDLE PARK. (1971) A graphic, frightening trip into the world of drug addicts in New York, Jerry Schatzberg's film pulls no punches. Nor, unlike a lot of other drug movies of the time, does it stop for a homily. Instead, there is nothing left to say after Al Pacino has done with an addict who, in the name of a twisted love, drags a girl down with him.

★★★

D: Jerry Schatzberg; W: Joan Didion and John Gregory Dunne; Ph: Adam Holender.
Cast: Al Pacino, Kitty Winn, Alan Vint, Richard Bright.

PANIC IN THE STREETS. (1950) In New Orleans, a city medical official makes the appalling discovery that a man who has been shot is also carrying bubonic plague and has —with poetic justice—infected his killers. Elia Kazan made judicious use of the locations and built to a strong climax as the police hunt the contagious hoods.

★★★

D: Elia Kazan; W: Richard Murphy; Ph: Joe MacDonald; M: Alfred Newman.
Cast: Richard Widmark, Paul Douglas, Barbara Bel Geddes, Jack Palance.

PANIC IN THE YEAR ZERO. (1962) Although Ray Milland's look at post-nuclear survival is painfully naive in its depiction of conditions, he offers an intriguing account of a man coping with the breakdown of law and order. When he steals a gun to protect his newly nuclear family, he writes a check for the amount. They, along with everyone else, flee Los Angeles after the bomb and try to fend off hungry and horny looters. Try it if you like to believe there'll be a day after.

★★★

D: Ray Milland; W: John Morton and Jay Simms; Ph: Gil Warrenton; M: Les Baxter.
Cast: Ray Milland, Jean Hagen, Frankie Avalon, Joan Freeman.

THE PAPER CHASE. (1973) John Houseman made his reputation the old fashioned way, earning it with such roles as the Harvard Law professor with a snide aside for every occasion. Houseman is so good that a rather average film about the pressures of ambition and college life has an over-rated reputation itself. Timothy Bottoms is the midwesterner who falls for Houseman's daughter. The film formed the basis for the television series in which Houseman starred between commercials.

★★★

D and W: James Bridges; Ph: Gordon Willis; M: John Williams.
Cast: John Houseman, Lindsay Wagner, Timothy Bottoms, Graham Beckel.

PAPILLON. (1973) The title means butterfly and they aren't free in this grim chronicle of the adventure of Henri Charriere. He was sentenced to Devil's Island, which would never be mistaken for summer camp. Franklin Schaffner loads on the brutality in an attempt to make the viewer feel the harshness of life in the French penal colony. When the escape comes, it is welcome as a liberation for the audience as well as Steve McQueen.

R. ★★★

D: Franklin J. Schaffner; W: Dalton Trumbo and Lorenzo Semple, Jr.; Ph: Fred Koenekamp; M: Jerry Goldmsith.
Cast: Steve McQueen, Dustin Hoffman, Don Gordon, Anthony Zerbe.

PARADISE. (1982) A teen couple lost in the wastes of Arabia proves that when you take the water out of *The Blue Lagoon* you wind up with just desert. Standard "make-out" fare with much ogling of Phoebe Cates and other elements of nude travelogue. The kids are orphaned and then hounded across the desert by Arab brigands.
R. ★
D and W: Stuart Gillard; Ph: Adam Greenberg; M: Paul Hoffert.
Cast: Phoebe Cates, Willie Aames, Richard Curnock, Tuvia Tavi.

PARADISE ALLEY. (1979) Sylvester Stallone even croaked out the title song in the course of tripping over his ego. The three Carbone brothers try to make it out of New York's Hell's Kitchen after World War II with one of them becoming a pro wrestler. There are shades of Rocky Balboa, but Stallone's direction is undisciplined and often incomprehensible and the attempt at raucous humor falls flat.
PG. ★★
D and W: Sylvester Stallone; Ph: Laszlo Kovacs; M: Bill Conti.
Cast: Sylvester Stallone, Armand Assante, Kevin Conway, Anne Archer.

THE PARALLAX VIEW. (1974) Not for the paranoid, Alan Pakula's gripping thriller was a harbinger of *All the President's Men*. This time, an investigative reporter tries to uncover the truth about the assassination of a presidential candidate at the Seattle space needle. The witnesses—he is one—begin dying "natural" deaths and the trail leads him to the doors of the sinister Parallax Corporation. Well-made but ultimately depressing.
R. ★★★★
D: Alan Pakula; W: Lorenzo Semple, Jr. and David Giler; Ph: Gordon Willis; M: Michael Small.
Cast: Warren Beatty, Paula Prentiss, William Daniels, Hume Cronyn.

PARASITE. (1982) In 1992 the only available food is Campbell's soup in a film that is "M-M-M-bad." A scientist creates two parasites who take it out on bad actors. Theatrically released in 3-D and not worth the time in any dimension.
R. ★
D: Charles Band; W: Alan Adler, Michael Shoob and Frank Levering; Ph: Chris Condon; M: Richard Band.
Cast: Robert Glaudini, Demi Moore, Luca Bercovici, James Davidson.

PARDON MON AFFAIRE. (1977) Jean Rochefort's klutzy attempts to commit adultery lead him to a window ledge high above Paris with a large crowd and television cameras looking on. An inventive and amusing comedy of a mid-life crisis that owes more to the panache Rochefort brings to the role than the sometimes corny ideas in the screenplay. Gallic froth.
PG. ★★★
D: Yves Robert; W: Robert and Jean-Loup Dabadie; Ph: Rene Mathelin; M: Vladimir Cosma.
Cast: Jean Rochefort, Anny Duperey, Guy Bedos, Pierre Brasseur.

THE PARENT TRAP. (1961) A double helping of Hayley Mills that gets into trouble by mixing summer camp antics with a more complicated and less comic look at the way parental separation affects kids. For that reason, it remains timely, if optimistic. Mills plays identical twins with different personalities and she does it very well as the children plot various ploys to get father and mother back together.
★★
D and W: David Swift; Ph: Lucien Ballard; M: Paul J. Smith.
Cast: Hayley Mills, Maureen O'Hara, Brian Keith, Charlie Ruggles.

PARTNERS. (1982) A heterosexual detective and a gay cop are ordered to live together to solve the murders of several homosexual models. Not the most offensive Hollywood gay movie—that honor belongs to *Cruising*—but one that still laughs both at and with homosexuals—depending on the scene. Ryan O'Neal is a very uncomfortable straight man.
R. ★★
D: James Burrows; W: Francis Veber; Ph: Victor J. Kemper; M: Georges Delerue.
Cast: Ryan O'Neal, John Hurt, Kenneth McMillan, Robyn Douglass.

THE PASSAGE. (1979) Not just another terrible movie with Anthony Quinn doing his simple-peasant-communing-with-surly-sheep routine. For bad measure, Malcolm McDowell does a manic turn as an SS officer with a swastika emblazoned on his jock strap. He pursues a scientist and his family trying to reach the safety of Spain in World War II.
R. ★
D: J. Lee Thompson; W: Bruce Nicolaysen; Ph: Mike Reed; M: Michael J. Lewis.

Cast: Anthony Quinn, James Mason, Malcolm McDowell, Patricia Neal.

THE PASSENGER. (1975) Michelangelo Antonioni couched some familiar themes —the alientation of modern man and the aridity of contemporary life—in what is, for him, a plot. Jack Nicholson, a disgruntled TV journalist, gets the chance to change his life by assuming the identity of a businessman who looks like him. Visually arresting, but the story loses cohesion and Nicholson spends much time exchanging ambiguities with the other characters.
PG. ★★★
D: Michelangelo Antonioni; W: Antonioni, Mark Peploe and Peter Wollen; Ph: Luciano Tovoli; M: Ivan Vandor.
Cast: Jack Nicholson, Maria Schneider, Jenny Runacre, Ian Hendry.

PATERNITY. (1981) Buddy Evans (Burt Reynolds) manages Madison Square Garden and wants a child without the burden of a wife. He hears a lecture on the emu, a species of bird in which the male raises the young. It's not very emusing. Buddy tries his girlfriends and then hires a trumpet player to carry his tune. Beverly D'Angelo, in a potentially demeaning role, carries off the film without blowing her own horn too obviously.
PG. ★★
D: David Steinberg; W: Charlie Peters; Ph: Bobby Burne; M: David Shire.
Cast: Burt Reynolds, Beverly D'Angelo, Paul Dooley, Norman Fell.

PAT GARRETT AND BILLY THE KID. (1973) Bob Dylan sings along with Sam Peckinpah and even appears as one of Billy's buddies. Billy is a woefully miscast Kris Kristofferson pursued by another friend, Pat Garrett. This being Peckinpah, Garrett is the sell-out and everything is offered with a great deal of remarkably composed violence.
R. ★★
D: Sam Peckinpah; W: Rudolph Wurlitzer; Ph: John Coquillon; M: Bob Dylan.
Cast: Kris Kristofferson, James Coburn, Jason Robards, Bob Dylan.

PATHS OF GLORY. (1957) In the war to end all wars, Stanley Kubrick set an anti-war film to end all anti-war films. It remains the film against which other attacks on militarism are measured and it established Kubrick as a major talent. *Paths of Glory* pits a colonel who refuses to see his men die in a futile attack on a German stronghold against the generals who planned the assault. Three of the reluctant men are singled out for court martial and executed. The technique is masterly and the tone impasssioned.
★★★★★
D: Stanley Kubrick; W: Kubrick, Calder Willingham and Jim Thompson; Ph: George Krause; M: Gerald Fried.
Cast: Kirk Douglas, Ralph Meeker, Adolphe Menjou, George Macready.

PATTON. (1970) From the immortal opening speech to the troops to the moving conclusion, George C. Scott's reading of the life and mind of General George Patton is an indelible screen portrait. Patton's volatile temperament, his ego and his tactical genius lend the film an extraordinary nervous energy. This is not a war film shot from the trenches, but a remarkably insightful look at command. For all his flaws, Patton seems heroic when measured against the schemers at Allied Command. His exploits, both private and public, are set forth honestly.
★★★★★
D: Franklin Schaffner; W: Francis Ford Coppola and Edward H. North; Ph: Fred Koenekamp; M: Jerry Goldsmith.
Cast: George C. Scott, Karl Malden, Michael Bates, Stephen Young.

PEEPER. (1975) What is Michael Caine doing as a British private eye in Los Angeles in 1947? Good question and one that Peter Hyams' weak spoof of the genre never answers satisfactorily. This is not the kind of light material in which you would expect Hyams to be comfortable and that's how it turns out. Besides Sam Spade and his ilk have taken so many satiric punches that *Peeper* becomes no more than a slap on he wrist. Caine is hired to find a millionaire's daughter.
★★
D: Peter Hyams; W: W.D. Richter; Ph: Earl Rath; M: Richard Clements.
Cast: Michael Caine, Natalie Wood, Kitty Winn, Thayer David.

PENITENTIARY II. (1982) Hanging's too good for James Fanaka, the perpetrator of an awful sequel to *Penitentiary*. Too Sweet Gordon is out of the slammer and not interested in resuming his boxing career. Events, none of them credible or even palatable, force him back into the ring. The title is misleading since the action does not take place in jail.
R. ★

D and W: James Fanaka; Ph: Steve Posey; M: Jack Wheaton.
Cast: Leon Isaac Kennedy, Glyn Turman, Ernie Hudson, Mr T.

THE PEOPLE THAT TIME FORGOT. (1977) You can too. The only recorded instance of an actor declaring, "We're being followed by a volcano!" A sequel to the equally memorable *The Land That Time Forgot* that has the intrepid explorers returning to their fantasy island, which teems with dinosaurs, cavemen and soldiers who look like extras from *Alexander Nevsky* in drag. They try to rescue an overweight Doug McClure from same. Dime store special effects, including a pterodactyl that looks like a paper airplane made by a drunk.
PG. ★
D: Kevin Connor; W: Patrick Tilley; Ph: Alan Hume; M: John Scott.
Cast: Patrick Wayne, Doug McClure, Sarah Douglas, Dana Gillespie.

PEOPLE WILL TALK. (1951) And they still do about Joseph Mankiewicz's daring mixture of comedy and almost flagrant melodrama. Cary Grant is at his urbane best as Dr. Pretorius, a physician who alarms the medical establishment by arguing that a patient's psychological welfare is also the responsibility of the doctor. This outrageous view is, of course, contested by the quacks.
★★★★
D and W:: Joseph L. Mankiewicz; Ph: Milton Krasner; M: Alfred Newman.
Cast: Cary Grant, Jeanne Crain, Hume Cronyn, Finlay Currie.

A PERFECT COUPLE. (1979) The relationship of two people who have little to say to each other and, it emerges, Robert Altman has nothing to add to the subject. Paul Sorvino is a scion of a very traditional Greek family and she is a rock singer and they meet through a dating service called Great Expectations. Modest hopes are dashed because Altman milks their differences for humor and then insists they're compatible.
PG. ★★
D: Robert Altman; W: Altman and Alan Nicholls; Ph: Edmond L. Koons; M: Alan Nicholls.
Cast: Paul Dooley, Marta Heflin, Titos Vandis, Belita Moreno.

PETE KELLY'S BLUES. (1955) Jack Webb blows his own trumpet and, let's face it, nobody's about to do it for him. He directs himself as a jazz musician in the twenties but the non-Dragnet environment did nothing to loosen up his arthritically stiff acting. He becomes involved with gangsters and Peggy Lee.
★★
D: Jack Webb; W: Richard Breen; Ph: Hal Rosson; M: Sammy Cahn.
Cast: Jack Webb, Peggy Lee, Edmond O'Brien, Janet Leigh.

PETE 'N TILLIE. (1972) An odd and quite effective hybrid of wit and tear-jerker that is well above the average. That can be attributed to the predictably suave playing of Walter Matthau and the remarkable screen debut of Carol Burnett. They are ordinary people who have to cope with the death of their only son. The humor in the movie is a self-defense mechanism for people dealing with tragedy and it never seems misplaced.
PG. ★★★
D: Martin Ritt; W: Julius J. Epstein; Ph: John Alonzo; M: John Williams.
Cast: Walter Matthau, Carol Burnett, Geraldine Page, Barry Nelson.

PETER IBBETSON. (1935) Even in its own day, Henry Hathaway's assertion that death is not the end of love was greeted with sneers by the critics. The years have not been kind to it. Gary Cooper endures several Gothic setbacks, but his love is sustained in dreams and these still have an odd haunting quality in Hathaway's reading of the George du Maurier novel.
★★★
D: Henry Hathaway; W: Waldemar Young, Vincent Lawrence, Constance Collier John Meehan and Edward Justus Mayer; Ph: Charles Lang and Gordon Jennings; M: Ernst Toch.
Cast: Gary Cooper, Ann Harding, John Halliday, Ida Lupino.

PETER PAN. (1953) Peter Pan whisks three children off to adventures in Never-Neverland and the unwelcome attentions of Captain Hook. No one would claim the animation to be among Disney's greatest creations, but it is very well executed and worthy of the Barrie story, which retains its hold on children.
★★★★
D: Wilfred Jackson, Hamilton Luske, Clyde Geronimi; M: Oliver Wallace.
Cast: (Voices) Bobby Driscoll, Kathyrn Beaumont, Hans Conried, Bill Thompson.

PETE'S DRAGON. (1977) Comedian Charlie Callas does the voice of Elliott, an animated dragon whose antics are combined with live action and actors in a Disney musical fantasy. The film takes up the familiar children's story of the secret friend that nobody else knows about. The 19-ft. dragon helps a little boy evade mean foster parents and get back to the light-house where he belongs. Someone called Steven Spielberg did this a little better in *E.T.*, but the cast takes to the songs and their parts with zest.

G. ★★★
D: Don Chaffey; W: Malcolm Marmorstein; Ph: Frank Phillips; M: Irwin Kostal.
Cast: Jim Dale, Mickey Rooney, Red Buttons, Sean Marshall.

THE PETRIFIED FOREST. (1936) The contrivance of pitting animal man against intellectual man probably worked better on the stage and that was where Humphrey Bogart originated the role of Duke Mantee. It became his first major screen part and his Mantee overcomes the staginess and burdensome philosophy of Robert Sherwood's play. Mantee, an escaped convict, holds people hostage in an Arizona diner.

★★★
D: Archie Mayo; W: Charles Kenyon and Delmer Daves; Ph: Sol Polito; M: Leo F. Forbstein.
Cast: Humphrey Bogart, Bette Davis, Leslie Howard, Genevieve Tobin.

PEYTON PLACE. (1957) With the sexual candor now common to daytime television, it may be hard to credit the scandalous reputation Grace Metalious' book enjoyed in the fifties. As an exercise in soap opera—the tireless search for sexual and personal fulfilment in a small New England town—Mark Robson's work is quite passable and the acting is not as overwrought as you find in the many later films influenced by *Peyton Place*.

★★★
D: Mark Robson; W: John Michael Hayes; Ph: William Mellor; M: Franz Waxman.
Cast: Lana Turner, Hope Lange, Lee Philips, Lloyd Nolan.

THE PHANTOM OF LIBERTE. (1974) Surrreal comedy from Luis Bunuel that inverts situations and takes them to absurdist extremes. A loosely assorted arrangement of gibes at his favorite targets —church, state and other institutional hypocrisies. Priests play cards with religious medals as chips, the police investigate the kidnapping

of a child who is present throughout the film and a sniper becomes a celebrity. Not among his best.

★★
D and W: Luis Bunuel; Ph: Edmond Richard.
Cast: Adriana Asti, Julien Bertheau, Jean-Claude Brialy, Adolfo Celi.

THE PHANTOM OF THE PARADISE. (1974) An often funny send-up of two very different worlds—rock music and horror movies. Brian De Palma, who is not especially noted for satire, takes a broadsword to dissect groupies, superstars, rapacious record companies and pushers. The pastiche of *The Phantom of the Opera* has a mad rock composer seeking vengeance against the promoter who stole his material.

PG. ★★★
D and W:: Brian De Palma; ; Ph: Larry Pizer; M: Paul Williams.
Cast: Paul Williams, William Finley, Jessica Harper, George Memmoli.

THE PHILADELPHIA STORY. (1940) One of the landmarks in Katherine Hepburn's career casts her as Tracy Lord and plays off her Main Line hauteur. On the eve of her second marriage, Tracy's first husband shows up and so does a reporter. The witty screenplay turns on their disruption of Tracy's nuptials and the twitting of her snobbery.

★★★★
D: George Cukor; W: Donald Ogden Stewart; Ph: Joseph Ruttenberg; M: Franz Waxman.
Cast: Katharine Hepburn, James Stewart, Cary Grant, Ruth Hussey.

PICK-UP ON SOUTH STREET. (1953) A pickpocket picks up a lot more than he bargained for when the loot turns out to be a microfilm sought by both the FBI and communist agents. Cult director Sam Fuller brings his visceral flair for violence and tension to the proceedings and Richard Widmark does a variation of his nutty hood in *Kiss of Death*.

★★★
D and W: Sam Fuller; Ph: Joe MacDonald; M: Lionel Newman.
Cast: Richard Widmark, Thelma Ritter, Jean Peters, Richard Kiley.

PICNIC. (1955) A drifter comes to a small town in Kansas and disrupts the rhythm and relationships. Adapted from William Inge's play and once considered quite steamy, *Picnic* is more interesting for William Holden's work than its rather glib assertions about provincial life.

★★★

D: Joshua Logan; W: Daniel Taradash; Ph: James Wong Howe; M: George Dunning.
Cast: William Holden, Kim Novak, Susan Strasberg, Rosalind Russell.

PICNIC AT HANGING ROCK. (1979) Peter Weir's very mystifying mystery deals with the disappearance of a party of Australian schoolgirls on St. Valentine's Day, 1900. It is full of images of innocence arrayed against malevolent natural backdrops. The girls vanish at Hanging Rock, a volcanic formation. Weir is more taken with tone painting than delving into what really happened. It is based on an actual event.

PG. ★★★

D: Peter Weir; W: Cliff Green; Ph: Russell Boyd.
Cast: Rachel Roberts, Dominic Guard, Helen Morse, Vivean Gray.

THE PICTURE OF DORIAN GRAY. (1945) An elegant and literate rendering of Oscar Wilde's clever invention with glittering performances from Hurd Hatfield, the gentleman who lives a life of tireless debauchery without even a mild hangover to show for it, and George Sanders, the suitably nasty nobleman. While Dorian remains eternally young, the portrait upstairs shows his years.

★★★★

D and W: Albert Lewin; Ph: Harry Stradling; M: Herbert Stothart.
Cast: George Sanders, Hurd Hatfield, Donna Reed, Angela Lansbury.

A PIECE OF THE ACTION. (1977) Sidney Poitier and Bill Cosby resumed their partnership for a third go-round. Poitier directs in a way that suggested the film he felt commericially obliged to make intruded on the one that was in his heart. The movie is a comedy about two rich felons blackmailed into doing public service with unemployed ghetto kids. It becomes a public service commercial. There is certainly nothing wrong with addressing a vital national problem, but it does not work in this context.

PG. ★★

D: Sidney Poitier; W: Charles Blackwell; Ph: Don Morgan; M: Curtis Mayfield.
Cast: Bill Cosby, Sidney Poitier, James Earl Jones, Denise Nicholas.

PINK FLOYD: THE WALL. (1982) Depending on your point of view—and very possibly your age—Alan Parker's colorful rock opera depicts either a profound and sym-

bolic psychological crisis or a whining adolescent outburst. Either way, it is a depressing nihilist essay on the alienation of western youth. The songs are from the group's 1979 album.

R. ★★★

D: Alan Parker; W: Roger Waters; Ph: Peter Bizou; M: Pink Floyd.
Cast: Bob Goldof, Christine Hargreaves, James Laurenson, Eleanor David.

THE PINK PANTHER. (1963) The Pink Panther is a priceless diamond and so is Peter Sellers in the comedy that established Inspector Clouseau and his inimitable capacity for wreaking havoc but somehow muddling through. There isn't much to it apart from Sellers and David Niven's suave jewel thief, but they are more than enough. It was this collaboration with Sellers that rescued Blake Edwards' faltering career and allowed him eventually to fashion some wonderful comedies beyond this enormously lucrative series.

★★★

D: Blake Edwards; W: Edwards and Maurice Richlin; Ph: Philip Lathrop; M: Henry Mancini.
Cast: Peter Sellers, David Niven, Capucine, Claudia Cardinale.

THE PINK PANTHER STRIKES AGAIN. (1976) The highlight finds Inspector Clouseau storming across a castle moat to get at Herbert Lom and a deadly weapon that threatens the world. As usual, every inanimate object is a threat to Clouseau and the film is a deft mix of expertly done slapstick and puerile jokes. By this time, Sellers had refined Clouseau and wore the role like a perfectly tailored suit. Better than its dawdling, immediate predecessor, *Return of the Pink Panther*.

PG. ★★★

D: Blake Edwards; W: Edwards and Frank Waldman; Ph: Harry Waxman; M: Henry Mancini.
Cast: Peter Sellers, Herbert Lom, Colin Blakely, Burt Kwouk.

PINKY. (1949) Elia Kazan's groundbreaker on race relations can claim an honorable place in raising consciousness over an issue that was barely discussed. Jeanne Crain, a light skinned black girl, goes back to the south and eventually becomes involved in a bitter dispute over her inheritance from the rich white woman she has nursed. Emotionally forceful with Kazan laying particular emphasis on the consequences of prejudice for blacks.

★★★

D: Elia Kazan; W: Philip Dunne and Dudley Nichols; Ph: Joe MacDonald; M: Alfred Newman.
Cast: Jeanne Crain, Ethel Barrymore, Ethel Waters, William Lundigan.

PINOCCHIO. (1940) One of the finest offerings from the heyday of the Disney animators. From the smallest detail—the movement of Jiminy Cricket's eyes—to the vividly imagined Pleasure Island and the monstrous whale, this is animation that ranks with *Fantasia* and *Snow White*. 750 artists labored for two years to produce it.

G.

★★★★★

D: Ben Sharpsteen and Hamilton Luske; M: Leigh Harline.

PIPE DREAMS. (1976) Singer Gladys Knight is Pipless in a pointless movie about the Alaska pipeline. She goes to Alaska to make it up with her husband, a black macho type who confuses women and property. It contains the immortal line "That all out there is called the tundra," but little else. Sloppy and amateurish in every department.

PG.

★

D and W: Stephen Verona.
Cast: Gladys Knight, Barry Hankerson, Bruce French, Sherry Bain.

PIRANHA. (1978) Joe Dante went on to *The Howling* and *Gremlins* and some people think that all the blood-letting here should be forgiven because of the occasional humor. But it's still men women and children being ripped up by carnivorous fish. They are loosed into supposedly safe waters in a military experiment.

R.

★★

D: Joe Dante; W: John Sayles; Ph:Jamie Anderson; M: Pino Donaggio.
Cast: Bradford Dillman, Heather Menzies, Kevin McCarthy, Bruce Gordon.

THE PIRATE MOVIE. (1982) Can a Gilbert and Sullivan opera be turned into a teen romance? Ken Annakin's inept attempt at this odd coupling comes a cropper, complete with soft-rock ballads to supplement the score of *The Pirates of Penzance*. The idea comes from the Linda Ronstadt success in the New York production of the opera. Terrible dialogue, "in" movie jests and awful dirty jokes.

PG.

★

D: Ken Annakin; W: Trevor Farrant; Ph: Robin Copping; M: Terry Britten, Kit Hain, Sue Shifrin and Brian Robertson.
Cast: Kristy McNichol, Christopher Atkins, Ted Hamilton, Bill Kerr.

THE PIRATES OF PENZANCE. (1983) Only the third attempt to put Gilbert and Sullivan on the screen and, for all the bonhomie and cleverness, it's easy to see why the stage is preferable for their light operas. This is a faithful translation of Joseph Papp's Broadway production and it is best taken as a record of a fun evening in the theater than as a movie despite the high energy level.

G.

★★★

D and W: Wilford Leach; Ph: Douglas Slocombe; M: Sir Arthur Sullivan(Adapted by William Elliott).
Cast: Kevin Kline, Linda Ronstadt, Angela Lansbury, George Rose.

PIXOTE. (1981) In Brazil, half the population is under 21 and at least three million children are homeless urban nomads. Hectro Babenco's look at the consequences is as punishing as the movies get. It is filled with gang rape, murder and despair and centers on children without the slightest chance of becoming anything more than they are. The indictment of Brazilian society and the system that condones the ghastly conditions is the more powerful for its tone of matter-of-fact understatement. It isn't rated, but it is definitely not for kids or adults with weak stomachs.

★★★★

D: Hector Babenco; W: Babence and Jorge Duran; Ph: Rodolfo Sanches; M: John Neschling.
Cast: Fernando Ramos da Silva, Marilla Pera, Jorg Juliao, Gilberto Moura.

THE PLAINSMAN. (1936) This being a Cecil B. de Mille western, there is nothing at all plain about it. The fanciful biography of Wild Bill Hickock (Gary Cooper) is crammed with action and quite well mounted spectacle that now has a certain quaintness. Cooper's astonishing authority on the screen is far more absorbing than the dated trappings.

★★★

D: Cecil B. de Mille; W: Waldemar Young, Lynn Riggs and Harold Lamb; Ph: Victor Milner; M: George Anthheil.
Cast: Gary Cooper, Jean Arthur, James Ellison, Charles Bickford.

PLANET OF THE APES. (1968) The fact that the series deteriorated in simian sequels takes nothing away from the originality of this skilled mixture of adventure and arch social commentary. Charlton Heston leads a party of astronauts after a crash-landing on what seems to be a distant planet. They discover that a sophisticated ape society rules and humans are a sub-class. There are many witty inversions woven into the story and the make-up artists did their work so well that you accept the premise. ★★★★
D: Franklin J. Schaffner; W: Rod Serling and Michael Wilson; Ph: Leon Shamroy; M: Jerry Goldsmith.
Cast: Charlton Heston, Roddy McDowall, Kim Hunter, Maurice Evans.

PLAYERS. (1979) World class tennis reduced to a love match and it's a long time between sets. The film tries to avoid the sports climax syndrome of *Rocky* by putting the big event at the beginning, but it finds nothing noteworthy to substitute in the relationship of a young tennis hustler and an older woman. Several tennis stars were recruited and, alas, allowed to speak.
PG. ★
D: Anthony Harvey; W: Arnold Schulman; Ph: James Crabe; M: Jerry Goldsmith.
Cast: Ali MacGraw, Dean-Paul Martin, Maximilian Schell, Pancho Gonzalez.

POLICE ACADEMY. (1984) The screenwriters suffer from an acute case of arrested development as an assortment of racial and sexual stereotypes make life hard on the instructors. One of the latter is hurled from a motorcycle and is impacted in the rear end of a horse, where he was able to read the rest of the script.
R. ★
D: Hugh Wilson; W: Wilson, Neal Israel and Pat Profit; Ph: Michael Margiules; M: Robert Folk.
Cast: Steve Guttenberg, Kim Cantrall, G.W. Bailey, Bubba Smith.

POLLYANNA. (1960) You can be forgiven for being a cockeyed pessimist about what Disney would do with the world's most optimistic orphan. Actually, the gushiness is at a minimum and Eleanor Porter's story of the girl who is a past master of the "glad game" and who infects others with her good cheer comes across very well. The story was filmed once before, in 1920, with Mary Pickford in the role played by Hayley Mills. ★★★

D and W: David Swift; Ph: Russell Harlan; M: Paul J. Smith.
Cast: Hayley Mills, Jane Wyman, Richard Egan, Karl Malden.

POLTERGEIST. (1982) Ghosts are supposed to be the causes of psychological disturbances, not its victims. *Poltergeist* suffers from a split personality. dividing itself between trying to scare the audience and poking fun at suburbia. Tobe Hooper is the director of record but Steven Spielberg's fingerprints are all over the picture. The special effects are first-class, but the dreadful secret that besets a middle class family isn't that dreadful.
PG. ★★★
D: Tobe Hooper; W: Steven Spielberg, Michael Grais and Mark Victor; Ph: Matthew Leonetti; M: Jerry Goldsmith.
Cast: Craig T. Nelson, Jobeth Williams, Beatrice Straight, Dominique Dunne.

POLYESTER. (1981) In the compass of one movie, John Waters and his 300-pound transvestite managed to offend four of the senses—sight, hearing, smell and, most of all, taste. Patrons at the theatrical run were given cards, which emitted the appropriate smell for the screen action. Your nose will be spared but not your eyes. Waters' target is suburban bad taste but his own is far worse than anything he criticizes.
R. ★
D and W: John Waters; Ph: David Insley; M: Chris Stein.
Cast: Divine, Tab Hunter, Edith Massey, Mink Stole.

POOR LITTLE RICH GIRL. (1936) The perennial problem of how to get Shirley Temple on a stage was here solved by having her nanny lose her. Two hoofers pick her up and put her into their act. The music is a cut above the norm for a Temple tuner. ★★
D: Irving Cummings; W: Sam Hellman, Gladys Lehman and Harry Tugend; Ph: John Seitz; M: Louis Silvers.
Cast: Shirley Temple, Alice Faye, Gloria Stuart, Jack Haley.

THE POPE OF GREENWICH VILLAGE. (1984) Vincent Patrick adapted his own hilarious novel, but a lot of the humor never made it to the screen. Partly that's the medium's fault but there's also a conscious attempt to darken the tone. Two losers, one of them street-dumb, make the mistake of

stealing money from the Mafia. A rich New York atmosphere and powerful lead performances.
R. ★★★
D: Stuart Rosenberg; W: Vincent Patrick; Ph: John Bailey; M: Dave Grusin.
Cast: Mickey Rourke, Eric Roberts, Daryl Hannah, Kenneth McMillan.

POPEYE. (1980) Robert Altman's capacity for indulging himself and his actors shipwrecked an idea that was beyond salvage in the first place. You can turn real people into comic book characters —as in *Smokey and the Bandit*—but it rarely works in the opposite direction. Large stretches of the dialogue are mercifully unintelligible. Popeye adopts a child and searches for his father. Topped off with atrociously inept singing.
PG. ★
D: Robert Altman; W: Jules Feiffer; Ph: Giuseppe Rotunno; M: Harry Nilsson.
Cast: Robin Williams, Shelley Duvall, Ray Walston, Paul Dooley.

PORK CHOP HILL. (1959) Although this unsung Korean war film concludes with a conventional epilogue about men dying for freedom, what precedes it makes some pungent points about the way the grunts are abused and killed by mindless superiors. The hill which costs American lives assumes more importance at the armistice talks than in reality. One of those film's that uses Peck's decency and humanity to great advantage.
★★★★
D: Lewis Milestone; W: James R. Webb; Ph: Sam Leavitt; M: Leonard Rosenman.
Cast: Gregory Peck, Harry Guardino, Woody Strode, George Shibata.

PORKY'S. (1982) Like *Animal House*, this unspeakable piece of pandering has exercised great influence through the many imitations it has prompted. For some reason, kids took to a mixture of voyeurism, stupidity and every adolescent bad joke you can think of in numbers that astonished the industry. Six boys get involved with a redneck who runs a dive in Florida.
R. ★
D and W: Bob Clark; Ph: Reginald Morris; M: Carl Zittrer.
Cast: Dan Monahan, Wyatt Knight, Tony Ganios, Mark Herrier.

PORTNOY'S COMPLAINT. (1972) That Richard Benjamin and Lee Grant have survived a humiliation of this order is a testament to their durability and talent. Philip Roth's novel is impossible to film, as Ernest Lehman wastes little time in demonstrating.
★
D and W: Ernest Lehman; Ph: Philip Lathrop; M: Michel Legrand.
Cast: Richard Benjamin, Lee Grant, Jill Clayburgh, Jeannie Berlin.

THE POSEIDON ADVENTURE. (1972) A ship for fools and the kind of disaster film that has you rooting for the sea over the characters. On New Year's Eve, the ocean goes wild and overturns a luxury liner crammed with everyone from Gene Hackman's turtle-necked clergyman to Shelley Winters' whining Jewish mother. Battling flood, fire and fatness the survivors struggle to last until help comes.
PG ★
D: Ronald Neame; W: Stirling Silliphant and Wendell Mayes; Ph: Harold Stine; M: John Williams.
Cast: Gene Hackman, Ernest Borgnine, Shelley Winters, Red Buttons.

POSSE. (1975) A post-Watergate western that demonstrated what a climate of public cynicism did to the genre. Kirk Douglas is a law and order Texas marshal running for the U.S. Senate and the distance between his speeches and the truth is wider than the Rio Grande. He makes a public issue of capturing an outlaw, inventively played by Bruce Dern. The modern political sourness and the more traditional western elements occasionally collide, but *Posse* is a worthwhile reflection of its two times.
PG. ★★★
D: Kirk Douglas; W: William Roberts and Christopher Knopf; Ph: Fred Koenekamp; M: Maurice Jarre.
Cast: Kirk Douglas, Bruce Dern, Bo Hopkins, James Stacy.

THE POSSESSION. (1981) Almost an hour of the running time was cut for the American market and the remaining 128 minutes deserved the same fate. A pretentious attempt to dignify the sleazy horror film genre. Isabelle Adjani lives in a run-down tenement with a disgusting creature and they do not take kindly to visitors. It's hard to see how the film could be anything but nauseating at any length.
R. ★
D and W: Andrzej Zulawski; Ph: Frederic Tuten.

Cast: Isabelle Adjani, Sam Neil, Heinz Bennent.

THE POSTMAN ALWAYS RINGS TWICE.
(1981) Bob Rafelson offers a convincing case for the argument that a film can and should be made more than once. Liberated from the limits of censorship, he wisely chose to keep the story in its original Depression context. Jack Nicholson is brilliant as the drifter Frank Chambers and Jessica Lange finally got people to start taking her seriously with her sexually charged Cora. Rafelson rightly claimed that his, rather than the 1947 version, was the one that is faithful to the James M. Cain story.

R. ★★★★
D: Bob Rafelson; W: David Mamet; Ph: Sven Nykvist; M: Michael Small.
Cast: Jack Nicholson, Jessica Lange, John Colicos, Michael Lerner.

THE PREMONITION.
(1975) Set in that hotbed of parapsychological research, Mississippi, the movie lives up to its title. You feel something awful is going to happen and it certainly does. An exercise in extra-sensory perception that is short on extra sense. A detective shambles around muttering "I'm sorry to discommode you" to a cripple and "There's too many weird things going on here" to everyone else. A little girl is kidnapped and telepathy is used to find her. No sign of further thought, transmitted or otherwise.

PG. ★
D: Robert Allen Schnitzer; W: Schnitzer and Anthony Mahon; Ph: Victor C. Milt; M: Henry Mollicone.
Cast: Sharon Farrell, Richard Lynch, Jeff Corey, Edward Bell.

THE PRESIDENT'S LADY.
(1953) Like John Ford's *Young Mr. Lincoln*, the film takes up the more private years of a U.S. President before he reached the White House. The similarity ends there. Charlton Heston is quite forceful as Andrew Jackson, a man who suffered mightily from the moral strictures of the time when he married Rachel. They later discover that her divorce from her first husband is not valid and she dies without the pleasure of seeing him elected President.

★★★
D: Henry Levin; W: John Patrick; Ph: Leo Tover; M: Alfred Newman.
Cast: Charlton Heston, Susan Hayward, John McIntire, Fay Bainter.

PRETTY BABY.
(1978) You would think the subject of child prostitution in a New Orleans brothel after World War I would elicit an opinion, if not a moral judgment from Louis Malle. Instead, he is downright diffident and the film is anemic. The girl is played by Brooke Shields, who, at the time, had the body of 12-year-old and the eyes of a three-time divorcee.

R. ★★★
D: Louis Malle; W: Polly Platt; Ph: Sven Nykvist; M: Jerry Wexler.
Cast: Brooke Shields, Susan Sarandon, Keith Carradine, Frances Faye.

THE PRIDE OF ST. LOUIS.
(1952) The career of the great Cardinals pitcher Dizzy Dean is seen through rose-colored glasses masquerading as a microscope. Dean was obviously a more amusing fellow than Dan Dailey is allowed to be in a so-so biography. After winning the World Series, Dean has to face forced retirement and finds a new challenge as a sportscaster.

★★
D: Harmon Jones; W: Herman J. Mankiewicz; Ph: Leo Tover; M: Arthur Lange.
Cast: Dan Dailey, Joanne Dru, Richard Hylton, Richard Crenna.

PRIEST OF LOVE.
(1981) Ian McKellen brings D.H. Lawrence to the screen but not really to life. Once again, the essential impenetrability of the writer's art defies the camera. Matters are not helped by the attempt to encompass some of Lawrence's cosmic and confused philosophical theories. The work covers the highly controversial author's life and loves from the publication of his first novel to his untimely death from tuberculosis. For all its flaws, *Priest of Love* is one of the more successful films about the creative writing process.

R. ★★★
D: Christopher Miles; W: Alan Pater; Ph: Ted Moore; M: Joseph James.
Cast: Ian McKellen, Janet Suzman, Ava Gardner, Penelope Keith.

THE PRIME OF MISS JEAN BRODIE.
(1969) An eccentric teacher at a private girls school in Edinburgh in the thirties exercises a mesmerizing influence over her pupils. Maggie Smith extends that influence to the audience in a *tour de force* that quite deservedly won her the Oscar. She holds forth on life and love with a blithe nuttiness that is captivating, but the structure of the film supporting her is rather weak. Based on the Muriel Spark novel.

★★★

D: Ronald Neame; W: Jay Presson Allen; Ph: Ted Moore; M: Rod McKuen.
Cast: Maggie Smith, Pamela Franklin, Robert Stephens, Gordon Jackson.

THE PRINCE AND THE PAUPER. (1937) The first version of Mark Twain's story (it was remade in 1978 as *Crossed Swords*) is faithful to its spirit and can boast Errol Flynn to liven up the action. Prince Edward exchanges places with a beggar boy and creates havoc in the realm. Lavishly mounted and with a better sense of period than most of its costume rivals.

★★★

D: William Keighley; W: Laird Doyle; Ph: Sol Polito; M: Erich Wolfgang Korngold.
Cast: Errol Flynn, Claude Rains, Billy and Bobby Mauch, Henry Stephenson.

THE PRINCE AND THE SHOWGIRL. (1957) It takes place at the coronation of George V and it is in no danger of being listed among the crowning achievements of Laurence Olivier's career. He directs himself and Marilyn Monroe—one of the screen's odder couples—and she seems more comfortable than he is. He is a prince from Ruritania who falls for a chorine and it's as slight as it sounds.

★★

D: Laurence Olivier; W: Terence Rattigan; Ph: Jack Cardiff; M: Richard Addinsell.
Cast: Laurence Olivier, Marilyn Monroe, Sybil Thorndike, Richard Wattis.

PRINCE OF FOXES. (1949) A handsome version of Samuel Shellabarger's historical novel that allows Orson Welles to impose his considerable screen authority on the person of Cesare Borgia. Welles is more arresting as the acquisitive potentate than the hero (Tyrone Power). Power works for Borgia as a sort of Renaissance advance man, setting up new lands for conquest, before learning the error of his ways and leading a revolt against his master. Some rousing action and Henry King's sense of ceremony make *The Prince of Foxes* one of Power's better swashbucklers.

★★★

D: Henry King; W: Milton Krims; Ph: Leon Shamroy; M: Alfred Newman.
Cast: Tyrone Power, Orson Welles, Wanda Hendrix, Marina Berti.

PRINCE OF THE CITY. (1981) Sidney Lumet brought a new level of sophistication and moral subtlety to the police film in a study of man stranded in the criminal justice system. Notions of right and wrong have lost their currency. The law is not an ass so much as an out-of-control rogue elephant. Treat Williams gave the performance of his career as a detective on an elite drug squad who talked to the Knapp Commission. No one can put New York cops on the screen like Lumet and here he brought off an edge-of-the-seat drama that owes nothing to car chases. It is a rewarding study of guilt, greed and conflicts of loyalty.

R. ★★★★★

D: Sidney Lumet; W: Lumet and Jay Presson Allen; Ph: Andrzej Bartkowiak; M: Paul Chihara.
Cast: Treat Williams, Jerry Orbach, Richard Fornly, Don Billett.

PRINCE VALIANT. (1954) As a Viking prince, Robert Wagner has all the elan of a prune Danish. Historical nonsense without the redeeming quality of entertainment and only James Mason, as the Black Knight, escapes with his armor and reputation intact. Drawn from the comic strip, where the story belongs.

★

D: Henry Hathaway; W: Dudley Nichols; Ph: Lucien Ballard; M: Franz Waxman.
Cast: James Mason, Robert Wagner, Janet Leigh, Sterling Hayden.

THE PRISONER OF SECOND AVENUE. (1975) Jack Lemmon comes apart at the seams after losing his advertising agency job and suffering the assorted miseries that are the lot of Mahattanites. Neil Simon, adapting his play, provides an uneasy mixture of one-liners and pathos with Lemmon succumbing to a nervous breakdown. The ultimate liberation of the prisoner is a resolution of a situation and not what one would expect from the character.

PG. ★★

D: Melvin Frank; W: Neil Simon; Ph: Philip Lathrop; M: Marvin Hamlisch.
Cast: Jack Lemmon, Anne Bancroft, Gene Saks, Elizabeth Wilson.

THE PRISONER OF SHARK ISLAND. (1936) When Dr. Samuel Mudd saved the life of a wounded man he ruined his own. The man turned out to be John Wilkes Booth, the murderer of Lincoln. In the ensuing climate of vengeance, Dr. Mudd was given a life sentence even though he did not know his patient's identity. John Ford, with a keen eye for the moral issues of the story, directed eloquently and Warner Baxter is memorable and moving as Mudd.

★★★★

D: John Ford; W: Nunnally Johnson; Ph: Bert Glennon; M: Louis Silvers.
Cast: Warner Baxter, Gloria Stuart, Claude Gillingwater, Arthur Byron.

THE PRISONER OF ZENDA. (1979) A send-up of the Anthony Hope story that never gets off the ground and of interest only to devout Peter Sellers fans. Sellers, who was disgusted enough to disassociate himself from the finished picture, plays the role of Rudolph and Syd, a London cabbie and Rudolph's exact double. Sluggishly directed and a weak parody that wastes a good cast.
PG. ★★
D: Richard Quine; W: Dick Clement and Ian La Frenais; Ph: Arthur Ibbetson; M: Henry Mancini.
Cast: Peter Sellers, Lionel Jeffries, Elke Sommer, Jeremy Kemp.

PRIVATE BENJAMIN. (1980) After her new husband succumbs to a heart attack while they are making love on the bathroom floor, a Jewish American princess joins the army. Partly a very basic training comedy and partly a spoiled brat learning to stand on her own feet once they are shod in combat boots. For all her charm, Goldie Hawn can't hold *Private Benjamin* together and the ending is insufferable.
R. ★★
D: Howard Zieff; W: Nancy Meyers, Charles Shyer and Harvey Miller; Ph: David M. Walsh; M: Bill Conti.
Cast: Goldie Hawn, Eileen Brennan, Armand Assante, Robert Webber.

PRIVATE LESSONS. (1981) Sylvia Kristel becomes as available as pubic education for a rich kid played by Eric Brown. She is blackmailed into initiating the lad into sex by a chauffeur (none other than Howard Hesseman). Subsequent movies in the same vein make it seem rather tame and it is by no means the worst of the series spawned by the unlikely liaison.
R. ★★
D: Alan Myerson; W: Dan Greenburg; Ph: Jan DeBont; M: Eric Clapton.
Cast: Sylvia Kristel, Howard Hesseman, Eric Brown, Ed Begley, Jr.

THE PRIVATE LIFE OF HENRY VIII. (1933) If you prefer histrionics to history, sit back and revel in Charles Laughton's regal hamminess as England's most denigrated

great king. His public achievements are somewhere under the pile of bones that Laughton tosses from the royal table. Various episodes from Henry's life are touched upon. Laughton's acting may seem as dated as the Tower of London, but it's enormously vital on its own terms.

★★★

D: Alexander Korda; W: Lajo Biro and Arthur Wimperis; Ph: Georges Perinal; M: Kurt Schroeder.
Cast: Charles Laughton, Robert Donat, Binnie Barns, Merle Oberon.

THE PRIVATE LIVES OF ELIZABETH AND ESSEX. (1939) Elizabeth I would have sent the screenwriters to the Tower of London for a prompt beheading if she had seen their blithe and unhistorical fiction. But she would surely have admired Bette Davis, catty and regal as the Virgin Queen. Errol Flynn knew how to wear a sword, but he was otherwise out of his depth and wisely left the pyrotechnics to Davis. The story covers the queen's jealousy over her handsome courtier.

★★★

D: Michael Curtiz; W: Norman Reilly Raine and Aeneas Mackenzie; Ph: Sol Polito; M: Erich Wolfgang Korngold.
Cast: Bette Davis, Errol Flynn, Donad Crisp, Olivia De Havilland.

PRIVATE SCHOOL. (1983) In the opening, a girl steps on a bag of horse manure and after ten minutes of this teenage sex fantasy you know exactly how she feels. The girls in the school go everywhere in their underwear so the boys from the neighboring academy can press their noses to the window and pant. Lots of nudity and snickering sex jokes and one of those cynical efforts that is rated R but really aimed at the early teen audience.
R. ★
D: Noel Black; W: Dan Greenburg and Suzanne O'Malley; Ph: Walter Lasally; M: Various artists.
Cast: Phoebe Cates, Betsy Russell, Matthew Modine, Michael Zorek.

PRIVILEGE. (1967) Peter Watkins' biting and frenzied satire evisaged a Britain where the media adoration of rock stars would be taken one step further and turn them into messianic figures. A sinister authority would then control the youth of the country through its false idols. A pungent commentary on manipulation well suited to Watkins' highly individual style.

★★★

D: Peter Watkins; W: Norman Bogner; Ph: Peter Suschitsky; M: Mike Leander.
Cast: Jean Shrimpton, Paul Jones, Mark London, Max Bacon.

THE PRIZE FIGHTER. (1980) Tim Conway and Don Knotts are paired once more as two fools separated only by differing levels of gullibility. It's a severely limited partnership and it takes a dive before the first fight. Conway is a hopeless fighter who wins the championship because his opponents also take dives. Weak family entertainment.
PG.

★★

D: Michael Preece; W: Tim Conway and John Myhers; Ph: Jacques Haitkin; M: Peter Matz.
Cast: Tim Conway, Don Knotts, Robin Clark, David Wayne.

.THE PRODUCERS. (1967) Say you had to create a play that would be a guaranteed bomb on Broadway. How about *Springtime for Hitler* with singing and dancing Nazis? Of course, things backfire and it doesn't flop. Neither does Mel Brooks' first try at directing. He has a tendency to let things—and Gene Wilder—ramble on too much, but stretches of it are hysterically funny.

★★★

D and W: Mel Brooks; Ph: Joseph Coffey; M: John Morris.
Cast: Zero Mostel, Gene Wilder, Kenneth Mars, Dick Shawn.

THE PROFESSIONALS. (1966) For sheer profesionalism, you would have to look long and hard for anything better in the macho adventure department. Ralph Bellamy recruits four soldiers of fortune with different military credentials to resue his wife from a bandit stronghold in Mexico. It may not sound much more than *Mission Impossible*, but Brooks and a stand-out cast do everything possible to make it exciting.

★★★★

D and W: Richard Brooks; Ph: Conrad Hall; M: Maurice Jarre.
Cast: Burt Lancaster, Lee Marvin, Robert Ryan, Jack Palance.

THE PROMISE. (1979) Two young lovers have the misfortune to survive an auto accident and live on into this ludicrous tear-jerker. The man's ruthless mother offers to buy the girl a new face if she'll get out of his life. Then things start to get seriously silly.
PG.

★

D: Gilbert Cates; W: Garry Michael White; Ph: Ralph Woolsey; M: David Shire.
Cast: Kathleen Quinlan, Stephen Collins, Beatrice Straight, Laurence Luckinbill.

PROM NIGHT. (1980) An axe-murderer hacks his way through the high school seniors in an unusually revolting Canadian hack horror outing that plagiarizes *Halloween* and *Carrie*. His motive is revenge for an accident that took place six years before.
R.

★

D: Paul Lynch; W: William Gray; Ph: Robert New; M: Paul Zaza and Carl Zittrer.
Cast: Jamie Leigh Curtis, Leslie Nielsen, Casey Stevens, Eddie Benton.

PROVIDENCE. (1977) Alain Resnais' preoccupation with memory and the passage of time yields an unmemorable movie that is partially redeemed by the acting of Dirk Bogarde and John Gielgud. Gielgud is Clive Langham, a 78-year-old novelist dying without dignity and in great pain. His ramblings deal with the characters he wishes to place in his next novel and they are all people close to him. They are presented as Langham perceives them. "He's not dying," sneers Bogarde, as Langham's son. "He's merely having a long, drawn-out tantrum." In the end we are given no chance to measure Langham's perceptions against what might be the truth.
R.

★★

D: Alain Resnais; W: David Mercer; Ph: Ricardo Aronovich; M: Miklos Rosza.
Cast: John Gielgud, Dirk Bogarde, Ellen Burstyn, David Warner.

PSYCHIC KILLER. (1975) Jim Hutton has nightmares about the death of his mother, or perhaps his presence in the film. Wrongly incarcerated in a lunatic asylum, he uses psychic energy to avenge himself on those responsible. The director could use some too. The movie degenerates into the usual mix of death and dumb dialogue and wastes a cast of B-film veterans that deserves something better.
PG.

★

D: Ray Danton; W: Greydon Clark, Mike Angel and Danton; Ph: Herb Pearl; M: William Kraft.
Cast: Jim Hutton, Julie Adams, Aldo Ray, Neville Brand.

PSYCHO. (1960) One of the shrewdest and certainly the most influential psychological thriller in all movies. Alfred Hitchcock put together a masterful blend of horror and suspense and served it with a generous helping of black humor. Tony Perkins never escaped his identification with the role of Norman Bates, the denizen of the strange motel to which a fugitive Janet Leigh comes. The murder in the shower is a brilliant and celebrated piece of cinema that lasted but 70 seconds and endured as a permanent example to legions of directors.

★★★★★

D: Alfred Hitchcock; W: Joseph Stefano; Ph: John L. Russell; M: Bernard Herrmann.
Cast: Anthony Perkins, Janet Leigh, Vera Miles, John Gavin.

PSYCHO II. (1983) A little better than the cheap rip-off you might expect. Norman Bates, allegedly cured after the mass murders at the Bates motel, is let out of the asylum over the opposition of the bereaved relatives. It is 22 years later and it's still business as usual at the motel. Quite stylish and reverential toward the original and with some pertinent points to make about our attitudes to insanity and responsibility for crimes. More graphically violent than Hitchcock's film.

R ★★★

D: Richard Franklin; W: Tom Holland; Ph: Dean Cundey; M: Jerry Goldsmith.
Cast: Anthony Perkins, Vera Miles, Robert Loggia, Meg Tilly.

PT 109. (1963) The honorable tradition of Hollywood pre-presidential biographies (*Young Mr. Lincoln, Sunrise at Campobello*) sank under the weight of hero worship. Given the time it was made, that is perhaps understandable. The subject is the war-time career of John F. Kennedy during which he skippered a PT boat against the Japanese. He was surely more of a tearaway than Cliff Robertson suggests in the lead.

★★

D: Leslie Martinson; W: Richard Breen; Ph: Robert Surtees; M: William Lava.
Cast: Cliff Robertson, Ty Hardin, James Gregory, Robert Blake.

PUBLIC ENEMY. (1931) The writers wanted to call it *Beer and Blood* and its notoriety lives on in the immortal grapefruit scene where Jimmy Cagney shows his displeasure with the hapless Mae Clark. A classic of the gangster genre, *Public Enemy* took the trouble to begin at the beginning—in the boyhood of Tom Powers—and show the gradual calibrations of wrong-doing. It makes a complete and cohesive portrait enriched by the searing power of Cagney, who exudes the desperation of the slums.

★★★★★

D: William Wellman; W: John Bright and Kubec Glasmon; Ph: Dev Jennings.
Cast: James Cagney, Edward Woods, Jean Harlow, Joan Blondell.

PUMPING IRON. (1977) Based on the successful book by Charles Gaines, the documentary is an engrossing look at the sub-culture of body-builders. Essentially a portrait of muscleman Arnold Schwarzenegger and his rivals for the Mr. Olympia crown. The film skirts issues of homosexuality and narcissism, but it is often amusing and avoids the temptation to ridicule its subject.

PG. ★★★

D: George Butler and Robert Fiore; Ph: Robert Fiore; M: Michael Small.
Cast: Arnold Schwarzenegger, Lou Ferrigno, Matty Ferrigno.

THE PURPLE HEART. (1944) An unusual and powerful war film that raised—and of course patriotically refuted—the notion that Americans could be guilty of war crimes. The crew of a flying fortress is shot down in Japan and then tortured, tried and executed. Directed with honed tension by Lewis Milestone, it remains a moving work.

★★★

D: Lewis Milestone; W: Jerry Cady; Ph: Arthur Miller; M: Alfred Newman.
Cast: Dana Andrews, Richard Conte, Farley Granger, Kevin O'Shea.

PURPLE RAIN. (1984) Most rock stars run into heavy weather when they try movies. The usual preference is a concert film or a star vehicle. Prince's debut is autobiographical and a straightforward piece of storytelling dealing with the creative troubles of a musician on the brink of the big time. It's technically interesting and he is secure in the lead.

R. ★★★

D: Albert Magnoli; W: Magnoli and William Blinn; Ph: Donald Thorin; M: Prince.
Cast: Prince, Morris Day, Jerome Benton, Brenda Bennett.

THE PURSUIT OF D.B. COOPER. (1981) D.B. Cooper became a minor folk legend by

hijacking a Boeing airliner in 1971 and bailing out of the rear exit with a parachute and a $200,000 ransom. Roger Spottiswoode's film begins in the middle and we are not given the motives and planning of the daring, highly publicized crime. Since no one has heard from Copper since, any speculation goes. The idea that his old army sergeant should turn out to be the pursuing insurance agent is wildly implausible. The chases are sandwiched between slices of Americana.
PG.   ★★★
D: Roger Spottiswoode; W: Jeffrey Allan Fiskin; Ph: Harry Stradling; M: James Horner. Cast: Robert Duvall, Treat Williams, Kathryn Harrold, Ed Flanders.

PYGMALION. (1938) George Bernard Shaw himself contributed to the script for what was to be re-filmed almost thirty years later as *My Fair Lady*. This production is far preferable for its wit and the calibre of the acting. The Shavian ideas emerge more forcefully when freed from musical inflation.
★★★★
D: Leslie Howard and Anthony Asquith; W: W.P. Lipscomb, Cecil Lewis and Asquith; Ph: Harry Stradling; M: Arthur Honegger. Cast: Leslie Howard, Wendy Hiller, Wilfred Lawson, Marie Lohr.

Q

Q. (1982) What's monstrous, preys on innocent people and makes an outrageous living in New York? No, not room service at the Plaza Hotel, but a winged serpent that devours Manhattanites at an alarming rate and lives on top of a skyscraper. Larry Cohen tries to leaven the gore with humor, but the joke is on anyone who tries *Q* with an IQ in double figures.

R.   ★
D and W: Larry Cohen; Ph: Fred Murphy; M: Robert Ragland.
Cast: David Carradine, Michael Moriarty, Candy Clark, Richard Roundtree.

QUADROPHENIA. (1979) Based on the 1973 album by the Who but a lot more than just another rock concert movie. Franc Roddam's highly charged direction brings the England of the early sixties to life in sound and image and deals with the conflicts between mods and rockers. Beneath all the flashiness is a pointed comment on alienation and the need to belong to something.

R.   ★★★
D: Franc Roddam; W: Roddam, David Humphries and Martin Stellman; Ph: Brian Tufano; M: John Entwhistle and Peter Townshend (directors).
Cast: Phil Daniels, Mark Wingett, Leslie Ash, Garry Cooper.

QUERELLE. (1983) The last film of Rainer Werner Fassbinder —he committed suicide during its editing—amounts to graffiti on his tombstone. An adaptation of Jean Genet's novel, *Querelle de Brest*, it brings out the worst in Fassbinder. A sailor drifts into a portside brothel which is mostly given over to sodomy and sadism among participants who insist they are not gay.

R.   ★
D and W: Rainer Werner Fassbinder; Ph: Xaver Schwarzenberger; M: Peer Raben.
Cast: Brad Davis, Jeanne Moreau, Gunther Kaufmann, Franco Nero.

QUEST FOR FIRE. (1982) A shining example of what can be done to overcome the cumulative cliches in movies about primitive man. Jean-Jacques Annaud grasps the viewer with the language and gestures worked out for the actors and also with a sense of humor. Here, alongside the discovery of fire, is the first joke. Life is short and brutal and four rival tribes vie for supremacy. Three warriors go off in search of fire when their tribe's flame is extinguished. An absolutely fascinating film that younger children might find too violent.

R.   ★★★★
D: Jean-Jacques Annaud; W: Gerard Brach; Ph: Claude Agostini; M: Philippe Sarde.
Cast: Everett McGill, Ron Perlman, Rae Dawn Chong, Nameer El Kadi.

THE QUIET MAN. (1952) The Ireland conjured by John Ford exists only in the minds of nostalgic Irish Americans and you will have a hard time finding a tape of this charmer around St. Patrick's Day. Ford knew the real Ireland, as he proved in *The Informer*. His *billet-doux* gave John Wayne one of his best light roles as Sean Thornton, a man seeking his Irish roots and trying to live down a violent past in the American boxing ring. The quiet man meets a very loud one, Victor McLaglen, and a spirited woman, Maureen O'Hara. Sentimental and thoroughly irresistible.

           ★★★★
D: John Ford; W: Frank Nugent; Ph: Winton Hoch; M: Victor Young.
Cast: John Wayne, Maureen O'Hara, Victor McLaglen, Barry Fitzgerald.

THE QUILLER MEMORANDUM. (1966) Harold Pinter turned Adam Hall's thriller into a defiance of the Bond market in spy movies and he was very much ahead of his time. George Segal is betrayed at every turn when he tries to track down a new Nazi leader in Berlin. Adult, intelligent and written with Pinter's uncanny ear for speech.

           ★★★
D: Michael Anderson; W: Harold Pinter; Ph: Erwin Hiller; M: John Barry.
Cast: George Segal, Alec Guinness, Max Von Sydow, Senta Berger.

QUINTET. (1978) Robert Altman at his most exasperating and impenetrable in an apocalyptic vision that has one wishing for the end. As a new Ice Age encroaches, the remnants of humanity play a game called quintet. Its rules and meaning are a secret closely guarded by Altman. A woman shows up at one point with a spike rammed through her head, a fitting image for the effect of the movie.

R.   ★★
D: Robert Altman; W: Altman and Frank Barhydt; Ph: Jean Boffety; M: Tom Pierson.
Cast: Paul Newman, Vittorio Gassman, Fernando Rey, Bibi Andersson.

R

RABBIT TEST. (1978) What would happen if a man became pregnant? An aborted comedy that delivers nothing in the hands of Joan Rivers. She's a very good stand-up comedian and she compensates for the limited potential of the film's idea with an assortment of zingers from her club routines. They have nothing to do with the gist of the movie.
PG. ★
D: Joan Rivers; W: Rivers and Jay Redack. Cast: Billy Crystal, Joan Prather, Imogene Coca, Paul Lynde.

RABID. (1977) There are two accidents here: a motorcycle mishap that puts porn star Marilyn Chambers in the hands of plastic surgeons and the one that cast her in this movie. David Cronenberg, the cult director of *Scanners* and *Videodrome*, serves up slick gore with Chambers starting a rabies-like plague in Montreal. The real sickness is to be found in minds that like this sort of thing. Strictly for the strong of stomach and weak of head and the raincoat brigade will be disappointed to find Chambers limited to mere nude scenes.
R. ★
D and W: David Cronenberg; Ph: Rene Verzier; M: Ivan Reitman.
Cast: Marilyn Chambers, Frank Moore, Joe Silver.

RACE FOR YOUR LIFE, CHARLIE BROWN. (1977) The third theatrical feature developed from the "Peanuts" comic strip by Charles M. Schulz. The economics of animation and the fact that comic strip characters have to be brought to life dictate that much of what adults savor in "Peanuts" is missing. This is much more an adventure for kids than a film in which children are burdened with adult hang-ups. On its level, it is quite good. Charlie Brown copes with summer camp bullies and enters a raft race.
G. ★★★
D: Bill Melendez; W: Charles M. Schulz; M: Ed Bodgas.

RACE WITH THE DEVIL. (1975) *The Exorcist Goes to the Indianapolis 500* would be a more accurate title. Satanism laced with STP. Peter Fonda and Warren Oates find their vacation trip thwarted when they chance upon some good ole country devil worshippers. Much fire and brimstone and godless pickup trucks chasing a mobile home.
PG. ★
D: Jack Starrett; W: Wes Bishop and Lee Frost; Ph: Robert Jessup; M: Leonard Rosenman.
Cast: Peter Fonda, Warren Oates, Loretta Swit, Lara Parker.

RAFFERTY AND THE GOLD DUST TWINS. (1975) A road movie that hits a dead-end in the first reel. Alan Arkin drinks his lunch between testing California drivers for their licenses. He is kidnapped and forced to drive Sally Kellerman and Mackenzie Phillips to New Orleans. Films that take this much-traveled route depend almost entirely on our interest in the travelers. This one is more monotonous than the nearest interstate.
R. ★
D: Dick Richards; W: John Kaye; Ph: Ralph Woolsey; M: Artie Butler.
Cast: Alan Arkin, Sally Kellerman, Mackenzie Phillips, Alex Rocco.

RAGE. (1972) George C. Scott's first attempt at directing tries to combine a fairly standard revenge melodrama with contemporary paranoia about technology. A sheep farmer in Utah loses both his son and his flock when the Army accidentally releases some nerve gas. His response is predictable and totally at odds with the point *Rage* wishes to make. A cold and uninvolving piece.
PG. ★★
D: George C. Scott; W: Philip Friedman and Don Kleinman; Ph: Fred Koenekamp; M: Lalo Schifrin.
Cast: George C. Scott, Richard Basehart, Martin Sheen, Barnard Hughes.

RAGGEDY ANN AND ANDY. (1977) Accomplished piece of animation for younger children supervised by Richard " Pink Panther" Williams. The songs by Joe Raposo, of *Sesame Street* note, are run of the mill Broadway but the two main characters are well-realized and kids should like Greedy, a self-consuming lava pit of chocolate and other sweets.
PG. ★★★
D: Richard Williams; W: Patricia Thackray, Max Wilk; M: Joe Raposo.

RAGGEDY MAN. (1981) Sissy Spacek is a divorced woman trying to raise two sons in

Texas in 1944 and she has every right to sue her director for non-support. He happens to be her real-life husband and his debut is an instance of a picture that starts well and then capitulates to perceived commercial considerations. Spacek's work is as fascinating as ever in the part of a woman who becomes the center of a small-town scandal, but *Raggedy Man* meanders into a climax that would shame a Gothic novelist.
PG.   ★★★
D: Jack Fish; W: William Witliff; Ph: Ralf Bode; M: Jerry Goldsmith.
Cast: Sissy Spacek, Sam Shepard, Eric Roberts, William Sanderson.

RAGING BULL. (1980) For sheer primal force, there has never been anything quite like Robert De Niro's portrait of Jake La Motta. The champion is seen as a tragic figure whose rage sustains him inside the ring and destroys him in life outside. Machismo becomes paranoid anger. The film does not so much tell La Motta's story as release his pent-up fury and watching it is like standing on the slope of a volcano. The boxing sequences are a technical knockout.
R.   ★★★★★
D: Martin Scorsese; W: Paul Schrader and Mardik Martin; Ph: Michael Chapman.
Cast: Robert De Niro, Cathy Moriarty, Joe Pesci, Frank Vincent.

RAGTIME. (1981) There are so many threads woven through the tapestry of E.L. Doctorow's novel that "Cut!" is what the director has to say to the script-writer instead of the cameraman. Milos Forman's intelligent and beautifully realized version evicts some popular characters and concentrates on Coalhouse Walker, a black nightclub pianist and prototypical urban terrorist. Forman sees the book as a view of turn-of-the century society and its notions of justice at opposite ends of the social scale. The transformation of Walker is set against an upper crust murder. The playing is revelatory and James Cagney admirers—who isn't?—should not miss his menacing account of Police Commissioner Rheinhold Waldo.
PG.   ★★★★★
D: Milos Forman; W: Michael Weller; Ph: Miroslav Ondricek; M: Randy Newman.
Cast: Howard Rollins, James Cagney, Elizabeth McGovern, Mary Steenburgen.

THE RAID. (1954) Based on a true and absorbing Civil War story. Van Heflin leads an escape of Confederate prisoners north to Canada. From there, they plan to destroy a Vermont town in retaliation for the burning of Atlanta and in an effort to divert Union troops away from the south. Heflin poses as a businessman to mastermind the attack.
                                                          ★★★
D: Hugo Fregonese; W: Sydney Boehm; Ph: Lucien Ballard; M: Roy Webb.
Cast: Van Heflin, Anne Bancroft, Richard Boone, Lee Marvin.

RAIDERS OF THE LOST ARK. (1981) A terrific fusion of technical skill and precisely judged humor that moves so fast it makes the Indianapolis 500 seem like a funeral cortege. Steven Speilberg and George Lucas dredged their memories of Saturday matinee serials and put them on the screen with exemplary panache. Harrison Ford's Indiana Jones has just the right touch of humor and lightness and there is no camp to be found here. He never runs out of cliffs from which to hang as an archeologist battling the Nazis for possession of the sacred ark and its mystical powers.
PG.   ★★★★★
D: Steven Spielberg; W: Lawrence Kasdan; Ph: Douglas Slocombe; M: John Williams.
Cast: Harrison Ford, Karen Allen, Wolf Kahler, Paul Freeman.

THE RAIN PEOPLE. (1969) The "road" movie is a form that can bring out the worst in directors and writers. Francis Ford Coppola did both chores here and showed what could be done. His central character is a woman, whose problems are charted with an accuracy that looks forward to the seventies. Bored with life in Long Island, she heads westward and takes up with a hitch-hiker who turns out to be brain-damaged. An illuminating and thoughtful work.
                                                          ★★★★
D and W: Francis Ford Coppola; Ph: Wilmer Butler; M: Ronald Stein.
Cast: Shirley Knight, James Caan, Robert Duvall, Tom Aldredge.

THE RAINS CAME. (1939) The earthquake and flood at the climax seem a richly merited retribution for the silliness that precedes the disaster. Tyrone Power, in a piece of casting only Darryl Zanuck (the producer) would dare, is an Indian physician who goes home to tend to the natives in Ranchipur and the needs of an Englishwoman.
                                                           ★★
D: Clarence Brown; W: Philip Dunne and Julien Josephson; Ph: Arthur Miller; M: Alfred Newman.

Cast: Tyrone Power, Myrna Loy, George Brent, Brenda Joyce.

THE RAINS OF RANCHIPUR. (1955) A flood of drivel descends upon the unwary heads of Richard Burton and Lana Turner in a remake of *The Rains Came*. They have nothing to add to the the affair of a Hindu doctor and the woman of consequence. The viewer will share the anger of Mother Nature at the characters which culminates in several disasters at the climax. These were better done in the original.

★★

D: Jean Negulesco; W: Merle Miller; Ph: Milton Krasner; M: Hugo Friedhofer.
Cast: Richard Burton, Lana Turner, Fred MacMurray, Joan Caulfield.

RAISE THE TITANIC. (1980) Beyond salvage despite the expenditure of $36 million. The Russians, displaying rare prescience about the nuclear age, stored something called byzanium aboard the doomed ship. Jerry Jameson moves the film at the pace of a crippled tramp steamer and the vaunted effects seem to have been shot in a bath-tub. The actual raising and the potentially fascinating technology is dismissed in a couple of sentences. A case of yo-ho-hum.
PG. ★
D: Jerry Jameson; W: Adam Kennedy; Ph: Matthew Leonetti; M: John Barry.
Cast: Jason Robards, Richard Jordan, David Selby, Anne Archer.

RANCHO DE LUXE. (1975) Frank Perry's attempt at a modern western is not especially at home on the range. The cowgirls consume more grass—albeit of a different variety— than the cows, and the humor is broad and affectionate. Jeff Bridges and Sam Waterston, as the inevitably superior Indian, shake down a cattle baron by stealing his prize bull and demanding ransom. Slim Pickens livens things up as an ancient detective, but in this case De Luxe turns out to be second class.
R. ★★
D: Frank Perry; W: Thomas McGuane; Ph: William A. Fraker; M: Jimmy Buffett.
Cast: Jeff Bridges, Clifton James, Sam Waterston, Slim Pickens.

RASHOMON. (1950) A landmark in Akira Kurosawa's career and, after its bow at the Venice Film Festival, the vehicle that put Japanese cinema on the map. Set in the fifteenth century, it proposes a bestial crime —the murder of a nobleman and the rape of his wife. Kurosawa, by having different participants offer their version of the event, produced a brilliant essay on whether absolute truth really exists and a knowing account of how men and women warp it to their own ends.

★★★★★

D: Akira Kurosawa; W: Kurosawa and Shinobu Hashimoto; Ph: Kazuo Miyagawa; M: Fumio Hayasaka.
Cast: Toshiro Mifune, Masayuki Mori, Machiko Kiyo, Takashi Shimura.

RASPUTIN—THE MAD MONK. (1966) Just as he did with Dracula, Christopher Lee put his distinctive and personal imprint on a role that has turned other actors into bug-eyed hams. The script has very little to do with what actually happened at the Russian court and Rasputin's eerie influence. A neat little horror film capped by a stylish exit by Lee.

★★

D: Don Sharp; W: John Elder; Ph: Michael Reed; M: Don Banks.
Cast: Christopher Lee, Barbara Shelley, Richard Pasco, Francis Matthews.

THE RAVEN. (1935) A raving mad plastic surgeon whose hobbies include Poe worship and a house filled with torture devices. Hell hath no fury like a doctor scorned. Besides working off his tensions, Bela Lugosi gets to redo Boris Karloff's face. It has its moments.

★★★

D: Lew Landers; W: David Boehm; Ph: Charles Stumar .
Cast: Bela Lugosi, Boris Karloff, Irene Ware, Samuel Hinds.

THE RAVEN. (1963) Horror heavyweights Vincent Price and Boris Karloff are joined by Peter Lorre in a rather lightweight black comedy of magicians spelling one another in the fifteenth century. Richard Matheson's script keeps it going and there is the added pleasure of watching Jack Nicholson (as Lorre's son) in the days when he still had to worry about paying the rent.

★★★

D: Roger Corman; W: Richard Matheson; Ph: Floyd Crosby; M: Les Baxter.
Cast: Boris Karloff, Vincent Price, Peter Lorre, Hazel Court.

RAWHIDE. (1951) Also known as *The Desperate Siege* and a worthwhile western. Outlaws descend on a lonely stage depot, kill the manager and lock up Tyrone Power and Susan Hayward. The bandits quarrel among themselves as they wait for a gold shipment on the next stage. Strong leads and taut direction.

★★★

D: Henry Hathaway; W: Dudley Nichols; Ph: Milton Krasner; M: Lionel Newman.
Cast: Tyrone Power, Susan Hayward, Hugh Marlowe, Dean Jagger.

REAR WINDOW. (1954) The ultimate voyeur movie that found Alfred Hitchcock's genius for exploring the philosophical implications of tension in full flower. He always cast a bleak eye on the frailty of humanity and here he makes a covenant with the viewer. We share the perspective of the hero—a wheel-chair bound photographer—in a way that makes him ambivalent. A broken leg transforms the photographer from an active to a passive observer. We see the unfolding of a possible murder from the window of his apartment, but we see it slightly differently. The dialogue is sparse, the technique dazzling and this is one window you can peer through again and again without quite exhausting its mysteries.

★★★★★

D: Alfred Hitchcock; W: John Michael Hayes; Ph: Robert Burks; M: Franz Waxman.
Cast: James Stewart, Grace Kelly, Raymond Burr, Thelma Ritter.

REBECCA OF SUNNYBROOK FARM. (1938) Nothing to do with the children's story of the same title by Kate Douglas Wiggin. The idea is to show that you can't keep Shirley Temple down on the farm. She is dispatched to the country to stay with an aunt who doesn't want her to sing. Randolph Scott rides to the rescue as a talent scout.

★★

D: Allan Dwan; W: Karl Tunberg and Don Ettlinger; Ph: Arthur Miller; M: Arthur Lange.
Cast: Shirley Temple, William Demarest, Helen Westley, Randolph Scott.

REBEL WITHOUT A CAUSE. (1955) The issues raised in Nicholas Ray's study of youth and disenchantment became a rallying cry in the sixties and then no less than the assumptions of personal freedom. Thus it is easy to pass over the work as dated and merely acknowledge it as James Dean's launching pad. His barely articulated frustration with the smugness of his parents and his world distilled the feelings of a generation into one movie and he is mesmerizing on the screen. *Rebel Without a Cause* was not only

a daring venture. It is a touching and even wrenching film about friendship and the generation gap (before the term was even coined).

★★★★

D: Nicholas Ray; W: Stewart Stern; Ph: Ernest Haller; M: Leonard Rosenman.
Cast: James Dean, Natalie Wood, Sal Mineo, Jim Backus.

RECKLESS. (1984) A teenager plays a cliff-top game of chicken on his motor bike. He avoids self-destruction, which is more than one can say for *Reckless*. It covers the same mill-town desperation of the infinitely better *All the Right Moves* but makes the mistake of sharing the perspective of the whining teenager who wants to escape. James Foley's notion of steaming up an erotic scene is to place it in a high school boiler room.

R.   ★★

D: James Foley; W: Chris Columbus; Ph: Michael Ballhaus; M: Thomas Newman.
Cast: Aidan Quinn, Daryl Hannah, Kenneth McMillan, Cliff De Young.

THE RED BADGE OF COURAGE. (1951) The uncivil war over the film was a famous controversy in Hollywood and a dispute between art and commerce. At a time of fierce cold war patriotism, the studio didn't care for John Huston's views on bravery and war, especially since he was using all-American hero Audie Murphy. The mutilated movie runs only 69 minutes and the editing completely altered Huston's argument. What's left is fascinating, but Huston has disowned it.

★★★

D and W: John Huston; Ph: Harold Rosson; M: Bronislau Kaper.
Cast: Audie Murphy, Bill Mauldin, John Dierkes, Royal Dano.

THE RED BALLOON. (1955) A little Parisian boy finds a balloon and tries to keep it. Soon the balloon, like a favored pet, and the boy are inseparable. From these modest ingredients comes a captivating fantasy that will immediately take children for an enthralling ride. It only lasts 35 minutes but the director's absolute assurance in dealing with the emotions and fears of children ranks with Steven Spielberg's understanding in *E.T.*

★★★★★

D and W: Albert Lamorisse; Ph: Edmond Sechan; M: Maurice le Roux.
Cast: Pascal Lamorisse, Sabine Lamorisse, Michel Pezin.

RED DAWN. (1984) Pour yourself a glass of John Birch beer and stare in disbelief at John Milius' paranoid scenario which posits a land invasion of the United States by the Russians and their Latin American allies. It's another of his noble warrior fantasies of violence and vengeance. A bunch of high school kids become guerrillas and slaughter the occupying troops, who respond by shooting their parents. The picture of Genghis Khan used by a history teacher is a likeness of Milius. Nothing could be more appropriate. Milius' bloody outburst had the dubious distinction of being the first film to be rated PG-13.
PG-13. ★
D: John Milius; W: Milius and Kevin Reynolds; Ph: Ric Waite; M: Basil Poledouris.
Cast: Patrick Swayze, C. Thomas Howell, Lea Thompson, Charlie Sheen.

RED RIVER. (1948) With Montgomery Clift's coiled spring edginess and John Wayne's Tom Dunson, *Red River* has a mesmerizing personal conflict that gives Howard Hawks' epic western an emotional core that is so often missing from films conceived on this scale. The contentious relationship of a cattle baron and his foster son is set against the opening of the Chisholm Trail. One of the writers later said he had merely transplanted *Mutiny on the Bounty* to Texas, but the love-hate ties between Clift and Wayne are far more intricate. The film belongs on any responsible short-list of the great westerns.
★★★★★
D: Howard Hawks; W: Borden Chase and Charles Schnee; Ph: Russell Harlan; M: Dmitri Tiomkin.
Cast: John Wayne, Montgomery Clift, Joanne Dru, Walter Brennan.

REDS. (1981) Warren Beatty's sprawling and absorbing account of the experiences of American radical John Reed, the author of *Ten Days That Shook The World*. Its size and budget belies its anti-capitalist sentiments and the cleverest aspect of the epic is the way it uses our knowledge of what became of Russia after the heady days of the revolution. It places too much focus on the relationship of Reed and Louise Bryant as the lovers caught up in political tumult and nobody can make the nit-picking debates of communist idealogues interesting. But this is daring and literate film-making and the all too brief cameos are wonderful.
PG. ★★★★
D: Warren Beatty; W: Beatty and Trevor Griffiths; Ph: Vittorio Storaro; M: Stephen Sondheim.
Cast: Warren Beatty, Diane Keaton, Jack Nicholson, Edward Herrmann.

THE REINCARNATION OF PETER PROUD. (1975) Seems to take several lifetimes to sit through. A reincarnated professor looks up the wife who murdered him—with a few well-deserved blows of an oar—and falls in love with his daughter by the earlier marriage. Then things really get dumb. Propelled by such lines as "Life is one big Karma trip."
R. ★
D: J. Lee Thompson; W: Max Ehrlich; Ph: Victor J. Kemper; M: Jerry Goldsmith.
Cast: Michael Sarandon, Jennifer O'Neill, Margot Kidder, Cornelia Sharpe.

THE REMARKABLE MR. PENNYPACKER. (1959) A totally unremarkable comedy about bigamy. Clifton Webb marries twice, but if you can find one laugh in a lumbering adaptation of the stage play, you are easily pleased.
★★
D: Henry Levin; W: Walter Reisch; Ph: Milton Krasner; M: Leigh Harline.
Cast: Clifton Webb, Dorothy McGuire, Charles Coburn, Jill St. John.

REMBRANDT. (1936) Another of Alexander Korda's historical dramas. It was made in the wake of the enormous success of *The Private Life of Henry VIII* and it is a far superior work. Charles Laughton gives a rounded and touching account of the artist as an older man and the film is often arresting visually.
★★★★
D: Alexander Korda; W: Carl Zuckmayer; Ph: Georges Perinal; M: Geoffrey Toye.
Cast: Charles Laughton, Gertrude Lawrence, Elsa Lanchester, John Bryning.

REPORT TO THE COMMISSIONER. (1975) Michael Moriarty is Bo Lockley, a New York detective of astonishing naivete. After he accidentally kills an undercover cop (Susan Blakely), the cover-up begins. A clumsy exercise in the *Serpico* vein that doesn't work because Lockley is a character whose fate arouses pity rather than anger. Another film that was deeply influenced by the Watergate climate.
PG. ★★
D: Milton Katselas; W: Abby Mann and Ernest Tidyman; Ph: Mario Tosi; M: Elmer Bernstein.

Cast: Michael Moriarty, Susan Blakely, Yaphet Kotto, Hector Elizondo.

REPULSION. (1965) A study of madness that prizes images over speech and it turns into an apt way of framing the kind of derangement at issue. In his first venture into the always treacherous shoals of directing a film in another language, Roman Polanski keeps the English to a minimum and shows a fine hand for escalating tension. Catherine Deneuve is a young Belgian girl whose fear and loathing of sex reduces her to terrified reaction.

★★★

D: Roman Polanski; W: Polanski and Gerard Brach; Ph: Gilbert Taylor; M: Chico Hamilton.
Cast: Catherine Deneuve, Ian Hendry, John Fraser, Patrick Wymark.

RETURN FROM WITCH MOUNTAIN. (1978) The telekinetic kids from outer space in a sequel to *Escape to Witch Mountain*. The adults who want to use their powers include Christopher Lee and Bette Davis, whose stint makes the movie worthwhile. First-rate Disney special effects to perk things up.
G. ★★★

D: John Hough; W: Malcolm Marmorstein; Ph: Frank Phillips; M: Lalo Schifrin.
Cast: Bette Davis, Christopher Lee, Ike Eisenmann, Kim Richards.

THE RETURN OF A MAN CALLED HORSE. (1976) A rarity in that the sequel is better than the original which inspired it. It picks up Sir John Morgan, captured and adopted by the Indians, in the empty splendor of his English mansion. He returns to ordain the spiritual regeneration of a band of Indians.
PG. ★★★

D: Irvin Kershner; W: Jack de Witt; Ph: Owen Roizman; M: Laurence Rosenthal.
Cast: Richard Harris, Gale Sondergaard, Geoffrey Lewis, Bill Lucking.

THE RETURN OF FRANK JAMES. (1940) Since Henry Fonda stole the film in *Jesse James*, it seemed natural to make him the focus of a sequel that is the equal of its illustrious predecessor. Frank waits for justice to execute his brother's killers and takes the law into his own hands when they are pardoned. Gene Tierney, in her first movie, is a reporter who falls for the subject of her story.

★★★

D: Fritz Lang; W: Sam Hellman; Ph: George Barnes; M: David Buttolph.

Cast: Henry Fonda, Gene Tierney, Jackie Cooper, John Carradine.

THE RETURN OF MARTIN GUERRE. (1983) We live in an age where the rules governing the area between perceived moral obligation and personal desire have changed and even vanished in some cases. Daniel Vigne's thoroughly engrossing work sets some contemporary issues—a woman abandoned and forced to raise a son by herself, a family torn apart by self-interest—in the world of sixteenth century French peasants. A man returns and says he is the husband, touching off a fascinating chain of ambiguities that are beautifully handled by Vigne and his players.

★★★★★

D: Daniel Vigne; W: Vigne and Jean-Claude Carriere; Ph: Andre Neau; M: Michel Portal.
Cast: Gerard Depardieu, Nathalie Baye, Roger Planchon, Maurice Jacquemont.

RETURN OF THE DRAGON. (1973) Bruce Lee had a way of rising above the kung-foolery of his movies. He was a terrific athlete and he had a sense of humor. In his penultimate movie, he defends a Chinese restaurant in Rome from a syndicate and takes on Chuck Norris in the Coliseum. This was their only appearance together.

★★

D and W: Bruce Lee.
Cast: Bruce Lee, Chuck Norris, Nora Miao.

RETURN OF THE FLY. (1959) A sequel that amounts to little more than a fly in the ointment. The scientist's son starts meddling with same formula that got his old man swatted and turns into a partial fly. Vincent Price comes to the rescue.

★★

D and W: Edward L. Bernds; Ph: Brydon Baker; M: Paul Sawtell.
Cast: Vincent Price, Brett Halsey, David Frankham, John Sutton.

RETURN OF THE PINK PANTHER. (1974) The theft of the famous Pink Panther diamond allows Peter Sellers to steal the show again in the fourth Inspector Clouseau film. The parts are funnier than the whole and the film has a dated sixties look. Nevertheless, the individual moments—Sellers lecturing a blind beggar and his "minkey"—make it worthwhile. This is one series that, unlike most, got better until Sellers' untimely death. The action pits him against the diamond thief and his boss, played by Herbert

Lom with his usual aplomb.

G. ★★★
D: Blake Edwards; W: Frank Waldman and Edwards; Ph: Geoffrey Unsworth; M: Henry Mancini.
Cast: Peter Sellers, Herbert Lom, Christopher Plummer, Catherine Schell.

RETURN OF THE SECAUCUS SEVEN. (1980) The directing debut of the multi-talented John Sayles is a precursor of the more famous *The Big Chill*. Sayles brings together a cadre of sixties anti-war activists to muse and mope through a weekend of friendship and wondering where it all went wrong. His strong points are a shrewd eye and and a very good ear for revelatory dialogue.
★★★★
D and W: John Sayles; Ph: Austin De Besche; M: Mason Daring.
Cast: Mark Arnott, Maggie Cousineau-Arndt, Gordon Clapp, Brian Johnston.

THE RETURN OF THE SEVEN. (1966) Inarguable proof that you can't go home again, especially when it's really only the return of the one (Brynner). On a scale of seven, this is a two that lacks the charisma and chemistry of the magnificent original cherished by fans of the western. It also lacks the sense of civilization encroaching on the gunmen. Brynner recruits a new and equally outnumbered band to go back to the village in Mexico, which is once again being terrorized by bandits.
★★
D: Burt Kennedy; W: Larry Cohen; Ph: Paul Vogel; M: Elmer Bernstein.
Cast: Yul Brynner, Robert Fuller, Claude Akins, Warren Oates.

RETURN TO MACON COUNTY LINE. (1975) Nick Nolte has a fuel-injected Chevy but the film runs out of gas amost as soon as it crosses the infamous Macon County line. There the cops are still pigs and the waitresses keep a suitcase packed in case a couple of drifters come in to whisk them off to Hollywood and movie stardom. Sex, inane car chases and vindictive troopers and bad enough to keep the nation's waitresses a long way from Los Angeles.
PG. ★
D and W: Richard Compton; Ph: Jacques Marquette; M: Robert O. Ragland.
Cast: Nick Nolte, Don Johnson, Robin Mattson, Eugene Daniels.

RETURN TO PEYTON PLACE. (1961) Further proof that you can't go home again.

A young author does, only to find that the randy townsfolk are miffed at the way they were depicted. A bungled sequel whose flaws are not hidden by high-gloss production.
★★
D: Jose Ferrer; W: Ronald Alexander; Ph: Charles Clarke; M: Franz Waxman.
Cast: Carol Lynley, Jeff Chandler, Eleanor Parker, Mary Astor.

REVENGE OF THE CREATURE. (1955) Like the third *Jaws* film in that a desperate scriptwriter decides that you can always toss the monster into a Florida marine park in lieu of a good idea for a sequel. The creature from the black lagoon is all gills and scales and as horny as ever in his pursuit of the ladies. He is confined to the tank in Florida for scientific studies and objects. If that lab technician looks familiar, you're right. It's Clint Eastwood's movie debut.
★★
D: Jack Arnold; W: Martin Berkeley.
Cast: John Agar, John Bromfield, Lori Nelson, Nestor Paiva.

REVENGE OF THE NERDS. (1984) Frontal nerdism that won a following and some admiring reviews because the state of youth-oriented comedy made it look passable. The nerds—quite amusingly led by Robert Carradine and Tim Busfield—are the downtrodden of Adams College. WASP girls disdain them and the jocks make life miserable. The R is for some mild nudity and the humor is less offensive than the competition, which isn't saying much.
R. ★★
D: Jeff Kanew; W: Steve Zacharias and Jeff Buhai; Ph: King Baggot; M: Thomas Newman.
Cast: Robert Carradine, Tim Busfield, Anthony Edwards, Curtis Armstrong.

REVENGE OF THE NINJA. (1983) A sort of Oriental *The Quiet Man* with a Japanese hero who has forsworn the deadly arts of the Ninja and become an art dealer in Salt Lake City. Still directed at morons rather than Mormons, it involves a nasty American hero-in dealer who cons the Japanese.
R. ★
D: Sam Firstenberg; W: James Silke; Ph: David Garfinkel.
Cast: Sho Kosugi, Keith Vitali, Virgil Frye, Arthur Roberts.

REVENGE OF THE PINK PANTHER. (1978) A marked falling-off in invention in this installment, but Sellers had brought Inspector Clouseau to a point where familiarity breeds anticipation. Clouseau earns the enmity of a mob kingpin who decides to prove the strength of his French connections and impress the American Mafia by knocking off the world's greatest detective. Dyan Cannon makes a fine addition.

PG. ★★★
D: Blake Edwards; W: Edwards, Frank Waldman and Ron Clarke; Ph: Ernie Day; M: Henry Mancini.
Cast: Peter Sellers, Robert Webber, Dyan Cannon, Herbert Lom.

RHAPSODY IN BLUE. (1945) There's no reason to wax rhapsodic or even enthusiastic about a biography of Gershwin that insists on turning the life of America's foremost composer into a cautionary tale about the miseries of success. Robert Alda is out of tune in the title role and the only element to survive with any dignity is the music. Paul Whiteman and his orchestra do the title piece. Of this account of his life and times, Gershwin could justly say, "It ain't necessarily so."

★★
D: Irving Rapper; W: Elliot Paul and Howard Koch; Ph: Sol Polito; M: Music of Gershwin.
Cast: Robert Alda, Joan Leslie, Alexis Smith, Charles Coburn.

RHINESTONE. (1984) Inspired, to use the word loosely, by Glen Campbell's hit *Rhinestone Cowboy*. However, the man doing the singing, to use the word very loosely, is Sylvester Stallone and nails on a blackboard sound more pleasant. It would be tolerable if there were anything to Bob Clark's redundantly vulgar production. Dolly Parton has to turn Stallone, a New York cab driver, into a country singer to win a bet involving her virtue. The film has none.

PG. ★
D: Bob Clark; W: Phil Alden Robinson and Sylvester Stallone; Ph: Timothy Galfas; M: Dolly Parton.
Cast: Sylvester Stallone, Dolly Parton, Ron Liebman, Richard Farnsworth.

RICH AND FAMOUS. (1981) A friendship of two women authors, one a devout feminist and the other a peddler of lurid best-sellers. The popular writer (Candice Bergen) wants the esteem that the other (Jacqueline Bisset) has achieved and their relations grow more strained through the years. So does Gerald Ayres' script which veers between a view of wealth and its trappings and a serious stab at the real and imagined penalties of literary fame. In the scenes that give her a chance, Bisset is excellent.

R. ★★★
D: George Cukor; W: Gerald Ayres; Ph: Don Peterman; M: Georges Delerue.
Cast: Jacqueline Bisset, Candice Bergen, David Selby, Hart Bochner.

RICHARD PRYOR—HERE AND NOW. (1983) One of the targets of Pryor's scathing and scatalogical wit is Pryor himself. That he is here at all after his celebrated accident is a wonder to him and a boon to his fans. The funniest part of this 90-minute concert are his thoughts on the bad old days of drugs and drinking.

R. ★★★
D and W: Richard Pryor.
Cast: Richard Pryor.

RICHARD PRYOR—LIVE ON THE SUNSET STRIP. (1982) The comedian was, of course, lucky to be live on the strip or anywhere else after his notorious accident. It is now part of his routine and the second Pryor concert film is 82 minutes devoted to the travails of a unique personality. His reminiscences of working in a Mafia night club where the boss used to rub his head for luck are a riot.

R. ★★★
D: Joe Layton; W: Richard Pryor; Ph: Haskell Wexler.

RICHARD III. (1955) Laurence Olivier's third Shakespeare film enshrines one of the most memorable performances in all of movies. It is an adage of drama that evil is more fascinating than good and rarely has that seemed truer than in the Richard Olivier brings to vivid life here. From his soliloquy we are plunged into the winter of discontent that becomes a maelstrom. Work of such hypnotic magnetism makes everything else secondary. Through Olivier's unrivalled gift we come to share Lady Anne's mixture of revulsion and fascination for the monster who pursues her.

★★★★★
D: Laurence Olivier; W: Alan Dent (Adaptor); Ph: Otto Heller; M: William Walton
Cast: Laurence Oliver, Claire Bloom, John Gielgud, Ralph Richardson.

RICH KIDS. (1979) Divorce and its aftermath in upper middle class families perceived through the eyes of two precocious 12-year-olds. The view from there is understandably naive and the complex emotional and social issues involved in the sundering of the family are given a consequently superficial treatment. In fact, the kids are so rich that the usual economic imperatives that operate in most divorces are not even heard from.

PG. ★★
D: Robert M. Young; W: Judith Ross.
Cast: Trini Alvarado, Jeremy Levy, John Lithgow, Kathryn Walker.

RIDE THE HIGH COUNTRY. (1962) John Wayne said farewell with *The Shootist* and Joel McCrea and Randolph Scott ended their careers with almost equal distinction. Sam Peckinpah used his skill at visual composition to provide a beautiful framework for the two stalwarts of western acting. They are down-at-heel, sometime lawmen who confront temptation separately when they are invited to escort a gold shipment. It's all the more poignant because of the elegiac quality imparted by the two stars and the cumulative image they had built over their long careers.

★★★★
D: Sam Peckinpah; W: N.B. Stone, Jr.; Ph: Lucien Ballard; M: George Bassman.
Cast: Joel McCrea, Randolph Scott, Edgar Buchanan, Mariette Hartley.

RIFIFI. (1955) A crime classic whose ideas have been stolen countless times. Jules Dassin had to leave the United States in the McCarthy years and he set the jewel robbery in Paris where four men undertake a daring theft. The 35-minute sequence that documents the robbery set the standard and tone for years to come. After the theft, the criminals pay dearly in a way that owes more to morality than reality.

★★★★
D: Jules Dassin; W: Dassin, Rene Wheeler and Auguste Le Breton; Ph: Philippe Agostini; M: Georges Auric.
Cast: Jean Servais, Karl Mohner, Robert Manuel, Jules Dassin.

THE RIGHT STUFF. (1983) Philip Kaufman's exhilarating celebration of the dawn of the space age in America is patriotic in the best sense. It is about the American spirit, a can-do kind of heroism called "the right stuff." And it is much more. In telling the story of the Mercury astronauts, Kaufman made them human and showed how politicians and the media go about making heroes. And how the heroes have to live with it. Their deeds are spectacularly re-created and there is a streak of insouciant humor that makes the film a delight.

PG. ★★★★★
D and W: Philip Kaufman; Ph: Caleb Deschanel; M: Bill Conti.
Cast: Sam Shepard, Ed Harris, Scott Glenn, Dennis Quaid.

RINGS ON HER FINGERS. (1942) Henry Fonda is the victim of con artists who think he is rich. He's actually broke and an innocent girl recruited for the scam falls for him. As flimsy as it sounds, but the cast gives it some substance.

★★
D: Rouben Mamoulian; W: Ken Englund; Ph: George Barnes; M: Cyril J. Mockridge.
Cast: Henry Fonda. Gene Tierney, Spring Byington, Laird Cregar.

RIO BRAVO. (1959) A western that doesn't quite earn the bravos and praise it has received over the years. Howard Hawks and John Wayne said they wanted to contest the craven response of the civilians in *High Noon* and in trying to they did not make a picture in the same class. Wayne is a sheriff trying to hold off the friends of a killer in his jail with the help of a drunk, a cripple and a kid. The climax is literally dynamite, but the film takes its own sweet time getting there.

★★★
D: Howard Hawks; W: Leigh Brackett and Jules Furthman; Ph: Russell Harlan; M: Dmitri Tiomkin.
Cast: John Wayne, Dean Martin, Rick Nelson, Angie Dickinson.

RIO GRANDE. (1950) Once again, John Ford rides to the rescue of the cavalry movie with his troop of regulars. The relationships and conflicts inside and outside the troop are well conceived and prompt a broad range of responses. John Wayne is a commander on the Mexican border just after the Civil War. He wants to cross and have it out with the Apaches.

★★★★
D: John Ford; W: James K. McGuiness; Ph: Bert Glennon; M: Victor Young.
Cast: John Wayne, Maureen O'Hara, Ben Johnson, Claude Jarman.

RIO LOBO. (1970) Howard Hawks' last film rehashes some of the ingredients of *Rio Bravo* with John Wayne as a Yankee officer helping a couple of Confederate soldiers clean up a Texas town after the Civil War. It even ends with the same dynamite-tossing fight that climaxes *Rio Bravo* with less than explosvie results. The movie's sense of humor and self-deprecation has been praised, but it is a tired walk-through for both Hawks and Wayne, who did the same kind of thing much better elsewhere.

★★★

D: Howard Hawks; W: Leigh Brackett, Burton Wohl; Ph: William Clothier; M: Jerry Goldsmith.
Cast: John Wayne, Jennifer O'Neill, Jorge Rivero, Chris Mitchum.

THE RISING OF THE MOON. (1957) More Hiberniana from John Ford. He directed members of the Abbey Theater company of Dublin in three short stories and their presence cuts down on the encrustations on the Blarney Stone and sentimentality common to American-Irish film-making. The best of the tales is the one of the title and deals with an escape.

★★★

D: John Ford; W: Frank Nugent; Ph: Robert Krasker; M: Eamonn O'Gallagher.
Cast: Maureen Connell, Eileen Crowe, Cyril Cusack, Maureen Delany.

RISKY BUSINESS. (1983) Paul Brickman's flashy debut at least took a risk in a teen market where Hollywood rarely gambles. But underneath the original veneer is the same dreary sexism. If it had been played as a black comedy that demolishes notions of capitalism and greed, it might have worked. But Brickman doesn't have any real point of view. The film chooses prostitution as a metaphor and asks us to root for a kid who becomes a pimp to get what he wants out of life. Tom Cruise is amusing as the youth who sets up the scheme to service his school friends, but the same piggish notions you find in *Porky's* are beneath the surface here.

R. ★★

D and W: Paul Brickman; Ph: Reynaldo Villalobos and Bruce Surtees; M: Tangerine Dream.
Cast: Tom Cruise, Rebecca De Mornay, Curtis Armstrong, Bronson Pinchot.

THE RITZ. (1976) The gay bath-house where this one-joke comedy takes place may be fit for a queen but not for a farce. Rita Moreno, Jack Weston and Jerry Stiller repeated their Broadway roles with Weston hiding out from the Mafia in the bath-house that turns into a flop-house in the film version. "If there's one thing I can't stand, it's a queer without a sense of humor," says one character. The movie earns the same opinion and you don't have to be gay to despise it.

R. ★

D: Richard Lester; W: Terence McNally; Ph: Paul Wilson; M: Ken Thorne.
Cast: Rita Moreno, Jerry Stiller, Jack Weston, Kaye Ballard.

THE RIVER NIGER. (1976) Acting of uncommon depth is not enough to rescue an essentially shallow film based on Joseph Walker's play. The adaptation from the stage is clumsy and magnifies the work's inept mixture of political attitude and soap opera. Conflicts in a black family with James Earl Jones as a house painter who would rather write poetry and Cicely Tyson as his his wife, a cancer victim.

R. ★★

D: Krishna Shah; W: Joseph Walker; Ph: Michael Marguiles; M: War.
Cast: James Earl Jones, Cicely Tyson, Lou Gossett, Glynn Turman.

RIVER OF NO RETURN. (1954) A meandering western that proved that Otto Preminger was wise not to try the genre again. The splendid scenery includes Marilyn Monroe, who is caught between a homesteader and a worthless gambler of a husband.

★★

D: Otto Preminger; W: Frank Fenton; Ph: Joseph La Shelle; M: Cyril Mockridge.
Cast: Robert Mitchum, Marilyn Monroe, Rory Calhoun, Tommy Rettig.

THE ROAD WARRIOR. (1982) George Miller takes a back seat to no one, including Steven Spielberg, when it comes to laying on a chase. In a post-nuclear world where gasoline is more precious than blood, he concocts a bleakly witty contemporary tale. Mel Gibson, reprising his *Mad Max* role, is not just a burned out hero. He's incinerated. He comes to the aid of survivors who must ward off marauding gangs. Miller balances arch humor with a brilliantly rendered adventure. It's also very violent.

R. ★★★★

D: George Miller; W: Miller, Terry Hayes and Brian Hannant; Ph: Dean Serrier; M: Brian May.
Cast: Mel Gibson, Bruce Spence, Vernon Wells, Mike Preston.

THE ROARING TWENTIES. (1939) Made when the sound of the previous decade was still fresh and the end of Prohibition was an event when everyone could still recall his personal hangover. Raoul Walsh's gangster film says nothing particularly original but it says it with style. James Cagney pulled out all the stops for Eddie Bartlett, a war veteran who shuns an honest living for the riches of bootlegging.

★★★★

D: Raoul Walsh; W: Jerry Wald, Robert Rossen and Richard Macaulay; Ph: Ernest Haller.
Cast: James Cagney, Humphrey Bogart, Priscilla Lane, Jeffrey Lynn.

THE ROBE. (1953) A pious and opulent rendering of Lloyd Douglas' novel about the tribune who supervised the execution of Christ and who wins his robe in a dice game. Richard Burton, as Tribune Gallio, and Jean Simmons have to compete against the measured tread of the direction. Together they are converted to Christianity and pay the price of their new faith. *The Robe* was the first Cinemascope picture.

★★★

D: Henry King; W: Philip Dunne; Ph: Leon Shamroy; M: Alfred Newman.
Cast: Richard Burton, Jean Simmons, Victor Mature, Michael Rennie.

ROBERT ET ROBERT. (1980) Claude Lelouch's satirical salute to American "buddy" movies in general and *The Odd Couple* in particular. Halfway through the film he decides that two is not enough company and throws in a crowd. A Parisian cab driver and a trainee gendarme search for an ideal mate through a dating service. There are some hilarious individual scenes, but the movie falters in its ambivalent view of the single life as both desperate and funny.

★★★

D and W: Claude Lelouch; Ph: Jacques Lefrancois; M: Francis Lai.
Cast: Charles Denner, Jacques Villeret, Jean-Claude Brialy, Germaine Montero.

ROBIN AND MARIAN. (1976) Precious little merriment among the men of Sherwood in an unmasking of the legend of Robin Hood. Sean Connery, in one of his finest performances, gives us a middle-aged Robin of Locksley, returned from the crusades. He is a man of modern preoccupations in a medieval setting as he resumes his dalliance with Marian and confronts the Sheriff of Nottingham for the last time. A wistful, mellow and poignant movie, which, for once gives us an accurate King Richard. Richard Harris plays him as the bloody-minded twit he was.
PG. ★★★★

D: Richard Lester; W: James Goldman; Ph: David Watkin; M: John Barry.
Cast: Sean Connery, Audrey Hepburn, Robert Shaw, Richard Harris.

ROBIN AND THE SEVEN HOODS. (1964) Nelson Riddle wrote the now standard "My Kind of Town" for this amiable and overlong twist to the Robin Hood theme. How much you care for it depends on whether Frank Sinatra and his friends are your kind of people. Their work has the suggestion that we are deeply privileged to share in their in jokes. Here they are Chicago gangsters who rob the rich to help the poor. The poverty of the screenplay is beyond such help.

★★

D: Gordon Douglas; W: David Schwartz; Ph: William Daniels; M: Nelson Riddle.
Cast: Frank Sinatra, Dean Martin, Sammy Davis, Jr., Bing Crosby.

ROBINSON CRUSOE ON MARS. (1964) Crusoe is an astronaut stranded on the Red Planet and his Man Friday is a being who who helps him survive in a very hostile environment. Don't look for the underlying philosophical discourse of Defoe; it's played as a straight adventure and it's not at all bad on its own terms. Death Valley does service as Mars.

★★★

D: Byron Haskin; W: Ob Melchior and John C. Higgins; Ph: Winton Hoch; M: Van Cleave.
Cast: Paul Mantee, Vic Lundin, Adam West.

ROB ROY, THE HIGHLAND ROGUE. (1954) The kind of highlander you want to fling down the stairs. The *Sword and the Rose* team went north of the border minus director Ken Annakin and he was sorely missed. A dull story of Scots rebellion against the English in the eighteenth century told with the grace of a man tossing the cable. One of Disney's worst pseudo-historical adventures.

★

D: Harold French; W: Lawrence E. Watkins; Ph: Guy Green; M: Muir Mathieson.
Cast: Richard Todd, Glynis Johns, James Roberston Justice, Michael Gough.

ROCK AROUND THE CLOCK. (1956) The meteoric rise of Bill Haley and the Comets is recounted with flimsy plot. Nothing matters here but the music and it's a baedeker to the early days of rock and roll. The excitement the new music inspired in the young is amply caught even if much of the movie now seems quaint. Haley does some of his landmark numbers and other artists include the Platters offering "The Great Pretender".

★★

D: Fred Sears; W: Robert Kent and James Gordon; Ph: Benjamin Kline; M: Various artists.
Cast: Bill Haley and the Comets, the Platters, Little Richard, Freddie Bell and the Bellboys.

ROCKY. (1976) The punch-drunk sequels tend to detract from the simple charm and appeal of the first round. Stallone was fresh and—a necessity for him—someone else was directing. He wrote a movie about a Philadelphia club fighter who takes on the world champ in a way that is both derivative and original. Rocky's unlikely climb is given a conviction by the gritty Philadelphia settings and speech and the bluntness of the characters' emotions. It was released at a time when movies were very short on optimism and hope and it has never lost the exuberant vitality that touched so many people.

PG. ★★★★

D: John Avildsen; W: Sylvester Stallone; Ph: James Crabe; M: Bill Conti.
Cast: Sylvester Stallone, Talia Shire, Burgess Meredith, Burt Young.

ROCKY II. (1979) Punchdrunk sequel to the Oscar winner that repeats the formula by returning the Italian Stallion to bumhood and resurrecting him all over again. Rocky has a son, thereby paving the way for *Rocky XV* at the turn of the century, and his wife lies in a post-natal coma. In the dreary warm-up to the climactic fight, you'll feel like joining her. The fight is well-staged, but Stallone shouldn't direct himself and this is the weakest of the three *Rocky* pictures.

PG ★

D and W: Sylvester Stallone; Ph: Bill Butler; M: Bill Conti.
Cast: Sylvester Stallone, Talia Shire, Burgess Meredith, Burt Young.

ROCKY III. (1982) The scorecard for this series reads a knockout, a loss and—being charitable—a draw. Many of Sylvester Stallone's feelings about Hollywood and success crept into his thoughts on Rocky and much of it has a false ring. Rocky takes on stiffs and his manager accuses him of pounding hamburger. Then Burgess Meredith has a heart attack, presumably at the prospect of *Rocky IV.* Enter Mr. T. for the rousing climax.

PG. ★★

D and W: Sylvester Stallone; Ph: Bill Butler; M: Bill Conti.
Cast: Sylvester Stallone, Talia Shire, Burgess Meredith, Mr. T.

ROLLERBALL. (1975) Norman Jewison firmly rejected the chance to say something about the role of sports and violence in our society. Instead, he made a boring and very violent parable, warning—to the point of tedium—about the menace of multi-national corporations. Rollerball has replaced war in the 21st century. James Caan, often mumbling unintelligibly, is the star of the sport. Courageous, if pointless stunt-work.

R. ★★

D: Norman Jewison; W: William Harrison; Ph: Douglas Slocombe; M: Andre Previn.
Cast: James Caan, John Houseman, Ralph Richardson, Maud Adams.

ROLLER BOOGIE. (1980) Requires you to believe that Linda Blair is a flute virtuoso on her way to Julliard and take an interest in a California roller-skating rink. The latter is threatened with conversion to a shopping mall. Half-hearted and sloppy and only for those who like to watch kids dancing on roller skates.

★★

D: Mark Lester; W: Barry Schneider; Ph: Dean Cundey; M: Bob Esty.
Cast: Linda Blair, Beverly Garland, Roger Perry, Jim Bray.

ROLLERCOASTER. (1977) Like a visit to a mobbed theme park, James Goldstone's film features spectacular rides interspersed with long and boring waits. Released theatrically in Sensurround, a deafening technique that puts a wall of sound between the viewer and the indifferent action. This involves an extortionist who has threatened to blow up the nation's major rollercoasters. George Segal turns in a performance of easy skill as the Federal agent pursuing the case. Nobody thinks of simply shutting down the rollercoasters and in the end it's the audience that is taken for a ride.

PG. ★★

D: James Goldstone; W: Richard Levinson, William Link; Ph: David M. Walsh; M: Lalo Schifrin.
Cast: George Segal, Timothy Bottoms, Richard Widmark, Susan Strasberg.

ROLLING THUNDER. (1977) Paul Schrader's interest in blood-letting and vengeance triumphs over a potentially interesting study of a Vietnam POW who finds less than a welcome when he comes home. Schrader, who went on to directing films like *Cat People*, cooks up a gang that murders the hero's family and the rest is routine and predictable revenge redeemed by better acting than you normally find in this kind of movie.

R. ★★
D: John Flynn; W: Paul Schrader and Heywood Gould; Ph: Jordan Croneweth; M: Barry DeVorzon.
Cast: William Devane, Tommy Lee Jones, Linda Haynes.

ROLLOVER. (1981) Jane Fonda, who is what might be called a "cause celebrity," put her production company behind a brave attempt to make a statement about international banking. Specifically, it addresses the possible fiscal calamity that could stem from the shift in global wealth to the Middle East. Fonda takes control of her late husband's company and comes across a mysterious account number locked in a computer. The climax is a bewildering cop-out.

PG. ★★★
D: Alan Pakula; W: David Shaber; Ph: Giuseppe Rotunno; M: Michael Small.
Cast: Jane Fonda, Kris Kristofferson, Hume Cronyn, Josef Sommer.

ROMANCING THE STONE. (1984) Steven Spielberg borrowed a lot of ideas from old-fashioned cliff-hangers for *Raiders of the Lost Ark* and his protege, Robert Zemeckis, borrowed a lot of ideas from Steven Spielberg. Despite the plagiarism, it's fun in its own right. A New York woman novelist goes to South America in search of her sister and runs into all manner of rough company and hair-raising adventure.

PG. ★★★
D: Robert Zemeckis; W: Diane Thomas; Ph: Dean Cundey; M: Alan Silvestri.
Cast: Michael Douglas, Kathleen Turner, Danny DeVito, Zack Norman.

ROMAN HOLIDAY. (1953) Audrey Hepburn made the most of her first starring role and time has taken nothing from the spontaneous gaiety of William Wyler's light comedy. She is a princess going the pauper route —or at least looking for the experience of ordinary people. She finds it with an American newsman (Gregory Peck) and the two of them make one oblivious to the obvious situations that arise.

★★★
D: William Wyler; W: Ian McLellan Hunter and John Dighton; Ph: Franz Planer; M: Georges Auric.

Cast. Audrey Hepburn, Gregory Peck, Eddie Albert, Hartley Power.

THE ROMAN SPRING OF MRS. STONE. (1961) Vivien Leigh and Tennessee Williams have done better elsewhere by the middle-aged woman desperately facing the passage of years and the absence of love. This adaptation of his short novel finds Leigh, as an actress well past her prime, discovering that money can't buy love in the person of Warren Beatty, an Italian gigolo.

★★
D: Jose Quintero; W: Gavin Lambert; Ph: Harry Waxman; M: Richard Addinsell.
Cast: Vivien Leigh, Warren Betty, Lotte Lenya, Jeremy Spenser.

ROMANTIC COMEDY. (1983) Bernard Slade's play has a very optimistic title and fails to deliver. Dudley Moore is strait-jacketed in the guise of a successful Broadway playwright who takes on a new collaborator. Their success complicates his marriage. If this sounds more like Neil Simon, you're right. The trouble is that he didn't write the script.

PG. ★★
D: Arthur Hiller; W: Bernard Slade; Ph: David Walsh; M: Marvin Hamlisch.
Cast: Dudley Moore, Mary Steenburgen, Frances Sternhagen, Ron Leibman.

ROOM AT THE TOP. (1958) A look at social stratification in England with a great deal of class. Laurence Harvey's Joe Lampton is a familiar movie figure—the ambitious social climber who elbows his way to some perceived room at the top. England and its class system—seen through its entrenchment in a provincial Northern city—has rarely seemed so depressing. The compassionate older woman is superbly done by Simone Signoret.

★★★★
D: Jack Clayton; W: Neil Paterson; Ph: Freddie Francis; M: Mario Nascimbene.
Cast: Laurence Harvey, Simone Signoret, Heather Sears, Donald Wolfit.

ROOSTER COGBURN. (1975) A sad and depressing experience with two great stars in a formula western that asks them to perform feats of action beneath their years and dignity. John Wayne trotted out his Oscar-winning marshal, first seen in *True Grit*, to help Katharine Hepburn find the killers of her father. He was 70 and she was 66 when this was made and it shows. The film is an intru-

sion on happier memories of both of them.
PG. ★★
D: Stuart Millar; W: Martin Julien; Ph: Harry Stradling, Jr.; M: Laurence Rosenthal.
Cast: John Wayne, Katharine Hepburn, Richard Jordan, Anthony Zerbe.

THE ROOTS OF HEAVEN. (1958) An early plea for enviromental sanity that falls prey to its own rhetoric. Trevor Howard is an idealist who rounds up a motley bunch of adventurers to help save a herd of elephants in French Africa. They also trampled over the script before John Huston started filming and he did not find the material amenable. Errol Flynn does another drunk in his last signficant outing and it's a sad sight.
★★
D: John Huston; W: Romain Gary and Patrick Leigh-Fermor; Ph: Oswald Morris; M: Malcolm Arnold.
Cast: Errol Flynn, Trevor Howard, Juliette Greco, Eddie Albert.

ROPE OF SAND. (1949) Strands a good cast in a predictable adventure with some references to *Casablanca*. The intrigue, which isn't very intriguing, surrounds diamonds located in Diamondstad, South Africa. Burt Lancaster is a great white hunter who squares off against Paul Henreid, the police chief.
★★
D: William Dieterle; W: Walter Doninger; Ph: Charles Lang; M: Franz Waxman.
Cast: Burt Lancaster, Claude Rains, Paul Henreid, Peter Lorre.

THE ROSE. (1979) An account of the desperate last days of a rock star to which Bette Midler makes the same kind of redeeming contribution that Diana Ross brought to *Lady Sings the Blues*. The character is closely modeled on Janis Joplin, but the social and political context of the time is missing along with any real attempt to elaborate on the star's relationships. Midler is fine in the concert sequences and even finer off-stage in her first film.
R. ★★★
D: Mark Rydell; W: Bill Kerby and Bo Goldman; Ph: Vilmos Zsigmond; M: Paul Rothchild.
Cast: Bette Midler, Alan Bates, Frederic Forrest, Harry Dean Stanton.

ROSEBUD. (1975) The daughters of five immensely wealthy men are kidnapped and the ransom is an economic embargo of Is-
rael. Otto Preminger turns this into a garrulous and inept potboiler that finds Peter O'Toole, as a CIA man posing as a *Newsweek* correspondent, on the trail of the women. The bizarre casting includes John Lindsay, the former mayor of New York, and Richard Attenborough muttering in a Lebanese cave as an Arab fanatic.
PG. ★★
D: Otto Preminger; W: Erik Lee Preminger; Ph: Denys Coop; M: Laurent Petitgerard.
Cast: Peter O'Toole, Richard Attenborough, Cliff Gorman, John Lindsay.

ROSEMARY'S BABY. (1968) That rarity, an intelligent possession movie. The Dakota Apartments, which face Central Park and house a galaxy of star tenants serve as the location and they are not as exclusive as one might think. Mia Farrow and her actor husband, John Cassavetes, move in and discover they don't know which is witch. Roman Polanksi brings off one of the most startling pregnancies in the movies with a considerable panache and all the imitations only make his work look better. Ruth Gordon took an Oscar as Farrow's neighbor.
★★★★
D and W: Roman Polanski; Ph: William Fraker; M: Krzysztof Komeda.
Cast: Mia Farrow, John Cassavetes, Ruth Gordon, Sidney Blackmer.

ROSE OF WASHINGTON SQUARE. (1939) A wilted flower of a musical that is worth a listen rather than a look because of Al Jolson's reprise of some of his twenties hits. The star-is-born formula has Alice Faye as a singer on the way up despite the weight of a boyfriend on the way down. She makes it as a star of the Ziegfeld Follies.
★★★
D: Gregory Ratoff; W: Nunnally Johnson; Ph: Karl Freund; M: Louis Silvers.
Cast: Alice Faye, Tyrone Power, Al Jolson, William Frawley.

ROUGH CUT. (1980) Burt Reynolds' attempt to revive the polished gentleman thief is remarkably listless, especially with a director like Don Siegel in charge. It was made with much on-set rancor and that must have been where all the energy went since there's none on the screen. Reynolds is blackmailed out of retirement for a big heist in Holland.
PG. ★★
D: Don Siegel; W: Francis Burns; Ph: Frederick Young; M: Nelson Riddle.
Cast: Burt Reynolds, Lesley-Anne Down, David Niven, Timothy West.

ROUSTABOUT. (1964) Middling Elvis Presley with Barbara Stanwyck. She runs a carnival and takes on Elvis so that he can learn about life. He learned little about acting from her, but he is in good voice in almost a dozen songs.

★★

D: John Rich; W: Allan Weiss and Anthony Lawrence; Ph: Lucien Ballard; M: Joseph Lilley.
Cast: Elvis Presley, Barbara Stanwyck, Sue Ann Langdon, Joan Freeman.

ROYAL FLASH. (1975) Richard Lester and novelist George MacDonald Fraser, who collaborated on the *Three Musketeers*, combine for a raucous Victorian comedy. Harry Flashman, a randy coward and a British officer, keeps emerging as a hero in assorted adventures. Lester sustains the joke very well as Flashman becomes embroiled with Otto Von Bismarck.
PG.   ★★
D: Richard Lester; W: George MacDonaldFraser; Ph: Geoffrey Unsworth; M: Ken Thorpe.
Cast: Malcolm McDowell, Alan Bates, Oliver Reed, Florinda Bolkan.

RUNNING. (1979) A lot of the film consists literally of running time. Besides the usual sports cliches of training, sacrifice and setbacks before the athlete proves himself in the big finish, there is an attempt at character study. Michael Douglas is a runner who has failed in marriage and career as well as on the track. His relationships make very little sense.
PG.   ★★
D and W: Steven Hilliard Stern; W: Ph: Laszlo George; M: Andre Gagnon.
Cast: Michael Douglas, Susan Anspach, Lawrence Dane, Eugene Levy.

RUNNING BRAVE. (1983) Native Americans put up the money to make the story of Billy Mills but stuck themselves with a wooden Indian in the title role. Robby Benson lacks the presence and range to flesh out Mills, the Indian runner who pulled off one of the great upsets in Olympic history by winning the 10,000 meters in Tokyo in 1964. He ran into a lot of bigotry on the way there as an athlete at the University of Kansas and that makes a repetitive dramatic conflict. Uplifting family entertainment.
PG.   ★★★
D: D.S. Everett; W: Henry Bean and Shirl Hendryx; Ph: Francois Protat; M: Mike Post.
Cast: Robby Benson, Pat Hingle, Claudia Cron, Jeff McCracken.

RUBY. (1977) A horror movie filled with departed spirits, including the liquor consumed by Piper Laurie. Hopelessly confused mayhem with a gangster returning to exact revenge on his enemies and persuade Laurie, a soused motel owner, to join him. Stuart Whitman snarls to the inevitable parapsychologist, "Come on, doc, don't give me any $10 words." The movie, which is very gory, stays within that intellectual budget.
R.   ★
D: Curtis Harrington; W: George Edwards and Barry Schneider; Ph: Brice Mack; M: Don Ellis.
Cast: Piper Laurie, Stuart Whitman, Roger Davis, Janet Baldwin.

RUBY GENTRY. (1952) Jennifer Jones is a girl from the Carolina swamps who grows up to become a woman scorned and spends the rest of a steamy, hysterical movie exacting her revenge. Dead husbands, mad brothers and a beleaguered Charlton Heston as her boyfriend.

★★

D: King Vidor; W: Sylvia Richards; Ph: Russell Harlan; M: Heinz Roemheld.
Cast: Jennifer Jones, Charlton Heston, Karl Malden, Tom Tully.

S

SABRINA. (1954) Not Billy Wilder's finest hour and largely a criminal waste of the talent recruited. Audrey Hepburn, the daughter of the chauffeur of a rich Long Island family, falls for the son and the resolution of the romance is downright silly.

★★

D: Billy Wilder; W: Wilder, Samuel Taylor and Ernest Lehman; Ph: Charles Lang, Jr.; M: Frederick Hollander.
Cast: Audrey Hepburn, William Holden, Humphrey Bogart, John Williams.

THE SAD SACK. (1957) A bumbler joins the army and reduces the military comedy to the ranks of private. Jerry Lewis without Dean Martin is even heavier than Jerry Lewis with Dean Martin. Peter Lorre shows up as an Arab. Lewis fans claim this is one of his better solo flights.

★★

D: George Marshall; W: Edmund Beloin and Nate Monaster; Ph: Loyal Griggs; M: Walter Scharf.
Cast: Jerry Lewis, David Wayne, Peter Lorre, Phyllis Kirk.

SAHARA. (1942) Humphrey Bogart's tank becomes a magnet for various stray soldiers as he makes his way through hostile territory. Bogart's fine characterization has to fight a war of its own with the preachy tone of the movie, but he wins and it's a perceptive look at life at the grunt level in war.

★★★

D: Zoltan Korda; W: Korda and John Howard Lawson; Ph: Rudolph Mate; M: Miklos Rozsa.
Cast: Humphrey Bogart, Lloyd Bridges, Bruce Bennett, Rex Ingram.

THE SAILOR WHO FELL FROM GRACE WITH THE SEA. (1976) Yukio Mishima, the right-wing Japanese novelist, committed suicide shortly before the film of his book was released, possibly out of a premonition of how bad it would be. His work is transferred to an English seaport and the tragic love story pairs a widow and a sailor who is torn between the lure of the sea and his ardor. Gamely acted, but as monotonous as a long voyage on a tramp steamer.
R.

★★

D and W: Lewis John Carlino; Ph: Douglas Slocombe; M: John Mandel.
Cast: Kris Kristofferson, Sarah Miles, Jonathan Kahn, Margo Cunningham.

SAINT JACK. (1979) Ben Gazzara brings off a real contradiction—a likeable pimp who services Singapore whites with Oriental girls. Peter Bogdanovich's film, set in the early seventies, is an all but plotless character study that is rich in a sense of time and place and teeming with well-turned paradoxes in a multi-racial society where the whites no longer dominate.
R.

★★★

D: Peter Bogdanovich; W: Bogdanovich, Paul Theroux and Howard Sackler; Ph: Robby Muller.
Cast: Ben Gazzara, Denholm Elliott, James Villiers, Joss Ackland.

SAINT JOAN. (1957) Otto Preminger plucked Jean Seberg from obscurity to play the lead in George Bernard Shaw's interpretation of the saint and her visionary career. Shaw's understanding of Joan and the way she functioned in a political context is lost on Seberg and Preminger. All she conveys is a sort of lofty naivete.

★★

D: Otto Preminger; W: Graham Greene; Ph: Georges Perinal; M: Mischa Spoliansky.
Cast: Jean Seberg, Richard Widmark, John Gielgud, Richard Todd.

THE SALZBURG CONNECTION. (1972) A missing link among espionage movies and a bungled translation of Helen MacInnes' thriller. A convention of international spies shows up at scenic locations to compete for some incriminating Nazi papers. It would help one's understanding of the twisted plot if they wore name-tags. Barry Newman is the American lawyer who becomes involved.

★

D: Lee H. Katzin; W: Oscar Millard; Ph: Wolfgang Treu; M: Lionel Newman.
Cast: Barry Newman, Anna Karina, Klaus-Maria Brandauer, Karen Jensen.

SAME TIME, NEXT YEAR. (1978) A chronicle of adultery, from 1951 to 1977, a period that saw it change from a reprehensible sin to an alternative life-style. Valiant work by Alan Alda and Ellen Burstyn, as the two married lovers who meet once a year in a California hotel, but they are written as chameleons who reflect changing social attitudes rather than as real people.
PG.

★★

D: Robert Mulligan; W: Bernard Slade; Ph:

Robert Surtees; M: Marvin Hamlisch.
Cast: Alan Alda, Ellen Burstyn.

SAN ANTONIO. (1945) Errol Flynn almost died with his boots on in a lavishly produced and empty-headed western. He takes on cattle thieves in Texas in a series of incidents that could have been randomly assembled from other westerns. Not among his best rides in the genre.

★★

D: David Butler; W: Alan le May and W.R. Burnett; Ph: Bert Glennon; M: Max Steiner.
Cast: Errol Flynn, Alexis Smith, Victor Francen, Paul Kelly.

THE SAND PEBBLES. (1966) Some critics discerned a commentary on our growing involvement in Southeast Asia in Robert Wise's sprawling epic and it does touch on the ever-pertinent issue of self-interested intervention in the affairs of another country. An American gunboat in the Yangtze River in 1926 has to contend with turbulence on shore and malaise below decks. Steve McQueen holds the film together as a stubbornly independent sailor.

★★★

D: Robert Wise; W: Robert Anderson; Ph: Joseph MacDonald; M: Jerry Goldsmith.
Cast: Steve McQueen, Candice Bergen, Richard Crenna, Richard Attenborough.

THE SATAN BUG. (1965) John Sturges and James Clavell are two old hands and one would expect them to get a lot more from the germ of a good idea. George Maharis must track down a purloined and a lethal virus that a deranged scientist plans to use against the world. Solid, but strangely lacking in suspense.

★★

D: John Sturges; W: James Clavell and Edward Anhalt; Ph: Robert Surtees; M: Jerry Goldsmith.
Cast: George Maharis, Richard Basehart, Anne Francis, Dana Andrews.

SATURDAY NIGHT FEVER. (1977) One sign of a really good movie is its ability to survive the fad surrounding it. Disco, mercifully, is dead, but the movie that immortalized it and made it a craze is as vital and visceral as ever. Travolta, who became a star with his stunning performance, is a Brooklyn dancer, a kid of 19 who can find both identity and release in his protean skills on the floor of the disco on Saturday night. Not much of a script, but a true account of kids of a certain class and time with universal appeal. It is no wonder it has held its own through the years as an exemplary piece of popular entertainment.

R.

★★★★

D: John Badham; W: Norman Wexler; Ph: Ralph D. Bode; M: David Shire, the Bee Gees.
Cast: John Travolta, Karen Gorney, Barry Miller, Joseph Cali.

SATURN 3. (1980) On Saturn's third moon Kirk Douglas and Farrah Fawcett take showers and pop pills—activities that are inexplicably vital to saving the people back on Earth. A murderer arrives and both character, motive and a believable social context are lost in space. Stanley Donen, in his one and only piece of science fiction, resorts to the usual horror tricks. The production design is quite handsome.

R.

★★

D: Stanley Donen; W: Martin Amis; Ph: Billy Williams; M: Elmer Bernstein.
Cast: Kirk Douglas, Farrah Fawcett, Harvey Keitel, Douglas Lambert.

THE SAVAGE IS LOOSE. (1974) A couple and their son are marooned on a desert island and the catastrophe turns into one of those Oedipus wrecks. The pair try to raise their son in a civilized fashion, but as he grows up there is only one woman in sight and no hope of rescue resolving the situation. Flea-brained, pompous and too contrived to have anything of interest to add to the subject of incest

R.

★

D: George C. Scott; W: Max Erlich and Frank de Felitta; Ph: Alex Phillips; M: Gil Melle.
Cast: George C. Scott, Trish Van Devere, John David Carson, Lee H. Montgomery.

SAVAGE SAM. (1963) A sequel to Disney's much admired *Old Yeller* that discards the themes which sustained the original in favor of a canine reprise of *The Searchers*. Two young neighbors are kidnapped by Indians and when the trail cools only Sam, the trusty hound, can sniff out the tribe's whereabouts.

★★

D: Norman Tokar; W: Fred Gipson and William Tunberg; Ph: Edward Colman; M: Oliver Wallace.
Cast: Brian Keith, Tommy Kirk, Kevin Corcoran, Jeff York.

SAVANNAH SMILES. (1983) Grown-ups are more likely to wince and only the youngest kids are likely to respond to the kind of sentimentality that engulfs this family movie. It is of an order that would embarrass Disney with two lovable croooks and a cute six-year-old on the lam from her career obsessed father.

PG. ★★
D: Pierre DeMoro; W: Mark Miller; Ph: Stephen W. Gray; M: Ken Sutherland.
Cast: Mark Miller, Bridgette Andersen, Donovan Scott, Peter Graves .

SAYONARA. (1957) Although there are antecedents in Puccini's *Madam Butterfly*, the Americans here are a more sensitive lot in their dealings with the Japanese. Marlon Brando and Red Buttons are excellent in what is essentially a high-toned soap opera about the perils of lovers who try to bridge two cultures. The film traces their affairs and the very different outcomes. Buttons revealed his Oscar-winning talent and briefly escaped his comedian identification.
★★★
D: Joshua Logan; W: Paul Osborn; Ph: Ellsworth Fredericks; M: Franz Waxman.
Cast: Marlon Brando, Red Buttons, Miyoshi Umeki, Miiko Taka.

SAY ONE FOR ME. (1959) Bing Crosby put on the dog collar again as a Broadway priest and he should have said a Requiem mass over a dog of a musical. He prays for the souls of his showbiz parishioners while trying to save the body of Debbie Reynolds from the attentions of Robert Wagner.
★
D: Frank Tashlin; W: Robert O'Brien; Ph: Leo Tover; M: Lionel Newman.
Cast: Bing Crosby, Debbie Reynolds, Robert Wagner, Ray Walston.

SCANNERS. (1980) Not much to look at. Canadian cult director David Cronenberg dreamed up the ultimate headache —heads that literally explode when subjected to advanced telepathic powers. He is famous for such gimmicks, but his inventiveness always seems to run out when it comes to basic plotting. Scanners are people with psychic power and an evil one wants to take over the world.
R. ★★
D and W; David Cronenberg; Ph: Mark Irwin; M: Howard Shore.
Cast: Patrick McGoohan, Stephen Lack, Jennifer O'Neill, Michael Ironside.

SCARECROW. (1973) A trip across America and you could not ask for better company than Gene Hackman and Al Pacino. They are drifters hitching their way East where Hackman dreams of opening his own car-wash and only the clumsy end of the journey is disappointing. Made at a time when the buddy film was becoming an industry to itself, *Scarecrow* is among the leaders because of its leads.
R. ★★★
D: Jerry Schatzberg; W: Garry Michael White; Ph: Vilmos Zsigmond; M: Fred Myrow.
Cast: Gene Hackman, Al Pacino, Dorothy Tristan, Ann Wedgeworth.

SCARFACE. (1983) If the *Godfather* movies invite us to think about justice and what it has meant in various chapters in American history, *Scarface* doesn't ask us to think about anything at all. Brian De Palma's flashy look at the Miami cocaine trade and a Cuban hood who rises to the top of it is a peek into a sewer. Tony Montana has the scruples of a piranha. De Palma doesn't romanticize him, but he is so repulsive and one-dimensional that his gruesomely detailed decline and violent fall have the impact of watching a rat cornered and killed. Foul-mouthed and extremely violent.
R. ★★
D: Brian De Palma; W: Oliver Stone; Ph: John A. Alonzo; M: Giorgio Moroder.
Cast: Al Pacino, Michelle Pfeiffer, Steven Bauer, Mary Elizabeth Mastrantonio.

SCAVENGER HUNT. (1979) Slim pickings. A tycoon's will ordains that his relatives engage in a scavenger hunt around San Diego, procuring various items of junk. The biggest turns out to be the movie.
PG. ★
D: Michael Schultz; W: Steven A. Vail and Henry Harper; Ph: Ken Lamkin; M: Billy Goldenberg.
Cast: Richard Benjamin, James Coco, Scatman Crothers, Cloris Leachman.

SCENES FROM A MARRIAGE. (1974) Originally made for television and abbreviated for theatrical release, Ingmar Bergman's film is an excruciatingly accurate depiction of what men and women do to each other in the name of marriage. It remains an unrivalled dissection of the subject. The couple, both lawyers, begin in outward contentment and Bergman traces all the guilts and gambits deployed on both sides as their union comes apart with wrenching pain. The acting is unforgettable and no one who has been or is married is likely to be unaffected by the insights of a great artist.
★★★★★

D and W: Ingmar Bergman; Ph: Sven Nyk-vist.
Cast: Erland Josephson, Liv Ullmann, Bibi Anderson, Jan Malmsjo.

SCOTT OF THE ANTARTIC. (1948) John Mills is Robert Scott, the British explorer who finished second in the race to the Pole behind a Norwegian in 1912. The Antartic scenery is handsome, but Charles Frend is not really disposed to go much beyond chronicling heroism that could be construed as rashness and the English penchant for treating life as a game.

★★★

D: Charles Frend; W: Walter Reader and Ivor Mongue; Ph: Jack Cardiff *et al.*; M: Ralph Vaughan Williams.
Cast: John Mills, Harold Warrender, Derek Bond, James Robertson-Justice.

THE SEA CHASE. (1955) A German freighter with an odd roster and Lana Turner on board for the ride tries to make it to safety. The greatest oddity in an otherwise hum-drum adventure is the casting of John Wayne, who had slaughtered more Germans than anyone else, on the screen, as the cap-tain.

★★

D: John Farrow; W: John Twist and James Warner Bellah; Ph: William Clothier; M: Roy Webb.
Cast: John Wayne, Lana Turner, David Far-rar, Lyle Bettger.

THE SEA GYPSIES. (1978) A boat sinks, making Alaskan castaways of a widower, his family and a woman journalist. Family fare that floats along harmlessly enough on the strength of the animals they encounter and the handsome scenery.
G.   ★★
D and W: Stewart Raffil; Ph: Thomas McHugh; M: Fred Steiner.
Cast: Robert Logan, Mikki Jamison-Olsen, Heather Rattray, Shannon Saylor.

THE SEARCHERS. (1956) John Ford's beautifully composed and influential film is one of the enduring achievements of the western genre. John Wayne's Ethan Ed-wards is a surly Civil War veteran who em-barks on a five-year search for two neices captured by Indians. The movie draws its strength from its celebration of frontier life and its hardships and the fact that the two searchers — Ethan and his half-breed companion — are both loners outside the structure of family life. Their search is for

something they can never have and Ford makes it a powerful motive.

★★★★★

D: John Ford; W: Frank S. Nugent; Ph: Wil-liam C. Hoch; M: Max Steiner.
Cast: John Wayne, Ward Bond, Jeffrey Hunter, Natalie Wood, Vera Miles.

SEA WIFE. (1957) Exceptionally obtuse and pompous exercise in unrequited love. After the fall of Singapore in 1942, four people are cast adrift in a lifeboat, ma-rooned on an island and eventually rescued. The woman is a nun, but she doesn't tell the man who falls for her. Current admirers of Joan Collins may find some amusement in this unhabitual casting.

★★

D: Bob McNaught; W: George K. Burke; Ph: Ted Scaife; M: Kenneth V. Jones.
Cast: Richard Burton, Joan Collins, Basil Sydney, Cy Grant.

THE SEA WOLF. (1941) Among portraits of maritime madness from Captain Bligh to Captain Queeg, Edward G. Robinson's Captain Wolf Larsen, master of the *Ghost*, deserves a place on the bridge. Equally, Michael Curtiz's filming of Jack London's powerful story far outsails its rivals. Survivors of a boating accident are given shelter and much more than they expected when they climb aboard Larsen's ship. Richly atmo-spheric and inventively scored by Korngold.

★★★★

D: Michael Curtiz; W: Robert Rossen; Ph: Sol Polito; M: Erich Wolfgang Korngold.
Cast: Edward G. Robinson, John Garfield, Alexander Knox, Ida Lupino.

THE SEA WOLVES. (1981) A 50-year-old Roger Moore is the youngster among the stars in a bland retelling of a true story. A group of over-the-hill British officers relive their glory days by planning an assault on a transmitter aboard a freighter in the neutral port of Goa. The script is cumbersome and no one in the cast could decide whether this was a straight adventure or a comedy. It would have fared better as the latter.
PG.   ★★
D: Andrew V. McLaglen; W: Reginald Rose; Ph: Tony Imi; M: Roy Budd.
Cast: Gregory Peck, David Niven, Trevor Howard, Roger Moore.

SECOND CHANCE. (1953) A boxer trying to forget his past and a gangster's moll try-ing to escape hers in South America. It was an early exercise in 3-D and is now only noteworthy for a struggle in a cable car that used the technique quite impressively.

★★

D: Rudolph Mate; W: Sidney Boehm and Oscar Millard; Ph: William Snyder; M: Roy Webb.
Cast: Robert Mitchum, Jack Palance, Linda Darnell, Reginald Sheffield.

SECOND HAND HEARTS. (1981) When Hal Ashby's film was released, the publicists, in obvious desperation, called it, "a recession comedy." It's as funny as a farm foreclosure and the actors were visibly as desperate as the publicists. Robert Blake and Barbara Harris are two losers making their way from Texas to California. Their playing borders on the obnoxious and why Hal Ashby ever chose to make the movie is one of life's continuing mysteries.
PG. ★★
D: Hal Ashby; W: Charles Eastman; Ph: Haskell Wexler; M: Willie Alan Ramsey.
Cast: Robert Blake, Barbara Harris, Collin Boone, Amber Rose Gold.

THE SECRET AGENT. (1936) Not one of Hitchcock's greatest—as he himself pointed out—but still an instance of the way his skill could elevate the most unpromising material. It is based on Somerset Maugham's novel *Ashenden* and revolves around a secret agent who is dispatched to Switzerland to kill a spy. He dispatches an innocent man by mistake.

★★★

D: Alfred Hitchcock; W: Charles Bennett; Ph: Bernard Knowles; M: Louis Levy.
Cast: Madeleine Carroll, Peter Lorre, John Gielgud, Robert Young.

THE SECRET LIFE OF AN AMERICAN WIFE. (1968) An attempted satire on the middle class that is scarcely middling. Anne Jackson exchanges domestic drudgery for the life of a call girl to test her allure. Her husband is a press agent for a film star, who turns out to be her first client. Not as funny as it sounds.

★★

D and W: George Axelrod; Ph: Leon Shamroy; M: Billy May.
Cast: Walter Matthau, Anne Jackson, Patrick O'Neal, Edy Williams.

THE SECRET LIFE OF WALTER MITTY. (1947) A comedy to be savored for Danny Kaye more than James Thurber. The latter's priceless and timeless essay on man's capacity for fantasy is a Kaye star turn and certainly one his best pictures. In reality, he is a proofreader, but in his mind there is no limit to his heroics.

★★★

D: Norman McLeod; W: Ken Englund and Everett Freeman; Ph: Lee Garmes; M: David Raksin.
Cast: Danny Kaye, Boris Karloff, Virginia Mayo, Florence Bates.

THE SECRET OF NIMH. (1982) Don Bluth led a defection from the Disney studio and said he wanted to restore animation to the halcyon days of classics like *Fantasia*. His first effort is one of the great pieces of postwar animation, alive with exhilirating technique and full of honest truths for kids. It tells the story of some field mice who rescue rats from an experimental laboratory and it doesn't pull any punches.
G. ★★★★★
D and W: Don Bluth; M: Jerry Goldsmith.
Cast: (Voices) Hermione Baddeley, John Carradine, Dom DeLuise, Elizabeth Hartman.

THE SECRET POLICEMAN'S OTHER BALL. (1982) A concert on behalf of Amnesty International featuring the Monty Python troupe and other British comedians in an assortment of mostly prime material. Rock stars such as Eric Clapton are also featured.

★★★

D: Julian Temple; Ph: Julian Temple.
Cast: John Cleese, Michael Palin, Peter Cook, Graham Chapman.

THE SEDUCTION OF JOE TYNAN. (1979) Alan Alda wrote a knowing portrait of a liberal senator attempting to keep a southern conservative off the Supreme Court. Enjoyable and very astute in dealing with the senator's public struggles, it loses steam in his private troubles. These were added to make things more seductive to a large audience, but they detract from the film's savvy political observations.
PG. ★★★
D: Jerry Schatzberg; W: Alan Alda; Ph: Adam Holender; M: Bill Conti.
Cast: Alan Alda, Meryl Streep, Barbara Harris, Melvyn Douglas

THE SEDUCTION OF MIMI. (1974) Pointed, funny and a raunchy dissection of sex and the singular Sicilian from Lina Wertmuller. Mimi is a Sicilian quarry worker who goes to Turin looking for work and who is fired for his left-wing views. He returns to Sicily and sets up two households, thus allowing Wertmuller to demolish male notions of honor and posturing machismo. A few slack moments, but Giancarlo Giannini's comic gifts make this one of Wertmuller's most seductive works.

★★★★

D and W: Lina Wertmuller; Ph: Blasco Giurato; M: Pietro Piccioni.
Cast: Giancarlo Giannini, Mariangela Melato, Agostina Belli, Elena Fiore.

SEEMS LIKE OLD TIMES. (1980) Neil Simon, the past master of urbane contemporary comedy, tried to rekindle the spirit of the thirties screwball movies. His effort is more of an oddball that finds Chevy Chase seeking the protection of his ex-wife, an attorney, after he is framed for a bank hold-up. Simon milks the situation inventively enough, but Goldie Hawn is shamefully underused and Chase's acting is a collection of mugging shots.

PG. ★★★

D: Jay Sandrich; W: Neil Simon; Ph: David M. Walsh; M: Marvin Hamlisch.
Cast: Chevy Chase, Charles Grodin, Goldie Hawn, Robert Guillaume.

SEMI-TOUGH. (1977) Dan Jenkins' uproarious pro football novel puts a film-maker in a third and long situation before he starts. The monologue from Billy Clyde Puckett, cheerfully racist lecher and running back, is missing and now he's just one of three characters. The movie also substitutes the build-up to the big game—this is, after all, a football story—with an emphasis on a minor romance that should have been kept on the bench. Ritchie's sardonic view of winning and losing holds one's interest.

R. ★★★

D: Michael Ritchie; W: Walter Bernstein; Ph: Charles Rosher; M: Jerry Fielding.
Cast: Burt Reynolds, Jill Clayburgh, Kris Kristofferson, Robert Preston.

THE SENDER. (1982) Thoroughly forgettable fare about an amnesiac. He is in a mental hospital and he is able to transmit his nightmares to other people who don't have return postage. The director did the sets for *Star Wars* and this is flashy, largely incoherent drivel that demeans Kathryn Harrold, cast as the sympathetic shrink.

R. ★★

D: Roger Christian; W: Thomas Baum; Ph: Roger Pratt; M: Trevor Jones.
Cast: Kathryn Harrold, Zeljko Ivanek, Shirley Knight, Paul Freeman.

THE SENTINEL. (1977) A New York model finds a dream apartment in a Brooklyn Heights brownstone and life turns into a predictable nightmare. An abortive imitation of *Rosemary's Baby* with a motley assortment of neighbors trying to drive the girl crazy and thereby open the portals of hell. The stampede for the exits starts before that. Oh yes, there's a blind priest upstairs. Very gory.

R. ★

D and W: Michael Winner; Ph: Dick Kratina; M: Gil Melle.
Cast: Cristina Raines, Chris Sarandon, Burgess Meredith, Martin Balsam.

SERENADE. (1956) Mario Lanza, the fine Philadelphia tenor who sacrificed his serious career and himself to Hollywood, in full voice. The story, if you care, comes from a James M. Cain novel about a California vineyard worker who reaches stardom as an opera singer. The usual price-of-success clichés, but a must for Lanza fans.

★★

D: Anthony Mann; W: Ivan Goff, Ben Roberts and John Twist; Ph: Peverell Marley; M: Ray Heindorf (md).
Cast: Mario Lanza, Joan Fontaine, Sarita Montiel, Vincent Price.

THE SERGEANT. (1968) Rod Steiger's performance has weathered the years a lot better than the gingerly way the film tiptoes around his homosexuality. For its time, *The Sergeant* was a courageous if not especially perceptive treatment of a subject that was more or less off-limits as a dramatic theme. Steiger, in an army camp in the early fifties, has to struggle with his desire for a young private who does not reciprocate.

★★★

D: John Flynn; W: Dennis Murphy; Ph: Henri Persin; M: Michel Mayne.
Cast: Rod Steiger, John Philip Law, Frank Latimore, Ludmila Mikael.

SERGEANT PEPPER'S LONELY HEARTS CLUB BAND. (1978) Sacrilege. The thirty great songs from the Beatles' most influential album are done by Peter Frampton, the Bee Gees and others and often mangled or abbreviated. The songs, which have nothing to do with each other, are made to fit into a silly fantasy about Heartland. U.S.A., and a threat to destroy love and joy. There is a feeble swipe at the pop music business, whose cynicism is best represented by the film itself.

PG. ★

D: Michael Schultz; W: Henry Edwards; Ph:

Owen Roizman; M: The Beatles.
Cast: Peter Frampton, the Bee Gees, George Burns, Steve Martin.

SERGEANT RUTLEDGE. (1960) The theme of bigotry and injustice has inspired John Ford to better efforts elsewhere. The flashback format is not helpful to the argument in a story of a black cavalryman accused of rape and a white officer trying to prove him innocent. Woody Strode brings a grave dignity to the title role.
★★
D: John Ford; W: James Warner Bellah; Ph: Bert Glennon; M: Howard jackson.
Cast: Woody Strode, Jeffrey Hunter, Constance Towers, Willis Bouchey.

SERGEANT YORK. (1941) More than the flag-waver the heroic story might initially suggest. York was a hick from Tennessee with more intelligence than education and a stubborn sense of principle. He eventually compromised on his pacifism and became a national hero when he single-handedly captured 132 Germans in World War I. York himself insisted that Gary Cooper relive his exploits and how right he was. Cooper won the Oscar for his account of a man who comes to grasp that some things are worth fighting for. Howard Hawks' evocation of rural Tennessee suggests what some of those things are.
★★★★
D: Howard Hawks; W: Abem Finkel, Harry Chandler, Howard Koch and John Huston; Ph: Sol Polito; M: Max Steiner.
Cast: Gary Cooper, Joan Leslie, Walter Brennan, George Tobias.

SERIAL. (1980) Cyra McFadden's devastating satire on Marin County trendies and their liberal ennui is reduced to a sex comedy of modest attainments. The deadpan narrator—the source of most of the humor—is gone and only a few broad laughs remain. Martin Mull is the hero, behind his neighbors in fashionable acquistions and beneath the contempt of his wife.
R. ★★
D: Bill Persky; W: Rich Eustis and Michael Elias; Ph: Rexford Metz; M: Lalo Schifrin.
Cast: Martin Mull, Tuesday Weld, Sally Kellerman, Jennifer McAllister.

THE SERPENT'S EGG. (1977) This movie is set in Berlin in 1923, with starving people scavenging flesh from dead horses and tossing aside rats. The narrator says they have "lost faith both in the future and the present." And so had Bergman, through many personal problems, when he made this movie. Carradine is a trapeze artist who seeks out a cabaret singer in this Dantean milieu. Bergman gives us a vision of embryonic fascism and barbarity without having much to say about it. He called it a horror story. The horror is there, but not the story that would give it perspective.
R. ★★★
D and W: Ingmar Bergman; Ph: Sven Nykvist; M: Rolf Wilhelm.
Cast: David Carradine, Liv Ullmann, Gert Froebe, Heinz Bennent.

THE SERVANT. (1963) Harold Pinter's masterly script and Joseph Losey's attuned direction are merely the beginning. Dirk Bogarde has never been more coolly sinister as the co-operative cockney valet whose attentions finally make him his master's voice. Edward Fox is equally riveting in his slide into boozy oblivion. A taut drama and a very sly commentary on English class relationships and their frail assumptions.
★★★★
D: Joseph Losey; W: Harold Pinter; Ph: Douglas Slocombe; M: Johnny Dankworth.
Cast: Dirk Bogarde, Edward Fox, Sarah Miles, Wendy Craig.

THE SET-UP. (1949) In the aptly named town of Paradise City, Stoker Thompson is a washed up fighter who can still stand on his dignity. Robert Wise's tough-minded and widely admired film makes much of the brutal implications outside the ring. Robert Ryan had one of his best roles as Stoker, who refuses to take a dive.
★★★
D: Robert Wise; W: Art Cohn; Ph: Milton Krasner; M: C. Bakaleshnikoff.
Cast: Robert Ryan, Audrey Totter, George Tobias, Alan Baxter.

SEVEN BEAUTIES. (1976) Lina Wertmuller's masterly film can be admired for its consummate artistry and despised for its moral vision. Her interest in sex and politics reaches its perverse ultimate in a concentration camp and the dealings of a grotesque woman commandant and an inmate. A wide-ranging and multi-themed film that addresses depravity and the will to survive at any cost. There is not one beauty here, let alone seven, and in the end there is only an impenetrable darkness.
★★★★
D and W: Lina Wertmuller; Ph: Tonio Delli-Colli; M: Enzio Ianacci.

Cast: Giancarlo Giannini, Fernando Rey, Shirley Stoler, Mario Conti.

SEVEN BRIDES FOR SEVEN BROTHERS. (1954) Hollywood has a long and understandable tradition of letting a musical earn its wings on Broadway before seeing if it will fly as a movie. Stanley Donen's exuberant and sweet-natured musical was written without a Broadway tryout and it has stood the test of time. The brothers come looking for suitable spouses and opportunities to strut their stuff in such sequences as the barn-raising scene that still brings the house down. The choreography is the creation of Michael Kidd.

★★★

D: Stanley Donen; W: Frances Goodrich and Albert Hackett; Ph: George Folsey; M: Adolph Deutsch.
Cast: Howard Keel, Jane Powell, Russ Tamblyn, Jeff Richards.

SEVEN DAYS IN MAY. (1964) A stimulating exercise in paranoia that raises the simple issue of what would happen if the American high command started behaving in the pre-emptive fashion so dear to coup-happy countries. Enraged by what he believes is a sell-out to the Soviets in a nuclear arms treaty, Burt Lancaster schemes to overthrow the President and Kirk Douglas is the loyal opposition. Frankenheimer and the cast play for tension and there is a pleasing disdain for rhetoric in Rod Serling's excellent script.

★★★★

D: John Frankenheimer; W: Rod Serling; Ph: Ellsworth Fredericks; M: Jerry Goldsmith.
Cast: Burt Lancaster, Kirk Douglas, Frederic March, Edmond O'Brien.

THE SEVEN PERCENT SOLUTION. (1976) Herbert Ross's thoughtful and invigorating film gives us a Holmes of our own—the great detective beset by contemporary fears and very much addicted to cocaine—while retaining the Victorian element. The Holmes-Watson relationship is also far more complex than the genius-buffoon partnership of Basil Rathbone and Nigel Bruce. The adroit script merges Holmes' struggle with the drug with his efforts to solve the kidnapping of a beautiful woman. Excellent ensemble acting and a keen sense of elegant depravity behind the lace curtains.

PG. ★★★★

D: Herbert Ross; W: Nicholas Meyer; Ph: Oswald Morris; M: John Addison.
Cast: Nicol Williamson, Robert Duvall, Va-

nessa Redgrave, Laurence Olivier, Alan Arkin.

1776. (1972) A light touch from director Peter Hunt and the presence of Howard Da Silva and William Daniels in the roles they did on Broadway makes for a pleasant adaptation of the musical. The material is unlikely—the events surrounding the signing of the Declaration of Independence—but the spirit is there. Da Silva's Ben Franklin remains a fetching creation and one of the film's attainments is its humanizing of the Founding Fathers.

G. ★★★

D: Peter Hunt; W: Peter Stone; Ph: Harry Stradling, Jr.; M: Sherman Edwards.
Cast: Howard Da Silva, William Daniels, Ken Howard, Blythe Danner.

SEVENTH HEAVEN. (1937) James Stewart and Simone Simon in the remake of the celebrated 1927 film prove that silence is golden. Stewart is miscast as the sewer worker who marries a destitute woman and finds happiness before marching off to war. He comes back blinded. The original starred Charles Farrell and Janet Gaynor to better effect.

★★

D: Henry King; W: Melville Baker; Ph: Merritt Gerstad; M: Louis Silvers.
Cast: Simone Simon, James Stewart, Jean Hersholt, Gregory Ratoff.

THE SEVENTH SEAL. (1955) Ingmar Bergman's father was a pastor and the boy used to let attention wander to the mediaeval paintings during the long church services. Life in the Middle Ages was short and brutal and death an everyday fact of life. He used the period to ask the urgent questions that beset contemporary man in a unique context and *The Seventh Seal* is a triumphant masterpiece. A knight returning from the crusades plays a game of chess with Death and seeks answers to the eternal questions. There aren't any, but the questions have rarely been raised with such eloquence.

★★★★★

D and W: Ingmar Bergman; Ph: Gunnar Fischer; M: Erik Nordgren.
Cast: Max Von Sydow, Gunnar Bjornstrand, Nils Poppe, Bibi Andersson.

THE SEVENTH VOYAGE OF SINBAD. (1958) And one of the liveliest for the much traveled sailor. Sinbad's girl-friend has been reduced to a midget and he has to find a roc's egg to break the spell imposed by an evil magician. Ray Harryhausen's monsters, often an unpredictable lot, don't lay an egg and it's all topped off with a sweeping Bernard Herrmann score.

★★★

D: Nathan Juran; W: Kenneth Kolb; Ph: Wilie Cooper; M: Bernard Herrmann.
Cast: Kerwin Mathews, Kathryn Grant, Torin Thatcher, Richard Eyer.

THE SEVEN-UPS. (1973) The first directing effort of Philip D'Antoni, the producer of *Bullitt* and *The French Connection*, so the presence of a first-rate car chase is no surprise. There isn't much else to *The Seven Ups*, an undercover police squad specializing in serious career criminals. Roy Scheider reprises his *The French Connection* cop, but the material isn't up to his talent.

PG. ★★

D: Philip D'Antoni; W: Albert Ruben and Alexander Jacobs; Ph: Urs Furrer; M: Don Ellis.
Cast: Roy Scheider, Tony LoBianco, Victor Arnold, Jerry Leon.

THE SEVEN YEAR ITCH. (1955) Tom Ewell is liberated into temporary singledom when his wife takes a trip. To the normal sexual fantasy humor that results, Billy Wilder appends Marilyn Monroe. She had a lot of fun with her gossip column image by playing a knockout who is unaware of the cataclysmic effect she has on neighboring libidos. She made the most of the part and it is one of her best sustained screen roles. Wilder, to his credit, also sustains the joke.

★★★★

D: Billy Wilder; W: Wilder and George Axelrod; Ph: Milton Krasner; M: Alfred Newman.
Cast: Marilyn Monroe, Tom Ewell, Evelyn Keyes, Sonny Tufts.

SHADOW OF A DOUBT. (1942) Alfred Hitchcock had no doubt about this film's place in his canon. He said that he ranked it at the very top of his work in America, even though a good number of his other movies have commanded a wider following. The villain is that Hitchcock perennial—the wife-killer who is outwardly the soul of virtue. He visits relatives in a small town and the niece begins to suspect. The tension is unrelenting and underscored by the mundane pulse of life in the town.

★★★★★

D: Alfred Hitchcock; W: Thornton Wilder, Alma Reville and Sally Benson; Ph: Joseph Valentine; M: Dmitri Tiomkin.

Cast: Joseph Cotten, Teresa Wright, MacDonald Carey, Patricia Collinge.

SHADOW OF THE HAWK. (1976) The Devil takes Alger's advice and goes west in this inept attempt at sagebrush occult. It deserves to be put out of its misery like a horse with a broken leg. An Indian sorceress —don't the Indians ever get a break from Hollywood?—comes back after a couple of centuries to take her revenge on an Indian village.

PG. ★

D: George McCowan; W: Norman Thaddeus Vane and Herbert J. Wright; Ph: Alan Zenuk; M: Robert McMullin.
Cast: Jan-Michael Vincent, Marilyn Hassett, Chief Dan George.

THE SHAGGY DOG. (1959) A really shaggy dog story that gives its plot a dangerously long leash. A ring falls into a boy's pants cuff and turns him into a sheepdog, allowing a lot of overdone slapstick and much silliness involving spies. This was the first of Fred MacMurray's paternal twit routines that became such a burden to Disney films.

★★

D: Charles Barton; W: Bill Walsh and Lillie Hayward; Ph: Edward Colman; M: Paul J. Smith.
Cast: Fred MacMurray, Jean Hagen, Tommy Kirk, Annette Funicello.

SHAMPOO. (1975) A razor-sharp sex farce that takes the common joke about the gaiety of hairdressers and inverts it. Warren Beatty is an airheaded Beverly Hills hairdresser commuting between bedrooms on his motor cycle. He says things like, "I've been cutting too much hair lately. I'm losing my concept." Set in 1968 on Presidential election night, it falters in trying to link sexual hypocrisy with the Nixonian kind we were given in the following six years. It's still one of the best American sex comedies of its time .

R. ★★★★

D: Hal Ashby; W: Warren Beatty and Robert Towne; Ph: Laszlo Kovacs; M: Paul Simon.
Cast: Warren Beatty, Julie Christie, Goldie Hawn, Lee Grant.

SHANE. (1953) Of all the great westerns, George Stevens' superlative film comes closest to defining the genre's capacity to lend a mythic quality to story-telling while exploring subtle human responses to harsh conditions. The stranger with a past and no future (Alan Ladd) befriends a homesteading family and finds himself emotionally entangled with husband, wife and small son for different reasons. He takes their side against the hired guns brought in by ranchers who wish to drive them from the land. There is an equal entanglement of religious and secular myths woven through the story and it musters a rare and haunting power.

★★★★★

D: George Stevens; W: Jack Sher and A.B. Guthrie, Jr; Ph: Loyal Griggs; M: Victor Young.
Cast: Alan Ladd, Jean Arthur, Van Heflin, Jack Palance.

SHARK'S TREASURE. (1975) Old-fashioned treasure hunt updated with a Mexican homosexual as the villain who demands, "You think I don't know what means sadist?" Blithe melange of competing plots about the recovery of a treasure in Honduras, mutiny, mean sharks and meaner convicts. For good measure, there is a stern lecture on the evils of tobacco and booze. The underwater sequences are quite good.
PG.   ★★
D and W: Cornel Wilde; Ph: Jack Atcheler and Al Giddings; M: Robert O. Ragland.
Cast: Cornel Wilde, Yaphet Kotto, John Neilson, David Canary.

SHE. (1935) Before she became Richard Nixon's favorite congresswoman Helen Gahagan starred in a lavish and slightly inane version of H. Rider Haggard's fantasy. Much loved by camp followers, She features a woman whose powers will fade if she succumbs to love—a typically Victorian sentiment.
★★★
D: Irving Pichel; W: Ruth Rose; M: Max Steiner.
Cast: Helen Gahagan, Randolph Scott, Nigel Bruce, Helen Mack.

SHE. (1965) Ursula Andress thinks she recognizes an old flame in John Richardson and wants to sample the fire that promises eternal youth. A mere flicker of the original spectacle, the Hammer Films remake is ponderous and slow-witted and if you like camp, you're better off with the 1935 version.
★★
D: Robert Day; W: David Chantler; Ph: Harry Waxman; M: James Bernard.
Cast: Ursula Andress, Peter Cushing, Christopher Lee, John Richardson.

SHEENA. (1984) The Variety reviewer noted that the PG rating, rather than the then new PG-13 designation, made a joke of the revised system because of an extended nude scene. The joke is actually on the viewer who is asked to accept Tanya Roberts, a refugee from Charlie's Angels as a wilderness woman. The conception and acting owe much to Bo Derek's dopey Tarzan. Sheena is raised by an African tribe and saves their spiritual home. The dialogue is rudimentary and the primal menace of the jungle so artfully captured in Hugh Hudson's Greystoke is missing.
PG.   ★
D: John Guillermin; W: David Newman and Lorenzo Semple, Jr.; Ph: Pasqualino De Santis; M: Richard Hartley.
Cast: Tanya Roberts, Ted Wass, Donovan Scott, France Zobda.

SHEILA LEVINE IS DEAD AND LIVING IN NEW YORK. (1975) And the viewing isn't worth it. Gail Parent helped adapt her wry novel about a Jewish girl trying to land a doctor husband in the competitive world of singledom in Manhattan. So she has only herself to blame for the film, which turns the story into a fantasy about love and perseverance conquering all—including a man's resistance.
PG.   ★
D: Sidney J. Furie; W: Kenny Solms and Gail Parent; Ph: Donald M. Morgan; M: Michel Legrand.
Cast: Jeannie Berlin, Roy Scheider, Rebecca Dianna Smith, Janet Brandt.

THE SHERIFF OF FRACTURED JAW. (1959) Kenneth More is an English gunsmith who journeys west and finds himself the law in a wild town after a poker game. The western comedy depends on the single humorous idea of More's English aloofness contrasting with frontier loudness and the joke expires before the movie. More is quite amusing under the circumstances.
★★
D: Raoul Walsh; W: Arthur Dales; Ph: Otto Heller; M: Robert Farnon.
Cast: Kenneth More, Jayne Mansfield, Henry Hull, Bruce Cabot.

SHE WORE A YELLOW RIBBON. (1949) In a part that ranks in the top half dozen from his long career, John Wayne ages himself gracefully and convincingly to give us Captain Nathan Brittles. He is slated for retirement against his will and unwilling to step down when so much is left to be done against the Indians. Wayne turns this into a touching portrait of a man who is reluctant to let go because his life is so intertwined with his livelihood. John Ford peopled the cavalry outpost with draftees from his stock company and the ensemble work is a joy to watch.

★★★★

D: John Ford; W: Laurence Stallings and Frank Nugent; Ph: Winton Hoch; M: Richard Hageman.
Cast: John Wayne, Joanne Dru, John Agar, Ben Johnson.

THE SHINING. (1980) Stanley Kubrick opens his venture into the low-rent district of horror film with the chords of the *Dies Irae* and he makes the viewer feel he is eating popcorn in a cathedral. Kubrick has replenished other genres with his genius, but here his strong points—the measured pace, the immaculate composition—work against him. He loses his characters in straining for cosmic utterance. A boozy writer changes for the worse when he and his family move into the Overlook Hotel, which is burdened with the mandatory curse.

R.   ★★★

D: Stanley Kubrick; W: Kubrick and Diane Johnson; Ph: John Alcott; M: Music of Bartok.
Cast: Jack Nicholson, Shelley Duvall, Danny Lloyd, Scatman Crothers.

SHOCK TREATMENT. (1983) Coming up with a movie worse than *The Rocky Horror Show* is no small achievement. Those who thought it couldn't be done are welcome to sit through the wretched antics in the sequel to the cult favorite. Terrible music interrupted by infantile comedy about television game shows and drugs.

PG.   ★

D: Jim Sharman; W: Sharman and Richard O'Brien; Ph: Mike Molloy; M: Richard Hartley.
Cast: Jessica Harper, Cliff De Young, Richard O'Brien, Patricia Quinn.

THE SHOOTIST. (1976) John Wayne could have left no more fitting valedictory than this moving portrait of a cancer-ridden gunfighter who has outlived his usefulness. His last film is full of references, both pointed and oblique, to his own career, and the myths of the west become entwined with his own screen legend. His last film gives us the final week of the gun fighter's life. It is the last great western and, some would argue, the crowning glory of Wayne's life and the western genre.

PG.   ★★★★★

D: Don Siegel; W: Miles Hood Swarthout and Scott Hale; Ph: Bruce Surtees; M: Elmer Bernstein.
Cast: John Wayne, James Stewart, Lauren Bacall, Ron Howard.

SHOOT THE MOON. (1981) The husband sits in his tuxedo in the study, listening to the happy clamor of his wife and four daughters while tears stream down his cheeks. Thus begins one of the finest American films about the disintegration of a marriage, precisely written and eloquently acted. Albert Finney is a successful author making the wrenching decision after fifteen years. This is one film that acknowledges the fact that children should be heard as well as seen and its special quality arises from the guilt they create in the departing father. Alan Parker, known for flashier fare before *Shoot the Moon*, directs with great sensitivity.

R.   ★★★★★

D: Alan Parker; W: Bo Goldman; Ph: Michael Sereskin.
Cast: Albert Finney, Diane Keaton, Karen Allen, Peter Weller.

SHORT EYES. (1977) Filmed in the Manhattan House of Detention, popularly known as the Tombs, this powerful version of Miguel Pinero's play resounds with the desperate cries of prisoners. In sight, sound and sense of volcanic despair, the movie ranks as one of the most unsparing prison films ever made. The story focuses on the prisoners' attitude toward a child molester who has the misfortune to be thrown into their company.

R.   ★★★★

D: Robert Young; W: Miguel Pinero; Ph: Peter Sava; M: Curtis Mayfield.
Cast: Bruce Davison, Jose Perez, Nathan George, Don Blakely.

SHOUT AT THE DEVIL. (1976) They don't make films like this any more and it's pretty clear why. An old-fashioned African epic with Moore as a smooth old Etonian and Marvin marinating in gin and wild schemes. Set in Zanzibar in 1913, the film pits the pair against a cartoon German commissioner. Lots of action and a plot that moves with the grace of an elephant.

PG.   ★★

D: Peter Hunt; W: Wilbur Smith, Stanley Price, Alastair Reid; Ph: Mike Reed; M: Maurice Jarre.
Cast: Roger Moore, Lee Marvin, Barbara Parkins, Ian Holm.

THE SIGN OF ZORRO. (1960) Inept splicing of episodes from the Disney TV series that shows its origins by reaching a climax and lurching on to the next incident. Guy Williams is a passable Don Diego/Zorro who repeatedly makes a fool of the commandant in California in 1820.

★★

D: Norman Foster and Lewis Foster; W: Norman Foster; Ph: Gordon Avil; M: William Lava.
Cast: Guy Williams, Henry Calvin, Gene Sheldon, Britt Lomond.

THE SILENCERS. (1966) The less said about Dean Martin's forays into espionage as Matt Helm the better. Perhaps his storied fondness of the bottle can be explained by repeated exposure to his own Helmsmanship. A rudderless film pits Helm against an organization called the Big O, an apt name for a film that registers as a big zero. Martin goes through the entire movie with a leer and an arched eyebrow.

★

D: Phil Karlson; W: Oscar Saul; Ph: Burnett Guffey; M: Elmer Bernstein.
Cast: Dean Martin, Stella Stevens, Victor Buono, Daliah Lavi.

SILENT MOVIE. (1976) Not up to Mel Brooks' high standards of parody in *Young Frankentstein* and *Blazing Saddles* and not because it actually is a silent movie. A loose collection of sight gags, some hilarious and some excruciating. Can Mel Funn save Big Picture Studios from the conglomerate, Engulf and Devour? Not a valentine to silent movies so much as a decanting of Brooks' febrile mind.

PG. ★★★

D: Mel Brooks; W: Brooks, Barry Levinson, Ron Clark, Rudy DeLuca; Ph: Paul Lohmann; M: John Morris.
Cast: Mel Brooks, Dom DeLuise, Marty Feldman, Bernadette Peters.

SILENT RAGE. (1982) Chuck Norris is a sheriff on the path of a superhuman killer who owes his tremendous strength to a botched DNA experiment. DNA stands for Does Not Act in Norris' case and it shows even more here because he has cut down on his karate. His fans will enjoy his exemplary way of clearing out a bikers' bar.

R. ★

D: Michael Miller; W: Joseph Fraley; Ph: Robert Jessup; M: Peter Bernstein.
Cast: Chuck Norris, Ron Silver, Steven Keats, Tony Kalem.

SILENT RUNNING. (1972) Douglas Trumbull's futuristic fantasy is very much of its own time. It is suffused with flower-child music from Joan Baez and a self-consciously precious attitude toward environmental issues. Perhaps the overbearing presence of these elements accounts for the film receiving less than its due. The fact that it preceded the *Star Wars* boom in sci-fi didn't help either. *Silent Running*, with convincing rather than spectacular effects, is one of the most provocative science fiction films ever made. Bruce Dern is exceptional as a botanist charged with keeping the only surviving Earth vegetation alive on a space station near Saturn. When the home office orders the greenery destroyed, he retaliates. A thoughtful discussion of a serious issue before the kids and their concerns took over the genre.

PG ★★★★

D: Douglas Trumbull; W: Deric Washburn, Michael Cimino and Steve Bochco; Ph: Charles Wheeler; M: Peter Schickele.
Cast: Bruce Dern, Cliff Potts, Jesse Vint, Ron Rifkin.

SILKWOOD. (1983) On her way to meet a *New York Times* reporter to discuss safety violations at the nuclear plant where she worked, Karen Silkwood died in a car accident of a very suspicious nature. Mike Nichols' moving film draws its strength from the fact that it is about some issues of vast importance and also about a complex young woman. In Meryl Streep's richly textured performance we have a core of nuclear power that discusses what the work-place and its attitudes can do to us. The film has a point of view but its opinion of Karen is honest and there is no attempt at beatification.

R. ★★★★

D: Mike Nichols; W: Nora Ephron and Alice Arlen; Ph: Miroslav Ondricek; M: Georges Delerue.
Cast: Meryl Streep, Cher, Kurt Russell, Craig T. Nelson.

THE SILVER CHALICE. (1954) We all have to start somewhere and it was Paul Newman's misfortune to be left holding the cup that runneth over with biblical cliches. In his first movie, Newman certainly looked good, but he had to speak the inferior lines of Lesser Samuels. He played a Greek slave who is freed so that he can design a stand for the chalice Jesus used at the Last Supper. Happily, his career survived.

★

D: Victor Saville; W: Lesser Samuels; Ph: William Skall; M: Franz Waxman.
Cast: Paul Newman, Pier Angeli, Virginia Mayo, Jack Palance.

SILVER STREAK. (1976) Set aboard a train bound from Los Angeles to Chicago and full of the meandering nonchalance we associate with that mode of travel, the film tries for both comedy and suspense without mustering much of either. Wilder, as a publisher involved with vital documents, is asked to reconcile a romantic lead with his trademark hysterics. Off-track most of the time, but Richard Pryor livens things up when he tries to disguise Wilder as a black.
PG.   ★★
D: Arthur Hiller; W: Colin Higgins; Ph: David M. Walsh; M: Henry Mancini.
Cast: Gene Wilder, Jill Clayburgh, Patrick McGoohan, Richard Pryor.

SIMON. (1980) Marshall Brickman, Woody Allen's long-time collaborator, thought up a think tank which persuades Alan Arkin to think he's from another planet. Arkin remarks that you can move the world with an idea, but first you have to think of one. The same rule applies here. Arkin goes on to found a religion, but Brickman loses his grasp of a very good satirical idea and *Simon* is full of missed opportunities.
PG.   ★★★
D and W: Marshall Brickman; Ph: Adam Holender; M: Stanley Silverman.
Cast: Alan Arkin, Madeleine Kahn, Austin Pendleton, Judy Graubert.

A SIMPLE STORY. (1980) Claude Sautet's study of a woman's mid-life crisis is not at all simple. Romy Schneider is an unalloyed pleasure as Marie, a woman trying to decide whether she should go back to her husband. The plot is languid and Sautet has a tendency to let the film drift away from Marie and into peripheral characters. It won the French Academy Award.
★★★
D: Claude Sautet; W: Sautet and Jean-Loup Dabadie; Ph: Jean Boffety; M: Phillipe Sarde.
Cast: Romy Schneider, Bruno Cremer, Claude Brasseur, Arlette Bonnard.

SINBAD AND THE EYE OF THE TIGER. (1977) A pacifier rather than a challenger for kids that features lurid over-acting and dated special effects from Ray Harryhausen, who by this time was being shown up by *Star Wars* and other fantasies. Pat Wayne (John's son) and Taryn Power (Tyrone's daughter) are likable enough in an adventure which finds Sinbad freeing a city from a witch's spell.
PG.   ★★
D: Sam Wanamaker; W: Beverly Cross; Ph: Ted Moore; M: Roy Budd.
Cast: Patrick Wayne, Taryn Power, Margaret Whiting, Jane Seymour.

THE SINGER NOT THE SONG. (1962) The actor, not the part, is what's at fault. Dirk Bogarde is woefully out of place in Mexico, where he creaks around in his leather, and has a strangely ambivalent relationship with a priest. John Mills is equally out of his element in a cassock. There is much pretension and guarded hints at homosexuality.
★★
D: Roy Baker; W: Nigel Balchin; Ph: Otto Heller; M: Philip Green.
Cast: Dirk Bogarde, John Mills, Mylene Demongeot, John Bentley.

SINGIN' IN THE RAIN. (1952) The most delightful of all American musicals is a high-spirited and witty Hollywood production that debunks Hollywood. Judiciously set at the dawn of the sound era in movies, it moves at an exuberant clip and blends song and dance with a satisfying comic plot. It is built around a silent star whose first sound production requires her to talk attractively and to sing. She can't and Debbie Reynolds is recruited to become her secret voice. The tone of the movie is unique, balanced delicately between the overtly conflicting elements of nostalgia and satire.
★★★★★
D: Stanley Donen and Gene Kelly; W: Adolph Green and Betty Comden; Ph: Harold Rosson; M: Nacio Herb Brown.
Cast: Gene Kelly, Donald O'Connor, Debbie Reynolds, Jean Hagen.

SINK THE BISMARCK. (1960) A cerebral war movie centering on the battle of wits that led to the successful attack on the German battleship. Kenneth More is in top form as a newly widowed and bitter intelligence chief masterminding the campaign. The producers used German newsreel film of the launching of the Bismarck, but then were content to employ models that look like bath toys. It doesn't seriously detract from the drama.
★★★
D: Lewis Gilbert; W: Edmund H. North; Ph: Christopher Challis; M: Muir Mathieson.

Cast: Kenneth More, Dana Wynter, Carl Mohner, Laurence Naismith.

SISTERS. (1972) Brian De Palma's love of Alfred Hitchcock yielded much better and more assured results later in his career. In his sixth feature he emerged from the underground to pay homage to *Psycho* and even got Bernard Herrmann to write the score. The music is a lot better than the movie. Jennifer Salt is a standard reporter who witnesses a murder and sets off to learn the truth. Technique pre-empts the basic requirements of story-telling in an opaque thriller.

★★
D: Brian De Palma; W: De Palma and Louisa Rose Youell; Ph: Greg Sandor; M: Bernard Herrmann.
Cast: Margot Kidder, Jennifer Salt, Charles Durning, William Finley.

SIX PACK. (1982) A noisy stock car provides a vehicle for Kenny Rogers' stab at translating his singing popularity to the screen. It needs a major overhaul. He has several country miles to go before he can carry a film like this, which uses the idea of a bunch of kids bringing out the better side in a curmudgeonly adult. Rogers is simply too nice a guy to make it convincing and there is no convincing transition in the character.
PG. ★★
D: Daniel Petrie; W: Alex Matter and Mike Marvin; Ph: William J. Crebber; M: Charles Fox.
Cast: Kenny Rogers, Diane Lane, Erin Gray, Barry Corbin.

SIX WEEKS. (1982) A sadistically miscast tear-jerker about a little girl dying from leukemia and playing matchmaker. She dreams of uniting her mother and Dudley Moore, who is running for political office in California. Mary Tyler Moore, whose reticence was ideal for *Ordinary People*, looks miserable. The other Moore is at less than his best in absurdly implausible circumstances.
PG. ★★
D: Tony Bill; W: David Seltzer; Ph: Michael D. Margulies; M: Dudley Moore.
Cast: Dudley Moore, Mary Tyler Moore, Katherine Healy, Shannon Wilcox.

SKY RIDERS. (1976) A gimmick in search of a movie. Terrorists kidnap the wife and children of a wealthy businessman in Greece and spirit them away to an inaccessible mountain fortress. The plot fell into the Mediterranean and its political theme gives way to a familiar sexual triangle. The gimmick itself, a hang glider assault on the fortress, is a two-dramamine special and very well executed.
PG. ★★
D: Douglas Hickox; W: Jack DeWitt; Ph: Ousama Rawi; M: Lalo Schifrin.
Cast: James Coburn, Susannah York, Robert Culp, Charles Aznavour.

THE SLAP. (1976) A humane and wittily observed French movie. Claude Pinoteau probes a father and a daughter caught in separate life crises. Their efforts to resolve them, however, are inextricably linked by their complex relationship. Lino Ventura is a divorced teacher now facing the departure of his mistress. His daughter is 18 and making decisions that loom large and seem small later on. Thoughtful and rewarding.
★★★★
D: Claude Pinoteau; W: Pinoteau and Jean-Loup Dabadie; Ph: Jean Collomb; M: Georges Delerue.
Cast: Isabelle Adjani, Lino Ventura, Annie Girardot, Francis Perrin.

SLAP SHOT. (1977) A riotous comedy about minor league hockey with language that consists entirely of blue lines. Like one of those interminable fights that afflict the sport, not all the punches thrown are on target. When the movie sticks to what it has to say about sports and winning, it's a winner. When it tries to decide what it all *means*, it loses its exuberance. Paul Newman's aging jock, leading a losing team through the season, is wonderful and he holds the film even when it starts getting serious about the violence it has laughed at in the early scenes.
R. ★★★★
D: George Roy Hill; W: Nancy David; Ph: Victor Kemper, Wallace Worsley; M: Elmer Bernstein.
Cast: Paul Newman, Michael Ontkean, Lindsay Crouse.

A SLAVE OF LOVE. (1978) The days of silent film-making are celebrated—in Russia. A small film company in the Crimea goes about its work and intrigues while the Russian Revolution builds inexorably around it. Moscow has fallen to the Bolsheviks. The images of proletarian woe are blunt—this is a Soviet film after all—and the other contrasts stark. Elena Solovei, as the actress changed by events, gives the film needed focus.

★★★

D: Nikita Mikhalkov; W: Friedrich Gorenstein and Andrie Mikhalkov-Konchalovsky; Ph: Pavel Lebeshev; M: Eduard Artemiev.
Cast: Elena Solovei, Rodian Nakhapetov, Alexander Kalyagin, Konstantin Grigoryev.

SLEEPAWAY CAMP. (1983) The place is Camp Arawak and unless you haven't seen a horror film for the last ten years, you've slept through this plot before. Teenagers meet the murderer and depart amid the usual gore.

R.   ★
D and W: Robert Hitzik; Ph: Benjamin Davis; M: Edward Billous.
Cast: Felissa Rose, Jonathan Tiersten, Karen Fields, Christopher Collet.

SLEEPING BEAUTY. (1959) Disney was taken to task for over-producing a simple story, but this ambitious piece of animation has come to stand with the pre-war classics. It contains some of the studio's most elaborate work, such as the "Hail the Princess Aurora" opening that takes us into the palace. The customary shrewd mix of suspense of horror and humor, but the film is a little more grown-up in its conception than *Snow White.*

                                    ★★★★★
D: Clyde Geronimi; W: Erdman Penner; M: Tchaikovsky(adapted by George Bruns).
Cast: (Voices) Mary Costa, Bill Shirley, Eleanor Audley, Verna Felton.

SLEEPING DOGS. (1982) Roger Donaldson posits a New Zealand plunged into a civil war between the government and guerrilla insurgents. But he makes very little effort to explain how such a turn of events might come about in a quiet corner of the world. A loner leaves wife and child to live on an island and to evade the authorities. The action is well staged but the digressions are more interesting than the main plot.

                                    ★★★
D: Roger Donaldson; W: Ian Mune and Arthur Baysling; Ph: Michael Seresin; M: Murray Grindlay.
Cast: Sam Neill, Melissa Donaldson, Ian Mune, Warren Oates.

SLEUTH. (1972) You might expect the staginess of Anthony Shaffer's play, with its delight in the conventions of the traditional whodunit, to be magnified into creakiness by the screen. But the movie works surprisingly well, thanks to the zest Laurence Olivier and Michael Caine bring to their alternating roles as cat and mouse. A knighted mystery writer

schemes against a hairdresser who has cuckolded him. The two actors make the most of the clash of upper and working class that propels the dialogue.

PG.   ★★★★
D: Joseph L. Mankiewicz; W: Anthony Shaffer; Ph: Oswald Morris; M: John Addison.
Cast: Laurence Olivier, Michael Caine.

THE SLIPPER AND THE ROSE. (1976) A sumptuous retelling of the Cinderella story with pleasantly unmemorable songs by Richard and Robert Sherman. The story is told from the perspective of the prince, which permits a more mature narrative than one might expect. Cinderella is a popular Christmas pantomime in England and childhood memories may have influenced Forbes' sometimes staged direction. Chamberlain is no singer and Gemma Craven (Cinderella) no great actress, but they make affecting lovers.

G.   ★★★
D: Bryan Forbes; W: Forbes, Robert and Richard Sherman; Ph: Tony Imi; M: Robert and Richard Sherman.
Cast: Richard Chamberlain, Gemma Craven, Michael Hordern, Kenneth More .

SLOW DANCING IN THE BIG CITY. (1978) A New York newspaper columnist, hard of nose but soft of heart, falls for a ballerina. She fights muscle problems, while he scuffles around the city curing Puerto Rican drummers of drug problems and scrounging up other column material. Paul Sorvino is a fine actor confronted with insurmountable odds and Jimmy Breslin ought to have sued the screenwriter for libel.

PG.   ★★
D: John Avildsen; W: Barra Grant; Ph: Ralf Bode; M: Bill Conti.
Cast: Paul Sorvino, Anne Ditchburn, Nicholas Coster, Anita Dangler.

SLUMBER PARTY MASSACRE. (1982) Not the sleeper you might suspect from the two women responsible for the direction and screenplay. If they intended satire they fall terribly short and the film confirms that they yield to no men in their ability to shovel out the schlock. The killer has a drill and the victims are the girl's basketball team. Bloody, crude and tedious.

R.   ★
D: Amy Jones; W: Rita Mae Brown; Ph: Steve Posey; M: Ralph Jones.
Cast: Michele Michaels, Robin Stille, Michael Villela, Andre Honore.

SMALL CHANGE. (1976) Truffaut's superb film is without the condescension of most children's movies which are too often afflicted with adult perceptions of how kids ought to be. The director becomes a companion of youth as he strings together a series of exquisitely done vignettes of children in a quiet provincial town. Full of humor and wry observation, the movie is both a celebration and a defense of the world of kids.
PG.   ★★★★★
D: Francois Truffaut; W: Truffaut and Susan Schiffman; Ph: Pierre-William Glenn; M: Maurice Jaubert.
Cast: Georges Desmouceaux, Claudio Deluca, Philippe Goldman.

A SMALL CIRCLE OF FRIENDS. (1980) Harvard students evade the draft and their whining sounds both repulsive and elitist when you recall that Vietnam claimed such an absurdly disproportionate number of minority kids and lower-class whites. It is also a very simplistic view of the domestic protest movement in the sixties.
PG.   ★★
D: Rob Cohen ; W: Ezra Sacks .
Cast: Brad Davis, Karen Allen, Jameson Parker, John Friedrich.

SMASH PALACE. (1982) A part-time race driver runs a scrapyard filled with rusty autos and endures an equally dilapidated marriage. Roger Donaldson's look at the couple's problems is as rough hewn and inarticulate as the husband is in places, but it boasts a basic honesty and an unusual setting— New Zealand.
R.   ★★★
D: Roger Donaldson; W: Donaldson, Peter Hansard and Bruno Lawrence; Ph: Graeme Cowley; M: Sharon O'Neill.
Cast: Anna Jackson, Bruno Lawrence, Greer Robson, Keith Aberdein.

SMILE. (1975) The essential ugliness of the assumption behind beauty pageants is dissected with cruel and devastating wit by Michael Ritchie. A small-town contest in California allows him to scrutinize the naive bitchiness of the competitors and the silliness of the officials. In the talent section, one girl tells the judges she wants to be "either a veterinarian or a nun." Ritchie lets the awfulness speak for itself throughout.
PG.   ★★★★
D: Michael Ritchie; W: Jerry Belson; Ph: Conrad Hall; M: Daniel Osborn.
Cast: Bruce Dern, Barbara Feldon, Michael Kidd, Geoffrey Lewis.

SMITHEREENS. (1982) A punk variation on advertisements for myself and something of a send-up of *A Star is Born*. Wren is from New Jersey and desperate to make it in the New Wave world. She crashes parties and clubs and slaps portraits of herself on the wall with the provocative question "Who is This?" The answer is tersely funny and the milieu of Manhattan punkdom and its denizens archly captured.
                                          ★★★
D: Susan Seidelman; W: Ron Nyswaner and Peter Askin; Ph: Christine El Khadem; M: Glen Mercer and Bill Million.
Cast: Susan Berman, Brad Rinn, Richard Hell, Roger Jett.

SMOKY. (1946) The tale of a cowboy's love for his horse, who starts out as a free stallion and ends up as a broken down nag hauling a junkman's cart. Of course, they're reunited and the film has held up well as children's entertainment.
                                          ★★★
D: Louis King; W: Lily Hayward, Dwight Cummins and Dorothy Yost; Ph: Charles Clarke; M: David Raksin.
Cast: Fred MacMurray, Anne Baxter, Burl Ives, Bruce Cabot.

SMOKY. (1966) No effort was made to update the story for a new generation and the ingredients are faithfully in place. Fess Parker does a presentable job in the Fred MacMurray role.
                                          ★★
D: George Sherman; W: Harold Medford; Ph: Jack Swain.
Cast: Fess Parker, Diana Hyland, Katy Jurado, Hoyt Axton.

SMOKEY AND THE BANDIT. (1977) Car chases and crashes and CB radio slang are directed at those with their "ears on" and their brains in neutral. An amiable cast with Burt Reynolds smirking at the wheel of his souped-up Pontiac and Jackie Gleason fuming in pursuit. People in the movie keep saying things are "negatory," and the whole thing is sheer purgatory for anyone interested in more than auto wrecks.
PG   ★★
D: Hal Needham; W: James Lee Barrett, Charles Shyer, Alan Mandel; Ph: Bobby Byrne; M: Bill Justis, Jerry Reed, Art Feller.
Cast: Burt Reynolds, Sally Field, Jackie Gleason, Jerry Reed.

SMOKEY AND THE BANDIT II. (1980) Better stunts, worse language, but this still

turned out to be a bad new movie from the good old boys. This time, the sheriff is chasing a pregnant elephant instead of a truckload of beer, but nothing saves this production from being an all-out turkey. Two Texans commission the bandit to transport the pachyderm for $400,000. Money is also the only reason for the existence of this sequel.
PG. ★
D: Hal Needham; W: Jerry Belson, Brock Yates; Ph: Michael Butler; M: Snuff Garrett.
Cast: Burt Reynolds, Sally Field, Jerry Reed, Jackie Gleason.

SMOKEY AND THE BANDIT—PART 3.
(1983) In the opening credits we see Burt Reynolds laughing hysterically and Jackie Gleason picking up a dog dropping on a beach. Reynolds is laughing because he's not in the rest of the movie and Gleason is wincing at a discovery that symbolizes the witless shambles that follows. How you can make a Smokey film without the bandit is beyond me. And beyond the scriptwriters, who served their apprenticeship scrawling on the wall of a bus station washroom.
PG. ★
D: Dick Lowry; W: Stuart Birnbaum and David Dashey; Ph: James Pergola; M: Larry Cansler.
Cast: Jackie Gleason, Jerry Reed, Paul Williams, Pat McCormick.

SMURFS AND THE MAGIC FLUTE.
(1983) An eighty-minute cartoon feature originally made for television in Europe. The smurfs look for a magic flute in a story set in medieval times. Quite pleasant, but the animation is fairly low-budget.
G. ★★
D and W: John Rust; M: Michel Legrand.

THE SNAKE PIT. (1948) Although madness is a staple convenience of Hollywood plots, mental institutions are another matter. *The Snake Pit* went behind the walls and faced up to the way the mentally ill were treated. The attitudes and techniques espoused seem as primitive as they are sincere. Olivia De Havilland is a married woman who becomes unhinged but whose mind is rescued by a psychiatrist.
★★★
D: Anatole Litvak; W: Frank Partos and Millen Brand; Ph: Leo Tover; M: Alfred Newman.
Cast: Olivia De Havilland, Leo Genn, Mark Stevens, Celeste Holm.

THE SNOWS OF KILIMANJARO. (1952)

The reflections of a wounded hunter on his life become a series of flashbacks. The memories are culled from several Hemingway novels and poorly mixed and it is the masculine posturing and rambling discourses on the writer's art and purpose that are given emphasis. A prostrate Gregory Peck is done in by the approach.
★★
D: Henry King; W: Casey Robinson; Ph: Leon Shamroy; M: Bernard Herrmann.
Cast: Gregory Peck, Susan Hayward, Ava Gardner, Hildegarde Neff.

SNOW WHITE AND THE SEVEN DWARFS. (1937) It took three years, 570 artists, 250,000 drawings and a vision on Walt Disney's part to prove that there was an audience for feature length animation. It has been there in huge numbers ever since. The animation, especially in the encounter of Snow White with the dwarfs, is superb and it set the Disney standard. For all his reputed penchant for cuteness, Disney here left the grimness in the Grimm Brothers fairy tale.
★★★★★
D: Walt Disney; M: Larry Morey and Frank Churchill.
Cast: (Voices) Adriana Caselotti, Lucille La Verne, Roy Atwell, Billy Gilbert.

SNUFF. (1976) A disgusting hoax that capitalized on press reports that a "snuff" film, in which an actress was killed and dismembered on camera, had been made in Argentina. This is an awful South American movie with a simulated murder at the end that the promoters tacked on and pretended was the real thing. It got reams of publicity. What it says about the people who would want to watch it does not bear contemplation.

S.O.B.(1981) Blake Edwards answers all those "Hooray for Hollywood" sentiments with a devastating Bronx cheer. His weapon of choice is a meat cleaver and he wields it mercilessly at the many available targets in Tinseltown. The humor is nasty enough to make *Shampoo* seem like a mild spoof. Robert Vaughn stands out as a studio chief with the scruples of a wharf rat and William Holden is wonderful as a boozy, nymphet-chasing director.
R. ★★★★
D and W: Blake Edwards; Ph: Harry Stradling; M: Henry Mancini.
Cast: William Holden, Julie Andrews, Richard Mulligan, Robert Vaughn.

SODOM AND GOMORRAH. (1963) You will not be turned into a pillar of salt if you make it through an often hilarious biblical epic. Stewart Granger finds it his unhappy lot to play Lot, who leads his cohorts away from much righteously depicted sin. Robert Aldrich directed like a confirmed atheist.

★★

D: Robert Aldrich; W: Aldrich and Giorgio Prosperi; Ph: Mario Montuori; M: Miklos Rozsa.
Cast: Stewart Granger, Pier Angeli, Stanley Baker, Rosanna Podesta.

SO FINE. (1981) Ryan O'Neal accidentally designs a new line of jeans for women with transparent rear panels. They're a sensation and they lend new meaning to the word hindsight. When the movie is taking the scissors to Seventh Avenue and the pretensions of fashion, it's very funny and Jack Warden is in inspired form as O'Neal's desperate father. Unfortunately, the bite is blunted by the film's preference for standard sex farce.
R. ★★★
D and W: Andrew Bergman; Ph: James Contner; M: Ennio Morricone.
Cast: Ryan O'Neal, Jack Warden, Mariangela Melato, Richard Kiel.

SOLARIS. (1976) "My God! What is all this talk?" demands a space station cosmonaut in this turgid and over-rated Russian entry into science fiction. A cosmonaut's mission—and unfortunately he decides to accept it—is disrupted when a life force on the planet Solaris reaches his mind. It has the ability to turn memories and thoughts into human reality. The movie doesn't. Wretched dubbing and actors who behave as if they were on their way to a labor camp.
★
D: Andrei Tarkovsky; W: Tarkovsky and Friedrich Gorenstein; Ph: Vadim Yusov; M: Eduard Artemyev.
Cast: Danatis Banionis, Natalya Bondarchuk, Yuri Jarvet.

THE SOLDIER. (1982) For people who like travelogues where tourist spots are blown up and for anyone who thinks the Joint Chiefs of Staff are a bunch of closet liberals. An elite CIA squad takes on terrorists bent on blowing up the world's oil supply. Dumb nonsense from the director of the even worse The Exterminator.
R. ★
D and W: James Glickenhaus; Ph: Robert M. Baldwin; M: Tangerine Dream.

Cast: Ken Wahl, Alberta Watson, Jeremiah Sullivan, William Prince.

SOLDIER OF FORTUNE. (1955) Ernest K. Gann, known chiefly for his aviation novels, hit the ground with a thud in a screen adaptation of his book. Clark Gable goes through the motions as a smuggler helping Susan Hayward find her husband in Red China. Routine and tainted by Cold War rhetoric.
★★
D: Edward Dmytryk; W: Ernest K. Gann; Ph: Leo Tover; M: Hugo Friedhofer.
Cast: Clark Gable, Susan Hayward, Gene Barry, Michael Rennie.

SOMEBODY UP THERE LIKES ME. (1956) Robert Wise had already established his primacy in the field with The Set-Up and his dramatization of the life of Rocky Graziano is a follow-up punch that also lands on target. Paul Newman is Graziano and it's an honest and involving piece of work that surmounts the occasional up-from-the-streets contrivance inherent in this kind of story. Graziano made it all the way to the middleweight championship of the world.
★★★★
D: Robert Wise; W: Ernest Lehman; Ph: Joseph Ruttenberg; M: Bronislau Kaper.
Cast: Paul Newman, Anna Maria Pierangeli, Eileen Heckart, Everett Sloane.

SOME KIND OF HERO. (1982) As in so many other areas of life, Vietnam veterans deserve better than this shabby and clumsy piece of mediocrity. Richard Pryor comes home after a stint as a prisoner of the Viet Cong and the many painful truths he must face are lost in broad comedy that is entirely inappropriate to the subject. Where a darkly absurdist humor might work, Pryor is busy wetting his pants in a bank hold-up.
R. ★★
D: Michael Pressman; W: Robert Boris and James Kirkwood; Ph: King Baggot; M: Patrick Williams.
Cast: Richard Pryor, Ray Sharkey, Margot Kidder, Ronny Cox.

SOME LIKE IT HOT. (1959) Jack Lemmon, in drag, tells his rich suitor that he's a man. "Nobody's perfect," is the famous riposte. Billy Wilder's uproarious comedy is close to perfection. The pace is exuberant, the laughter non-stop and Wilder's judgement of how long to milk each gag and situation is unfailing. Jack Lemmon and Tony Curtis disguise themselves as women to escape the vengeance of a gangster in the twenties. They travel with an all-girl band that includes Marilyn Monroe, who is all woman throughout the picture.

★★★★★

D: Billy Wilder; W: Wilder and I.A.L. Diamond; Ph: Charles Lang, Jr.; M: Adolph Deutsch.
Cast: Jack Lemmon, Tony Curtis, Marilyn Monroe, George Raft.

SOMETHING WICKED THIS WAY COMES. (1983) It would be hard to imagine an odder couple than Ray Bradbury and Walt Disney, but the collaboration proves very effective in this thematically rich and tautly rendered ghost story. A carnival arrives in a small town and tempts the citizens by offering to fulfill their deepest desires. Two boys find the awful truth. Puritanical in tone, but it's a pleasure to find children as heroes instead of victims, which has become the norm for horror films. The acting is also well above the usual for this genre
PG. ★★★
D: Jack Clayton; W: Ray Bradbury; Ph: Stephen H. Burum; M: Dennis Ricotta.
Cast: Jason Robards, Jonathan Pryce, Vidal Peterson, Shawn Carson.

THE SONG OF BERNADETTE. (1943) In the nineteenth century a French peasant girl, Bernadette Soubirous, claims that she has seen the Virgin Mary at Lourdes. Hollywood's treatment is for the incurably religious, but Jennifer Jones, who won the Oscar, is a redeeming presence in the film. Henry King was more inclined to genuflect than direct, which did not stop the movie becoming a huge success.

★★

D: Henry King; W: George Seaton; Ph: Arthur Miller; M: Alfred Newman.
Cast: Jennifer Jones, William Eythe, Charles Bickford, Vincent Price.

SON OF FLUBBER. (1963) Flabby sequel to *The Absent-Minded Professor* which repeats the gags that barely stood up the first time around. The invention this time is "dry rain" and the comic consequences of using it. The basketball game in the original is replaced by a football contest involving the use of "flubbergas." The film suffers from similar inflation.

★★

D: Robert Stevenson; W: Bill Walsh and Donald Da Gradi; Ph: Edward Colman; M: George Bruns.

Cast: Fred MacMurray, Nancy Olson, Tommy Kirk, Keenan Wynn.

SON OF FURY. (1942) Tyrone Power is mad at his uncle for cheating him out of his inheritance and sails off to the South Seas where he finds a girl and a lot of pearls which enable him to finance his legal fight back home. This one is no great gem, but a good instance of Power's way with an adventure.

★★★

D: John Cromwell; W: Philip Dunne; Ph: Arthur Miller; M: Alfred Newman.
Cast: Tyrone Power, Gene Tierney, George Sanders, Frances Farmer.

SON OF SINBAD. (1955) The Catholic League of Decency decried what used to be called cheesecake packed into the junior Sinbad's adventures, mostly having to do with saving Baghdad. Otherwise as dopey as Hollywood Arabian nights usually get. Vincent Price throws in some camp lines as Omar the Tentmaker.

★★

D: Jack Pollexfen; W: Aubrey Wisberg; Ph: Ted Tetzlaff; M: Victor Young.
Cast: Dale Robertson, Vincent Price, Sally Forrest, Lili St. Cyr.

SONS AND LOVERS. (1960) A sensitive and rewarding translation of D.H. Lawrence's autobiographical novel to the screen. Trevor Howard, in one of his outstanding roles, is the gruff, coal-miner who disdains the artistic ambitions of his son. Jack Cardiff framed strong acting with a view of Nottinghamshire that makes you understand the strength of the urge to get out.

★★★★

D: Jack Cardiff; W: Gavin Lambert and T.E.B. Clarke; Ph: Freddie Francis; M: Mario Nascimbene.
Cast: Trevor Howard, Dean Stockwell, Wendy Hiller, Mary Ure.

THE SONS OF KATIE ELDER. (1965) A rollicking and not especially challenging western that convenes four sons at the grave of their mother. The father is already dead and it's time to settle some scores in town. The movie stays in a predictable rut, but it is cheerfully without airs.

★★

D: Henry Hathaway; W: William Wright, Alan Weiss and Harry Essex; Ph: Lucien Ballard; M: Elmer Bernstein.
Cast: John Wayne, Dean Martin, Martha Hyer, Earl Holliman.

SOPHIE'S CHOICE. (1982) William Styron's novel confronts the adaptor with a bewildering array of options and Alan Pakula made all the right choices. He found the heart of the story in its major contrasts. A young southern writer of little experience but much imagination meets Sophie, a survivor from Warsaw, in New York after the war. She has suffered things beyond imagining. Secondly, having escaped the madness and barbarity of the camps, she finds more insanity in the New World in the person of her lover Nathan. Pakula ranges back and forth to unfold the terrible truth and the choice that confronted Sophie. It is work of exquisite acting and calibrated tension.

R.   ★★★★★
D and W: Alan Pakula; Ph: Nestor Almendros; M: Marvin Hamlisch.
Cast: Meryl Streep, Peter MacNicol, Kevin Kline, Rita Karin.

SORCERER. (1977) William Friedkin's rather garbled remake of Henri-Georges Clouzot's classic *The Wages of Fear* places four strangers in a primitive South American jungle town. Their only way out is by driving trucks loaded with nitroglycerine along rough roads. Friedkin isn't always in the driver's seat as he tries to create tension visually. Despite the investment of $20 million and a laconic contribution from Roy Scheider, he merely increases one's regard for the French original.

PG.   ★★
D: William Friedkin; W: Walon Green; Ph: John M. Stephens; Cast: Roy Scheider, Bruno Cremer, Francisco Rabal.

SORRY, WRONG NUMBER. (1948) Originally a radio play and not an especially original one at that, this is something that is better heard than seen. For all Anatole Litvak's energy with the camera and the use of sound to frighten, it's a humdrum melodrama in the helpless woman vein. Barbara Stanwyck, confined to bed, picks up the phone and overhears a plot to kill her.

                                            ★★
D: Anatole Litvak; W: Lucille Fletcher; Ph: Sol Polito; M: Franz Waxman.
Cast: Barbara Stanwyck, Burt Lancaster, Ann Richards, Wendell Corey.

THE SOUND AND THE FURY. (1959) A weird version of William Faulkner's novel that is melodramatic and crammed with the various forms of decadence that are *de rigueur* for this kind of southern family. Yul Brynner is miscast as the family head and Joanne Woodward is a young woman trying to find love outside the troubled household.

                                            ★★
D: Martin Ritt; W: Irving Ravetch and Harriet Frank, Jr.; Ph: Charles Clarke; M: Alex North.
Cast: Yul Brynner, Joanne Woodward, Margaret Leighton, Stuart Whitman.

SOUTHERN COMFORT. (1981) A clumsy parable of Vietnam that only seems valid after one has consumed a generous quantity of the booze for which the movie is named. In 1975, a squad of Louisiana National guardsmen stray into Cajun swamp country and provokes the wrath of the natives. Underneath the pretentious imagery, it's a poor cousin to *Deliverance*.

R.   ★★
D: Walter Hill; W: Hill, David Giler and Michael Kane; Ph: Andrew Laszlo; M: Ry Cooder.
Cast: Keith Carradine, Powers Booth, Les Lannom, Carlos Brown.

SOUTH PACIFIC. (1958) Nellie, the American nurse, and Emile, the French planter may not feel that age makes a difference but the years have not been notably kind to the screen version of the Rodgers and Hammerstein hit. Mitzi Gaynor's effervescence tends to be flattened out by Rossano Brazzi's low-keyed performance and the supporting players are more arresting than the leads. It no longer makes one feel younger than springtime, but the production is very handsome.

                                            ★★★
D: Joshua Logan; W: Paul Osborn; Ph: Leon Shamroy; M: Richard Rodgers.
Cast: Mitzi Gaynor, Rossano Brazzi, John Kerr, Ray Walston.

SOYLENT GREEN. (1973) In another four decades, New York will have more than gridlock and George Steinbrenner to worry about. Richard Fleischer sees the future and it doesn't work with pollution and overcrowding removing any real quality from life. His film doesn't work totally because of its portentous tone. Charlton Heston is one of New York's finest and he discovers the terrible truth about how the government is feeding people when a friend dies. The film was Edward G. Robinson's valedictory and a less than fitting end to a wonderful career.

PG.   ★★★
D: Richard Fleischer; W: Stanley Greenberg; Ph: Richard H. Kline; M: Fred Myrow.
Cast: Charlton Heston, Edward G. Robinson, Leigh Taylor-Young, Chuck Connors.

SPACEHUNTER. (1983) Peter Strauss is a sort of interplanetary garbage man in a cheerfully trashy tale of an adventurer's efforts to rescue three stranded women on a plague-ridden planet. The movie, which was released in 3D, features a villain called Overdog, part-man, part-robot and all histrionics. Very much a cartoon with no sympathy for the Overdog allowed. It took no particular advantage of its added dimension and the production values are shabby. Andrea Marcovicci walks off with the acting honors and she plays a robot.
PG. ★★
D: Lamont Johnson; W: Edith Rey, David Preston, Dan Goldberg and Len Blum; Ph: Frank Tidy; M: Elmer Bernstein.
Cast: Peter Strauss, Michael Ironside, Molly Ringwald, Andrea Marcovicci.

SPARKLE. (1976) All that glitters is not gold in a movie that blows a chance to be good. The film conveys its setting—Harlem in the late fifties—well enough. It then opts for lurid melodrama about three sisters who form an act and make it to the top of the charts. Personal complications set in as the girls try to overcome their ghetto origins. A soap opera that doesn't wash. Admirers of Curtis Mayfield will like the score.
PG. ★★
D: Sam O'Steen; W: Joel Schumacher; Ph: Bruce Surtees; M: Curtis Mayfield.
Cast: Philip M. Thomas, Irene Cara, Lonette McKee, Dwan Smith.

A SPECIAL DAY. (1977) Ettore Scola makes this special by taking pains with the ordinary details of life. Reminiscent of *Brief Encounter*, the film brings together two lost souls in 1938 in Mussolini's Italy. Sophia Loren is married to a lout whose idea of a celebration is to impregnate her with yet another child. Marcello Mastroianni is a bachelor clerk and homosexual. For one day, they find refuge with each other in the political chaos around them. Low-key and unpretentious and admirable for the quiet eloquence of the acting
★★★
D: Ettore Scola; W: Ruggero Maccari, Ettore Scola, Maurizio Costanzo; Ph: Pasqualino De Santis; M: Armando Travailoli.
Cast: Sophia Loren, Marcello Mastroianni, John Vernon, Francoise Berd.

SPECIAL SECTION. (1975) Costa-Gavras could have made one of his pulsating political thrillers, but he went after something much deeper. After the assassination of a

German naval officer in Occupied France, the Vichy government has to execute six dissidents as scapegoats. But first they must be convicted in kangaroo court. The film judges the judges and becomes a potent study of hypocrisy and venality when they try to rationalize and justify their conduct.
PG. ★★★★★
D: Costa-Gavras; W: Costa-Gavras and Jorge Semprun; Ph: Andreas Winding; M: Eric Demarsan.
Cast: Michel Lonsdale, Ivo Garrani, Louis Seigner, Francois Maistre.

SPHINX. (1981) Franklin Schaffner opens in ancient Egypt with grave-robbers being torn apart by wild horses and his rendition of Robin Cook's sloppy novel disintegrates with the same abruptness. A thriller that plays like a travelogue, it has Frank Langella hounding antique smugglers and Lesely-Anne Down posing next to pyramids.
PG. ★★
D: Franklin Schaffner; W: John Byrum; Ph: Ernest Day; M: Michael J. Lewis.
Cast: Frank Langella, Lesley-Anne Down, John Gielgud, Maurice Ronet.

THE SPIRIT OF ST. LOUIS. (1957) Not even a flier of Charles Lindbergh's credentials could find a way to soar over the inherent problem of dramatizing a solo flight. A man sitting in a cockpit for 33½ hours and 3600 miles is hardly the kind of thing to keep you glued to the edge of your seat. James Stewart, re-creating Lindbergh's historic 1927 transAtlantic flight, does much to ease the boredom of the journey.
★★★
D: Billy Wilder; W: Wilder and Wendell Mayes; Ph: Robert Burks; M: Franz Waxman.
Cast: James Stewart, Murray Hamilton, Marc Connelly, Patricia Smith.

SPITFIRE. (1942) An instance of a film remembered more for its score than its dramatic content. Walton's music lives on as *Spitfire Prelude and Fugue* and it catches the courageous spirit of R.T. Mitchell. He designed the Spitfire, the fighter plane that helped the Royal Air Force prevail over the Luftwaffe in the Battle of Britain. Mitchell's belief in his unique aerodynamic design, beginning in the twenties, is presented as a triumph of perseverance over conservative prejudice. Patriotic without being overbearing.
★★★
D: Leslie Howard; M: William Walton.
Cast: Leslie Howard, David Niven, Anne Firth, Roland Culver.

SPLENDOR IN THE GRASS. (1961) Elia Kazan imposed some needed restraint on the volatile ingredients and his treatment of young lovers in Kansas during the twenties is passionate without being overblown. They suffer mightily when they meet with parental opposition and although the film reaches out to the emerging youthful protest of the time, it does not pander to it. Wiliam Inge's screenplay won the Oscar and Warren Beatty made his debut.

★★★

D: Elia Kazan; W: William Inge; Ph: Boris Kaufman; M: David Amram.
Cast: Natalie Wood, Warren Beatty, Pat Hingle, Audrey Christie.

SPRING BREAK. (1983) The director of this vile piece of teen exploitation is Sean Cunningham, who made his dubious reputation in horror films like *Friday the 13th*. He decided to branch out into a movie that was merely horrible in this outing. The film combines the plot of an old beach movie with the kind of snickering vulgarity and sexual explicitness found in *Porky's* and its ilk. Four young men go to Fort Lauderdale for a mindless time and that's just what the film offers. Strictly for jiggle voyeurs.

R.   ★

D: Sean Cunningham; W: David Smilow; Ph: Stephen Poster; M: Harry Manfredini.
Cast: David Knell, Steve Bassett, Perry Lang, Paul Land.

S*P*Y*S . (1974) As the asterisks suggest, the idea was to reteam Elliott Gould and Donald Sutherland and cash in on the success of *M*A*S*H*. Irvin Kershner would doubtless like to forget this spy spoof and that's easy since there isn't a memorable moment in it. Gould and Sutherland are Paris-based CIA agents who bungle the defection of a Russian athlete who has been promised a date with Linda Lovelace. It all ends up with a microdot code in a pooch's contact lens. The picture itself is simply a dog.

PG.   ★

D: Irvin Kershner; W: Malcolm Marmorstein and Lawrence J. Cohen; Ph: Gerry Fisher; M: John Scott.
Cast: Elliott Gould, Donald Sutherland, Joss Ackland, Kenneth Griffith.

THE SPY WHO LOVED ME. (1977) The tenth James Bond film lacks a crucial ingredient — Ian Fleming. The movie uses Fleming's recipe without his skill as Bond pursues a villain who kidnaps nuclear submarines. It sticks to the formula of cunning gadgets and stunning women, but, like Bond drawing his Walther PPK, the movie always reaches for the automatic. It marked Moore's third effort as Bond and the series was already beginning to be overwhelmed by its own technology.

PG.   ★★

D: Lewis Gilbert; W: Christopher Wood, Richard Maibaum; Ph: Claude Renoir; M: Marvin Hamlisch.
Cast: Roger Moore, Curt Jurgens, Barbara Bach, Richard Kiel.

STAGECOACH. (1939) The characters aboard the most celebrated single vehicle in western movies have suffered the flattery of almost compulsive imitation down through the years. John Ford's classic is best enjoyed by remembering that it was once an original conception. The doctor on the bottle, the tart with the golden heart, the decent outlaw and the hypocritical businessman emerge in vivid portraits. The human squabbles are enclosed in the tiny passenger compartment and contrasted with the majesty of Monument Valley in a way that Ford makes increasingly ironic. The action scenes are justly renowned and Thomas Mitchell won an Oscar for his drunk.

★★★★★

D: John Ford; W: Dudley Nichols; Ph: Bert Glennon; M: Richard Hageman.
Cast: John Wayne, Claire Trevor, Thomas Mitchell, George Bancroft.

STAGECOACH. (1966) Alex Cord tries on John Wayne's boots and finds them many sizes too large in an all-star remake of the 1939 classic. The action is more plentiful but the faces of the newcomers pale in comparison with the characters in the original. Bing Crosby, in his last movie, did the best turn as the drunken doctor.

★★

D: Gordon Douglas; W: Joseph Landon; Ph: William Clothier; M: Jerry Goldsmith.
Cast: Alex Cord, Ann-Margret, Bing Crosby, Robert Cummings.

STAGE DOOR. (1937) Katharine Hepburn won her first Oscar for her aspiring actress in *Morning Glory* and she does much the same kind of part here. The difference is the bitchy dialogue, mostly between Hepburn and Ginger Rogers. It's peppery and funny and moves the film past the usual cliches about making it on Broadway.

★★★

D: Gregory LaCava; W: Morris Ryskind and

Anthony Veiller; Ph: Robert de Grasse; M: Roy Webb.
Cast: Katharine Hepburn, Ginger Rogers, Adolphe Menjou, Gail Patrick.

STAGE STRUCK. (1958) A not especially striking remake of *Morning Glory*, the movie about an aspiring Broadway actress that had the real-life impact of propelling Katharine Hepburn to stardom. Susan Strasberg takes the Hepburn role of Eva Lovelace, but the shoes are several sizes too large for her to fill. The cast is a good one if you can put up with the theater movie banalities.
★★★
D: Sidney Lumet; W: Ruth and Augustus Goetz; Ph: Franz Planer; M: Alex North.
Cast: Susan Strasberg, Henry Fonda, Christopher Plummer, Joan Greenwood.

STAIRCASE. (1969) For its time, the study of two aging homosexuals was at least a step in the right direction, even though Stanley Donen lays on the sentimentality with a trowel. Originally a two-man play, it was opened up for Richard Burton and Rex Harrison as two old queens discovering their need for each other in a cruel world. Burton's edgy, whining performance is splendid.
★★
D: Stanley Donen; W: Charles Dyer; Ph: Christopher Challis; M: Dudley Moore.
Cast: Richard Burton, Rex Harrison, Cathleen Nesbitt, Beatrix Lehmann.

STALAG 17. (1953) William Holden won the best actor Oscar for his Sefton, a prisoner of war who seems to be a selfish loner and a German informer and the very antithesis of the escapist hero of the standard POW movie. The smooth mixing of comedy and suspense plays off stereotypes and shows what the behavior of the men behind the barbed wire was really like.
★★★
D: Billy Wilder; W: Wilder and Edwin Blum; Ph: Ernest Laszlo; M: Franz Waxman.
Cast: William Holden, Don Taylor, Robert Strauss, Harvey Lembeck.

STANLEY AND LIVINGSTONE. (1939) The tale behind the famous question, "Dr. Livingstone, I presume?" Spencer Tracy is the American journalist who undertook one of history's most grueling assignments when his editor dispatched him to find the lost Scottish missionary. Henry King spliced in a great deal of location footage to make the quest realistic.
★★★

D: Henry King; W: Philip Dunne and Julien Josephson; Ph: George Barnes; M: Louis Silvers.
Cast: Spencer Tracy, Nancy Kelly, Richard Greene, Walter Brennan.

STAR. (1968) Gertrude Lawrence would have a hard time recognizing herself in what turns out to be a star vehicle for Julie Andrews. It badly needs an overhaul, but the format at least allows the inclusion of a wide range of songs from the likes of George Gershwin and Noel Coward. Backstage and outside the theater, it's another matter with Andrews rising from music hall obscurity to Broadway stardom.
★★
D: Robert Wise; W: William Fairchild; Ph: Ernest Laszlo; M: Lennie Hayton.
Cast: Julie Andrews, Daniel Massey, Richard Crenna, Michael Craig.

STAR CHAMBER. (1983) What would happen if judges, disgusted with the nitpicking legalisms of the modern court system, took the law—or more acurately justice—into their own hands? Peter Hyams' answer is fascinating and provocative but it begins in the middle when Michael Douglas joins the Star Chamber. Our curiosity about the founding of the secret court is never satisfied. Douglas is a young jurist converted to the extreme measures of his seniors with dramatic consequences. The issues here are usually confined to *Death Wish* movies and it is satisfying to see them intelligently aired.
R.   ★★★
D: Peter Hyams; W: Hyams and Roderick Taylor; Ph: Richard Hannah; M: Michael Small.
Cast: Michael Douglas, Hal Holbrook, Yaphet Kotto, Sharon Gless.

STARDUST MEMORIES. (1980) Instead of discussing the problems of being Woody Allen, the font of his great movies, Woody Allen takes up the problem of being as famous as Woody Allen. He is withering in his scorn for film buffs, critics, groupies, studio exectuvies and other deserving victims. It takes place on one of those meet-the-film-maker weekends that directors and stars masochistically attend. There is a note of arrogance in Woody's wailing about the cross he has to bear and it's something he would skewer in one of his characters.
PG.   ★★★
D and W: Woody Allen; Ph: Gordon Willis .
Cast: Woody Allen, Charlotte Rampling, Jessica Harper, Marie-Christine Barrault.

STAR 80. (1983) Film and reality become inseparable. Dorothy Stratten was murdered by her jealous and pyschopathic husband after appearing in Peter Bogdanovich's *They All Laughed*. The husband apparently suspected an affair between his wife and the director, killed her and then committed suicide. Bob Fosse recreates this harrowing story with a great deal of style but evinces no substantive conclusions about its implications. The revulsion one feels towards the sleazy husband undermines both the structure and impact of the film.
R.   ★★★
D and W: Bob Fosse; Ph: Sven Nykvist; M: Ralph Burns.
Cast: Mariel Hemingway, Eric Roberts, Cliff Robertson, Carroll Baker.

A STAR IS BORN. (1954) Studio hacks cut 37 minutes from this Hollywood classic to appease exhibitors worried about the running time. The footage was recently restored for a reissue and you should seek out the full version. Judy Garland was born with the talent to play Esther Blodgett and she lived a life that allowed her to invest the role with a touching conviction. James Mason's Norman Maine is more than equal to Garland's strong presence and *A Star is Born* remains one of the definitive works on the Hollywood dream machine and its victims.
                                            ★★★★★
D: George Cukor; W: Moss Hart; Ph: Sam Leavitt; M: Ray Heindorf (md).
Cast: Judy Garland, James Mason, Charles Bickford, Jack Carson.

A STAR IS BORN. (1976) The third version of the story proves Barbra Streisand's greatness as a singer while magnifying her deficiencies as an actress. The writing is full of lines like "If you die, I'll kill you" to burden the players. In placing the familiar ingredients in a rock setting, the movie makes us hope for a reappraisal and updating of the story. It's still just a remake of the price-of-success theme that does not translate to contemporary terms or recognize changes in public attitudes to stardom between Garland and Streisand.
R.   ★★
D: Frank Pierson; W: John Gregory Dunne, Joan Didion; Ph: Robert Surtees; M: Paul Williams.
Cast: Barbra Streisand, Kris Kristofferson, Paul Mazursky.

STARS AND STRIPES FOREVER. (1952) Hollywood marches roughshod over the truth in a sentimental biography of John Philip Sousa. Even so, Clifton Webb is an engaging Sousa, the march king, who left the marines and whose flair for bouncy tunes won him international fame. The bouyancy of the 1890s is there and so, more importantly, is the music.
                                            ★★
D: Henry Koster; W: Lamar Trotti; Ph: Charles Clarke; M: Alfred Newman(arr.).
Cast: Clifton Webb, Debra Paget, Robert Wagner, Ruth Hussey.

THE STARS LOOK DOWN. (1939) Carol Reed's version of A.J. Cronin's novel yields very little to *How Green Was My Valley* as a stirring and socially conscious study of the plight of miners. In Northeast England, a miner's son goes to university, returns to the aptly named Sleesdale and makes a disastrous marriage. The conditions under which miners were forced to work provide the pivotal action.
                                            ★★★★
D: Carol Reed; W: J.B. Williams; Ph: Mutz Greenbaum; M: H. May.
Cast: Michael Redgrave, Margaret Lockwood, Emlyn Williams, Nancy Price.

STARTING OVER. (1979) Neither Burt Reynolds nor Alan Pakula found what might be better titled *An Unmarried Man* to be material congenial to their talents. Reynolds wife walks out and he spends his time deciding if he should pursue her or his new girlfriend. Some funny moments, especially a divorced men's support group discussion, but Pakula is too low-key and *Starting Over* finishes limply.
R.   ★★
D: Alan Pakula; W: James L. Brooks; Ph: Sven Nykvist; M: Marvin Hamlisch.
Cast: Burt Reynolds, Jill Clayburgh, Candice Bergen, Charles Durning.

STAR TREK—THE MOTION PICTURE. (1980) Robert Wise was widely pilloried for the slow pace and tendency to stop and admire his own effects and gadgetry. Indeed the ride up to the *Enterprise* is interminable, but you don't have to be a trekkie to admire the willingness to try for an intelligent story and the way the characters are fleshed out. Kirk, now an admiral, leaves his boring desk job to resume command of the star-ship when a force of unprecedented power moves toward Earth.
G.   ★★★
D: Robert Wise; W: Harold Livingston; Ph: Richard H. Kline; M: Jerry Goldsmith.

Cast: William Shatner, Leonard Nimoy, Stephen Collins, DeForest Kelley.

STAR TREK II—THE WRATH OF KHAN.
(1982) The second big screen outing of the Enterprise—like the old television series—was under severe budget limits by contemporary sci-fi standards. Nicholas Meyer gives us a cinematically scaled treatment of a lesser episode from the series. Its more interesting element deals with the creation of life in something called Project Genesis, but that takes a back seat to a tired vengeance melodrama. As Khan, Ricardo Montalban looks like Sid Vicious on Social Security. This one, however, moves faster and is not in awe of its own hardware.
PG. ★★★
D: Nicholas Meyer; W: Jack Sowards; Ph: Gayne Rescher; M: James Horner.
Cast: William Shatner, Leonard Nimoy, Ricardo Montalban, DeForest Kelley.

STAR TREK III—THE SEARCH FOR SPOCK.
(1984) Ending feverish Spockulation on what happened to the world's favorite Vulcan, Leonard Nimoy also directed a first class piece of science-fiction. He shunned the occasionally ponderous tone of the first adventure and the campiness of the second and intuitively brought out the strengths of Gene Roddenberry's initial ideas. He deals with issues of loyalty and moral choice with considerable sophistication and emotional power when Captain Kirk and company take matters into their own hands to find out the truth about Spock's fate.
PG. ★★★★
D: Leonard Nimoy; W: Harve Bennett; Ph: Charles Correll; M: James Horner.
Cast: Leonard Nimoy, William Shatner, DeForest Kelley, Christopher Lloyd.

STAR WARS.
(1977) George Lucas renewed the science fiction genre and redefined what people expect of it in a film so successful that it is part of our popular culture. The moment the space cruiser passes overhead at the beginning establishes a level of technical brilliance and a sense of absolute reality never before seen in a space adventure. Lucas cunningly mined the best of the B movies for a quest in which a young man, a cynical pilot and a fugitive princess take on the evil forces of the empire. The film has also had enormous influence on the economics of film-making and has persuaded Hollywood to pursue blockbusters at the expense of smaller pictures, but that's not Lucas' fault.
PG. ★★★★★
D and W: George Lucas; Ph: Gilbert Taylor; M: John Williams.
Cast: Mark Hamill, Carrie Fisher, Harrison Ford, Alec Guiness, Peter Cushing.

STATE FAIR.
(1945) The reason for remaking the Will Rogers picture was musical. And since the men behind the music were Rodgers and Hammerstein, it was a pretty good reason. Hammerstein also wrote the screenplay, which was not such a good idea. The Frake family win prizes and lovers at the Iowa state fair and you can enjoy songs like *It Might as Well be Spring*.
★★★
D: Walter Lang; W: Oscar Hammerstein; Ph: Leon Shamroy; M: Richard Rodgers and Oscar Hammerstein.
Cast: Jeanne Crain, Dana Andrews, Dick Haymes, Vivian Blaine.

THE STATE OF THINGS.
(1982) Wim Wenders' statement on the ancient conflict between art and money in the film world. He had the failure of his first English-language film, *Hammett*, to fuel his argument. He chooses a film-within-a film format that is quite effective in the early going. A stranded director and his company have to deal with treachery back in Hollywood. An intriguing, if rather contrived addition to an old debate.
★★★
D: Wim Wenders; W: Wenders and Robert Kramer; Ph: Henri Alekan and Fred Murphy; M: Jurgen Knieper.
Cast: Patrick Bachau, Paul Getty, 3d, Sam Fuller, Allen Goorwitz.

THE STATIONMASTER'S WIFE.
(1977) A bizarre combination of satire and melodrama that confirms the view that the brilliant Rainer Werner Fassbinder was a better director when he was not exorcising private demons. The stationmaster is an unlovable slob who is cuckolded and then brought down by his neighbors. In his scornful rendering of a simple story, Fassbinder speaks volumes through this Bavarian microcosm about the climate that made Nazism possible.
★★★★
D and W: Rainer Werner Fassbinder; Ph: Michael Ballhaus; M: Peer Raben.
Cast: Kurt Raab, Elisabeth Trissenaar, Bernhard Helfrich.

STAVISKY. (1974) Alain Resnais' witty and beautifully mounted re-creation of the Stavisky scandal which shook France in the thirties. Directed in Resnais' free-form enigmatic style, the film wanders back and forth over the principals and events in Stavisky's international fraud schemes. Jean-Paul Belmondo is memorable as the spinner of this intricate web and corruption was never so stylish.

★★★★

D: Alain Resnais; W: Jore Semprun; Ph: Sacha Vierny; M: Stephen Sondheim.
Cast: Jean-Paul Belmondo, Charles Boyer, Anny Duperey, Francois Perier .

STAY HUNGRY. (1976) Charles (*Pumping Iron*) Gaines wrote the novel which offers a strange conflict between the nouveau riche of the new south and body builders in a seedy gym that stands in the way of development. Bob Rafelson's film version is at its best in studying the coming of age of an aimless and rich young man. Overburdened and ambitious and sorely in need of a sense of discipline and order.

R. ★★

D: Bob Rafelson; W: Charles Gaines; Ph: Victor Kemper; M: Bruce Langhorne and Byron Berline.
Cast: Jeff Bridges, Sally Field, Arnold Schwarzenegger, R.G. Armstrong.

STAYIN' ALIVE. (1983) In the sequel to *Saturday Night Live* the gritty blue collar atmosphere not to mention the blue language of the original is gone and John Travolta is transformed into an aerobic Rocky. Tony Manero is now an aspiring dancer on Broadway, but the story plays like *42d Street*. Travolta's charisma cannot carry the film past the deficiencies of a feeble script and a weaker score. He is torn between his girlfriend and the star of the show. The heavy hand of director Sylvester Stallone doesn't help either.

PG. ★

D: Sylvester Stallone; W: Stallone and Norman Wexler; Ph: Nick McClean; M: The Bee Gees and Frank Stallone.
Cast: John Travolta, Cynthia Rhodes, Finola Hughes, Steve Inwood.

THE STEPFORD WIVES. (1975) The modest clay of Ira Levin's novel turns into mud in the hands of usually reliable William Goldman. Something is rotten in the state of Connecticut—the women are perfectly content to be wives and obedient lovers. Katharine Ross, a new arrival, tries to find out why they are so mindlessly obliging. There was an opportunity here to combine a thriller with some pointed comments on male chauvinism. It was missed.

PG. ★★

D: Bryan Forbes; W: William Goldman; Ph: Owen Roizman; M: Michael Small.
Cast: Katharine Ross, Paula Prentiss, Nanette Newman, Peter Masterson.

STEVIE. (1981) The lives of poets are not generally congenial to the cinema, but this study of Stevie Smith is an exception. Glenda Jackson is predictably forceful as the British poet, who lived with a maiden aunt. The latter is memorably done by Mona Washbourne, as she moves from supporting her niece to depending on her with the passing years. A study of a relationship spiced with a dash of wit from Smith's poems and observations.

★★★

D: Robert Enders; W: Hugh Whitemore; Ph: Freddie Young; M: Patrick Gowers.
Cast: Glenda Jackson, Mona Washbourne, Alec McCowen, Trevor Howard.

STILL OF THE NIGHT. (1982) Robert Benton's salute to Hitchcock has an unmystifying mystery that has you counting the references to the maestro instead of watching the film as a whole. Meryl Streep is a Hitchcockian ice goddess who shows up in a psychiatrist's office after her lover is murdered. The doctor is drawn into the dark intrigues surrounding her. Is she a murderer or the victim of her own past? Since there are only two suspects, it's not much of a question and that puts too much emphasis on the skimpily written relationship of the shrink and his patient.

R. ★★★

D and W: Robert Benton; Ph: Nestor Almendros; M: John Kander.
Cast: Roy Scheider, Meryl Streep, Jessica Tandy, Joe Grifasi.

STILL SMOKIN'. (1983) Cheech and Chong go Dutch, but the audience ends up paying the bill. Even by their witless standards, the film sets a new low in how to fill 90 minutes with vulgarity, dope jokes, marijuana smoke and saying "man" five times in every sentence. Easily the funniest comedy duo since Leopold and Loeb, the pair goes to the Amsterdam Film Festival. This was not an entry.

R. ★

D: Thomas Chong; W: Cheech Marin and

Chong; Ph: Harvey Harrison; M: George S. Clinton.
Cast: Cheech Marin, Tommy Chong, Susan Hahn.

STINGRAY. (1978) Shot in St. Louis and guaranteed to give the blues to anyone over the age of ten. Two pals buy a red Corvette without knowing that there is a cache of heroin in the trunk. Sherry Jackson leads the gang pursuing them. Lamebrained action, tasteless humor and quite bloody.
PG. ★
D and W: Richard Taylor; Ph: Frank Miller; M: Murray MacLeod.
Cast: Chris Mitchum, Sherry Jackson, Les Lannom, Bill Watson.

STIR CRAZY. (1980) A comedy about doing time that expends most of its length marking time. A lot of the humor depends on how funny you find the harsh realities of life in our prisons—rape, violence and corruption. Gene Wilder and Richard Pryor (his last film before the celebrated accident) are a pair of New Yorkers who are wrongly imprisoned for a bank robbery in the southwest. Much of what ensues borrows heavily from *The Longest Yard*.
R. ★★
D: Sidney Poitier; W: Bruce Jay Friedman; Ph: Fred Schuler; M: Tom Scott.
Cast: Gene Wilder, Richard Pryor, George Stanford Brown, Jobeth Williams.

ST. IVES. (1976) For Charles Bronson, this is non-violence of Gandhiesque dimensions, but unfortunately it's not much else. Bronson is an aspiring novelist and people keep coming up to ask "How's the book?" He responds with a manly shrug and goes off to retrieve some incriminating diaries that belong to a tycoon. It asks acting rather than action of Bronson and, for all his menacing presence, that is a mistake.
PG. ★★
D: J. Lee Thompson; W: Barry Beckerman; Ph: Lucien Ballard; M: Lalo Schifrin.
Cast: Charles Bronson, John Houseman, Jacqueline Bisset, Maximilian Schell.

STORMY WEATHER. (1943) A musical that is both unusual and rewarding with a dazzling array of black entertainers in a loosely connected string of numbers. Lena Horne sings the title song and she is joined by the likes of Fats Waller and Cab Calloway.
★★★
D: Andrew Stone; W: Frederick Jackson and Ted Koehler; Ph: Leon Shamroy; M: Emil Newman.
Cast: Lena Horne, Bill Robinson, Cab Calloway, Fats Waller.

THE STORY OF ADELE H. (1975) An exercise in Gothic passion with the daughter of Victor Hugo following a British officer to Nova Scotia and suffering from unrequited love and eventual madness. The subject is at odds with Francois Truffaut's objectives. He wants a distance between the audience and Adele but Isabelle Adjani, who was only 20 when she played Adele, blows Truffaut's coolness with a powerful and emotional performance. She won a deserved Oscar nomination for it.
★★★
D: Francois Truffaut; W: Truffaut, Jean Grualt and Suzanne Schiffman; Ph: Nestor Almendros; M: Maurice Jaubert.
Cast: Isabelle Adjani, Bruce Robinson, Sylvia Marriott.

THE STORY OF ALEXANDER GRAHAM BELL. (1939) One of the roles for which Don Ameche is fondly recalled. A more or less accurate account of the young teacher of the deaf who devised the telephone. He falls in love with a deaf girl and has to fend off a rival corporation. A little mawkish, but still enjoyable.
★★★
D: Irving Cummings; W: Lamar Trotti; Ph: Leon Shamroy; M: Louis Silvers.
Cast: Don Ameche, Loretta Young, Henry Fonda, Charles Coburn.

THE STORY OF G.I. JOE. (1945) Ernie Pyle was the most celebrated war correspondent in World War II and a journalist who furnished unembellished reports from the trench level. He saw the war from the viewpoint of the men who fought it rather than the generals who planned it. The film, with Burgess Meredith in a stirring account of Pyle, shares that perspective in tracing the campaign in Italy. Pyle was killed later while covering Okinawa.
★★★
D: William Wellman; W: Leopold Atlas, Guy Endore and Philip Stevenson; Ph: Russell Metty; M: Ann Ronell and Louis Applebaum.
Cast: Burgess Meredith, Robert Mitchum, Freddie Steele, Wally Cassell.

THE STORY OF LOUIS PASTEUR. (1936) The general thrust in the biography of the scientist is to uplift and educate rather than titillate. Given the life in question it could hardly be otherwise. What makes the difference is Paul Muni's humanizing presence as Pasteur, who developed a cure for rabies and did the pioneer work in the field of bacteriology. Occasionally as slow and dogged as scientific research, but equally rewarding for the patient.

★★★★

D: William Dieterle; W: Sheridan Gibney and Pierre Collins; Ph: Tony Gaudio.
Cast: Paul Muni, Josephine Hutchinson, Anita Louise, Donald Woods.

THE STORY OF MANKIND. (1957) Before he took up the manufacture of all-star disaster movies like *The Towering Inferno*, Irwin Allen concocted one of the all-time cinematic disasters. Should mankind be destroyed? While the debate rages upstairs, snippets of history acted out by a parade of screen luminaries who would dearly love to forget this epic are offered. If the film were the only evidence of human achievement, the debate would be very short.

★

D and W: Irwin Allen; Ph: Nicholas Musuraca; M: Paul Sawtell.
Cast: Ronald Colman, Vincent Price, Cedric Hardwicke, the Marx Brothers.

THE STORY OF O. (1975) The underground porn novel about sado-masochism is all Masters and no Johnson in a truly loathsome picture. A young woman proves her love by letting her man's friends abuse her. There is genuine obscenity in the way women are whipped and otherwise chastised and the film is probably the only one in existence that consists entirely of rough cuts. Its magazine glossiness makes it even more revolting.
X.
D: Just Jaeckin; W: Sebastien Japrisot; M: Pierre Bachelet.
Cast: Corinne Clery, Udo Kier, Anthony Steel, Jean Gaven.

THE STORY OF ROBIN HOOD. (1952) Ken Annakin admits to peeking at the classic Errol Flynn version before having a go at the legend for Walt Disney. His work stands up quite well with all the familiar incidents in place, handsome scenery and an expanded view of the love of Robin and Marian. Richard Todd is a pleasant Robin, if lacking in Flynn's elan.

★★★

D: Ken Annakin; W: Laurence E. Watkin; Ph: Guy Green; M: Clifton Parker.

Cast: Richard Todd, Joan Rice, James Hayter, Hubert Gregg.

THE STORY OF WILL ROGERS. (1952) The life of the entertainer and populist wit is given with a respect bordering on reverence that he might have questioned loudly. Rogers is played with affection by his son and the film traces his rise from folksy obscurity to the crash that killed him in 1935. But not before he had earned his place in American folklore.

★★★

D: Michael Curtiz; W: Frank Davis and Stanley Roberts; Ph: Wilfrid Cline; M: Victor Young.
Cast: Will Rogers, Jr., Jane Wyman, James Gleason, Eddie Cantor.

STRANGE BREW. (1983) The Mackenzie Brothers, of SCTV fame, save the world from a threat to its beer supply. The humor that makes them so amusing in television sketches on "The Great White North," Canada's dumbest talk show, doesn't stretch to the length of a feature. The script could also have used a few more drafts.
PG. ★★
D: Dave Thomas and Rick Moranis; W: Thomas, Moranis and Steve De Jarnatt; Ph: Steven Foster; M: Charles Fox.
Cast: Rick Moranis, Dave Thomas, Paul Dooley, Max Von Sydow.

A STRANGER IS WATCHING. (1981) Sean Cunningham sank even lower than his *Friday the 13th*. To the cellar underneath the oyster bar in Grand Central station to be precise. A violent, disgusting and consistently stupid horror flick about a little girl who witnesses her mother's rape and murder and who is subsequently kidnapped. By guess who?
R. ★
D: Sean Cunningham; W: Eric Mae Rauch and Victor Miller; M: Lalo Schifrin.
Cast: Rip Torn, Kate Mulgrew, James Naughton, Shawn von Schreiber.

STRANGERS ON A TRAIN. (1951) Alfred Hitchcock got Raymond Chandler to help out on the screenplay and the results put the director's career back on track. All his protean technical resources are marshalled for an elegant thriller in which a tennis star gets more than he bargained for in his dealings with a suave psychotic on a train.

★★★★★

D: Alfred Hitchcock; W: Raymond Chandler

and Czenzi Ormonde; Ph: Robert Burks; M: Ray Heindorf.
Cast: Farley Granger, Robert Walker, Ruth Roman, Leo G. Carroll.

STREAMERS. (1983) The title is paratrooper slang for a parachute that doesn't open and Robert Altman had grounds for feeling a similar lack of support in David Rabe's play. Three soliders—an urban black, a boy mildly ashamed of his education and sexual tendencies and a homosexual—await their orders for Vietnam in a Virginia barracks. Rabe has not resolved the perennial problem of writing for characters who are unaware of themselves and he offers declamatory statements where a subtle, revelatory line would serve. The soldiers lives are tragically disrupted by the intrusion of a troubled young black who hates the army.
R. ★★★
D: Robert Altman; W: David Rabe; Ph: Pierre Mignot.
Cast: Matthew Modine, Michael Wright, Mitchell Lichtenstein, David Alan Grier.

A STREETCAR NAMED DESIRE. (1951) Although the Oscars went to Vivien Leigh and others, this searing adaptation of Tennessee Williams's play (by the playwright) is now more celebrated for Marlon Brando's Stanley Kowalski. Brando's animal and brutal vigor and Leigh's vulnerability to it proved to be a once-in-a-lifetime fusion of talent and they were directed with faultless craft by Elia Kazan. Brando is so magnetic that it is possible to overlook the skill of the other actors. A good enough reason to see a treasured and very moving film again and again.
★★★★★
D: Elia Kazan; W: Tennessee Williams; Ph: Harry Stradling; M: Alex North.
Cast: Marlon Brando, Vivien Leigh, Karl Malden, Kim Hunter.

STREET PEOPLE. (1976) Rarely climbs out of the gutter and its only claim to attention is a piece of whimsical casting. Roger Moore plays a Sicilian, a role that leaves him with no defense. Otherwise, a typical movie made on the "buddy" system that pairs Moore with Stacy Keach in a search for heroin smugglers.
R. ★
D: Maurice Lucidi; W: Ernest Tidyman and Randall Kleiser; M: Luis Enriquez.
Cast: Roger Moore, Stacy Keach, Ivo Garrani, Ettori Manni.

STREETS OF FIRE. (1984) Walter Hill has a penchant for forgetting that it is hard to worry about what happens to someone you have not been made to care about. In what he styled a rock and roll fable, he achieved a failure of mythic proportions. In an unspecified time and place in the future, a man seeks to rescue his girlfriend who has been kidnapped by a punk gang. Heavily laden atmosphere encloses a vacuum and it's quite violent.
PG ★★
D: Walter Hill; W: Hill and Larry Gross; Ph: Andrew Laszlo; M: Ry Cooder.
Cast: Michael Pare, Diane Lane, Rick Moranis, Amy Madigan.

STRIPES. (1981) A juvenile service comedy that's as amusing as a draft notice in the morning mail. Everyone you expect—the maniacal tough drill sergeant, the idiot captain and the overdecorated general—is on parade. It is designed as a vehicle for Bill Murray and it's about as subtle as an armored personnel carrier trying to get out of a swamp.
R. ★
D: Ivan Reitman; W: Reitman, Bill Murray and Harold Ramis; Ph: Bill Butler; M: Elmer Bernstein.
Cast: Bill Murray, Harold Ramis, Warren Oates, Sean Young.

STROKER ACE. (1983) Having reached the end of the road in the *Smokey and the Bandit* series, Hal Needham and Burt Reynolds elected to go round in circles in a stock-car film. The *car*-toon is best watched with the brain idling at low revs. Ned Beatty, a fast-food tycoon, chews chicken and scenery in conning Reynolds into wearing a humiliating chicken suit for sales promotions. The whole dreary enterprise amounted to a humiliation for the star.
PG. ★
D: Hal Needham; W: Needham and Hugh Wilson; Ph: Nick McLean; M: Al Capps.
Cast: Burt Reynolds, Ned Beatty, Loni Anderson, Jim Nabors.

THE STRONGEST MAN IN THE WORLD. (1975) So-so Disney fare about college kids who discover a formula that gives superhuman strength. The movie is pretty much a formula proposition too with Phil Silvers and Eve Arden as rival cereal company magnates trying to steal the secret from the students.
G. ★★
D: Vincent McEveety; W: Joseph L. McEveety and Herman Groves; Ph: Andrew Jackson; M: Robert F. Brunner.

Cast: Kurt Russell, Joe Flynn, Eve Arden, Phil Silvers.

STROSZEK. (1977) An alcoholic German migrates to Wisconsin with all the usual hopes of an immigrant in one of Herzog's less esoteric efforts. Herzog can't decide whether the main character is a figure of honorable simplicity or mere pathos and the movie has nothing to add to many and better observations of American life. ★★
D and W: Werner Herzog; Ph: Thomas Mauch; M: Chet Atkins and Sonny Terry.
Cast: Bruno S., Eva Mattes, Clemens Scheitz.

STRYKER. (1983) A strike out. In a post-nuclear society, the most precious commodity is fresh water, but it takes a stiff drink to make it through a flagrant steal of the ideas in *The Road Warrior*. The latter was cheerfully derivative but brilliantly executed. *Stryker* is simply derivative. ★
R.
D: Howard Cohen; W: Leonard Hermes.
Cast: Steve Sandor, Andria Savio, William Ostrander, Michael Lane.

THE STUD. (1978) A prodgiously endowed dumb waiter rises to the top of the London disco scene by servicing Joan Collins, the wife of a club owner. Collins has only her sister Jackie to blame for concocting soft-core porn for the soft of head. Actually, the film is like a teenager boasting to his friends—a lot of talk but very little action. ★
R.
D: Quentin Masters; W: Jackie Collins; M: Biddu.
Cast: Joan Collins, Oliver Tobias, Sue Lloyd, Mark Burns.

A STUDY IN TERROR. (1965) John Neville and Donald Huston enter the highly competitive Holmes-Watson sweepstakes and they make a good team. As in the later and excellent *Murder by Decree*, the idea is to pit Holmes against Jack the Ripper. It's bloodier than the Holmesian norm, but intelligently presented. ★★★
D: James Hill; W: Donald and Derek Ford; Ph: Desmond Dickinson; M: John Scott.
Cast: John Neville, Donald Huston, John Fraser, Robert Morley.

THE STUNT MAN. (1980) More riddles than the sphinx asked, virtuoso variations on an enigma and a film that constantly risks tripping over its own cleverness. The best stunt is pulled off by Richard Rush who keeps this brilliant and ironic work on a tightrope. A convict escapes and is offered refuge by an overtly mad movie director in return for performing a dangerous stunt. *The Stunt Man* views this situation through a prism of constantly changing angles by choosing a figure whose job is to make illusion seem real. Capped by a classically manic performance from Peter O'Toole as the director. ★★★★★
R.
D: Richard Rush; W: Lawrence B. Marcus; Ph: Mario Tosi; M: Dominic Frontiere.
Cast: Peter O'Toole, Steve Railsback, Barbara Hershey, Alan Goorwitz.

THE ST. VALENTINE'S DAY MASSACRE. (1967) A routine rehash of Chicago's most famous shooting enhanced by a sobering view of Al Capone from Jason Robards. Roger Corman made more than a low budget quickie, but he got nervous and opted for gun battles instead of the characterization the talent on hand invited. ★★
D: Roger Corman; W: Howard Browne; Ph: Milton Krasner; M: Fred Steiner.
Cast: Jason Robards, George Segal, Ralph Meeker, Jean Hale.

SUBMARINE PATROL. (1938) John Ford admirers—and who isn't?—will be grateful that he's in command of the World War I action. In this warm-up for *Stagecoach*, Preston Foster takes over a dilapidated rustbucket anti-submarine ship and harries the crew back to efficiency before they sail off on a mission to the Adriatic. Ford handled the action with his usual aplomb. ★★★
D: John Ford; W: Rian James, Jack Yellen and Darrell Ware; Ph: Arthur Miller; M: Arthur Lange.
Cast: Preston Foster, Richard Greene, Nancy Kelly, George Bancroft.

SUBURBIA. (1983) Not the world of quiet tree-lined streets, but the home of a commune of teenagers in the shadows of the roaring freeways of Los Angeles. Penelope Spheeris' vision of their life is as depressingly well-done as *Over the Edge*. She concentrates on the tension between the punks and a nihilism expressed by the way they live and the "normal" people who have to deal with them. ★★★
R.

D and W: Penelope Spheeris; Ph: Timothy
Suhrstedt; M: Alex Gibson.
Cast: Chris Pedersen, Bill Coyne, Jennifer
Clay, Timothy Eric O'Brien.

SUDDEN IMPACT. (1983) The fourth
Dirty Harry outing has Clint Eastwood point
his .44 Magnum at a suspect who is reaching
for a gun and inviting him to "Make my day,
punk." Unless you're somewhere to the right
of Attila the Hun, who probably said something similar at the gates of Rome, this round
of police brutality is pretty heavy going. The
main plot involves a woman artist who takes
an extremely dim view of the men who raped
her and her sister and exacts a bloody vengeance.
R.   ★★
D: Clint Eastwood; W: Joseph Stinson; Ph:
Bruce Surtees; M: Lalo Schifrin.
Cast: Clint Eastwood, Sondra Locke, Pat
Hingle, Bradford Dillman.

SUEZ. (1938) The building of the Suez
Canal reduced to Tyrone Power's divided
loyalty to Annabella and Loretta Young.
Ferdinand De Lesseps, the French engineer
responsible for the massive undertaking,
was in his sixties. Hollywood knocked forty
years off his age for the convenience of
romance. Good spectacle helps atone for
blithely rewritten history.
                                              ★★
D: Allan Dwan; W: Philip Dunne and Julien
Josephson; Ph: Peverell Marley; M: Louis
Silvers.
Cast: Tyrone Power, Annabella, Loretta
Young, J. Edward Bromberg.

THE SUGARLAND EXPRESS. (1974) The
bountiful talent that would see Steven Spielberg become such a force in Hollywood in
the following ten years is very much in evidence here. He takes a true story of a wife
who springs her husband from jail so they
can retrieve their baby from its adoptive
parents and fashions a movie that is exciting
and touching. The chase—with a cavalcade
of police cars in pursuit of the couple and
the state trooper they kidnap—is played as
a media event as much as a pursuit. Goldie
Hawn's performance as the mother is especially winning.
PG.   ★★★★
D: Steven Spielberg; W: Hal Barwood and
Matthew Robbins; Ph: Vilmos Zsigmond; M:
John Williams.
Cast: Goldie Hawn, William Atherton, Ben
Johnson, Michael Sacks.

SULLIVAN'S TRAVELS. (1941) Preston
Sturges emulated his protagonist with delightful results. It deals with a Hollywood
director, who tires of the lightweight musicals that have made him rich and decides to
disguise himself as a tramp to discover the
real America and the lives of the poor. What
he finds is what you might expect, but what
happens to him gives the movie a biting irony.
                                            ★★★★
D and W; Preston Sturges; Ph: John Seitz; M:
Leo Shuken.
Cast: Joel McCrea, Veronica Lake, Robert
Warwick, William Demarest.

SUMMER LOVERS. (1982) The ancient
statues used as backdrops outplay the actors in Randal Kleiser's soft-headed celebration of a *menage a trois* in the Aegean islands.
The movie even has a credit for "Greek Director of Photography." Lots of nudity, but
rather tame sexually, the film goes for travel
poster exoticism rather than eroticism. Kleiser
takes his kids absolutely seriously, which
provides much unintended mirth but probably explains his success.
R.   ★★
D and W: Randal Kleiser; Ph: Timothy Galfas; M: Basil Poledouris.
Cast: Peter Gallagher, Daryl Hannah, Valerie
Quennessen, Barbara Rush.

THE SUN ALSO RISES. (1957) The sun
was also setting on the flamboyant career of
Errol Flynn, but he is the one character
worth watching in an unwieldly adaptation of
Hemingway's arguably unfilmable novel.
Flynn is an hilarious lush brightening the
attempt to catch the flavor of life for Ameri-
cans in Paris after World War I.
                                              ★★
D: Henry King; W: Peter Viertel; Ph: Leo
Tover; M: Hugo Friedhofer.
Cast: Tyrone Power, Ava Gardner, Mel Fer-
rer, Errol Flynn.

SUNBURN. (1979) The high point is a car
chase in Mexico that ends up with a bull
attacking Farrah Fawcett's car and thus
proving himself an impeccable judge of
movies. La Fawcett, in her second attempt
at movie stardom, joins a private eye in attempting to uncover the mystery of a millionaire's death.
PG.   ★★
D: Richard Sarafian; W: John Daly, Stephen
Oliver and James Booth; Ph: Alex Phillips,
Jr. M: John Cameron.

Cast: Farrah Fawcett, Charles Grodin, Art Carney, Joan Collins.

SUNDAY LOVERS. (1981) The NATO alliance goes to the movies. Four directors, from the U.S., Italy, France and England, offer four stories loosely united by the theme of weekend romance. Too many cooks spoil an already thin broth and the only tale worth a second look is Ugo Tognazzi's turn as a middle-aged man looking up his old girlfriends while his wife is away.
R.   ★★
D: Gene Wilder, Bryan Forbes, Edouard Molinaro, Dino Risi; W: Wilder, Leslie Bricusse and Frances Veber; Ph: Gerald Hirschfeld, et. al..
Cast: Gene Wilder, Roger Moore, Lino Ventura, Ugo Tognazzi.

SUNNYSIDE. (1979) Just about every cliche and convention of the teen gang film about a kid who wants justice leaving Queens and heading for Manhattan. That, metaphorically, is what Joey Travolta attempted in his film debut. The Big Apple eludes John's younger brother in a slapdash and off-hand effort.
R.   ★
D: Timothy Galfas; W: Galfas and Jeff King; Ph: Gary Graver; M: Alan Douglas and Harold Wheeler.
Cast: Joey Travolta, John Lansing, Stacey Pickren, Andrew Rubin.

SUNRISE AT CAMPOBELLO. (1960) The early lives of presidents long before they ever reach the White House have yielded several worthwhile films. The timing allows character study without political cant. Ralph Bellamy's marvelous portrait of Franklin Roosevelt has a natural dramatic center in his struggle to overcome the crippling effects of polio. He repeated his stage role with few lingering traces of the theater and it's a fine blend of fortitude and resilience.
★★★★
D: Vincent Donehue; W: Dore Schary; Ph: Russell Harlan; M: Franz Waxman.
Cast: Ralph Bellamy, Greer Garson, Hume Cronyn. Ann Shoemaker.

SUNSET BOULEVARD. (1950) When Gloria Swanson declaims her famous defense—"I am big. It's the pictures that got small."—she cannot include Billy Wilder's mordant examination of Hollywood. To this day, it has very few rivals in assessing how the dream factory works and how it affects

the custodians of illusion. Swanson does Norma Desmond, the silent era star planning a comeback, with the conviction of experience. William Holden, the young scriptwriter who strays into her decaying mansion, is extraordinary as Joe Gillis. Fittingly, this shattering vision of Tinseltown is narrated by a corpse.
★★★★★
D: Billy Wilder; W: Wilder, Charles Brackett and D.M. Marshman, Jr.; Ph: John Seitz; M: Franz Waxman.
Cast: Gloria Swanson, William Holden, Erich Von Stroheim, Nancy Olson.

THE SUNSHINE BOYS. (1975) You might call this Neil Simon effort *The Old Couple*. It made one of the better Simon films with George Burns and Walter Matthau as members of a vaudeville act who hate each other. They are forced back together by a television special. George Burns, in a role orginally intended for Jack Benny, is wonderfully understated and a good foil to Walter Matthau's cantankerous presence. The movie has its fun with growing old but also celebrates defiance in the twilight.
PG.   ★★★
D: Herbert Ross; W: Neil Simon; Ph: David M. Walsh; M: Harry V. Lojewski.
Cast: George Burns, Walter Matthau, Richard Benjamin, Carol Arthur.

SUPERMAN. (1978) The playing ranges from absolutely sober (Marlon Brando as Superman's father) to high camp (Gene Hackman's Lex Luthor) and what keeps things aloft and in balance is the under-rated playing of Christopher Reeve. His Clark Kent is diffident without being timid and his Superman is perfectly judged offering of straight-faced humor. Superman is raised by earthly parents and takes on Lex and his henchmen. The airborne effects are good enough to sustain the illusion of human flight and the technical credits are first-rate.
PG.   ★★★
D: Richard Donner; W: Marion Puzo, David and Leslie Newman and Robert Benton; Ph: Geoffrey Unsworth; M: John Williams.
Cast: Christopher Reeve, Margot Kidder, Marlon Brando, Gene Hackman.

SUPERMAN II. (1981) Richard Lester took over the direction from Richard Donner and the production problems, lawsuits and bad blood don't show up on the screen in the best of the trilogy. Lester brought his trademark aplomb and wit to the action sequences and persuaded the cast to play in

a consistent style. Reeve was given room to amplify the conflicts in his character as Superman takes on three powerful rebels from Krypton. Bang-up action and an enjoyable love story.
PG. ★★★
D: Richard Lester; W: Mario Puzo, David Newman and Leslie Newman; Ph: Geoffrey Unsworth; M: Ken Thorne.
Cast: Christopher Reeve, Margot Kidder, Gene Hackman, Terence Stamp.

SUPERMAN III. (1983) Superman fights a war between good and evil within his own being, a rich theme that is undermined by the comic strip framework Richard Lester gives it. As before, Christopher Reeve is the one responsible for holding the film in some kind of balance and the addition of Richard Pryor ensures that it is the funniest of the trilogy. Pryor is a computer whiz recruited by a corrupt tycoon to corner the world oil market. He obtains some kryptonite that brings out the worst in the man of steel.
PG. ★★★
D: Richard Lester; W: David and Leslie Newman; Ph: Robert Paynter; M: Ken Thorne.
Cast: Christopher Reeve, Richard Pryor, Robert Vaughn, Annette O'Toole.

SUPPORT YOUR LOCAL GUNFIGHTER. (1971) James Garner is an itinerant gambler who shows up in the town of Purgatory and is mistaken for a notorious gunslinger. The humor in this attempt to capitalize on the popularity of *Support Your Local Sheriff* is often in limbo and there is much slow going between the laughs.
★★
D: Burt Kennedy; W: James Edward Grant; Ph: Harry Stradling, Jr.; M: Jack Elliott.
Cast: James Garner, Suzanne Pleshette, Joan Blondell, Jack Elam.

SUPPORT YOUR LOCAL SHERIFF. (1969) Among the few really successful western comedies. It turns around many of the sainted cliches and plot devices, most notably the one about the stranger who comes to town and reluctantly agrees to protect it from bad elements. In this case it's James Garner, who has few peers in this kind of humor. The people who are actually reluctant to do the supporting are equally diverting, especially Joan Hackett.
★★★★
D: Burt Kennedy; W: William Bowers; Ph: Harry Stradling, Jr.; M: Jeff Alexander.

Cast: James Garner, Joan Hackett, Walter Brennan, Jack Elam.

SURF II. (1983) Surf's down in a parody sequel to a non-existent original. An inbred Hollywood joke that is as funny as an oil slick on an innocent beach, it has something to do with the high school jerk exacting his revenge on the surfers who wronged him.
R. ★★
D and W: Randall Badat; Ph: Alex Phillips, Jr.
Cast: Cleavon Little, Eddie Deezen, Linda Kerridge, Ruth Buzzi.

SUSPICION. (1941) Alfred Hitchcock's second American venture explores the proximity of love and hate at a more superficial level than he evinced later. Joan Fontaine is a woman who makes a bad marriage that seems a lot worse when her husband apparently is bent on murdering her.
★★★
D: Alfred Hitchcock; W: Samson Raphaelson, Joan Harrison and Alma Reville; Ph: Harry Stradling; M: Franz Waxman.
Cast: Cary Grant, Joan Fontaine, Nigel Bruce, Cedric Hardwicke.

SWAMP THING. (1982) When somebody lops off the creature's arm, Adrienne Barbeau asks him if it hurts. "Only when I laugh," he replies. There's little danger of the audience joining in for a camped-up comic book tale. A scientist drinks the formula that amplifies the essence of life and turns into an ambulatory blob.
PG ★
D and W: Wes Craven; Ph: Robin Goodwin; M: Harry Manfredini.
Cast: Adrienne Barbeau, Louis Jourdan, Ray Wise, David Hess.

SWANEE RIVER. (1939) Don Ameche in a biography of Stephen Foster that stretches the truth, but not to the breaking point. The song-writer falls under the spell of the South and its belles and his music celebrates the region's charms before the Civil War intervenes. Al Jolson plays E.P. Christy, the minstrel who made Foster's music the toast of America.
★★★
D: Sidney Lanfield; W: Philip Dunne and John Taintor Foote; Ph: Bert Glennon; M: Louis Silvers.
Cast: Don Ameche, Andrea Leeds, Al Jolson, Felix Bressart.

THE SWARM. (1978) A bungled bee movie. Any credits that include the notation "Fred MacMurray as Clarence" are harbingers of doom. Death's sting arrives with the bees from Brazil. Michael Caine lends his cockney accent to the cockeyed story as a Princeton entomologist tracking the northward flight of the bad news bees. Every so often someone pipes up with "Oh my God, bees, bees, millions of bees." A long drone.
PG. ★
D: Irwin Allen; W: Stirling Silliphant; Ph: Fred J. Koenekamp; M: Jerry Goldsmith.
Cast: Michael Caine, Richard Widmark, Katharine Ross. Richard Chamberlain.

SWASHBUCKLER. (1976) Shunning the parody that was fashionable at the time, James Goldstone chose to make a boisterous romantic comedy that offered a bracing and briny contrast to prevailing cynicism. Robert Shaw is the swashbuckler and Peter Boyle, a homosexual governor, provides the opposition as the swishbuckler. The bad guys wear black and there are no grey areas in an enjoyable, escapist entertainment. Topped off with a fine score by John Addison
PG. ★★★
D: James Goldstone; W: Jefrey Bloom; Ph: Philip Lathrop; M: John Addsion.
Cast: Robert Shaw, Beau Bridges, Peter Boyle, Genevieve Bujold.

SWEET REVENGE. (1977) Stockard Channing as a car thief who steals only to realize her ambiton of owning a Ferrari in an exercise that exacts a terrible vengeance on the viewer. If this strikes you as an extremely flimsy and ill-considered premise for a movie, you are not alone. One spends most of the dreary running time wondering why she doesn't simply steal the Ferrari instead of making payments on it. When her lawyer looks at a wrecked car at the end and asks, "Was that really necessary?," he is really referring to the film.
PG. ★
D: Jerry Schatzberg; W: B.J. Perla, Marilyn Goldin; Ph: Vilmos Zsigmond; M: Paul Chihara.
Cast: Stockard Channing, Sam Waterston, Richard Doughty, Norman Matlock.

SWEPT AWAY. (1975) Lina Wermuller reworked *The Admirable Crichton*, but her customary wit is missing in a film as subtle as a Maoist poster. A rich bitch and a crewman from her yacht are marooned, allowing for a predictable role reversal. When she argues that lower class women should diet, he retorts, "They're on a constant diet. It's called poverty." Such rhetoric overburdens the film, which nonetheless has its pungently satiric moments.
R. ★★★
D and W: Lina Wertmuller; Ph: Giulio Battifierri; M: Piero Piccioni.
Cast: Giancarlo Giannini, Mariangela Melato.

SWING SHIFT. (1984) The pivotal era in our social history when women went to the factories in World War II and Rosie the Riveter became a national symbol. Goldie (Hawn) is less than riveting and the post production arguments over content with director Jonathan Demme show up in the inconsistency and occasional incoherence of the narrative. Her husband joins the navy, leaving Goldie to confront temptation. There is more feminist hindsight than insight and it would surely have worked better as a straightforward Goldie vs. the men comedy.
PG. ★★
D: Jonathan Demme; W: Rob Morton; Ph: Tak Fujimoto ; M: Patrick Williams.
Cast: Goldie Hawn, Kurt Russell, Christine Lahti, Ed Harris.

THE SWISS FAMILY ROBINSON. (1960) The family that strays together stays together. The Disney penchant for defanging classic children's tales was much in evidence here in a muted, toned down version of Johann Wyss' story. The hair-raising sense of danger you are supposed to feel when the family tries to defend itself against pirates is all slapstick and booby traps. Otherwise, it's smoothly done and unexceptionable and a calm sea that needs a storm.
★★★
D: Ken Annakin; W: Lowell S. Hawley; Ph: Harry Waxman; M: William Alwyn.
Cast: John Mills, James MacArthur, Dorothy McGuire, Janet Munro.

THE SWORD AND THE ROSE. (1953) The team that made Disney's version of Robin Hood was reunited to rewrite English history. Based on Charles Major's *When Knighthood Was in Flower*, the quite lavish costume epic is about the intrigues of Mary Tudor at the court of Henry VIII and her love for the captain of the guard. Factually ridiculous, but good fun.
★★★

D: Ken Annakin; W: Lawrence E. Watkin; Ph: David Harcourt; M: Clifton Parker.
Cast: Richard Todd, Glynis Johns, James Robertson Justice, Michael Gough.

THE SWORD IN THE STONE. (1963) Walt Disney's version of the wonderful T.H. White rendering of the boyhood of King Arthur is a little short on wonder. The film recounts Arthur's humble origins and the lessons about responsibility that he learns from Merlin before he pulls Excalibur from the stone. The moral lessons tend to be a little belabored, but there is some fine animation—especially a fight between two wizards who can change themselves into different animals. This one wears its age lightly, and while not a Disney classic, it remains solid children's fare.
G.   ★★★
D: Wolfgang Reitherman; W: Bill Peet; M: George Burns (Songs by the Sherman brothers).

THE SWORD OF SHERWOOD FOREST. (1960) When a television series found great popularity in the U.S. in this period, few producers could resist the temptation to chuck together often unrelated episodes and pass it off as a feature film. Witness Disney's *Davey Crockett*. Richard Greene had a vast British following for his Robin Hood and the makers had the class to make an all-new feature. It's a feather in his cap and Greene's is as good a Hood as you'll find. Once again, he has to shoot down a nefarious scheme cooked up by the Sheriff of Nottingham.
                                                      ★★★
D: Terence Fisher; W: Alan Hackney; Ph: Ken Hodges; M: Alan Hoddinott.
Cast: Richard Greene, Peter Cushing, Richard Pasco, Niall MacGinnis.

SVENGALI. (1931) Not one of the great profile's most hypnotic performances. John Barrymore, hidden behind a black slouch hat leers at the camera and the lines roll lovingly off his tongue. You could play the Super Bowl in the time it takes him to say "Go a-w-a-y." *Svengali* was his last picture at Warner Brothers before he went on to greater things, like *A Bill of Divorcement*, the following year.
                                                      ★★
D: Archie Mayo; W: J. Grubb Alexander; Ph: Barney McGill.
Cast: John Barrymore, Marian Marsh, Luis Alberni, Lumsden Hare.

T

TABLE FOR FIVE. (1983) The setting is the Mediterranean where the death of the mother provokes an emotional custody fight between the father and step-father over the right to bring up the children. It is an issue of urgency and interest to many sundered couples, but the writing is woeful and David Seltzer's script predictably settles for tears that ultimately engulf the inherent drama of the situation.
PG. ★★
D: Robert Lieberman; W: David Seltzer; Ph: Vilmos Zsigmond.
Cast: Jon Voight, Richard Crenna, Marie-Christine Barrault, Millie Perkins.

TAKE A HARD RIDE. (1975) Take a long walk in the other direction. A western filmed in, of all places, the Canary Islands. An inarguable turkey resulted with Jim Brown and Fred Williamson involved in trying to safely shepherd $86,000 to a widow in Mexico. They make a compelling case for confining ex-jocks to broadcasting booths—or anywhere but a movie screen.
PG. ★★
D: Anthony M. Dawson; W: Eric Bercovici and Jerry Ludwig; Ph: Riccardo Pallotini; M: Jerry Goldsmith.
Cast: Jim Brown, Fred Williamson, Lee Van Cleef, Jim Kelly.

TAKE THIS JOB AND SHOVE IT. (1981) A labored film rendering of Johnny Paycheck's hit anthem for working stiffs. Robert Hays is a brewery executive who returns to his hometown of Dubuque with a mandate to galvanize the workers into better productivity. The opportunity for some sharp comedy about factory boredom is lost in the bar fights and other stand-bys of pictures that owe their origins to country and western songs.
PG. ★★
D: Gus Trikonis; W: Barry Schneider; Ph: James Devis; M: Billy Sherrill.
Cast: Robert Hays, Art Carney, Barbara Hershey, David Keith.

THE TAKING OF PELHAM ONE TWO THREE. (1974) New York, where any urban catastrophe is instantly credible, is one of the stars of Joseph Sargent's taut account of the hijacking of a subway car and its occupants. The ransom is $1.5 million and a hostage will be shot every hour if it is ignored. Sargent cuts back and forth between the

two camps and uses the abrasiveness of the Big Apple to great advantage. Robert Shaw is as excellent as usual in leading the quartet of crooks.
R. ★★★
D: Joseph Sargent; W: Peter Stone; Ph: Owen Roizman; M: David Shire.
Cast: Robert Shaw, Walter Matthau, Martin Balsam, Hector Elizondo.

A TALE OF TWO CITIES. (1936) Hollywood had both the resources and the willingness to do justice to Dickens' crowded depiction of the Reign of Terror that claimed so many lives in the French Revolution. The film has an epic scale but the cast—especially Ronald Colman as Sydney Carton—is too good to be overwhelmed and the picture teems with vitality and fascinating characters we want to know better.
★★★★
D: Jack Conway; W: W.P. Lipscomb and S.N. Behrman ; Ph: Oliver Marsh; M: Herbert Stothart.
Cast: Ronald Colman, Elizabeth Allan, Basil Rathbone, Edna May Oliver.

TALES OF TERROR. (1962) An anthology of Edgar Allen Poe stories mounted in macabre style by Roger Corman. He contrived to recruit Basil Rathbone and Peter Lorre. The stories include "Morella" and "The Black Cat."
★★★
D: Roger Corman; W: Richard Matheson; Ph: Floyd Crosby; M: Les Baxter.
Cast: Vincent Price, Basil Rathbone, Peter Lorre, Debra Paget.

THE TALL MEN. (1955) *Red River* reduced to a muddy trickle. The cattle drive is led by a crusty Clark Gable through assorted Indian and natural threats, but the lavish production only shows up the weakness of the script on the way from Texas to Montana.
★★
D: Raoul Walsh ; W: Frank Nugent and Sydney Boehm; Ph: Leo Tover; M: Victor Young.
Cast: Clark Gable, Jane Russell, Robert Ryan, Cameron Mitchell.

THE TAMARIND SEED. (1974) Blake Edwards directing his wife in material that is not particularly amenable to either of them. Julie Andrews, a British embassy secretary, and Omar Sharif, a Soviet attache, have an

affair that has espionage implications. Edwards, quite wrongly, discards the minimal suspense to concentrate on the boring romance.
PG. ★★
D and W: Blake Edwards; Ph: Freddie Young; M: John Barry.
Cast: Julie Andrews, Omar Sharif, Anthony Quayle, Daniel O'Herlihy.

TARANTULA. (1955) There is no web of intrigue to get in the way of a straightforward mutated monster on the loose. The mad professor fiddles with Mother Nature while trying to concoct artificial food. Result: one 100-ft. tall spider with an appetite for cattle and people. Discreet effects keep it from looking too artificial and *Tarantula* still has a scary moment or two.
★★★
D: Jack Arnold; W: Martin Berkeley and Robert Fresco; Ph: George Robinson; M: George Gershenson.
Cast: Leo G. Carroll, John Agar, Mara Corday, Nestor Paiva.

TARGETS. (1968) An on-target, provocative horror film and the debut of the erratic Peter Bogdanovich. Here he makes the most of an intriguing notion—the way in which unstable minds are so influenced by movies that the distinction between fantasy and reality becomes blurred. A young sniper, after killing his family, holes up at a drive-in and is confronted by an old horror film star. Boris Karloff plays the latter with great aplomb.
★★★
D and W: Peter Bogdanovich; Ph: Laszlo Kovacs.
Cast: Boris Karloff, Tim O'Kelly, James Brown, Sandy Baron.

TARZAN, THE APE MAN. (1981) The level of a pricelessly daft Bo Derek adventure is set when Richard Harris tells his long-lost daughter what birth pangs did to her mother. "Your conception almost killed her," he intones. You spend the rest of the move wondering what happened at the actual delivery. Not a film, so such as a cinematic wet T-shirt night. Tarzan spends the film with the expresssion of a very dumb linebacker listening to a half-time pep talk from his coach. The other characters keep falling into any available body of water.
R. ★
D: John Derek; W: Tom Rowe and Gary Goddard; Ph: John Derek; M: Perry Botkin.

Cast: Bo Derek, Richard Harris, John Phillip Law, Miles O'Keefe.

TATTOO. (1981) Of all the loonies Bruce Dern has ranted his way through, none comes close to the madman he was asked to flesh out in *Tattoo*. Bob Brooks' film is so daft that it seems pointless to needle it. Someone called Karl Kinski likes to leave his mark on beautiful women but *Tattoo* doesn't have an inkling about how to make it believable. It is mostly given over to longing shots of Maud Adams, the unwilling victim of Kinski's kinkiness.
R. ★
D: Bob Brooks; W: Joyce Bunuel; Ph: Arthur Ornitz; M: Barry Devorzon.
Cast: Bruce Dern, Maud Adams, Rikke Borge, Leonard Frey.

TAXI DRIVER. (1976) A work of riveting impact with Robert De Niro driving the mean streets. His Travis Bickle, a Vietnam veteran, is tormented by sublimated sexual urges he cannot acknowledge and filled with a brooding insanity that no one else notices. He drives exhausting shifts and his rage against his seamy world accumulates through the film until it explodes in almost orgasmic violence. This bleak, brilliant film later earned notoriety through the John Hinckley case. It deserves its place as one of the landmark movies of the seventies and De Niro's work is one of the greatest studies of madness ever committed to the screen.
R. ★★★★★
D: Martin Scorsese; W: Paul Schrader; Ph: Michael Chapman; M: Bernard Herrmann.
Cast: Robert De Niro, Jodie Foster, Cybil Shepherd, Peter Boyle.

TELEFON. (1977) Soviet agents, planted during in the U.S. when the Cold War was at its chilliest, are dispatched years later on sabotage missions. There is some unplanned obsolescence in the movie since the targets they choose are out-of-date. Charles Bronson trudges through the film as a Russian agent trying to stop the plot. The movie's plot grinds to a halt early and time is passed in meaningless killings and explosions. Don Siegel does better with a hero with a code of honor rather than a KGB man with an area code and a number.
PG ★★
D: Don Siegel; W: Peter Hyams, Stirling Silliphant; Ph: Michael Butler; M: Lalo Schifrin.
Cast: Charles Bronson, Donald Pleasence, Lee Remick, Tyne Daly.

TELL ME A RIDDLE. (1980) An ambitious attempt to blend the memories of a dying woman with her present circumstances. Under Lee Grant's direction—this marked the actresses' debut—flashbacks are used arbitrarily and the drama becomes as diffuse as the recollections themselves. Melvyn Douglas is an effective complement as the woman's husband.
PG. ★★★
D: Lee Grant; W: Joyce Eliason and Alev Lytle; Ph: Fred Murphy; M: Sheldon Shkolnik.
Cast: Melvyn Douglas, Lila Kedrova, Brooke Adams, Dolores Dorn.

THE TEMPEST. (1982) Paul Mazursky's ambitious and fascinating translation of Shakespeare's play is a serio-comic study of a modern mid-life crisis. Prospero becomes Phillip, a troubled Manhattan architect who has recurring dreams about death and tries to escape to the Greek Islands. He brings along his mistress and teenaged daughter. Mazursky's point in this fluently acted piece is that you cannot escape emotional commitments and moral obligations wherever you go.
PG. ★★★
D: Paul Mazursky; W: Mazursky and Leon Capetanos; Ph: Don McAlpine; M: Stomu Yamashta.
Cast: John Cassavetes, Gena Rowlands, Susan Sarandon, Molly Ringwald.

THE TENANT. (1976) The previous tenant left the apartment by jumping out the the window and comes back to haunt the current occupant. Despite Polanksi's credentials in this kind of movie, The Tenant is a creaking bore that is not helped by atrocious dubbing. Polanski plays the lead with an understatement that reduces the character to a hopeless blandness
R. ★★
D: Roman Polanski; W: Polanski and Gerard Brach; Ph: Sven Nykvist; M: Philippe Sarde.
Cast: Roman Polanski, Melvyn Douglas, Isabelle Adjani, Shelley Winters.

THE TEN COMMANDMENTS. (1956) The script reads as if it were written on ten tablets and you'll need a couple of aspirin after 219 minutes of the Bible acording to Cecil B. de Mille. In his seventies, de Mille remade his silent classic and, perhaps because he felt closer to God, decided to dub His voice. For all that, the sprawling epic is as grand as it is pompous and film-making on such a scale is no longer feasible. Despite de Mille, Charlton Heston as Moses and Yul Brynner as the plague-ridden Pharoah put some emotion into their parts. The movie is cherished for the parting of the Red Sea and it's still a marvelous piece of legerdemain.
★★★
D: Cecil B. de Mille; W: Aeneas Mackenzie, Jesse Lasky, Jack Guriss, Fred Frank; Ph: Loyal Griggs; M: Elmer Bernstein.
Cast: Charlton Heston, Yul Brynner, Edward G. Robinson, Anne Baxter.

TENDER IS THE NIGHT. (1962) The novels of Scott Fitzgerald, not to mention films about him, have had an unhappy history on the screen. *Tender is the Night* is one of the better attempts, which is damning with faint praise. Jason Robards is a doctor who marries his patient and becomes part of the world of rich Americans in Europe in the twenties.
★★★
D: Henry King; W: Ivan Moffatt; Ph: Leon Shamroy; M: Bernard Herrmann.
Cast: Jennifer Jones, Jason Robards, Joan Fontaine, Tom Ewell.

TEN GENTLEMEN FROM WEST POINT. (1942) In the early 1800s the first class of cadets at the U.S. Military Academy undergo training so harsh that only ten of them last through it. They go off to chastise Tecumseh and his Indians, thereby earning the grudging admiration of the curmudgeon of a commandant. Historical nonsense but fun.
★★
D: Henry Hathaway; W: Richard Maibaum; Ph: Leon Shamroy; M: Alfred Newman.
Cast: George Montgomery, Maureen O'Hara, Laird Cregar, John Sutton.

TEN LITTLE INDIANS. (1975) Ten strangers are invited to a millionaire's mansion and find their numbers dwindling rapidly. So does the viewer's interest in the third movie version of Agathie Christie's popular whodunit. The actors are as bored as anyone else and behave as if they can't wait to meet their comeuppance and get out of the picture.
PG. ★
D: Peter Collinson; W: Peter Welbeck; Ph: Fernando Arribas; M: Bruno Nicolai.
Cast: Oliver Reed, Elke Sommer, Richard Attenborough, Stephane Audran.

TEN NORTH FREDERICK. (1958) A version of the John O'Hara novel that insists on politics taking a back seat to its more maudlin inventions. The damage is severe but not fatal. Gary Cooper seemed visibly uncomfortable as the businessman who makes some unsurprising discoveries about politics and succumbs to a younger woman. ★★

D and W: Philip Dunne ; Ph: Joe MacDonald; M: Leigh Harline.
Cast: Gary Cooper, Diane Varsi, Suzy Parker, Gerladine Fitzgerald.

TERMINAL MAN. (1974) A terminal bore claimed by its makers to be a picture to be viewed "not as science fiction, but as chilling facts." The facts lie there like a corpse on a morgue slab. George Segal is a scientist who submits to a brain operation in which electrodes will be implanted to control his outbursts of madness. Inevitably, things go wrong and *The Terminal Man* is little more than Frankenstein dressed up in modern scientific ideas and cloaked with a new pretension.
PG. ★★
D and W: Mike Hodges; Ph: Richard H. Kline; M: Music of J.S. Bach.
Cast: George Segal, Joan Hackett, Richard A. Dysart, Jill Clayburgh.

TERMS OF ENDEARMENT. (1983) Look past the shower of Oscars heaped on James Brooks and you find flaws that were hidden by the dazzling glare of the acting, notably from Shirley MacLaine and Jack Nicholson. The film spans three decades in a mother-daughter relationship and two very different moods. It begins with fine comic brio before turning to manipulations worthy of the worst kind of soap opera. The tears are earned by the players in spite of rather than because of the screenplay.
R. ★★★
D and W: James Brooks; Ph: Andrzej Bartkowiak; M: Michael Gore.
Cast: Shirley MacLaine, Debra Winger, Jack Nicholson, John Lithgow.

TERROR TRAIN. (1980) Rolls down the much beaten track with a group of young people being creatively murdered by a mad killer. A fraternity leases the train for a New Year's Eve party. This marked the directing debut of Roger Spottiswoode, who went on to make the splendid *Under Fire*.
R. ★
D: Roger Spottiswoode; W: T.Y. Drake; Ph: John Alcott; M: John Mills-Cockle.
Cast: Ben Johnson, Jamie Lee Curtis, David Copperfield.

TESS. (1979) Roman Polanski found a way of rendering Thomas Hardy's doom-laden novel for contemporary eyes. He defused the emotional detonations in the tragic story of a peasant girl who ruins and is ruined by two men. Thus, we have a thoughtful treatment of Hardy's belief in a force outside good and evil that governs our lives instead of Gothic melodrama. In Polanski's hands, the reticent approach builds with inexorable force that is devastating when it is finally unloosed. The cinematography is breath-taking.
PG. ★★★★★
D: Roman Polanski; W: Polanski, Gerard Brach and John Brownjohn; Ph: Geoffrey Unsworth and Ghislain Cloquet; M: Philippe Sarde.
Cast: Nastassja Kinski, Leigh Lawson, Peter Firth, John Collin.

TESTAMENT. (1983) All the ink went to *The Day After*, the television view of the nuclear aftermath that was in circulation at the same time. This modestly scaled independent production boasts the anchoring and noble presence of Jane Alexander as a mother watching her community and her family die of radiation after a nuclear attack on the United States. Much of it is precious and antiseptic, but the power of the subject matter makes it moving.
PG. ★★★
D: Lynne Littman; W: John Sacret Young; Ph: Steven Poster; M: James Horner.
Cast: Jane Alexander, William Devane, Ross Harris, Roxanna Zal.

TEX. (1982) The problems of two youths facing life without father in rural Oklahoma. Sponsored by the Disney studio in its continuing effort to find suitable mature material, it is sensitively acted and unsentimentally directed by Tim Hunter. The major flaw is the sheer number of problems shoehorned into the production.
PG. ★★★
D: Tim Hunter; W: Hunter and Charles Haas; Ph: Ric Waite; M: Pino Donaggio.
Cast: Matt Dillon, Jim Meltzer, Meg Tilly, Bill McKinney.

THE TEXAS CHAINSAW MASSACRE. (1974) An appalling and very influential piece of trash about a group of young campers who fall into the hands of a family of demented sadists. The film established an audience taste—or lack thereof—for very specific bloodslinging and encouraged innu-

merable imitations that went even further. Watching this you will find it hard to believe that any movie could sink any lower.
R.
D: Tobe Hooper; W: Hooper and Kim Henkel; Ph: Daniel Pearl; M: Hooper and Wayne Bell.
Cast: Marilyn Burns, Allen Danziger, Paul Partain, William Vail.

THANK GOD IT'S FRIDAY. (1978) One night in a Los Angeles disco where even the humblest nerd will find true love. Cynical Hollywood packaging aimed at selling a soundtrack so that the movie is an afterthought that displays no sign of thinking. Even if you liked disco, this is a movie that should be heard and not seen.
PG.   ★
D: Robert Klane; W: Barry Armyan Bernstein; Ph: James Crab; M: Marc Paul Simon.
Cast: Hilary Beane, The Commodores, John Friedrich, Jeff Goldblum.

THANKS A MILLION. (1935) Thirties musicals are hardly celebrated for their satiric content, but thanks to the acerbic contribution from Fred Allen *Thanks a Million* works. Nunnally Johnson's sardonic script finds a group of entertainers visiting a small town political rally. Dick Powell takes over when the original candidate gets too plastered to deliver his speech and winds up running for office. There are some arch connections between the business of politics and show business.
                                              ★★★
D: Roy Del Ruth; W: Nunnally Johnson; Ph: Peverell Marley; M: Arthur Lange.
Cast: Dick Powell, Fred Allen, Ann Dvorak, Patsy Kelly.

THAT CHAMPIONSHIP SEASON. (1982) Jason Miller returned to his home town to make the film of his hit play and the results are not of championship caliber. The claustrophobia of the stage that is necessary to this drama of bitter revelations is missing. Middle-aged failures of various persuasions reunite to celebrate a single moment of glory in their youth when they won the state basketball championship. The rancor is predictable and the pace that of a four-corners offense used to stall a basketball game.
R.   ★★
D and W: Jason Miller; Ph: John Bailey; M: Bill Conti.
Cast: Robert Mitchum, Bruce Dern, Stacy Keach, Martin Sheen.

THAT NIGHT IN RIO. (1941) Carmen Miranda belts out "Chica, Chica, Boom Chic," but there's nothing especially chic or memorable about this remake of *Folies-Bergere*. Incredibly involved identity crises for Don Ameche who is both a night club impersonator in Rio de Janeiro and a nobleman.
                                              ★★
D: Irving Cummings; W: George Seaton, Bess Meredyth and Hal Long; Ph: Leon Shamroy; M: Alfred Newman.
Cast: Alice Faye, Don Ameche, Carmen Miranda, J. Carrol Naish.

THAT'S ENTERTAINMENT! (1974) A magical musical tour, with guides like Gene Kelly and Frank Sinatra, through the vaults of MGM. The studio celebrated its 50th anniversary with this delightful anthology of scenes and songs from 100 musicals made between 1929 and 1958. It amounts to a history of the genre and offers everything from Clark Gable singing "Puttin' on the Ritz" to Kelly's classic sortie through the puddles in *Singin' in the Rain*.
G.   ★★★★
D and W: Jack Haley, Jr.; Ph: (Additional) Gene Polito, Ernest Laszlo, Russell Metty; M: (Additional) Henry Mancini.
Cast: (Narrators) Frank Sinatra, Gene Kelly, Fred Astaire, Bing Crosby.

THAT'S ENTERTAINMENT PART 2. (1976) MGM raided its own vaults for the second time and the results were almost as good as the scintillating predecessor. Gene Kelly and Fred Astaire dance and chat and introduce a rich array of clips—everything from early Rooney and Garland up to Doris Day in *Love Me or Leave Me*. A feast for film lovers.
G.   ★★★★
D: Gene Kelly; W: Leonard Gershe; M: Nelson Riddle.
Cast: Gene Kelly, Fred Astaire.

THEATER OF BLOOD. (1973) A Shakesperean actor is raving mad about his reviews and in a fantasy that will be dear to anyone who has suffered the slings and arrows of outraged criticism, he retaliates. What makes this a delightful horror piece is the method of his madness. He seeks the inspiration of the Bard and every murder has a precedent in the Shakespeare canon. Vincent Price has a glorious time as the actor.
                                              ★★★
D: Douglas Hickox; W: Anthony Greville-Bell; Ph: Wolfgang Suschitzky; M: Michael Lewis.

Cast: Vincent Price, Diana Rigg, Ian Hendry, Harry Andrews.

THEM! (1954) Don't be put off by the exclamation mark. *Them!* is a low-key and gripping little sci-fi thriller that is widely regarded as one of the finest monster-on-the-loose movies of the fifties. And rightly so. Radiation creates 12-ft high ants who make their way to the sewers of Los Angeles. The actors behave as if it were really happening instead of just another monster movie.
★★★★
D: Gordon Douglas; W: Ted Sherdemann; Ph: Sid Hickox; M: Bronislau Kaper.
Cast: Edmund Gwenn, James Whitmore, James Arness, Joan Weldon.

THERE'S NO BUSINESS LIKE SHOW BUSINESS. (1954) You may be muttering "Thank God there isn't" by the end of two hours with Ethel Merman as a vaudeville matriarch. She and Dan Daily reflect on a life in the business. Marilyn Monroe raised the temperature with "Heat Wave," but this is pretty grim going despite Berlin's songs.
★★
D: Walter Lang; W: Phoebe and Henry Ephron; Ph: Leon Shamroy; M: Irving Berlin.
Cast: Ethel Merman, Dan Dailey, Marilyn Monroe, Donald O'Connor.

THEY CAME TO CORDURA. (1959) An officer who has been branded a coward winds up leading a squad of soldiers, who have demonstrated exceptional bravery, and Rita Hayworth on a perilous journey to a military post in Mexico in 1916. Robert Rossen tries to combine adventure and action with a discussion of valor that is rather obvious in asserting that heroisim is inspired by often bewildering motives. Cooper gives the film needed substance.
★★★
D: Robert Rossen; W: Rossen and Ivan Moffat ; Ph: Burnett Guffey; M: Elie Siegmeister.
Cast: Gary Cooper, Rita Hayworth, Van Heflin, Richard Conte.

THEY DIED WITH THEIR BOOTS ON. (1941) There was more than a little of Errol Flynn in General George Armstrong Custer and the shoe fits in a biography that purports to trace its hero's life from West Point to Little Big Horn. Hollywood never let the facts get in the way of a good story in this period and what many consider Flynn's best western is both rousing entertainment and historical rubbbish. Even though there is a strain of light comedy before the tragic last stand, Raoul Walsh made it fit together nicely.
★★★
D: Raoul Walsh; W: Wally Kline and Aeneas Mackenzie; Ph: Bert Glennon; M: Max Steiner.
Cast: Errol Flynn, Olivia de Havilland, Charles Grapewin, Arthur Kennedy.

THEY LIVE BY NIGHT. (1947) It's not hard to see why Nicholas Ray's debut as a director quickly developed a cult following. Within the confines of a gangster film —three men on the run plotting a robbery— he placed two young lovers looking for a way out and a chance at a normal life. There is none and the movie touches some of the pent-up resentment that made Ray's *Rebel Without a Cause* so popular with kids in the fifties.
★★★
D: Nicholas Ray; W: Charles Schnee; Ph: George Diskant; M: Leigh Harline.
Cast: Cathy O'Donnell, Farley Granger, Howard Da Silva, Jay C. Flippen.

THEY WON'T FORGET. (1937) As memorable as Fritz Lang's *Fury*, which was released in the previous year. Claude Rains is a Southern prosecutor with more ambition than scruple. He sees an opportunity in a murder to advance himself and by accusing a teacher. Mervyn Le Roy makes subsequent events another harrowing essay in crowd psychology after the governor commutes the sentence and the mob takes over.
★★★★
D: Mervyn Le Roy; W: Aben Kandel and Robert Rossen; Ph: Arthur Edeson; M: Adolph Deutsch.
Cast: Claude Rains, Gloria Dickson, Edward Norris, Otto Kruger.

THIEF. (1981) A pounding, relentless and expert crime thriller and James Caan makes off with the honors. He is an expert jewel thief who lives for his aspirations rather than by a code. After life in an orphanage and a penitentiary, he yearns for the domesticity of wife and family—a satisfaction that has been stolen from him by fate. Although *Thief* views its subject as a victim, there is no public defender liberalism here. It is gritty, street-smart and very exciting.
R. ★★★★
D and W: Michael Mann; Ph: Donald Thorin; M: Tangerine Dream.
Cast: James Caan, Tuesday Weld, Willie Nelson, James Belushi.

THE THIEF OF BAGHDAD. (1940) Of the seemingly 1001 movies inspired by the Arabian Nights tales, Alexander Korda's spectacular production remains the champion by a wide margin. There are magic carpets and winged horses and the whole undertaking is one of the blithest flights of fancy in films. Conrad Veidt is the nasty magician and Sabu tries to help a king regain his throne.

★★★★★

D: Michael Powell, Ludwig Berger and Tim Whelan; W: Lajos Biro and Miles Malleson; Ph: Georges Perinal and Osmond Borradaile; M: Miklos Rozsa.
Cast: Conrad Veidt, Sabu, John Justin, June Duprez.

THE THIEF OF BAGHDAD. (1978) Benighted Arabian tale that does not knock the 1940 Ludwig Berger version off its magic carpet. Two suitors, the hero and an indestructible opponent, set out to find the most valuable thing in the world. The former is told he will be turned into stone if he strays, but that happens to the acting shortly after the opening credits. The bottled genie and the other special effects are strictly non-vintage.
PG. ★★
D: Clive Donner; W: A.J. Carothers; Ph: Denis Lewiston; M: John Cameron.
Cast: Peter Ustinov, Roddy McDowall, Terence Stamp, Kabir Bedi.

THIEVES. (1977) Adaptation of Herb Gardner's play that tries to mix a sepia-toned look at a disintegrating marriage with a vision of New York teeming with beggars, crazy taxi drivers and assorted nuts with philosophies. The results are truly wretched and make one appreciate Neil Simon's facility in this kind of humor. Charles Grodin is long-suffering as the husband and Marlo Thomas, largely because of the writing, merely insufferable. One of the cameos is done by Bob Fosse as a mugger who is easily scared off and the content of the film has much the same effect.
PG. ★
D: John Berry; W: Herb Gardner; Ph: Arthur J. Ornitz, Andrew Lazlo.
Cast: Marlo Thomas, Charles Grodin, Irwin Corey, Hector Elizondo.

THIEVES LIKE US. (1974) The title refers to the sentiment among Depression era criminals and their many supporters that capitalists were "thieves like us." Robert Altman does for the gangster film what he brought off more effectively in *McCabe and Mrs. Miller*. He offers his usual, sardonic view of the American dream in the context of bank robbers whose crimes are justified by the system that holds them down. He embellishes this familiar Hollywood theme with a view that is ironic and unromantic and *Thieves Like Us* has a strong sense of a period and its attitudes.
R. ★★★
D: Robert Altman; W: Calder Willingham, Altman and Joan Tewkesbury; Ph: Jean Boffety. .
Cast: Keith Carradine, Shelley Duvall, Bert Remsen, John Schuck.

THE THING. (1982) John Carpenter's ferocious remake of the fifties classic is not the same old *The Thing*. It is an *Alien* on ice that uses the situation of the embattled polar expedition for imaginative blood-slinging and nothing more. The creature in this case is literally what it eats and assumes the form of its last meal. Carpenter knows every horror trick in the book, but the overall impact is like a walk through a slaughter-house.
R. ★★
D: John Carpenter; W: Bill Lancaster; Ph: Dean Cundey; M: Ennio Morricone.
Cast: Kurt Russell, A. Wilford Brimley, T.K. Carter, David Clennon.

THINGS ARE TOUGH ALL OVER. (1982) Cheech and Chong, the worst pair of comedians in movies, boasted that this one had had a plot. So does your neighborhood cemetery and it's certainly a lot more amusing. They are pursued by rich Arabs and the jokes run to herpes and flatulence. Chong also eats a horse dropping, doubtless mistaking it for the next scene in the screenplay.
R. ★
D: Thomas Avildsen; W: Richard Marin and Thomas Chong; Ph: Bobby Byrne; M: Gaye Delorme.
Cast: Richard Marin, Thomas Chong, Shelby Fiddis, Rikki Marin.

THINGS TO COME. (1936) H.G. Wells adapted his own book and if things didn't come to pass in the way he envisioned his bleak vision of the future is still required viewing. It is often compared to *Metropolis*, but it is a unique picture and fascinating for its evidence of what the world looked like to a prescient man of the thirties. He rightly predicted World War II and his speculation of its consequences has its own logic. The story covers a century and traces the consolidation of the populace into vast underground cities. The sets and the production values are stunning.

★★★★

D: William Cameron Menzies; W: H.G. Wells; Ph: Georges Perinal; M: Arthur Bliss.
Cast: Raymond Massey, Ralph Richardson, Cedric Hardwicke, Edward Chapman.

THE THIRD MAN. (1949) A pulp novelist in post-war Vienna sets out to discover the truth about his friend Harry Lime, who may or may not be dead and who may or may not be a black market crook. Graham Greene, who is anything but a pulp novelist, peopled his elaborate intrigue with a gallery of memorable characters and Carol Reed brought it off with great aplomb. Reed found the zither player, Anton Karas, by accident in a Vienna cafe and commissioned one of the most famous themes in movies.

★★★★★

D: Carol Reed; W: Graham Greene; Ph: Robert Krasker; M: Anton Karas.
Cast: Joseph Cotten, Orson Welles, Trevor Howard, Alida Valli.

13 RUE MADELEINE. (1947) A quartet of OSS agents goes to the address, which houses the Gestapo in Paris, to steal the plans to a Nazi rocket site and save lives in the imminent invasion. The style is documentary, but James Cagney's presence as the leader of the espionage ring livens things up.

★★★

D: Henry Hathaway; W: John Monks and Sy Bartlett; Ph: Norbert Brodine; M: Alfred Newman.
Cast: James Cagney, Annabella, Richard Conte, Frank Latimore.

—30—. (1959) When newspaper reporters still typed their stories they would write "-30-" at the bottom of the last page to indicate the end. There wasn't much point in beginning Jack Webb's idea of a night at a big city newspaper. It belongs in the back with the truss ads. Suspense is supposed to build as the staff worries about a little girl lost in the sewers of Los Angeles. Hold the presses on this one and get me rewrite on the script.

★★

D: Jack Webb; W: William Bowers; Ph: Edward Colman; M: Ray Heindorf.
Cast: Jack Webb, William Conrad, David Nelson, Whitney Blake.

THE THIRTY-NINE STEPS. (1959) That Kenneth More should turn out to be less than Robert Donat isn't much of a surprise. Nor, for that matter, is it really his fault. Ralph Thomas chose to follow in some pretty big foot-steps and turned out what amounts to a facsimile of Hitchcock's witty creation. As with most copies, the original is to be preferred on all counts.

★★

D: Ralph Thomas; W: Frank Harvey; Ph: Ernest Steward; M: Clifford Parker.
Cast: Kenneth More, Taina Elg, Barry Jones, Faith Brook.

THIS ABOVE ALL. (1942) A superior and shrewd piece of wartime propaganda in which an airwoman falls in love with a deserter and persuades him that English society is worth saving from the Nazi hordes. One of his reasons for dissenting is a belief that he is being forced to fight for the upper classes, an issue that still has some pertinence in Britain. A smoothly disguised sermon.

★★★

D: Anatole Litvak; W: R.G. Sheriff; Ph: Arthur Miller; M: Alfred Newman.
Cast: Tyrone Power, Joan Fontaine, Thomas Mitchell, Henry Stephenson.

THIS IS ELVIS. (1981) Elvis Presley made enough bad movies in his lifetime to deserve something better from a posthumous biography. The ill-advised mixing of clips of Presley himself and actors impersonating him at various stages in his career doesn't work. The singer's family contributed its blessing and some home movies and, not surprisingly, objectivity and the hard questions go by the board. A tantalizing life is recounted but not really examined.

PG. ★★

D and W: Malcolm Leo and Andrew Solt; M: Walter Scharf.
Cast: Elvis Presley, Joe Esposito, Linda Thompson, Johnny Harra.

THIS ISLAND EARTH. (1955) First-class science-fiction with a commendable disdain for sensationalism and silliness. It deals with aliens contacting the earth—via a complex kit that arrives at the laboratory of a scientist. When he assembles it, he eventually finds himself embroiled in the affairs of an alien planet. The special effects were state of the art for their time.

★★★

D: Joseph Newman; W: Franklin Coen and Edward O'Callaghan; Ph: Clifford Stine; M: Joseph Gershenson.
Cast: Rex Reason, Jeff Morrow, Faith Domergue, Lance Fuller.

THOSE LIPS, THOSE EYES. (1980) Frank Langella, of Draculan note, is doing summer stock in Cleveland in 1951, a stint he describes as "10 weeks in an open grave." While Langella awaits the big Broadway break that will never come—he's not good enough—a young medical student succumbs to the lure of the theater. Langella is far more noteworthy than the main coming-of-age theme.
R.   ★★★
D: Michael Pressman; W: David Shaber; Ph: Bobby Byrne; M: Michael Small.
Cast: Frank Langella, Glynnis O'Connor, Thomas Hulce, Kevin McCarthy.

THOSE MAGNIFICENT MEN IN THEIR FLYING MACHINES. (1965) A family comedy that really flies despite the generous length of the trip. A happy fusion of first-class aerial footage and inventive slapstick prompted by a London newspaper's offer of a reward for the winner of a London-to-Paris air race. The machines celebrate the mad bravery of the early days of aviation.
                                          ★★★
D: Ken Annakin; W: Annakin and Jack Davies; Ph: Christopher Challis; M: Ron Goodwin.
Cast: Stuart Whitman, Sarah Miles, James Fox, Terry Thomas.

THREE BROTHERS. (1982) Francesco Rosi's beautifully composed and elegiac consideration of family conflicts and the way the death of a parent imposes a sense of personal mortality as well as loss on grown children. The brothers, who have gone their separate ways and followed different ideologies and ambitions, come back to their village for the funeral of their mother. The film is both an exquisitely insightful look at family conflicts and a protest against disruptive social and political change in Italy.
                                          ★★★★
D and W: Francesco Rosi; Ph: Paqualino de Santis; M: Piero Piccioni.
Cast: Philippe Noiret, Charles Vanel, Michele Placido, Vittorio Mezzogiorno.

THREE COINS IN THE FOUNTAIN. (1954) Many more coins went into box office cash registers as movie-goers responded to the slight romance. Three American girls see their amorous wishes come true after tossing money in the Trevi fountain. Superior travelogue footage of the wonders of Rome and a tuneful score make it go down easily.
                                          ★★
D: Jean Negulesco; W: John Patrick; Ph: Milton Krasner; M: Victor Young.

Cast: Cliffton Webb, Dorothy McGuire, Jean Peters, Louis Jourdan.

THREE DAYS OF THE CONDOR. (1975) First-rate, elliptically structured thriller that reflected post-Watergate cynicism about government institutions. Exposures of Central Intelligence Agency machinations in real life made the story of a lower echelon researcher, who becomes a man who knows too much, very believable. Robert Redford is appropriately low-keyed and there is a fine sense of the way personal and professional entanglements can become entrapments.
R.   ★★★★
D: Sydney Pollack; W: Lorenzo Semple, Jr., and David Rayfiel; Ph: Owen Roizman; M: Dave Grusin.
Cast: Robert Redford, Faye Dunaway, Cliff Robertson, Max Von Sydow.

THE THREE FACES OF EVE. (1957) Alistair Cook narrates the experience of a schizophrenic woman, but it's not masterpiece cinema. Joanne Woodward won the Oscar for her triple threat account of a woman who has three entirely different personalities. Lee J. Cobb drags her back to mental health through hypnosis, but the overall treatment of the subject is glib.
                                          ★★★
D and W: Nunnally Johnson; Ph: Stanley Cortez; M: Robert Emmett Dolan.
Cast: Joanne Woodward, David Wayne, Lee J. Cobb, Edwin Jerome.

THREE GODFATHERS. (1948) John Ford filmed this story as a silent called *Marked Men* and his second version of the tale of three outlaws who adopt an orphaned baby in the desert and take care of it has its boosters. It is laden with religious symbolism of dubious relevance to the narrative and often wallows in sentimentality.
                                          ★★★
D: John Ford; W: Laurence Stallings and Frank Nugent; Ph: Winton Hoch; M: Richard Hageman.
Cast: John Wayne, Pedro Armendariz, Harry Carey, Jr., Ward Bond.

THE 300 SPARTANS. (1962) One of the grandest stands in all of history that saw 300 legendary Spartan soldiers hold off the entire Persian army at Thermopylae in 480 B.C. They paid with their lives but won some vital time. The small-scaled epic was filmed in Greece and one wishes the writing and acting were up to the setting.
                                          ★★

D: Rudolph Mate; W: George St. George; Ph: Geoffrey Unsworth; M: Manos Hajidakis.
Cast: Richard Egan, Ralph Richardson, Diane Baker, Barry Coe.

THE THREE MUSKETEERS. (1974) All-star send-up of swashbuckling movies that keeps its balance through a deliciously judged sense of humor and the vitality of Richard Lester's direction. Satirical slapstick is by no means easy, but Lester and his cast are masters of it. The devious Cardinal Richelieu plots to steal the Queen's diamonds. Charlton Heston plays him straight and it's an effective foil to the the musketeers, who are something less than romantic heroes. Lester also took the trouble to make the period come to life with a gritty realism that anchors the movies high spirits.
PG. ★★★★
D: Richard Lester; W: George MacDonald Fraser; Ph: David Watkin; M: Michel Legrand.
Cast: Michael York, Oliver Reed, Richard Chamberlain, Charlton Heston.

THE THREE STOOGES FOLLIES. (1974) "Violent is the Word for Curley" is one of the episodes and dumber than usual is the word for this compilation form the tedious threesome. Columbia, which cobbled together stoogery from the late thirites and forties, threw in a Buster Keaton two reeler called "Nothing But Pleasure." It's from the days when he was broke and desperate and contains but a flash or two of his comic genius.
G. ★★
Cast: Moe Howard, Larry Fine, Curley Howard, Buster Keaton.

3:10 TO YUMA. (1957) The wait for a train has rarely been as tense and nerve-wracking as it is in Delmer Daves' ticking clock drama. Van Heflin is a farmer desperate for money who takes on the job of escorting a prisoner to the penitentiary. Glenn Ford does the killer with a mocking charm that is never quite supercilious. Outside, his men, led by Richard Jaeckel, circle like jackals. The film's debt to *High Noon* is considerable, but so is its innate quality.
★★★★
D: Delmer Daves; W: Halsted Welles; Ph: Charles Lawton; M: George Duning.
Cast: Van Heflin, Glenn Ford, Felicia Farr, Richard Jaeckel.

THREE THE HARD WAY. (1974) A white nutcase millionaire and squads of fascists want to poison the water supplies of three cities with a substance that only affects blacks. Paranoid black fantasy with Jim Brown, Jim Kelly and Fred Williamson beating up on everything.
R. ★
D: Gordon Parks; W: Eric Bercovici and Jerry Ludwig; Ph: Lucien Ballard; M: Richard Tufo.
Cast: Jim Kelly, Jim Brown, Fred Williamson, Sheila Frazier.

THREE WOMEN. (1977) Robert Altman had a dream but are dreams the stuff from which memorable films are made? The answer here is a heavily qualified yes. The director switches from dreamy vision to the gritty reality and keen eye and ear that enrich his best work. It may all be of a piece to Altman, but it is difficult for the viewer to follow him in and out of the lives of a desert painter, a psychotherapist and her co-worker.
PG. ★★★
D and W: Robert Altman; Ph: Charles Rosher; M: Gerald Busby
Cast: Shelley Duvall, Janice Rule, Sissy Spacek.

THE THREE WORLDS OF GULLIVER. (1959) The greatest satire in the English language goes to kiddie city. Jonathan Swift's world can be treated on many levels and, even at the lowest—with its brilliant moral arguments excised—it still works. The first two books, dealing with Gulliver's adventures among the little people of Lilliput and the giants of Brobdingnag are given the Ray Harryhausen treatment.
★★
D: Jack Sher; W: Sher and Arthur Ross; M: Bernard Herrmann.
Cast: Kerwin Matthews, Basil Sydney, Mary Ellis, Jo Morrow.

THRESHOLD. (1983) A half-hearted attempt to dramatize a pioneer operation involving the implanting of the first artificial heart. It was upstaged by real-life developments. The emphasis is on the surgeons and the technical detail, which is sometimes difficult to follow, rather than the patient. More could have been done with the ethical and philosophical implications of perpetuating life with technology.
PG. ★★
D: Richard Pearce; W: James Salter; Ph: Michael Brault; M: Micky Erbe.
Cast: Donald Sutherland, Jeff Goldblum, Allan Nichols, Sharon Acker.

THUNDERBALL. (1965) The fourth James Bond adventure and one of the weaker efforts from Sean Connery's tenure. Connery is submarined by a story that puts him underwater for long stretches as Bond takes on SPECTRE and its dastardly plan to pinch a plane armed with atomic bombs. The target is Miami and the ransom must be paid in gems.

★★★

D: Terence Young; W: Richard Maibaum and John Hopkins; Ph: Ted Moore; M: John Barry.
Cast: Sean Connery, Adolfo Celi, Claudine Auger, Luciana Paluzzi.

THUNDERBOLT AND LIGHTFOOT. (1974) Michael Cimino's first outing as a director (he subsequently went on to the notoriety of *Heaven's Gate*) is two films that are barely worth the price of one. Clint Eastwood restages a robbery to satisfy the men who believe themselves cheated out of the loot the first time. The other motif is his paternal relationship with a young drifter who saves his life that is potentially of more interest, but goes undeveloped because of the noisier requirements of the movie.

R. ★★

D and W: Michael Cimino; Ph: Frank Stanley; M: Dee Barton.
Cast: Clint Eastwood, Jeff Bridges, George Kennedy, Geoffrey Lewis.

THUNDER ROAD. (1958) A high-spirited tribute to the moonshine trade and a B movie that has always and quite deservedly had a loyal following. Robert Mitchum does the driving and even the composing of the title song. He is at his liveliest as Doolin, who smuggles the booze over the objections of gangsters and feds.

★★★

D: Arthur Ripley; W: James Arlee Phillips and Walter Wise; Ph: Alan Stensvold; M: Jack Marshall.
Cast: Robert Mitchum, Gene Barry, Jacques Aubuchon, Keely Smith.

THX 1138. (1971) George Lucas is now so indelibly associated with the massive spectacle and essentially optimistic vision of *Star Wars* that the unwary viewer is in for a surprise. In his first film he expanded on a student project and took his cameras into the warren of the still uncompleted tunnels that were to become San Francisco's BART system. There he proved that you don't need a lot of money to achieve a chilling reality. Robert Duvall rebels against a fascist society that keeps the people in control with drugs. There are hints of *Star Wars*—the precur-

sors of the storm troopers for instance—but the view is one of unrelieved gloom. As a debut, it is nothing short of astonishing.

★★★★

D: George Lucas; W: Lucas and Walter Murch; Ph: Dave Meyers; M: Lalo Schifrin.
Cast: Robert Duvall, Donald Pleasence, Pedro Colley, Maggie McOmie.

TICKET TO HEAVEN. (1981) A harrowing ride to a psychological hell, the powerful Canadian drama studies the process through which an outgoing youth gradually is drawn to a religious cult. The subsequent attempt to deprogram him becomes a struggle for his soul. The description of his recruitment is especially strong and the film is only weakened by a stance that is, in its own way, fundamentalist black and white.

R. ★★★

D and W: R.L. Thomas; Ph: Richard Leiterman; M: Mickey Erbe.
Cast: Nick Mancuso, Saul Rubinek, Meg Foster, R.H. Thomson.

A TICKET TO TOMAHAWK. (1950) The rivalry of a stage line and a railroad in Colorado is the inspiration of a western spoof that doesn't quite go the distance. Rory Calhoun, the stage line owner, keeps putting various obstacles like a theatrical company in the way of his opposition. Good fun.

★★★

D: Richard Sale; W: Sale and Mary Loos; Ph: Harry Jackson; M: Lionel Newman.
Cast: Rory Calhoun, Dan Dailey, Anne Baxter, Walter Brennan.

TIDAL WAVE. (1975) Silly combination of disaster movies with the special effects found in tacky Japanese sci-fi efforts like *Godzilla Eats Benihana* and those other staples of late night TV. The land of the Rising Sun is sinking and, after the earthquakes, a tidal wave engulfs Tokyo. Hopelessly unconvincing.

PG. ★

D: Shiro Moritani and Andrew Meyer.
Cast: Lorne Greene, Keiju Kobayashi, Rhonda Leigh Hopkins.

TIGER BAY. (1959) Hayley Mills witnesses a murder and steals the film. She is a lonely little girl full of romantic dreams and the movie plays very cleverly on the possibilities. The seaman sought for the crime wants to ensure her silence and a bond forms between them. Mills was later forced into much pap, but she did extraordinary things with her character's yearnings in this off-beat thriller.

★★★

D: J. Lee Thompson; W: John Hawkesworth and Shelley Smith; Ph: Eric Cross; M: Laurie Johnson.
Cast: Hayley Mills, Horst Buchholz, John Mills, Megs Jenkins.

TIGHTROPE. (1984) The later Dirty Harry movies found Clint Eastwood blasting away with his .44 Magnum in works of progressively lower calibre. As Wes Block, troubled New Orleans detective, he did a cop who is a man of flesh as well as blood and it's one of the performances of his often maligned career. Block hunts a maniacal killer and, as the investigation proceeds, finds out much about himself that he would rather not know. The plot is basic telemovie fare with liberal amounts of sex. The character, however, gives Eastwood a chance to explore the effect of constant exposure to depravity and murder on a cop.

R.   ★★★

D and W: Richard Tuggle; Ph: Bruce Surtees; M: Lennie Niehaus.
Cast: Clint Eastwood, Genevieve Bujlold, Dan Hedaya, Alison Eastwood.

TILL MARRIAGE DO US PART. (1974) Flimsy Franco-Italian production that posits a half-brother and sister who get married in ignorance of their consanguinity. Instead of seekng an annulment, they decide to live together platonically and the rest is given over to the various sexual adventures of Laura Antonelli. She is remarkably unchanged as a woman by her progress from total naivete to experience and such a development is necessary to the film.

★★

D: Luigi Comencini; W: Comencini and Ivo Perilli; Ph: Tonino delle Colli; M: Feorenzo Carpi.
Cast: Laura Antonelli, Alberto Lionello, Jean Rochefort, Michele Placido.

TIM. (1979) A rather weak-minded chronicle of the love between an older woman and a mentally retarded young man. One can understand the stilted lines given to Mel Gibson, but the same style infects the dialogue Piper Laurie is supposed to utter. Michael Pate's effort is even more mawkish than the topic requires.

★★

D and W: Michael Pate; Ph: Paul Onorata; M: Eric Jupp.

Cast: Mel Gibson, Piper Laurie, Alwyn Kurts, Deborah Kennedy.

TIME AFTER TIME. (1979) A stylish fantasy that propels H.G. Wells, who is best known for his visionary novels, in a time machine from Victorian London to contemporary San Francisco. His quarry is Jack the Ripper, who has used the machine to escape and wreak havoc in the future. Deftly handled and enriched by the theme of Wells' obsession with finding the ideal woman and the idea of the great futurist actually confronting the future.

PG.   ★★★

D and W: Nicholas Meyer; Ph: Paul Lohmann; M: Miklos Rozsa.
Cast: Malcolm McDowell, Mary Steenburgen, David Warner, Kent Williams.

TIME BANDITS. (1981) Because the Universe was slapped together in seven days, a gang of midgets keeps slipping through holes in time and showing up at various points in human history. They take along an English boy on their riotous journey and every kid should go along for the ride. Some of the humor is Pythonesque and beyond the grasp of children—John Cleese does Robin Hood as a sort of doddering Margaret Thatcher—but *Time Bandits* is a richly imaginative fantasy.

PG.   ★★★★

D: Terry Gilliam; W: Gilliam and Michael Palin; Ph: Peter Biziou; M: Ray Cooper.
Cast: John Cleese, Sean Connery, Shelley Duvall, David Warner.

THE TIME MACHINE. (1960) In what could have been the most satisfying film inspired by H.G. Wells, the past turns out to be more preferable to the future. Things begin auspiciously with Rod Taylor burning with curiosity and finding his friends skeptical of his scientific dabbling. His machine hurtles him into the far future and much inanity involving Morlocks and downtrodden humanity. A fine start is largely wasted.

★★★

D: George Pal; W: David Duncan; Ph: Paul C. Vogel; M: Russell Garcia.
Cast: Rod Taylor, Yvette Mimieux, Alan Young, Sebastian Cabot.

TIME RIDER. (1982) A California corporation is trying a time travel experiment with a rhesus monkey. Instead, a biker is sent back to the old West by accident. The film would have been better off sticking with the monkey. Folks around town keep wondering who that helmeted man was as he roars around the frontier. His adventures wouldn't pass for an episode in a Lone Ranger serial.

PG. ★

D and W: William Dear; M: Michael Nesmith. Cast: Fred Ward, Belinda Bauer, Peter Coyote, Ed Lauter.

TIMES SQUARE. (1980) A movie attached to a soundtrack—20 New Wave songs. Two teenage girls from opposite sides of the tracks run away from home and finally make it as the singing Sleaze Sisters. A tacky bore.

R. ★

D: Alan Moyle; W: Jacob Brackman; Ph: James A. Contner; M: Greg Sheldon. Cast: Trini Alvarado, Ti Curry, Robin Johnson, Peter Coffield.

TIME WALKER. (1983) A mummy movie that's a grave error and one that trips over its bandages on its way out of the pyramid. A shameless rip-off of *E.T.*, it tries to combine bits of the mummy motif with a vision of benign aliens—two elements that the desperate screenwriters cannot reconcile. The alien has been sleeping under wraps until scientists rudely awaken him for predictable horror hijinks.

PG. ★

D: Tom Kennedy; W: Tom Friedman and Karen Levitt; M: Richard Band. Cast: Ben Murphy, Nina Axelrod.

TIN PAN ALLEY. (1940) Before World War One, two struggling songwriters try to make it on music publishing's tough street. Lots of complications involving two singing sisters—Alice Faye and Betty Grable—and a lively score and a musical that has retained its effervescence.

★★★

D: Walter Lang; W: Robert Ellis and Helen Logan; Ph: Leon Shamroy; M: Alfred Newman.
Cast: Betty Grable, Alice Faye, Jack Oakie, John Payne.

THE TIN STAR. (1957) It is the stars who elevate Anthony Mann's picture above the common run of westerns. Anthony Perkins is the nervous but determined lawman confronted with a villain played with animal menace by Neville Brand. Henry Fonda marshals his awesome expertise in the part of a one-time lawman turned bounty hunter who reluctantly teaches Perkins how to stay alive.

★★★★

D: Anthony Mann; W: Dudley Nichols, Barney Slater and Joel Kane; Ph: Loyal Griggs; M: Elmer Bernstein.
Cast: Henry Fonda, Anthony Perkins, Betsy Palmer, Neville Brand.

TITANIC. (1953) Not a film to remember in its account of the disaster that befell the ocean liner in 1912. A sinking feeling sets in early with cheap dramatics surrounding a father learning some hard truths about his son and achieving reconciliation on the way down. As *A Night to Remember* so vividly demonstrates, truth is stronger than fiction in re-creating such catastrophes.

★★

D: Jean Negulesco; W: Charles Brackett, Walter Reisch and Richard Breen; Ph: Joe MacDonald; M: Lionel Newman.
Cast: Clifton Webb, Barbara Stanwyck, Robert Wagner, Audrey Dalton.

TOBACCO ROAD. (1941) Erskine Caldwell's novel of impoverished rural whites became a long-running Broadway play before John Ford filmed it. In Jeeter Lester and the gang, Ford saw more comic opportunities than the chance for deeply felt commentary and it's not among his more memorable efforts.

★★★

D: John Ford; W: Nunnally Johnson; Ph: Arthur Miller; M: David Buttolph.
Cast: Charley Grapewin, Marjorie Rambeau, Gene Tierney, William Tracy.

TO BE OR NOT TO BE. (1942) Ernst Lubitsch's brilliant comedy was widely misunderstood as humor that was misplaced in wartime. In fact, it is a savage demolition of Nazism and its assumptions that uses the theater as a metaphor of illusion and reality to particularly telling effect. Jack Benny, in his best screen performance, and Carole Lombard, in her last one before her fatal plane crash, lead a Warsaw theater company in an effort to help out the Polish underground by impersonating Hitler.

★★★★

D: Ernst Lubitsch; W: Edwin Justus Mayer; Ph: Rudolph Mate; M: Werner Heymann.
Cast: Jack Benny, Carole Lombard, Robert Stack, Stanley Ridges.

TO BE OR NOT TO BE. (1983) Mel Brooks abandoned his usual spoofing and parody's loss was our gain in a surprisingly satisfying remake of the Lubitsch film. Even though the usual route for a good remake —updating the material—was obviously impossible, Brooks managed a slick mix of satire and farce and had the time of his life playing Hitler. It's his second screen outing as the Fuhrer. The highlight is the Brooks' rendering of "Sweet Georgia Brown" with Anne Bancroft. In Polish.

PG. ★★★
D: Alan Johnson; W: Ronny Graham and Thomas Meehan; Ph: Gerald Hirschfeld; M: John Morris.
Cast: Mel Brooks, Anne Bancroft, Tim Matheson, Charles Durning.

TO CATCH A THIEF. (1955) Grace Kelly was to catch a husband in the principality of Monaco where Alfred Hitchcock found himself in a more light-hearted mood than usual. He discovers some sensuality in Kelly and is content to prefer sophisticated banter and handsome scenery over mystery and psychological depth. Cary Grant rather than Kelly is the saving grace of the film for his John Robie, a worldly jewel thief forced out of retirement to refute suspicions that he is responsible for a string of Riviera robberies.
★★★
D: Alfred Hitchcock; W: John Michael Hayes; Ph: Robert Burks; M: Lyn Murray.
Cast: Cary Grant, Grace Kelly, Jessie Royce Landis, John Williams.

TO HAVE AND HAVE NOT. (1945) It does not have much to do with the Hemingway story. What it does have is Humphrey Bogart and the debut of Lauren Bacall. When she said "Anybody got a match?" with that sensual voice, Warner Brothers knew it certainly did in Bogie and Bacall. The location of the story was moved to Martinique and embroils Bogart, a fishing boat captain, in intrigues involving the Nazis. The real intrigue is between him and Bacall.
★★★
D: Howard Hawks; W: Jules Furthman and William Faulkner; Ph: Sid Hickox; M: Franz Waxman.
Cast: Humphrey Bogart, Lauren Bacall, Hoagy Carmichael, Walter Brennan.

TOM HORN. (1980) Steve McQueen's last western contrasts encroaching civilization with the wide vistas of Wyoming. The familiar theme was handled with more sophistication in John Wayne's valedictory, *The Shootist.* McQueen gives a laconic account of Horn, a gunfighter and trapper, hired by some ranchers to stamp out rustling. He becomes an encumbrance to them and they plot against him.
PG. ★★★

D: William Wiard; W: Thomas McGuane and Bud Shrake; Ph: John Alonzo; M: Ernest Gold.
Cast: Steve McQueen, Linda Evans, Richard Farnsworth, Slim Pickens.

TOMMY. (1975) The hero of Ken Russell's lurid and ludicrous rock opera is blind, deaf and dumb. He is thus at an advantage over anyone who has to sit through *Tommy* with faculties intact. Russell turned from trashing the memories of classical composers to heaping perverse symbolism on the story of a child of the blitz who rises to head a new religion. Roger Daltry plays the kid with vacuous conviction and the soundtrack is earboggling. Tommyrot.
PG. ★
D and W: Ken Russell; Ph: Dick Bush; M: Pete Townshend and the Who.
Cast: Roger Daltrey, Jack Nicholson, Elton John, Ann-Margret.

TONKA. (1958) George Armstrong "They're all bad Indians!" Custer rants and raves before receiving his come-uppance. Before Little Big Horn, there is a meandering story of a young brave (Sal Mineo) capturing and taming a wild horse that is quite personable. The film drifts rather aimlessly after the cavalry takes the horse, but its heart is in the right place in noting the injustices suffered by the Indians.
★★
D: Lewis R. Foster; W: Foster and Lillie Hayward; Ph: Loyal Griggs; M: Oliver Wallace.
Cast: Sal Mineo, Philip Carey, Jerome Courtland, Rafael Campos.

TONY ROME. (1967) The years have not been kind to Frank Sinatra's detective and the same can be said about the movie. He lives on a boat in Biscayne Bay and goes up against assorted Miami toughs in his efforts to recover a jewel. Self-consciously hardboiled.
★★
D: Gordon Douglas; W: Richard Breen; Ph: Joseph Biroc; M: Billy May.
Cast: Frank Sinatra, Jill St. John, Richard Conte, Gena Rowlands.

TOOTSIE. (1982) Sydney Pollack's exhilarating comedy could easily have settled for farce in exploiting the transformation of Michael Dorsey, a truculent and unemployed actor, into Dorothy Michaels, soap opera superstar. But Pollack and Dustin Hoffman turned *Tootsie* into an ironic and compas-

sionate exploration of sexual confusion in the eighties. Hoffman is superb in both parts and his Dorothy isn't a man in drag but a highly persuasive impersonation. The film is set in the now blurred middle ground between the sexes, a terrain it probes with much perception and wit. It is one of those works that can be enjoyed on many levels.
PG. ★★★★★
D: Sydney Pollack; W: Larry Gelbart and Murray Schisgal; Ph: Owen Roizman; M: Dave Grusin.
Cast: Dustin Hoffman, Jessica Lange, Teri Garr, Dabney Coleman.

TOPKAPI. (1964) One of the better elaborate robberies because Peter Ustinov is on hand to steal the film as Arthur Simpson, a low-life British expatriate whose cowardice is matched by his greed. Many caper movies ripped off Jules Dassin's influential *Rififi* and since Dassin made this one it turns into a diamond theft that is a cut above the rest. The target is an elaborately guarded jeweled dagger, the music is loud, the playing rather forced, but it's still a thriller to be reckoned with.
★★★
D: Jules Dassin; W: Monja Danischewsky; Ph: Henri Alekan; M: Manos Hajidakis.
Cast: Robert Morley, Peter Ustinov, Maximilian Schell, Melina Mercouri.

TOP SECRET. (1984) A crash landing for the team that created *Airplane!* The movie style they parody this time—old spy films unaccountably mixed with rock and roll references—isn't amenable to the same treatment. It gets the same shotgun gag approach, but most of them are off-target. The tedious intrigue has to do with an attempt to reunite the two Germanys.
PG. ★★
D: Jim Abrahams, David and Jerry Zucker; W: Abrahams, the Zuckers and Marilyn Burke; Ph: Christopher Challis; M: Maurice Jarre.
Cast: Omar Sharif, Jeremy Kemp, Warren Clarke, Tristram Jellinek.

TORA! TORA! TORA!. (1970) Subsequent revelations of who knew what and when date a plodding account of the attack on Pearl Harbor. There is strong evidence that the day of infamy was not such a surprise to some in the American government. On its own terms, Richard Fleischer's re-creation of the attack is far more interesting than the even-handed explanation of the prelude. It is told from both the Japanese and American point of view.
★★
D: Richard Fleischer; W: Larry Forrester; Ph: Charles Wheeler; M: Jerry Goldsmith.
Cast: Martin Balsam, Jason Robards, Joseph Cotten, James Whitmore.

TORSO. (1974) For necrophiliacs who like amputees, Carlo Ponti offers film footage without feet and other appendages. An Italian answer to *The Texas Chainsaw Massacre*, but who asked the question? The coeds at a summer school are carved up in gruesome detail. A thoroughly vile enterprise.
R.
D: Sergio Martino; W: Martino and E. Gastaldi; Ph: Giancarlo Farrando.
Cast: Suzy Kendall, Tina Aumont, Luc Merenda, John Richardson.

TO SEE SUCH FUN. (1982) A compilation of a dizzying number of clips from British screen comedy from the arrival of sound to the *Carry On* series. There is too much of the tiresome George Formby and too little of the brilliant Tony Hancock, but it's an amusing anthology if you're fond of the more raucous vein of British humor.
★★★
D: Jon Scofield .
Cast: George Formby, Norman Wisdom, Tony Hancock, Charlie Drake.

TOUGH ENOUGH. (1983) A competition to find the toughest man in America. He is undoubtedly the one who can sit through all of Richard Fleischer's dreadful combination of country and western singing and boxing. Dennis Quaid enters the contest as the "Country and Western Warrior." War is indeed hell.
PG. ★
D: Richard Fleischer; W: John Leone; Ph: James Contner; M: Michael Lloyd and Steve Wax.
Cast: Dennis Quaid, Warren Oates, Carlene Watkins, Stan Shaw.

THE TOWERING INFERNO. (1974) A tall story and a typical disaster movie in its insistence that a fire singles out people for incineration solely on the basic of moral conduct. Sub-standard wiring begins the blaze in the world's tallest building and traps a cast of caricatures on the top floor. Sub-standard screenplay makes the movie a very slow burn. Good special effects if you're a pyromaniac.
PG. ★★

D: John Guillermin; W: Stirling Silliphant; Ph: Fred Koenekamp; M: John Williams.
Cast: Paul Newman, Steve McQueen, William Holden, Faye Dunaway.

TOWER OF LONDON. (1939) Richard III would probably drown the print in a butt of malmsey wine if he could get his hands on it. Certainly, Basil Rathbone doesn't give a pat on the hunchback to the king who has endured a bad press for centuries. All kinds of atrocities go on in the Tower and are supervised by Boris Karloff as the the executioner willing to chop off anything that moves. An off-beat item for connoisseurs of horror.
★★★
D: Rowland Lee; W: Robert Lee; Ph: George Robinson; M: Charles Previn.
Cast: Basil Rathbone, Boris Karloff, Vincent Price, Barbara O'Neil.

THE TOY. (1982) The PG here stands for "Pryor Grounded." Anyone used to listening to Richard Pryor's blue tirades will be amazed to find him lecturing a little kid on the meaning of love. *And* respect for women! In a remake of Francis Veber's *Le Jouet*, Pryor is a janitor taken home by a millionaire's kid. The film has the same effect as a toy that already bores a kid the day after Christmas. It's expensive and outlives its amusement value.
PG.
★★
D: Richard Donner; W: Carol Sobieski; Ph: Laszlo Kovacs; M: Patrick Williams.
Cast: Richard Pryor, Jackie Gleason, Ned Beatty, Scott Schwartz.

TRACKS. (1976) Dennis Hopper is a paranoid Vietnam veteran escorting the body of soldier on a train bound for the latter's home town. He communes with representatives of civilian life and lapses into fantasies done in an overwrought style by Henry Jaglom. The actors have to surmount Jaglom's eccentric attempt to write like Harold Pinter, but Hopper's work lingers in the memory.
R.
★★★
D and W: Henry Jaglom; Ph: Paul Glickman.
Cast: Dennis Hopper, Taryn Power, Dean Stockwell, Michael Emil.

TRADING PLACES. (1983) A sardonic look at old money capitalism that has some wickedly funny moments, but also some overstated farce. Ralph Bellamy and Don Ameche bet one dollar that Eddie Murphy, a poor black, can move into the boardroom. This involves ousting Dan Aykroyd, who, in his muted way, is sometimes more amusing than Murphy. They both would have benefitted from a director with less fondness for broad humor.
PG.
★★★
D: John Landis; W: Timothy Harris and Herschel Weingrod; Ph: Robert Paynter; M: Elmer Bernstein.
Cast: Eddie Murphy, Dan Aykroyd, Jamie Lee Curtis, Ralph Bellamy.

TRAFFIC. (1972) Admirers of Jacques Tati will like his variation on *Modern Times*, but the automobile has supplanted M. Hulot at the center of the comedy. Since Hulot is funnier than the traffic jams, breakdowns and hostile machines, it is a mistake to leave him on the sidewalk. Some of Tati's struggles with technology are funny, but his point has been made countless times and *Traffic* is not on a creative par with his earlier work.
G.
★★★
D: Jacques Tati; W: Tati and Jacques Lagrange; Ph: Marcel Weiss and Edward Van der Enden; M: Bernard Gerard.
Cast: Jacques Tati, Maria Kimberly, Marcel Fravel, Honore Bostel.

TRAIL OF THE PINK PANTHER. (1982) Was Peter Sellers' last film *The Fiendish Plot of Fu Manchu* or this miserable clip job? It will be a trivia question years from now and certainly both are trivial films. Blake Edwards resurrected unused footage from the Pink Panther series and slapped them together with a plot about a reporter trying to find out the truth about Clouseau's disappearance. It would have worked better as a simple anthology of out-takes.
PG.
★★
D: Blake Edwards; W: Edwards, Frank Waldman, Geoffrey Edwards and Tony Waldman; Ph: Dick Bush; M: Henry Mancini.
Cast: Peter Sellers, David Niven, Herbert Lom, Robert Mulligan.

THE TRAIN. (1965) Non-stop and tightly orchestrated excitement in which John Frankenheimer uses black and white photography with great ingenuity to create a period atmosphere. The treatment of the French Resistance is equally black and white. The most interesting character in the story of a Nazi attempt to make off with French art treasures as the Allies approach Paris is Paul Scofield's German officer who cares more for Monet than the men at the front.
R.
★★★★
D: John Frankenheimer; W: Walter Bern-

stein, Franklin Coen, Frank Davis; Ph: Jean Tournier, Walter Wottitz; M: Maurice Jarre.
Cast: Burt Lancaster, Paul Scofield, Jeanne Moreau, Michael Simon.

TREASURE ISLAND. (1950) Stevenson's classic story is both a great children's adventure and a lesson in the ambivalence of evil. In the latter regard, Robert Newton's Long John Silver has no rivals and he remains one of the most likeable rogues to ever stride before a camera. The Disney film is good-looking and faithful to the story of Jim's adventures with the treasure-seeking pirates.

★★★★

D: Byron Haskin; W: Lawrence Edward Watkin; Ph: Freddie Young; M: Clifton Parker.
Cast: Robert Newton, Bobby Driscoll, Walter Fitzgerald, Basil Sydney.

TREASURE ISLAND. (1972) The third and easily the worst film version is overwhelmed by Orson Welles's incredibly pompous and pretentious reading of Long John Silver. The charm of the character which is so pivotal to Jim Hawkins' relationship with him is completely lost and the supporting roles are nondescript.

G. ★★

D: John Hough; W: Orson Welles and Wolf Mankowitz; Ph: Cecilio Paniagua; M: Natal Massara.
Cast: Orson Welles, Kim Burfield, Walter Slezak, Lionel Stander.

THE TREASURE OF MATECUMBE. (1976) Rather dated Disney family fare with a couple of boys trying to save their Southern plantation by finding buried treasure in the 1860s. This comes from a time when the studio was still looking for the map that would guide it through the changing taste of American children. Shades of *Huckleberry Finn* but ne'er the twain shall meet in this totally predictable story.

G. ★★

D: Vincent McEveety; W: Don Tait; Ph: Frank Phillips; M: Buddy Baker.
Cast: Robert Foxworth, Joan Hackett, Peter Ustinov, Vic Morrow.

THE TREASURE OF SIERRA MADRE. (1948) Along with *The Maltese Falcon*, this movie treasure stands as one of the definitive examinations of the consequences of unbridled greed. Its special distinction lies in its study of the differing but equally damaging effects on the characters. A good case can be made for choosing Humphrey Bogart's Fred Dobbs, a character who degenerates from the Bogie forties archetype to something far less palatable, as his finest performance. John Huston's fascination with this particular theme becomes a shared experience. We are drawn inexorably into the fate of three American drifters in Mexico who prospect for gold.

★★★★★

D and W: John Huston; Ph: Ted McCord; M: Max Steiner.
Cast: Humphrey Bogart, Walter Huston, Tim Holt, Alfonso Bedoya.

THE TREASURE OF THE FOUR CROWNS. (1983) The movie is a *Raiders* rip-off whose only claim to attention when it was released theatrically was its 3-D format. The characters remain one-dimensional and the story of an attempt to recover treasure guarded by members of a religious cult even dafter than usual. Four crowns maybe, but only one star.

PG. ★

D: Ferdinando Baldi; W: Lloyd Battista, Jim Bryce, Jerry Lazarus; Ph: Marcello Masciocci; M: Ennio Morricone.
Cast: Tony Anthony, Ava Obregon, Gene Quintano.

TREASURE OF THE GOLDEN CONDOR. (1953) Delmer Daves dug up *Son of Fury* for a tarnished remake. Cornel Wilde takes the Tyrone Power role as a young Frenchman who is cheated by his uncle. He goes off to Guatemala to find his fortune and love (Constance Smith).

★★

D and W: Delmer Daves; Ph: Edward Cronjager; M: Sol Kaplan.
Cast: Cornel Wilde, Constance Smith, Finlay Currie, Walter Hampden.

A TREE GROWS IN BROOKLYN. (1945) A superb and rewarding study of an Irish family coping with poverty in Brooklyn in the early years of the century. James Dunn is an alcoholic who, like any optimist, believes the bottle is half full rather than half empty and Dorothy McGuire is equally good as the woman trying to hold the family together in rough times. Elia Kazan invested the story with sharp observations of domestic tension.

★★★★★

D: Elia Kazan; W: Frank Davis and Tess Slesinger; Ph: Leon Shamroy; M: Alfred Newman.

Cast: Dorothy McGuire, Joan Blondell, James Dunn, Lloyd Nolan.

THE TREE OF WOODEN CLOGS. (1979) A year in the life of peasant families in turn-of-the-century Lombardy that uses small events to touch larger feelings. Measured, beautifully photographed and acted by real-life peasants. The unsentimental story makes the point that to produce more a farmer needs a big family of helpers and that creates more mouths to feed. The perspective is socialist without being polemical.

★★★★

D and W: Ermanno Olmi; Ph: Ermanno Olmi; M: Music of J.S. Bach.
Cast: Luigi Ornaghi, Francesca Moriggi, Omar Brignoli, Teresa Brescianini.

TRENCHCOAT. (1983) In its endless and uncertain quest to break out of the mold, the Disney studio tried to be a little more adult in a private eye spoof. Chronologically and mentally, the results are pre-teen with Margot Kidder as an ingenue tourist and would-be mystery writer who gets mixed up in the real thing while vacationing on Malta. Kidder is far too hip and funny for the character she's playing. Her performance is enjoyable, if out of context. The movie, like so many of Disney's post-Walt productions, is simply out of step.

PG. ★★

D: Michael Tuchner; W: Jeffrey Price, Peter Seaman; Ph: Tonino Delli Colli; M: Jack Wadsworth.
Cast: Margot Kidder, Robert Hayes, David Suchet, Daniel Faraldo.

THE TRIAL OF BILLY JACK. (1974) Tom Laughlin's laughable wooden Indian returns in a sequel to the enormously succesful *Billy Jack*. The same simple-minded appeal to the anger of the young is apparent with re-hashings of Kent State, My Lai and Watergate. It centers on the hostility of the authorities toward a freedom school on Indian land in Arizona and Billy Jack's efforts to defend the students. To be watched with grave reservations and considerable stamina. It runs 170 often incoherent minutes in its uncut theatrical form.

PG. ★

D: Frank Laughlin; W: Frank Laughlin and Teresa Christina; Ph: Jack A. Marta; M: Elmer Bernstein.
Cast: Tom Laughlin, Delores Taylor, Victor Izay, Teresa Laughlin.

TRIBUTE. (1980) If there is any tribute to

be paid, it is to Jack Lemmon's portrait of a man facing death with drollery rather than dignity. His Scottie Templeton is a fine effort on behalf of a poor film. Bob Clark's adaptation of the play is literal-minded and claustrophobic. Before using his last few one-liners, Scottie must reconcile with his son and the movie rests on the questionable contention, also found in *On Golden Pond*, that the prospect of death removes a lifetime's worth of rancor and guilt.

PG. ★★

D: Bob Clark; W: Bernard Slade; Ph: Reginald Morris.
Cast: Jack Lemmon, Robbie Benson, Lee Remick, Colleen Dewhurst.

TRON. (1982) A video game masquerading as a movie, it is visually arresting but guilty of reducing its characters to mere blips on a screen. An intriguing premise—computer programmers, or their alter egos, who become stranded inside a vast computer—is lost in a very muddled plot. The main trouble with the Disney fantasy is that it begins in the middle of the story. A master programmer has concluded a Faustian pact with the giant computer, but we learn of it in a couple of allusions. The illusions inside the computer are very vivid.

PG. ★★★

D and W: Steven Lisberger; Ph: Bruce Logan; M: Wendy Carlos.
Cast: Jeff Bridges, Bruce Boxleitner, David Warner, Cindy Morgan.

TRUE CONFESSIONS. (1981) Confession is a vehicle for both the detective and the priest and in this richly ironic work the question is whether it really matters if the truth is confessed. Robert Duvall is the cop and Robert De Niro the ambitious priest and each brother becomes the keeper of the other's conscience during a murder investigation. The case is merely the spring-board for a discussion of power and hypocrisy in both professions and Robert De Niro and Robert Duvall bring it to vivid life. The corrupt climate of Los Angeles in the early forties is also well realized.

R. ★★★★

D: Ulu Grosbard; W: John Gregory Dunne and Joan Didion; Ph: Owen Roizman; M: Georges Delerue.
Cast: Robert De Niro, Robert Duvall, Charles Durning, Ed Flanders.

TRUE GRIT. (1969) John Wayne, emerging from his bout with cancer, played a character of the right age instead of lumbering around in sometimes embarrassing reprises of earlier heroics on the screen. His Rooster Cogburn, a crusty and truculent old lawman who helps a little girl find the killers of her father, won the Oscar that should have been his much sooner. It was given in sentimental acknowledgement of his true grit in beating cancer, but there is much to savor in the humor of the performance. Wayne has fun at his own expense and the only serious lapse in the movie is the casting of Glen Campbell, who is a pathetic actor, as a gambler.

★★★

D: Henry Hathaway; W: Marguerite Roberts; Ph: Lucien Ballard; M: Elmer Bernstein.
Cast: John Wayne, Kim Darby, Glenn Campbell, Dennis Hopper.

TUDOR ROSE. (1936) Like *La Nuit de Varennes*, Robert Stevenson's pageant proves that great events are often best seen from the sidelines. In this instance, the view is that of a young chambermaid at the English court in the struggle for power after the death of Henry VIII.

★★★

D: Robert Stevenson; W: Miles Malleson; Ph: Mutz Greenbaum.
Cast: Cedric Hardwicke, John Mills, Felix Aylmer, Leslie Perrins.

TUNNELVISION. (1976) The deodorant commercial offers "the smells. of five great American cities." The soap opera is about a family of repulsive gypsies. It is a vision of television in the future with the excesses of today pushed to greater extremes of vulgar commercialism. Some good skits, but mostly off-the-mark.
R.

★★

D: Brad Swirnoff, Neil Israel; W: Israel and Michael Mislove;
Cast: Chevy Chase, Larraine Newman, Howard Hesseman.

THE TURNING POINT. (1977) One-time choreographer Herbert Ross' splendid ballet film pivots on three views of perfection assigned to three characters. The story traces a young dancer's struggle to attain it, a fading star's desperate reaching back for it and a mother's regret in retiring from the search to raise a family. Filled with an intimate knowledge of the world of ballet and surmounting the potential "star-is-born" triteness of its theme, the movie is only weakened by the wooden contribution of Leslie Brown. Some wonderfully catty and high powered work from Bancroft and MacLaine.
PG.

★★★★

D: Herbert Ross; W: Arthur Laurents; Ph: Robert Surtees; M: John Lanchbery.
Cast: Anne Bancroft, Shirley MacLaine, Leslie Brown, Mikhail Baryshnikov.

TWELVE ANGRY MEN. (1956) Sidney Lumet's jury-room drama is—beyond any reasonable doubt—a definitive exercise in courtroom drama. Henry Fonda is an architect and Juror number 8. He is also on the short end of an 11 to 1 count when a vote is taken on the guilt of a Puerto Rican defendant. Lumet makes you part of the agonizing process as what seemed like an open and shut case is shown to be far more complicated. The camera work inside the room is both revelatory and a prime ingredient in the escalating tension.

★★★★

D: Sidney Lumet; W: Reginald Rose; Ph: Boris Kaufman; M: Kenyon Hopkins.
Cast: Henry Fonda, Lee J. Cobb, E.G. Marshall, Jack Warden.

TWELVE O'CLOCK HIGH. (1949) Henry King's riveting study of the agonizing strain of leadership has remained high on the list of the great war films. Derived from the true experiences of General Frank Armstrong, the film examines the plight of a man who must send flight after flight of airmen to their death. He is torn between guilt over what he does and his inability to allow himself to become too involved with the bombardiers. The movie soars far above the usual exercises in this vein and it offers one of Peck's finest roles.

★★★★

D: Henry King; W: Sy Bartlett and Beirne Lay, Jr.; Ph: Leon Shamroy; M: Alfred Newman.
Cast: Gregory Peck, Hugh Marlowe, Gary Merrill, Dean Jagger.

TWENTY MILLION MILES TO EARTH. (1957) William Hopper chases one of Ray Harryhausen's monsters around Rome. It stows away on a space-ship returning to earth and finds the atmosphere so congenial that it grows just by breathing. The guest in this traditional sci-fi tribute to the military industrial complex is sedated by electric current in the Rome Zoo. The Italian utilities perform predictably, allowing Hopper to utter the unforgettable cry, "Get that elephant out of there!" when the monster breaks out and threatens an innocent pachyderm .

★★

D: Nathan Juran; W: Bob Williams and Chris

Knopf; Ph: Irving Lippmann; M: Mischa Bakaleinikoff.
Cast: William Hopper, Joan Taylor, Frank Puglia, John Zaremba.

20,000 LEAGUES UNDER THE SEA. (1954) First class adaptation of the Jules Verne fantasy and one of the Disney studio's most admired ventures in live action. James Mason attracts considerable sympathy toward Captain Nemo, the mad genius in command of the submarine Nautilus, and Kirk Douglas makes a light-hearted hero. The special effects —including an attack by a giant squid—are smoothly integrated into a well-told story. ★★★★
D: Richard Fleischer; W: Earl Felton; Ph: Franz Planer; M: Paul J. Smith.
Cast: James Mason, Kirk Douglas, Paul Lukas, Peter Lorre.

TWENTY THOUSAND YEARS IN SING SING. (1933) "Crime doesn't pay" was the staple theme of the movies, but the thrust of this melodrama is paying for someone else's crime. Spencer Tracey's Tom Connors is a hood with a redeeming streak of decency who winds up in Sing Sing's hot seat to protect his girlfriend. The only teaming of Tracy and Bette Davis. It was remade seven years later as *Castle on the Hudson*. ★★★
D: Michael Curtiz; W: Brown Holmes and Wilson Mizner; Ph: Barney McGill; M: Bernhard Kaun.
Cast: Spencer Tracy, Bette Davis, Arthur Byron, Lyle Talbot.

TWENTY THREE PACES TO BAKER STREET. (1956) An exciting walk with Van Johnson. He is thoroughly convincing as a blind playwright who overhears a kidnapping plot in a London pub. He obdurately insists on tracking down the criminals despite his handicap and the refusal of the authorities to believe his claims. ★★★
D: Henry Hathaway; W: Nigel Balchin; Ph: Milton Krasner; M: Leigh Harline.
Cast: Van Johnson, Vera Miles, Cecil Parker, Patricia Laffan.

TWILIGHT'S LAST GLEAMING. (1977) A liberal army general may sound like a contradiction in terms, but Burt Lancaster makes him reasonably convincing. The taking of a U.S. missile silo is done with flair and Aldrich is at home with the fright-mongering,

Fail Safe aspects of the movie. But when the general tries to blackmail the White House into damaging political admissions that turn out to be less than a bombshell, the movie becomes pompous. A fine Charles Durning contribution as the President.
R. ★★★
D: Robert Aldrich; W: Ronald M. Cohen, Edward Huebsch; Ph: Robert Hauser; M: Jerry Goldsmith.
Cast: Burt Lancaster, Burt Young, Charles Durning, Melvyn Douglas.

THE TWILIGHT ZONE—THE MOVIE. (1983) The twilight's last gleaming—the fourth and final segment directed by Australian George Miller—is easily the best. The homage to the celebrated television series lavishes both reverence and contemporary technology on the four 25-minute stories. John Landis offers a plodding and pompous piece about a racist who finds the tables turned. Steven Spielberg turns in a good-natured but unprepossessing tale of old people who are given their youth again. Things improve when Joe Dante throws an entertaining change-up at the kid with secret powers cliche. But the hands-down winner is Miller's flashy account of a paranoid on an airplane. The film is notorious for the accident on location that killed Vic Morrow, the star of the Landis story, and two children.
PG. ★★
D: 1. John Landis. 2. Steven Spielberg. 3. Joe Dante. 4. George Miller; W: 1. John Landis. 2. George Clayton Johnson, Richard Matheson, Josh Rogan. 3 and 4. Richard Matheson ; Ph: 1. Steve Larner. 2 and 4. Alan Daviau. 3. John Hora ; M: Jerry Goldsmith.
Cast: John Lithgow, Kathleen Quinlan, Vic Morrow, Scatman Crothers.

TWINKLE, TWINKLE KILLER KANE. (1980) Something of an obsession for William Peter Blatty, author of *The Exorcist*. It is a rambling and largely pointless essay on sanity and other matters. Servicemen who may or may not be feigning madness to avoid Vietnam combat are sent to an institution where the truth will out. Also released under the title *The Ninth Configuration*.
R. ★★
D and W: William Peter Blatty; Ph: Gerry Fisher; M: Barry DeVorzon.
Cast: Stacey Keach, Jason Miller, Scott Wilson, Neville Brand.

TWO AGAINST THE WORLD. (1936) Although it is unpersuasively relocated in a radio station, the minor Bogart opus is really a remake of *Five Star Final*. There is a lot more hand-wringing over the issue of journalistic ethics in re-opening an old criminal case and it's a generally poor second edition.

★★

D: William McGann; W: Michael Jacoby; Ph: Sid Hickox; M: Heinz Roemheld.
Cast: Humphrey Bogart, Beverly Roberts, Helen MacKellar, Henry O'Neill.

TWO FOR THE ROAD. (1967) An uncommonly perceptive and wry look at a marriage over the course of a dozen years. Through flashbacks and on return vacations to France we come to know an architect and his wife. Most of the sophisticated humor arises from the way the partners change more than the partnership and Hepburn does the transitions very well. For Finney, this was the brighter side of his brilliant *Shoot the Moon*.

★★★★

D: Stanley Donen; W: Frederic Raphael; Ph: Chris Challis; M: Henry Mancini.
Cast: Albert Finney, Audrey Hepburn, William Daniels, Eleanor Bron.

TWO-MINUTE WARNING. (1976) A sniper esconced in the peristyle of the L.A. Coliseum during a football game provokes profound psychology ("Don't try to get logical with one of these kooks.") and deeper questions ("Who would want to kill an assistant professor of botany?") and cogent answers ("Some nut, I guess"). Despite all this, the killer remains a faceless presence so the film can concentrate on the blood-letting as he opens fire during a football game.

R. ★

D: Larry Peerce; W: Edward Hume; Ph: Gerald Hirschfeld; M: Charles Fox.
Cast: Charlton Heston, Martin Balsam, John Cassavetes.

TWO MULES FOR SISTER SARA. (1970) Shirley MacLaine as a prostitute posing as a nun who gets to be a habit with Clint Eastwood. He guns down would-be rapists to save her and even for a Don Siegel-Eastwood collaboration, the western is unduly violent.

★★

D: Don Siegel; W: Albert Maltz and Budd Boetticher; Ph: Gabriel Figueroa; M: Ennio Morricone.
Cast: Clint Eastwood, Shirley MacLaine, Manolo Fabregas, Alberto Morin.

TWO OF A KIND. (1983) John Travolta and Olivia Newton-John's attempt to repeat the chemistry of *Grease* hit the skids. An attempt at gossamer fantasy of the sort popular in the thirties with God deciding to do in the human race unless two losers change their behavior. Film-making of this ineptitude only gives Him an excuse to end it all.

PG. ★

D and W: John Herzfeld; Ph: Fred Koenekamp ; M: Patrick Williams.
Cast: John Travolta, Olivia Newton-John, Charles Durning, Beatrice Straight.

TWO RODE TOGETHER. (1961) James Stewart, a jaded lawman, and Richard Widmark, a cavalryman, are the riders and John Ford directs it as if he were just along for the ride. It has the Ford look, but not much else. They venture into Commanche territory in an attempt to retrieve white prisoners. Perhaps Ford inwardly felt that he had done the definitive movie on this topic in *The Searchers* and there was nothing much to add. If so, he was right.

★★

D: John Ford; W: Frank Nugent; Ph: Charles Lawton; M: George Duning.
Cast: James Stewart, Richard Widmark, Shirley Jones, Linda Cristal.

U

ULYSSES. (1955) The Italian passion for trashing Greek and Roman myths produced some hilarious epics and triumphs of dubbing over dialogue. Despite that, Kirk Douglas's exuberant portrayal of Homer's hero who wants only to go home is a great deal of fun. Parts of the script are silly, but the set piece adventures like the battle with the Cyclops and the wicked wiles of Circe are surprisingly well done.

★★★

D: Mario Camerini; W: Camerini, Franco Brusati *et. al.*; Ph: Harold Rosson; M: Alessandro Cicognini.
Cast: Kirk Douglas, Silvana Mangano, Anthony Quinn, Rosanna Podesta.

ULZANA'S RAID. (1972) Turns into something of a mounted sermon on prejudice while giving a violent depiction of its consequences. Burt Lancaster is in top form as the scout who has seen it all and Bruce Davison complements him as the naive cavalry officer. Together they pursue a renegade band of Indians and the words flow as freely as the blood. The handsome production makes up for the preaching.

★★★

D: Robert Aldrich; W: Alan Sharp; Ph: Joseph Biroc; M: Frank de Vol.
Cast: Burt Lancaster, Bruce Davison, Jorge Luke, Richard Jaeckel.

UNCLE JOE SHANNON. (1978) An attempt to make you cry over the uncle and a kid dying of bone cancer. Burt Young stars as a downtrodden musician and he wrote this appalling wallow in mawkishness to touch the same emotions as *Rocky*. The bum also rises theme has never been more clumsily handled.
PG ★
D: Joseph C. Hanwright; W: Burt Young; Ph: Bill Butler; M: Bill Conti.
Cast: Burt Young, Doug McKeon, Madge Sinclair, Jason Bernard.

UNCOMMON VALOR. (1983) A dirty half-dozen goes to Laos to rescue prisoners held by the communists long after the end of the Vietnam War. Gene Hackman, a colonel whose son is among the prisoners, gives a peculiar speech asserting that America hates Vietnam veterans because they lost the war. Apart from this specious argument, it's a male-bonding piece with Hackman rounding up his son's buddies for the assault. The action is well-staged.
R. ★★
D: Ted Kotcheff; W: Joe Gayton; Ph: Ric Waite and Steven Burum; M: James Horner.
Cast: Gene Hackman, Robert Stack, Reb Brown, Fred Ward.

THE UNCONQUERED. (1947) Cecil B. de Mille was, if nothing else, a showman, and that's about all there is to this fatuous epic that pits settlers against Indians in 18th century America. He went for spectacle as usual but the attitude to Indians displayed by the film tends to prevent one savoring its dumbness.

★★

D: Cecil B. de Mille; W: Jesse Lasky, Jr., Charles Bennett and Frederic Frank; Ph: Ray Rennahan; M: Victor Young.
Cast: Gary Cooper, Paulette Goddard, Boris Karloff, Howard da Silva.

THE UNDEFEATED. (1969) Roman Gabriel, who tasted defeat many times as the quarterback of the Philadelphia Eagles, fares no better on the screen. He and Merlin Olsen are supporting players in a tedious, unwieldy story that defeats Andrew McLaglen. John Wayne, in one of his lesser late westerns, and Rock Hudson are Civil War officers embroiled with rebels and the army in Mexico.

★★

D: Andrew V. McLaglen; W: James Lee Barrett; Ph: William Clothier; M: Hugo Montenegro.
Cast: John Wayne, Rock Hudson, Roman Gabriel, Tony Aguilar.

UNDERCOVERS HERO. (1975) The British are inordinately fond of bedroom farces with schoolboy dirty jokes, but their taste—or lack of it—doesn't travel well. Set in a Paris brothel during World War II and full of single entendres about "the German rear" and "strategic withdrawal." Peter Sellers does six roles but this one should have stayed under wraps. Released in England as *Soft Beds, Hard Battles*.
R. ★
D: Roy Boulting; W: Leo Marks and Boulting; M: Neil Rhoden.
Cast: Peter Sellers. Curt Jurgens, Beatrice Romand, Lila Kedrova.

UNDER FIRE. (1983) An insightful and incisive consideration of the ethics and re-

sponsibilities of modern news reporting. Three journalists covering the turmoil in Nicaragua are news nomads drifting from one civil war to the next. Through their personal relationships and their different reactions from the sidelines of the front line, *Under Fire* scrutinizes the difficulty, if not impossibility, of staying objective. It is also the most vivid depiction of this kind of warfare ever put on film.
R. ★★★★
D: Roger Spottiswoode; W: Ron Shelton and Clayton Frohman; Ph: John Alcott; M: Jerry Goldsmith.
Cast: Gene Hackman, Nick Nolte, Joanna Cassidy, Ed Harris.

UNDERGROUND. (1976) An informative documentary on the Weather Underground with such campus radicals as Bernadine Dohrn holding forth while still fleeing the law. For that reason they are masked by a gauze curtain. An interesting perspective is marred by the failure to ask tough questions or even to follow up on the soft ones.
★★★
D: Haskell Wexler, Emile De Antonio, Mary Lampson.
Cast: Kathy Boudin, Bernadine Dohrn, Jeff Jones, Billy Ayers.

UNDER THE RAINBOW. (1981) And beneath contempt. Somebody had the idea of making a comedy about the midgets recruited to play roles in the production of *The Wizard of Oz* and a studio was short-sighted enough to put up the money. Dwarfs swing from chandeliers and squirt each other with Budweiser. A giant pothole in the yellow brick road and one of the most pathetic movies made in the last ten years.
PG. ★
D: Steve Rash; W: Pat McCormick, Harry Hurwitz, Martin Smith, Pat Bradley and Fred Bauer Ph: Frank Stanley; M: Joe Renzetti.
Cast: Chevy Chase, Carrie Fisher, Bill Barty, Eve Arden.

UNDER THE RED ROBE. (1937) Vitality and a sense of humor liven up a tale of a duellist who reluctantly signs up with Cardinal Richelieu and agrees to capture the leader of the Huguenots. Romantic complications set in. A superior period piece with Massey in eminent form as the scheming cardinal.
★★★
D: Victor Seastrom; W: Lajos Biro and Philip Lindsay; Ph: Georges Perinal.

Cast: Conrad Veidt, Raymond Massey, Annabella, Romney Brent.

UNDER THE VOLCANO. (1984) John Huston's marvelous rendering of the Malcolm Lowry masterpiece that was long considered unfilmable. His approach is to cut away the imagery and offer an objective study of a terminal alcoholic on the last day of his life. Albert Finney, the doomed British consul in Cuernevaca in 1938, is quite breath-taking in a chilling portrait of self-destruction. It is the most accurate —and surely the most tragic—drunk ever committed to film. The consul's wife returns, offering hope of a new life elsewhere to a man whose nature forces him to choose the abyss instead.
R. ★★★★
D: John Huston; W: Guy Gallo; Ph: Gabriel Figueroa; M: Alex North.
Cast: Albert Finney, Jacqueline Bisset, Anthony Andrews, Katy Jurado.

UNDER TWO FLAGS. (1936) Far-fetched Foreign Legion fare. A jealous commandant sends Ronald Colman out on a dangerous mission and hopes he won't come back. Colman turns on the charm as a man torn between a camp girl and a visiting high society lady.
★★
D: Frank Lloyd; W: W.P. Lipscomb and Walter Ferris; Ph: Ernest Palmer and Sidney Wagner; M: Louis Silvers.
Cast: Ronald Colman, Claudette Colbert, Victor McLaglen, Rosalind Russell.

UNFAITHFULLY YOURS. (1948) Preston Sturges knocks a vain conductor off the podium with a devilishly funny study of jealousy and marriage. Rex Harrison's egocentric maestro is a joy. He thinks his pretty wife is having an affair with his assistant and plots his revenge while waving his baton over the orchestra. Harrison's character is said to be a parody of Sir Thomas Beecham.
★★★★
D and W: Preston Sturges; Ph: Victor Milner; M: Alfred Newman.
Cast: Rex Harrison, Linda Darnell, Barbara Lawrence, Rudy Vallee.

UNFAITHFULLY YOURS. (1984) Dudley Moore, after a string of movies that left him open to charges of conduct unbecoming his comic talent, returned to top form as the jealous symphony conductor. The idea of an all-consuming and ultimately murderous

jealousy allows him a full measure of slow, burns, byzantine misunderstandings and opportunities for physical comedy. He is a born farceur and Howard Zieff's remake has the sense to allow him to turn the proceedings into a one-man show.
PG. ★★★
D: Howard Zieff; W: Valerie Curtin, Barry Levinson and Robert Klane; Ph: David Walsh; M: Bill Conti.
Cast: Dudley Moore, Armand Assante, Nastassja Kinski, Albert Brooks.

UNIDENTIFIED FLYING ODDBALL. (1979) A lively Disney film that hurls a NASA engineer and his double (a robot) back to Camelot for a variation on Twain's *A Connecticut Yankee in King Arthur's Court*. There they become involved in court intrigues and, of course, save the king.
G. ★★★
D: Russ Mayberry; W: Don Tait; Ph: Paul Beeson; M: Ron Goodwin.
Cast: Dennis Dugan, Jim Dale, Ron Moody, Kenneth More.

UNION CITY. (1980) The director was two years old when the fifties began and his notion of that drab decade is limited to neon signs flashing over cars of the correct vintage. There is no special reason for setting the dreary tale of a put-upon housewife and her accountant husband in the fifties. He is obsessed with finding out who is stealing the morning milk from outside their apartment. Why we should be is a secret still guarded by Mark Reichert.
PG. ★★
D and W: Mark Reichert; Ph: Edward Lachman; M: Chris Stein.
Cast: Deborah Harry, Dennis Lipscomb, Irina Maleeva, Everett McGill.

UNION PACIFIC. (1939) Some of Cecil B. de Mille's epics have all the order and excitement of a train wreck. So here, he outdid himself with a locomotive collision that still stops the show in its tracks. The rails must go through in a cheerful hymn to free enterprise that brims with action as the lines from east and west are finally linked in Utah. As usual, de Mille is as subtle as the man hitting the last spike, but it doesn't much matter ★★★
D: Cecil B. de Mille; W: Walter de Leon, Jesse Lasky and C. Gardner Sullivan; Ph: Victor Milner; M: Sigmund Krumgold.
Cast: Joel McCrea, Barbara Stanwyck, Robert Preston, Brian Donlevy.

AN UNMARRIED WOMAN. (1978) A lot of newly unmarried women familiar with the many economic hardships of divorce chastised Paul Mazursky for the upscale separation in which Jill Clayburgh has to worry about her $90-an-hour shrink bill. But Mazursky rescued the topic from soap opera and directed an uncompromising and painfully accurate portrait of the break-up of a seemingly secure marriage and the wife's struggle to find her way in a changed world. Jill Clayburgh's Erica is the high point of her acting career.
R. ★★★★
D and W: Paul Mazursky; Ph: Arthur Ornitz; M: Bill Conti.
Cast: Jill Clayburgh, Michael Murphy, Alan Bates, Cliff Gorman.

THE UNQUIET DEATH OF JULIUS AND ETHEL ROSENBERG. (1975) Alvin Goldstein makes no effort to hide his sympathy for the Rosenbergs, who were executed after the most controversial espionage trial in American history. The documentary is lucid, thoroughly researched. It presents the views of both sides and is commendable for those who want something more than the thinly disguised fiction in *Daniel*.
★★★
D and W: Alvin Goldstein.

UP. (1976) Russ Meyer, still whistling "Thanks for the Mammary," wallows in the blood-and-boobs sexual violence that is his hallmark. The usual prodigiously endowed women cavort through this fantasy in which the sex is interrupted by castrations and disembowelments with a chain saw. Some people think Meyer is a self-parodist, but his tongue is always in someone else's cheek. The star makes you realize why they invented twin theaters.
X. ★
D: Russ Meyer; W: R. Callern; Ph: Russ Meyer; M: William Loose and Paul Ruhland.
Cast: Robert McLane, Edward Schaaf, Mary Gavin, Elaine Collins.

UP PERISCOPE. (1959) But there's nothing much worth seeing. Edmond O'Brien and James Garner in a thrice-familiar conflict between officers aboard a submarine. Garner's mission is to go ashore in enemy territory and break a code. The film is conscientious in its avoidance of originality.
★★
D: Gordon Douglas; W: Richard Landau; Ph: Carl Guthrie; M: Ray Heindorf.

Cast: Edmond O'Brien, James Garner, Alan Hale, Jr., Carleton Carpenter.

UP THE CREEK. (1984) A description of the state of film comedy as much as a title. The makers deserve to be paddled and sent to stand in the corner. The four worst students in America enter a whitewater raft race. Apparently, they wrote the screenplay before leaving. Otherwise, a routine *Animal House* clone.
R. ★
D: Robert Butler; W: Jim Kouf; Ph: James Glennon; M: William Goldstein.
Cast: Tim Matheson, Jennifer Runyon, Stephen Furst, Dan Monahan.

UP THE DOWN STAIRCASE. (1967) Although the problems of the students and some of the attitudes that surface here may seem either innocuous or dated, Robert Mulligan's consideration of some of the issues in a tough New York high school is still thought-provoking. Its main point is that these problems worsen when people—the students, teachers, educators and parents—keep passing the buck. Sandy Dennis is excellent as a young teacher trying to cope.
★★★
D: Robert Mulligan; W: Tad Mosel; Ph: Joseph Coffey; M: Fred Karlin.
Cast: Sandy Dennis, Patrick Bedford, Eileen Heckart, Ruth White.

UP THE SANDBOX. (1972) Garbled mixture of fantasy and reality about a Manhattan housewife who is unhappy with her lot. The facts of her life, including a meddlesome mother and a boring husband, are a lot funnier than the flights of fancy. These include a seduction scene with Fidel Castro and a black militant plot against the Statue of Liberty. Worthwhile for one of Barbra Streisand's more restrained and low-key performances.
R. ★★
D: Irvin Kershner; W: Paul Zindel; Ph: Gordon Willis; M: Billy Goldenberg.
Cast: Barbra Streisand, David Selby, Jane Hoffman, Ariane Heller.

UPTOWN SATURDAY NIGHT. (1974) A black comedy in the best sense of the word. Sidney Poitier and Bill Cosby, a couple of working stiffs, lose a winning lottery ticket and the recovery takes them past a gallery of underworld types. A jerry-built but often funny outing with Richard Pryor and Flip Wilson in fine form as, respectively, an inept private eye and a preacher.
PG. ★★★
D: Sidney Poitier; W: Richard Wesley; Ph: Fred J. Koenekamp; M: Tom Scott.
Cast: Bill Cosby, Sidney Poitier, Harry Belafonte, Richard Pryor.

URBAN COWBOY. (1980) A slice of life masquerading as the whole loaf. James Bridges is at his best when he looks at the fantasy life of oil workers who come to Gilley's saloon to ride the mechanical bull and posture as cowboys. But for long stretches he shares the fantasy and that blunts the point. Typically, he introduces the bull in a sardonic way and then gets caught up in John Travolta's efforts to conquer it. The more asbsorbing consequence of the fantasy—the way it colides with life outside and attitudes to women—is lost in the schizophrenia.
PG. ★★★
D: James Bridges; W: Bridges and Aaron Latham; Ph: Ray Villalobos; M: Ralph Burns.
Cast: John Travolta, Debra Winger, Scott Glenn, Madolyn Smith.

URGH! A MUSIC WAR. (1980) Ugh. 23 punk rock acts, ranging from the then relatively obscure Police to something called Oingo Boingo. The Police open and close the show and it's very uneven going in between, even if you are a devout punkophile.
PG. ★★
D: Derek Burbridge.
Cast: (Acts) The Police, X, the Go-Gos, Echo.

USED CARS. (1980) A pre-owned lemon that begins with the inarguable contention that there is no difference between used car salesmen and politicians. Bob Zemeckis heaps scorn on the business tactics and scruples of the former in his ambition to become one of the latter. Then he does a U-turn and tries to make the salesman a sympathetic figure. Jack Warden takes two roles as twin brothers who hate each other.
R. ★★
D: Bob Zemeckis; W: Zemeckis and Robert Gale; Ph: Donald M. Morgan; M: Patrick Williams.
Cast: Jack Warden, Kurt Russell, Deborah Harmon, David Lander.

V

THE VALACHI PAPERS. (1972) The sort of Mafia movie where everyone adds "capisce?" to the end of their sentences. The adaptation of Peter Maas' book about the inner workings of the underworld labors under the criminal penalty of Charles Bronson as Joe Valachi. Whatever drama there is in the conflicts of loyalty and ensuing peril in Valachi's story is lost behind his impenetrable countenance. The story, told in flashbacks, is mostly violent killings by cartoon gangsters. Capisce?
R. ★
D: Terence Young; W: Stephen Geller; Ph: Aldo Tonti; M: Riz Ortolani.
Cast: Charles Bronson, Lino Ventura, Fred Valleca, Gerald S. O'Loughlin.

VALDEZ IS COMING. (1971) Burt Lancaster is one of the few stars of his generation to have expanded his horizons in the seventies. The versatility that made that transition possible is obvious in what could have been a throwaway western. Like his character in *Atlantic City*, he's a man who's seen better days in his profession and who is forced to do more than remember them by the turn of events. He seeks justice for the widow of an innocent man and it turns into a one-man war.
★★★
D: Edwin Sherin; W: Roland Kibbee and David Rayfiel; Ph: Gabor Pogany; M: Charles Gross.
Cast: Burt Lancaster, Susan Clark, Jon Cypher, Barton Heyman.

VALENTINO. (1977) Ken Russell, who believes nothing succeeds like excess, opens with the great lover in a coffin besieged by mourning women. Nothing that follows breathes life into an intriguing figure. As an actor, Nureyev is a great ballet dancer and no one seems to have thought of the fact that he would have to speak as the silent star. Russell disdains direct biography in the sensational events leading to Valentino's death in 1926 and indulges himself in lurid visions of the star as a protean sex symbol.
R. ★★
D: Ken Russell; W: Russell and Mardik Martin; Ph: Peter Suschitzsky; M: Ferde Grofe.
Cast: Rudolf Nureyev, Leslie Caron, Michelle Phillips, Carol Kane.

VALLEY GIRLS. (1983) Because a woman with some solid credentials in documentaries directed this foray into the San Fernando Valley and its strange young denizens, considerable and rather rash claims were made for it. While not enough to provoke a cry of "gag me with a spoon," it's an innocuous tale of young love sundered by two cultures—Valleyspeak and Hollywood punk. The brief fad for Valleyisms had long since passed by the time it was released.
R. ★★
D: Martha Coolidge; W: Wayne Crawford and Andrew Lane; Ph: Frederick Elmas; M: Various Artists.
Cast: Nicolas Cage, Deborah Foreman, Elizabeth Daily, Heidi Holicker.

VALLEY OF THE DOLLS. (1967) Once is more than enough if you're watching this rendering of Jacqueline Susann's best-seller. Trash on such an inspired level has a certain chutzpah that yields many a good laugh and *Valley of the Dolls* is fun if approached in such a spirit. Three women learn that there's no business like show business.
★
D: Mark Robson; W: Helen Deutch and Dorothy Kingsley; Ph: William Daniels; M: John Williams.
Cast: Sharon Tate, Barbara Parkins, Patty Duke, Paul Burke.

VENOM. (1981) Klaus Kinski leads a group of kidnappers who take a small boy hostage in a London house and engage in a battle of wills with the cops. You are invited to believe in a 15-foot black mamba slithing around the heating ducts and having a sense of rough justice. The actors are far too good for this sort of nonsense.
R. ★★
D: Piers Haggard; W: Robert Carrington; Ph: Gilbert Taylor; M: Michael Kamen.
Cast: Sterling Hayden, Nicol Williamson, Klaus Kinski, Sarah Miles.

VERA CRUZ. (1954) In 1860s Mexico two adventurers have to escort a consignment of gold and a lady and deal with their desire for both. Burt Lancaster and Gary Cooper make the trip with trademark mannerisms, but it's a lavishly mounted if slightly mindless production.
★★
D: Robert Aldrich; W: Borden Chase, James R. Webb and Roland Kibbee; Ph: Ernest Laszlo; M: Hugo Friedhofer.

Cast: Gary Cooper, Burt Lancaster, Denise Darcel, Cesar Romero.

VERDI. (1974) Crude and unintentionally funny Italian biography of the great composer. It purports to trace his life from his arrival in Milan in 1838 to his deathbed. We have Verdi walking the snowy streets declaring, "I am disillusioned, bitter, empty," and other nonsense. A disservice to genius that is not accurate, it turns a fascinating life into a soap opera.

G.   ★
D: Rafallo Matarazzo.
Cast: Pierre Cressay, Anna Maria Ferrero, Gaby Andre, Mario Del Monaco.

THE VERDICT. (1946) One of the pleasures of movies is in looking into the early work of a director for the signs of talent and individuality that separate the good ones from mediocrity. Don Siegel showed his stuff in his debut and he was lucky enough to have the unbeatable combination of Peter Lorre and Sidney Greenstreet. The latter is a retired Scotland Yard detective in Victorian London who won't give up on a case.

★★★
D: Don Siegel; W: Peter Milne; Ph: Ernest Haller; M: Frederick Hollander.
Cast: Sidney Greenstreet, Peter Lorre, Joan Lorring, George Coulouris.

THE VERDICT. (1982) Frank Galvin is the kind of lawyer whose only call to the bar is for another round of Irish whiskey. Paul Newman gives him a sleazy charm and does well by a rather belabored story of Galvin's redemption through his jousts with the medical and legal establishment in a malpractice case. The talent mustered on both sides of the camera for several implausible legal developments is rather like having F. Lee Bailey defend a parking ticket.

R.   ★★★
D: Sidney Lumet; W: David Mamet; Ph: Andrzej Bartkowiak; M: Johnny Mandel.
Cast: Paul Newman, Milo O'Shea, Charlotte Rampling, James Mason.

VERONIKA VOSS. (1982) The last of the trilogy Rainer Werner Fassbinder devoted to Germany in the fifties was his penultimate film before his death at the age of 36. The tone is merciless and the mood one of unrelieved gloom. Footsteps echoing from *Sunset Boulevard* can be heard in the musings of an over-the-hill, drug addicted movie star. A reporter becomes fascinated with her and

uncovers corruption around her. But this is Fassbinder and the rich inherit Germany, if not the rest of the earth.

R.   ★★★
D: Rainer Werner Fassbinder; W: Peter Marthesheimer and Pea Frohlich; Ph: Xaver Schwarzenberger; M: Peer Raben.
Cast: Rosel Zech, Hilmar Thate, Cornelia Froboess, Annemarie Duringer.

VERTIGO. (1958) Alfred Hitchcock plunged into the very depths of his own fears to reach the dizzy heights attained in one of his masterpieces. It is a work of extraordinary power that functions on several levels: an elaborate mystery, a complex and symbol-laden psychological study and a compelling and deeply disturbing essay on the fears that surround love and death. There isn't a frame in the film that has only one meaning. James Stewart is superb as a prisoner of more than the phobia in the title. In this beautifully constructed picture, his search for the thing he fears most—love— leads him to a mysterious woman who is prey to her own form of vertigo.

★★★★★
D: Alfred Hitchcock; W: Alec Coppel and Samuel Taylor; Ph: Robert Burks; M: Bernard Herrmann.
Cast: James Stewart, Kim Novak, Barbara Bel Geddes, Tom Helmore.

VICTORIA THE GREAT. (1937) A decorous biography of the queen who reigned longer than any British monarch and a sincere title performance from Anna Neagle. The work is stately rather than dramatic and draws from her early life and final years.

★★★
D: Herbert Wilcox; W: Robert Vansittart and Miles Malleson.
Cast: Anna Neagle, Anton Walbrook, H.B. Warner, Walter Rilla.

VICTOR/VICTORIA. (1982) Blake Edwards' scintillating blend of satire and keen, humane observation has a cabaret scene where a costuming trick allows men to become women by turning around. His point is that such changes are easier than we think. Julie Andrews abandons inhibition to play a woman who becomes the toast of Paris in the thirties by posing as a man who is a female impersonator. Got it? Edwards explores both the earthy farcical possibilities and the way we cling to images of ourselves.

R.   ★★★★

D and W: Blake Edwards; Ph: Dick Bush; M: Henry Mancini.
Cast: Julie Andrews, Robert Preston, Lesley Ann Warren, James Garner.

VICTORY. (1981) Soccer stars, held captive in a German prison camp, have to dribble their way around cliches dear to the ecapist genre. They often trip up and John Huston's effort falls flat on its face because it stretches credibility in trying to make a wartime version of *The Longest Yard*. The prisoners have to play the German national squad and with Sylvester Stallone in goal it's mostly *Rocky Goes to Stalag 17*. All the prison stockade characters are in place and the soccer played is anachronistic. If Pele, one of the captives, were ever let loose among players of this era his team's scores would be in triple figures.
PG.   ★★
D: John Huston; W: Evan Jones and Yabo Yablonsky; Ph: Gerry Fisher; M: Michel Polnareff.
Cast: Michael Caine, Sylvester Stallone, Max Von Sydow, Pele.

VIDEODROME. (1983) A piece of videocy from Canadian horror director David Cronenberg. Here is a move for those who been kept awake nights wondering whether a television set can have an orgasm. A programmer for a soft porn cable channel finds a "snuff" show being broadcast from Pittsburgh and investigates. Cronenberg wants to say something about television controlling the lives of people addicted to it but his sleazy creation only shows how much worse it could get.
R.   ★
D and W: David Cronenberg; Ph: Mark Irwin; M: Howard Shore.
Cast: James Woods, Sonja Smits, Deborah Harry, Peter Dvorsky.

VIGILANTE. (1983) Not as repulsive as the same director's *Maniac*, but what is? A standard helping of revenge with Fred Williamson helping out a man whose son has been murdered by thugs let loose by a judge.
R.   ★
D: William Lustig; W: Robert Vetere; Ph: James Lemmo; M: Jay Chattaway.
Cast: Fred Williamson, Robert Forster.

VILLAGE OF THE DAMNED. (1960) One of the finest British science-fiction movies, this chilling piece musters a surprisingly intelligent attitude to intelligence from another world. Made long before possessed children became a raging fashion, *Village of the Damned* is based on John Wyndham's *The Midwich Cuckoos*. The aliens are born as super-bright children who communicate with each other through telepathy and confound their parents. There is a fine contrast of natural maternal feelings and the unnatural truth.
                                    ★★★★
D: Wolf Rilla; W: Rilla, Stirling Silliphant and George Barclay; Ph: Geoffrey Faithfull; M: Ron Goodwin.
Cast: George Sanders, Barbara Shelley, Michael Gwynn, Martin Stephens.

THE VILLAIN. (1979) A road runner western cartoon with live actors taking the pratfalls and it runs out of gas soon after the credits. Ex-stuntman Hal Needham allows ex-strongman Arnold Schwarzenegger to speak, which is invariably a mistake. Kirk Douglas chases Schwarzenegger and Ann-Margret and the jests are as funny as Boot Hill.
PG.   ★
D: Hal Needham; W: Robert G. Kane; Ph: Bobby Byrne; M: Bill Justis.
Cast: Kirk Douglas, Ann-Margret, Arnold Schwarzenegger, Paul Lynde.

VILLA RIDES! (1968) But not very well and it's one trip you can safely pass up. Yul Brynner, in an exotic piece of casting, is Pancho Villa minus the punch. Robert Mitchum is an American pilot who becomes involved in both the revolution and a remarkably confused screenplay.
                                      ★★
D: Buzz Kulik; W: Robert Towne and Sam Peckinpah; Ph: Jack Hildyard; M: Maurice Jarre.
Cast: Robert Mitchum, Yul Brynner, Charles Bronson, Grazia Bucetta.

VIOLETTE. (1978) In 1933, a young woman poisoned her stiffly bourgeois parents in a murder that became a sensation in France. The erratic Claude Chabrol was never better in making us privy to the workings of her twisted mind. His approach is understanding rather than sympathetic and Isabelle Huppert is expert in giving us a woman full of emotions and devoid of scruples.
                                    ★★★★
D: Claude Chabrol; W: Odile Barski, Herve Bromberger and Frederic Grendel; Ph: Jean Rabier; M: Pierre Jensen.

Cast: Isabelle Huppert, Stephane Audran, Jean Carmet, Jean-Francois Garreaud.

VINCENT, FRANCOIS, PAUL AND THE OTHERS. (1976) A very successful film about failure, as it intrudes upon the personal and professional lives of three men in mid-life. Vincent, bankrupt businessman in a small town, loses both wife and mistress and turns for emotional sustenance to two friends with many problems of their own. An effortless work that moves gracefully and observantly between the three lives and one that brings out the best in Yves Montand.
★★★★★
D: Claude Sautet; W: Jean-Loup Dabadie, Claude Neron and Sautet; Ph: Jean Boffety; M: Philippe Sarde.
Cast: Yves Montand, Stephane Audran, Michel Piccoli, Serge Reggiani.

VIRGINIA CITY. (1940) The team responsible for *Dodge City* the previous year took on a muddled script about various parties trying to commandeer a gold shipment. Errol Flynn and Randolph Scott have it out and Humphrey Bogart made a demeaning contribution as a Mexican bandit with an allegedly Spanish accent. Nobody had much fun making this and it shows.
★★
D: Michael Curtiz; W: Robert Buckner; Ph: Sol Polito; M: Max Steiner.
Cast: Errol Flynn, Randolph Scott, Miriam Hopkins, Humphrey Bogart.

THE VIRGINIAN. (1929) A western to be savored for the slightly gawky decency of Gary Cooper's ranch foreman in a much-admired version of Owen Wister's book. It is now cherished for its often misquoted line—"If you want to call me that, smile." Cooper courts an Eastern schoolmarm and has to dispense some painful justice on the way to a finely realized gunfight at the end. *The Virginian* was one of the first sound westerns to become a box office hit and it proved an early landmark in the genre.
★★★★
D: Victor Fleming; W: Edward E. Paramore, Jr., Howard Estabrook; Ph: J. Roy Hunt.
Cast: Gary Cooper, Walter Huston, Richard Arlen, Mary Brian.

THE VIRGIN QUEEN. (1955) Bette Davis' second royal progress has nothing much to do with the actual relationship between Elizabeth I and Sir Walter Raleigh. He introduces himself by throwing his cloak over a puddle in the queen's path and the ensuing drama is merely a muddle of romance and intrigue. Davis had more to do in her first Elizabeth I opposite Errol Flynn in *Elizabeth and Essex*.
★★★
D: Henry Koster; W: Harry Brown and Mindret Lord; Ph: Charles Clarke; M: Franz Waxman.
Cast: Bette Davis, Richard Todd, Joan Collins, Jay Robinson.

THE VISIT. (1964) An unwelcome guest that drains the savagery of Friedrich Duerrenmatt's play and wastes a strong cast. Ingrid Bergman is the woman who comes home with vast wealth and buys up the town. What she really wants is for the townspeople to kill the seducer who ruined her. She is never really at home in the part.
★★
D: Bernhard Wicki; W: Ben Barzman; Ph: Armando Nannuzzi; M: Hans-Martin Majewski.
Cast: Ingrid Bergman, Anthony Quinn, Irina Demich, Paolo Stoppa.

VISITING HOURS. (1982) Since this kind of horror film represents a form of mental illness, it is appropriately set in a Canadian hospital. In it, real fears—such as the size of the bill when you emerge from the operating room—are replaced by the killer skulking around and murdering nurses. An example of the calamitous slide in Canadian film-making.
R. ★
D: Jean Claude; W: Brian Taggert; Ph: Rene Verzier; M: Jonathan Goldsmith.
Cast: Lee Grant, William Shatner, Michael Ironside, Linda Purl.

VIVA KNIEVEL. (1977) Unwittingly hilarious fictional tribute to the mad heroics of Evel Knievel. It describes the same trajectory as one of his more ill-advised jumps—resolutely downward and pointless anyway. Evel becomes involved with drug smugglers, Lauren Hutton ("Are you a woman or a Ms.?" he asks her with touching gallantry) and Gene Kelly. Kelly is Evel's mechanic and drinks a lot. Understandably.
PG. ★
D: Gordon Douglas; W: Antonio Santillan, Norman Katkov; Ph: Fred Jackman; M: Charles Bernstein.
Cast: Evel Knievel, Lauren Hutton, Red Buttons, Gene Kelly.

VIVA ZAPATA! (1952) Elia Kazan and Marlon Brando, together again after *A Streetcar Named Desire*, and with no less than John Steinbeck writing the screenplay. The dream teaming did not produce a dream movie and Steinbeck took a few liberties in chronicling the life of a Mexican apostle of freedom. Brando and Anthony Quinn are marvelous as Zapata rises from obscure peasant protest to political leadership. Steinbeck has some pertinent observations on the way power corrupts even the best intentions.

★★★★

D: Elia Kazan; W: John Steinbeck; Ph: Joe MacDonald; M: Alex North.
Cast: Marlon Brando, Jean Peters, Anthony Quinn, Joseph Wiseman.

VOICES. (1978) The boy's band is called the New Jersey Turnpike and sounds like it. The girl is deaf, but wants to be a ballerina. When you hear the script you'll envy her. Michael Ontkean and Amy Irving give the improbable love affair a diligent try but are done in by the overwhelming phoniness around them.
PG. ★★
D: Robert Markowitz; W: John Herzfeld; Ph: Alan Metzger; M: Jimmy Webb.
Cast: Michael Ontkean, Amy Irving, Alex Rocco, Barry Miller.

VON RYAN'S EXPRESS. (1965) One of the finest and certainly among the most exciting prisoner-of-war movies. The familiar conflict between the duty to escape and the urge to sit the war out is refreshed by Frank Sinatra and Trevor Howard. Sinatra is an American colonel interested in the welfare of his men while Howard is an escapist of devout and dangerous resolve. The climax belongs with *The Train* for its unscheduled and heart-stopping tension.

★★★★

D: Mark Robson; W: Wendell Mayes; Ph: William H. Daniels; M: Jerry Goldsmith.
Cast: Frank Sinatra, Trevor Howard, Raffaella Carra, Brad Dexter.

VORTEX. (1983) Punk singer Lydia Lunch is amusingly cast as a punk gumshoe in high heels. An independent movie made on a budget that wouldn't keep a self-respecting punk in staples and safety pins for very long. Lunch grapples with a dastardly defense contracting firm in a film whose attitude to "the System" borders on outright paranoia. Visually, it has some striking scenes.

★★★

D and W: Scott B. and Beth B.; Ph: Steven Fierber; M: Lydia Lunch.
Cast: Lydia Lunch, James Russo, Bill Rice, Haouli Montaug.

VOYAGE OF THE DAMNED. (1976) Sometimes the fate of the few encompasses the vast issues confronting the many and such was surely the case with the Jewish refugees who left Hamburg in 1939 aboard the liner *St. Louis*. Sometimes the wrong people get to make movies about such events. For commercial reasons, the film concentrates on the pawns instead of the game of kings and the journey turns into an odyssey of rejection and the voyage becomes a facile melodrama.
PG. ★★
D: Stuart Rosenberg; W: Steve Shagan, David Butler; Ph: Billy Williams; M: Lalo Schifrin.
Cast: Faye Dunaway, Max Von Sydow, Malcolm McDowell, James Mason.

VOYAGE TO THE BOTTOM OF THE SEA. (1961) Before the television series submerged the idea under a tide of repetition, there was a movie and a pretty diverting one at that. Admiral Nelson commands an advanced submarine which takes a party of contentious scientists on a mission to save the earth. Fine effects underwater.

★★★

D: Irwin Allen; W: Allen and Charles Bennett; Ph: Winton Hoch; M: Paul Sawtell.
Cast: Walter Pidgeon, Joan Fontaine, Barbara Eden, Peter Lorre.

W

THE WAGES OF FEAR. (1952) Much has been written about the philosophical underpinnings, but this incredibly—sometimes unbearably—tense French thriller is one of those movies that carry rewards at several levels. Four desperate men—and they are desperate in every sense—agree to drive trucks loaded with nitro-glycerine over crude roads to an oil well fire 300 miles away. Each bump could be their last. The suspense of the ride is excruciating and there is much symbolism in both their plight and their response.

★★★★★
D: Henri-Georges Clouzot; W: Clouzot and Jerome Geronimi; Ph: Armand Thirard; M: Georges Auric.
Cast: Yves Montand, Charles Vanel, Folco Lulli, Peter Van Eyck.

THE WAGONMASTER. (1950) John Ford had a special affection for this western and it is easy to share his judgement. It is a simple, rather traditional plot presented in a simple, traditional manner and sets out the tribulations of a Mormon wagon train beset by outlaws on its way to a new settlement in Arizona.

★★★★
D: John Ford; W: Frank S. Nugent and Patrick Ford; Ph: Bert Glennon and Archie Stout; M: Richard Hageman.
Cast: Ben Johnson, Harry Carey, Jr., Joanne Dru, Ward Bond.

THE WALKING DEAD. (1936) Michael Curtiz and Boris Karloff were on hand to breath life into the macabre tale of a man who is unjustly sent to the electric chair and who is resurrected by a scientist. His first order of business is to settle accounts with those responsible for his execution. A neatly turned piece of horror and a typical Karloff vehicle.

★★★
D: Michael Curtiz; W: Ewart Adamson and Peter Milne; Ph: Hal Mohr.
Cast: Boris Karloff, Edmund Gwenn, Marguerite Churchill, Ricardo Cortez.

WALKING TALL. (1973) The inimitably named Sheriff Buford Pusser cleans up the county in Tennessee with club and gun. Enormously successful and based on a true story. Joe Don Baker is resolute and one-dimensional as he takes on racketeers who make moonshine and run dens of gambling and prostitution. Really an updated western for those who don't like the Supreme Court.

★★
D: Phil Karlson; W: Mort Briskin; Ph: Jack Marta; M: Walter Scharf.
Cast: Joe Don Baker, Elizabeth Hartman, Gene Evans, Noah Beery.

WALKING TALL, PART TWO. (1975) Buford Pusser was supposed to play himself in the sequel, but he died in a car crash. Bo Svenson took over the Joe Don Baker role and did it better in a less melodramatic and more sentimental story. Pusser pursues moonshiners who are backed by the mob and dodges several attempts on his life.
PG. ★★
D: Earl Bellamy; W: Howard B. Kreitsek; Ph: Keith Smith; M: Walter Scharf.
Cast: Bo Svenson, Luke Askew, Noah Beery, John Chandler.

A WALK IN THE SUN. (1945) A premium grade war film that places a platoon of ordinary men from Texas in the unenviable predicament of having to clear out a deeply entrenched German position. The film's superiority arises from its attention to detail and character and its refusal to wave the flag.

★★★★
D: Lewis Milestone; W: Robert Rossen; Ph: Russell Harlan; M: Frederic Efrem Rich.
Cast: Dana Andrews, Richard Conte, George Tyne, John Ireland.

WALK PROUD. (1979) Robby Benson is absurdly miscast as a Chicano gang leader in the Los Angeles barrio who falls for a girl from the other side of the yacht basin in Marina del Rey. His manner suggests that he practised for the part by watching Ricardo Montalban Chrysler comercials. Oddly, the film argues that a strong family life and gang membership are not incompatible despite all the evidence to the contrary.
PG. ★★
D: Robert Collins; W: Evan Hunter; Ph: Bobby Byrne; M: Don Peake.
Cast: Robby Benson, Sarah Holcomb, Henry Darrow, Pepe Serna.

THE WANDERERS. (1979) A charged, volatile gang movie that borrows liberally from its predecessors all the way back to

West Side Story and musters some of the spirit of *American Graffiti*. Philip Kaufman has a voice and style of his own with three kids tangling with rival gangs and wrestling with girls not ready to go "all the way." A strong sense of the early sixties.
R. ★★★
D: Philip Kaufman; W: Philip and Rose Kaufman; Ph: Michael Chapman.
Cast: Ken Wahl, John Friedrich, Karen Allen, Toni Kalem.

WARGAMES. (1983) A kid who prefers computers for company gains access to the one that controls our nuclear missiles. John Badham's taut drama is at its best when he simply unfolds the story and allows us to draw our own inferences. They are terrifying enough without the set speeches from the overdrawn military-industrial characters. And don't laugh at the premise. There was a real life precedent when a computer in Colorado Springs ordered a nuclear alert in 1979.
PG. ★★★
D: John Badham; W: Lawrence Lasker and Walter F. Parkes; Ph: William A. Fraker; M: Arthur Rubinstein.
Cast: Matthew Broderick, Dabney Coleman, John Wood, Ally Sheedy.

WARLOCK. (1959) A western with an unusual twist to the standard plot of the lawman cleaning up a troubled town. The citizens get more than they bargained for when they hire Henry Fonda, but there are too many twists and digressions in the story and the natural force of its confrontations is sapped. A powerhouse cast compensates.
★★★
D: Edward Dmytryk; W: Robert Alan Aurthur; Ph: Joe MacDonald; M: Leigh Harline.
Cast: Henry Fonda, Anthony Quinn, Richard Widmark, Dorothy Malone.

WARLORDS OF ATLANTIS. (1978) Doug McClure has made a career out of getting lost and this time it is the misfortune of Atlantis to find him. A diving bell submerges in a sea of idiocy at the bottom of which—in every sense of the word—lies the mythical city. The scriptwriter had the gall to take it all seriously. Admirers of truly hilarious monster costumes will not be disappointed by the dime-store assemblage paraded here.
PG. ★
D: Kevin Connor; W: Brian Hayles; Ph: Alan Hume; M: Mike Vickers.
Cast: Doug McClure, Peter Gilmore, Shane Rimmer, Lea Brodie.

WAR OF THE WORLDS. (1953) A well-mounted and pompously written version of the H.G. Wells story of the invasion of the world by unstoppable Martians. When the U.S. Army rides to the rescue—the staple of invasion movies of the period—its weapons are useless. Things look bleak until more natural defenses take over. It could do without the superfluous sermons, but it's a decent example of period paranoia.
★★★
D: Byron Haskin; W: Barre Lyndon; Ph: George Barnes.
Cast: Gene Barry, Ann Robinson, Les Tremayne, Bob Cornthwaite.

THE WARRIORS. (1955) The swagger had gone out of Errol Flynn's swashbuckling by the time he picked up the sword for his final costume adventure. There is nothing much else to take up the slack. He is Edward III's son, a.k.a. the Black Prince, involved in saving Joanne Dru from rapacious French barons. Nobody mentions the fact that the English were even more rapacious.
★★
D: Henry Levin; W: Daniel B. Ulman; Ph: Guy Green; M: Cedric Thorpe Davie.
Cast: Errol Flynn, Joanne Dru, Peter Finch, Yvonne Furneaux.

THE WARRIORS. (1979) A stylized piece on gang warfare in New York that was justly criticized for creating as much violence outside theaters as there was on the screen. And there was plenty of the latter. A gang trying to make its way across the hostile turf of its rivals provides most of the action. *The Warriors* never interests itself in what prompts youths to join the armies of the night or ever suggests they might find better uses for their time. Instead it preys upon gullible minds and remains contemptible.
R. ★
D and W: Walter Hill; Ph: Andrew Laszlo; M: Barry De Vorzon.
Cast: Michael Beck, James Remar, Thomas Waites, Dorsey Wright.

THE WAR WAGON. (1967) John Wayne staked his claim to stardom in *Stagecoach*, but the one careening across the screen here is impenetrably armored and passengers are not welcome. Part vengeance and part comedy—in an amiable mixture. Wayne has to assemble an unlikely crew to try and take what is rightfully his from a prototype of the Brinks Truck.
★★★

D: Burt Kennedy; W: Clair Huffaker; Ph: William Clothier; M: Dmitri Tiomkin.
Cast: John Wayne, Kirk Douglas, Bruce Cabot, Howard Keel.

WATERSHIP DOWN. (1978) Martin Rosen's exemplary version of the Richard Adams fable about a tribe of rabbits seeking a better life occasionally trips up on its own symbolism. It's a tough-minded movie that doesn't shirk from some unpleasantness and younger viewers might finds segments a little frightening. The rabbits have human qualities but they move like rabbits, not people.
PG. ★★★★
D and W: Martin Rosen; M: Art Garfunkel.
Cast: (Voices) Ralph Richardson, Roy Kinnear, Zero Mostel, Michael Hordern.

WATUSI. (1959) Harry Quartermain's son in the dark continent in what amounts to a remake of *King Solomon's Mines.* It never finds the mother lode. Some footage that was left over from the 1950 film was used here and the whole batch is about as appetizing as left-overs usually are.
★★
D: Kurt Neumann; W: James Clavell; Ph: Harold Wellman.
Cast: George Montgomery, Taina Elg, David Farrar, Rex Ingram.

THE WAY AHEAD. (1944) A superior exercise that argued the necessity of duty and preparation in World War II. Carol Reed followed a group of civilians as they make the wrenching adjustments to military life after the debacle at Dunkirk. The precisely observed detailing of the characters make it one of the wartime propaganda films that has survived its original purpose on merit.
★★★
D: Carol Reed; W: Eric Ambler and Peter Ustinov; Ph: Guy Green; M: William Alwyn.
Cast: David Niven, Raymond Huntley, William Hartnell, Stanley Holloway.

WAY OF A GAUCHO. (1952) A "southern" is what you call a western shot in Argentina. Rory Calhoun is a deserter who rounds up a band of misfits to oppose the railroad and a police chief (Richard Boone). Familiar stuff set off by the sweeping scenery.
★★
D: Jacques Tourneur; W: Philip Dunne; Ph: Harry Jackson; M: Sol Kaplan.
Cast: Rory Calhoun, Richard Boone, Gene Tierney, Hugh Marlowe.

THE WAY TO THE STARS. (1945) The Battle of Britain as seen from the ground, a terrain that allows Anthony Asquith to explore the relationships of the pilots and how they are affected by the daily threat of death. Under such circumstances, is it fair to marry and have a family? The response is thoughtful. The movie is also known under the title *Johnny in the Clouds.*
★★★
D: Anthony Asquith; W: Terence Rattigan; Ph: Derek Williams; M: Nicholas Brodszky.
Cast: Michael Redgrave, John Mills, Rosamund John, Douglas Montgomery.

THE WAY WEST. (1967) An attempt to make the definitive wagon train movie that goes around in circles of irrelevant digression and has you wishing fervently for the arrival of the Indians. The fault is not with the stars—even here Robert Mitchum acquits himself well—but with Andrew Mclaglen's understandable uncertainty with how to cram all the screenwriter's trite ideas into two hours. The film is based on a a good novel by A. B. Guthrie, Jr.
★★
D: Andrew V. McLaglen; W: Ben Maddow and Mitch Lindemann; Ph: William Clothier; M: Bronislau Kaper.
Cast: Robert Mitchum , Kirk Douglas, Richard Widmark, Lola Albright.

W.C. FIELDS AND ME. (1976) Rod Steiger gives us a portrait and no mere impersonation of the comedian and the film avoids many of the common pitfalls of Hollywood biographies. However, the account of Fields' years with his mistress—the movie is based on her memoir—concentrates on the wrong things. It begins with Fields as both a star and a lush without examining how he became either. It also favors the consequences of his alcoholism over the discussion of his comic genius.
PG. ★★★
D: Arthur Hiller; W: Bob Merrill; Ph: David M. Walsh; M: Henry Mancini.
Cast: Rod Steiger, Valerie Perrine, John Marley, Jack Cassidy.

A WEDDING. (1978) If *Nashville* is an American tapestry, *A Wedding* is Robert Altman's patchwork quilt. It is seamlessly woven together from bits and pieces culled from the lives of 48 characters. The action is encompassed on the day of a wedding that unites two families who don't care for each other

and the overall effect is like walking through a crowded party.
PG. ★★★
D: Robert Altman; W: Altman, John Considine, Patricia Resnick, Allan Nicholls; Ph: Charles Rosher; M: Tom Walls.
Cast: Carol Burnett, Amy Stryker, Paul Dooley, Mia Farrow.

WEEKEND PASS. (1984) Veterans will recall those training films that warned the sexually careless serviceman of all the diseases he could catch. Any one of them is better—not to mention funnier—than this numbskull chronicle of four sailors on leave in Los Angeles. The director has all the routine vulgarities at his fingertips, but the picture plays like the reminscences of a sailor waking up in the brig on Monday morning and trying to piece together what happened.
R. ★
D and W: Lawrence Bassoff; Ph: Bryan England; M: John Baer.
Cast: Chip McAllister, Peter Ellenstein, Patrick Houser, D.W. Brown.

THE WESTERNER. (1940) The life and times—and more importantly—the contradictions to be found in the person of Judge Roy Bean. In an Oscar-winning performance, Walter Brennan brought out these complexities in his dispute with a drifter (Gary Cooper) hauled before his kangaroo court. Cooper gets off by telling a tall one about the judge's favorite, Lily Langtry. Their conflict makes a rich entertainment of a handsomely done traditional plot about homesteaders and cattlemen.
★★★★
D: William Wyler; W: Niven Busch and Jo Swerling; Ph: Gregg Toland; M: Dmitri Tiomkin.
Cast: Gary Cooper, Walter Brennan, Doris Davenport, Fred Stone.

WESTERN UNION. (1941) A western whose action and actors—with the exception of Randolph Scott—never quite matched the epic conception Fritz Lang had for the story of the opening of telegraph lines between Nebraska and Utah. Scott rises above his normal impassivity and Barton MacLane's hamming makes him look even better. They are two brothers torn apart by the coming of the telegraph.
★★★
D: Fritz Lang; W: Robert Carson; Ph: Edward Cronjager; M: David Buttolph.
Cast: Randolph Scott, Robert Young, Dean Jagger, Virginia Gilmore.

WESTWARD HO THE WAGONS. (1956) The wagons hauled Mouseketeers from the TV show popular at the time and they get into various scrapes. Fess Parker is around to right matters as the trusty scout Doc Grayson. Long for a Disney picture and only fitfully interesting, but there are some reliable battle scenes supervised by the incomparable Yakima Canutt.
★★
D: William Beaudine; W: Tom Blackburn; Ph: Charles Boyle; M: George Bruns.
Cast: Fess Parker, Kathleen Crowley, Jeff York, David Stollery.

WESTWORLD. (1973) Michael Crichton is a film-maker who excels in making technology both comprehensible and menacing. Here he came up with a very clever idea—a millionaire's resort where androids allow the guests to live out their fantasies in historical settings. "There is no way to get hurt here," says the host. "Just enjoy yourself." That applies to the film, too, which misses excellence because the themes Crichton raises go undeveloped. *Futureworld* was the sequel to this one.
★★★
D and W: Michael Crichton; Ph: Gene Polito; M: Fred Karlin.
Cast: James Brolin, Yul Brynner, Richard Benjamin, Norman Bartold.

WHATEVER HAPPENED TO BABY JANE? (1962) A garish and diverting horror film that—at the time— answered the question of whatever happened to Bette Davis and Joan Crawford. They responded with a vengeance. Davis is Baby Jane Hudson, a former child star who lives in a Hollywood mansion and gets her kicks from tormenting Crawford, who is crippled. The two stars, abetted by actual clips from their old movies, act up a storm in the grand manner.
★★★
D: Robert Aldrich; W: Lukas Heller; Ph: Ernest Haller; M: Frank de Vol.
Cast: Bette Davis, Joan Crawford, Victor Buono, Anna Lee.

WHAT PRICE GLORY? (1952) A remake of the popular silent film (1926) that found John Ford going for boisterous humor and downplaying the harsher aspects. James Cagney's Captain Flagg and Dan Dailey's Sergeant Quirt punch each other out between fights with the Germans. Corinne Calvet is the girl they both want.
★★★
D: John Ford; W: Phoebe and Henry Ephron; Ph: Joe MacDonald; M: Alfred Newman.

Cast: James Cagney, Dan Dailey, Corinne Calvet, William Demarest.

WHAT'S UP DOC? (1972) Peter Bogdanovich later hit a very wrong note in his salute to the muscial in *At Long Last Love* and this is another and more enjoyable homage to pictures of the past. The object of his affection is the screwball comedy of the thirties, but putting Ryan O'Neal in a Cary Grant role is like standing a glass of flat club soda next to a bottle of Dom Perignon. He's a bumbling scholar and Barbara Streisand is the girl who gets him in trouble. The film has an energy and love for the the old days that is disarming.

★★★
D: Peter Bogdanovich; W: Buck Henry, David Newman and Robert Benton; Ph: Laszlo Kovacs; M: Artie Butler.
Cast: Ryan O'Neal, Barbra Streisand, Kenneth Mars, Madeleine Kahn.

WHEN A STRANGER CALLS. (1979) A slick horror offering that touches all the right panic buttons by preferring realistic fears to the occult and outlandish that was in vogue at the time. A baby-sitter, alone with her charges, is stalked by a berserk merchant seaman.
R. ★★★
D: Fred Walton; W: Walton and Steve Feke; Ph: Don Peterman ; M: Dana Kaproff.
Cast: Carol Kane, Charles Durning, Rutanya Alda, Carmen Argenziano.

WHEN COMEDY WAS KING. (1960) A good anthology of aptly chosen clips from the heyday of silent comedy including the work of the Keystone Kops and Buster Keaton.

★★★
W: Robert Youngson; M: Ted Royal.
Cast: Harry Langdon, Buster Keaton, Laurel and Hardy, Fatty Arbuckle.

WHEN DINOSAURS RULED THE WORLD. (1970) A sequel to *One Million Years B.C.* that is neanderthal in conception and yet quite presentable in the execution of its special effects. Raquel Welch is a conspicuous absentee and her designer pelt is inherited by Victoria Vetri. There is very little dialogue and, given the cast, that's a blessing.

★★
D and W: Val Guest; Ph: Dick Bush; M: Mario Nascimbene.
Cast: Victoria Vetri, Patrick Allen, Robin Hawdon, Patrick Holt.

WHEN WORLDS COLLIDE. (1951) When they do—with the imminent collision of the Earth with a star called Bellus—the issue is who will board a spaceship version of Noah's Ark and restart the human race on another planet. Spectacle takes precedence over an interesting moral dilemma that is advanced in pretty simplistic terms. A selfish and crippled capitalist tries to play God while saving himself. A little naive but a compelling end-of-the-world entry.

★★★
D: Rudolph Mate; W: Sydney Boehm; Ph: John Seitz and W. Howard Greene; M: Leith Stevens.
Cast: Richard Derr, Barbara Rush, Larry Keating, Peter Hanson.

WHERE THE BOYS ARE. (1984) Where the brains aren't is anywhere near an atrocious remake of George Hamilton's 1960 movie. Four actresses who are far too old for the parts play the co-eds on spring break in Fort Lauderdale, which one of them describes as "a supermarket of sex." The stupidity leaves you supine in disbelief.
R. ★
D: Hy Averback; W: Jeff Burkhart and Stu Kreiger; Ph: James Contner; M: Sylvester LeVay.
Cast: Lynn-Holly Johnson, Lorna Luft, Lisa Hartman, Russell Todd.

WHIFFS. (1979) Elliott Gould is a private who has spent fifteen years at an army chemical warfare center as a guinea pig. "We don't want to kill you. We just want to make you a little sick," says his colonel. The movie, very much a missed *M.A.S.H.*, has that effect.
PG. ★
D: Ted Post; W: Malcolm Marmorstein; Ph: David Walsh; M: John Cameron.
Cast: Elliott Gould, Eddie Albert, Harry Guardino, Godfrey Cambridge.

THE WHITE BUFFALO. (1977) Among the worst of the *Jaws* ripoffs. It would be hard to imagine a more blameless and ill-used animal than the buffalo and the one here looks like an obese sheep wearing a floor mop. Charles Bronson, as Wild Bill Hickock, has bad dreams and killing the buffalo is the only way to stop it roaming through his head. Notable for his rejection of a hooker played by Kim Novak with the excuse, "One of your scarlet sisters dosed me proper."
PG. ★
D: J. Lee Thompson; W: Richard Sale; Ph: Paul Lohman; M: John Barry.

Cast: Charles Bronson, Will Sampson, Kim Novak, Jack Warden.

THE WHITE DAWN. (1974) A thoughtful adventure film that makes the stranding of three whalers among a tribe of Eskimos in the 1890s a forum for considering the clash of two cultures. The style is documentary and the screenplay informative as the three men react to their situation in different ways. The ending is inevitable and slightly didactic. **R.** ★★★
D: Philip Kaufman; W: James Houston and Tom Rickman; Ph: Michael Chapman; M: Henry Mancini.
Cast: Timothy Bottoms, Lou Gossett, Jr., Warren Oates, Simonie Kopapik.

WHITE HEAT. (1949) With James Cagney at the center as Cody Jarrett the temperature is kept at the promised level. Jarrett winds up shouting "Made it, Ma! Top of the world!" and that's where this performance belongs. To evade a murder conviction Jarrett, a killer with a mother fixation, goes to jail on a minor rap. Edmond O'Brien is the undercover agent who sets him up in a tale that unfolds with operatic intensity. ★★★★★
D: Raoul Walsh; W: Ivan Goff and Ben Roberts; Ph: Sid Hickox; M: Max Steiner.
Cast: James Cagney, Edmond O'Brien, Margaret Wycherly, Virginia Mayo.

WHITE LINE FEVER. (1975) Director Jonathan Kaplan tried to travel two roads by combining a standard B movie about violence in the trucking industry with an essay on the crushing boredom of blue collar life. He ended up stuck on the median strip. Jan-Michael Vincent is the put-upon Vietnam veteran who takes on corrupt trucking interests in the Southwest.
PG. ★★
D: Jonathan Kaplan; W: Ken Friedman and Kaplan; Ph: Fred Koenekamp; M: David Nichtern.
Cast: Jan-Michael Vincent, Kay Lenz, Slim Pickens, L.Q. Jones.

WHITE WILDERNESS. (1958) The bleak majesty of the Arctic and its animal life is imposingly captured in one of the best of the Disney True-Life nature films. The usual over-cute narration is annoying, but the documentary is honest in showing some cruel killings by a wolverine and striking in a sequence devoted to the mass suicide of lemmings. They leap off a cliff in the misguid-ed belief that they only have a narrow stretch of water to cross.
★★★
D and W: James Algar; Ph: James R. Simon et al., M: Oliver Wallace.
Cast: Winston Hibler (narrator).

WHO IS KILLING THE GREAT CHEFS OF EUROPE? (1978) Ted Kotcheff's decision to turn the mystery into a Cook's tour of lavish continental locations and kitchens produces a feast for the eye instead of food for thought. Robert Morley is a legendary, dying gourmet who thinks up a unique form of revenge against those whom he feels responsible for his terminal gluttony. He also steals the film with one of his finest comic performances.
PG. ★★★
D: Ted Kotcheff; W: Peter Stone; Ph: John Alcott; M: Henry Mancini.
Cast: George Segal, Jacqueline Bisset, Robert Morley, Jean-Pierre Cassel.

WHO'LL STOP THE RAIN? (1978) An absorbing but not entirely successful version of Robert Stone's Dog Soldiers. The venting of anger over Vietnam and the scars the war left on the men who fought in it shares space with some fierce action. Nick Nolte smuggles drugs for a friend and then flees with the man's wife while government agents and crooks give chase.
R. ★★★
D: Karel Reisz; W: Judith Roscoe and Robert Stone; Ph: Richard H. Kline; M: Laurence Rosenthal.
Cast: Nick Nolte, Tuesday Weld, Michael Moriarty, Anthony Zerbe.

WHOLLY MOSES. (1980) An anemic parody of The Ten Commandments that Dudley Moore would doubtless like to see dumped in the Red Sea. If you don't know the original, you will miss a lot of the humor. If you do, you will notice there isn't much to miss. Moore is Herschel, who was cast adrift in a basket at the same time as Moses.
PG. ★
D: Gary Weis; W: Guy Thomas;.
Cast: Dudley Moore, James Coco, Paul Sand, Jack Gilford.

WHO'S AFRAID OF VIRGINIA WOOLF? (1965) Don't be put off by the years of Liz and Dick publicity. Elizabeth Taylor gives what is arguably her finest screen performance and Richard Burton tops it in Mike Nichols' painfully good adaptation of Edward Albee's play. George and Martha hurt themselves as much as each other in lacerating exchanges. The language broke new ground in what could be said on the screen and Albee furnished an uncannily accurate chart of one couple's relationship. It is for the latter reason that the film remains potent cinema.

D: Mike Nichols; W: Ernest Lehman; Ph: Haskell Wexler; M: Alex North.
Cast: Richard Burton, Elizabeth Taylor, George Segal, Sandy Dennis. ★★★★

WHOSE LIFE IS IT ANYWAY? (1981) The real question raised with heart-wrenching eloquence is what happens when the will to live becomes the determination to die. In one of the most memorable pieces he has ever committed to the screen, Richard Dreyfuss is a sculptor whose hope of recovery after a car accident gives way to the realization that he is condemned to spend the rest of his days as a quadriplegic on a dialysis machine. The argument rages back and forth between lawyers, doctors and the patient. The strength of the film lies in the compassion—rather than condemnation—it extends to everyone involved.
R. ★★★★
D: John Badham; W: Brian Clark and Reginald Rose; Ph: Mario Tosi; M: Arthur B. Rubinstein.
Cast: Richard Dreyfuss, John Cassavetes, Christine Lahti, Bob Balaban.

WHY NOT. (1979) In this shrill French film, a *menage a trois* becomes a *menage a quatre* and it's a case of three's company and four is a crowd. The foursome sleep with each other and live in a house that is, with bludgeoning signficance, fenced off from the bourgeois world. Coline Serreau's impassioned political views interfere with the potential drama of men and women exploring non-familial ways to live.
★★
D and W: Coline Serreau; Ph: Jean-Francois Robin; M: Jean-Pierre Mas.
Cast: Sami Frey, Mario Gonzalez, Christine Murillo, Nocile Jamet.

WHY SHOOT THE TEACHER? (1980) The worst of times in the Depression in rural Saskatchewan where even the best of times are never easy. The farmers grudgingly agree to hire a teacher (Bud Cort), but are too poor or reluctant to pay him. Lightertoned and more humorous than most Depression movies.
PG. ★★★

D: Silvio Narizzano; W: James Defilice; Ph: Marc Champion; M: Rick Hyslop.
Cast: Bud Cort, Samantha Eggar, Chris Wiggins, Gary Reineke.

WHY WOULD I LIE?. (1980) Cletus Hayworth is a chronic liar who dreams up "fabrications" because the truth is boring. So is this nice effort which is almost puppyish in its need to be liked. Hayworth lies his way into a job as a welfare caseworker and becomes entangled with a young boy's problems.
PG. ★★
D: Larry Peerce; W: Peter Stone; Ph: Gerald Hirschfeld; M: Charles Fox.
Cast: Treat Williams, Lisa Eichhorn, Gabriel Swann, Valerie Curtin.

THE WICKED LADY. (1983) A sort of peeping *Tom Jones* that comes across as Restoration travesty. Absurdly overcast with big names in nothing roles to a degree that suggests asking the 82d Airborne to serve as school crossing guards. I doubt if the actors knew that Michael Winner would spice up the feeble story of a bitchy social climber with porn interludes for the international market.
R. ★★
D: Michael Winner; W: Winner and Leslie Arliss; Ph: Jack Cardiff; M: Tony Banks.
Cast: Faye Dunaway, Alan Bates, John Gielgud, Denholm Elliott.

WIFEMISTRESS. (1978) An Italian sex comedy that's as frothy as cold cappucino. A frigid wife who believes her philandering husband is dead finds out about his affairs and pays him back in kind. He becomes a powerless witness. The feminist point is lost in the non-stop coupling.
★★
D: Marco Vicario; W: Vicario and Rodolfo Sonego .
Cast: Laura Antonelli, Marcello Mastroianni, Leonard Mann, Gaston Moschin.

THE WILBY CONSPIRACY. (1975) Wellmeaning thriller about race relations in South Africa that turns into a crashing Boer in italicising its message. Security Chief Nicol Williamson chain-smokes and worries about "hoodlums 20 years out of the trees." He pursues Sidney Poitier, the leader of the black insurgents, and Michael Caine, an engineer who becomes unwittingly and unwillingly involved.
PG. ★★
D: Ralph Nelson; W: Rod Amateau and

Harold Nebenzai; Ph: John Coquillon; M: Stanley Myers.
Cast: Sidney Poitier, Michael Caine, Nicol Williamson, Saeed Jaffrey.

THE WILD BUNCH. (1969) Although *Ride the High Country* is arguably the better Peckinpah western, *The Wild Bunch* has undoubtedly proved the more influential both inside and outside the western form. The way in which violent death is lyrically and almost lovingly portrayed in slow detail and bloody eruptions rewrote the methods of action direction. The story of a bunch of killers in Mexico in 1913 is one that is tailored to Peckinpah's admiration for the gesture that is at once noble and nihilistic. They have no claim to our sympathy but the picture is so shrewdly made that it is their due by the time the finale arrives. John Sturges borrowed *The Seven Samurai* for *The Magnificent Seven*, but *The Wild Bunch* is the closest an American director has come to a Kurosawa vision of a warrior's honor.

★★★★

D: Sam Peckinpah; W: Peckinpah and Walon Green; Ph: Lucien Ballard; M: Jerry Goldsmith.
Cast: William Holden, Robert Ryan, Ernest Borgnine, Edmond O'Brien.

THE WILD DUCK. (1977) An engrossing version of Ibsen's play that, quite rightly, does not try to open up its pent-up emotions for the screen. The direction is straightforward and stresses Ibsen's subtle working of the way illusion and reality intrude upon one another. A somewhat dotty inventor presides over a family riven by revelations from the past. Released theatrically in German with English subtitles.

★★★

D and W: Hans Geissendorfer (from the play by Henrik Ibsen); Ph: Harry Nap; M: Nils Janette Walen.
Cast: Jean Seberg, Peter Kern, Bruno Ganz, Anne Bennett.

THE WILD GEESE. (1978) A band of white mercenaries is recruited to rescue a deposed African leader from his captors. Killing for hire is an unsavory trade and the film tries to make these literal soldiers of fortune palatable by assuring us of their virtue and viewing them as pawns in the hands of even more dubious men higher up. It also keeps stopping for simplistic sermons on racial harmony and other issues confronting contemporary Africa.

R.   ★★

D: Andrew V. McLaglen; W: Reginald Rose; Ph: Jack Hildyard; M: Roy Budd.
Cast: Richard Burton, Richard Harris, Roger Moore, Hardy Kruger.

WILD IN THE COUNTRY. (1961) The Pelvis takes up the pen as a country boy saved from delinquency by a social worker who thinks he can become a great writer. Elvis sings a few songs to atone for the idiocy of this idea and *Wild in the Country* is one of his tamest movies.

★★

D: Philip Dunne; W: Clifford Odets; Ph: William C. Mellor; M: Kenyon Hopkins.
Cast: Elvis Presley, Hope Lange, Tuesday Weld, Millie Perkins.

WILD IN THE STREETS. (1968) In a satirical fantasy typical of its era, a pop star becomes President of the United States when the voting age is lowered to fourteen. An IQ in that neighborhood is behind the treatment of the idea and very few of the jibes work. Everyone over 30 is sent to camps and forced to take LSD. The movie's a bad trip and nobody should be forced to watch the wretched excesses of Shelly Winters as the singer's mother.

★

D: Barry Shear; W: Robert Thom; Ph: Richard Moore; M: Les Baxter.
Cast: Christopher Jones, Shelley Winters, Diane Varsi, Hal Holbrook.

THE WILD ONE. (1953) A notorious movie in its day and one that was even banned in England in the fear that it might give native bikers the wrong ideas. Marlon Brando's way of wearing a cap was imitated by youth around the world and his work is as inimitable as ever. He is the leader of a motorcycle gang which roars into a small town and takes over. The adult world found the sentiments expressed quite frightening but, given what goes on in your neighborhood Hells Angels' clubhouse today, these guys aren't that wild.

★★★

D: Laslo Benedek; W: John Paxton; Ph: Hal Mohr; M: Leith Stevens.
Cast: Marlon Brando, Lee Marvin, Mary Murphy, Robert Keith.

THE WILD PARTY. (1974) An occasion with little life, no soul and an hors d'oevre that consists of an indigestible amount of ham tendered by James Coco. A silent film comedian's career is ruined when an orgy

ends in scandal and death. Set in 1929 and based on the sad fate of Fatty Arbuckle.
R. ★
D: James Ivory; W: Walter Marks; Ph: Walter Lassally; M: Larry Rosenthal.
Cast: James Coco, Raquel Welch, Perry King, Tiffany Bolling.

WILD RIVER. (1960) Elia Kazan was a little too prone to invest the collision of progress and old values with symbolism, but *Wild River* is still a thoughtful and moving drama. Its issues certainly remain relevant. Montgomery Clift represents the Tennessee Valley Authority in its proposal to flood lands over the loud objections of the owners.
★★★★
D: Elia Kazan; W: Paul Osborn; Ph: Ellsworth Fredericks; M: Kenyon Hopkins.
Cast: Montgomery Clift, Jo Van Fleet, Lee Remick, Albert Salmi.

WILD STYLE. (1984) Very little style of any kind. Rap music that inspires little rapture and break dancing that breaks down. The film has a certain nervous energy that is vitiated by an uncommonly dumb story of a kid whose graffiti is taken seriously by the New York art crowd. But then, what isn't?
PG. ★★
D and W: Charlie Ahearn; M: Cold Crush Brothers.
Cast: Lee Quinones, Fred Braithwaite, Patty Astor.

WILLARD. (1971) The heartwarming saga of a boy and his rats. For some inexplicable reason, the world was ready for Willard, a rat-fink office boy, who finds a way of taking it out on his enemies, and the movie was a hit. He trains rats to kill them. The set must have been a lot of fun, especially for Ernest Borgnine who gets rattled. Apart from the rodent novelty, it's a third-rat horror film.
★
D: Daniel Mann; W: Gilbert Ralston; Ph: Robert Hauser; M: Alex North.
Cast: Bruce Davison, Elsa Lanchester, Ernest Borgnine, Sondra Locke.

WILLIE AND PHIL. (1980) Paul Mazursky's flair for chronicling the way social and moral changes in society affect people struggling to find some rules of behavior surfaces once again. Two inseparable friends who love the same woman try to make a threesome work. Mazursky has crowded in too many themes that are worth films to themselves. It's a very American version of Truffaut's *Jules et Jim*.
R. ★★★

D and W: Paul Mazursky; Ph: Sven Nykvist; M: Claude Bolling.
Cast: Michael Ontkean, Margot Kidder, Ray Sharkey, Jan Miner.

WILL PENNY. (1968) Charlton Heston, cast against heroic stereotype, is a cowboy for whom getting by is a full-time occupation. What turns out to be one of his most satisfying performances and deserves to be framed in a better film. His laconic, understated acting and an equally gratifying piece from Joan Hackett as a frontier stalwart get lost in the hysterics of Donald Pleasence and Bruce Dern. They behave as if they're in another picture and they certainly shouldn't be in this one.
★★★
D and W: Tom Gries; Ph: Lucien Ballard; M: David Raksin.
Cast: Charlton Heston, Bruce Dern, Joan Hackett, Donald Pleasence.

WINCHESTER '73. (1950) Despite it's modest black and white look, Anthony Mann's film is one of the best westerns of the fifties and it played a part in renewing the form's popularity before television repetition did so much damage. James Stewart does some splendid work as a man who loses his treasured new rifle and recovers it through the turns of an old vengeance plot. The film is rightly noted for the brilliantly staged duel in its finale.
★★★★
D: Anthon Mann; W: Borden Chase and Robert Richards; Ph: William Daniels; M: Frank Skinner.
Cast: James Stewart, Dan Duryea, Shelley Winters, Stephen McNally.

THE WIND AND THE LION. (1975) Sweeping, well-made adventure on the old Hollywood scale with the same rewriting of history for the convenience of the box office. Thus one fat Englishman kidnapped by a Berber chief in Morocco in fact becomes the ravishing Candice Bergen in fiction. Teddy Roosevelt, as macho here as the Marlboro man, is alleged to have sent in the Marines. He did not. John Milius also overlaid some opaque comments on the U.S. penchant for military adventurism abroad.
PG. ★★
D and W: John Milius; Ph: Billy Williams; M: Jerry Goldsmith.
Cast: Sean Connery, Candice Bergen, Brian Keith, John Huston.

WINDOWS. (1980) Cinematographer Gordon Willis' debut achieved the impossi-

340

ble—a film about homosexuals that is even viler than *Cruising*. The screenplay, a demented men's locker room fantasy masquerading as a script, has a lesbian arranging to have a woman she fancies raped. This will turn her off men. The picture is a turn-off with much of it devoted to Elizabeth Ashley panting into a telescope trained on her beloved's apartment.
R.
D: Gordon Willis; W: Barry Seigel; Ph: Gordon Willis; M: Ennio Morricone.
Cast: Talia Shire, Elizabeth Ashley, Joseph Cortese, Kay Medford.

WINDWALKER. (1980) Given the years of Hollywood stereotyping and slander of the American Indian, Keith Merrill's conscientious reconstruction of life before the arrival of the white man offers considerable redress. Near death, a Cheyenne chief recalls the tragedies of his life and his futile quest to recover a son kidnapped by a rival tribe. Handsomely made, but the Great Spirits are poured too liberally at the finale.
PG.   ★★★
D: Keith Merrill; W: Ray Goldrup; Ph: Reed Smoot; M: Merrill Jensen.
Cast: Trevor Howard, Nick Ramus, James Remar, Serene Hedin.

WINGED VICTORY. (1944) Moss Hart wrote the script from his stage play and the stars were mostly actors who were given leave from active duty to appear. Otherwise, George Cukor did his best with a routine rite-of-passage story that sees the young airmen in training and eventually in combat.
                                                   ★★
D: George Cukor; W: Moss Hart; Ph: Glen MacWilliams; M: David Rose.
Cast: Lon McCallister, Jeanne Crain, Edmond O'Brien, Jane Ball.

THE WINSLOW BOY. (1948) Anyone wrongly accused of some trespass at school will envy the defense the boy receives here. A father is outraged by the expulsion of his son for petty theft and takes on the system. It culminates in court when Robert Donat leading the defense. Proof, in Terence Rattigan's hands, that you don't need a sensational crime to discuss serious issues.
                                                   ★★★
D: Anthony Asquith; W: Terence Rattigan and Anatole De Grunwald; Ph: Frederick Young; M: William Alwyn.
Cast: Robert Donat, Cedric Hardwicke, Neil North, Margaret Leighton.

WITHOUT A TRACE. (1983) Producer Stanley Jaffe's directing debut addresses the emotional issue of missing children. It begins with a fierce honesty and ultimately capitulates to Hollywood notions of what an audience can take. It is further weakened by the need to dramatize anguish at considerable length. Kate Nelligan turns in a bravura performance as the grief-stricken mother and the film airs a matter that cannot be raised too often.
PG.   ★★★
D: Stanley Jaffe; W: Beth Gutcheon; Ph: John Bailey; M: Jack Nitzsche.
Cast: Kate Nelligan, David Dukes, Judd Hirsch, Stockard Channing.

WITNESS FOR THE PROSECUTION. (1957) Enjoyable if slightly convoluted courtroom drama that translates Agatha Christie's stage play to the screen. Its main asset is Charles Laughton, a barrister who takes on a man accused of murdering a widow for her money, despite the overwhelming evidence on the prosecutor's side.
                                                   ★★★
D: Billy Wilder; W: Wilder and Harry Kurnitz; Ph: Russell Harlan; M: Matty Malneck.
Cast: Charles Laughton, Tyrone Power, Marlene Dietrich, Elsa Lanchester.

THE WIZ. (1978) An all-black musical version of *The Wizard of Oz* that places the Yellow Brick Road along Harlem's 125th street. The midwestern pieties of the original don't sit well with the hip setting. Garish and overblown, it lurches from one production number to the next.
PG.   ★★
D: Sidney Lumet; W: Joel Schumacher; Ph: Oswald Morris; M: Quincy Jones.
Cast: Diana Ross, Michael Jackson, Nipsey Russell, Lena Horne.

THE WIZARD OF BABYLON. (1983) A documentary about Rainer Fassbinder and the making of his dreadful last film, *Querelle*. It holds a macabre fascination for an interview with the director filmed only a dozen hours before his death from a drug overdose at the age of 36. He is in worse shape than his film and the mesmerizing force that his actors see in him is not much in evidence.
                                                   ★★
D: Dietor Schidor; Ph: Carl-Friedrich Koschnik; M: Peer Raben.

THE WIZARD OF OZ. (1939) A magical movie experience that has never lost its spellbinding quality. For many years, most critics agreed that nothing on either side of the rainbow could equal Dorothy's adventures in the Land of Oz. Then *E.T.* came along. Both movies show a profound understanding of what captivates and what challenges children and how art can help them cope with natural fears. Judy Garland's Dorothy is spirited away from Kansas to a fantasy world of strange characters like the Cowardly Lion and the Tin Man. This was arguably one of the most perfectly cast movies in the history of the screen and the enchanting score and effortless direction are equally impressive.

★★★★★

D: Victor Fleming; W: Noel Langley, Florence Ryerson, Edgar Allan Woolf; Ph: Harold Rosson; M: (Songs) E. Y. Harburg and Harold Arlen.
Cast: Judy Garland, Margaret Hamilton, Bert Lahr, Ray Bolger.

WIZARDS. (1977) Ralph Bakshi, the man who made animation grow up, returned to the sword-and-sorcery milieu as a precursor to his rendering of Tolkien's *Lord of the Rings*. Some startlingly good technical work only shows up a simplistic story of a clash of wizards millions of years in the future. The conflict is between the forces of technology and the beauty of nature.
PG. ★★
D and W: Ralph Bakshi; Ph: Ted C. Bellimer; M: Andrew Belling.

WOLFEN. (1981) Albert Finney, ending a long absence from the screen, returned as a detective charged with solving some macabre goings on in the South Bronx. The creatures responsible only cry wolf when they are threatened and Michael Wadleigh, the man who made *Woodstock*, has some intelligent things to add to a basically formulaic structure. The philosophy ultimately undermines the tension, but his work is an elevation of the form.
R. ★★★
D: Michael Wadleigh; W: Wadleigh and David Eye; Ph: Gerry Fisher; M: James Horner.
Cast: Albert Finney, Diane Venora, Edward James Olmos, Gregory Hines.

THE WOLF MAN. (1940) The movie that started all the howling. Lon Chaney, Jr., is bitten and starts behaving strangely when the moon comes out. He had to do something until *Frankenstein Meets the Wolf Man* two years later, so he stalks around Wales looking for prey. Claude Rains is very good as Chaney's father and horror addicts rank

The Wolf Man in the classic division, even though it is slow and very stylized.

★★★★

D: George Wagner; W: Curt Siodmak; Ph: Joseph Valentine; M: Hans Salter and Frank Skinner.
Cast: Lon Chaney, Jr., Claude Rains, Ralph Bellamy, Warren William.

THE WOMAN IN RED. (1984) She is the object of Gene Wilder's by no means obscure desires. He falls prey to temptation in middle age and most of the humor is built on his consistent incompetence as an adulterer. It's a remake of the French hit *Pardon Mon Affaire* and Wilder, who is given to outrageous overplaying when he's directing himself, has things well in hand.
PG-13. ★★★
D and W: Gene Wilder; Ph: Fred Schuler; M: John Morris.
Cast: Gene Wilder, Gilda Radner, Charles Grodin, Joseph Bologna.

THE WOMAN IN THE WINDOW. (1944) The woman is in a portrait and it is the misfortune of a psychology professor to find the model who posed for it. It leads him into a nightmare that begins when he kills the woman's lover as an act of self-defense and then follows a course of action that had, until that time, seemed a remotely academic issue. Fritz Lang's direction is as expert as his view of humanity is bleak and *The Woman in the Window* is generally considered to be one of the best films he made in this country.

★★★★

D: Frtiz Lang; W: Nunnally Johnson; Ph: Milton Krasner; M: Arthur Lang.
Cast: Edward G. Robinson, Joan Bennett, Dan Duryea, Raymond Massey.

THE WOMAN NEXT DOOR. (1981) Francois Truffaut shows what a major director can do with a volatile Gothic theme. Two lovers who married different spouses wind up living next door to each other years later and have to keep their separate marriages going while their illicit ardor heats up. Everything is done with a delicacy and precision that never allows the situation to degenerate into melodrama. It makes the final detonation truly shattering.

★★★★

D: Francois Truffaut; W: Truffaut, Suzanne Schiffman and Jean Aurel; Ph: William Lubtchansky; M: Georges Delerue.
Cast: Gerard Depardieu, Fanny Ardant, Henri Garcin, Michele Baumgartner.

A WOMAN UNDER THE INFLUENCE.
(1974) One of John Cassavetes' best works.
Gena Rowlands gives an uncompromisingly
honest account of a woman brought to the
brink of madness by the collision between
her unarticulated aspirations and her lot as
the wife of a contented construction worker.
The episodic film also benefits from Peter
Falk's perceptive account of a husband who
loves but does not understand his wife.
★★★★
D and W: John Cassavetes; Ph: Mitch Breit;
M: Bo Harwood.
Cast: Gena Rowlands, Peter Falk, Matthew
Cassel, Matthew Laborteaux.

THE WONDERFUL CROOK. (1975) Gerard Depardieu inherits a failing furniture
factory and takes to genteel bank robbery to
help meet the payroll. Claude Goretta, who
excels at fashioning large statements from
small subjects, doesn't go for the easy satirical targets and the Robin Hood side of the
story. Beneath the superficial and flawlessly
handled comedy is an eloquent essay on the
relationships of fathers and sons and hus-
bands and wives.
★★★★
D and W: Claude Goretta; Ph: Renato Berta;
M: Arie Dzierlatka.
Cast: Gerard Depardieu, Marlene Jobert,
Dominique Labourier, Philippe Leotard.

**THE WONDERFUL WORLD OF THE
BROTHERS GRIMM.** (1962) A children's
picture that's pretty grim going for adults in
tow. The story-telling brothers' lives are
recounted, but the better part of the movie is
given over to the reason for their fame. The
best of the three fairy tales offered is *the
Singing Bone* with Terry-Thomas and Buddy
Hackett.
★★
D: Henry Levin; W: David Harmon, Charles
Beaumont and William Roberts; Ph: Paul
Vogel; M: Leigh Harline.
Cast: Laurence Harvey, Karl Boehm, Claire
Bloom, Barbara Eden.

**WON TON TON, THE DOG WHO SAVED
HOLLYWOOD.** (1976) Strictly Alpo. More
than seventy luminaries from Hollywood's
past and present crowd into this flimsy piece
of slapstick that is meant to celebrate the
silent era. Madeline Kahn is a starlet and the
only human the dog will obey. You spend
most of your time muttering, "God, I thought
she was dead." with each new walk-on
cameo.
PG. ★

D: Michael Winner; W: Arnold Schulman and
Cy Howard; Ph: Jack Asher; M: Neal Hefti.
Cast: Madeline Kahn, Art Carney, Bruce
Dern, Ron Leibman.

WOODSTOCK. (1970) Here you can find
what movies like *The Big Chill* discussed
with such a sense of loss. A dizzy array of the
great names in the music of the time in a
work that is far more than a concert film. It is
a celebration of an event whose spirit and
unity passed with the sixties—the gathering
of half a million young people in Woodstock,
N.Y., in the summer of '69. A prodigious feat
of editing got the concert down to a man-
ageable length.
★★★★
D and Ph: Michael Wadleigh.
Cast: Joan Baez, Joe Cocker, The Who,
Crosby, Stills and Nash, *et al.*

WORD IS OUT. (1978) Twenty-six homosexuals reminisce about their experiences
for two hours in a sincere documentary. The
interviewers offer a shoulder to cry on instead of penetrating questions and there is
a great deal of verbosity. For those willing to
put up with the windiness, there are individual moments of candor and humor.
★★
D: The Mariposa Film Group; Ph: Amanda
Pope and Ann Hersey; M: Buena Vista.

THE WORLD ACCORDING TO GARP.
(1982) A wealth of talent tried to cope with
the complexities of John Irving's sprawling
book. The author took a cameo role as a
wrestling referee, but his narrative voice—a
key presence in the book—is sorely missed.
The story is stripped down and it plays as an
absurdist comedy of lust, mortality and fate.
The acting, especially Glenn Close's Jenny,
is of a high order.
R. ★★★
D: George Roy Hill; W: Steve Tesich; Ph:
Miroslav Ondricek; M: David Shire.
Cast: Robin Williams, Glenn Close, Mary
Beth Hurt, John Lithgow.

THE WORLD'S GREATEST LOVER.
(1977) Easily one of the world's worst movies in its time. It combines the staged neuro-
ses and mannerisms of Gene Wilder and the
boisterous hysterics of Dom De Luise in a
pastiche of Hollywood in the silent era. The
film, to its lasting cost, has a soundtrack and
has something to do with a search for a new
Valentino. The level of humor finds Wilder
sticking out his tongue when he loses his

nerve. Slapstick and sentimental romance.
PG. ★

D and W: Gene Wilder; Ph: Gerald Hirschfeld; M: John Morris.
Cast: Gene Wilder, Carol Kane, Dom De Luise, Fritz Feld.

THE WORLD, THE FLESH AND THE DEVIL. (1958) The world has ended in a mushroom cloud, the flesh shows up in a boring romantic triangle that has no place in this kind of movie and things go to the devil long before the end. Harry Belafonte emerges from a mine cave-in to find a dreadful new world and roams a deserted Manhattan. When he encounters Mel Ferrer and Inger Stevens, the film becomes predictable and loses its dramatic impulse. It's hard to be ultimately boring on the subject, but George Englund managed it.

★★

D: George Englund; W: Ranald MacDougall; Ph: Harold Marzorati; M: Miklos Rozsa.
Cast: Harry Belafonte, Inger Stevens, Mel Ferrer.

WORLD WITHOUT END. (1955) There are no end of variations on the theme and this piece of science fiction is one of the more passable attempts. A spaceship on its way to Mars enters a time warp and brings its crew down to Earth in the 26th century long after a nuclear war has wiped out civilization.

★★★

D and W: Edward Bernds; Ph: Ellsworth Fredericks; M: Leith Stevens.
Cast: Rod Taylor, Nancy Gates, Hugh Marlowe.

THE WRECKING CREW. (1968) There could be no more apt title for Dean Martin's final foray into the espionage spoof. His fourth Matt Helm film was his last. The tiresome plot sends Helm to make sure a shipment of gold bullion is protected from Nigel Green and his antics. Pure dross.

★

D: Phil Karlson; W: William McGivern; Ph: Sam Leavitt; M: Hugo Montenegro.
Cast: Dean Martin, Nigel Green, Sharon Tate, Elke Sommer.

WRONG IS RIGHT. (1982) Sean Connery is a television superstar who orchestrates world events to suit the needs of his news operation and even holds up invasions for three minutes of commercials. In a loud, incoherent absurdist comedy, Richard Brooks has some fun with the media, but

he's flogging a long-dead horse. The newsman becomes involved with Middle Eastern terrorists and various sub-plots.
R. ★★

D and W: Richard Brooks; W: Fred J. Koenekamp; Ph: Art Kane.
Cast: Sean Connery, George Grizzard, Robert Conrad, Katharine Ross.

WUTHERING HEIGHTS. (1939) Understandably the most popular version of Emily Bronte's novel. Olivier's Heathcliff is a figure of brooding power who is intentionally asked to dominate the film as he extracts his revenge. The atmosphere, with artificial Yorkshire moors, is doom-laden and madness and passion flourish. Much of the Bronte subtext is missing, but it could hardly be otherwise. We could also have been spared the heavenly choir ending.

★★★★

D: William Wyler; W: Ben Hecht and Charles MacArthur; Ph: Gregg Toland; M: Alfred Newman.
Cast: Laurence Olivier, Merle Oberon, David Niven, Flora Robson.

WUTHERING HEIGHTS. (1953) Luis Bunuel made his version during his Mexican period and despite the lurid Latin actors he was stuck with, the results are fascinating. He moved the story to rural Mexico with the lovers defying Catholic morality and macho behavior. It is a tale made for a surrealist sensibility and Bunuel exalts in the mad passion while giving a wry running commentary.

★★★★

D: Luis Bunuel; W: Bunuel, Arduino Maiuri and Julio Alejandro de Castro; Ph: Augustin Jimenez; M: Wagner.
Cast: Irasema Dilian, Jorge Mistral, Ernesto Alonso, Lilia Prado.

W.W. AND THE DIXIE DANCE KINGS. (1975) Burt Reynolds' trademark mannerisms are rather anachronistic in this fond recreation of the south in the peace and quiet of the early sixties. He lives in a '55 Oldsmobile, holds up gas stations and eventually takes a country singer and her band under his wing. Lots of chases, slapstick, southern drawling and country and western bawling.
PG. ★★

D: John Avildsen; W: Thomas Rickman; Ph: James Crabe; M: Dave Grusin.
Cast: Burt Reynolds, Art Carney, Conny Van Dyke, Jerry Reed.

X

XICA. (1983) A sloppy rendering of a Brazilian folk tale about a slave who used her body to become mistress of all she surveyed in the country's days as a Portuguese colony. We keep hearing a strangled and unexplained noise from the bedrooms where Xica does her stuff. It sounds like a man in mid-orgasm who has just been told his tax returns are to be audited. The Brazilian film made quite a splash, but all it has in its favor is a crude vitality.

★★

D: Carlos Diegues; W: Diegues and Joao Felicio; Ph: Jose Medeiros; M: Roberto Menescal.
Cast: Zere Motta, Walmor Chagas, Jose Wiker.

X—THE MAN WITH X-RAY EYES. (1963) The eyes have it when Dr. Xavier (Ray Milland) tries dropping something a lot stronger than Visine. Milland can see through everything and the science-fiction thriller is an enjoyable low-rent trip until his vision encompasses more than he bargained for. And, yes, the guy at the carnival *is* Don Rickles.

★★

D: Roger Corman; W: Robert Dillon and Ray Russell; Ph: Floyd Crosby; M: Les Baxter.
Cast: Ray Milland, Diana Van Der Vlis, Harold Stone, Don Rickles.

Y

THE YAKUZA. (1975) Yakuza films about the underworld brotherhood are as popular in Japan as westerns once were in this country. A properly brought up Yakuza makes an apology by cutting off his little finger and giving it to the offended party. So finger-pointing at Sydney Pollack's effort is dangerous. Robert Mitchum, looking as if someone had just slapped him awake after a three-day bender, goes to Japan to rescue the daughter of a friend from a Yakuza clan. Extremely bloody.

R. ★★
D: Sydney Pollack; W: Paul Schrader and Robert Towne; Ph: Duke Callaghan and Okazaki Kozo; M: Dave Grusin.
Cast: Robert Mitchum, Takakura Ken, Brian Keith, Kishi Keilo.

YANKEE DOODLE DANDY. (1942) With the country at war, Michael Curtiz decided that his evocation of the life and spirit of Broadway showman George M. Cohan should come wrapped in a flag. The biography is vivid, affectionate and unabashedly patriotic. The star amid the stripes is, of course, James Cagney, whose galvanic portrait of Cohan won an Oscar. Some of the happiest hoofing in movies is housed in this much loved film and it is a monument to Cagney's astonishing versatility.

★★★★
D: Michael Curtiz; W: Edmund Joseph and Robert Buckner; Ph: James Wong Howe; M: (songs) George M. Cohan.
Cast: James Cagney, Walter Huston, Joan Leslie, Rosemary de Camp.

A YANK IN THE R.A.F. (1941) At a time when American intervention on England's side against Hitler was a considerable and controversial issue, Tyrone Power played a feisty yank who joins the R.A.F. to be near his girl-friend in London. There's a good deal of actual footage of air combat as he learns the error of his arrogance and the film amounts to what might be called pre-war propaganda for Americans. It was a hit in its day.

★★★
D: Henry King; W: Darrell Ware and Karl Tunberg; Ph: Leon Shamroy; M: Alfred Newman.
Cast: Tyrone Power, Betty Grable, John Sutton, Reginald Gardiner.

YANKS. (1979) John Schlesinger understands that on the homefront World War II was a liberating experience for many English men and women as well as a fight for survival. He studies the change through the relationships of three Anglo-American couples at different class levels. The material is familiar—the collision of two cultures—but it is rendered with sensitivity and affection. Wartime England is also captured with great precision.

R. ★★★★
D: John Schlesinger; W: Walter Bernstein and Colin Welland; Ph: Dick Bush; M: Richard Rodney Bennett.
Cast: Richard Gere, Lisa Eichhorn, Vanessa Redgrave, William Devane.

THE YEAR OF LIVING DANGEROUSLY. (1983) Peter Weir has many original ideas on what can be done within the framework of lovers caught up in the sweep of great events—in this instance the fall of the Sukarno regime in Indonesia in 1965. The Third World is a living presence in the film, not a backdrop, and a humble mother and son are as poignant as the other characters. *The Year of Living Dangerously* is also a brilliant study of how journalists are affected by the misery they cover as well as what they will do in pursuit of a story. Linda Hunt is astonishing as the dwarf who bridges the world of the reporters and the teeming masses.

PG. ★★★★
D: Peter Weir; W: Weir, C.J. Koch and David Williamson; Ph: Russell Boyd; M: Maurice Jarre.
Cast: Mel Gibson, Sigourney Weaver, Linda Hunt, Bill Kerr.

YELLOWBEARD. (1983) An all-star comedian roster spoofs the pirate movie and an all-points bulletin for worthwhile jokes is in order. For pirate parody try *Swashbuckler.* This overloaded boat belongs in Davey Jones' locker and the presence of some of the Monty Python crew amounts to less than truth in advertising. Sadly, the picaresque tale that becomes picayune in its wit was Marty Feldman's last movie. He died while shooting it.

PG ★★
D: Mel Damski; W: Peter Cook, Graham Chapman and Bernard McKenna; Ph: Gerry Fisher; M: John Morris.

Cast: Graham Chapman, Peter Boyle, Richard Marin, Marty Feldman.

YELLOW SKY. (1949) Outlaws come to a ghost town whose only inhabitants are an old prospector and his beautiful granddaughter. They learn of a cache of gold and the inevitable dishonor among thieves erupts when Gregory Peck, the leader, falls for the girl. William Wellman shared John Huston's flair for documenting the dire results of greed and turned an unoriginal plot into a strong character study.

★★★

D: William Wellman; W: Lamar Trotti; Ph: Joe MacDonald; M: Alfred Newman.
Cast: Gregory Peck, Anne Baxter, Richard Widmark, Robert Arthur.

YENTL. (1983) It took Barbra Streisand 15 years to bring the Isaac Bashevis Singer story about a girl who poses as a boy to study the Torah to the screen. She wasn't about to let anyone get a look in once the production started. She directed, produced, starred and sang the twelve songs. The results are as charming as they are egocentric and the Eastern Europe at the turn fo the century is conjured emotionally as well as physically. The music is often painfully inspirational.
PG. ★★★
D: Barbra Streisand; W: Streisand and Jack Rosenthal; Ph: David Watkin; M: Michel Legrand.
Cast: Barbra Streisand, Amy Irving, Mandy Patinkin, Nehemiah Persoff.

YES, GIORGIO. (1982) Luciano Pavarotti, the worlds premier tenor, opens his dramatic film debut with Schubert's *Ave Maria*, but he needs more than a song and a prayer to make it in movies. Genuinely quaint and reminiscent of Mario Lanza's efforts, *Yes Giorgio* casts him as a great singer romancing a woman doctor. Whenever he bursts into a song, he is invariably cut short by the need to get on with the movie. Frustrating for his fans.
PG. ★★
D: Franklin J. Schaffner; W: Norman Steinberg; Ph: Fred Koenekamp; M: Michael J. Lewis.
Cast: Luciano Pavarotti, Kathryn Harrold, Eddie Albert, Emerson Buckley.

YOR. (1983) The days of Yor were numbered at the box office and only the hardened connoisseur of the epically dreadful is advised to spend any time with the caveman hero. The script includes lines like "Yor, you're so different from the other men." Yor searches for his past while knocking off monsters and then the film plunges into the future.
PG. ★
D: Anthony Dawson; W: Dawson and Robert Bailey; Ph: Marcello Masciocchi; M: John Scott.
Cast: Reb Brown, Corinne Clery, John Steiner, Carole Andre.

YOU CAN'T HAVE EVERYTHING. (1937) You can have a reasonably good time with Alice Faye and the Ritz Brothers in a stage door musical. Faye writes a play and falls for Don Ameche. Amid romantic complications, he turns it into a smash hit musical.
★★
D: Norman Taurog; W: Harry Tugend, Jack Yellen and Karl Tunberg; Ph: Lucien Andriot; M: David Buttolph.
Cast: Alice Faye, Don Ameche, the Ritz Brothers, Charles Winninger.

YOU CAN'T TAKE IT WITH YOU. (1938) Another of Frank Capra's good-natured arguments that you're really better off being poor. Adapted from George Kaufman's Broadway hit, it proved that you can take a couple of Oscars with you (Best Picture and Director). A millionaire's son wants to marry a poor girl from a family where eccentricity is the norm.
★★★★
D: Frank Capra; W: Robert Riskin; Ph: Joseph Walker; M: Dmitri Tiomkin.
Cast: Jean Arthur, Lionel Barrymore, James Stewart, Edward Arnold.

YOU LIGHT UP MY LIFE. (1977) Didi Conn makes her way through the prostrate emotions of one of the truly dumb films of the seventies with the look of a bewildered otter. As the daughter of a third-rate vaudeville comedian, she does a children's show on television that does not amuse the kids. Joseph Brooks came to this film from writing commercial jingles and his script has the same mindless patness. He has packed every conceivable banality about show business and making it into a gruesome ninety minutes.
PG. ★
D and W: Joseph Brooks; Ph: Eric Saarinen; M: Joseph Brooks.
Cast: Didi Conn, Joe Silver, Michael Zaslow, Stephen Nathan.

YOUNG AND INNOCENT. (1937) Alfred Hitchcock is several floors below the level of *The Thirty Nine Steps* but he brings his customary technique to the plight of a man who—once again—is unjustly accused of murder. A policeman's daughter helps him track down the real killer and Hitchcock has a field day with the single clue—the murderer's eye keeps twitching. Also known as *The Girl Was Young*.

★★★

D: Alfred Hitchcock; W: Charles Bennett and Alma Reville; Ph: Bernard Knowles; M: Louis Levy.
Cast: Derrick de Marney, Nova Pilbeam, Percy Marmont, Edward Rigby.

YOUNGBLOOD. (1978) A promising beginning on the pressures that lead black kids to join gangs, but then Noel Nosseck allows it to degenerate into the predictable exploitation. Lawrence-Hilton Jacobs leads the troops against syndicate drug pushers.

R. ★★

D: Noel Nosseck; W: Paul Carter Harrison ; Ph: Robin Greenberg; M: War.
Cast: Lawrence-Hilton Jacobs, Bryan O'Dell, Tony Allen, Vince Cannon.

THE YOUNG DOCTORS. (1961) Frederic March is an old one who resists innovative ideas represented by Ben Gazzara. He is a pathologist and most of the ideas in this hospital drama are old enough to warrant an autopsy. Even so, the acting and the central situation surrounding March's stubbornness are more than enough to compensate.

★★★

D: Phil Karlson; W: Joseph Hayes; Ph: Arthur Ornitz; M: Elmer Bernstein.
Cast: Frederic March, Ben Gazzara, Dick Clark, Eddie Albert.

YOUNG DOCTORS IN LOVE. (1982) The writers of this medical *Airplane* think your funny bone is located much lower than the position shown in *Gray's Anatomy*. The humor is off-the-wall, but, unfortunately, it's a bathroom wall and most of it is as amusing as your doctor's bill. Hospital soap operas are satirized and there are a lot of redundant "in" jokes about other movies.

R. ★

D: Garry Marshall; W: Michael Elias and Rich Eustis; Ph: Don Peterman; M: Maurice Jarre.
Cast: Michael McKean, Sean Young, Harry Dean Stanton, Patrick MacNee.

YOUNG FRANKENSTEIN. (1974) Dr. Frankenstein's train pulls alongside the platform and he hails an urchin with, "Pardon me boy, is this the Transylvania station?" With that we are off to a merrily vulgar spoof of horror films in one of Mel Brooks best parody efforts. As Gene Wilder assembles a prodigiously endowed monster, Brooks tears apart every creaking cliche in the genre. Erratic, but mostly very funny.

PG ★★★★

D: Mel Brooks; W: Brooks and Gene Wilder; Ph: Gerald Hirschfeld; M: John Morris.
Cast: Gene Wilder, Marty Feldman, Madeline Kahn, Peter Boyle.

THE YOUNG LIONS. (1958) As Christian Diestl, a ski instructor who takes up Nazism and then has second thoughts, Marlon Brando dominated his segments of the adaptation of Irwin Shaw's novel. His gradual disillusionment is more compelling than events on the other side of the line, which trace the war experiences of a Jew and an entertainer. The movie shuttles back and forth rather frenetically, but it is invested with a thoughtful irony that makes the climax—which brings the three men together—moving rather than contrived.

★★★

D: Edward Dmytryk; W: Edward Anhalt; Ph: Joe MacDonald; M: Hugo Friedhofer.
Cast: Marlon Brando, Dean Martin, Montgomery Clift, Hope Lange.

YOUNG MAN WITH A HORN. (1950) Kirk Douglas didn't blow his own trumpet—Harry James dubbed it—but he can certainly take a lot of credit for his account of a musician who is obsessed with his music. The movie is very freely based on the life of Bix Beiderbecke and its rise and fall structure is helped by Lauren Bacall's suitably bitchy contribution.

★★★

D: Michael Curtiz; W: Carl Foreman and Edmund North; Ph: Ted McCord; M: Ray Heindorf.
Cast: Kirk Douglas, Doris Day, Lauren Bacall, Hoagy Carmichael.

YOUNG MR. LINCOLN. (1939) The private and early years that forged the country's greatest President. The subject allows John Ford to show the man behind the legend. He does not canonize Lincoln and Henry Fonda brings a stalwart decency to the character of the young attorney. The film covers the decade that saw Lincoln rise to prominence as a lawyer who defends two men accused of murder. After the death of his fiancee, he takes up with Mary Todd and enters Illinois politics.

★★★★

D: John Ford; W: Lamar Trotti; Ph: Bert Glennon; M: Alfred Newman.
Cast: Henry Fonda, Alice Brady, Marjorie Weaver, Arleen Whelan.

YOUNG WARRIORS. (1984) *Death Wish* for college kids. A bunch of fraternity brothers abandon honest pleasures like surfing to make waves in the barrios of Los Angeles. Their motive is that one of them has a sister who was raped and murdered and everyone in the slums looks alike. Nastier than it sounds.

R. ★

D: Lawrence Foldes; W: Foldes and Russell Colgin; M: Ron Walsh.
Cast: James Van Patten, Ernest Borgnine, Anne Lockhart, Richard Roundtree.

YOUNG WINSTON. (1972) Richard Attenborough excels in making history live and finding themes of contemporary relevance in the past—witness *Gandhi* and *A Bridge Too Far.* His biography of Winston Churchill's early years is more traditional, but still a superior exercise. This is not the British Lion rallying the people during the Blitz, but a young man finding his way and coming to terms with his overbearing father. In those years, he had enough adventures in the Boer War to make the picture exciting as well as thoughtful.

PG. ★★★

D: Richard Attenborough; W: Carl Foreman; Ph: Gerry Turpin; M: Alfred Ralston.
Cast: Simon Ward, Anne Bancroft, Robert Shaw, Jack Hawkins.

YOU ONLY LIVE TWICE. (1967) Sean Connery decided that you really only live once and there must be something more to life than playing James Bond. He quit after this trip to Japan to disrupt a SPECTRE plan to start World War III. He came back again a few years later for *Diamonds Are Forever* and again in 1983 with *Never Say Never Again. You Only Live Twice* is one of the lesser films in his first quintet. It has the trappings of a Bond film and then some, but the traps that propel 007 are not up to snuff.

★★★

D: Lewis Gilbert; W: Roald Dahl; Ph: Freddie Young; M: John Barry.
Cast: Sean Connery, Tetsuro Tamba, Akiko Wakabayashi, Mie Hama.

Z

ZARDOZ. (1974) John Boorman's vision of the world in 2293 divides it between a barbarian hunting society and a group of insulated intellectuals who have discovered the secret of eternal life. A wild mix of styles and themes and you can take you pick in believing it to be an allegory or a parody. Sean Connery is the natural force who becomes an avenging angel among the atrophied immortals and he is a strong physical presence in the film.
R. ★★
D and W: John Boorman; Ph: Geoffrey Unsworth; M: David Munrow.
Cast: Sean Connery, Charlotte Rampling, Sara Kastelman, Sally Anne Newton.

ZELIG. (1983) In this brilliant fake documentary, Woody Allen offers us a stand-up chameleon and a new form of humor —the historically funny comedy. It is a totally spurious account of the career of one Leonard Zelig, who became physically like the people he was with because he wanted to be liked. A superb hoax where every joke has a function beyond its immediate humor in a screenplay of masterly precision. Beneath the non-stop barrage of gags is a mordant essay on celebrity, media hype and a society that worships a personality who is barely a person. It's set in the twenties, with spliced newsreels making the falsehood absolutely real, but it's about the way we live today.
PG. ★★★★★
D and W: Woody Allen; Ph: Gordon Willis; M: Dick Hyman.
Cast: Woody Allen, Mia Farrow, Susan Sontag, Bruno Bettelheim.

ZIGGY STARDUST. (1973) David Bowie made this concert film in 1973, but it wasn't released for ten years. In the interim, he went on to establish himself as an interesting presence in films. His fans will revel in it, but by today's standards of slick visuals, *Ziggy Stardust* shows signs of gathering dust.
PG. ★★
D: F.S. Pennebaker; Ph: James Desmond.
Cast: David Bowie, Angie Bowie, Mick Ronson, Mick Woodman.

ZORBA THE GREEK. (1964) The part Anthony Quinn was born for and, happily, got to play. His Zorba is a figure of earthy exuberance and inexhaustible energy who defies hidebound convention and acts as a catalyst for a questing young English writer. It is the kind of performance that sweeps aside criticism of the weaker aspects of the movie.
★★★
D and W: Michael Cacoyannis; Ph: Walter Lassally; M: Mikis Theodorakis.
Cast: Anthony Quinn, Alan Bates, Irene Papas, Lila Kedrova.

ZORRO, THE GAY BLADE. (1981) George Hamilton scores a couple of points above the mark of zero you might expect from the maker of the awful *Love at First Bite*. The idea of Don Diego, savior of the California peasantry, suffering an injury that forces him to hand over to his foppish brother has possibilities. They remain largely unrealized in a cruel shortage of rapier wit. Hamilton encourages the rest of the cast into shameless hamming.
PG. ★★
D: Peter Medak; W: Hal Dresner, Greg Alt, Bob Randall and Don Moriarty; Ph: John Alonzo; M: Ian Fraser.
Cast: George Hamilton, Lauren Hutton, Brenda Vaccaro, Ron Leibman.

Comments

Comments

Comments

Comments

Comments

Comments

Comments

Comments

Comments

Comments